NETWORK NATION

NETWORK NATION

Inventing American
Telecommunications

RICHARD R. JOHN

The Belknap Press of Harvard University Press

Cambridge, Massachusetts

London, England

2010

For Nancy,

who makes it all worthwhile

Copyright © 2010 by the President and Fellows of Harvard College
All rights reserved
Printed in the United States of America

Library of Congress Cataloging-in-Publication Data

John, Richard R., 1959–
Network nation : inventing American telecommunications /
Richard R. John.
p.   cm.
Includes bibliographical references and index.
ISBN 978-0-674-02429-8 (alk. paper)
1. Telecommunication—United States—History.   I. Title.
TK5102.3.U6J64   2010
384—dc22   2009050825

CONTENTS

ILLUSTRATIONS AND TABLES

Illustrations

Tables

INTRODUCTION: INVENTING AMERICAN TELECOMMUNICATIONS

This book is a history of the formative era of the first electrical communications media in the United States. It considers how they worked and why they mattered. Its theme is the influence on these media of the structuring presence of the state, or what nineteenth-century contemporaries called the political economy. The first electrical communications media—the telegraph and the telephone—were products not only of technological imperatives and economic incentives, but also of governmental institutions and civic ideals.

The telegraph and the telephone are often associated with eponymous inventors: the telegraph with Samuel F. B. Morse, the telephone with Alexander Graham Bell. This association is understandable. The Morse code was long the most widely used telegraphic signaling language, and the Bell System was for many decades the largest telephone network in the United States. Although Morse and Bell make frequent appearances in the pages that follow, they are not the major protagonists. The invention of American telecommunications involved far more than the invention of novel technical contrivances. Even more fundamental was the scaling up of these contrivances into the spatially extensive and temporally intensive communications networks that have become a hallmark of modernity. Invention is not innovation, and for the historian of communications, the institutionalization of the fruits of invention is the more compelling theme.

The telegraph and the telephone have dual identities as channels of communications and as powerful institutions. The telegraph used electricity to circulate written information; the telephone used electricity to amplify the human voice. In the formative era of American telecommunications, the dominant telegraph network was operated by Western Union,

1

and the dominant telephone network was operated by the federation of operating companies that held licenses from and that were largely owned by American Bell and, after 1900, the American Telephone and Telegraph Company (AT&T).

The origins of telecommunications date back to the 1790s with the invention of the optical telegraph in France; its most recent phase began in the 1990s with the commercialization of the Internet in the United States. Its most revolutionary period spanned the eight decades between 1840 and 1920, an epoch that witnessed the emergence of the United States as an economic giant and a world power. These years also marked the formative era of American telecommunications. Each of these dates coincided with a landmark event: the granting of the first telegraph patent to Samuel F. B. Morse in 1840 and the first radio broadcasts in 1920.

The communications revolution that the telegraph and telephone set in motion was the second communications revolution to occur in the United States. The first began in 1792 with the restructuring of the mail to facilitate the low-cost circulation of information on public affairs; the second began in 1845 with the almost simultaneous commercialization of the electric telegraph and the further restructuring of the mail to facilitate the low-cost circulation of information on personal matters. This revolution entered a new phase around 1900 with the popularization of the telephone, it crested in 1910 with the popularization of the telegraph, and it ended in 1920 with the invention of radio broadcasting.

The last telegram bearing the logo of the once-formidable telegraph giant Western Union was transmitted in 2006, making the telegraph one of the few electrical communications media to have become obsolete. Although the telegraph has disappeared, its memory lives on in the admiring accounts of journalists, media scholars, and sociologists, who have variously hailed it as the "Victorian Internet," the prototype of all later electrical communications media, and the harbinger of the present-day "Information Age."

Each of these three characterizations is misleading. The telegraph followed a very different trajectory from that of the telephone, and, as an organizational form, it had less influence on telephone network builders than the mail. In no sense was the telegraph a "Victorian Internet." To the exasperation of network critics, during its first sixty-five years it remained a specialty service for an exclusive clientele, and not until 1910 would it be recast as a mass service for the entire population.

Present-day interest in the telegraph owes much to its motive power. The telegraph was the first communications medium to rely on electricity, a form of energy that has long intrigued historians of technology. In 1934, for example, Lewis Mumford hailed the telegraph for facilitating the real-time, or "instant," circulation of information; a half-century later, the organizers of a long-running exhibit on the "Information Age" at the Smithsonian Institution's Museum of American History afforded it pride of place in their genealogy of information technology innovations.[1] The fixation on instantaneity has complicated the task of locating the telegraph in its historical milieu. The harnessing of electricity to convey information at high speed over long distances was an impressive feat. Yet in only a narrowly technical sense was the telegraph something new under the sun.[2] Invention is not innovation: to contend that the invention of the telegraph led in some predetermined way to the establishment of a particular organizational form obscures the historical process by imputing agency to electrical equipment, batteries, and wires.

The telephone is less often mythologized, at least in part because it is better known. Here, too, however, misleading stereotypes persist. It is often assumed, for example, that the telephone was envisioned as a mass service from the opening of the first telephone exchange in 1878. Like the telegraph, the telephone was originally designed as a specialty service for an exclusive clientele; it would not be reconfigured as a mass service for the entire population until around 1900, and then only for local calls. In no sense did the telephone make a "neighborhood of a nation," as AT&T public relations announcements proclaimed following the commercialization of transcontinental telephone service in 1915. Long-distance calls were expensive and would not become a mass service until after the Second World War.

Most historical accounts of the formative era of American telecommunications tell the story backward from the present. This book, in contrast, takes as its starting point events that occurred in the half century before Samuel F. B. Morse secured his first telegraph patent in 1840. In selecting themes for emphasis, the primary criterion has been the priorities of contemporaries. Issues of compelling concern to earlier generations, such as the evils of stock watering, are duly considered, even though their significance is often discounted today.

Like most historical writing, this book is based on the paper trail of its protagonists. Sources include trade journals, newspapers, magazines, pamphlets, petitions, government publications, personal correspondence, and the records of government agencies at the federal, state, and municipal levels. Of particular value have been the business archives of Western Union, the Chicago Telephone Company, and AT&T.

Access to these business archives has been much affected by the recent churning in the telecommunications sector. Western Union's business records have been open to researchers since the mid-1990s at the Smithsonian Institution, a tribute to the intrepid museum staffers who rescued them from almost certain destruction following the collapse of the telegraph business. The business records of a wide array of telephone operating companies have been assembled in one location by a far-sighted corporate archivist committed to ensuring their preservation following the merger boom that followed the Telecommunications Act of 1996; they have been available for consultation since 2002 at the AT&T Archives and History Center in San Antonio, Texas. *Network Nation* is the first history of early American telecommunications to systematically mine these remarkable collections.

1

MAKING A NEIGHBORHOOD OF A NATION

> There can be but few great developments in the future of
> which the beginnings have not been made or have not been
> foreshadowed.... In "intercommunication" the signal lights
> of the Middle Ages gave way to the semaphore of the eighteenth
> century—the electric telegraph of the early, supplemented by
> the telephone in the late nineteenth century.
>
> *Theodore N. Vail, 1916*

Three events, reflected the 78-year-old historian Henry Adams in 1906, had thrown into an "ash-heap" the "old universe" into which he had been born. These events were the arrival of the first regularly scheduled transatlantic steamship in Boston harbor in 1840; the opening of the first interregional rail link between Boston and Albany in 1841; and the first telegraphic news dispatch in 1844.[1]

Adams's reminiscence highlights the enormous significance one thoughtful American gave to a communications revolution that he experienced as a youth. Adams's memory was selective. Oddly absent from his catalogue of famous firsts was any allusion to the federal legislation that had inaugurated the era of "cheap postage" in 1845, an event that remained well known when Adams wrote his memoir.[2] Equally puzzling was the omission of any acknowledgment of the fact that each of the innovations Adams hailed had been dependent on government support: the steamship had been subsidized by the British admiralty, the railroad by the Massachusetts legislature, and the telegraph by Congress. Adams's myopia was particularly curious since, as Adams well knew, his own grandfather, John Quincy Adams, had vigorously championed government funding for public works during his long and distinguished public career.

From 1906 until the present, several generations of historians, social theorists, and cultural critics have echoed Henry Adams by downplaying

the influence of governmental institutions and civic ideals on major technological innovations. Only in the mid-twentieth century, in their view,
would the political economy catch up with the technological torrent.
This belief is mistaken. From the eighteenth century to the present, technology and politics have been inextricably linked.

The United States has long boasted an impressive array of facilities for
circulating information regularly and reliably over vast distances and at
high speed. By 1840, the mail linked thousands of localities in a single
countrywide network, while line-of-sight, or optical, telegraphs hastened
ship-to-shore communications in several of the country's largest seaports. By 1920, the United States had become integrated into a global
telegraph network and boasted the world's largest and most intensively
patronized federation of telephone exchanges.

The telegraph and the telephone exerted a far-reaching influence on
American life. The telegraph established new conventions of simultane-
ity; the telephone severed the age-old link between propinquity and the
spoken word. By 1920, the two media had become the central nervous
system of the city.[3] The influence of the telegraph and the telephone on
American society is well known; often overlooked, however, is the influence of American society on the telegraph and the telephone.

In the years between 1840 and 1920, the proposition that the entire
population had a right to a certain basic level of telegraph or telephone
service was the subject of a long and sometimes acrimonious public
debate. In 1840, almost no one anticipated that the entire population
might one day communicate electrically by wire. By 1920, few doubted
that the operators of the nation's telegraph and telephone networks had
a social responsibility to provide the entire population with facilities
to send a telegram across the continent or make a local telephone call.
How and why did the telegraph and the telephone shift from a specialty
service for an exclusive clientele to a mass service for the entire population? The answer to this question involves an exploration not only of
technology and economics, but also of politics and culture.

The telegraph had not been designed to accommodate the entire
population, and for many years it did not. In fact, the dominant network
provider would not reconfigure the medium for the mass market until
1910, sixty-five years after the opening of the first fee-for-service telegraph line in 1845. Prior to 1910, the telegraph had, with a few minor

exceptions, remained a specialty service for an exclusive clientele of merchants, lawmakers, and journalists. Telegraph leaders regarded this circumstance as inevitable. Fewer than 10 percent of the American people would prefer the telegraph to "letter communication," predicted Western Union president Norvin Green in 1890, even if the cost were identical.[4] Green may have underestimated the popular demand for a low-cost telegraph. Even so, the mail remained the principal long-distance communications medium for all but the few. If operating revenue is used as a rough proxy for public demand, Green had a point. Western Union operated the largest telegraph network in the United States; in 1890 it generated $20 million in revenue, and the Post Office Department, three times as much (see Table 1).

Although the telegraph and the telephone differed in many ways, each evolved through three stages. In the first stage—commercialization—the network was established; in the second stage—popularization—the network was scaled up from a specialty service into a mass service; and in the third stage—naturalization—the network was depoliticized through the constant repetition of the seductive dogma that existing institutional arrangements were rooted in technology and economics rather than politics and culture. The telephone was commercialized in the 1870s, popularized around 1900, and naturalized during the First World War. In the case of the telegraph, the sequencing of the second and third stages was reversed. The telegraph was commercialized in the 1840s, naturalized in the 1880s, and popularized in 1910.

Table 1. Annual operating revenue of the Post Office Department, Western Union, and the Bell System, 1866–1920.

Year	Operating revenue (millions of dollars)		
	Post Office Department	Western Union	Bell System
1866	14.4	4.6	0.0
1870	18.9	6.7	0.0
1880	33.3	10.6	3.1
1890	60.9	20.1	16.2
1900	102.4	22.8	46.1
1910	224.1	30.7	164.2
1914	287.9	45.9	224.5
1920	437.2	n.a.	448.2

Source: Historical Statistics of the United States (Cambridge: Cambridge University Press, 2006), tables Dg 19, Dg 69, and Dg 182.

The political economy of communications in the early republic was highly centralized, fostering the presumption that the telegraph should be operated by a federal government agency. This federally oriented political economy was partly supplanted in the 1840s by a state-oriented political economy that encouraged competition between rival telegraph network providers chartered as private corporations. Patent rights remained the domain of the federal government; in most other realms, the states prevailed. Beginning in the 1880s, this state-oriented political economy came into conflict with a municipally oriented political economy that hastened the consolidation of telephone corporations and their mutation from private enterprises into public utilities. Political structure shaped business strategy. The competitive political economy glorified the equal rights of network providers and vilified government-granted special privilege; the consolidationist political economy idealized the public utility that networks provided their users and deplored the unnecessary waste that competition entailed.

The word "network" has become a ubiquitous metaphor for any phenomenon that includes some combination of links and nodes. People network to find jobs, improve their social status, and stay well informed. The mass media abounds with references to social networks, business networks, and, tragically, terrorist networks. The Internet is, literally, a network of networks, or internetwork. To make sense of this reality, social theorists have devised a science of networks.[5] No longer is the basic economic unit an organization such as a government agency or a private corporation; rather, it has become the network in which organizations interact.[6]

One of the most distinctive features of the science of networks is the hypothesis that the value of a network for its users increases as the network expands. This relationship is called a network "externality" or "effect." Network effects do not exist in every enterprise that might be characterized as a network: they are absent, for example, in gas plants and water works. If a gas plant or water works increases in scale, the value of a unit of gas or water for its consumers remains the same. In contrast, if a communications network is scaled up, the value of the facilities it provides for each of its users is presumed to increase because it is now possible to interconnect more intensively with a larger number of users over a more spatially extensive domain.[7]

The hypothesis that networks become more valuable as they expand has colored much of the historical writing on the telegraph and the telephone. Unfortunately, this hypothesis is assumed rather than demonstrated. In practice, telegraph and telephone network builders only gradually became aware of the relationship between network size and network value; indeed, in some instances they had cause to doubt that any relationship existed. In writing the history of early American telecommunications, it is important not to anachronistically conflate the prescriptions of twenty-first-century network theorists with the conduct of nineteenth-century network builders.

The science of networks is new, but the word "network" is not. The first networks were intricate, densely textured handicrafts made from metal or lace. Over time the word came to denote interconnected artifacts that were more spatially extensive, such as the telegraph, the mail, and the telephone. The telegraph was a "network of nerves of iron wire," reflected one journalist in 1845.[8] The mail was "weaving a network" of "social, intellectual, and commercial intercourse," observed one lawmaker in 1851.[9] The telephone was a "network of invisible wires," opined a publicist in 1913.[10]

The network metaphor highlights the spatiality of early American telecommunications.[11] Though the telegraph spanned the nation, the mesh remained porous, and many localities were excluded. The telegraph remained a loosely coupled combine, or what Europeans called a cartel, rather than a tightly coupled system. The telephone was equally variegated. Thousands of operating companies competed, many head-on, while few users wished or desired to communicate over a distance that exceeded the boundaries of a city or town.

The heterogeneity of the telephone network is worth underscoring because it is often assumed that, beginning around 1908, every single telephone operating company in which the American Telephone and Telegraph Company had made a substantial investment was part of a seamless web dubbed by telephone executive Theodore N. Vail the "Bell System." In fact, the telephone network remained a federation of operating companies that were organizationally distinct. To the extent that a genuine system existed, it was localized in the nation's largest cities. Operating companies maintained their own corporate identities, published their own magazines, designed their own advertising, issued their own securities, and even built their own headquarters buildings. Among the most architecturally significant skyscrapers of the 1920s were the headquarters buildings for the Bell-associated operating companies in New York City and San Francisco.

Just as the "system" metaphor can mislead, so too can the claim that the telegraph and the telephone transformed the nation into a "neighborhood." Metaphor is inescapable in telecommunications, and the relationship of network, neighborhood, and nation was complex. The conceit that communications could create community originated long before the twentieth-century media critic Marshall McLuhan proclaimed that television was fast transforming the world into a "global village." McLuhan himself hinted that he derived the inspiration for this metaphor from a bit of dialogue that he had encountered in an 1851 novel by Nathaniel Hawthorne in which one of the characters exulted that the telegraph had transformed the "round globe" into a "vast head, a brain, instinct with intelligence!"[12] The "neighborhood" metaphor even antedated the commercialization of electricity. The mail had made the United States "one great neighborhood," reflected moralist William Ellery Channing in 1829, more than a decade before the opening of the first electric telegraph line in the United States.[13]

The nation-building potential of the telegraph and the telephone was a frequent boast of network promoters. In the case of the electric telegraph, this boast went back at least as far as 1838, several years before the opening of the first telegraph line. "It would not be long," predicted telegraph inventor Samuel F. B. Morse, before the "whole surface of this country" would be "channeled" for those "*nerves*" that were to "diffuse, with the speed of thought, a knowledge of all that is occurring throughout the land; making, in fact, *one neighborhood* of the whole country."[14] As long as the slavery issue loomed, the political implications of the telegraph remained contested. Following the abolition of slavery during the Civil War, the linkage of network and nation became a cliché.

In the case of the telephone, the indispensability of the network to the nation was harder to sustain. The overwhelming majority of telephone calls were limited to the confines of a city or town, and few had the need or the desire to communicate over vast distances. Even so, telephone boosters did their best. The railroad and the steamship had done much to unite the American people, reflected one telephone publicist in 1910, yet the telephone was the "keystone of the arch": it was the "one last improvement" that enabled an "interdependent nation" to "handle itself and to hold together."[15] Transcontinental telephone service—boasted a public relations announcement for the nation's leading telephone network provider in 1915—was "Making a Neighborhood of a Nation."[16]

The actual relationship of the telegraph and the telephone to the nation was far from obvious. The telegraph was originally intended not to unite the country, but, rather, to link in a vast transnational arc the cotton factories of Manchester, England, with the cotton ports of the American South. Prior to the completion of the Atlantic cable in 1866, one segment in this circuit remained nonelectric: to transmit information across the ocean, merchants relied on the regularly scheduled steamships that plied the North Atlantic. Even the Pacific telegraph—a cherished symbol, along with the transcontinental railroad, of national integration—was originally conceived of not only as a nation-spanning project, but also as a link in a transnational circuit linking the United States and Europe by way of Alaska, the Bering Strait, and Siberia.

The relationship of the telephone and the nation was even more strained. The telephone network in its formative era was an archipelago of mostly self-contained exchanges, many of which did not interconnect. Ninety-seven percent of all telephone calls in 1920 remained confined within a city or town.[17] Today it is by no means uncommon to call a distant friend or relative for a casual conversation; as recently as the 1970s, however, this practice remained a luxury for all but the well-to-do. Despite the steady stream of corporate public relations advertising that trumpeted the possibilities of regional, interregional, and even transcontinental telephone service, the most relevant spatial unit for telephone service long remained neither the nation, nor even the region, but the locality. Telephone publicists were so fixated on long-distance service that they overlooked the space-conquering triumphs that were closer to home.

A similar misunderstanding has swirled around the oft-made claim that the telegraph "annihilated" space and time. Like the "neighborhood" metaphor, the "annihilation" metaphor is often linked with the electric telegraph. In fact, it originated long before its commercialization and seems to have been the brainchild of the eminently quotable late eighteenth-century English poet Alexander Pope.[18] The "annihilation" Pope referred to was the elimination by divine intervention of the physical distance that kept two lovers apart: "Ye Gods! annihilate but space and time, and make two lovers happy." Not until the opening decades of the nineteenth century would it become customary to presume that mere mortals could wield such a power. And when it did, contemporaries invoked the metaphor to characterize not only the electric telegraph, but also the mail and the optical telegraph. "Time and distance are annihilated," exclaimed one essayist in 1831, in describing the experience of opening a letter sent through the mail from a childhood friend, and "we are *there*."[19] The imagination was "overpowered," gushed one optical telegraph enthusiast several years later, in contemplating the possibilities of the medium: "Distance is annihilated."[20] Little wonder that one journalist saw fit to predict in 1838 that time and space would be "almost annihilated" should the electric telegraph prove a success: by this time, the annihilation of distance had become little more than a stale metaphor.[21]

Today it is customary to lump together the telegraph and the telephone as telecommunications. Though this pairing is understandable, in a strict sense it is anachronistic. The word "telecommunications" is a surprisingly recent invention. The neologism was coined in 1904 by Edouard Estaunié in a manual for postal administrators—*Traité Pratique de Telecommunication Électrique*. Estaunié was a French postal administrator much admired as a prose stylist.[22] To avoid confusion with the nonelectric telegraph, Estaunié left open the possibility that a telegraph might be optical: it was for this reason that he qualified "telecommunication" with "électrique." Although this usage is unusual today among engineers, it remains conventional among historians. The "essence of telecommunications" had nothing to do with motive power, one eminent historian of communications has explained; rather, it involved the transmission of information between two points at a speed significantly faster than the message could be physically transported. By this criterion, the electric telegraph was a "less dramatic improvement" than the optical telegraph because it merely speeded up the dissociation of transportation and communication that the optical telegraph had pioneered.[23]

Words have a way of carrying their etymologies with them forever, and telecommunications is no exception. From the beginning, the word comingled phenomena that remained in basic ways distinct. In 1904, these phenomena were the telegraph and the telephone; in the 1930s, the telegraph and radio. The identification of telecommunications with radio received its official imprimatur in 1932 when the Swiss-based International Telegraph Union expanded its mandate to embrace the new medium. To highlight this change, the organization renamed itself the International Telecommunication Union (ITU). For the first time, explained one American government administrator, all the nations of the world had officially adopted a single word to refer simultaneously to the telegraph, the telephone, and radio, as well as any other system of "electric or visual (semaphore) signaling."[24] Interestingly, the original mandate of the ITU did not embrace the telephone: the ITU was an international organization, and few telephone networks crossed national borders. Today, "telecommunications" is often used to refer to the convergence of the telephone and the computer. Ironically, this usage excludes both the telegraph and radio, two of the first media to which it had been applied.

The word "telecommunications" only slowly found its way across the Atlantic. In the period before 1920, it was unknown. Not until 1934 would the word appear in the *New York Times* and the *Wall Street Journal;* in both instances, in references to developments in Europe.[25] Not until 1936 would the word grace the title page of an academic monograph.[26] Not until after the Second World War would it become conventional in the United States to use the word to denote a communications medium rather than a government agency like the ITU. Prior to that time, contemporaries who wished to refer simultaneously to the telegraph and the telephone had no choice but to fall back on clumsy circumlocutions such as the "electrical means of communication," "electrical communication," or the "wire system." The word "telecommunications" remained so unfamiliar that when Congress established an administrative body in 1934 to oversee the telegraph, the telephone, and radio, it named it the Federal Communications Commission rather than the Federal Telecommunications Commission.

"Telecommunications" may not have come into common usage in the United States before the Second World War, yet the vision of media convergence that it presumed had long intrigued network builders, lawmakers, and network critics. The name of the nation's first long-distance telephone network provider—the American Telephone and Telegraph Company—anticipated the merger of the telephone and the telegraph. So, too, did the popularization by its president, Theodore N. Vail, of a "universal service" that would combine the telephone and the telegraph in a single interactive medium.

Of the various precursors to the electric telegraph, few were more influential than the optical telegraph that the French government built in the 1790s to facilitate high-speed communication between the capital and the provinces. This project inspired the invention of the word "telegraph," a neologism coined by a French government administrator. The word "telegraph" meant, in Greek, "writing-at-a-distance," a locution that few nineteenth-century Americans saw reason to improve upon. The French optical telegraph relied on specially trained operators to relay coded messages along a chain of towers spaced at intervals of between 10 and 20 miles: the maximum distance by which an operator could interpret a signal using the telescopes of the day. If the weather were good, the only limitation on the distance a message could be transmitted was the number of towers in the network. The new medium, an encyclopedist aptly noted in 1803, was a "machine" for conveying messages from "one extreme point to another" be they "ever so distant."[27]

The French optical telegraph remained in operation even after the electric telegraph had gone into operation in Great Britain and the United States. It reached twenty-nine cities in 1852 in a hub-and-spoke configuration radiating out of Paris that linked 556 towers and extended over 2,900 miles. In good weather, operators could transmit twenty characters per minute from tower to tower, a speed that present-day electrical engineers have compared favorably with the earliest electric telegraphs.[28]

The French optical telegraph was well known in the United States. Some form of the word "telegraph" appeared on the masthead of over forty American newspapers by 1820; the word also furnished the title for the official campaign newspaper of presidential candidate Andrew Jackson in 1828.[29] All of these variants referred to the optical telegraph: the electric telegraph had yet to be invented. Even electric telegraph enthusiasts found the optical telegraph impressive. Among the "various systems of the moderns," observed one admirer in 1844, the French optical telegraph "may be mentioned in the first rank."[30] Following the commercialization of the electric telegraph, the optical telegraph gradually faded from memory; even so, it lived on long enough in the popular imagination to be hailed as a precursor to the telephone. "Napoleon's Visual Telegraph," proclaimed one telephone public relations announcement in 1912, was "The First Long Distance System."[31]

Among the most eloquent champions of the optical telegraph was the linguist John Pickering. The optical telegraph was unquestionably one of the "greatest improvements of modern times," Pickering announced in 1833 in a public lecture before the Boston Marine Society: "no means of conveying intelligence can ever be devised that shall exceed or even equal [its] rapidity . . . for with the exception of the scarcely perceptible delay at each station, its rapidity may be compared with that of

From an old print in La Telegra"e Historique.

Napoleon's Visual Telegraph
The First Long Distance System

Although the optical telegraph was abandoned following the commercialization of the electric telegraph, it lived on in the popular imagination. In this 1912 public relations announcement, Bell publicists hailed the French optical telegraph as the "first long distance system"—a precursor to Bell's own long-distance telephone network. "Napoleon's Visual Telegraph: The First Long Distance System," January 1912, AT&T Archives and History Center, Warren, N.J.

light itself." Unfortunately, Pickering lamented, many of its features remained little-known: "Every one of us hears and reads of news by the [optical] telegraph, from day to day, without ever considering, much less understanding any thing of the principles of this mode of communicating intelligence."[32] Although everyone regarded the optical telegraph as a major technical advance, not everyone hailed its French incarnation as benign. The French optical telegraph, warned one journalist in 1846, was one of the "mightiest of the agents" by which the French general Napoleon Bonaparte had transformed himself into a military despot.[33]

The possibility that the federal government might build an optical telegraph on the French model appealed to lawmakers troubled by the vulnerability of the country's ports to seaborne invasion. An optical telegraph would provide the military with an early warning system in case of foreign attack. Congress debated the propriety of establishing an optical telegraph in 1807, a year in which the possibility of war with France or Britain loomed large. Supporters secured a favorable vote in the House for a bill to fund a 1,200-mile-long chain of optical telegraph towers between New York City and New Orleans. In the end, however, the project was shelved, and the New York City–New Orleans optical telegraph remained unbuilt.[34] Following Napoleon's defeat at Waterloo in 1815, the construction of a telegraphic early warning system seemed less pressing. Yet the idea was not forgotten. In 1833, for example, Andrew Jackson's secretary of state Edward Livingston endorsed the establishment by the federal government of "telegraphic communication" between the seat of government and those points on the seaboard that were "most exposed to invasion."[35] Four years later, a similar proposal received the endorsement of optical telegrapher Samuel C. Reid.

Optical telegraph enthusiasts hailed the potential of the new medium in peace as well as war. The linkage of North and South America by optical telegraph, speculated polymath William Thornton around 1800, would facilitate the political consolidation of the two continents by empowering the "supreme government" to obtain any communication from the "remotest bounds of this vast empire" in less than a day.[36] There was "no country," declared Reid in 1837, in which the optical telegraph would bring "greater benefits and advantages to the public at large," and most especially to the "*mercantile* class of the community."[37] Once the federal government had built an optical telegraph between New York City and New Orleans, it would become possible to transmit vitally important messages between these two far-flung cities in a mere two hours.[38]

Nothing like the French optical telegraph was ever built in the United States. Yet modest ship-to-shore optical telegraphs were established in several cities. The first optical telegraph in the United States went into operation in 1801; 72 miles in length, it linked the North Atlantic shipping lanes with Boston. This venture was abandoned in 1807, a victim of the commercial dislocations that followed President Thomas Jefferson's embargo of overseas trade.[39] Another early optical telegraph linked the North Atlantic shipping lanes with New York City. Chronically underfunded, it gained fleeting renown during the War of 1812 when it warned nervous New Yorkers of the nearby presence of a hostile British frigate.[40]

The most successful optical telegraphs to be built in the United States were established in New York City and Boston in the years immediately following the War of 1812. The New York City telegraph was established by Reid, and the Boston telegraph by John R. Parker. Each transmitted messages to the city from the offing, the furthest point on the horizon that was visible by telescope. The final destination for each was a specially designated room in the downtown business district known as the "exchange." The mainstay of the business was time-sensitive information on ship arrivals. In the fifteen-month period between October 1833 and December 1834, Parker's optical telegraph reported the arrival in Boston harbor of 2,104 vessels.[41] Each arrival was duly recorded in a bound book, after it had been telegraphed from the shipping lanes to Parker's Boston office by way of an elaborate numerical code that could be deciphered using Parker's *United States Telegraph Vocabulary*, a 12,000-phrase compendium of common expressions used at sea.[42] Both telegraphs relied for funding primarily on an annual user fee. In return for the payment of this fee, users—primarily marine insurers, merchants, ship owners, and journalists—obtained access to the information the telegraph conveyed.[43]

The optical telegraph presented electric telegraph promoters with an obvious challenge. How would they differentiate their invention from a medium that already existed? One promoter floated the name "Morsegraph" in honor of telegraph inventor Samuel F. B. Morse.[44] Most people retained the older name—"telegraph"—at least in part to trade on its familiarity. To avoid confusion, electric telegraph promoters highlighted the novel motive power of the new medium and its superior reliability. The new medium, they contended, was an "electric telegraph," an "electro-magnetic telegraph," or a "recording telegraph." The qualifier "recording" highlighted the ability of the electric telegraph to generate a transcript automatically, a feature that, though soon abandoned, was always regarded by Morse as an essential element of his invention.

Optical telegraphers confronted the analogous challenge of distinguishing their medium from its electrical rival. To highlight this distinction, they borrowed from the British the word "semaphore," which had been coined during the Napoleonic wars to describe an optical signaling method used primarily by ships at sea.[45]

The U.S.-based optical telegraphs left little imprint on the popular imagination. In fact, in 1928, one government administrator went so far as to erroneously contend that none had ever been built.[46] Even so, their memory lives on today in place names such as San Francisco's "Telegraph Hill."

While the optical telegraph quickly gave way to the electric telegraph, the mail was a more enduring rival. The mail assumed its modern form in the years immediately following the enactment of the Post Office Act of 1792, a landmark in American communications and one of the most far-reaching pieces of legislation enacted in the early republic. This law established several precedents assuring that the mandate of the Post Office Department would be broad, dynamic, and open-ended. In particular, it hastened the rapid extension of the mail into the hinterland and the large-scale conveyance through the mail of newspapers and magazines, then the principal source of time-sensitive information on public affairs. Each of these innovations was expensive, and as long as the mail remained self-sustaining, each was paid for by patrons through an elaborate array of spatial and format-based cross-subsidies. The existence of these cross-subsidies helps to explain why many contemporaries characterized the mail as a "system": like Henry Clay's "American system," the mail system balanced different interests to perpetuate the union.

Since the Second World War, the word "information" has acquired a wealth of meaning that no contemporary in 1840 or even 1920 could possibly have anticipated. Indeed, an entire branch of scientific inquiry, known as information theory, has emerged to define its properties and to predict its behavior. For many scientists, information has become, like energy and matter, a fundamental building block of the natural world. "I think of my lifetime in physics" as being divided into three periods, observed one eminent physicist in his memoir: in the first phase, everything was particles; in the second, everything was fields; and now he was "in the grip of a new vision, that Everything is Information."[47]

In the early republic, the meaning of the word "information" was less expansive. It referred neither to data regarding natural phenomena nor even to the insights that one might glean from a book. Rather, it denoted the time-sensitive "intelligence" about public affairs and market trends that was commonly called news. Information was news for a spatially dispersed population that would never meet face to face; its circulation presupposed the establishment of institutional arrangements to keep this population well informed.[48]

For most of human history, political, religious, and military leaders have labored mightily, often with considerable success, to prevent ordinary people from securing access to information about the wider world. Few indeed were the individuals who—like the sixteenth-century Spanish monarch, Philip II—could plausibly be said to have suffered from "information overload."[49] Not until the sixteenth century would large numbers of laypeople successfully challenge the authority of the Catholic Church to limit their access to the Bible. And as late as the eighteenth century, the suppression of popular access to information about public affairs remained a cornerstone of government policy in France.[50]

The founders of the United States chose a different path. If the people were sovereign, as the federal Constitution proclaimed, then it seemed indisputable that the government had an obligation to provide them with regular broadcasts on public affairs from the seat of power. No longer was access to information about public affairs a privilege; rather, it now became a right, or, more precisely, a practical necessity for a government whose legitimacy rested in the sovereignty of the people. The mail, declared one lawmaker in 1792, had been established for "no other purpose" than the "conveyance of information" into "every part of the Union."[51]

The circulation of information in a country as spatially extensive as the United States entailed the establishment of a large-scale enterprise, or what sociologists call a bureaucracy. In the United States, this bureaucracy was the Post Office Department, a government agency that, early on, was often known as simply the "Post Office," the "Post," or the "Mail."

The federal government's mandate to circulate information was seldom questioned; on only rare occasions was it even debated. At least in part this was because contemporaries presumed the benefits of information circulation to be not only political but also economic. To stimulate the desire for exchange, explained the American political economist Francis Wayland in the first edition of an influential textbook published in 1837, lawmakers had at their disposal only a limited number of tools. Among the most effective was legislation to foster the physical means for the "dissemination of knowledge and intelligence" through the establishment of an "efficient and cheap post office system" that should pervade every portion of the country and bring to "every man's door" all of the "information" that was circulating "throughout the civilized world."[52]

The Post Office Department's mandate proved to be remarkably capacious. In 1857, for example, Illinois senator Stephen A. Douglas invoked it to support federal funding for a transatlantic telegraph. The proposed legislation was a "post office arrangement," Douglas explained: "It is for the transmission of intelligence, and that is what I understand to be the function of the Post Office Department."[53] A few years later, Ohio congressman James A. Garfield invoked this mandate to justify a congressional buyout of the entire telegraph network. Should Congress conclude that it was expedient to graft the telegraph network onto the Post Office Department, Garfield would not object, since the telegraph was in the "line of transmitting intelligence," which he took to be the object of the Post Office Department.[54]

The civic mandate for the mail presupposed an intricate set of cross-subsidies to facilitate the low-cost circulation of newspapers and magazines throughout the length and breadth of the United States. The "complete transmission" of "intelligence" to the "most distant points," reflected jurist C. C. Nott in 1873, was one of the "conditions of civilization." Should lawmakers eliminate these cross-subsidies, Nott feared for the future: "One could hardly imagine what would be the condition of national affairs, if the greater part of our population, cut off from letters and newspapers, knew little more of the affairs in Washington than the returning members chose to tell them." The Post Office Department could never be dispensed with. Echoing Wayland, Nott termed it the "one agency of government" that came "impartially" to "every man's door."[55]

Postal cross-subsidies elicited little public debate, primarily because they were uncontroversial. The tax that a large proportion of Americans paid every time they sent a letter, explained one government statistician in 1900, had the "unanimous approval" of the people, since it was widely understood to be necessary to ensure that access to "intelligence" would be cheap and convenient in localities in which remunerative rates were prohibitively high. There was "scarcely a scintilla of evidence" that New Yorkers objected to the transfer of postage generated in New York to cover the cost of mail delivery in Texas and Alaska, even though New Yorkers paid far more in postage than they received in postal facilities.[56] The "post office principle," explained political economist Henry C. Adams in 1918, in summarizing what had by that time become the conventional wisdom, subsidized different sections and classes to provide every citizen with access to the mail "on equal terms."[57]

The kinds of information that the Post Office Department had a civic mandate to circulate repeatedly expanded. In the 1790s, this mandate was confined primarily to information on public affairs; by 1825, it embraced information on market trends. It was "essential" to the "reputation of the mail," declared Postmaster General John McLean in defending this new mandate, for the Post Office Department to convey newspapers as rapidly as letters.[58] Newspapers carried time-sensitive information on the price of agricultural staples in overseas markets; McLean presumed that the federal government had an obligation to ensure that the owners of agricultural staples obtained up-to-date information about the value of their crops. "On all the principles of fair dealing," the "holder of property should be apprised of its value before he parts with it." Should the Post Office Department fail to outpace private carriers, speculators could purchase agricultural staples from producers at prices far below the going European rate. And this was unfair. For a speculator to purchase an article at "one-half or two-thirds of its value" on the basis of information known to the buyer, yet "carefully concealed from the seller," was "in opposition" both to the "principles of law and sound morality."[59]

McLean's gospel of speed raised thorny legal issues for the promoters of communications media intent on outpacing the mail. Judges routinely prosecuted merchants under common law for shady business practices. Now that McLean had committed the Post Office Department to outpacing private carriers, it suddenly seemed plausible for a litigant to accuse the proprietor of a high-speed mail carrier—such as, for example, a horse express or an electric telegraph—for conspiring against trade. It was "unquestionably" true, declared one early telegraph historian, in reflecting on an abortive electric telegraph built by inventor Harrison G. Dyar in 1827, that Dyar had abandoned the project when threatened with prosecution for circulating information "in advance of the mail."[60] Public outrage at insider trading had been inflamed by the recent conspiracy trial of a prominent New York banker, and it was hard to predict whom the courts might go after next. "Public prejudice" against the transmission of "secret intelligence" was intense, Dyar reminisced, while many of his friends had warned him that his electric telegraph was "not a lawful enterprise."[61]

McLean's gospel of speed posed a major operational challenge. Newspapers were heavy, and their conveyance was expensive. Even so, sympathetic lawmakers remained undeterred. It "should not be permitted"— proclaimed Tennessee senator Felix Grundy in 1835, in justifying a Post Office Department horse express—for an individual to establish a "mode of communication" by which "intelligence" could be "received and acted upon" by him before the "community at large" could have the "benefit of

it" through the "medium of the government mails."[62] This new, more capacious mandate for the mail received a legal imprimatur in 1843 when
the attorney general issued an open letter in which he explicitly defined
the news to embrace information not only on public affairs but also on all
manner of "passing events," including market trends.[63]

Not everyone approved. The high-speed circulation of information
was expensive, and its benefits redounded to the few. "The design of the
post," contended Portsmouth, New Hampshire, postmaster Jeremiah
Libbey in 1792, was "for the convenience of the inhabitants of the state
in general" and the larger the number of persons it accommodated the
better it answered the "end design'd." In writing specifications for mail
contracts, it would be undesirable to confine mail contactors to the
densely settled coastal town. "Expedition," Libbey postulated, was "not
of equal consequence with convenience," and lawmakers should instruct
the contractors to follow whatever route served the "largest number of
inhabitants," even if the route happened to be circuitous and slow.[64]

The high speed–limited access trade-off received detailed attention in a
thoughtful essay on the "post office system" that Congregationalist minister Leonard Bacon published in 1843. The proper mandate of the Post
Office Department, Bacon contended, was the "equal accommodations" of
"all the members" of society. It was "not necessary" for the mail to "out-
strip every possible conveyance." The speed of the "most rapid ordinary
traveling" on a given route was all the public required: "If a more rapid
transmission is attempted, it will be found that cheapness is sacrificed to
speed, and the mail, instead of affording equal accommodations to all the
members of society, is a convenience only to those who can afford to pay
high postage."[65]

The commercialization of the electric telegraph as a private enterprise
doomed McLean's gospel of speed. Yet it did nothing to diminish Bacon's
conviction that the federal government had a civic mandate to provide
"equal accommodations" to the entire population. In the years to come,
this mandate would prove remarkably enduring. Throughout the entire
"civilized world," explained one close student of postal affairs in 1869,
the transportation of the mail was an exclusive government monopoly,
for the "simple reason" that no statutes could so "regulate and control the
institution in private hands" as to give "fit and proper accommodation,
confidence, and security to the public."[66] In the United States, "proper accommodation" remained the ideal. "It is difficult," observed one political
commentator in 1874, to "get too exaggerated an idea of the vastness of

this great governmental institution for the diffusion of intelligence among the people."[67] The Post Office Department, exulted essayist Edward Everett Hale in 1891, was the "most majestic system of public education which was ever set on foot anywhere."[68]

In the formative era of American telecommunications, network building followed no single logic and had no fixed destination. Network builders highlighted certain organizational forms and ignored others. Only occasionally did they make analogies with networks that—like the telegraph and the telephone—relied on electricity as a motive power. Electric telegraph network builders had no electrical prototype and drew inspiration from the optical telegraph, package carriage, and the mail. Telephone network builders combined organizational forms derived from the telegraph, the mail, the gaslight plant, and the electric power station.

Enthusiasm is an emotional trait that is rarely associated with network building. Yet it aptly characterized the mind-set not only of the inventors of the telegraph and the telephone but also of the network builders who scaled up their inventions into self-sustaining innovations. The construction of a global telegraph network pitted Hiram Sibley and Cyrus Field against each other in an epic contest. The transformation of the nationwide telegraph network into an enduring institution consumed William Orton. The popularization of the telephone inspired in Angus Hibbard an almost evangelical zeal. The consolidation of every known electrical communications medium in a single interactive network became for Theodore N. Vail an unrealized dream. Enthusiasts like Sibley, Field, Orton, Hibbard, and Vail promoted not only profit-making business ventures but also visions of the future. For these virtuosos, as well as for the many others who followed their lead, network building transcended mere material considerations and became an epic quest to remake the world.

2

PROFESSOR MORSE'S LIGHTNING

This power of giving thought the distinctive, legible embodiment of language from any given point to any other given point in the Union, however distant, INSTANTANEOUSLY, is indeed sublime, and worthy the adoption of an energetic government like our own.

Francis O. J. Smith, 1845

In February 1837, Treasury secretary Levi Woodbury requested information from the "most intelligent sources" to help him prepare a report to Congress on the propriety of establishing a "system of telegraphs" for the United States. Of the eighteen responses that Woodbury received, seventeen assumed that the telegraph would be optical and that its motive power would be human. This had been Woodbury's assumption and also the assumption of Samuel C. Reid, the optical telegrapher whose petition to Congress had set in motion the chain of events that led to Woodbury's request. The only respondent to envision a different motive power was Samuel F. B. Morse, a painter-turned-professor who had been long intrigued by the moral implications of technical advance. Morse proposed, instead, a new kind of telegraph of his own devising that would transmit information not by sight but, rather, by electrical impulses transmitted by wire.[1]

Woodbury's request inspired Morse to build a demonstration project, which Morse completed in May 1844. Morse's project took the form of a 40-mile electric telegraph line between Washington, D.C., and Baltimore. The line was funded by Congress, which had awarded Morse a $30,000 grant the previous year. Morse's telegraph was not the first of its kind. By May 1844, the British telegraph promoters Charles Wheatstone and William F. Cooke had installed special-purpose electric telegraphs on several railroads in Great Britain. Yet the Washington–Baltimore line was the first electric telegraph in the United States. Following its transfer to the Post Office Department in 1845, it became the first electrical communications network in the world to be open to the public on a fee-for-service basis. Although the future disposition of Morse's invention remained uncertain, it was hailed from the outset as an epochal technical advance that was destined to have vast consequences for American business, politics, and public life.

The history of Morse's demonstration project is a case study in the unanticipated consequences of technological innovation. Morse had neither the inclination nor the temperament to scale up his demonstration project into a spatially extensive network. Rather, he conceived of himself as an inventor who owned the rights to a valuable invention for which he hoped to find a suitable buyer. The rights Morse owned were the rights that he had obtained from the Patent Office for a patent he had been granted for his invention in 1840. The buyer that Morse had in mind was Congress. If Morse had prevailed, the demonstration project that Congress transferred to the Post Office Department in 1845 would have become the first link in a spatially extensive telegraph network built around Morse's 1840 patent. It may seem odd that the owner of the patent rights to an invention widely hailed by contemporaries as a powerful agent of change would try to sell his invention to Congress so that it might be commercialized by a federal government agency. Yet this was what happened. The very extravagance of the claims advanced on behalf of Morse's invention strengthened the case for federal control. A congressional buyout of Morse's patent rights had the endorsement not only of Morse, but also of Morse's primary financial backers; the patent commissioner; several of the country's most influential newspapers; and a smattering of lawmakers, including the 1844 Whig presidential contender, Henry Clay. Only after Morse had failed to sell his patent rights to Congress would the telegraph become a quintessential private enterprise. This was an eventuality that Morse had worked to forestall for almost a decade and that would continue to trouble thoughtful critics of the telegraph business from the 1840s until the First World War.

Morse's faith in federal control was a corollary of certain assumptions that he made about how his invention would be scaled up from a demonstration project into a spatially extensive network. Like all inventors,

Morse relied on analogies between the known and the unknown. In envisioning how his telegraph would be operated, he compared it with two long-distance communications networks with which he was familiar: the French optical telegraph and the American mail. Both of these networks enjoyed a panoply of special privileges that included a legally protected monopoly over the circulation of information on market trends, and so Morse assumed, by no means implausibly, that his telegraph should too.

The French optical telegraph and the American mail were not the only organizational forms Morse might have chosen. The American optical telegraphs in New York City and Boston also circulated information at high speeds, as did the package carriers that sprang up on the highly trafficked routes in New England the Mid-Atlantic states following the Panic of 1837. So too did the British electric telegraphs. Yet Morse never seriously considered any of these organizational forms, presumably because of his conviction that his telegraph should remain under federal control: the American optical telegraphs and package carriers were proprietorships and the British electric telegraphs were private corporations. Morse proved equally reluctant to award territorial licenses for his patent rights to operators other than the federal government. Every early licensing agreement to which Morse assented included a clause requiring the licensee to sell its assets to Congress should Congress agree to buy Morse out.

The French optical telegraph had intrigued Morse ever since he had observed it firsthand during a visit to France in the early 1830s. To demonstrate the superiority of his telegraph over its optical precursor, Morse assumed that it must, at a minimum, transmit a signal to a receiver over a distance of 10 miles; "visual telegraphs," as his assistant Alfred Vail explained, were "usually at that distance apart."[2] Once Morse attained this performance standard, he set out to invent a machine to relay signals from receiver to receiver, by analogy with the French optical telegraph, which employed human operators known as "mutes" or "telegraphs" to manually relay signals from tower to tower.

To solve this problem, Morse invented an electromagnetic relay, which contemporaries and historians of technology alike regard as his most significant technical feat.[3] Morse's invention mimicked the work of the "mutes" by automatically relaying a signal from receiver to receiver. Had Morse known nothing about the French optical telegraph, he would still have had to find some way to relay signals over vast distances. Yet it was the French optical telegraph that provided him with the mental map that he relied on to surmount this technical challenge.

Morse's familiarity with the French optical telegraph also helps to explain his single most disastrous misjudgment in building his demonstration project, namely, his decision to bury wires without adequate knowledge of insulation. Not until after this experiment had failed would Morse string wires overhead, establishing a precedent that would soon be emulated throughout the United States.

The vulnerability of overhead wires to sabotage was a favorite theme of Ennemond Gonon, a French optical telegraph expert who had also responded to Woodbury's request for information in 1837.[4] Gonon's warning echoed Morse's own concerns. Morse freely conceded that it would be cheaper to string wires overhead, yet he denied that the resulting cost-savings counterbalanced the risk that "mischievously disposed persons" might "injure the circuit."[5] Morse's misgivings were reinforced in the late 1830s by a Russian official's objections to Morse's proposal to build for the czar an electric telegraph linking Moscow and Warsaw. Although Morse's telegraph might be faster than an optical telegraph, it was harder to protect against sabotage. This was a decisive disadvantage, given the uncertain loyalty of the population through whose territory it would traverse.[6]

Morse's fear of sabotage was exacerbated by a habit of mind that he inherited from his father Jedidiah. Like Jedidiah, Samuel was haunted by the specter that insidious conspirators were subverting the republic. And like his father, Samuel presumed that he had an obligation to alert his countrymen to the danger that these conspirators posed. Countersubversion was a Morse family tradition: Jedidiah had published sermons warning about a notorious cabal of European freethinkers known as the Bavarian illuminati; Samuel raised the alarm about reactionary Catholic priests and fanatical abolitionists. Telegraph saboteurs were but one more peril that Samuel felt impelled to combat.[7]

For Morse to translate electrical impulses into intelligible messages, he had to adopt a signaling code. Like the operators of the French optical telegraph, he had two basic choices. He could adopt an alphabetical code that substituted symbols for letters, or a numerical code that substituted symbols for words and phrases.

French optical telegraphers rejected alphabetical codes as outmoded, and, initially, Morse did too. Alphabetical codes, explained the Boston optical telegrapher John R. Parker in 1832, in articulating a common view, were slow and clumsy, whereas numerical codes eliminated the "tedious process of spelling."[8] Determined to emulate the best practice among optical telegraphers, Morse spent many months in the winter of 1837 devising a numerical code that featured 30,000 different combinations. Morse alluded to a numerical code in the preliminary patent for his telegraph that he obtained in 1837 and used a numerical code in the first public demonstration of his telegraph in the Capitol in 1838.[9] The first telegraph message that Morse sent on this occasion was "The enemy is near," a martial warning suggested by President Martin Van Buren and included by Morse in his numerical codebook.[10] Morse could presumably have emulated Parker and licensed the numerical code that had been patented by James M. Elford.[11] Yet Morse did not, conceivably because he had hoped to generate revenue from a numerical code of his own devising.

Alphabetical codes had their defenders, and by 1844 Morse concluded that certain of their features made them especially well suited for his telegraph. To designate letters, numbers, and punctuation marks, he employed two kinds of signals: a short signal, or dot, and a long signal, or dash. To minimize transmission delays, Morse's assistant Alfred Vail studied the distribution of letters in a printer's case and assigned the simplest signals to the most commonly used letters. Morse was not the first to translate the alphabet into binary signals, having been anticipated by the eighteenth-century German scholar Johann Bergsträsser.[12] Yet Morse's binary code was the first to be widely adopted. Its most obvious advantage was flexibility. A binary code was not restricted to the entries in a numerical codebook, but could transmit any message that could be rendered in an alphabetical form. Morse relied on his alphabetical code to send the first message over the newly completed Washington–Baltimore line, the biblical exhortation "What Hath God Wrought." The paper tape on which this message was embossed remains today among Morse's papers at the Library of Congress.

For telegraphers in the United States and abroad, the mastery of Morse's binary code quickly became a point of pride.[13] With minor modifications, it survived the transition from wired to wireless telegraphy, and it was widely adopted in the early twentieth century by wireless telegraphers around the world. The familiar maritime distress signal "S.O.S."—which, in Morse's code, was rendered by three dots, three dashes, and three dots—remained the worldwide wireless standard until 1999. Morse's code became so well known that it may help explain his posthumous reputation as an eponymous inventor. That is, Morse's renown may have owed as much to his association with a telegraphic language—the "Morse code"—as to his invention of the equipment for which this language had been devised. Morse code was relatively easy to learn and facilitated the proliferation of specialized cipher codes, a major consideration for users worried about confidentiality. Unfortunately for Morse, it did not require the publication of a proprietary codebook, the sale of which, in other circumstances, might have provided Morse with a steady income.

Although Morse looked to the optical telegraph as a prototype for his electric telegraph, he never doubted the superiority of the electric telegraph as a means of communication. The optical telegraph was confined to daylight and favorable atmospheric conditions; the electric telegraph could operate night and day and in any kind of weather.[14] Morse also assumed that his telegraph was faster, a presumption that, early on, was not necessarily true.[15]

The most decisive advantage of the electric telegraph over the optical telegraph for Morse was neither its superior speed nor even its superior reliability. Rather, it was its transparency. Morse's receiver included a stylus that imprinted dots and dashes onto a moving paper tape. Although these imprints remained coded, they left a permanent record, and, for Morse, this was what mattered. The literal meaning of the word "tele-graph," he never tired of repeating, was "writing-at-a-distance": by this definition, the optical telegraph was not a telegraph at all. The decisive advantage of Morse's telegraph over that of its rivals, explained his official biographer, was its combination of the "grandeur" of the "thought of writing" with a thousand-mile-long pen: "the thought of a postal system without the element of time."[16]

In theory, Morse's receiver automatically generated a perfect transcription of every telegraph message; in practice, it was slow, often malfunctioned, and was quietly abandoned. The vast majority of all the messages sent on Morse equipment by the 1850s generated no permanent record and were decoded exclusively by sound.[17]

The superiority of the electric telegraph over the optical telegraph was for Morse not only technical but also political. The medium was the message: the optical telegraph was monarchical, the electric telegraph republican. The optical telegraph was "in harmony" with the "genius" of a monarchy like France in which the government was sovereign and lawmakers all-powerful, since its carrying capacity was so limited that its operators restricted its facilities to official dispatches: "Were our mails used solely for the purposes of the government and private individuals forbidden to correspond by them, they would furnish a good illustration of the operation of the common [optical] European telegraphic systems." The electric telegraph, in contrast, was well suited to a republic like the United States, in which the people were sovereign and lawmakers' powers limited, because its carrying capacity was large enough to make its facilities accessible to the entire population. The superior carrying capacity of the electric telegraph was one of the two main reasons that Morse dubbed it the "American telegraph," the other reason being that a native-born American (that is, Morse himself) had been its inventor. Unlike the optical telegraph, the electric telegraph was "more in consonance" with the country's civic ideals because, like the mail system, it could "diffuse its benefits alike" to the many and the few.[18]

The affinities Morse discerned between his telegraph and the mail extended beyond their carrying capacity. The electric telegraph, he believed, was but "another mode" of accomplishing the "principal object" for which the Post Office Department had been established: that is, the "rapid and regular transmission of intelligence." The *mail system* had been founded on the "universally admitted principle" that the "greater the speed" with which "intelligence" could be transmitted from point to point, the greater the benefit to the "whole community." The only question that remained, therefore, was: which of the two modes of communication—the mail or the telegraph—was "best calculated" to "effect this desirable end?"[19]

The postal-telegraphic analogy shaped Morse's understanding of how the federal government would operate his telegraph network if Congress bought him out. If Congress wished, it could emulate the French and establish a special-purpose telegraph network that was restricted to the circulation of official dispatches.[20] Yet it would be unrepublican if the Post Office Department did not also operate a parallel public telegraph network that was open to the entire population. Morse's commitment to open access is worth recalling because historians have mistakenly conflated Morse's support for a government telegraph with the presumption that the telegraph should be used exclusively for government communications.

While Morse lobbied Congress to put the telegraph under federal control, he rejected the corollary that it should be operated exclusively by a government agency. Rather, he envisioned a hybrid public–private network that combined government ownership of Morse's patent rights with corporate ownership of individual telegraph lines. Although the ownership of the network would rest with the Post Office Department, its operation would devolve upon territorially based "private telegraphs" that held licenses from the Post Office Department regulating their rate structure, development strategy, and performance standards. Government ownership invested Congress with the authority to regulate telegraph corporations; private operation encouraged a "general competition" between would-be licensees that would hasten network expansion. Given the "enterprising character" of the American people, it was not "visionary" to suppose that before long the entire country would be "channeled" for those *"nerves"* that were to "diffuse" with the "speed of thought" a knowledge of everything occurring "throughout the land."[21]

Morse's vision built on long-standing assumptions about how best to coordinate a spatially extensive enterprise in a country in which authority remained divided between the federal government and the states. Precursors included the territorially based licensing arrangements that inventors relied on to commercialize their patent rights and the contracting protocols that postal administrators had adopted to transport the mail. Although Morse's plan was not implemented, it prefigured the regulations that the Federal Communications Commission devised in the twentieth century to regulate radio and television.

Morse admired the "enterprising character" of the American people, but he feared the evils that would ensue should Congress fail to put the telegraph under federal control. Only the federal government could ensure the proper coordination of the network and guard against speculative abuse. Federal control actually furnished the *only* preventive of the "evil effects" certain to ensue if the telegraph became a "monopoly of a company."[22] Should Congress decline to purchase his patent rights, this "instrument of immense power" would almost certainly become a tool for speculators intent on defrauding the public by using their exclusive access to advance information on market trends to purchase agricultural staples at below-market rates. And when then they did, the telegraph would become the means of enriching a "corporation" at the cost of the "bankruptcy of thousands."[23]

Morse's fear of the telegraph's "immense power" extended even to federal control. If a corporation's monopolization of the telegraph threatened the bankruptcy of thousands, its operation as an exclusive government agency also risked "vast mischief" to the republic. Only a hybrid public–private network that combined the oversight of federal control with the energy of private enterprise could guarantee the "checks and preventives of abuse" necessary to prevent the misuse of this "otherwise dangerous power."[24]

For Morse, federal control also had a personal dimension. Morse had supported himself for many years as an artist, which meant, in practice, that he obtained the bulk of his income by painting the portraits of wealthy patrons. Like many nineteenth-century artists, Morse yearned for a lucrative government grant that would permit him to undertake a more ambitious composition. Shortly before he lobbied Congress to fund his demonstration project, he had tried unsuccessfully to obtain a commission from Congress to paint a monumental tableau for the Capitol rotunda depicting the landing of the Pilgrims. Morse was bitterly disappointed by his failure to obtain this commission and hoped for better luck as an inventor. His telegraph was, as it were, his latest masterpiece that, for a suitable honorarium, he would share with a grateful world.

Morse's preoccupation with federal control may seem idiosyncratic and even bizarre. After all, it is widely assumed that the federal government in the early republic was either weak or nonexistent. This assumption says more about historians' preconceptions about the nineteenth-century political economy than it does about the political economy in Morse's day. In fact, Morse's priorities echoed, and were almost certainly indebted to, a related proposal presented to Congress in 1837 by Samuel C. Reid, the optical telegrapher whose trial balloon had first brought Morse's invention to public attention.

Reid's proposal took the form of an open letter to Congress in which he urged Congress to build a chain of optical telegraphs linking New York City and New Orleans. Reid sent his open letter in January 1837 on the eve of Martin Van Buren's inauguration. Reid and Van Buren were both New Yorkers, and Reid seems to have assumed that the incoming president would find merit in his ideas. The optical telegraph that Reid proposed was basically a scaled-up version of the optical telegraph that Reid himself had established in 1821 to link the North Atlantic shipping lanes to New York City. When built, Reid predicted that his New York City–New Orleans optical telegraph could transmit a twenty-word message from New York City to Washington in twenty-five minutes and from Washington to New Orleans in under two hours.[25]

Reid was the first prophet of telegraph regulation. It was Reid, and not Morse, who first popularized the convention that the telegraph should come under federal control, and it was Reid who proposed that the telegraph, like the mail, should be open to the public under the jurisdiction of the Post Office Department on a fee-for-service basis. When Reid sent his letter to Congress, the Post Office Department was running a large annual surplus, raising the possibility that Reid's New York City–New Orleans line would not require an appropriation from the general treasury. "The rapid diffusion of intelligence" was of "great importance" in "our busy country," declared Postmaster General Amos Kendall, in endorsing Reid's proposal, while a "portion" of the country's "abundant public funds" could not be "more usefully employed" than in the "attainment" by the government of that object.[26]

Reid is forgotten today, yet in the early republic he enjoyed a formidable reputation as a military hero. As the captain of an armed brig during the War of 1812, he launched a courageous assault on a flotilla of three British warships in the Portuguese port of Fayal. Reid's assault was widely credited with playing a critical role in Andrew Jackson's victory at the battle of New Orleans, a huge symbolic victory that helped propel Jackson to the presidency in 1828. Had Reid not killed and wounded so many British soldiers, contemporaries believed, the flotilla would have crossed the Atlantic several days earlier and the British army would have taken New Orleans long before Andrew Jackson's troops "by any possibility" could have arrived. The fact that Reid's brig was a privateer licensed to prey on British merchant shipping rather than a naval vessel outfitted for armed combat only made his conduct all the more meritorious.[27]

Reid's wartime exploits led Congress to honor him with the privilege of redesigning the American flag, which, then as now, consisted of an array of stars and stripes. Like the naval pennants that the British fleet had recently adopted, or the optical telegraph signals that Reid would design soon thereafter for his ship-to-shore optical telegraph in New York City, Reid's American flag was intended to be easily recognizable from afar, an important consideration for ships at sea. To improve its legibility, Reid arranged the stars into a single five-point cluster and reduced the number of stripes to thirteen. Congress rejected Reid's five-point cluster, yet approved his stripe proposal, a fixture of the American flag ever since.[28]

Reid's renown helps explain why Morse met with little resistance when Morse recommended that the federal government operate the electric telegraph just as it operated the mail. Yet even had Reid never petitioned Congress, Morse's recommendation still would not have been surprising. The mandate of the Post Office Department over the circulation of information was broad, dynamic, and open-ended, and since 1825 had come to embrace the circulation of information at the highest possible speed. Under the circumstances, it would have been more of an innovation to operate the telegraph as a private enterprise than as a government agency. The gospel of speed was so uncontroversial that, in the period between the opening of the Washington–Baltimore line in 1845 and the first congressional debate on the merits of a congressional buyout in the following year, only one prominent journalist and a handful of lawmakers questioned the wisdom of retaining federal control over the electric telegraph.

The public–private telegraph that Morse envisioned hinged on a congressional buyout of Morse's patent. And this was not easily arranged. Morse's invention was novel, untested, and easily ridiculed. Postmaster General Charles Wickliffe felt so certain that Morse's demonstration project would fail that he pointedly refrained from mentioning it in either of the two annual reports that he prepared when the Washington–Baltimore line remained under his jurisdiction.[29]

Prior to obtaining his congressional grant, Morse had relied for funding on a small number of investors. His first financial backers were New Jersey ironmaster Stephen Vail and Maine congressman Francis O. J. Smith. Vail loaned Morse money and permitted Morse to experiment with electrical transmission at a factory complex that Vail owned in Morristown, New Jersey. He had learned about Morse's invention from his son Alfred, who had met Morse while attending New York University, where Morse held a faculty appointment as a professor of design. Alfred soon became Morse's assistant. Smith first encountered Morse in 1838, when Morse made his initial request for government funding. Smith chaired the House committee to which Morse's request had been referred, and prepared a glowing report on the potential of Morse's invention in an unsuccessful bid to obtain congressional funding for a demonstration project. To formalize his relationship with his backers, Morse divided his venture into sixteen shares: nine for Morse, four for Smith, and two for the Vails. The remaining share went to Leonard Gale, a chemist at New York University who had provided Morse with technical advice. Henceforth, Morse and his backers became known as the Morse proprietors; their principal asset was the patent rights that Morse had obtained in 1840.[30]

Like most proprietorships, the proprietorship that Morse established with Smith, the Vails, and Gale presupposed that no proprietor could make a major decision without obtaining the assent from every other proprietor. Morse rarely encountered dissent from the Vails or Gale; Smith, however, was more independent-minded. Had Morse and Smith not been business partners, these differences might have been finessed. Yet they *were* business partners, and, thus, from a legal standpoint they were joined at the hip, a circumstance that would cause them both a great deal of grief in the years to come.

Had Morse lived in Great Britain, he could probably have obtained all the funding he needed from private investors. In 1845, for example, a consortium of venture capitalists purchased a major stake in the Wheatstone–Cooke telegraph for £115,000 in the expectation that they would license it to British railways for a sizable fee.[31] In the United States, however, venture capital was scarce. Under the circumstances, Congress was one of the only organizations in the country—public or private—to which Morse could plausibly turn to buy him out.

Morse recruited Smith shortly before Smith delivered his report on Morse's invention, making Smith Morse's publicist. Smith's effectiveness was enhanced by the fact that his financial interest in Morse's invention remained secret. Although the Morse–Smith agreement was known to certain lawmakers as early as 1845, it would not become generally known until a disaffected telegraph promoter exposed it in 1848.

The Morse–Smith agreement yoked together two men with very different priorities. Morse expected to be handsomely remunerated for his invention, but his overriding goal was not fortune but fame. He yearned to be immortalized as a civic benefactor whose technical advance had fostered moral progress. Unlike Morse, Smith hungered for wealth and was determined to make as much money out of Morse's invention as he could. During the difficult winter of 1843–1844, when the future of the Washington–Baltimore demonstration project remained in doubt, the two business partners found themselves embroiled in a bitter dispute that would haunt them for the rest of their lives.

Smith knew nothing about electricity. Yet he had long worked as a journalist and understood the power of publicity, or what a later generation would call hype. In particular, he had mastered the fine art of filling a printed page with grandiose rhetoric that was emotionally compelling and politically astute. Should Morse's invention prove a success, Smith predicted in his 1838 congressional report, it would hasten a "revolution" that was "unsurpassed" in "moral grandeur" by any prior discovery in the arts and sciences from the "most distant period" to which "authentic history extends" to the present day.[32] The presumption that a mere technical advance could hasten moral progress would have struck many, if not most, Americans in the 1830s as implausible and even blasphemous.[33] Smith lent it credibility by invoking a religious metaphor that had intuitive appeal for the many lawmakers who viewed the world through an evangelical lens. If Morse's invention worked as Morse had contended, it would invest human beings for the first time with the "HIGH ATTRIBUTE OF UBIQUITY"—an awesome power that had been previously the exclusive prerogative of God and that the human mind had hardly dared to contemplate out of an "instinctive feeling" of "religious reverence" toward a power of "such awful grandeur."[34]

Morse relied on Smith not only as a publicist, but also as a promoter. The nature of their relationship shone forth in the sheaf of plaintive letters that Morse wrote Smith during a fund-raising trip that Morse took to Europe in 1839. "I am at a loss how to act," Morse confessed at one point: "I fear that I am a child in business matters. I can invent and perfect the invention, and demonstrate its use and practicality, but 'further the deponent saith not.' "[35]

Morse's reliance on Smith increased after Morse obtained congressional funding for his demonstration project in 1843. Morse, lacking the business acumen to oversee the construction of the Washington–Baltimore line, appointed Smith as his general contractor. Smith's first assignment was to bury the telegraph wires underground. Terrified of sabotage, Morse was unwilling to risk the possibility that the wires might be disrupted if he strung them overhead.

Smith did his best to follow Morse's directive. To bury the wires, Smith recruited Ezra Cornell, an itinerant plow salesman whom Smith had met in Maine. Although Cornell knew no more about electricity than Smith did, he had a good grasp of the fundamentals of trenching and quickly built a serviceable wire-laying plow. While Cornell's plow worked, the insulation sheathing the wires did not, rendering the wires useless. This put Morse in a quandary. How could he bury telegraph wires underground if he lacked an effective method of insulation? Unable to answer this question, Morse threw caution to the wind and in early 1844 instructed Cornell to string the wire overhead.[36]

Demonstration projects rarely go as planned, and Morse's wire-laying misadventure might seem to have been a minor setback. For Smith, however, it was a disaster. Smith had spent a large sum of money on a fine team of horses that he had ostensibly purchased to help Cornell lay wire. In actual fact, Smith intended to take the horses home with him to Maine to impress his neighbors once the demonstration project had been completed. Now that Morse had abandoned the underground method, Smith might have to pay for the horses himself. The Treasury Department, Smith predicted correctly, would never pay him the $6,000 that he claimed to be owed. When Smith implored Morse to intercede on his behalf at the Treasury Department, Morse refused: partly because he deplored Smith's prodigality, and partly because he feared that the appropriation might deprive him of the necessary funds to complete the line.[37] Prior to Morse's refusal, Smith had deferred to Morse's expertise in the conviction that, as Morse himself had informed Smith on countless occasions, no "scientific" problems remained.[38] Smith would never make that mistake again.

The nub of Smith's quarrel with Morse lay in Smith's conviction that, as a proprietor, he was entitled to a percentage of the money that Congress had allocated for the demonstration project. Smith regarded it as outrageous for Morse to put himself and Vail on the government payroll, while rejecting Smith's claim for the horses. Morse responded that the salaries that Congress paid out to himself and Vail had been intended to remunerate them not for their ownership of Morse's patent rights, but, rather, for their technical expertise. Smith was unconvinced. "In practical matters," he fumed, "I do not think there was ever yoked into one team a pair of more decidedly unteachable asses than the professor and himself." Morse and Vail were "feathering their nests" by drawing salaries that totaled almost one-third of the $30,000 appropriation, while Smith had received nothing for the money he had advanced. "I see not how I am ever to derive benefit from the concern," he exploded to Cornell, until Congress decided one way or the other whether it wished to purchase Morse's patent rights. If Congress purchased Morse's patent rights, Smith would obtain one-quarter of the appropriation; if it declined, he would no longer find himself stymied by the specter of a congressional buyout from building a telegraph network himself.[39]

To help Congress make up its mind, Smith staged an ingenious media event. Smith had recently undertaken for President John Tyler a covert journalistic campaign in which he almost single-handedly defused a potentially explosive diplomatic quarrel between United States and Great Britain over the northern boundary of Maine. Now that this crisis had been averted, Smith turned his attention to the selling of the telegraph.[40] In the spring of 1844, each of the country's major political parties held its presidential nominating convention in Baltimore, which was, fortuitously, the very city to which Morse's telegraph line was being extended. Morse does not seem to have appreciated the likely publicity value of this conjunction of events. For Smith, however, it was an obvious opportunity to keep Congress focused on Morse's invention. The broadcast of telegraphic news reports to Washington from the political conventions in Baltimore could not but "excite" the members of Congress, Smith explained to Cornell, and, in so doing, would increase the likelihood that a congressional buyout would find its way onto the national political agenda.[41]

As Smith predicted, the telegraphic news reports from the Baltimore conventions generated an enormous amount of favorable publicity. Morse's Washington telegraph office was thronged with visitors eager to obtain the latest information. When Morse's Washington office broadcast the news that the Democrats in Baltimore had nominated the little-known James K. Polk to be their presidential nominee, the crowd was astonished by the news.[42]

Whether or not Smith sincerely hoped that this media event would inspire Congress to vote Morse the necessary funds to scale up the Washington–Baltimore line is an open question. Smith was much more politically savvy than Morse and seems to have intuited that Congress was unlikely to buy Morse out. It is just as likely that Smith had decided that he could make more money from Morse's invention by raking off high profits on construction contracts. Yet it was one thing to favor private enterprise in private and quite another to tell the world, and Smith was too ingenious to let slip an admission that might somehow lower the value of his share of Morse's patent rights.

The enormous acclaim that greeted the completion of the Washington–Baltimore line encouraged Morse to assume that somehow he and Smith might temporarily set aside their quarrel and together press Congress to allocate the necessary funding to scale up the demonstration project by extending it northward to New York City. No one expected the Washington–Baltimore line to cover its costs. The two cities were only 40 miles apart and already boasted excellent postal facilities. Few residents of either city could be expected to pay a premium for the incremental advantage the telegraph provided. If, however, the telegraph were extended northward to New York City, it could be expected to make a better showing. To obtain the necessary congressional appropriation for the New York City extension, Morse and Smith twice lobbied Congress, first in June 1844 and then again in February 1845. Each time they failed, which was a major setback, for it raised troubling questions about the financial viability of Morse's invention.

The first New York City extension bill found its way to Congress in June 1844. The bill had the approval of both Morse and Smith and was transcribed by Cornell. It authorized the appropriation of government funds for the New York City extension and empowered Morse to oversee its construction in accordance with an accompanying plan that was itself not part of the bill.[43] To maximize congressional support, the bill specified that the line would pass through no fewer than five states—Maryland, Delaware, Pennsylvania, New Jersey, and New York—with intermediate offices in Wilmington, Philadelphia, and Trenton. The likelihood of the bill's enactment seemed certain. The Washington–New York City corridor was the most lucrative postal route in the country and, thus, seemed destined to become the "backbone line" of the country's telegraph network—or so Smith predicted shortly before it came up for a vote.[44] "Everybody seems to think that it must pass, without opposition if not by acclamation," confided Cornell to his wife. To keep congressional interest high, Cornell installed a telegraph office in the Capitol. The office was crowded, he gleefully reported, with "gaping spectators" whose faces were "not infrequently distorted" with "wonder and amazement."[45]

Cornell's optimism proved premature. The extension bill failed following the adoption of an amendment that set the licensing fee for the patent rights to Morse's telegraph at $50 per mile, a total Smith regarded as entirely too low. Although Smith himself was no longer in Congress, he was determined to block the amendment. To voice his objections, he made a dramatic late-night appearance at the Capitol, at which he threatened, or so an astonished Cornell confided to his wife, to "blow our appropriation sky high."[46]

Smith's fury was compounded when he discovered that the author of this amendment was the patent commissioner, Henry L. Ellsworth. To maintain appearances, Smith absolved Morse of any complicity with Ellsworth's machinations. Yet Smith understood that Morse had a far greater stake in the New York City extension than he did and took it for granted that Ellsworth would not have gone ahead without Morse's approval.[47]

Ellsworth's intervention highlighted his vested interest as patent commissioner. Were Morse to abandon his telegraph, as Morse had repeatedly threatened, his failure would reflect poorly on Ellsworth's judgment and might even discourage other inventors from applying for patents. The leasing of patent rights on a territorial basis had long been a conventional way for inventors to generate revenue and often provided them with the best opportunity for a steady financial return. Ellsworth knew this and proceeded accordingly. The precedent that Congress would establish by setting the licensing fee at a relatively low price was likely to generate a sizable financial return in the long term for the Morse proprietors, even if it failed in the short term to reap Smith the financial bonanza he desired.[48]

The defeat of the extension bill was a major disappointment for Cornell, who took it upon himself to mediate between the warring proprietors. Following a marathon "twenty-four hours siege," Cornell confessed defeat, and the bill was lost. "I can assure you," he informed his wife, "that it is no enviable position to occupy to stand between parties in the ownership of property that depends on the action of Congress for its improvement, which action cannot be had without their concurrence to plans, and themselves wholly unable to agree on any plan and entertaining the most perfect hatred towards each other."[49]

The financial shortcomings of the Washington–Baltimore line became manifest in 1845 when the Post Office Department opened it as a fee-for-service government agency under the Department's jurisdiction. In the first six months of its operation, the line cost the Post Office Department $3,244 while generating a mere $413. This was hardly a promising start, especially given the extravagant expectations Smith had raised for Morse's invention.[50]

The poor financial showing of the Washington–Baltimore line greatly troubled Smith, who feared quite plausibly that it might reduce the value of Morse's patent rights.[51] To make matters worse, Congress appropriated $8,000 to the Post Office Department to cover the cost of operating the line, a sum that had been "calculated," Smith warned the postmaster general, to prejudice Morse's invention in the public mind.[52] It was a "most outrageous fraud," Smith sputtered to Cornell, to presume that it cost $666 per month to operate a 40-mile telegraph line.[53] As if this were not bad enough, over one-quarter of the $8,000 appropriation went to pay salaries for Morse and Vail. For Smith this was simply unconscionable. Why not dispense with Morse and Vail and hire assistants at $800 per year? After all, the operation of the telegraph involved "neither mystery nor science" beyond the capacity of ordinary minds.[54]

Among the many issues about which Smith and Morse quarreled was the market value of Morse's invention. Neither Smith, nor Morse, nor anyone else had the slightest idea what Morse's patent rights might be worth. "If the whole right could be set down at $250,000, and we could be paid that by the government," Morse plaintively queried Smith in December 1844, "would you not be satisfied?"[55] It was a question to which Smith never gave a straightforward reply. If the telegraph were the greatest invention of the age—as Morse believed, and as Smith had done his best to convince the world—why should Smith content himself with any lump-sum payment, no matter how large?

Smith continued to praise Morse in public as a heroic inventor for several months after their blowup over the New York City extension, even though by this time he had come to despise Morse as a sanctimonious fraud. The reason for Smith's public silence was simple. Morse's patent rights had by now become a tradable asset that bore little relationship to Morse himself, and by virtue of his ownership of one-quarter of Morse's patent rights, Smith retained a huge financial stake in Morse's reputation. Morse was the "genius" who had inspired a great invention, Smith proclaimed in the following November, in a telegraph codebook that Smith dedicated to "Professor Samuel F. B. Morse, Inventor of the American Electro-Magnetic Telegraph." And it was to Morse, Smith elaborated, in a palpably self-serving tribute that even the notoriously vainglorious Morse found embarrassing, to whom was due the "substantial reward" that "inventive merit" too seldom obtained in the "shape of pecuniary independence."[56]

To keep the idea of a congressional buyout alive, Smith invented a novel, fiscal rationale for a government telegraph. He floated this idea in a two-part essay that ran in *Hunt's Merchant's Magazine* in December 1844 and February 1845. *Hunt's* was the country's most influential business magazine, and Smith's essay was widely reprinted and commented on in the press. Smith opened his essay by repeating the by-now conventional paeans to Morse's invention that Smith had featured in his 1838 congressional report. The "revolution" in business, society, politics, commerce, and industry that would be hastened by Morse's invention, he reiterated, was "gigantic and sublime" to the "contemplative mind." This revolution, he elaborated, was destined to be even more far-reaching in its consequences than the revolutions that had already been unleashed by the steam engine and the mariner's compass. To channel this revolution along a morally desirable path, it should remain under federal control, which would minimize the possibility that the telegraph might become the tool of a speculative cabal, and ensure that it would remain "open to all" and "monopolized by none."[57]

The novelty of Smith's argument lay in the additional rationale for federal control that he now proposed for the first time. To win over lawmakers untroubled by the potential evils of speculation, he hailed a congressional buyout as a solution to a crisis already underway. This crisis was the revenue shortfall at the Post Office Department, a deficit that he blamed on the sharp competition that the Post Office Department had encountered on several of the country's most lucrative postal routes from nongovernmental mail carriers known as "private expresses." If nothing were done, the Post Office Department would require from the general treasury an annual appropriation of thousands, if not millions of dollars. Such an alarming prospect might well compel lawmakers to raise the tariff, an outcome that Democrats resolutely opposed.

Whereas some lawmakers urged Congress to enact restrictive legislation to force the private expresses out of business, Smith took a different approach. Punitive legislation, in his view, was not only unconstitutional but also futile. A far better option was a technical fix. Only the "almost super-human agency" of "Professor Morse's lightning" could save the Post Office Department from ruin. If Congress bought Morse's patent rights and the Post Office Department operated a telegraph line along the routes over which the private expresses had been established, the private expresses would find it impossible to stay in business even if Congress "interposed" no penal laws to deter them. Before long, they would either fail financially or "retire" to the "package system," thereby restoring to the Post Office Department the lost revenue that their rivalry had caused.[58]

The audacity of Smith's publicity campaign was a by-product of the magnitude of the challenge that Morse confronted. In Great Britain, the scientist-promoter team of Wheatstone and Cooke had little trouble raising capital for their electric telegraph. As a consequence, they had no need to publicize it. In the United States, the situation was very different. Smith puffed up Morse so lavishly and so long precisely because Morse found it so hard to obtain financial support. Smith's publicity campaign helped ensure that Morse would be remembered as the inventor of the telegraph, even though by 1844 Smith himself had come to question the veracity of this claim. Ironically, the absence of a paper trail discouraged later British chroniclers from hailing Wheatstone, as American chroniclers would come to hail Morse, as among the greatest inventors of the age.[59]

Morse and Smith quarreled about many things; yet both believed that the federal government had an obligation to protect patent rights. Morse held two telegraph patents. The first patent, which he had obtained in 1840, covered the use of electricity to transmit signals over long distances; the second, which he had obtained in 1846, covered his electromagnetic relay.

Not everyone regarded the trafficking in patent rights with equanimity. The scientist Joseph Henry, for example, refused as a matter of principle to patent any of his inventions, proclaiming that they had been "freely given" to the world. In lieu of a pecuniary reward, Henry sought the pleasure of discovering new truths, the satisfaction of advancing science, and the enjoyment of the "scientific reputation" to which his discoveries entitled him.[60] Similarly, the manufacturer Peter Cooper declined to patent the ingenious railroad engine that he had designed. If Cooper had done so, railroad leaders might have been predisposed to pay more attention to the economic value as intellectual property of the most important piece of equipment on which they relied. Yet Cooper did not seek a patent, and railroad leaders followed his lead.[61] In contrast, the telegraph business congealed around patents, of which the most important were the patents that Morse obtained in 1840 and 1846.

The confidence that Morse and Smith placed in Morse's patent rights built on, and was reinforced by, a quiet legal revolution inside the Patent Office that had been set in motion by the Patent Office Act of 1836. This law stipulated that government administrators must certify the patents that the federal government issued. This was a tricky matter, for it required the Patent Office to render an informed judgment about the merits of the invention. Following the enactment of the Patent Act of 1790, Secretary of State Thomas Jefferson had tried briefly to certify personally every invention for which an inventor sought a patent. Such a system soon proved unworkable, and he gave up in 1793. Between 1793 and 1836 anyone could obtain a patent upon the payment of a fee. If two patents overlapped, the federal executive left it up to the courts to adjudicate.

Beginning in 1836, the Patent Office began once again to examine every single patent filing to determine not only whether the submission had merit, but also whether the prospective patent infringed on any other patent that the Patent Office had already issued. In so doing, the Patent Office erected a filter between the inventor and the legal system that enhanced the value of patents that made it through the mesh by defining the rights of the patent holder. In the absence of the certification requirement, the scope of an inventor's patent remained uncertain, making it vulnerable to a court challenge by rival inventors. Following the establishment of the certification requirement, patent rights became tradable assets that, like land titles or government securities, could be bought or sold. To capitalize on their value, promoters bundled together patents for related inventions into cartels known as "pools." The leading telegraph patents were pooled in 1859; telephone patents were pooled in 1879; radio patents in 1919.

No other government in the world at this time had instituted a comparable certification requirement. This gave Morse's patents a moral authority that set them apart not only from the patents issued to American inventors before 1836, but also from the patents issued to inventors in Great Britain and France.[62]

The transformation of the American Patent Office reinforced the seductive, yet still-controversial, notion that self-interest could spur the technical advances that would foster moral progress. This syllogism received a classic formulation in 1859 when, in a popular lecture on "discoveries and inventions," the Illinois lawyer-turned-politician Abraham Lincoln praised the country's patent laws for ensuring that the "fuel of *interest*" would stoke the "fire of genius." The surviving draft of Lincoln's lecture left it ambiguous as to whether he regarded the telegraph as an agent of progress. Yet he was unequivocal in his judgment that the patent system deserved to be ranked with the invention of writing and printing and the discovery of America as one of the four greatest inventions in human history.[63] By creating financial incentives for inventors, contended British telegraph engineer William Preece in 1877, the American Patent Office had turned inventing into a "profession." This happy result, in Preece's view, was a product of the country's patent laws: "Every new thing is freely published, and the patent laws are sound and within the reach of all."[64]

The high regard Americans and foreigners alike had for the certification requirement came at a cost. By fostering the presumption that inventions sprang more or less unassisted from the brow of uniquely talented individuals, it seriously distorted the history of invention.[65] Morse's 1840 patent granted the inventor the rights not only to a particular method of electrical communications but also to any device that used electromagnetism to transmit "intelligence" between distant points.[66] Although the U.S. Supreme Court would eventually rule this latter claim to be invalid, it was a testament to Morse's self-assurance—and to the encouragement he received from the Patent Office—that it had found its way into the patent at all. Morse's exaltation reached its apotheosis in 1862, when the painter Christian Schussele unveiled his "Men of Progress," a group portrait of illustrious nineteenth-century American inventors in which Schussele assigned Morse an honored place among the greatest inventors of the age. Even today, it is conventional to identify Morse as the eponymous inventor of the most important technical advance in communications since the invention of printing.

The veneration of Morse as a heroic inventor owed much to popular conventions regarding electricity. In the popular imagination, the motive power that Morse harnessed was far more than merely the chemical reactions in the batteries that he employed. Rather, it was a mysterious force originating in the heavens that had been linked for millennia with the divine. To contend, as Smith did, that Morse had transformed an elemental force of nature—"lightning"—into a species of private property— "Professor Morse's lightning"—was extraordinarily presumptuous. Yet it was a conceit that few Americans who were not themselves rival telegraph promoters found occasion to doubt. That an American had harnessed lightning seemed only fitting, given the progressiveness of the country's political institutions and the purity of it citizens' morals. Franklin's kite experiment had earned him enormous renown, even though Franklin had not in fact been the first person to demonstrate that lightning was a form of electricity.[67] Morse's demonstration project made him Franklin's fitting successor. Franklin had captured lightning, and Morse put lightning to work. "And it needs not the gift of prophecy to foresee, nor the spirit of personal flattery to declare"—pontificated Smith, in a characteristic tribute—"that the names of FRANKLIN and MORSE are destined to glide down the declivity of time together—the equals in the renown of inventive achievements—until the hand of history shall become palsied, and whatever pertains to humanity shall be lost in the general dissolution of matter."[68]

Morse reveled in his reputation as a scientist who had unlocked one of the mysteries of God's universe. Actually, he had been neither the first individual nor even the first American to recognize the potential of electricity as a motive power.[69] The motive power that Morse relied on—namely, electromagnetism—had been discovered in 1820 by a Danish scientist, while the steady and reliable current that Morse employed had been made possible by the invention of a new kind of battery in 1836 by British chemist J. Frederick Daniell.[70] The British scientist-promoter team of Wheatstone and Cooke had installed an electrically powered signaling system on a number of railroads several years before Morse completed his demonstration project in 1844, while the American chemist Harrison Gray Dyar had built a demonstration project of a primitive yet workable electrical telegraph on Long Island as early as 1827. Had Dyar obtained the same level of support from the Patent Office in 1827 that Morse did beginning in 1837; had he had the advantage of the Daniell battery; and, perhaps above all, had he been able to take advantage of the certification requirement that Congress instituted in 1836, Dyar, rather than Morse, might be remembered today as the American inventor of the telegraph.[71]

Morse's scientific pretensions proved particularly troubling for insiders familiar with the actual history of the Washington–Baltimore line. Although the demonstration project succeeded, it had been a close call, as everyone closely associated with it knew well. "It is singular," reminisced Alfred Vail's assistant William Baxter, that a series of "mechanical and scientific failures" could have "given a man such a name and so proud a place in history." Morse was no scientist, Baxter elaborated: rather, he was an "ingenious, bold, and persistent diplomat" and a "projector" of "great enterprises." And it was a "peculiarity of the patent law," Baxter slyly added, that the Patent Office often accorded the originator of a single technical advance "no particular merit," while honoring the projector who combined two or more technical advances into a novel organizational form with the "issuance" of a patent. It would be no more logical to credit Morse with the telegraph, Baxter quipped, than it would be to exonerate a thief who had stolen both a horse and harness "with a view of *combining* them in use!"[72]

The American scientist Joseph Henry had a particularly jaundiced view of Morse's scientific pretensions. Morse was a man of "great ingenuity," Henry conceded to Wheatstone in 1846, yet he lacked not only the "scientific knowledge" but also the "habits of mind" that could lead to the discovery of "new principles."[73] Particularly distressing to Henry was Morse's refusal to credit him for the scientific insights that underlay Morse's electromagnetic relay. Morse had never made a "single original discovery" in "electricity, magnetism, or electro-magnetism" that was applicable to the telegraph, Henry huffed in a government report on the invention of the telegraph that the Smithsonian Institution issued in 1856. Morse derided Henry's assessment as outrageous; modern historians of technology, in contrast, find much merit in Henry's critique.[74]

Morse was a beneficiary not only of patent law, but also of the bureaucratic agenda of patent commissioner Henry L. Ellsworth. As patent commissioner, Ellsworth was determined to enhance the legitimacy of the certification requirement that Congress had institutionalized in 1836. For the Patent Office to be successful, Ellsworth recognized, he had to find some way to ensure that it remained sufficiently popular to perpetuate the operational autonomy he had come to enjoy. Although Congress was not likely to abolish the Patent Office altogether, the certification requirement was relatively new. For this reason, it was highly vulnerable to an antimonopoly assault of the kind that had prompted President Andrew Jackson to veto the rechartering of the Bank of the United States in 1832.

To build support for the certification requirement, Ellsworth launched an ingenious promotional campaign. Its centerpiece was the publication of a long, detailed annual report in which Ellsworth and his staff chronicled the inventions that had come to the Patent Office's attention in the previous year. Ellsworth's reports were highly laudatory and even fawning in their admiration for the ingenuity of the inventors whose inventions they described. The "advancement" in the arts that these inventions heralded "taxes our credulity," Ellsworth rhapsodized in his annual report for 1843, and presaged the arrival of an epoch when the progress of "human improvement" must cease.[75]

Ellsworth's reports were published in large runs that were much sought after throughout the country by artisans, engineers, and anyone who aspired to apply for a patent. Although these readers found the reports compelling, they accounted for a relatively small percentage of the population. Farmers remained the country's single largest occupational group, and, unless they had a penchant for invention, they would not likely find the descriptions of specific inventions of much relevance in their day-to-day lives. To provide farmers with a tangible benefit, Ellsworth appended to each report a mountain of data on agricultural production. Although this data had no obvious relationship to the patenting of new inventions, it curried political favor with a large and influential voting bloc that Ellsworth might well need to protect the Patent Office from hostile lawmakers. As a further sop to agriculturalists, he instituted a massive seed distribution program. In the next several decades, the Patent Office mailed millions of seeds to farmers free of charge. This initiative is customarily regarded as marking the beginnings of the Department of Agriculture.[76]

Of all the inventions that Ellsworth celebrated in his annual reports, few received more attention than Morse's telegraph. Among the "most brilliant discoveries of the age," Ellsworth proclaimed in his report for 1844, Morse's "electromagnetic telegraph" deserved a "conspicuous" place: "Distance is annihilated—thought has found a competitor."[77] By lifting up Morse's invention, Ellsworth praised not only the inventor himself, but also the government agency from which Morse had obtained the certification for his invention. Indeed, Ellsworth's laudatory reference to Morse's invention in his annual report was itself a kind of certification because it invested Morse's invention with the authority of the government agency that had granted him his patent rights.

The significance of Morse's invention was not only practical but also symbolic. Morse had been born and educated in the United States, a country not known for its scientific attainments, especially in a highly technical field such as electricity. Morse himself was highly sensitive to the possibility that a foreign inventor might steal his glory, and, in 1837, redoubled his efforts to build a working telegraph. The immediate catalyst was the public announcement that the French inventor Ennemond Gonon was at work on a similar invention. As it happens, Morse was mistaken: the telegraph Gonon proposed was not electric but optical. Yet had Morse not feared a foreign rival, his research might have been even further delayed. Ellsworth shared Morse's sensitivity about his country's scientific shortcomings and regarded Morse's telegraph as an eloquent rejoinder to the condescension of European savants. The first American patent for an electric telegraph had been awarded not to Morse, but to the British telegraphers Wheatstone and Cooke, and Ellsworth was determined to do what he could to ensure Morse's success.[78] "To a native citizen belongs the merit of the discovery," crowed Ellsworth, in promoting Morse's invention, "and it is hoped that the country of his birth will reward him accordingly."[79]

Ellsworth's nationalistic appeal resonated with at least one lawmaker, who invoked Wheatstone's priority as a reason to fund Morse's demonstration project.[80] It also resonated with Morse. Morse found highly troubling the recent immigration of large numbers of Irish Catholics to

New York City and, in 1836, had run unsuccessfully for mayor of New York City on an anti-immigrant ticket. Though he had failed to carry the day for native-born Americans at the polls, he remained hopeful that he might yet win a victory for them in the annals of discovery.

Ellsworth had a further, more personal reason to single Morse out for praise. When Ellsworth granted Morse his telegraph patent in 1840, the two men had known each other for over thirty years. Both had graduated from Yale College in the class of 1810; both hailed from politically prominent New England families; both were devout Congregationalists; and both had aligned themselves politically with Andrew Jackson—a decision that isolated them from many of their fellow New Englanders. Both were also the sons of men closely identified with the founding of the republic. Morse's father was Jedidiah Morse, the author of one of the first geographical compendia of the United States; Ellsworth's father was Oliver Ellsworth, the third chief justice of the Supreme Court.[81]

The assistance that Ellsworth provided Morse was, in retrospect, little short of astounding. To ensure Morse the maximum degree of freedom in shopping around his invention in Europe, Ellsworth granted him a preliminary patent known as a "caveat" in 1837. Following Morse's return to the United States, Ellsworth helped him obtain his first telegraph patent in 1840. In addition, when Morse journeyed to Washington in 1843 to lobby for federal funding for his demonstration project, Ellsworth helped him obtain technical information from the Patent Office, permitted him to store his equipment in the Patent Office, provided him with a place to stay, and hailed him as a benefactor to humanity in widely circulated government reports.[82] When Morse fell ill, Ellsworth's wife Nancy and daughter Anne took care of him. Following the completion of Morse's demonstration project, Ellsworth lobbied behind the scenes to obtain federal funding for the ill-fated New York City extension.

Ellsworth's friendship with Morse may help explain why neither Ellsworth nor his wife discouraged a potentially even more intimate bond between the two men: namely, the possibility that Ellsworth might become Morse's father-in-law. By 1844, Morse had fallen deeply in love with Ellsworth's daughter Anne—or "Annie" as Morse called her—and, in ways that only the lovestruck can fully comprehend, was determined to press his suit. Morse's courtship was in many ways improbable. He was a reclusive and financially strapped 53-year-old widower and father to a daughter several years older than Anne; Anne was a vivacious and eminently eligible 18-year-old girl. In fact, it is conceivable that Morse himself had courted Anne's mother several decades earlier when Morse had been a Yale undergraduate and Anne's mother the same age as Anne.[83]

Although no correspondence from Anne's parents from this period has come to light, it seems inconceivable that they knew nothing about her suitor's intentions. Morse was smitten and did little to conceal his suit. "I desire sincere love to dear Annie"—Morse wrote Ellsworth in February 1844, in offering Anne a gift as recompense for her labors in helping nurse Morse back to health following his illness—"to whom present for me the accompanying piece from my favorite Bellini, and the book on etiquette, after it shall have passed the ordeal of a mother's examination, as I have not had time to read it myself."[84] Morse's assistant, Alfred Vail, feared that Morse's infatuation prevented him from being an effective advocate for the proprietors. "The secret is," Vail explained to his brother, Morse was "so much in love he don't know what he is about half the time."[85] Morse's own daughter considered her father's marriage inevitable: "You seemed to be so attached to her," she reflected in a letter to her father that she wrote shortly after the completion of the Washington–Baltimore line.[86]

If Anne had the slightest intention of marrying Morse, her feelings have gone unrecorded. No correspondence in Anne's hand from this period is extant, while Anne's chaperone—her mother's sister, Julia G. Webster—did not list Morse among the eligible bachelors with whom Anne had been romantically linked.[87] Anne did save a love poem that Morse wrote her in March 1845; it was published many years later, after Morse's death, in *Scribner's Monthly*. Its publication presumably met with Anne's approval: her husband was the editor of the magazine in which it appeared.[88] It is hard to know how to interpret Anne's decision to save the poem and her husband's decision to publish it. Conceivably, Anne and her husband were discreetly poking fun at the temerity of the middle-aged inventor. Not until a half-century later would a contemporary who professed to be familiar with Anne's state of mind during the years of Morse's courtship reflect in print on Anne's feelings toward her suitor. The contemporary was Harriet White, the wife of an Indiana congressman who claimed to have been living in the same boarding house with the Ellsworths and Morse in 1843. Anne, White flatly declared, would never have married a man who was old enough to have been her father.[89]

The odd intertwining of the personal and the political in Morse's relationship with the patent commissioner casts a fresh light on one of the most celebrated episodes in the early history of Morse's invention. According to an oft-told story that began to circulate in print as early as August 1844, Morse gallantly gave Anne the honor of choosing the text of the first official telegraph message to be sent on the Washington–Baltimore line in gratitude for Anne's solicitude toward the inventor. Anne, or so the story went, had been the first person to inform Morse that Congress had appropriated funds to build the Washington–Baltimore line, having brought Morse the welcome news while he was eating breakfast on the morning of March 4.[90] At the opening ceremony, which took place in the Supreme Court Chamber of the Capitol on May 24, 1844, a telegrapher tapped out the text that Anne had selected—"What Hath God Wrought"—an evocative phrase, drawn from the Bible, that would forever after be associated with Morse's invention.

Anne always remained at the center of the story, but before long it became embellished with additional details intended to highlight Morse's mounting anxiety at the possibility that his bill might fail. The pivotal vote, it was said, occurred after Morse had left the Capitol in despair late on the evening of March 3, the final day of the congressional session.[91] Morse himself took considerable pains to ensure that the first telegraph message would be linked with Anne. Following the ceremony, for example, he carefully annotated the paper tape on which the message had been encoded by specifying that it had been "indited" by "my much loved friend, Annie G. Ellsworth." Morse presumably presented Anne the tape as a memento; it remained in her family until after her death.[92]

The Anne Ellsworth story has become firmly enshrined in American folklore, but certain details do not add up. To begin with, there is no first-hand newspaper account of the ceremony. This is a startling omission inasmuch as other telegraph-related events from the same months received lavish coverage in the press. Even more puzzling was Morse's insistence that Anne herself had chosen the text. Morse's authorized biographer assigned the honor to Anne's mother, Nancy, and there seems little reason to doubt the biographer's veracity. Anne's mother was known for her intense religiosity, and the text itself evinced an unquestioning faith in the power of divine intervention that an 18-year-old would not likely have associated with a new means of communication.[93]

Most problematic of all was the issue of timing. In most accounts of the ceremony, Anne is given the honor of sending the first message in recognition of the fact that she was the first person to inform Morse that his bill had been enacted. In reality, the final vote had not occurred near midnight on March 3—after Morse had supposedly left the Capitol in despair—but, rather, much earlier in the day. Morse himself duly noted the enactment of his bill on March 3 in letters that he wrote to Smith and Vail on that day. So, too, did Morse's friend, the sculptor Horatio Greenough, who was in Washington to help push through a bill of his own.[94]

If Anne had not brought Morse the initial news that his bill had been enacted, why, then, did Morse go to such lengths to give her an honored place at the Supreme Court ceremony? One explanation was that he hoped to link his invention with the woman with whom he had fallen in love and hoped to marry. If this were the case, it helps explain why the ceremony went unnoticed in the press. Journalists ignored it not because they failed to appreciate the significance of the telegraph (the invention had indeed received considerable press coverage by May 1844), but because it had not been promoted as a media event. Instead, Morse seems to have wanted the Supreme Court ceremony to be a private celebration for himself, Anne, her parents, and a few close friends. As a painter, Morse had gained renown for his artfully arranged tableaux of notable events; in the Supreme Court ceremony, he brought the tableau to life.[95] The setting itself was of special significance to Anne: the Supreme Court was the institution over which her grandfather had once presided.

In his annotation of the tape that Morse presented to Anne, Morse inserted a question mark at the end of the biblical text, so that it read "What Hath God Wrought?" Oddly, there was no question mark in either the biblical text or on the tape itself. Why Morse added the question mark is unknowable. Conceivably, he intended it as a term of endearment, or even as a marriage proposal. Many puzzles about the Supreme Court ceremony remain, yet one thing is certain. Anne's parents knew that Morse was courting their daughter, and they did nothing to break it off. If Morse by some miracle were to win Anne's heart, it had presumably occurred to them that Morse's patent rights would make a handsome dowry. Ordinarily, of course, a dowry was a gift from the bride's father to his daughter's betrothed; in this instance, the gift had already been bestowed.

Morse took it for granted that the primary users of the telegraph would be merchants engaged in long-distance trade. This was a plausible assumption. The export of cotton, wheat, and other agricultural staples was the biggest business in the country, and the export trade was dependent on the time-sensitive information on market trends known as "fresh news."

Federal control appealed to merchants for some of the same reasons it was compelling to Morse. Public outrage at financial chicanery had reached a fever pitch by the 1840s, having been aroused by a spate of riveting bank scandals in the 1820s, stimulated by President Andrew Jackson's veto of the rechartering of the Second Bank of the United States in 1832 and intensified by the land boom that culminated in the Panic of 1837.

If the telegraph were commercialized as a private enterprise, it was not hard to imagine merchants buying up agricultural staples from farmers and planters at prices they knew to be significantly below the current market rate. Today this practice might seem unexceptional, yet in the early republic, it was widely derided as immoral and unjust. "Beyond a doubt, the telegraph *ought* everywhere to be in the hands of the government," declared a prominent group of Boston merchants in 1845, "and independent of any individual interests." Among the merchants to endorse this position were Nathan Hale and Josiah Quincy Jr., the president and treasurer, respectively, of one of the largest railroads in the country.[96]

Government ownership also had the endorsement of Alexander Brown, a prominent Baltimore banker active in overseas trade. The federal government should not permit private expresses to beat out the Post Office Department day after day, Brown declared, in a petition to Congress that was signed by many of Baltimore's leading merchants. To guard against this evil, Brown urged Congress to purchase Morse's patent rights and put the telegraph under the jurisdiction of the Post Office Department. "The control of the entire commercial and news correspondence of the country" was a "tremendous power," Brown explained, and should be operated exclusively by the "most responsible public agents." And the only public agent that could be trusted with such a responsibility was the Post Office Department: "Its affinity to the post office, its agency in regulating commerce among the several states, and its obvious utility in directing most promptly the movements of armies and fleets, point unerringly to the government of the United States as the authority to which it ought to be entrusted."[97]

The likelihood that Morse's telegraph would be used for speculative purposes seemed incontrovertible. To outpace the mail, merchants

routinely established proprietary horse expresses on the New York City–
New Orleans route. In 1840 one merchant had established a chain of
optical telegraph towers between New York City and Philadelphia that
enabled him to circulate information from city to city in a mere thirty
minutes.[98] The New York City–Philadelphia telegraph had "no doubt
done good service to its owners," declared one journalist in 1846, upon
the occasion of its abandonment with the opening of an electric telegraph
line on the New York City–Philadelphia route: "It was a great affair
when first established, and many mysterious movements in the Philadelphia stock and produce market were laid at the door of the speculators
who worked the [optical] telegraph. No doubt the speculation paid them
well."[99]

The earnestness with which merchants as prominent as Hale, Quincy,
and Brown championed federal control underscored its respectability,
yet said little about the depth of commercial support for a congressional
buyout. Had merchants been seriously concerned about a privately
owned telegraph network, they could have flooded Congress with petitions calling for federal control, as one journalist recommended in December 1846.[100] Yet they did not. The only petition urging a congressional buyout that found its way into the voluminous files of the House
and Senate postal committees was the petition headed up by Alexander
Brown. And in all likelihood, Brown had prepared the petition out of his
personal regard for Morse.

The epicenter of the movement for federal control in the 1840s lay not
in merchants' counting houses, but, rather, in the editorial columns of the
principal daily newspapers originating in New York City, Philadelphia,
and Baltimore. To the extent that journalists in the rest of the country
followed the telegraph issue at all, they took their cues from newspapers
originating in these cities. With the notable exception of Jeremiah Hughes
of the Baltimore-based *Niles's Register,* no influential journalist in the
United States opposed a congressional buyout before December 1846,
when it was widely assumed that the issue would come before Congress.[101] "All the other public journals that expressed opinions," Hughes
declared the previous September, "appeared to urge the government to
make the telegraph a government monopoly."[102]

Journalistic support for a congressional buyout persisted even after
Morse licensees began to scale up the telegraph to the north, south, and
west of the Washington–Baltimore line. Private enterprise was rapidly
erecting telegraph lines in many directions, conceded James Gordon

Bennett of the *New York Herald* in April 1845. Yet the "public interest" would be "much more securely promoted" should the federal government "undertake the arrangement."[103] The issue came to a head in 1846 with the impending completion of a rudimentary telegraph network linking New York City with Boston, Buffalo, and Washington. "The wires are now nearly all laid," editorialized the *New York Sun* in February of that year, "and the question comes up, who should own the telegraph lines? The government or private companies?" For the *Sun*, the answer was plain: "We say, the government. The telegraph is as much a part of the postal facilities of the country as the old stage coach, the steamboat, or the modern railroad car; or as balloons would be, if in use for traveling purposes."[104]

The journalistic rationale for federal control reiterated arguments that Smith and Morse had previously advanced. The imminent financial collapse of the Post Office Department, warned the *Utica Daily Gazette*, picking up on an argument popularized by Smith, made it incumbent upon the federal government to adopt the telegraph or abandon postage and "for the safety of all concerned," the "sooner it is adopted the better."[105] The "monopoly of intelligence" that the telegraph created, warned James Brooks in the *New York Express*, echoing a favorite theme of Morse's, was too great an "element of power" to be vested in any human being. It had long been axiomatic, Brooks explained, that all human power ought to be checked. Yet with the telegraph there had suddenly emerged an "uncontrolled and illimitable power" before which all others "fade into insignificance and contempt." The potential evils of speculative abuse drove Brooks to distraction: "Stock gambling, bread gambling, or political gambling of the most frightful kind, may be carried on secretly by it, and successfully, too, often in the hands of adroit men, whose fortunes might be made by single operations."[106] In making the case for federal control, Brooks waxed poetic. It was a "settled principle," he proclaimed, that the ocean, the sea, and the rivers should "belong to no man, nay, to no one nation," since water was an "element" that belonged not to humanity but to God. For the same reason, the "lightning"—or any other equally powerful "element"—should be the "common property of all mankind" and "not the exclusive element of a single man."[107]

Federal control solved for Brooks a problem that was intrinsic to the structure of the American state. Telegraph corporations inevitably spanned state boundaries. And when they did, it was far from obvious under whose jurisdiction they fell. It had only been in 1839, after all, that the Supreme Court had first enumerated the conditions under which a state-chartered corporation might operate in a "foreign" out-of-state jurisdiction. In contrast, the Post Office Department derived its authority from the federal government, giving it legal standing in every state in the Union. The coordination of this "great instrument of THOUGHT and NEWS," Brooks declared, should be entrusted not to a multitude of rival state-chartered corporations, but to a single federal government agency.[108]

To drive his point home, Brooks reminded his readers of a recent controversy that pitted the Post Office Department against the railroads that it contracted with to carry the mail. Since these railroads had been chartered not by Congress but by state legislatures, they felt little compunction about charging the Post Office Department high rates—and there was nothing the Post Office Department could do about it. What was to prevent a state-chartered telegraph corporation from emulating the railroads' example by extorting its users should it too obtain from a state legislature "high corporative powers"? This legal dilemma had been forgotten amidst all of the hoopla that had surrounded the commercialization of the telegraph: "In our admiration of this discovery, and our enthusiasm for its success, we should not bind chains about us, as we did when the locomotive first came along, and ran over its road of iron."[109]

Brooks's endorsement of federal control was hardly disinterested. In the pretelegraphic era, the Post Office Department provided journalists with news reports free of charge by permitting every newspaper to exchange with every other newspaper an unlimited number of copies.[110] How journalists would obtain their news reports if the telegraph supplanted the mail, no one could say. If the Post Office Department were to retain control of the telegraph, it seemed likely that the exchange privilege would be retained. Yet if the telegraph were commercialized as a private enterprise, it might be abandoned. To stave off this eventuality, one Baltimore journalist urged Congress to enact legislation that would require state-chartered telegraph corporations to transmit to journalists "free of expense" all the information that was "important or interesting" to the "whole people." The cost of these news reports was to be paid for by those individuals who used the telegraph for "*private* benefit or speculation."[111] In so doing, lawmakers would help to ensure that the telegraph, like a public road, remained a "highway of thought" open to all.[112]

While journalists looked to the federal government to perpetuate privileges that they had long enjoyed, railroad leaders anticipated a financial bonanza. Congress "*will* & must eventually purchase the patent right," predicted one railroad investor in 1845, in a pointed letter to railroad president Erastus Corning, and when it did, it was certain to boost the value of the railroad's right-of-way. If, however, Corning's railroad were to grant a telegraph company access to its right-of-way without obtaining an equivalent, Corning might inadvertently undermine the railroad's bargaining position when the buyout occurred.[113]

Conspicuously missing from the calculations of early American railroad leaders was any recognition that the telegraph might be used to facilitate the scheduling of trains. Here, as in other respects, the telegraph business in the United States diverged from the telegraph business in Great Britain. In Great Britain, telegraphic train dispatching was the first major application of the telegraph, but in the United States it remained unusual until the Civil War. This was true even though American railroads were often single-tracked and even though it was well understood that telegraphic train dispatching could help minimize head-on collisions. The principal telegraph-related issue that American railroad leaders debated in the 1840s concerned not the possibilities of telegraphic train dispatching, but, rather, the perils that downed telegraph wires posed for passengers, railroad workers, and passersby.[114]

Merchants, journalists, and railroad leaders had obvious reasons to monitor the public debate over federal control. What other Americans thought about the issue—or even if they considered it at all—is an open question. This much is known. The enactment of legislation to provide the entire population with facilities to circulate handwritten letters over long distances at low cost was of pressing concern in the 1840s for thousands of Americans. The campaign for "cheap postage," as this reform movement came to be known, hastened the enactment of the Post Office Acts of 1845 and 1851. These landmarks in the history of American communications effectively eliminated cost as a barrier to long-distance personal communication.

The campaign for cheap postage is forgotten today, but in the 1840s and 1850s it attracted the attention of journalists and reformers in New York City, Boston, and several other cities. Postal reformers such as Joshua Leavitt wrote extensively, eloquently, and in detail about the federal government's obligation to provide the entire population with facilities to circulate information over long distances at low cost. Hundreds of petitions urging a reduction in the basic rate of letter postage have been dutifully preserved in the National Archives, many of them carrying dozens of signatures. Had Leavitt perceived a need for the high-speed facilities that Morse's invention promised, he could easily have added cheap telegraphy to his legislative wish list. Yet Leavitt does not seem to have turned his attention to the issue until 1872.[115] At no point did Leavitt—or, for that matter, any other prominent postal reformer in the 1840s or 1850s—so much as hint that the federal government had an obligation to provide the entire population with the facilities for high-speed, long-distance communications that the telegraph had made available to an exclusive clientele. In fact, in the vast corpus of printed material generated by the campaign for cheap postage in the period before the Civil War, it would be hard to point to a single pamphlet, or even a single newspaper article, that made more than an incidental reference to the telegraph at all. Large numbers of petitions urging Congress to cheapen the cost of telegraphy would not begin to find their way to Washington until 1875. Moreover, the trickle would not become a flood until after the notorious financier Jay Gould took over the country's largest telegraph corporation in 1881.

The reluctance of postal reformers to call for cheap telegraphy owed something to their realization that the facilities for the extra-high-speed long-distance communications that the electric telegraph promised were a priority only for the tiny percentage of Americans who dealt in agricultural staples and railroad securities. If high speed became a performance standard, postal reformers plausibly feared that its attainment might provide postal administrators with an excuse to keep up the cost of mailing a posted letter. As one upstate New York postmaster reminded Postmaster General Charles Wickliffe in 1841, merchants were the only class of postal patrons who demanded high-speed communications; for everyone else, low cost was key.[116]

The indifference of postal reformers to the popularization of communications facilities faster than the mail helps explain why Congress refused to endorse a congressional buyout of Morse's patent. Yet even had Americans in the 1840s deluged Congress with petitions for cheap telegraphy, Congress would still almost certainly have declined to buy Morse out. The United States in this period was in the midst of a revulsion against public works spending that had been triggered by the financial collapse of several state-sponsored canal projects following the Panic of 1837. Although the Whig presidential candidate Henry Clay did endorse a congressional buyout during the run-up to the 1844 presidential election, he did so in a personal letter that had little influence outside of the tiny circle of telegraph boosters to whom it had been addressed.[117] Under the circumstances, few lawmakers were willing to risk their constituents' wrath by embarking on costly new ventures that might run the federal government into debt.

In hindsight, Congress's refusal to buy Morse out is less surprising than its willingness to fund him at all. Morse was one of only two inventors in the early republic to obtain a direct congressional grant for a demonstration project. The other was Patent Office examiner Charles G. Page, to whom Congress granted a similar sum to build an electrically powered locomotive. Morse and Page had little in common other than a close personal relationship with the patent commissioner—raising the plausible suspicion that, in the allocation of federal funding for demonstration projects, political connections held the key to success.[118]

Although wartime exigency is often a catalyst for government spending on military logistics, Congress remained indifferent to Morse's invention even after it declared war on Mexico in May 1846. Should Congress build a telegraph network linking the country's major seaports, predicted one Washington journalist in the following December, the "timely intelligence" that it would provide military leaders could protect the country's seaports against a naval bombardment that might destroy millions of dollars of wealth.[119] Yet not even this frightening scenario spurred Congress to act. "With the expenses of a costly war on hand," reflected one telegraph insider in June 1846, "a majority of Congress cannot be found to authorize such an expenditure as the purchase and construction of the magnetic telegraph would involve."[120] No bill to fund a telegraph network could possibly find its way into law, the insider added, since, even if it received Congress's endorsement, it was certain to be vetoed by President James K. Polk. Like his mentor Andrew Jackson, Polk had long opposed federal funding for public works.[121]

The only member of Polk's cabinet to endorse a buyout of Morse's patent rights was Postmaster General Cave Johnson. For political insiders, Johnson's endorsement was a major surprise. A fiscal conservative whose hostility toward federal spending had earned him considerable notoriety, as a member of Congress Johnson had ridiculed Morse's invention as recently as 1843.[122] Now that he had witnessed Morse's demonstration project—and, perhaps more to the point, now that he himself had been appointed postmaster general—Johnson underwent a change of heart. The "business of transmitting intelligence," he affirmed in his first annual report, was an "important duty" that the federal Constitution had made "necessarily and properly" the "exclusive" prerogative of the Post Office Department. Johnson did not express an opinion as to whether a scaled-up telegraph network would break even. Yet, as a fiscal conservative, he could not fail to concede that the one telegraph line that was under his direct control had not covered its cost. "The operation of the telegraph between this city and Baltimore," reported Johnson in December 1845, "has not satisfied me that, under any rate of postages that can be adopted, its revenues can be made to equal its expenditures."[123]

Johnson emphatically rejected the presumption that the Post Office Department should abandon the telegraph just because he could not envision how it would cover its cost. The telegraph was an agent "vastly superior" to any that had been hitherto devised by the "genius of man" for the "diffusion of intelligence," and, thus, should not be evaluated merely with regard to the "probable income" that it might return. Rather—and here Johnson drew liberally on arguments that Smith and Morse had advanced—it was an "instrument" so "powerful for good or for evil" that it could not with "safety to the people" be "left in the hands of private individuals" who remained "uncontrolled by law." Precisely what kind of control Johnson envisioned he left unspecified. Yet if Congress were to permit Morse's invention to be commercialized by mere "individuals or associations," he warned ominously, it might become the "most potent instrument" in human history to "effect sudden and large speculations" that would rob the many of their "just advantages," and "concentrate" these advantages in the few.[124]

The 1840s contest over federal control of the telegraph became a point of reference in the post–Civil War public debate over the propriety of federal legislation to restrain Western Union. Western Union was a telegraph combine that had emerged during the Civil War as one of the country's largest and most powerful corporations. For Western Union critics, Morse's fervent endorsement of federal control made him a prophet of regulation. Samuel C. Reid's prior endorsement of a postal telegraph was quietly forgotten. No longer was Reid's military heroism so fresh in the public mind, and no longer was the optical telegraph such a relevant precursor for its electrical cousin.

Morse lived until 1872, and, as one of the most admired inventors of the age, his views on the future disposition of his invention commanded respect. He rarely missed an opportunity to take a stand on one of the leading issues of the day, and, shortly after Ulysses S. Grant's victory in the election of 1868, issued a public statement reminding his countrymen of his long support for a congressional buyout. Although Morse refrained from endorsing any current telegraph legislation, he could not resist pointing out that had Congress followed his advice a quarter century earlier, it could have acquired the rights to his invention for a mere $100,000. The editor who ran Morse's public statement was even more forthright: A congressional buyout of Western Union would realize part of Morse's "original intention."[125] Morse's endorsement of a congressional buyout attracted attention even after his death. The establishment of a "*national* system" of telegraphs under federal control had been one of Morse's most cherished goals, reminisced his old antagonist Francis J. Smith shortly after Morse's funeral.[126] Morse's endorsement of a plan for the "proper governmental control" of the telegraph, reflected Morse's son in 1911, anticipated the present-day movement to transform it into a "great public utility."[127]

The failure of lawmakers in the 1840s to buy out Morse impressed several post–Civil War lawmakers as a missed opportunity. The leasing of the Washington–Baltimore line in 1847 to private investors had cost the American people $100 million in excessive telegraph charges, estimated Colorado senator Nathaniel Hill in 1884, making it one of the most ill-advised pieces of legislation to have ever been enacted.[128] It had been an "evil hour" when Congress had permitted this "great agency" to pass into private ownership, declaimed North Carolina jurist Walter Clark a few years later, since it hastened the rise of Western Union, the "oldest trust" in the country. Among the dissenters were certain wise statesmen—Clark named Cave Johnson and Henry Clay— who had the foresight to warn against the "mischief" that would ensue if Congress abandoned this "essential government function" to a "private monopoly."[129]

To provide a historical perspective on federal telegraph regulation, journalists rummaged around for obscure documents pertaining to Morse's abortive venture. For example, when postal clerks scouring Post Office Department files in 1892 for a historical exhibit for the World's Columbian Exposition discovered that the federal government had never canceled its lease of the Washington–Baltimore line, a business journalist was so intrigued that he ran an article on the topic.[130] Similarly, Henry Clay's argument endorsing the "nationalizing" of the telegraph impressed the editors of the *North American Review* as sufficiently timely that in the same year they reprinted his letter in its entirety.[131] Western Union's critics had never before invoked Clay's name to support federal telegraph legislation, presumably because his 1844 letter had been forgotten.

Western Union apologists, in contrast, regarded Congress's refusal to buy out Morse as an object lesson in the folly of government intervention. Now that Western Union had emerged as one of the wealthiest corporations in the country, it seemed particularly shortsighted for the postmaster general to concede that he did not see how it could break even if it remained under federal control. Overlooked by Johnson's post–Civil War detractors were his misgivings about corporate ownership. That Johnson had questioned the financial viability of Morse's telegraph was enough for the political economist David A. Wells. In a pamphlet subsidized by Western Union, Wells ignored Johnson's anticorporate diatribe and implied, falsely, that Johnson had publicly urged Congress not to buy Morse out.[132] In fact, throughout his tenure as postmaster general Johnson had championed federal control—independent of the possible financial ramifications—in order to prevent the emergence of a corporate behemoth like Western Union.

Congress's refusal to purchase Morse's patents was a matter of public record, and for Western Union president Norvin Green this was the crux of the matter. Under the "advice" of Postmaster General Cave Johnson, Green reminded lawmakers in 1883—reiterating a falsehood that had by this time become the conventional wisdom among Western Union apologists—Congress had "relinquished and waived" its right to control the telegraph in favor of "private enterprise." Johnson's waiver was a turning point in the history of the telegraph business, since investors would not regard it prudent to build their own lines until after Congress had signaled its refusal to commercialize Morse's invention. In the absence of the capital that these investors "rashly invested" and on which they would for many years obtain no financial return, the telegraph would never have been "practically exploited."[133]

Morse's endorsement of a congressional buyout in the 1840s troubled Western Union insiders, giving rise to fears as to what the inventor might say next. To ingratiate themselves with Morse, Western Union staffers burnished his reputation as a heroic inventor. It did Morse an injustice, warned Western Union electrician George B. Prescott in 1869, to presume that he favored any of the telegraph bills with which Western Union was being "constantly menaced," because their enactment would hasten not only the "inevitable destruction" of all telegraph securities but also, very possibly, the "impoverishment" of the "great inventor himself."[134] Prescott's assertion was risky, for Morse was very much alive and could easily have issued a rebuttal. It was also disingenuous inasmuch as Prescott had flatly challenged Morse's pretensions as an inventor in a well-known history of the telegraph that Prescott had published in 1860. Morse resented Prescott's challenge and may well have linked Prescott with his arch-nemesis Francis O. J. Smith, for whom Prescott had long worked and to whose wife Prescott was almost certainly related.[135] Yet Morse remained silent in 1869, presumably because he relished the compliment, and very possibly because he had come by this time to identify his legacy with Western Union's. To curry favor with the famous inventor, Western Union's president William Orton had sponsored a lavishly publicized dinner in Morse's honor the previous December in New York City.[136] Shortly thereafter, Orton threw Western Union's support behind the erection of a full-sized statue of Morse in the city's recently completed Central Park. The Central Park statue was itself a highly flattering tribute to Morse. Even more remarkable was the fact that it had been installed prior to Morse's death, defying the informal convention that proscribed the erection of a full-sized monument to a living individual.

Western Union's wooing of Morse troubled Western Union critics. The public unveiling of Morse's statue had not been intended merely to celebrate a famous inventor, one critic charged, no matter what the distinguished guests whom Western Union had invited to witness the event might have assumed. Rather, it was part of a Western Union-backed public relations gambit. Morse's eulogists were mistaken to contend that Morse had invented the telegraph. Even worse, Morse should never have permitted himself to receive "unblushingly" the "almost divine honors" with which he had been showered and of which he was "equitably" due only the "most meager part." Most unforgivable of all, the assembled multitude had unwittingly permitted itself to become the "misinformed and beguiled instruments" of a cabal of "artful men" who had enlisted it to effect "certain ends of their own"—by which the critic presumably meant the boosting of the market price of Western Union shares and the derailing of federal legislation to bring the corporation under federal control.[137]

Congress's refusal to scale up Morse's demonstration project into a federally regulated telegraph network hastened the eclipse of the federally oriented political economy in which Morse's telegraph had been invented. Yet its legacy lived on in some unexpected ways. The bylaws devised by the Post Office Department to operate the Washington–Baltimore line became incorporated into the bylaws of state-chartered telegraph corporations, while federal legislation, federal court rulings, and federal patent law would continue to structure the telegraph business in the decades to come.

The most enduring legacy of Morse's demonstration project lay in its role in legitimating the transformation of patent rights into tradable assets, or what would soon become known as intellectual property. Henry L. Ellsworth is forgotten today. Yet it was under his leadership that the Patent Office became an engine of innovation. By encouraging the circulation of a vast amount of information about inventive activity, Ellsworth converted the Patent Office into a forum for the exchange of technical knowledge. And by legitimizing the certification requirement, Ellsworth enshrined the heroic inventor as a civic ideal.

3

ANTIMONOPOLY

It is true that a considerable portion of the business of the Post Office Department is likely to be superseded by the increasing facilities of telegraphing; but then the public will be incomparably better accommodated under a system of competition than with a government monopoly.

Scientific American, 1847

"Of one kind of monopoly I am in favor," editorialized Amos Kendall in September 1847, and that was a monopoly of "a man's own property." The property rights Kendall had in mind were the rights that the Patent Office had granted Samuel F. B. Morse for his telegraph. Morse had hired Kendall to manage his patent rights, and Kendall was determined to make the best case he could for his client. "Patent rights are as much private property as printing presses," Kendall explained, making an analogy that he hoped would strike a chord with readers troubled by special privilege and skeptical of monopoly grants.[1]

Kendall's vigorous defense of Morse's patent rights embroiled Kendall in a protracted and bitter contest with dozens of rival telegraph promoters, of whom the most successful was Hiram Sibley. Sibley was a founder of Western Union, a telegraph corporation that emerged during the Civil War as one of the largest and most powerful business enterprises in the country. Kendall and Sibley were representative figures of two successive generations of network builders. They operated in different political economies, envisioned the telegraph in different ways, and devised different business strategies to cope with the challenges that they confronted. Kendall entered the telegraph business at its beginning, when the political economy for network building remained federally oriented and centralized. Sibley rose to prominence at a time when the political economy had become state oriented and competitive. In ways that no one could have anticipated, the political economy that Sibley mastered and that Kendall never understood shaped not only how the telegraph evolved, but also how it would come to be remembered.

Morse hired Kendall in March 1845 shortly after Congress had refused for the second time to extend his Washington–Baltimore telegraph northward to New York City. Kendall managed Morse's patent rights from 1845 until 1859, when Kendall orchestrated their sale to a rival combine. Initially, Kendall tried to sell Morse's patent rights to Congress. When Congress declined, Kendall licensed Morse's patent rights on a territorial basis in an unsuccessful attempt to retain control over the network.

Kendall's management style reflected his personal background. Born in Massachusetts in 1789 in a family that lacked wealth and social connections, he moved to Kentucky as a young man, where he supported himself as a tutor and political journalist. In numerous editorials, Kendall attacked banking laws that bestowed special privileges on favored institutions. Kendall was an early and enthusiastic backer of Andrew Jackson's 1828 presidential campaign, which he actively supported; following Jackson's victory, he was rewarded for his support with a position in his administration. To help Jackson win reelection in 1832, Kendall ghostwrote Jackson's celebrated message vetoing the rechartering of the Bank of the United States. This message remains, over a century and a half later, one of the most biting indictments of government-sanctioned special privilege ever issued by a sitting president. The high point of Kendall's public career came in 1835, when Jackson appointed him postmaster general. The Post Office Department operated the largest and most spatially extensive network in the country. In managing Morse's patent rights, Kendall drew liberally on insights about information flows that he had gleaned while in office.

Although Kendall had no formal training as a lawyer and had never managed a patent, he had a reputation for moral rectitude that set him apart from Morse's previous business manager, Francis O. J. Smith. Kendall's personal background greatly impressed Morse and was probably the decisive factor in Morse's decision to hire him to manage his patent rights. Kendall's tenure as postmaster general had "fitted him" with "enlarged views" of the "public benefit," Morse explained to a prominent journalist in 1847.[2] Morse sometimes questioned Kendall's judgment, yet he never doubted his loyalty. Although Morse valued money, he coveted fame, and Kendall was a faithful guardian of Morse's reputation. Kendall possessed an additional qualification that may well have also figured in Morse's decision. Kendall was a loyal Democrat, and the Democratic Party in 1845 controlled not only the presidency but also the House and the Senate. Morse still intended to sell his patent to Congress and hoped that Kendall's political savvy would help close the deal.[3]

Kendall brought to the management of Morse's patent rights a political sensibility that combined a hatred of special privilege with a faith in government ownership as the ultimate remedy for abuses of power. Kendall had long distrusted state-spanning institutions like railroads and banks that remained outside of direct federal control. And as a champion of the equal rights of white men, he had a principled dislike for any institutional arrangement that empowered insiders to trade on advance information regarding market trends. Although Kendall had had no direct involvement with Morse's invention before 1845, he had attended the 1838 meeting that Morse had arranged in the Capitol to bring his telegraph to the attention of lawmakers. Greatly impressed with its potential, Kendall recommended that Congress put it under federal control, expanding on the endorsement that he had made in the previous year of Samuel C. Reid's proposal for a federally operated optical telegraph between New York City and New Orleans.[4]

Although federal control was compatible with Kendall's political beliefs, Morse's expansive conception of his patent rights was more problematic. Antimonopoly had long been for Kendall an article of faith, and Morse's patent rights were at their core a monopoly grant. Patent grants were uncontroversial, having been specifically enumerated in the federal Constitution as among the powers the framers reserved to Congress. Yet it remained an open question how broadly they should be construed. Had Morse not hired Kendall as his business manager, Kendall might well have joined the "liberalizers" intent on narrowing their scope.[5] The "true object" of government, Kendall declared in 1843, was to empower individuals to pursue their own happiness. Wealth accumulated through "honest pursuits" was legitimate; wealth acquired through "mere advantages" in the law was "legalized plunder." For Kendall to defend Morse's patent rights without compromising his political creed, he had to transmogrify Morse's monopoly grant into a fundamental right that the inventor had acquired through "honest pursuits" unbeholden to any "mere advantages in the law." And that would not prove to be easy.[6]

Kendall set forth his "plan of operations" in February 1845 in a remarkable letter to Morse in which Kendall enumerated the course of action that he would pursue should Morse hire him to defend his patent rights.[7] Kendall's letter provides a revealing glimpse of how Kendall envisioned the scaling up of Morse's invention from a standalone demonstration project into a spatially extensive network. In it, Kendall endorsed Morse's goal of a congressional buyout, explained how he would bring it about, and emphasized why he was peculiarly well qualified for the job.

Kendall endorsed a congressional buyout for three reasons. First, it minimized the likelihood that insiders could dupe unwary planters by trading on advance information on changing market trends—and, in so doing, overbalance the familiar objections to federal public works spending. Second, it liberated the Post Office Department from greedy railroad "monopolists" who charged huge sums to carry the mail on the most heavily trafficked routes. Newspapers were the heaviest component of the mail, and the carrying capacity of the railroad was far superior to a stagecoach, oxcart, or post rider. If the Post Office Department operated the telegraph, it could transmit news reports in advance of the mail, eliminating the demand for nonlocal newspapers and enabling it to shift from the railroad to less expensive modes of conveyance. And, third, it eliminated special privileges that favored journalists located in New York City. New York City journalists had long overloaded the mail with newspapers bound for distant locations. Kendall deplored this practice not only because it obliged the Post Office Department to contract with railroads, but also because it threatened the decentralized political culture that Kendall presumed to be a necessary precondition for perpetuation of the Union.[8]

Although Kendall had intended his plan for a congressional buyout to appeal to lawmakers of all political persuasions, it included several elements that were designed to appeal to lawmakers hostile to any augmentation in the organizational capabilities of the federal government. Federal control, these lawmakers warned, might put the institution of slavery at risk by upsetting the delicate sectional balance between the slaveholding and nonslaveholding states. To meet this objection, Kendall championed a political agenda that was antidevelopmental: that is, it focused not on how the telegraph might transform the republic, but, rather, on how it might perpetuate the compromises of the past.[9]

The government telegraph that Kendall envisioned was closely modeled on a high-speed horse express that he had operated as postmaster general between 1836 and 1839. Each had the same rationale: to curtail speculation, reduce government spending, and prevent media concentration.

Kendall justified the rationale for his horse express in a congressional report that he prepared in 1838. The recent augmentation in the mandate of the Post Office Department to outpace nongovernment carriers in the circulation of information, Kendall declared, had made his high-speed horse express a practical imperative. "It is the true interest of the country," Kendall conceded, for lawmakers to spread "intelligence" with the "greatest possible rapidity." Kendall presumed that his mandate obliged the Post Office Department to transport at high speed only news reports, and not the newspapers in which these news reports were customarily found.[10]

The distinction Kendall made between newspapers and news reports enabled him to uphold the Post Office Department's mandate to outpace nongovernment carriers without compelling post riders to carry newspapers in their portmanteaus. Newspapers were extremely heavy in bulk, and Kendall feared that their conveyance would slow his horse express to a crawl. In contrast, news reports were typically brief and could be printed on tissue paper to minimize their weight. By transmitting news reports to journalists by express, the Post Office Department could check speculation in agricultural staples and keep the citizenry informed of late-breaking political developments without straining the physical limitations of the mail.

Kendall justified his horse express as not only a check on speculation, but also a cost-cutting measure. The newsgathering capabilities of the New York City press exceeded those of any other city, and subscribers throughout the country had come to discover that the news reports in James Gordon Bennett's *New York Herald* were often more up-to-date than the news reports in newspapers published closer to home. To transport Bennett's *Herald* throughout the country, the Post Office Department found it necessary to contract with railroads. Specific railroad corporations enjoyed a de facto monopoly over particular routes, and the Post Office Department had to pay them whatever they charged. Had the railroads held federal charters, the Post Office Department could presumably have held them to account. Yet railroads held state charters, rendering them impervious to federal control. It was largely to solve this problem that Kendall instituted his horse express. If the Post Office Department decoupled the circulation of newspapers from the circulation of news reports, New York City–based newspapers would lose their allure with nonlocal subscribers, who would prefer, all things being equal, to subscribe to newspapers published closer to home. And a news report was just as valuable if it had been printed in a local newspaper than if it had been printed in a "foreign" newspaper originating in New York City.[11]

The decoupling of news reports and newspapers improved the relative position of the hundreds of small-town journalists known collectively as the country press. Henceforth, these journalists would no longer have to compete with newspapers originating hundreds or even thousands of miles away. As a further advantage, it minimized the likelihood that the press could become the tool of a speculative cabal. "One man, or a few, or one corporation or a few" might "buy up the principal presses" and hire the "most able writers," not to advocate the "rights of man" or the "cause of liberty" but, rather, to merely carry some "great point of ambition or speculation" that would undermine the "rights of the people" and the "general interests of society."[12]

The long-distance circulation of editorial commentary originating in New York City risked the even more serious danger of exacerbating the looming sectional conflict between the slaveholding and nonslaveholding states. This danger had been forcibly impressed on Kendall in 1835, when, as postmaster general, he had found himself thrust into the middle of a major political crisis that had been spurred by slaveholder outrage at the mass mailing to slaveholders of antislavery tracts by a group of New York City–based abolitionists. "Our nation is not one in relation to many subjects discussed in newspapers," Kendall reflected in 1838, in looking back on this event: "In many respects, we are twenty-six independent nations. Each of these has its separate interests, systems of legislation, jurisprudence, and police; and each requires a well-sustained local press to discuss local topics, represent its separate rights, and maintain its rank and importance among its confederates." The consolidation of the newspaper business in a single city not only increased the likelihood of speculative abuse, but diminished the "separate rights" of the states.[13]

Amos Kendall's tenure as postmaster general in the 1830s won him the admiration of telegraph inventor Samuel F. B. Morse, who hired Kendall in 1845 to manage Morse's patent rights. In this sympathetic 1838 "pen portrait," Kendall takes his political cues from a Southern newspaper while admiring the high-speed horse express that he had established to outpace the railroad, a venture Kendall would later hail as a prototype for Morse's telegraph. "Amos Kendall," *United States Magazine* 1 (March 1838): 402.

Although Kendall's 1838 report focused on his horse express, it included a brief and revealing allusion to Morse's telegraph, whose operations Kendall had recently witnessed at a public display Morse had organized for lawmakers at the Capitol. Why should the people be "taxed" to drag "masses" of newspapers over muddy roads by stagecoach or oxcart, if news reports might "fly to them" in half the time by horseback, or "instantaneously" along "electric wires"?[14] Long before Morse had completed his demonstration project, Kendall anticipated a major rationale for the founding of telegraphic newsbrokers like the New York Associated Press (NYAP).

The continuities between Kendall's 1838 congressional report and his 1845 "plan of operations" call into question the common contention among historians of technology that the electric telegraph had "no lineage" and did not respond to a "clear social need."[15] The motive power for Morse's telegraph was new; Kendall's plan for scaling it up from a demonstration project into a spatially extensive network was not. "The thorough knowledge which Mr. Kendall obtained of the *Post-Office System*" as postmaster general, declared one early telegraph promoter—and in particular the "opportunities" Kendall's position had given him to discern the "wants" of the "business community" for high-speed facilities like the "*Express Mails*'"—had qualified him "peculiarly" for judging the extent to which the "telegraph system" would be used in the United States for the "convenience of the people" in their "social and business relations."[16]

The influence of postal precedent on telegraph network building was pervasive and enduring. The physical appearance of the first telegraphic dispatches closely resembled the physical appearance of posted letters. Even the word "dispatch" was a postal carryover; the neologism "telegram" would not be coined until 1853.[17] Postal precedent was evident in the format of the telegraphic dispatch that Kendall sent from Baltimore to Washington on April 8, 1845, a mere seven days after the official opening of the Washington–Baltimore line. Kendall's dispatch is carefully preserved among the Post Office Department's records in the National Archives; it is almost certainly the oldest fee-for-service telegram in existence. Although Kendall's message had been transmitted electrically from Baltimore to Washington, the telegraph operator in Washington transcribed it in on a piece of stationary that was plainly meant to resemble a posted letter. The dispatch was neatly recorded in an elegant hand, and the stationary bore on its letterhead the hand-stamped header, "Telegraph.

Baltimore, April _____ 1845"—mimicking the letterhead on a posted letter that had been physically transported from city to city.[18]

For Kendall to mastermind a congressional buyout, he had to enlist the support not only of lawmakers but also of Morse's estranged partner Francis O. J. Smith. Smith retained a one-quarter share in Morse's patent rights, giving him the power to block any congressional initiative of which he disapproved. Here Kendall met with the first of several major reverses. Although Smith remained publicly committed to a buyout, by early 1844 he had privately cast his lot with private enterprise in the conviction that he would make more money stringing telegraph wire than waiting for Congress to buy Morse out. To win Smith over, Kendall wrote him numerous letters explaining the financial benefits of federal control. A congressional buyout, Kendall reminded Smith, had the virtue not only of simplicity but also of certainty. No one knew what Morse's patent rights were worth or how broadly the courts might construe them. Should Congress buy Morse out, Smith would "realize at once" all of the wealth a "human heart ought to desire" without having to fight for years through all manner of "perplexities" no matter how "brilliant in imagination" the potential.[19]

A congressional buyout had the further advantage of minimizing the risk that a rival group of promoters might emulate Morse's example and tap the "power of government" to demonstrate a superior telegraph. The risk that the Morse proprietors might find themselves confronting a rival became all the greater if they offended lawmakers by making extravagant financial demands. No matter what happened, Kendall lectured Smith, it was "all important" to keep open the possibility of a congressional buyout, if only to "keep public opinion with us."[20]

Kendall's correspondence with Smith provides insight into the mindset of two of the most politically astute leaders of the first generation of telegraph network builders. For both men, financial considerations loomed uppermost. "You and I have the same object in view," Kendall confided to Smith, shortly after Morse signed Kendall on as his business manager, to "make the most money in the shortest time that we honestly can out of the magnetic telegraph." Nothing, in Kendall's view, should interfere with this overriding goal: "Like you I have no special love for the people which in ordinary times would prevent my exacting from them the value of that which I propose to sell them."[21] Kendall himself placed his own financial "expectations" at $1 million, a princely sum in an age in which many artisans made $1 a day and Morse himself would have been willing to sell his patent rights to Congress for a far more modest price. Might it not make sense, Kendall privately mused, for the proprietors to negotiate with Congress some kind of contractual agreement that would guarantee them the payout to which they presumed themselves entitled? After all, Kendall reasoned, it was "not material" whether the sum that would "satisfy our desires" was to come from the government or the "people."[22]

Once it became obvious that Congress had no intention of buying Morse out, Kendall's relationship with Smith became more complicated. To minimize the conflicts that were certain to arise as long as the ownership of Morse's patent rights remained divided between two hostile proprietors, Kendall segmented the market. Smith would commercialize New England and Morse the rest of the country. The precise boundary between Smith's territory and Morse's territory remained hazy, especially in the northwest. Even so, this agreement remained in force until Smith and Kendall left the telegraph business in 1859.[23]

Having mollified Smith, Kendall set out to raise the capital necessary to build a telegraph network. Network building was expensive, and neither Kendall nor Morse had the financial resources to go it alone. Kendall's first stop was New York City, the home of some of the country's wealthiest financiers. Here Kendall met with another setback. Stiff and moralistic, Kendall lacked the bonhomie to entice wealthy New Yorkers to take a flyer on Morse's invention.[24] Even had Kendall excelled as a salesman, he would have found it hard to live down the journalistic salvos that he had lobbed at New York City bankers in years past. Yet Kendall was a poor promoter, and New Yorkers had little trouble poking holes in the arguments he advanced. Morse's line was certain to be destroyed by an "indignant public" following the "first important speculator" that could be attributed to its "agency," declared one skeptic in a letter to the editor of a New York City newspaper that catered to the business elite—"regardless of the penalties that may be fixed by the law."[25] Financier Jacob Little was reputed to have declared that he would help bankroll Morse's research, but that he would not invest a dollar in the telegraph, since he doubted that it could be adequately protected against sabotage: "There is no safety in those wires, nor in those posts. Anybody can tamper with them, and anybody can destroy them."[26] Other would-be investors found Kendall's terms unattractive. Morse had instructed Kendall to retain a 50 percent share of any licensing arrangement involving his patent rights. When a group of New York City investors demanded five-sixths, Kendall had no choice but to turn them down. Rather than accept an "interest so minute," one journalist reported, the proprietors preferred to build on a smaller scale.[27] Even had investors found Kendall's terms acceptable, a further problem remained. A "chief reason" that "capitalists" remained wary of investing in Morse's invention, one journalist explained, was the fear that "company patents" would prove to be an "insecure" investment.[28]

Having failed in New York City to recruit investors and in Washington to entice lawmakers, Kendall concluded ruefully that his only remaining option was to build a telegraph network himself. To get underway, Kendall chartered two telegraph corporations: the Magnetic Telegraph Company and the Washington and New Orleans Telegraph Company. The Magnetic linked New York City and Baltimore, and the Washington and New Orleans Company linked the two cities for which it had been named. In combination with the federally operated Washington–Baltimore line, these two companies connected New York City and New Orleans, the single most lucrative market for telegraphic information in the United States. "There is no other chance in the world," Kendall boasted in a public letter in 1846, "for creating so great a property by so small an expenditure."[29] The route Kendall settled on followed closely the southern route that postal administrators used to carry the mail. Intermediate points included Petersburg, Virginia; Raleigh, North Carolina; Columbia, South Carolina; and Augusta, Georgia. The alternative, western route that looped west to Cincinnati before turning south to Louisville, Kendall left for others to build.

Kendall's confidence in the financial potential of the New York City–New Orleans route built on first-hand knowledge of long-distance information flows that he had acquired as postmaster general. Kendall had established a horse express linking New York City and New Orleans on both the southern and the western routes in 1836, and Reid chose the southern route for the optical telegraph that he proposed in 1837.[30] The Washington–New Orleans telegraph line would be its successor. The horse express had been a "daily mail"; the electric telegraph would be an "all-day" mail.[31] In a single year, Kendall estimated, using postal data as a proxy, it would return 25 percent of the cost of its construction.[32] The horse express–electric telegraph analogy remained familiar for at least thirty years. The lightweight news reports that James Gordon Bennett had prepared in 1836 for Kendall's horse mail were the precursors to the "telegraphic news dispatches of the present," reported Bennett's longtime associate Frederic Hudson in his pioneering history of American journalism in 1873.[33]

The superiority of the electric telegraph over a horse express was not only technological but also political. With the exception of the Washington–Baltimore link, the New York City–New Orleans line would be operated as a private enterprise rather than a public agency. Kendall the postmaster general had been obliged under federal law to permit journalists to exchange an unlimited number of newspapers free of change, a special privilege that Congress had codified in federal law to facilitate the circulation of news.[34] Kendall the telegraph promoter was under no such constraint. Henceforth, Kendall reminded would-be investors, he would be free to charge users whatever the traffic would bear and anticipated that he would to obtain from journalists at least 10 percent of his total revenue.[35]

Neither of the corporations that Kendall chartered relied on railroad rights-of-way. South of Virginia a North–South railroad had yet to be built, and in New Jersey Kendall found it impossible to obtain a right-of-way from the railroad corporation that held the exclusive rights to the New York City–Philadelphia route. Unfazed, Kendall built a New York City–Philadelphia telegraph line along the public highway.[36] The reluctance of railroad leaders to accommodate the telegraph was due in part to their discovery that the benefits they obtained from the free use of the telegraph on their lines failed to compensate them for the nuisance of permitting the telegraph company to string wire on their right-of-way. Railroads made little use of the telegraph to dispatch trains, while fallen telegraph wires endangered passengers and rolling stock.[37] A further consideration was the personal repugnance that railroad leaders felt toward Kendall on account of his antirailroad polemics. Kendall had justified his 1836 horse express as a technical fix that would render the Post Office Department "measurably independent" of the railroad.[38] Following Kendall's resignation as postmaster general, he stepped up his antirailroad campaign; in one 1843 editorial, he went so far as to propose that the Post Office Department abandon the railroad altogether as a mode of conveyance.[39] Had Kendall not been such an outspoken railroad critic, he might have had less trouble obtaining the exclusive railroad-right-of-way contracts that proved so instrumental for second-generation network builders like Hiram Sibley.

The bylaws Kendall devised for the Magnetic Telegraph Company laid out certain principles that would soon be adopted by telegraph corporations throughout the United States. The telegraph was to be open to anyone willing to pay the standard fee on a first-come-first-served basis "without regard to sex, wealth or station."[40] Although it might seem self-evident that the telegraph would be operated on this basis, this was by no means a foregone conclusion. Certain traders had long operated private horse expresses on certain stretches of the route between New York City and New Orleans to provide themselves—and no one else—with advance information on sudden spikes in the price of cotton in overseas markets. The Philadelphia broker William C. Bridges, for example, had operated a private optical telegraph since 1840 between New York City and Philadelphia that provided him and his backers—and no one else—advance information on market trends.

Kendall deplored speculative ventures of this kind and assumed that most merchants did too. Even if he had not, he had little choice. The Post Office Department had operated the Washington–Baltimore line on a fee-for-service basis since April 1845. As long as the "Office of the Electro-Magnetic Telegraph" remained under federal control, open access remained a principle that no nongovernment line could ignore. The proprietors of Morse's patent rights, Kendall affirmed, would emulate the Post Office Department by making all of their lines a *"servant of the public"* rather than an "instrument of private speculation." In so doing, the telegraph would put down the "system" of carrier pigeons, signal fires, and private optical telegraphs that were now growing at an "alarming extent."[41]

Kendall conceded that it would be impossible to devise bylaws that would preclude the possibility of speculative abuse. Even so, he took great pride in having formulated rules that placed "all men on equality," even though no one could make them equal in the sagacity, industry, and enterprise that would enable them to use the telegraph "profitably to themselves." To fault telegraph companies for encouraging speculation was particularly unfair. Before the coming of the electric telegraph, merchants had operated an optical telegraph for several years between New York City and Philadelphia for the benefit of *"speculators exclusively,"* and no one had complained.[42]

Unmentioned in Kendall's bylaws were the special privileges, if any, that the Magnetic would offer the press for the transmission of news reports. Kendall had long supported himself as a journalist, and his fellow journalists assumed that he would carry over to the telegraph at least some of the perquisites that they had obtained from the mail. Kendall had other ideas. Although Kendall granted journalists preferential access to the telegraph at low rates, he did not retain the exchange privilege that newspaper editors had enjoyed when they had received their news reports in the mail.

Smith was even more unyielding in his relations with the press. To the outrage of journalists, Smith refused to grant journalists any special privileges whatsoever. Not until after Smith retired from the telegraph business would second-generation telegraph network builders negotiate an entente with the New York Associated Press that smoothed telegraph–press relations on the critical transatlantic route that linked the North Atlantic shipping lanes off Halifax, Nova Scotia, with the New York City–based journalists who owned the NYAP.[43]

Smith's recalcitrance infuriated journalists throughout New England; they responded in kind by ridiculing him mercilessly as greedy and unprincipled. To heighten the satire, they poked fun at his predilection for high-flown rhetoric by nicknaming him "Fog," a play on his initials— "F. O. J." The press campaign against Smith helps explain why Smith has come to be remembered not only as Morse's nemesis, but also as a poor promoter. It would be an exaggeration to award Smith chief credit for the "skillful management" by which the telegraph had been "forced upon" the "attention of the people" and "erected into a public necessity." Even so, this was how one well-informed post–Civil War chronicler described Smith's role in the early history of the telegraph business.[44] Yet Smith did organize and operate a telegraph network in New England that was far more extensive than any network that Morse himself had built and maintained.

The telegraph lines that Kendall operated between New York City and New Orleans and that Smith operated in New England were the only lines that the Morse proprietors controlled directly. The construction of the rest of the network became the responsibility of agents that Kendall and Smith licensed on a territorial basis. Morse licensees received an exclusive franchise to Morse's patent rights. Everything else they purchased in the open market: the Morse proprietors provided little technical guidance and had no financial stake in any telegraph equipment manufacturer. The "indispensable preliminary" to the construction of a telegraph line, reminisced one early telegraph promoter, was the purchase from Kendall or Smith of a territorially defined license. For a typical licensee, the cost of building a line was $300 per mile—$150 to the contractors and $150 to the proprietors of Morse's patent rights.[45]

Early telegraph promoters were a mixed bag. For the New York City–Albany–Buffalo route, Kendall chose John Butterfield, a veteran stage-coach contractor eager to diversify. Butterfield's partners included Henry Wells, Crawford Livingston, and Theodore S. Faxton. Each shared Butterfield's determination to try something new. None really had a choice: each had had his world turned upside down by the Post Office Act of 1845. Butterfield's stagecoach business relied heavily on postal subsidies that the postal law eliminated, whereas Wells, Livingston, and Faxton operated a private mail carriage business that the law legislated out of business. The telegraph line that Butterfield and his partners established—the New York, Albany, and Buffalo Telegraph Company—soon became one of the most profitable in the United States, as well as a major source of Morse's income. Morse owned stock in the company, and it was one of the few to pay a regular dividend.[46]

For the territory linking the North Atlantic shipping lanes to New York City's financial district, Kendall chose Samuel Colt and William Robinson.[47] Colt provided the technical expertise, Robinson the capital. Although this territory was small, it had a large financial potential: no news was more highly valued than European market reports, and the North Atlantic shipping lanes were the best place to obtain the timeliest information. Colt and Robinson opened for business in November 1845, making their telegraph the first to go into operation in New York City. Not until the following June would the city's financial district be linked in a regional network to Washington, Boston, and Buffalo.

To put their venture on a solid legal footing, Colt and Robinson obtained a special charter from the New York state legislature for a corporation that they styled the New York and Offing Telegraph Association. Offing was not a locality; it was, rather, the furthest point on the Atlantic horizon that was visible by telescope. Although the motive power that Colt and Robinson relied on was novel, their business strategy was not. Like the operators of the New York City optical telegraph that Samuel C. Reid had established, Colt and Robinson hired spotters to locate ships en route to New York City, and like Bennett and the other owners of the city's leading newspapers, they employed rowboats to obtain news reports from ships that remained out at sea.

To fund their telegraph, Colt and Robinson depended on annual subscriptions. Up-to-date news reports from every point in the compass would be "free and open to all alike" only to those individuals who paid an annual subscription for access to the books in which this information was recorded: $12 a year for merchants, $24 for journalists.[48] In public, Colt and Robinson reassured merchants that their telegraph would prevent speculators from deploying its "immense power" to obtain advance information on overseas market trends.[49] In private, they conceded that they intended to use it to speculate themselves. "For although we are not to allow any one to suppose that we shall use our information for that purpose," Robinson confided to Colt, "still I am convinced we shall have to do it when an opportunity offers." Optical telegraphs had not proved to be particularly lucrative, and neither would the electric telegraph: "The merchants will never give us an adequate support."[50]

Colt is remembered today as a manufacturer of small arms, including the famed "six-shooter" that the army used to subjugate the Indian tribes of the trans-Mississippi West. In the 1840s he was also known as the inventor of the "submarine battery," an electrically detonated underwater mine that the navy had paid him $15,000 to develop. Colt's submarine battery had been designed to destroy enemy warships; in essence, it was a telegraphic torpedo. To detonate it, an operator closed a circuit from a remote location to which the mine had been connected.[51]

Kendall had no interest in pyrotechnics, yet he valued Colt's expertise in underwater insulation. New York City's financial district was located on the southern tip of an island that was separated by water from the two most advantageous points from which to monitor the North Atlantic shipping lanes: Sandy Hook in New Jersey and Coney Island in Brooklyn.

Colt and Robinson's venture was significant less for what it accomplished than for what it portended. By publicizing the newsgathering potential of the electric telegraph, it challenged two powerful institutions: the Post Office Department and the New York City newspaper press.

Although Colt and Robinson courted journalists as potential subscribers, they hailed their telegraph less as a handmaiden to the press than as its successor. "It is evident," boasted a promotional pamphlet, "that the system of telegraphing news is destined to supersede, in a great degree, the publication of commercial newspapers in this and other northern cities." The collapse of the New York City newspaper press was, they felt certain, only a matter of time: "Who in New Orleans, for instance, would subscribe to New York newspapers, and wait eight or ten days for the receipt of commercial news brought by an Atlantic steamer, when they can be in possession of it in as many minutes by our telegraphic correspondence"?[52]

Among the journalists who took Colt and Robinson's challenge seriously was James Gordon Bennett. Bennett's *Herald* boasted one of the largest circulations of any newspaper in the country, partly because of the tidy business that he had built up over the years selling newspapers to subscribers outside New York City. Bennett had employed Kendall's 1836 horse express to send lightweight news reports to distant subscribers, and he had no intention of being upstaged by Kendall licensees. The threat was real: If Colt and Robinson succeeded, at least some of Bennett's nonlocal subscribers could be expected to shift their allegiance from the *Herald* to a locally published newspaper filled with telegraphic news reports that predated the news reports in their copies of the *Herald* that arrived in the mail.[53]

The implications of the electric telegraph for communications networks spurred a good deal of discussion in the press. The "astonishing" invention that Colt and Robinson had licensed, gushed one journalist shortly after their telegraph opened for business, threatened to supplant not only the Post Office Department, but also the proprietary horse expresses that speculators sometimes operated between New York City and New Orleans.[54] Now that it was possible to transmit news electrically, predicted a contributor to the *New York Daily Tribune,* newspapers like the *Herald* would have no choice but to abandon their traditional focus on national and international news and specialize either in local "'items'" or in the imponderable "philosophical" issues that presented themselves through the "mist" that "shrouds" the future. One thing was certain: the newspaper of the future would be "emphatically useless" as the "rapid and indispensable carrier" of news reports, since it would be anticipated at every point by the "lightning wings" of the telegraph.[55]

To reassert control over the newsgathering business, Bennett joined together with Moses Y. Beach of the *Sun* to organize a newsgathering combine that would soon come to be known as the New York Associated Press (NYAP).[56] If Bennett and his colleagues wrote up a formal agreement, it is no longer extant. Yet there can be little doubt that they found it expedient to meet the challenge that the telegraph posed. This challenge came from two directions: the south and the east. The challenge from the south was immediate. The United States and Mexico were at war, making it expedient for the New York press to join together to obtain news reports from the front. The challenge from the east was more amorphous. Colt and Robinson had obtained a territorial license to a new communications medium that, if properly managed, had the potential to give them control over the vitally important news reports from the North Atlantic shipping lanes. The NYAP had been founded not only to meet the technical challenge of obtaining news reports and the organizational challenge of coordinating their flow, but also to regain control over the newspaper business at a moment when its future seemed imperiled by a rival newsbroker. The newsbroker had gained control of a new means of communication by virtue of a special charter from a state legislature and a territorial franchise to federally guaranteed patent rights.[57]

Colt and Robinson soon moved on to other projects. More tenacious was Henry O'Rielly, a journalist whom Kendall licensed in 1845 to build telegraph lines in the West. O'Rielly had impressed Kendall with his ingenuity in hunting down mail robbers during his tenure as Rochester postmaster, and Kendall assumed that he would prove equally adept at building telegraph lines.[58] This was a colossal mistake. Hot-tempered and imprudent in money matters, O'Rielly failed at every business venture he undertook, and the telegraph proved to be no exception.

When Kendall signed his original contract with O'Rielly, Kendall thought that O'Rielly would build a limited number of lines between specific localities. O'Rielly had a more expansive vision. Temperamentally opposed to be anyone's agent, he aspired to build a vast and largely autonomous telegraph network that would stretch all the way from the Atlantic to the Pacific. By 1852, O'Rielly claimed to have built 6,000 miles of line, more than anyone else in the world.[59]

To highlight his autonomy, O'Rielly called his ventures "People's Lines." The word "people's" was meant to imply that O'Rielly relied on local funding; in fact, he obtained almost all of his financing from his friends and neighbors in Rochester, New York, a burgeoning upstate commercial center that was destined to play an oversized role in the early history of the telegraph business. "For all my expenses for the last twenty months," O'Rielly complained to a colleague early in 1847, not more than $9,000 had been paid by anyone other than his *"old & longtime friends"* in upstate New York.[60]

A typical O'Rielly line was built in great haste, capitalized at several times its actual cost, and strung along country roads rather than railroad rights-of-way. O'Rielly was not the only early telegraph promoter to employ slipshod construction methods, but because he built the largest number of lines, he received a disproportionate share of the public opprobrium when things went wrong, as they so often did. Faulty insulation posed a constant challenge. The wire on O'Rielly's Philadelphia–Baltimore line was insulated with a thin layer of tar; the wire on his Philadelphia–Lancaster line was insulated with beeswax and cotton cloth. Neither lasted much longer than the first rain.[61]

The transfer of messages from an O'Rielly to a non-O'Rielly line was problematic. Interconnection protocols had yet to be devised, and, after November 1846, Kendall and Smith refused to interconnect with O'Rielly on the grounds that his telegraph equipment violated Morse's patent rights. O'Rielly's assistant James D. Reid drew attention to the problem in a record book that he maintained as superintendent of O'Rielly's Pittsburgh office. Of the seventy-four messages that Reid sent from Pittsburgh to New Orleans in December 1849, only twenty-nine reached their intended destination: "The balance had been torn up and the money—$134.02—pocketed by the little villain through whose hands they passed!!" For Reid, the lesson was plain: "When you can give us New York at one end, with New Orleans and St. Louis on the other, united with the facilities we have, and each secure on our own lines, we need fear no competition, and we may put the O'Rielly lines against the world."[62]

O'Rielly's methods scared off potential investors and did much to earn the telegraph its unsavory reputation as a risky investment. "I found no encouragement in St. Louis," reported one would-be rival promoter in January 1851. O'Rielly had so entirely "'gulled'" the city's merchants that they had become "completely disgusted" with the telegraph as a potential investment, rendering it "next to impossible" to raise the necessary funds to build lines.[63]

The licensing of Morse's patent rights was a source of recurrent tension that frequently spilled into court. Kendall launched his legal campaign in 1846 when he got Morse a patent for an automatic telegraphic relay. Shortly thereafter Kendall obtained from the Patent Office a "reissue" of Morse's 1840 patent that broadened its scope.[64] Having bolstered Morse's patent rights, Kendall set his sights on patent infringers, known commonly as "pirates." The principal target of Kendall's legal campaign was O'Rielly, who, of course, had initially been a Morse licensee. Kendall canceled O'Rielly's contract in November 1846 on the grounds that O'Rielly had violated its terms by building lines in territory where O'Rielly had not yet been granted a license. O'Rielly saw things differently. Unfortunately for Kendall and O'Rielly, the language of their contract was so vague that it was hard to determine which interpretation was correct.

Unfazed by the cancellation of his contract, O'Rielly proceeded as if little had changed. The country was large, telegraph charters were easy to obtain, and telegraph equipment was cheap and easy to manufacture. To protect himself against lawsuits for patent infringement, O'Rielly modified slightly the telegraph equipment he had licensed from Morse—and kept right on building. Patent litigation was complex, and no one knew for certain how broadly the courts would construe Morse's patent rights.

The Kendall–O'Rielly contretemps came to a head over the perennially vexing issue of interconnection. The commercial potential of a telegraph network increased as it became longer and more intensively interconnected. For this reason, one might assume that Kendall would have welcomed the interconnection of Morse's lines with O'Rielly's. Yet Kendall refused: O'Rielly had violated federal patent law by using Morse equipment without a license and, thus, was guilty of patent infringement.[65] When O'Rielly switched to a nonelectromagnetic chemical telegraph patented by the British inventor Alexander Bain, Kendall sued him on the highly questionable ground that Morse's patents embraced every conceivable form of electrical communication. To O'Rielly's astonishment, Kendall's claim was sustained in court. Had Bain been American, O'Rielly might have won. Yet Bain had the misfortune of being British, and American judges were loath to rule in favor of non-American inventors. Bain had better not bring his own children to the United States, howled one journalist, lest Morse claim them as his own.[66]

Kendall and O'Rielly were both journalists, and so it was perhaps inevitable that their quarrel would find its way into print. Both were firmly convinced that their antagonist was in the wrong, and, as so often happened in such situations, their quarrel came to be waged with the ferocity of a religious crusade. Kendall ridiculed O'Rielly's oft-voiced claim that O'Rielly was the better antimonopolist because he relied on local capital to finance his lines. In reality, Kendall charged, O'Rielly was a mere shill for a grasping *"junta of speculators"* based in Rochester, New York. "The western people," Kendall sneered, "were to be *wheedled* into furnishing the money to build the lines and *amused* with local directories, but holding half or a majority of all the stock in all the companies, the confederates would choose their members, select their officers, and control every movement."[67]

O'Rielly scored a major publicity coup in 1848 when he exposed the Morse–Smith secret agreement of 1838. In a widely circulated open letter, O'Rielly demonstrated not only that Morse had granted Smith a share of Morse's still-to-be-issued telegraph patent—a fact that until then was little known—but also that this transaction had occurred several weeks before Smith had issued his euphoric congressional report on Morse's invention.

The Morse–Smith secret agreement was damning enough. Even worse was the "insidious scheme" of Morse and his "controllers" to obtain the necessary "governmental patronage" to build a vast telegraph network, a conspiracy "unparalleled"—O'Rielly charged, in a characteristic rhetorical fusillade—in the entire history of "any project in art or science."[68] The proprietors of Morse's patent claimed "universal control" over the "whole system" of electrical communications, complained O'Rielly to Boston mayor and fellow antimonopolist Josiah Quincy Jr., as if they could "really patent and monopolize a *General Principle!*" As a consequence, the "noblest enterprise" of the age had become "befogged"—a dig at Morse's partner, Francis O. J. Smith, whom journalists had dubbed "Fog."[69]

In our more jaundiced age O'Rielly's hyperbole might seem overblown. Yet his inference was sound. No matter how ingeniously Morse and his admirers tried to explain it away, Morse's secret agreement with Smith remained, as even historians sympathetic to Morse have acknowledged, one of the "most clear-cut cases of conflicts of interest on record."[70] The timing of the secret agreement was particularly incriminating, for it left no doubt that Morse had bribed a congressman by offering him a share of his invention in return for a favorable government report.

O'Rielly's correspondence with Quincy provides a glimpse of the early stirrings of a political movement that would later assume formidable proportions. The two men could not have been more different: O'Rielly was an Irish immigrant who had arrived in New York City at the age of 10, whereas Quincy was the scion of one of the oldest and most distinguished families in the country, who, as a boy, had spent many hours as a guest of former president John Adams at his Quincy, Massachusetts, homestead. Yet the two men found common cause in antimonopoly, an influential, if short-lived, reform movement designed to check the prerogatives of the railroad and telegraph corporations that had gained control of the channels of commerce.[71]

Antimonopolists derided railroad and telegraph leaders as "robber barons." The original robber barons were notorious medieval noblemen who defied the Holy Roman Emperor by laying chains across the Rhine River to collect tolls on passing vessels. The railroad leader–medieval nobleman analogy went back at least as far as the 1850s; the robber baron metaphor was current by 1869, when it was invoked by Charles Francis Adams Jr. in a personal letter to economist David A. Wells.[72] Beginning around 1865, Quincy used the metaphor or a variant— "feudal barons"—in several public addresses in which he criticized railroads for their high rates and low performance standards.[73] The presumption that certain favored individuals had illicitly obtained the power to dominate a channel of commerce was much older: in fact, it had been a major element in O'Rielly's assault on Morse's patent rights as early as 1848.

O'Rielly's revelations did little to tarnish Morse's reputation but posed a more serious problem for Kendall. Unable to shield himself behind the mantle of science, Kendall came in for a great deal of journalistic abuse. Kendall was actively lobbying to expand the scope of Morse's two patents, sputtered the editors of *Scientific American*. In addition, he had covertly recruited the patent examiners Leonard Gale and Charles G. Page to testify on Morse's behalf. The fact that Gale and Page both had a long-standing personal relationship with Morse only compounded the injustice. Gale had provided Morse with technical information about batteries and electromagnetism when he and Morse had been colleagues at New York University in the 1830s, and Page helped Morse obtain his 1846 patent for his automatic electromagnetic relay as an examiner in the Patent Office. Gale sold his interest in Morse's patent rights around the time he took a position in the Patent Office. Page, however, retained his shares in Morse's Magnetic Telegraph Company during the months he helped Morse obtain his 1846 patent.[74]

Kendall's legal campaign against O'Rielly culminated in January 1854, when the Supreme Court handed down its ruling in Morse's patent infringement suit against O'Rielly. In a majority opinion, Supreme Court Chief Justice Roger Taney endorsed Morse's contention that O'Rielly had infringed on Morse's patent rights and that Morse was the sole inventor of the electromagnetic telegraph. But Taney refused to extend Morse's patent rights to embrace every conceivable form of electromagnetic communication. It was permissible to patent a method of circulating information, Taney ruled—endorsing a distinction of

O'Rielly's—but it was impermissible to patent the underlying scientific principle on which this method relied.[75]

For Kendall, the Supreme Court ruling was a pyrrhic victory. Although it burnished Morse's ego, it opened the way for rivals who owned the patent rights to technical contrivances that, unlike O'Rielly's, were sufficiently different from Morse's to pass muster in the courts. It was hardly a ringing endorsement of Kendall's management skills that he had had to resort to the Supreme Court to settle a dispute with a licensee that had originated in a vaguely worded contract to which Kendall himself had been a party. Had Kendall provided licensees with technical support or bought the patent rights of Morse's rivals, it is conceivable that he might have fared better. Kendall did neither, and as a consequence, he failed to create the organizational capabilities necessary to transform Morse's patent rights into an enduring business.

Kendall's failure owed something to his overreliance on the postal-telegraphic analogy. The potential benefits of "unity" were so self-evident that Kendall spent little time figuring out how it might be realized. Just as the Post Office Department had been granted a broad range of special privileges by the federal Constitution, so, too, the telegraph should be invested with an analogous bundle of special privileges by virtue of Morse's patent rights. "It was the obvious interest of the country, as well as of the patentees," Kendall explained, "that the telegraph on the great lines of correspondence should, as far as practicable, be placed under one management. If, like the post office, the whole telegraph system for the United States could be managed by one energetic and honest directory, it would incalculably increase its utility and add to its profits."[76] To attain the "one management" ideal, Kendall looked to the courts. Taney's ruling spoiled his plans.

Among the many problems associated with Kendall's business strategy was his narrow conception of his mandate. The Post Office Department's special privileges were uncontroversial in large part because it was assumed that they were necessary to keep the citizenry well informed. Harder to justify were the special privileges that Kendall demanded for the telegraph corporations that had licensed Morse's patent rights. Kendall presumed that these corporations would cater to an exclusive clientele and actively discouraged the subsidization of thinly trafficked routes. "It is no part of our duty, and certainly not our policy," Kendall reminded one licensee in 1853, "to apply the proceeds of productive lines to keep up the unproductive lines for the convenience of the public."[77] Lacking a nonpecuniary justification for the special privileges to which he presumed himself entitled, Kendall had no alternative to trading on Morse's reputation—and this proved to be an inadequate foundation for establishing an interconnected telegraph network under a common set of regulations.

The limitations of Kendall's business strategy were highlighted by the failure of the American Telegraph Confederation (ATC). The ATC was an association of Morse licensees that Kendall organized in 1853 to facilitate cooperation between different telegraph corporations. Because the ATC lacked common protocols, it was often impossible to assign responsibility for messages that had been sent from one line to the next or even to prevent operators from threatening the integrity of Morse's code by tinkering with his dot-and-dash alphabet. "Multitudes abandon the use of the telegraph," explained one promoter, "not because their messages have been delayed or lost, but because they can obtain no satisfactory explanation of the cause."[78]

If the ATC had combined a substantial percentage of the country's largest telegraph corporations under a single legal framework, Kendall might have been able to bring some coherence to the telegraph business. Unfortunately for Kendall, however, the ATC linked together only those telegraph corporations that had obtained the rights to Morse's patents— which at this time represented but a fraction of the whole. Herein lay a dilemma. The ATC was not a patent pool like the sewing machine combine organized by sewing machine promoters in 1856 or the telegraph combine established by Morse's rivals the following year. A telegraph patent pool was anathema to Morse because he firmly believed that he alone had invented the telegraph; from his perspective, the rival patent holders who might be invited to join the pool had infringed on his rights. To remain Morse's manager, Kendall had no alternative to endorsing Morse's blinkered story line. Morse's stubbornness helped ensure Morse's immortality as a heroic inventor; at the same time, it doomed the business that Morse had hired Kendall to run.

The ATC was Kendall's last major attempt to contain the entrepreneurial juggernaut unleashed by the commercialization of the telegraph. Kendall, Smith, and the various other first-generation telegraph promoters had found it impossible to stabilize the market without resorting to the courts, a time-consuming, costly, and ultimately self-defeating expedient. The early history of the telegraph, concluded veteran promoter Ezra Cornell in 1853, was a "history of wars" between rival promoters, and the seemingly interminable wrangling would not cease until the "prime movers"—including Kendall and Smith—had left the field.[79] It was a shrewd assessment and can serve as an epitaph for Kendall's stewardship of Morse's patents. The demise of Morse's rickety telegraph network was swift. In 1859, Kendall and Smith sold their telegraph properties to the American Telegraph Company, a new entrant in the telegraph business that bore no relationship to Kendall's American Telegraph Confederation and that had not even existed when the Supreme Court had anointed Morse the inventor of the electromagnetic telegraph in 1854.

Kendall professed to be an antimonopolist, yet shared Morse's faith in federal control. Western Union's Hiram Sibley chose a different path and in so doing became what business analysts call a first mover—that is, a promoter who made the necessary investment in organizational capabilities to build an enduring institution. The corporation that Sibley built, and not the corporations that Kendall and Smith controlled, would dominate the telegraph business for the next hundred years.

Sibley succeeded where Kendall and Smith had failed by devising a business strategy that was peculiarly well suited to the state-oriented political economy that emerged after Morse failed to sell his patent rights to Congress. Business strategy followed political structure: to succeed in the state-oriented political economy, Sibley mastered the rules of the game.

In the state-oriented political economy, state legislatures retained broad authority over the corporate charters necessary to raise capital and obtain rights-of-way. In the early days of the telegraph business, state legislatures granted special charters that were more or less analogous to the special charters they had granted to the incorporators of turnpikes, canals, and railroads. Colt and Robinson had obtained just such a charter from the New York state legislature in 1846.[80] The granting of special charters raised the specter of monopoly and was swiftly abandoned. A contributor to the New York *Morning Courier* explained why. A special charter was a special privilege, and should the New York state legislature permit New York state senator Erastus Corning to operate telegraph lines on his railroad, his railroad–telegraph combine might become one of the "greatest and most mischievous monopolies" since the "creation of the world." The owners of the telegraph could use it to obtain advance information on sudden shifts in overseas markets, for the "exclusive use" of whoever had a "controlling influence" over its operation.[81]

To limit the potential for abuse, state legislatures in New York, Ohio, and several other states rejected special charters in favor of general incorporation. General incorporation institutionalized the principled antimonopolism that had long been a compelling civic ideal by popularizing the still-novel idea that federal control was not necessary to coordinate a business that transcended the boundaries of an individual state. No longer would the chartering of a telegraph corporation be a special privilege restricted to the favored few. Henceforth it would be a right accessible to all. No longer would telegraph promoters assume, as had Morse and Kendall, that the federal government would eventually establish some kind of permanent regulatory apparatus. Henceforth, competition would be an automatic regulator. The Post Office Department had a broad civic mandate to provide equal accommodations for the entire citizenry; telegraph network providers could limit their facilities to an exclusive clientele. To underscore this conceptual shift, contemporaries began to call telegraph start-ups chartered "private enterprises," a phrase that until then had been seldom used to characterize state-chartered corporations. Prior to general incorporation, an enterprise could be either private or corporate, but not both simultaneously. After general incorporation, it became customary to call even a large spatially extensive telegraph corporation a private enterprise.[82]

The principle of general incorporation was what nineteenth-century Americans meant when they invoked the eighteenth-century French doctrine of "laissez-faire." A laissez-faire political economy was neither an unregulated political economy nor a political economy in which the administrative apparatus of the state was small or insignificant. Rather, it denoted a political economy in which a promoter no longer needed to obtain a special charter to enter a business. Henceforth, entry to the telegraph business, and, by implication, access to the fruits of invention that were necessary to operate a successful telegraph corporation, would be open to all.[83]

Lawmakers hoped that general incorporation would hasten the release of huge reservoirs of entrepreneurial energy, and they would not be disappointed. Now that the state legislatures had opened the telegraph business to all comers, a multitude of corporations sprang up almost overnight to string lines along the most lucrative routes. Duplicate lines were common, as was the opportunistic price-cutting that competition encouraged. The freedom that American telegraph promoters enjoyed to build new lines had no counterpart in Great Britain, observed British engineer Joseph Whitworth in 1854. No private interest could oppose the erection of a telegraph line over any property, Whitworth marveled, making it unnecessary to hire counsel, call witnesses, or convene expensive hearings. If a telegraph line damaged someone's property, the corporation paid compensation, and that was that.[84]

The most influential general incorporation law, enacted by the New York state legislature in 1848, established the legal framework for two of the most important nineteenth-century telegraph corporations: Sibley's Western Union and Peter Cooper's American Telegraph Company. The American Telephone and Telegraph Company would also be chartered under its provisions, though not until 1885. The New York Telegraph Act of 1848 had two main provisions. First, it established a simple procedure for chartering telegraph corporations. And second, it empowered journalists to circumvent the first-come-first-served rule to transmit "intelligence" of "general and public interest."[85] Frequently amended to facilitate the extension of New York–based telegraph corporations across state lines, this law helped to ensure that New York would long remain the home of the largest and most powerful telegraph corporations in the country.[86]

The circumstances surrounding the enactment of the New York Telegraph Act of 1848 remain a matter of speculation because no transcripts of the debates that preceded its enactment have survived. In its solicitude for new entrants, it resembled the New York Banking Act of 1838. This landmark banking law, like the telegraph act, had been designed to limit the special privileges that lawmakers lavished on their friends.[87] Backers included individuals prominently associated with both the Democrats and the Whigs, which at the time were the state's two most important political parties. Democratic supporters included antimonopoly activist Henry O'Rielly; Whig backers included two influential journalists—Thurlow Weed of the *Albany Evening Journal* and James Brooks of the *New York Express*.[88]

For Brooks the necessity for some kind of government intervention was self-evident. Telegraph corporations were destined to become the only "*media* of communication" for price information on cotton, wheat, and provisions, giving their owners a "stupendous power" that it was "not in the nature of man not to abuse."[89] To minimize this danger, Brooks urged Congress to buy Morse out. When Congress declined, Brooks turned to the courts in the hope that they might declare the telegraph to be a common carrier under common law. If telegraph corporations remained unchecked by the "salutary restraints" of the common law of common carriers, they would soon possess a power that would give them control of "all we *think,* all we say, and all we communicate."[90]

Having failed in Congress and the courts, Brooks turned to the state legislature. Here he eventually met with success. To move things along, Brooks won a seat in the legislature for himself. To his chagrin, however, he failed to convince his fellow lawmakers to put telegraph corporations under the jurisdiction of the common law of common carriers. He could not even convince them to mount an inquiry into the expediency of regulating telegraph rates.[91] Yet Brooks did not come away empty handed. The New York Telegraph Act of 1848 limited the special privileges enjoyed by Morse licensees by simplifying the procedure for obtaining a telegraph charter. In addition, it created a special privilege for journalists, including Brooks himself, by giving journalists priority in the transmission of news reports.[92]

Hiram Sibley was what nineteenth-century Americans called a self-made man. Born in Massachusetts to parents of modest means, Sibley moved west as a young adult to a hamlet just south of Rochester, New York, a booming wheat-processing center on the Erie Canal. By dint of hard work, good luck, and a supportive Rochester-based social network, Sibley became a successful textile manufacturer. Following a chance encounter with telegraph inventor Royal E. House in 1847, Sibley shifted his focus from textiles to telegraphy. House convinced Sibley that the printing telegraph he had invented did not infringe on Morse's patent rights, and Sibley believed him. With the help of Rochester lawyers Henry R. Selden and Samuel L. Selden, Sibley convinced Supreme Court Justice Levi Woodbury to define House's patent rights broadly.[93]

Sibley's legal victory was yet another blow for Kendall's federally oriented business strategy. Unable to challenge House's invention on its merits, Kendall and Smith floated false rumors insinuating that House, a Vermont native, had in fact been born in England. Anti-British xenophobia ran high and had prejudiced the courts against Alexander Bain, another rival telegraph inventor who was, in fact, British. Yet it failed to derail House. House issued a pointed response in which he accused Kendall and Smith of trying to monopolize the telegraph business and emphasized that he, too, was a native-born American. Woodbury backed House, creating a market opportunity that Sibley was quick to exploit.[94]

House's telegraph was in theory a major advance over Morse's. Morse's telegraph transmitted signals that a skilled operator had to code and decode; House's printed the letters of the alphabet. In practice, House's telegraph was slower and more complicated than Morse's. It was rapidly abandoned whenever promoters obtained a license to Morse's patent rights.

Sibley believed that the most promising market for the telegraph lay in the West. If he could build an east-west line between Buffalo and St. Louis, Sibley assumed that he could negotiate advantageous contracts with more established lines back East. Unfortunately for Sibley, many other would-be network builders had the same idea. Following a brief building spree that took him as far west as Louisville, Sibley concluded that there was no substitute for a coherent business strategy. Like Kendall before him, he had discovered a basic principle of telegraph network building: "methodless enthusiasm" did not pay.[95]

Having rejected line building, Sibley shifted to line consolidating. The value of a telegraph network, Sibley hypothesized, increased as it became more extensive and interconnected. If he merged several formerly rival corporations into a single combine, the combine might make a profit even if the individual corporations had operated at a loss. Interconnection had the further benefit of decreasing the likelihood that a message would be delayed, garbled, or lost when transferred from one independent line to another.

To raise the necessary funds, Sibley turned to the people who had helped him rise from poverty to wealth. Through a combination of bluster, charm, and a boundless faith in the commercial possibilities of the telegraph, Sibley persuaded twenty prominent Rochesterians—including the Seldens—to invest an average of $5,000 each, for a grand total of $100,000—a major gamble for a city of Rochester's size. The $100,000 that Sibley obtained provided him with all the capital he needed to build up an enterprise that would soon become one of the largest corporations in the country.[96]

Sibley's appeal was heightened by the involvement of many Rochesterians in the telegraph business as investors and promoters. O'Rielly hailed from the city, as did Anson Stager and James D. Reid. Stager and

Reid both worked as telegraph operators on early O'Rielly lines, Stager in Lancaster, Pennsylvania, Reid in Pittsburgh. Stager left the telegraph business soon after O'Rielly's break with Kendall to take a more secure position in the U.S. Coast Survey, a federal government agency responsible for mapping the shoreline. He returned to the telegraph business in 1852 to work for Sibley and remained at Western Union until 1881. Reid worked for various telegraph corporations, first as an operator and then as a journalist. In 1879, he published a copiously detailed 846-page history of the telegraph business in the United States in which he gave due attention to his fellow Rochesterians, including O'Rielly, for whom Reid worked first as a clerk in the Rochester post office.

According to an oft-told story that, at least in its broad details, has the ring of authenticity, Sibley raised the $100,000 at a single meeting in which he assembled a large number of Rochesterians in a room and asked them point-blank to sign a contract that would commit them to purchase a certain number of shares. How, one naysayer wondered, could a merger of telegraph lines that had failed individually possibly succeed as a combine? Rather than answer this question directly, Sibley asked his friends and neighbors to demonstrate their confidence in him by purchasing telegraph stock.[97]

Sibley knew his audience, and so his gambit worked. For a quarter century Rochester had been at the epicenter of an outpouring of evangelical fervor known today as the Second Great Awakening. On countless occasions, revivalists importuned the city's business leaders to take personal responsibility for their decisions. Sibley's appeal fit into this time-honored tradition. Like the signing of a temperance pledge or an affirmation of spiritual rebirth, the purchase of telegraph stock became a profession of faith.

Flush with cash, Sibley earned the sobriquet "line gobbler" for his rapid acquisition of telegraph lines.[98] When Sibley built his Buffalo–Louisville line, there were between twenty and thirty different telegraph corporations in the United States.[99] Few made any money; several competed head-to-head; many came cheap. In one instance, Sibley bought a line originally valued at $240,000 for 2 cents on the dollar.[100] One of Sibley's greatest coups was his takeover, in 1855, of the Michigan-based telegraph network cobbled together by Morse licensee Ezra Cornell. With this acquisition, Sibley acquired hundreds of additional miles of line in the upper Midwest as well as the patent rights to Morse's invention for the territory Cornell controlled. In Reid's judgment, these patent rights proved to be far more valuable than all the miles of wire that Cornell had strung.[101] Sibley's buyout of Cornell hastened a change in corporate nomenclature. At Cornell's suggestion, Sibley decided to call his corporation "Western Union." Though Cornell came up with the name, the business strategy was Sibley's.

To consolidate his telegraph network, Sibley hit upon an ingenious legal expedient: the exclusive right-of-way contract. If Western Union were to thrive in a business in which entry was easy and fixed costs were low, Sibley had to find some way to segment the market. Exclusive right-of-way contracts provided Western Union with a competitive advantage on the most highly trafficked routes and gave it the dependable through connections necessary to ensure consistent performance standards. The "supreme value" of these contracts, explained Reid in reviewing their history, lay in the protection they afforded incumbents from new entrants.[102] The "great point gained," observed Anson Stager, in explaining their rationale, was to "secure the right of way" and "shut out other parties" even if the promoter had "no definite idea" as to the "plan of construction."[103]

A typical right-of-way contract guaranteed a telegraph corporation the exclusive right to operate its lines along a railroad right-of-way and gave the railroad free use of the line for its routine business. In so doing, it presumed a mutuality of interests between the telegraph and the railroad that was far closer than anything Amos Kendall attained or desired. How Sibley came up with this idea is uncertain. Among the likely models were the exclusive long-term contracts that package carriers had negotiated with the railroads over which they operated.

Right-of-way contracts were an ad hoc solution to the problem of operating a state-spanning business in a state-oriented political economy that glorified equal rights and vilified special privilege. The protection they afforded network providers was independent of whatever patent rights they possessed; patent rights protected the nodes in the network, whereas right-of-way contracts protected the links. Patent rights were federal monopoly grants; in a political economy that vilified special privilege, this made them vulnerable to legal challenges mounted by rival promoters. Right-of-way contracts were private agreements between consenting parties; in a political economy that glorified equal rights, this rendered them sacrosanct. This was true even though these contracts could plausibly be characterized as a restraint of trade, a business practice illegal under common law. Morse's patent rights had been challenged repeatedly from 1847 onward. The first successful legal challenge to Western Union's right-of-way contracts would not come until 1879.

Railroad-based telegraph lines limited the hazards that bedeviled network builders who strung wires along remote turnpikes and country roads. Foliage was a constant challenge, for it often damaged telegraph wires. Even in parts of the country where foliage was not a problem, railroad-based lines reduced maintenance costs: it was easier for work crews to reach a telegraph line that had been damaged by vandals, storms, or high winds from a railroad handcar than from a horse-drawn wagon.[104]

Had railroad corporations built their own telegraph lines, they might have found it easier to negotiate more favorable contracts with telegraph corporations, or even to supplant them altogether by establishing their own railroad-owned network. Sibley himself reached this conclusion in 1860.[105] Yet few railroads did, telegraph corporations filled the gap, and the opportunity was lost. As late as 1879, fewer than a half-dozen railroads owned any telegraph wires.[106] "Sublime" as the telegraph was, reminisced telegraph promoter Jeptha H. Wade, and "useful and indispensable" as it later became in the dispatching of trains, it was "wonderful" how slow railroad leaders were to "comprehend its importance" and how hard it proved to be to "get them to try it." It took a good deal of hard work to persuade Michigan Central president J. W. Brooks to string a telegraph line along his railroad right-of-way. Brooks protested that he would rather have a single handcar to keep his track in repair than all the telegraph lines Wade could build. If Wade's line became entangled with Brooks's rolling stock, it might endanger his crew. Wade persisted, Brooks reluctantly yielded the point, and the line was built.[107]

Railroad right-of-way contracts helped Western Union dominate the telegraph business in the states where it operated. Yet these contracts did nothing to prevent rivals from underbidding it in the rest of the country. Here the solution lay in negotiating a market-segmenting agreement between rival network providers that resembled a cartel.

Sibley negotiated his first market-sharing agreement in 1857. To formalize relations between network providers, Sibley persuaded six of the country's largest telegraph corporations to sign a pact known as the Treaty of Six Nations and to join a trade group that was known as the North American Telegraph Association (NATA).[108] The original Treaty of Six Nations had been signed in 1794 between the federal government and six powerful upstate New York Indian tribes to demarcate the territory allotted to each tribe. Sibley's consortium was a noncompete agreement between six of the country's largest and most successful telegraph corporations. To Kendall's chagrin, it assigned no special significance to Morse's telegraph patents. Sibley's agreement was for *"thirty years,"* Kendall fumed, and "no one would know from the face of the paper itself that such a man as Samuel F. B. Morse ever existed."[109]

The NATA segmented the telegraph market by mandating interconnection protocols and granting each of its signatories the patent rights to an improved printing telegraph invented by David Hughes. Its "chief object," its proceedings declared, was to end the rivalries between telegraph corporations that had proved "so destructive to their interests" and that had rendered the "large capital" invested in the telegraph business "comparatively profitless." Few rival lines had yielded a fair rate of return: "Experience has shown that no benefit or advantage results to the public by ruinous competition."[110]

Unlike Kendall's ATC, the NATA was a genuine patent pool rather than a mere alliance of Morse licensees. Before long, it gained control of the patent rights owned not only by Hughes, but also by Morse, House, and Bain. In so doing, reminisced one later chronicler, it became the "Supreme Court" of the business, from which there could be no appeal.[111] The six corporations that dominated the American telegraph business, O'Rielly lamented in 1860, had successfully insulated themselves from the wholesome laws of competition that he had tried to institutionalize in the New York Telegraph Act of 1848. Would the public interest be served, O'Rielly asked rhetorically, if the "post office system" had been divided up into six corporations and operated in an analogous way? For O'Rielly, the answer was plain: "Cheap postage and cheap telegraphing are alike important to a free people. The *first* is secured to the public by law; the *second* is controlled by a close monopoly, governed by no law but their own interests."[112]

Sibley's business strategy accommodated the state-oriented political economy fostered by the New York Telegraph Act of 1848. Yet it also remained mindful of those realms in which the federal government was still influential. These included the construction of large-scale ventures, such as an Atlantic cable between Great Britain and the United States and a Pacific telegraph between New York City and San Francisco. Federal lawmakers deemed these projects of such importance that they were willing to enact federal legislation to hasten their completion.

The Atlantic cable was a pet project of Cyrus Field, a wealthy paper manufacturer on the prowl for lucrative investment opportunities. To fund the venture, Field raised $1.5 million, mostly from a circle of well-to-do friends in New York City, which he supplemented with additional funds from British investors. Field's Atlantic cable worked briefly in 1858; almost immediately, it went dead. Not until 1866 would a British consortium establish a permanent telegraphic link between Great Britain and the United States.

The Atlantic cable received various kinds of government support. One of the most important was logistical. It was one thing to raise the funds to lay a cable across the Atlantic; it was quite another to figure out where the cable should be laid. This latter problem had been solved by the superintendent of the Naval Observatory, Matthew Maury. During a navy-sponsored mapping expedition of the North Atlantic, Maury located a calm and level ocean bed between Newfoundland and Ireland that he labeled the "Telegraphic Plateau." This plateau seems to have been "placed there especially," Maury explained, for the purpose of "holding the wires of a submarine telegraph" and "keeping them out of harm's way."[113]

Maury's report appeared at around the same time Field had begun to raise funds for his Atlantic cable. It emboldened not only Field, but also the British consortium that eventually succeeded where Field had failed. Funding for Maury's research, of course, had come not from private investors but from the federal government. In its absence, the Atlantic cable might have been even longer delayed.

Just as the federal government had supported the laying of the Atlantic cable, so, too, it hastened the completion of the first east-west telegraph to span the North American continent. A Pacific telegraph had long been a cherished dream of telegraph promoter Henry O'Rielly, but ultimately it was built not by O'Rielly but by Sibley. Sibley obtained a federal grant to build a Pacific telegraph in 1860 and completed the work in October 1861. For Western Union, its completion was a "vast accession" of "strength and prestige," reflected James D. Reid, that elevated it to an enviable position as one of the vastest and "most comprehensive" of all the private enterprises in the world.[114]

O'Rielly had first championed a Pacific telegraph in 1849 shortly after Mexico's cession of California to the United States. A rudimentary telegraph network linked most of the commercial centers east of the Mississippi River, yet the westward extension of this network to the Pacific remained a visionary dream. Relatively few pioneers had settled the vast territory that lay between the Great Plains and California, and much of this territory remained under the control of hostile Indian tribes. Undaunted by the challenge, O'Rielly convinced the attendees of a St. Louis commercial convention to endorse its construction in 1849.[115]

In the popular imagination today, the Pacific telegraph and the transcontinental railroad are inextricably linked. O'Rielly's contemporaries saw things differently. In the same year O'Rielly addressed the St. Louis convention, for example, Asa Whitney published a 112-page brief for a transcontinental railroad that ignored the telegraph altogether.[116]

To build public support for a Pacific telegraph, O'Rielly teamed up with Illinois senator Stephen A. Douglas. Douglas was a logical ally because he had already thrown his support behind a transcontinental railroad. True to his antimonopoly convictions, O'Rielly did not seek a federal subsidy to build his telegraph. Rather, he requested merely that the army protect his contractors in those parts of the trans-Mississippi West that remained vulnerable to Indian attack. Although Kendall's lawsuit had ruined O'Rielly financially, O'Rielly retained many friends in high places who pitied him as a bold and courageous promoter unfairly victimized by a vicious legal vendetta. O'Rielly might not be much of a financier, reported one of Sibley's informants, yet he had cultivated friendly personal relations with dozens of distinguished statesmen, journalists, and politicians who would take more pleasure in doing him a favor than "almost any man in the country."[117] In the end, however, Congress declined O'Rielly's proposal to build a Pacific telegraph on the grounds that O'Rielly could neither raise the necessary funds to complete the project nor obtain the necessary patent rights to stay out of court.[118]

Emboldened by the completion of the Pacific telegraph, Sibley turned his attention to the even grander project of linking the United States and Europe. To achieve this goal, Sibley rejected Field's direct route across the North Atlantic. Telegraph experts had concluded that it was impossible to span such an enormous body of water, and Sibley concurred.[119] As an alternative, Sibley set out to reach Europe in the opposite direction by way of Alaska, the Bering Strait, and Siberia. The trans-Siberian route offered the "only feasible and reliable" method of permanently connecting the United States and Europe, Sibley lectured Field in 1861, and was destined to become one of the most "paying investments" in the world. When completed, Sibley boasted, it would leave nothing more in "telegraphic communication" for "human enterprise" to achieve other than to "fill up the picture" with "lateral lines."[120]

Unfortunately for Sibley, the telegraph experts were wrong. Sibley's trans-Siberian telegraph remained unfinished in 1866 when a British consortium successfully laid an Atlantic cable that was cheaper to operate, and, thus, more profitable, than Sibley's trans-Siberian line. Sibley's Siberian work crews toiled on for a few more months, yet the die was cast. Sibley's boldest gamble had failed.

The trans-Siberian telegraph cost its investors several million dollars for which they received not a penny in return. To cushion the blow, Sibley arranged for his shareholders to swap their shares for Western Union bonds. The ethics of Sibley's financial legerdemain troubled Western Union investors and hastened Sibley's ouster as Western Union president in 1866. For Sibley's successor William Orton, it was nothing short of outrageous. By saddling Western Union with a $5 million loss, Orton fumed, Sibley had perpetrated a fraud that deserved to be classed with the notorious South Sea bubble and that would almost certainly have destroyed Western Union had it not been the beneficiary of windfall profits during the Civil War.[121]

The most enduring legacy of the trans-Siberian telegraph was the annexation of Alaska by the federal government. Alaska was a remote and sparsely populated wilderness that remained almost entirely unknown. One of the major factors that tipped the balance in favor of annexation was the detailed inventory of Alaska's natural resources compiled by a team of Smithsonian Institution scientists that accompanied Western Union's construction crew. The Smithsonian report helped Secretary of State William H. Seward persuade skeptical lawmakers that the United States would be well served if it acquired a territory widely derided as a wasteland. "The project of the Western Union Telegraph Company of an overland telegraph across Bering Straits to Europe was a failure," concluded one of the scientists who had taken part in the expedition, "but its greatest result was the annexation of Alaska."[122] Here, as in the case of the Atlantic telegraph, a federal government agency had generated knowledge that shaped the course of events.

Warfare is often a catalyst for innovation, and the Civil War was no exception. Secretary of War Edwin M. Stanton, having served before the war as a director of a Pennsylvania-based telegraph corporation, understood the value of the telegraph in coordinating complex military operations on a continental scale.[123] To operate the military telegraph, Stanton tapped Western Union's Anson Stager. Before the war, Stager had inveigled railroad leaders to permit telegraph corporations to string wire along their rights-of-way; now his job was to sell the telegraph to the military. "General orders are given, armies are moved, battles are planned and fought, and victories won"—Stager declared, in a characteristically laudatory official report—"with the assistance of this simple yet powerful aide-de-camp—the military telegraph."[124]

The 15,000 miles of telegraph lines Stager operated and the 6 million telegrams the military telegraph sent did much to keep supplies moving, troops positioned, and lawmakers informed.[125] The "genius of Morse," gushed a former military telegrapher in 1882, had laid the groundwork for the rapid military maneuvers of General Ulysses S. Grant.[126] The military telegrapher exaggerated: the military railroad had been even more indispensable in coordinating the movement of troops and supplies. Yet the military telegraph did play a major, if rarely noted, part in helping the Union win the war. The Union operated 15,000 miles of military telegraph lines; the Confederacy had a mere 1,000 miles. This was a remarkable disparity, especially given the enormous size of the territory that the Confederacy embraced.[127]

The contribution of the telegraph to the Union victory was by no means confined to logistics. By facilitating the circulation of countless news reports for individual newspapers and the NYAP, it was also instrumental in molding public opinion in the North. False and misleading news reports were a constant challenge. On one occasion, Lincoln briefly suspended publication of a New York City newspaper whose editors had published an incendiary news report that turned out to be a hoax. To monitor the news, the Lincoln administration established a censorship bureau headed up by American Telegraph Company president Edward S. Sanford. Sanford's bureau worked closely not only with telegraph corporations, but also with the NYAP, the country's most important newsbroker.[128]

Sanford's appointment was a tribute to the dominant position American Telegraph had attained in the critical North-South Atlantic seaboard market that linked the North Atlantic shipping lanes with New York City and Washington. The entente that Sanford's American Telegraph Company had negotiated with the NYAP consolidated NYAP control over the newsbroker business. This action made it relatively easy for Sanford to monitor news reports without imposing the draconian censorship that he might have found impossible to avoid had the newsbroker business been less tightly controlled.

Western Union's wartime profits enabled Sibley to make good on the promise he had made to his Rochester investors in 1854. While the rest of the country was riveted on news reports from the front, Rochester was gripped by a telegraph mania. Three times during the war—in 1862 and twice in 1863—Sibley paid out large bonuses to Western Union's shareholders by issuing them additional shares of Western Union stock. Since each share paid an annual dividend, these bonuses generated a financial bonanza for their owners. Immediately after Sibley announced the first bonus in December 1863, Western Union stock shot up to $225 a share, $125 above its par value of $100. Telegraph shares remained tightly held in Rochester, and, as the share price soared, Sibley's Rochester friends and neighbors sold pianos and furniture and took out second mortgages on real estate to buy up the shares that had come onto the market.[129]

Sibley's successors regarded his wartime financial maneuvering with a mixture of disgust and disdain. Sibley's bonuses were a "stupendous blunder," observed rival promoter Norvin Green in 1865, because they divorced Western Union's capitalization from the value of the assets to which its capitalization should have remained pegged, obliging it to pay out far more in dividends than its more prudently financed rivals.[130] Green might have had occasion to reconsider such a judgment in 1881 when as Western Union's president he himself acquiesced in an even more audacious shareholder giveaway orchestrated by the financier Jay Gould. Sibley did his best to justify his wartime financial record in an interview he gave at age 78 to a New York City newspaper in 1885. Wartime bonuses, Sibley insisted, had not severed the link between Western Union's assets and its capitalization. Rather, they had merely adjusted Western Union's capitalization upward to better reflect the actual value of the assets on which it had been based.[131]

Whether Sibley had blundered was beside the point. Since the 1840s, promoters had hailed the telegraph as the greatest invention of the age. Prior to Sibley, few figured out how to make it pay. The vast majority of telegraph lines had been established by a tiny clique of insiders in a "spirit of speculation," reminisced one telegraph promoter in 1859.[132] Even promoters who hunkered down for the long haul often ran afoul of ruinous competition. "I have seen strong men who had embarked their all in its success after years of severe struggling give up in despair," reminisced one Rochester-based Western Union investor shortly after the end of the Civil War: "Organization after organization became bankrupt, 'til it seemed that the whole enterprise would prove a most disastrous failure."[133]

Sibley had convinced his friends and neighbors to trust him with their money, and he had not let them down. Had an investor purchased 100 shares of Western Union stock in 1854 for $100,000 and held onto them until 1881, his investment would have netted him $963,400.[134] Unlike so many telegraph promoters, Sibley had built up "regularly organized companies," explained one early chronicler.[135] Sibley's Western Union flourished in a competitive state-oriented political economy that circumvented its antimonopoly logic by negotiating exclusive right-of-way contracts with some of the country's largest and most powerful railroads. Through a fortunate combination of realism, boldness, and luck, Sibley had beaten the odds.

The commercialization of the electric telegraph spawned a deluge of magazine articles, sermons, and editorials. In keeping with the antimonopoly logic of the state-oriented political economy, these tributes hailed the channel of communications, rather than the private corporations that had built the facilities on which telegraph users relied. The telegraph was the agent, and not the "founders, promoters, and noted men" whose achievements James D. Reid chronicled in exhaustive detail in his *Telegraph in America*.

Expansive tributes to the telegraph dated back to Francis O. J. Smith's 1838 congressional report; they proliferated within days of the completion of the first Washington–Baltimore line. "In the Midst of a Revolution," screamed one headline in James Gordon Bennett's *New York Herald* shortly after learning that Morse's demonstration project had been a success: "We are indeed on the dawn of a greater era in the history of human progress on this continent than, perhaps, even enthusiasm itself has dreamed."[136] By bringing the opposite extremes of a vast continent within the limits of an hour, Morse's invention had made it difficult for even the "most enthusiastic imagination" to exaggerate the "progress of the race during the next half century."[137]

Similar tributes echoed and reechoed for the next forty years. By demonstrating the commercial potential of electricity—that "great hidden force in nature"—opined one journalist in *Harper's New Monthly Magazine* in 1873, the telegraph marked the dawn of a new epoch in history.[138] The "grandeur," "beauty," and "beneficence" of its "mission" led journalists to proclaim the telegraph a "highway of thought," recorded Reid in his *Telegraph in America* a few years later.[139] The telegraph was the *only* modern contrivance that was so astonishing in its results, reflected another journalist in 1881, that not even the legendarily prescient seventeenth-century polymath Francis Bacon could have envisioned its invention.[140]

Among the features of the telegraph that preoccupied city dwellers living along the Atlantic seaboard was its utility as an early warning system in the event of a foreign naval attack. It is sometimes contended that the nineteenth-century United States had little to fear from the European great powers. In fact, New Yorkers and Philadelphians retained a lively apprehension of their vulnerability to naval bombardment. Should a foreign army threaten New York City, predicted James Brooks, the "whole armed population" of the free states could be brought to its defense with the "force of lightning": "A living fortress of a million armed men are now within hail. We touch the wires of the telegraph, and in an instant they spring to our rescue."[141] No foreign army could long maintain a foothold in the United States, reflected a Philadelphia journalist, now that the principal seaboard cities had become linked together in a communications network that was capable of arousing 3 million able-bodied fighting men at a "single touch of the wire."[142]

In an age conspicuous for its evangelical piety, any medium that enabled individuals to circulate ideas over large distances and at high speed was an invitation to theological reflection. God annihilated space and time and now, too, could mere mortals. "Newspapers vie with each other in gas and grandiloquence," sneered Cyrus Field's neighbor George Templeton Strong when he learned that Field had spanned the Atlantic. Journalists freely compared Field's cable to the angel in the Book of Revelation, while "moderate people" hailed it merely as the "greatest human achievement in history." All in all, Strong had had enough: "Has so extensive, simultaneous, vociferous, and insolent a bray been emitted by puffed-up humanity on any previous occasion?"[143]

The "annihilation" metaphor itself prompted critical reflection. Few found the word "annihilation" troubling, even though it had a decidedly foreboding ring. At least one journalist wondered whether the metaphor accurately characterized the consequences of the telegraph for everyday life. It was commonly said that the electric telegraph had annihilated time and space, conceded this journalist in 1873. In a "deeper sense," it had magnified both: "For it has been the means of expanding vastly the inadequate conception which we form of space and distance, and of giving a significance to the idea of time which it never before had to the human mind."[144] The journalist had a point. By hastening the rapid circulation of information in time and space, the telegraph proved instrumental for tasks ranging from the creation of a nationwide public opinion and the reconfiguration of a global market to the mapping of the earth, the seas, the atmosphere, and the heavens. None of these tasks annihilated time and space. Rather, they had amplified them by shifting cognitive frameworks and readjusting perceptual lenses.

The high cost of telegraphy raised related questions about its accessibility. The telegraph was so expensive that its users were necessarily restricted to the "wealthier classes," observed one postal reformer in 1856. In contrast, the mail—"cheap, uniform, and certain"—remained "emphatically" the "institution of the middling and poorer classes of the community."[145] The impersonality of the telegram was another cause for concern. Although moralists implied that telegraphic communication was transparent, in fact, every telegram bore unmistakable signs of a human intermediary. Unlike the mail, the telegraph was "incapable" of conveying the "private feelings and sentiments" of one friend to another, observed maverick inventor John W. Post in 1856. This was not only because telegrams bore no trace of the sender's handwriting, but also because their content had been revealed to the telegraph operators who coordinated their transmission. A superior alternative was an "atmospheric" telegraph, a steam-powered pneumatic pump that, if properly configured, had the capacity to propel "mail balls" containing letters at 1,000 miles per hour. Post's fanciful invention failed to impress lawmakers preoccupied with other things. Yet it underscored two of the telegraph's most basic limitations: the telegraph was impersonal, and it was not private.[146]

The most searching issue the telegraph critics raised concerned the implicit equation of its enthusiasts between technical advance and moral progress. Like most technical advances, naturalist Henry David Thoreau reflected in 1854, telegraphs were nothing but "pretty toys": an "improved means" to an "unimproved end" that distracted attention from "serious things." Americans were in "great haste" to build a telegraph from Maine to Texas, but what if Maine and Texas had nothing important to communicate?[147] The creation of a long-distance telegraph network elicited similar misgivings from Illinois lawmaker Abraham Lincoln. Like the transcontinental railroad, Lincoln reflected in a public lecture that he delivered in 1859, the Pacific telegraph was a dubious expedient beloved of "Young America," the impulsive and reckless band of adventurers whose imperial fantasies held no charms for soberminded "old fogies" like himself. Unmentioned in the surviving transcript of Lincoln's lecture was an additional objection to both the Pacific telegraph and the transcontinental railroad that any reasonably well-informed member of Lincoln's audience could have been expected to grasp: each was a pet project of Stephen A. Douglas, Lincoln's most bitter political foe.[148]

Few nightmares haunted lawmakers in the early republic more than the specter of disunion. Every schoolchild knew that no republic as spatially extensive as the United States had long endured. The only solution to the "inconveniences" and even the "dangers" posed by the enormous size of the United States, warned Treasury secretary Albert Gallatin in 1808, lay in the federal government's establishment of "speedy and easy communication" throughout the country: "No other single operation, within the power of government, can more effectually tend to strengthen and perpetuate that union, which secures external independence, domestic peace, and internal liberty."[149]

By "communication," Gallatin meant roads and canals; the now-familiar bifurcation between the conveyance of people, goods, and information had not yet been made. Even so, it did not require too great a leap of logic to hail the telegraph as the ultimate solution to the problem Gallatin had posed. The presumption that a spatially extensive telegraph network would ensure the perpetuation of the Union found frequent expression in the press. The impending telegraphic linkage of New York City and New Orleans, predicted James Gordon Bennett, would inexorably transform all of the intermediate cities into a single "vast metropolis" that "nothing could dissever."[150] And in that not-too-distant day when a telegraph network spanned the globe, war would be no more, and cannonballs and mortars would be locked up in museums as "curiosities and remnants of a barbarous age."[151] The political challenge of perpetuating a spatially extensive republic had greatly troubled James Madison, Thomas Ritchie reminded readers in 1847 in the *Daily Union,* the official organ of President James K. Polk. Yet even a statesman as prescient as Madison had failed to anticipate how the railroad, the steamboat, and the telegraph would one day solve the seemingly intractable political dilemma that distance had posed: "As every day adds to the rapidity of intercourse, it removes some objection to the extent of our territory."[152]

The relationship Bennett and Ritchie envisioned between the telegraph and territorial expansion was not merely theoretical. When Morse completed his demonstration project in 1844, the United States was poised to annex Texas; by the time Kendall linked Washington and New York City, Polk had declared war on Mexico. The prospect that the United States–Mexican War might extend the boundary of the United States southward heartened Bennett and Ritchie, who hailed it as proof of the country's providential "manifest destiny." The phrase "manifest destiny" was coined in 1845 by John L. O'Sullivan, a like-minded journalist who shared Bennett and Ritchie's enthusiasm not only for the telegraph, but also for the conquest of Mexico.[153] None of these journalists found it troubling that the telegraph was certain to foster the rapid incorporation into the United States of a vast expanse of territory well suited to slave-based plantation agriculture. Indeed, this was precisely the point. By expanding the slaveholders' republic, the telegraph was a tool of empire that would slow the insidious developmentalism that, if left unchecked, would endanger the republic by increasing the political power of the nonslaveholding states. When it became possible to send a message instantaneously from Texas to Maine, exulted Bennett in 1844, the southward extension of the republic to the "uttermost extremities" of the North American continent would become no less "natural, justifiable, and safe" than the northward march of New York City to the Harlem River.[154]

The linkage of the telegraph with the perpetuation of a slaveholders' republic was so common—and so plausible, given the north-south orientation of the principal telegraph lines—that it is unsurprising that its commercialization was greeted with enthusiasm not only by Bennett, Ritchie, and O'Sullivan, but also by James D. B. De Bow and George Fitzhugh. De Bow and Fitzhugh were proslavery apologists who combined a defense of the South with a highly selective approach to technical advance. Although Fitzhugh regarded many inventions as pernicious, he made an exception for Field's Atlantic cable.[155] By linking in a vast transatlantic arc the cotton textile manufacturers of Great Britain with the cotton planters of the South, it perpetuated a political economy founded on slave labor and sustained by the export of slave-labor-based agricultural staples. That its inventor was Morse, Fitzhugh would doubtless have found reassuring. Morse too was a stalwart anti-abolitionist. In fact, Morse continued to defend slavery in print as a positive good even after such arguments ceased to be fashionable among conservative northern Democrats with close ties to the South.[156]

The spatial geography of the telegraph had a political cast. Proslavery Democrats like Bennett, Ritchie, and O'Sullivan had little trouble envisioning the telegraph spanning the North American continent from north to south. Antislavery Whigs such as New York senator William Seward preferred to envision it spanning the continent from east to west. The telegraph had become "indispensable," declared Seward in 1849, in endorsing O'Rielly's Pacific telegraph, in "perfecting" the "integrity" of the nation.[157] A new generation was growing up on the Pacific Coast, observed the moderate antislavery Whig Millard Fillmore in 1853. When it matured, the bonds that linked it to the rest of the country could only be "equal" if there existed a "free and uninterrupted" east-west communication between the national capital and the furthest reaches of the republic.[158]

The telegraph failed to save the Union from the maelstrom of civil war. The enhanced facilities for circulating the news reports that it created exacerbated sectional tensions, just as Amos Kendall had feared. No longer could proslavery radicals like Jefferson Davis deliver one speech in Mississippi and another in Maine.[159] The sectional animosities that the telegraph engendered so unsettled President James Buchanan that it led him to wonder aloud on the eve of the war whether its "political evils" might overbalance its commercial advantages.[160] There could be "no more insidious" form of "treachery," warned one patriotic Unionist after the war had begun, than the "electric thrill of panic" that swept through the civilian population following the hourly transmission of misleading news reports to the home front that had been sent by irresponsible journalists from the theater of war.[161]

Not everyone was so pessimistic. Completion of the Pacific telegraph prompted California Supreme Court justice Stephen J. Field to send President Lincoln a telegram in which Field expressed the earnest hope that the line would strengthen the "attachment" of the people of California to the Union in its "day of trial."[162] Field's message furnished the theme for a *Harper's Weekly* cartoon that ran the following month. "May the Union Be Perpetual," proclaimed a scroll symbolizing Field's telegram, which an angel protectively clutched as she tiptoed along a telegraph line linking California with the East.[163] The "momentous fact" of instantaneous communication, reflected one journalist in the following year, was fostering a unity of public sentiment that was more impervious to falsehood than would have been conceivable in any previous age: "All are impressed at the same time with the same thoughts, or with such kindred ideas as will naturally arise from reflection upon the same facts. Rumor, with its thousand tongues, is hushed."[164] Left unmentioned by the journalist was the extent to which it was not only the fact of "instantaneous" communication, but also the efficacy of the Lincoln administration's wartime censorship bureau that had helped to ensure that "rumor" remained "hushed."

The presumption that technical advances like the telegraph could unite Americans in a single continent-spanning nation found expression in President Lincoln's 1862 annual message to Congress. The electric telegraph, steam power, and "intelligence" had created the institutional preconditions necessary to support a single "national family" in the territory embraced by the prewar United States, rather than the two or more "families" that the Confederacy envisioned.[165] No longer did Lincoln poke fun at the Pacific telegraph as he had as recently as 1859. On the contrary, he now envisioned it as a guarantor of the Union.

The linkage Lincoln made between network and nation received a powerful boost with the victory of the North over the South in 1865. The Confederate defeat helped to transform into a cliché the still somewhat novel idea that the country was no longer a "union" of largely autonomous states, but, rather, a single consolidated nation. In the absence of the "free and rapid communication" facilitated by the railroad, steamboat, and telegraph, declared the author of a civics textbook in 1872, it was inconceivable that a country as spatially extensive as the United States could have survived its civil war. With these technical advances, the country had become more compact than any country in any previous age that was one one-hundredth its size.[166] The "only reasonable expectation" that a people dispersed over so "vast and various" a territory as the United States would remain permanently one nation, declared a distinguished astronomer in 1881, hinged on the presumption that the daily nationwide circulation of identical news broadcasts would so "intermingle us and our ideas" that it would rid the country of "provincialism" and "sectional dissentions": "The boundary lines virtually contract and a continent becomes a country." One might question the benefit of news reports that were circulated so rapidly and that were so uniform. Yet no one could deny that their circulation had become a major, and even a "controlling," element in differentiating the mind-set of late nineteenth-century Americans from the mind-set of the founders of the republic.[167]

Nowhere was the space-binding potential of the telegraph more vividly imagined than in the visual iconography of the trans-Mississippi West. Prior to the Civil War, few artists envisioned the settlement of this region as an unproblematic chapter in the nation's "manifest destiny."[168] The political challenges were too intractable and the physical impediments too forbidding. The presence of powerful, hostile, and still largely autonomous Indian tribes remained a pressing concern, as did the bloody conflict in Kansas that pitted slaveholders against nonslaveholders. If these political challenges could somehow be overcome, emigrants still confronted the daunting physical impediment of the Rocky Mountains.

The Civil War transformed the visual iconography of the trans-Mississippi West. The violence in Kansas ended with the abolition of slavery, and the Indian threat receded now that the army was no longer tied down fighting the Confederacy. Although the Rocky Mountains still loomed, even this physical impediment became less forbidding following the completion of the Pacific telegraph and the transcontinental railroad. The Pacific telegraph crossed the Rockies in 1861, and the transcontinental railroad followed in 1869. The social consequences of these technical advances were prefigured by cartoonist Thomas Nast in an engraving that he made in 1867 for the frontispiece of a compendium of trans-Mississippi lore. Against a backdrop of a forbidding mountain range, Nast juxtaposed a telegraph wire linking New York City and San Francisco with a railroad engine roaring through a mountainous gorge.[169]

The completion of the transcontinental railroad furnished the theme for a further refinement in the visual iconography of the trans-Mississippi West. The best known rendering of this epochal event was Frances F. Palmer's color lithograph "Across the Continent: Westward the Course of Empire Takes Its Way." Palmer's lithograph depicted the settlement of the region as the inevitable by-product of the Pacific telegraph and the imminent completion of the transcontinental railroad. In the foreground, hardy pioneers built a civilization on the edge of the prairie. In the middle ground, the trans-Mississippi railroad blazed a trail to the West. Although the railroad dominated Palmer's landscape, it was paralleled by a telegraph for as far as the eye could see. No previous visual rendering of the region displayed such serene confidence in the relationship of technical advance to moral progress. No longer did hostile Indians, sectional conflict, or the Rocky Mountains impede the expansion of the American empire from coast to coast.

The technological triumphalism that Nast prefigured and that Palmer celebrated reached its apotheosis in John Gast's "American Progress" (1872). For Nast and Palmer the conquest of the trans-Mississippi West remained an unfolding drama; for Gast it had become an accomplished fact. Now that the transcontinental railroad had gone into operation, the settlement of the western half of the continent had become a foregone conclusion. To render this eventuality visually compelling, Gast depicted a diaphanously clad goddess hovering over a sturdy band of westward-bound pioneers. To fortify the settlers, the goddess bore in her hands familiar emblems of moral progress. In one hand she held a school book, in the other, the by now ubiquitous telegraph wire.

"American Progress" was the brainchild of George A. Crofutt, an enterprising publisher who had recently moved from Chicago to New York City to capitalize on the commercial possibilities of trans-Mississippi tourism. Now that well-to-do Americans could journey across the continent in the relative comfort of a railroad car, Crofutt recognized that money could be made in supplying them with reading matter. "American Progress" had been intended to cultivate this market. Its ostensible theme was settlement of the trans-Mississippi West; its actual theme was the transformation of the westward movement from heroic epic into touristic fantasy.[170]

"American Progress" is best known today as a painting. Crofutt commissioned it as a mock-up for an elaborate nineteen-color chromolithograph that he gave away as a promotion to subscribers to a travel magazine. To advertise this promotion, Crofutt included a black-and-white steel engraving as the frontispiece in a guidebook for California-bound railroad passengers.[171]

"American Progress" was "purely national" in its evocation of the "gigantic results" of "American brains and hands," Crofutt's guidebook explained. Its appeal was self-evident: "Who would not have such a beautiful token to remind them of our country's grandeur and enterprise, which have caused the mighty wilderness to blossom like a rose!"[172] The

AMERICAN PROGRESS. (See Annex No. 1.)   (1.)

This iconic engraving—"American Progress"—was one of the earliest illustrations of the trans-Mississippi West to depict the political and social transformations wrought by the Pacific telegraph, the Civil War, and the transcontinental railroad. To render these transformations visually compelling, it featured a goddess holding aloft two harbingers of progress: a schoolbook and a telegraph wire. The engraving was based on an 1872 painting by John Gast, and appeared shortly thereafter in several editions of a guidebook for California-bound railroad passengers. "American Progress," in George A. Crofutt, *Crofutt's New Overland Tourist and Pacific Coast Guide* (Chicago: Overland Publishing Company, 1878), frontispiece.

"grandeur and enterprise" of this continent-spanning project elided the distinction between technical advance and moral progress that had been so important to realists such as Thoreau and Lincoln. While unquestionably "progress," it bore at best an oblique relationship to the time-honored civic ideals of liberty, justice, and equal rights.

Emblematic of the technological triumphalism of "American Progress" was the goddess hovering over the scene. Nothing in Gast's painting or

Crofutt's explication linked the goddess with Columbia, the mythological goddess often invoked by nineteenth-century American artists to symbolize the continuities between the civic ideals of the modern American republic and its ancient Roman counterpart. Yet the resemblance would have been obvious to well-educated readers familiar with political iconography. To evoke these civic ideals, artists often adorned Columbia with a liberty cap, a symbol of political freedom. Gast's goddess, however, sported a pulsating "star of empire," an emblem not only of westward expansion, but also of the technical advances that nineteenth-century Americans increasingly conflated with moral progress.

Was Crofutt's technological triumphalism widely shared? It is entirely plausible that many, if not most, Americans regarded the telegraph in a spirit that owed less to Ritchie and O'Sullivan than to Thoreau and Lincoln. Among the skeptics was William Orton, the president of Western Union between 1867 and 1878. Orton was immensely proud of the telegraph network over which he presided. Yet he studiously refrained from waxing rhapsodic about its social consequences in the manner of telegraph publicist Francis O. J. Smith. Orton never even went so far as to boast of the contribution that Western Union had made to the Union victory in the Civil War.

Orton's rejection of technological triumphalism was a prudent response to the antimonopoly logic of the political economy in which Western Union emerged. The political economy in which the first-generation telegraph network builder Amos Kendall operated was federally oriented and centralized. In contrast, the political economy Orton inherited was state-oriented and competitive. Had Orton linked the telegraph with moral progress, he would have been hard pressed to rebut the small but insistent chorus of critics who contended that Western Union had become too powerful, and its facilities too essential to the conduct of business and public life, to be operated as a private corporation. To anticipate this critique, Orton downplayed the power of Western Union's network, emphasized its dependence on technological imperatives and economic incentives, and concealed its embeddedness in a particular configuration of governmental institutions and civic ideals. By characterizing the telegraph as a channel instead of an institution, Orton concealed the power of the network that Sibley had built.

4

THE NEW POSTALIC DISPENSATION

It is more difficult, and requires greater executive ability, to manage a large business with small profits on each item than to conduct a small business with large profits. It is in this that the difference between a corporate and a postal service consists.

Gardiner G. Hubbard, 1873

In January 1871, Western Union president William Orton sent a gloomy letter to Anson Stager, the head of the company's Chicago office. The time was not distant, Orton warned, when Congress would buy out Western Union and operate the telegraph network as a government monopoly. Orton deplored this eventuality. He was familiar with the civil service, having served as a high-level administrator in the Treasury Department during the Civil War, and had no desire to relinquish the greater operational autonomy and higher salary that he had come to enjoy as the president of a large and powerful corporation. Should Congress intervene, all was not lost. "If the government should buy all the telegraph lines and monopolize the transmission of messages," Orton reasoned, it would not necessarily interfere with the sale of market reports to stock exchanges and boards of trade or the leasing of telegraph lines to factories, offices, and residences. In fact, by cultivating these niche markets, it might be possible to establish a business that would be capable of "almost infinite expansion."[1]

The emergence of Western Union as the nation's dominant telegraph network provider in 1866 made it an inviting target for lawmakers troubled by the specter of monopoly. In an age in which small proprietorships were the norm and antimonopoly was a moral imperative, Western Union stood out. With the exception of a few major railroads, no corporation had a larger capitalization. Not even the Pennsylvania Railroad—the nation's largest private employer—operated on a more spatially extensive scale. While antimonopoly legislation often did more to undermine competition than to sustain it, the elimination of monopoly in American business remained a cherished civic ideal.

Western Union's most persistent critic was Gardiner G. Hubbard, a Massachusetts lawyer and municipal franchise promoter who unsuccessfully lobbied Congress for several years beginning in 1869 to charter a corporation to popularize the telegraph. Hubbard presumed that it would be relatively simple for a corporation enjoying a federal charter to lower rates and extend facilities to those parts of the country that were underserved by the existing telegraph corporations. Congress never enacted Hubbard's telegraph bill. Even so, his quixotic campaign familiarized lawmakers with the idea that the telegraph might be recast as a mass service.

To Hubbard's chagrin, Orton had no intention of following his lead. Yet Orton was diligent and capable, and during his twelve-year tenure as Western Union's president (1867–1878) he labored tirelessly to guarantee that the network over which he presided provided a fast and reliable specialty service for its exclusive clientele. Orton's legacy included a massive headquarters building that architectural historians hail as one of the world's first skyscrapers, and a string of technical advances in electrical communications, of which the best known today is the telephone.

Orton's role in the invention of the telephone was accidental. To improve the carrying capacity of a telegraph wire, Orton offered a financial reward for the invention of a device known as a multiplex. Among the inventors to respond to Orton's challenge were Alexander Graham Bell and Elisha Gray. Each invented a device that not only transmitted signals at many different frequencies simultaneously—the core idea of a multiplex—but that also transmitted the human voice. Orton obtained for Western Union the patent rights to Gray's invention but not to Bell's. If Orton had not died unexpectedly in 1878, Western Union might well have commercialized Gray's invention, and the world might remember Gray and not Bell as the inventor of the telephone.

Orton's primary legacy was organizational. To maintain the performance standards that he regarded as essential, he championed the operational autonomy of Western Union's management against investors, journalists, lawmakers, and upstart rivals such as Jay Gould. Although Orton fended off Congress, he failed to neutralize Gould. Gould gained control of Western Union in 1881, three years after Orton's death. Gould's takeover shifted the balance of power at Western Union from managers back to investors, a development that Orton would have deplored and that he had labored diligently during his tenure as Western Union president to prevent.

The political economy that Orton inherited as Western Union's president remained state-oriented, though with a pronounced federal tilt. The catalyst for this shift was the enactment of the National Telegraph Act of 1866. This law was the first legislative attempt to regulate the telegraph business at the federal level and one of the first federal laws of any kind to regulate a sector of the political economy in which the corporation had supplanted the proprietorship as the dominant organizational form.[2]

The National Telegraph Act had three main provisions. First, it granted telegraph corporations the privilege to string wire on any right-of-way that Congress had designated as a post road. Second, it empowered the postmaster general to set the rates that telegraph corporations could charge government agencies. And third, it limited the right-of-way grant to those corporations that agreed to permit Congress to buy them out at any point five years after its enactment. Since the law was enacted in July 1866, the congressional buyout clause took effect in July 1871. Should Congress authorize a buyout, the value of the corporation's assets were to be determined by "five competent, disinterested persons," two of whom would be selected by the corporations, two by the postmaster general, and one by mutual agreement.[3]

The National Telegraph Act had certain features in common with the Pacific Railroad Act of 1862 and the National Banking Act of 1863. Each law had been intended to coordinate networks that extended beyond the boundaries of the individual states, and each focused on a different economic sector: transportation in the case of the Pacific Railroad Act; finance in the case of the National Banking Act; and communications in the case of the National Telegraph Act. Although the National Telegraph Act did not, like the Pacific Railroad Act and the National Banking Act, authorize the chartering of federal telegraph corporations, it did mandate performance standards for whichever state-chartered corporations agreed to its provisions. Henceforth, telegraph corporations operated in a quasi-regulatory political economy in which the federal government promoted rivalry between network providers and mandated rate caps for telegraphic dispatches sent by government agencies.

Like the better-known Sherman Antitrust Act of 1890, the National Telegraph Act had been designed not to accommodate the emerging corporate order, but, rather, to restore the political economy that giant corporations had subverted. Its target was not John D. Rockefeller's Standard Oil, but Hiram Sibley's Western Union. In theory, the National Telegraph Act was supposed to foster rivalry between telegraph corporations throughout the United States, just as the New York Telegraph Act of 1848 had been intended to promote rivalry among telegraph corporations within New York. In practice, the 1848 law hastened the further consolidation of the telegraph business that culminated in Jay Gould's takeover of Western Union in 1881.

The National Telegraph Act opened the door to a flood of bills intended to regulate the telegraph business. During Orton's tenure as Western Union president, no fewer than twenty-eight different telegraph-related bills found their way to Congress.[4] Most of these bills, like the National Telegraph Act, had been designed to restrain Western Union. None came up for a vote. From the standpoint of hindsight, it might seem inevitable that these bills would fail. Yet no one knew this at the time. The nationalization of the British domestic telegraph network in 1868 impressed many contemporaries as a clear sign that a congressional buyout of Western Union was imminent. Even if Congress did nothing, the steady stream of hostile bills depressed the value of Western Union's shares on the market. "The possibility of governmental interference in the business of telegraphing," Orton informed Western Union shareholders in 1869, "has a direct and important bearing upon the value of our property."[5]

Orton's voluminous business correspondence shows that he himself took the threat of hostile legislation seriously. In letter after letter, Orton warned lawmakers and journalists about the perils of federal intervention. "The agitation in Congress is so threatening of the interests of the company," reflected Western Union manager Norvin Green in January 1869, that it was certain to "occupy" Orton's time "almost entirely" until Congress adjourned in March.[6]

Although the National Telegraph Act was enacted almost a quarter century before the Sherman Act, the two laws shared a common pedigree. Both were closely associated with Ohio senator John Sherman; both invoked widely accepted legal precedents to codify at the federal level the principled antimonopolism that was deeply rooted in Anglo-American law; and both presupposed that a decentralized, market-oriented economy offered the best institutional safeguard for the cherished civic ideal of equal rights. Equal rights in the nineteenth century referred not only to the political and civil rights of citizens, but also to the economic rights of promoters. Among these economic rights was the right of individuals to enter a business even if they possessed modest financial resources and lacked the special privileges conferred by the ownership of patent rights. By consolidating control over the telegraph business, Western Union limited opportunities for would-be rivals to enter the market.

The Ohio senator, remembered today primarily for the Sherman Antitrust Act of 1890, was ill during much of the congressional debate over its provisions and criticized the final version as inadequate.[7] In contrast, Sherman's involvement in the drafting of the National Telegraph Act is well documented in his personal papers, even though, oddly, he did not mention it in his memoir. In a letter to financier Jay Cooke that he wrote less than one week after its enactment, Sherman acknowledged that he would feel a "permanent pride and interest" in joining together with Cooke to charter a telegraph corporation that would take advantage of the right-of-way clause because "I was responsible for the law." Although Sherman had sponsored the law, he saw nothing wrong if he himself took advantage of its provisions: "I will, gladly, join with you and share with you in pecuniary loss or profit if you wish me to—the franchise being open to all mankind."[8] Shortly before its enactment, one Chicago journalist went so far as to term it the "Sherman National Telegraph Bill."[9] John's brother, William Tecumseh Sherman, had battled the slave power as a Union army general during the Civil War. By supporting the National Telegraph Act, John laid siege to a corporation that had gained a stranglehold over the circulation of high-speed information in the United States.

The National Telegraph Act's buyout clause had a venerable pedigree. The British Parliament included a similar clause in the Railway Act of 1844. Henceforth, Parliament decreed, the owners of every railway corporation chartered by Parliament had to permit Parliament to buy them out in accordance with stipulations intended to ensure that the owners obtained a fair return.[10] The English political economist John Stuart Mill defended this principle in the first edition of his influential *Principles of Political Economy* (1848). Just as it was justifiable for a govern-

ment to grant temporary patent rights, Mill declared, so too it was justifiable for it to grant a limited franchise to "public works" such as
railroads that had become "practical monopolies." If it did, the government should either reserve to itself a "reversionary property" to buy out
the railroad, or retain and "freely exercise" its right to fix maximum
rates and to change these rates over time.[11] Mindful of British precedent,
the Massachusetts legislature enacted shortly thereafter a law that permitted the legislature to buy every railroad it chartered after twenty
years. In 1867 the veteran antimonopolist Josiah Quincy Jr. tried to convince the state legislature to invoke this clause to buy out the state's
principal east-west railroad.[12] Once the state owned the railroad, Quincy
reasoned, the legislature could lease it to contractors whom the legislature held accountable for certain performance standards. To meet the
critique that the state government lacked the expertise to operate a railroad, Quincy ventured a nautical metaphor that he presumed would
resonate among lawmakers in a state that boasted a proud maritime
tradition: "A man is not obliged to navigate a vessel because he owns
her. He will charter the ship, and retain control by the conditions of his
charter party."[13]

Textbook authors, determined to keep their publications up to date,
took it for granted that Congress would soon buy out the country's principal telegraph corporations—including Western Union. At no "distant
time," predicted the author of a treatise on American railroad law in
1867, the telegraph would "engross" a large portion of ordinary correspondence. And when it did, the federal government would find itself
compelled to assume its "exclusive control" as a "postal agency."[14] The
federal government's "ultimate absorption" of the telegraph, observed
the authors of the first book-length legal treatise on American telegraph
law in the following year, was "only a question of time."[15]

One catalyst for the National Telegraph Act was Western Union's acquisition in the spring of 1866 of its two principal rivals, the American
Telegraph Company and the United States Telegraph Company. The
American Telegraph Company operated a once-thriving network on a
north-south axis along the Atlantic seaboard, and the United States Telegraph Company operated a small and financially precarious network on
an east-west axis in the trans-Mississippi West. Both corporations had
been capitalized far more conservatively than Western Union. Western
Union was capitalized at 9.2 times its gross receipts, American at 1.4,
and the United States at less than 6.[16]

Western Union's triumph over its rivals owed little to its superior technological virtuosity, economic efficiency, or organizational capabilities. The American Telegraph Company operated 23,000 miles of telegraph wire and had a capitalization of $2 million, which worked out to $87 per mile. The United States Telegraph Company operated 16,000 miles of telegraph wire and had a capitalization at $6 million, or $375 per mile. Western Union, in contrast, operated 44,000 miles of wire and had a capitalization of $22 million, or $500 per mile. Western Union provided its users no facilities to justify its large capitalization; in fact, as the oldest of the three corporations, its equipment was the least up to date.[17]

The United States Telegraph Company never lived up to its potential, a fact that Orton knew well, since he had served as its president prior to its buyout by Western Union. American, in contrast, was widely regarded as the best-operated telegraph corporation in the country.

Had circumstances been different, American might have bought Western Union. American dominated the lucrative Atlantic seaboard market, giving it a privileged position in the circulation of overseas news; in addition, it had close relations with the New York Associated Press (NYAP), the nation's most important newsbroker. Unfortunately for American, it lost much of its domestic market with the bifurcation of its north-south network during the Civil War and never obtained the revenue that its owners had counted on from the Atlantic cable, which, at the time of the merger, had yet to go into operation.

The Western Union mergers troubled many lawmakers. In Sherman's opinion, Western Union owed its dominant position in the telegraph business not to the superiority of its management, but, rather, to the hundreds of exclusive railroad right-of-way contracts that it had negotiated with railroads with the tacit approval of the courts. Although these contracts were consensual, Sherman regarded them as a pernicious restraint of trade, since they unfairly blocked new entrants from entering the telegraph business. He was therefore determined to enact federal legislation to restrain their scope.

The right-of-way clause in the National Telegraph Act was intended to establish at the federal level an institutional mechanism to eliminate the legal barriers that impeded new entrants from entering the telegraph business. It was "manifestly the interest of the government," Sherman contended, in justifying the right-of-way clause, to "build up" new rivals to "compete, if possible" with Western Union.[18]

Prominent among Sherman's allies was the financier Jay Cooke. Cooke had used the telegraph extensively to market government bonds during the Civil War. Indeed, in the war years he was one of the heaviest users of the telegraph in the country. As a result of this experience, Cooke had grown disgusted with the high rates and limited carrying capacity of the existing telegraph corporations. "There is a necessity for a reform forthwith in all telegraphic business," Cooke wrote Sherman while the telegraph act was still being debated. "The public are now *fleeced* and the companies themselves don't have one dispatch thru line where they would have twenty if the price was *cheapened* and there was *promptness* in the transmission and delivery of messages. There is not one reason why the wires should not be gradually extended to at least 5,000 of the 27,000 post offices and many reasons why they *should* be."[19]

Sherman's brief for competition failed to convince Missouri senator B. Gratz Brown. In theory, Brown conceded, competition was the best regulator; in practice, however, competition in the telegraph business was no longer realistic. As an alternative, Brown urged Congress to buy out the entire telegraph network and transfer its operations to the Post Office Department.

A government telegraph would have two advantages over the status quo. First, it would improve the quality of news reports by eliminating the collusive relationship that had emerged during the Civil War between telegraph corporations and the NYAP. The NYAP restricted its news reports to the relatively small number of newspapers that it had admitted to membership. This approach gave these newspapers a major competitive advantage because it was cheaper for a newspaper to obtain news reports from the NYAP than to obtain them in the open market. Western Union did not explicitly endorse this practice but implicitly condoned it by giving the NYAP highly preferential rates. This practice reeked of special privilege and limited the flow of information, encouraging the circulation of countless news reports that were a "travesty of the truth."[20]

A government telegraph had the further advantage of fostering the rapid extension of the telegraph network into the many thinly settled regions that the existing telegraph corporations refused to serve on account of the high cost of their operation. If the federal government owned the telegraph network, Brown predicted, Congress could set telegraph rates in accordance with the "post office principle" of transferring revenue from those sections of the country in which the network made a profit to sections of the country in which it did not. In this way, the entire country would be brought into the "telegraphic circuit."[21]

To take advantage of the right-of-way clause, telegraph corporations had to give their written assent to the National Telegraph Act. Most of the country's telegraph corporations did. Dozens of these documents survive today in the files of the Post Office Department at the National Archives in Washington. The principal holdout was Western Union. Its reticence is not surprising inasmuch as the law had been intended to limit its prerogatives. The new law was profoundly unfair, Orton protested shortly before its enactment, because it permitted Congress to override state law by invalidating with the stroke of a pen the exclusive right-of-way contracts Western Union had painstakingly obtained from railroads and other common carriers through "years of labor" and the payment of "large sums of money."[22]

Orton's protest failed to block the law's enactment, and in June 1867 Western Union agreed to its provisions. The only Western Union official to sign the document that gave Western Union's assent to the National Telegraph Act was its former president, Hiram Sibley. Why Sibley signed on is a matter of conjecture. Presumably he was acting at the behest of Western Union's remaining Rochester, New York–based shareholders, for whom a congressional buyout would mean yet another financial windfall of the kind they had enjoyed during the Civil War.[23]

In explaining Western Union's change of heart, Orton downplayed the potential appeal of the National Telegraph Act for Western Union shareholders. Far more important, in his view, was its utility in helping the corporation cope with a highly unstable and rapidly changing political economy. In the eleven months between enactment of the National Telegraph Act in July 1866 and Western Union's assent to its provisions in June 1867, Congress had wrested from President Andrew Johnson control over the readmission of former Confederate states into the Union. Dissatisfied with Johnson's moderate course, Congress enacted sweeping legislation reorganizing ten former Confederate states into five military districts under the jurisdiction of the army. In so doing, Congress raised thorny legal questions about the validity of the exclusive right-of-way railroad contracts that Western Union had entered into in these states. In such a fluid, uncertain, and unprecedented legal environment, Western Union leaders deemed it prudent to put their corporation under federal jurisdiction. The army was a federal institution, and, on balance, Orton explained in 1870, Western Union would have been imprudent not to claim its "protection" in the military districts so as to prevent any "interference" with Western Union property.[24] A further consideration that Orton did not mention was prudential. If Western Union had not signed on to the National Telegraph Act and if Congress had subsequently authorized a buyout of the nation's telegraph network, Western Union would have found itself in the unenviable position of owning assets that Congress barred it from operating and for which it could not find a credible buyer.

Although the buyout clause posed the gravest long-term threat to Orton's operational autonomy, the rate-setting clause raised a more immediate set of concerns. This clause required every consenting telegraph corporation—including, after June 1867, Western Union—to provide telegraphic facilities for government agencies at rates set by the postmaster general. Spurred by the perception that Western Union's rates were too high, a succession of postmasters general required Western Union to transmit messages for government agencies on extremely advantageous terms. The resulting rate schedules marked one of the first forays of a federal government agency into the regulation of big business. Congress had previously required the federally chartered Pacific railroads to transport goods for the government at highly advantageous rates and to set rate caps for messages on Sibley's transcontinental telegraph. Never before, however, had it extended its rate-setting authority to the entire domestic telegraph network.[25]

One of the first federal administrators to take advantage of the federally mandated rate cap was Albert J. Myer, a brigadier general in the army signal corps who was looking for new worlds to conquer following the Civil War. With the Confederacy vanquished, Myer declared the threat posed by hurricanes, tornados, and storms to be the most formidable "enemy" that the country faced. To combat this foe, in 1870 Congress authorized the establishment of a meteorological agency that would eventually become the National Weather Service. The administration of this agency devolved upon Myer; its first official name—the "Division of Telegrams and Reports for the Benefit of Commerce"—underscored its intimate relationship with the nation's telegraph network. Under Myer's leadership, the signal corps used the congressionally mandated rate caps to obtain the time-sensitive weather data from many different locations necessary to chart meteorological trends. Fortified with this data, Myer's staff forecast the weather with unprecedented accuracy, which the signal corps then broadcast throughout the country free of charge. Myer's broadcasts provided mariners and farmers with reliable advance warnings of adverse weather conditions, saving countless lives and millions of dollars of property. On the Great Lakes alone, Myer's storm warnings saved between $1 million and $4.5 million per year in lost shipping. No nongovernmental agency had either the organizational capabilities or the privileged access to the telegraph network to perform a comparable service.[26]

To improve the signal corps' ability to broadcast weather reports, Myer obtained congressional authorization to permit it to build a government-owned telegraph network. The first link in the government network was completed in 1873; it established telegraphic communications between the lighthouses that were owned and operated by the federal government between Sandy Hook, New Jersey, and Cape Hatteras, North Carolina. Shortly thereafter, Myer extended his network to Texas and the Southwest. At its peak in 1881, the army signal corps operated a telegraph network that extended over 5,000 miles.[27]

Myer was not the first government administrator to use the telegraph to gather data from far-flung locations. Joseph Henry of the Smithsonian Institution had used the telegraph to forecast the weather beginning in 1849, and Alexander Dallas Bache of the U.S. Coast Survey had used the telegraph as early as 1846 to obtain the time measurements that, in conjunction with astronomical data, enabled the Coast Survey to calculate the longitude with unprecedented precision.[28] The utility of the telegraph as a time-measurement tool remained important to government cartographers in the post–Civil War era. The data the Coast Survey needed to calculate the longitude was relatively limited; as a consequence, it would probably have been little affected had Congress never enacted the National Telegraph Act. The data that Myer needed to forecast the weather, however, was immense. Had Congress not inserted the rate clause in the National Telegraph Act, Myer would probably not have been able to obtain appropriations large enough to operate what one contemporary called a permanent "telegraphic *nervous system*" for the continental United States.[29]

The British Parliament's buyout in 1868 of the domestic telegraph network buoyed the determination of government ownership advocates in the United States. American lawmakers monitored British politics intently. Now that Parliament had taken the lead, many presumed it was only a matter of time before Congress would follow.

Prominent among the government ownership advocates was Wisconsin senator Cadwallader Washburn. A congressional buyout of Western Union, Washburn believed, would hasten the establishment of a "postal telegraph" under the jurisdiction of the Post Office Department, and a government telegraph would substantially cheapen the cost of circulating information for telegraph users.[30]

Washburn had no quarrel with private enterprise. He himself was one of the richest men in the Senate, having built up a large grain-milling business in Minneapolis that eventually became General Mills. When it came to the telegraph, however, Washburn made an exception. The telegraph had become a channel of commerce, and it was up to the federal government to coordinate its operation. To stabilize a waterfall on the Mississippi River that lay astride his mills, Washburn relied on the Army Corps of Engineers. To coordinate the circulation of high-speed information, Washburn looked to the Post Office Department.[31]

Washburn's proposal received the imprimatur of President Ulysses S. Grant in December 1871. "Education," Grant declared in his annual message to Congress, was the "groundwork" of "republican institutions," and the broadcast of news reports was a form of education. As a consequence, the federal government had a civic mandate to operate a telegraph network, for the telegraph had become indispensable to the circulation of "speedy news" from "all parts of the country."[32] Grant was the first president to support a government telegraph, yet his rationale was resolutely traditional. Education was one realm in which an activist government was beyond controversy. In fact, Grant closely followed the strictures on government intervention that Francis Wayland had set forth in 1837 in the first edition of his influential and widely taught *Elements of Political Economy*. A similar rationale for a government telegraph had been articulated in 1862 by the eminently conservative postmaster general Montgomery Blair.[33]

The novelty of Grant's proposal lay not in the presumption that government had an obligation to promote education but in his extension of this presumption to the federal government. The federal government had entered indirectly into the education business in 1862 with the Morrill Act, a law that gave lucrative tracts of federal land to colleges and universities. Beneficiaries ranged from Iowa State University to the Massachusetts Institute of Technology (MIT). Yet all but a handful of educational institutions in the United States remained state or locally funded. Exceptions included the Coast Survey, Myer's signal corps, the Smithsonian Institution, West Point, Annapolis, and the various federal government scientific bureaus. The telegraph was a different kind of educational institution. Like the Post Office Department, it did not create knowledge; rather, it circulated knowledge that others had created. Had Congress followed Grant's advice, the telegraph would have joined the Post Office Department in providing this educational service for the nation. The Post Office Department subsidized the press by circulating newspapers and magazines at low cost and permitting newspapers to exchange with each other an unlimited number of copies. A government telegraph would extend this civic mandate to a novel means of communication.

Even more expansive in his rationale for a government telegraph was Grant's postmaster general, John A. J. Creswell. Just as the American people had a right to pure water and pure air on the "best possible terms," Creswell declared in 1873, so too they had a right to the "best and cheapest means" of "communication and intercourse." No one had the right to extort the public by monopolizing a force of nature: "I believe that the electric current has been given by God for the benefit of the whole human race."[34]

Occupying the middle ground between government ownership and antimonopoly was a small yet hardy band of Western Union critics. These critics were determined to extend to the entire telegraph network the regulatory mechanism that Myer had harnessed so effectively to forecast the weather. By far the most persistent of these would-be regulators was Gardiner G. Hubbard. Hubbard is best known today as a founder of the National Geographic Society and the father-in-law of telephone inventor Alexander Graham Bell. In the 1860s and 1870s, he was recognized as the country's most prolific, determined, and persistent champion of "postal telegraphy." Hubbard's involvement in telegraphy dated back to 1850, when he had briefly backed a promotional venture organized around Alexander Bain's ill-fated chemical telegraph.[35] Following a long hiatus during which he became heavily involved in the promotion of water works, horse-car lines, and gas plants in and around his hometown of Cambridge, Massachusetts, Hubbard returned to the telegraph business in 1869. The immediate impetus for his revival of interest was Grant's victory in the 1868 presidential election, an event that Hubbard regarded as a favorable omen for civic-minded promoters like himself who aspired to bring Western Union under permanent federal control.

Postal telegraphy for Hubbard meant not a government-owned and -operated telegraph on the British model, but rather an investor-owned telegraph corporation that held a federal charter. In Hubbard's view, the telegraph's enormous potential for social as well as business communication remained untapped. To realize this potential, Hubbard proposed neither the restoration of competition nor the establishment of a government telegraph on the British model. Rather, he advocated the institutionalization of a permanent regulatory mechanism to ensure that the telegraph would become no less indispensable to urban, middle-class Americans than a water works, a horse-car line, or a gas plant.[36]

The telegraph of the future, Hubbard believed, would provide the entire population with low-cost, high-quality facilities to circulate information at high speed to localities large and small. In short, it would extend to the telegraph the same rate structure, development strategy, and performance standards that had long characterized the mail. To attain this ambitious goal, Hubbard proposed establishing a telegraph network that was more spatially extensive than the Western Union network and that circulated information at a substantially lower cost. The "greatest value" of the telegraph for its users would not be attained until it reached "every point in the country" and provided facilities for the circulation of information to the entire population, rather than merely to the exclusive clientele that Western Union served.[37]

Hubbard floated a number of legislative proposals in Congress and the press, making it difficult to generalize about precisely what he had in mind. Indeed, at one point he even flirted with the idea of a congressional buyout.[38] Most of Hubbard's proposals envisioned the chartering by Congress of a corporation—the "Postal Telegraph Company"—to recast the telegraph as a cheap and convenient point-to-point communications medium for the entire population. Congress had already granted charters to banks and certain railroads. Just as these corporations crossed state boundaries, so too would Hubbard's Postal Telegraph Company.

Hubbard's attitude toward corporate management of the telegraph was ambivalent. The "corporate system," Hubbard conceded, had many advantages over government ownership: corporations were the "lifeblood" of the country, and lawmakers should rely whenever possible on their "efficient executive officers and their skilled operators."[39] The problem with corporations lay not in their management, but rather in their investors' insistent demand for high dividends and short-term gains. As long as investors put their self-interest ahead of the public, this problem would persist: "It does not solve the question to say that government work is more expensive than corporate, but we must consider *for whose benefit* is the greatest economy. Do the people share in the benefit, or does it inure wholly to the stockholders of the corporation?" To pose the question was to answer it: "All experience shows that the same self-interest which compels a corporation to have its work done as cheaply as possible also leads it to get all it can out of the people. The statistics prove that telegraphic management in private hands *does not* result in either economy or efficiency of service to the public." Unregulated private management was particularly lamentable because telegraph corporations, being indispensable for the circulation of information, had become "public corporations" in which the investors' self-interest did not merit the "same consideration" as the "rights of the public."[40]

Hubbard prided himself on his civic mindedness, but he was hardly disinterested. If he could obtain a federal charter for his Postal Telegraph Company, Hubbard stood to make a tidy profit. A federal charter for a business with the potential to generate millions of dollars in revenue was extremely unusual, and Hubbard intended to be one of its owners.

In Orton's mind, this made Hubbard just one more speculator intent on making a killing at Western Union's expense. Should Hubbard prevail, Orton predicted to his brother in 1870, Hubbard would make as much as $1 million on the deal. If only "speculative patriots and philanthropists" like Hubbard would leave him alone, Orton huffed, he could build a telegraph network large enough and cheap enough to forestall all demands for federal legislation.[41] Particularly exasperating to Orton was the moralistic language Hubbard used to cloak his appeal. The "evangels" of the "new postalic dispensation," Orton sarcastically warned Hubbard, using a highly charged religious metaphor to underscore his disdain, would be well advised to desist from their misguided campaign to "frighten the Western Union into repentance." It was insulting for Hubbard to presume that he had been anointed to save Orton and his colleagues from the "error of their ways" caused by their refusal to provide the public with the low-cost facilities to which Hubbard presumed the people to be entitled.[42]

The telegraph was not a subject that "materially concerns the masses," Orton lectured a Chicago newspaper reporter shortly after a huge fire had devastated Chicago in 1871, "and it will always be so." No matter how low a "tariff" a telegraph corporation charged, it would "never succeed the mail system." For Orton it was simply inconceivable that large numbers of Americans would ever abandon the mail for the telegraph. High speed was the only advantage the telegraph enjoyed over the mail, and for most Americans this advantage did not offset the telegraph's impersonality, inelegance, and inflexibility as a communications medium. To contend that the federal government should operate a telegraph network was, therefore, to favor the few at the expense of the many. Why should the federal government lower telegraph rates for the "greedy Wall Street brokers" who were its principal users, when it did nothing to ease the distress of the 80,000 Chicagoans who had been left homeless by a devastating conflagration?[43]

Telegraph users had a mixed response to the prospect of further federal telegraph legislation. With the exception of government agencies and newsbrokers, the principal users of the telegraph were merchants, brokers, and manufacturers. To the extent that these groups had a collective voice, it found expression in the commercial organizations in the nation's largest cities. Federal telegraph legislation had the endorsement of the Chicago Board of Trade; the St. Louis Board of Trade; the Providence, Rhode Island, Board of Trade; and the San Francisco Chamber of Commerce.[44] These groups endorsed federal legislation primarily in order to lower telegraph rates. Opponents of federal legislation included the New York Chamber of Commerce, the Boston Board of Trade, and the National Board of Trade, a federation of trade groups that aspired to speak for merchants throughout the United States.[45] The Cincinnati Board of Trade rejected federal legislation by a narrow margin in 1868, following a personal appeal from the president of a would-be Western Union rival who endorsed the traditional argument for antimonopoly.[46]

The reluctance of commercial organizations to endorse federal legislation is somewhat puzzling, given the broad support for a government telegraph among commercial organizations in Great Britain. The parliamentary buyout of the British domestic telegraph network had the endorsement of dozens of trade groups, including the influential Edinburgh Chamber of Commerce, a major factor in its nationalization in 1868.[47] In the United States, trade groups differed with regard not only to the propriety of federal intervention, but also to the efficacy of specific legislative proposals. Although there is no simple explanation for the different outcomes in the two countries, it probably owed something to the structuring presence of the American state. The American state was decentralized, while the British state was centralized. As a result, American trade groups operated in a much larger number of political forums, militating against not only the embrace of a single political agenda, but also the crystallization of a consensus among like-minded trade groups as to how best to proceed.

Among the champions of federal telegraph legislation were several influential journalists, including Joseph Medill of the *Chicago Tribune* and George W. Curtis of *Harper's Weekly*. The telegraph was properly part of the country's "educational and postal systems," Medill declared in an open letter to Orton in 1872, since its "mission" was the "diffusion of thoughts, ideas and information among the people instantaneously." Western Union's management had left no doubt in Medill's mind that, if the federal government turned the Post Office Department over to private enterprise, it would be a "national calamity."[48] Public opinion, declared Curtis in the following year, with more self-assurance than the facts of the case would seem to justify, was "almost unanimous" in favor of melding together the telegraph and the mail into a single government agency. Curtis conceded that the respected economist David A. Wells had warned that a government telegraph brought with it certain political dangers. Even so, Curtis refused to be swayed. So many naysayers had warned about the evils of federal legislation that he had become convinced that the country could "run the risk" of trying the experiment, since, after all, American institutions were not "such gingerbread as some people think."[49]

Even though Medill and Curtis did their best to galvanize public support for federal intervention, the results were disappointing. The New York City–based *Independent* did not endorse federal telegraph regulation until 1872. The *Independent*'s endorsement impressed Hubbard as sufficiently propitious that he took note of it in a letter to his wife.[50]

The *Independent*'s long silence was revealing. The *Independent* was a politically oriented religious newspaper with a wide readership that was regarded as a bellwether of reform. Its managing editor, Joshua Leavitt, had been a leading publicist for the political and moral benefits of cheap postage for almost thirty years. If anyone should have made the link between cheap postage and cheap telegraphy it would have been Leavitt. Yet for many years he did not.[51] With the notable exception of the *New York Herald*—whose editor, James Gordon Bennett, remained no less committed to a government telegraph in 1870 than he had been in

1845—the need for additional federal telegraph legislation did not attract the sustained attention of journalists until after Jay Gould took over Western Union in 1881. Even the *Chicago Tribune* mostly ignored the issue, despite the enthusiastic public endorsement of a government telegraph by its editor, Joseph Medill.[52]

Labor leaders proved equally reluctant to press for federal legislation. In the period before Gould's takeover of Western Union in 1881, most urged lawmakers to stick with antimonopoly, or what its critics would later deride as laissez-faire. The principal exception was the National Typographical Union, which endorsed a government telegraph as early as 1869, convinced that it would increase facilities for newspapers to obtain the news reports, and, thus, employment opportunities for typographers.[53]

Few labor leaders joined C. Osbourne Ward in advocating a vastly expanded federal role in circulating information. Ward was a prominent American socialist who had written widely on topics related to social reform. Were the Post Office Department to operate the telegraph, Ward prophesied in 1878, ordinary people would soon be able to place orders for goods for as little as 1 cent. Cheap telegraphy would "abolish letter writing" and, with it, much of the rationale for the Post Office Department. All that stood in the way was the transfer of the telegraph from a private corporation to a government agency modeled on the Post Office Department. A government telegraph would provide inclusive facilities for 40 million Americans, instead of high profits for the forty businessmen who owned telegraph stock: "The bigotry that prevents the politico-economical application of inventions, on consideration of moral right, is as intolerant as the bigotry that imprisoned Galileo."[54]

Far more characteristic was the response of A. C. Cameron, editor of the *Workingman's Advocate*. If the government operated the telegraph, Cameron warned in 1871, government agents would use it to monitor worker protests.[55] Cameron's fears were realized during the railroad strike of 1877, when Albert Myer provided President Rutherford B. Hayes with a steady stream of reports on labor conditions from many scattered locations.[56] Had the federal government owned the telegraph, the opportunities for surveillance would have been enhanced. Antimonopoly had a particular appeal to telegraph operators, who plausibly assumed that they would earn higher wages if their employers remained divided.[57]

The rejection of laissez-faire was more congenial to large telegraph users frustrated by the high rates Western Union charged and the limited facilities it provided. Yet even telegraph users could not agree on a legislative remedy. For the rest of the population, federal telegraph legislation remained at best a peripheral concern. If petitions to Congress can be used as a proxy for public opinion, then it would seem that, prior to Gould's takeover of Western Union in 1881, the enactment of postal legislation—including the still further reduction of the already low letter rate—had more popular support than the enactment of any kind of federal telegraph legislation.[58] The absence of petitions for cheap telegraphy troubled Hubbard's wife, who interpreted it as evidence that her husband remained in advance of public opinion.[59] Relatively few Americans, it seems, yearned to substitute the low-cost extra-high-speed facilities for long-distance communications of a government telegraph for the low-cost and reasonably high-speed facilities of the Post Office Department.

The first large batch of postal telegraph petitions did not find its way to Congress until 1875. Their circulation had almost certainly been coordinated by Massachusetts congressman Benjamin F. Butler as part of an anti-Western Union campaign that played into the hands of the financier Jay Gould, very possibly with Gould's covert support.[60] Although Gould would not take over Western Union until 1881, he had for several years been actively speculating in Western Union shares. Gould found that he could make a good deal of money by selling its shares short if he could predict in advance when their price was likely to decline.

Among the petitioners to endorse a postal telegraph was a group of Ohioans who found the postal-telegraphic analogy compelling. Western Union had filed its assent to the National Telegraph Act, the petitioners observed, and should be "incorporated" into the Post Office Department and "worked" for the benefit of the "government and the people." Only the federal government could secure for the citizenry the "freedom of the press" and the "sanctity of private correspondence." And only the federal government could provide the people with "cheap telegraphy," as it had provided them with "cheap postage." Congress should enact legislation to guarantee them a "UNIFORM RATE, AS LOW AS 25 CENTS" for the United States, Great Britain, and Canada, in the expectation that, with an "increase of business" comparable to that which had followed the advent of cheap postage and postal cards, a "*still lower rate* can be made."[61]

The petitioners' reference to "cheap postage" serves as a reminder that in the 1870s the pre–Civil War reform movement to lower the cost of letter postage remained a living memory for many Americans. Henry O'Rielly had invoked cheap postage as a rationale for cheap telegraphy as early as 1860.[62] Petitions championing "cheap telegraphy," however, were virtually unknown before 1875, even though lawmakers and Western Union critics had been debating the issue since 1869. All in all, then, it is hard to discern a groundswell of popular outrage against Western Union until 1881, when the political landscape was transformed overnight after Gould took over. It was this event, and not the long and often lonely crusade that Hubbard and a small circle of like-minded Western Union critics had spearheaded since 1869, that for the first time elevated postal telegraphy to a prominent place on the national political agenda.

William Orton became Western Union's president in July 1867, one month after the corporation had filed its acceptance of the National Telegraph Act with the Post Office Department. For the next twelve years, Orton consolidated the rickety telegraph network that his predecessors had built. This task did not prove to be easy. The federal tilt in the political economy had emboldened investors, lawmakers, and rivals to challenge Orton's operational autonomy in ways that he strenuously disapproved of and did his best to meet.

As Western Union president, Orton combined a dogged earnestness that harkened back to his Puritan forebears with a strategic vision that anticipated the mind-set of the modern professional manager. Before the Civil War, Orton had acquired a solid reputation as a bookseller in New York City, one of the country's leading publishing centers. Shortly after the war began, Orton joined the small but influential band of New York City–based Republicans, who combined a fanatical hostility toward political corruption with a fervent admiration for the moral rectitude of Treasury secretary Samuel P. Chase.[63] Orton's party loyalty earned him an appointment in the Treasury Department, where he helped collect the first federal income tax in American history. Orton's dogged pursuit of tax cheats won him widespread praise in government circles and led to his appointment in 1865 as revenue commissioner for the United States. Orton held this office for only four months before he was handpicked to assume the presidency of the ill-fated United States Telegraph Company, an unsuccessful wartime start-up that was merged into Western Union in 1866.

As Western Union president, Orton retained certain habits of mind that he honed during his wartime stint in the Treasury Department. The federal government was a seedbed for corporate leaders, and the Treasury Department gave Orton a crash course in the administrative skills necessary to oversee a large and complex organization. Just as Amos Kendall had drawn on insights that he had gleaned at the Post Office Department in managing Morse's patent rights, so Orton profited from lessons that he had learned at the Treasury Department in managing Western Union.

Among these lessons was Orton's abiding skepticism toward financiers. Orton's jurisdiction as a revenue collector included Wall Street. This was a challenging assignment because New York City's financiers were renowned not only for their wealth but also their guile. Orton's skepticism reinforced the fervent anticorruptionism that he had imbibed as a Republican Party activist. Tax evasion was rampant among New York City's leading merchants, and Orton was determined to root it out.

Orton's anti-investor bias set him apart from both his predecessor, Hiram Sibley, and his colleague and eventual successor, Norvin Green. Sibley and Green relied on outside investments for much of their income. Orton, in contrast, rarely alluded in his business correspondence to outside investments of any kind. Although Western Union stock had fluctuated wildly during Orton's presidency, not even his most bitter detractors accused him of having manipulated its market price for personal gain, or for that matter, of trading on inside information. Like all men of "pure ambition" Orton had no taste for mere "money-grabbing," as an admiring eulogist recorded following his death, and for his income he relied solely on "capability."[64]

Orton's major source of income during his tenure as Western Union's president was his annual salary, which fluctuated between $20,000 and $25,000. Orton obtained an additional $5,000 beginning in 1873 as the president of a telegraph company linking the United States and Cuba.[65] Orton's salary was very large for the era. The average annual income for workers in New York State was under $1,000.[66] The collector of customs for New York City earned $12,000, which was a princely sum and yet less than half of Orton's salary.[67] Even so, Orton's salary paled in comparison to the investment income of the extremely wealthy clique of New York City–based financiers. Orton knew this well. After all, he had had frequent dealings with this clique when he had served as a revenue officer during the Civil War, and he had also come into frequent contact with them as Western Union president; several, in fact, had acquired large blocs of Western Union stock from the original Rochester investors.

The size of Orton's salary almost certainly helped to account for his prodigious work ethic. As a Republican, Orton inherited the "free labor" ideology that had proved so effective in popularizing the antislavery cause. Free laborites presumed a direct relationship between the work an individual performed and the reward that was due. To justify his huge salary, Orton worked continuously, never took a vacation, and preoccupied himself with every facet of the telegraph business. Orton's almost manic industriousness had a major impact on his health. Often unwell, he may have literally worked himself to death. He died of a stroke suddenly in April 1878, while engaged in delicate negotiations over telegraph rights-of-way and the commercialization of the telephone. He was only 52.

The rapid transfer of the ownership of Western Union shares from Rochester to New York City was a direct result of Hiram Sibley's inflation of Western Union's capitalization during the Civil War. As Western Union's capitalization increased, the market price of its securities plummeted, and as the market price declined, the Rochester merchants who had been Western Union's primary pre–Civil War investors unloaded their holdings to a clique of financiers dubbed by journalists the "Vanderbilt interest." It was widely believed that this consortium was headed up by railroad magnate Cornelius Vanderbilt; it definitely included, and was probably led by, Vanderbilt's ambitious son-in-law Horace C. Clark.[68]

Cornelius Vanderbilt's precise role in Western Union's management remains a matter of speculation. Vanderbilt was 76 years old in 1870, the year in which the remaining Rochester investors were finally ousted from Western Union's board of directors, and he remained heavily involved with his extensive railroad holdings. This much is known. Vanderbilt began buying up Western Union shares in 1863, obtained a berth on Western Union's executive committee by 1873, and was acknowledged as a large shareholder by Orton in 1875.[69]

Sibley's inflation of Western Union's capitalization posed a major problem for Orton, since it obliged him to pay out in dividends revenue that he might otherwise have used to make capital improvements and lower rates. It was an axiom of nineteenth-century corporate finance that the value of a corporation's securities should not exceed the cost of reproducing its physical plant. And no one—least of all Orton himself—believed that the current value of Western Union's tangible assets matched its capitalization. Western Union suffered from "grave defects," Orton confessed to an investor in 1870, the most crippling of which remained the enormous inflation in the size of Western Union's capitalization that Sibley had authorized during the Civil War.[70]

Orton's first priority as Western Union's president was to cut costs. To reduce the drain on Western Union's revenue occasioned by its huge annual dividend payments, Orton orchestrated the purchase of thousands of Western Union shares in the open market. Having bought up the shares, Orton promptly sequestered them in Western Union's vault. Clark and Vanderbilt backed Orton in the conviction that the buyback would increase the market price of their holdings. For the past dozen years, Orton confided to a colleague in 1878, he had worked tirelessly at "squeezing water out" and putting "substance" into the "original inflated capital of Western Union."[71] With the revenue Orton saved, he embarked on a major capital improvement program that doubled the size of Western Union's telegraph network and quadrupled its carrying capacity. Orton also purchased for Western Union the patent rights to several promising inventions and a large stake in a telegraph equipment manufacturer long known as Western Electric.

Orton's relationship with his investors became more problematic following Grant's endorsement of a congressional buyout of the telegraph network in 1871. Grant's endorsement sparked a flurry of journalistic speculation that Western Union's investors were angling to cash in on their shares and were poised to lobby Congress to buy them out.[72] According to one rumor, Grant had met earlier that year with prominent New York journalist Horace Greeley at the behest of Cornelius Vanderbilt to fix the price of the sale. The deal was to be closed immediately after the presidential election of 1872.[73] The *New York Herald* reported that Greeley performed the errand, even though he himself opposed the buyout as unwarranted "centralization."[74] The purchase price that Vanderbilt proposed hovered around $30 million, reported one journalist: $5 million for Western Union bonds, and between $20 and $25 million for Western Union's shares, a total well above Western Union's current market price.[75]

Whether Clark, Vanderbilt, and other large Western Union investors genuinely hoped that Congress would buy their shares is impossible to say. It is conceivable that the Greeley–Grant meeting never occurred and that the whole story was a hoax. And if the meeting had taken place, it may have been intended merely to boost Western Union's share price. When Grant endorsed a buyout in 1871, the market price of Western Union shares shot up a full 2 percent in a single day, a large spike duly noted both in Congress and the press.[76] The suspicion could not be repressed, editorialized the *New York Sun,* that Grant's endorsement of a government buyout had been made in the interest of the same "telegraph ring" that was trying to sell Western Union to the federal government at an "excessive" price.[77]

To forestall federal intervention, Orton popularized the still-unfamiliar notion that an organization that had come to dominate a spatially extensive communications channel was best operated as a private corporation rather than a government agency. When the National Telegraph Act raised the possibility of a congressional buyout, Orton was quick to respond. To tamp down the persistent rumors that Western Union's management was willing to sell out to Congress, Orton issued an announcement, or "card," in the *New York Times* in February 1868 in which he denied that Western Union was, in fact, for sale.[78] If only Congress would give him five years to lower rates and increase performance standards, Orton pleaded to lawmakers two years later, he would provide the public with facilities for long-distance communications that were so "satisfactory" that it would end all calls for further legislation.[79]

To make the case for private enterprise, Orton testified in several government hearings, conducted a public debate with Chicago editor Joseph Medill, and hired economist David A. Wells to explain the economic rationale for corporate control. Orton's antigovernment ownership publicity campaign was less extensive than the better-known antigovernment ownership campaign mounted by the American Telephone and Telegraph Corporation during the first presidential administration of Woodrow Wilson (1913–1917). Yet it was more elaborate than any previous campaign of its kind, and it did much to accustom Americans to the still-novel idea that a private corporation could operate a major channel of commerce as effectively as a government agency. Among the most effective Western Union publicists was telegraph expert George B. Prescott. In a thoughtful and candid essay in the trade press in 1866, Prescott made the case against government ownership. He expanded on his position in an unsigned antigovernment ownership pamphlet that he prepared for Orton in 1869.[80] The fact that Prescott had for many years prior to 1869 publicly endorsed government ownership only enhanced his credibility. Ohio congressman James A. Garfield credited him with convincing him of the inadvisability of a congressional buyout of the telegraph network.[81]

The effectiveness of Orton's publicity campaign is underscored by a comparison of the American telegraph network with the domestic telegraph networks in Europe. The British government nationalized its domestic telegraph network in 1868, during the second year of Orton's tenure as Western Union president. The French telegraph network had always been operated as a government agency, as was the telegraph network in Germany. In the United States the domestic telegraph network remained corporately owned and corporately operated, with the brief exception of a one-year interval between 1918 and 1919, until it collapsed in the 1980s.

The only major telegraph corporations outside of the United States to remain investor owned coordinated the transnational telegraph network. Much of this network was laid under water—which required that it be very well insulated—prompting contemporaries to dub it the "cable" network. Although cable corporations remained privately owned, they retained close financial and operational ties with governments, of which the most important was Great Britain. The close involvement of the British government with the U.S. cable business troubled lawmakers during the First World War, who regarded it as a challenge to American sovereignty. Orton, in contrast, took the subordinate position of the United States in transnational communications for granted. Like most Americans of his day, he was accustomed to operating in an international political economy in which Great Britain dominated center stage and the United States hovered in the wings. Although he acquired a major financial stake for Western Union in a United States–Cuba cable in 1873, Western Union would not enter the North Atlantic cable business until several years after his death.[82]

Western Union critics routinely complained that telegraph rates were excessive. To answer this criticism, Orton tried various expedients. First, he cut rates in half between 1867 and 1875. Next, to utilize facilities that would otherwise be idle, Orton introduced cheap night rates for messages that did not have to be delivered at the highest possible speed.[83] In certain businesses, rate cuts often increased profits. Unfortunately for Orton, the telegraph business was not among them. The night rate proved equally disappointing. Few Americans were willing to pay a premium for a service that was little faster than the mail.[84]

Orton's rate cuts reinforced the conventional wisdom among telegraph experts that high rates led to high profits and low rates to low profits. "Dreamers" like Hubbard, Orton informed the editor of Western Union's company magazine in 1869, were mistaken in assuming that the cost of telegraphy could be radically reduced. This error, Orton suggested, originated in the treatment of ideas and the "intangible processes" of their transmission to a "distant point," as "physical things" to be disposed of "in bulk" by the "application" of "mechanism and power."[85] The notion, Orton explained in a newspaper interview, that the telegraph business at some point in the future could be conducted profitably on the low-cost "postal card plan" favored by Postmaster General Creswell was one of the "absurdities" that he did not care to discuss. The telegraph business involved the "writing" by telegraph operators of a vast number of "short letters" for the public. The Post Office Department could make money at low rates because, unlike Western Union, it did not have to pay for the cost of writing the letters. If, therefore, Western Union cut rates, it would inevitably see its profits decline: the traffic increase that a rate cut could be expected to bring would not offset the cost of providing the service: "One man can only write a given number of letters in a given time, be they long or short. The cost of writing is not reduced by an increase in the number written, because when the number exceeds the capacity of the present staff, additional writing or operating assistants must be employed."[86]

The high rates–high profits dogma had the endorsement of James Anderson, a highly respected sea captain who had commanded the successful cable-laying expedition that established the first permanent telegraphic link between Great Britain and the United States. To settle the issue of whether a reduction in telegraph rates was compatible with high profits, Anderson undertook an elaborate statistical analysis of the various government telegraphs in Europe. "The benefits, resulting from a great quantity of operations," Anderson concluded, "are less in telegraphy than in any industry." Anderson refrained from taking a stand on the propriety of the recent parliamentary buyout of the British telegraph network. He left little doubt, however, that a government telegraph would charge less than an investor-owned telegraph, since it cost less to operate a "self-supporting system" than a "dividend-paying system."[87] Investor-owned telegraph corporations had to be particularly wary of spending large sums to extend their facilities to thinly settled regions that were unlikely to generate enough revenue to cover the cost of the extension. A corporation that failed to heed this advice might find itself "burdened" by the cost of remotely situated routes and "attacked" on its "productive sections only" by a new company that combined a "small capital" with a determination to enter the business.[88]

Anderson's high rates–high profits dogma was well known in the United States. It was widely cited as authoritative not only by Western Union critics such as Hubbard, but also by journalists skeptical of federal telegraph legislation.[89] It would therefore be a mistake to assume that Orton cut rates to mobilize the organizational capabilities of Western Union's telegraph network. Far more pressing were the interrelated threats of hostile legislation and upstart rivals. Rate cutting, Orton explained to George B. Prescott in 1876, had the dual benefit of reducing the clamor for hostile federal legislation and discouraging new entrants from preventing Western Union from "monopolizing" the business. The public would not be frightened of a monopoly that rendered an "essential service" in a satisfactory manner at rates so low that no rival could match them.[90]

The political challenge that Orton confronted was by no means confined to hostile legislation. Equally troubling was the constant danger that the courts might subject telegraph corporations to the same strict "common carrier" liability standards they had long imposed on railroads and package carriers. Few denied that telegraph corporations had an obligation to perform certain tasks required of common carriers. Telegraph corporations, for example, could not refuse the use of their facilities to an individual willing to pay the standard fee. Nor were they supposed to discriminate between users by charging different rates for an identical service. The principal exception was the NYAP, which Western Union favored with much lower rates than those of any of its rivals. This controversial practice outraged journalists unable to obtain the NYAP's time-sensitive news reports.

Telegraph corporations accepted the obligation of providing equal facilities to all users, but they rejected the strict liability standards demanded of common carriers under common law. If a railroad or package carrier mishandled a shipment in transit, it was obliged to reimburse the shippers for its full value. Western Union, its critics charged, should be held to an identical standard. If a sell order failed to go through in a collapsing market, it could cost the sender thousands of dollars. Why, then, was not Western Union liable for this loss?

Orton strenuously resisted the presumption that telegraph corporations should be required to meet the strict common carrier liability standards of a railroad or package carrier. Although it was relatively easy to determine the value of a shipment of cotton or wheat, the value of a telegram was subject to a variety of considerations that were unrelated to the fee the sender had paid for its transmission. To complicate matters even further, senders had no obligation to reveal the presumed value of their telegrams in advance, making it impossible for Western Union operators to take unusual precautions for a particular message. The value of a given telegram, Orton's colleague Norvin Green dryly observed, was something that their senders "generally take great pains to conceal."[91]

The uncertainty surrounding liability standards prompted a good deal of litigation. Merchants who sued Western Union for commercial messages that had gone astray could in certain circumstances obtain large cash payments. Even noncommercial errors could sometimes result in substantial financial payouts if they caused what the courts called "mental anguish."[92] The father of a girl attending boarding school, for example, obtained a cash settlement from Western Union after a judge ruled that a Western Union telegraph operator had incorrectly transcribed a telegram from a boarding school administrator. The telegram was supposed to have read "your daughter had a chill last night." The operator, however, mistakenly altered the second "l" in "chill" to a "d," which, the judge ruled, had caused the girl's father mental distress for which Western Union was liable.[93]

To shield Western Union from liability for missent messages, Orton popularized a legal convention that became known as the intangibility doctrine. Western Union, Orton contended, was not a common carrier because the messages it transmitted were inherently different from items sent by railroads or package carriers. To call Western Union a common carrier was a "judicial fallacy." The intrinsic character of the telegraph business precluded it: "A common carrier is one to whom is entrusted a physical thing." Western Union, however, transmitted only an "intangible idea," and the "slightest quiver of atmospheric electricity" could alter its transmission and garble its meaning.[94]

To rebut the plausible contention that federal telegraph legislation was constitutional, since telegraphy was a form of commerce, Western Union counsel Grosvenor P. Lowrey challenged the premise. Telegraphy

was not a form of commerce, Lowrey argued, because it merely aug-
mented the "sense of hearing" of the "human voice." Commerce involved
the conveyance of tangible goods. Telegrams lacked physicality and, like
speech, were a form of "direct intellectual intercourse" that should never
be regulated by a government that professed to be a republic. Only a
despotism would assume the "exclusive control" of all the means by
which citizens might "interchange" ideas.[95]

Although Orton found it expedient for legal purposes to characterize
telegraphic dispatches as intangible, he prided himself on the accuracy
of the information that Western Union transmitted and the pains it took
to minimize the possibility that insiders might use its facilities to obtain
advance information on market trends. "The policy of the Western
Union Company" was to enable its users to "trade upon certainties."[96]
To discourage speculators from bribing telegraph operators to delay the
circulation of market information, Orton hired private detectives from
the Pinkerton Detective Agency to spy on his staff.[97] It was nothing
short of outrageous, in Orton's view, for critics to imply that Western
Union somehow favored certain traders with advance information
about market trends. If Western Union had shown such favoritism, the
nation's merchants could have been expected to rise up in protest: "Is it
likely that a company going into every state, and every territory but
one, should be carrying on the business of enriching one portion of the
traders in every community on this continent without a howl being
raised from one end of the country to the other? Do you not suppose
that telegrams would be here from the board of trade from all of those
cities?"[98]

Orton's commitment to impartiality was undercut by his corporation's
conduct during times of great political excitement such as the run-up to
the election of 1876.[99] Orton maintained good relations with key Republican leaders, and Orton's office in Western Union's headquarters building became, in the words of one party insider, the "resort of politicians"
who employed Orton on the "most delicate missions."[100] At no point did
Orton reflect on, or even so much as acknowledge, the conflict of interest
between his political activism and his leadership role in a corporation
that played a major role in circulating information on public affairs. That
Western Union had provided more than advice to Republican Party operatives was assumed by Democratic journalist Henry Watterson. In his
memoir Watterson credibly alleged that, during the 1876 presidential
campaign, Republican Party operatives intercepted and read confidential

dispatches that Watterson had sent to Democratic presidential nominee Samuel J. Tilden.[101]

Orton's partisanship compounded his disgust at the willingness of Republican lawmakers to provide Albert Myer with the special privileges he demanded from Western Union to compile his weather reports. "My indignation is so great at the outrage which the administration has permitted" that he had scant desire to help Myer succeed, Orton complained to Republican Party leader and Western Union director Edwin D. Morgan in July 1872. The complicity of Republican Party leaders not only in backing Myer, but also in championing all kinds of federal telegraph legislation, only made matters worse. "I am as good a Republican as anybody," Orton protested: "But my first and highest duty is to our stockholders, and there is small comfort in the recollection that it was Republicans who pushed the Washburn scheme, that Republicans only are pushing the Hubbard job, and that a Republican president endorsed the gross blunder of the postmaster general and recommended a government telegraph in his annual message. Not a single Democrat on the contrary has espoused that side—and the strongest opponent among the press has been the organ of the Democratic candidate—the [New York] Tribune."[102]

Orton's partisan ties may help explain how, shortly after the 1876 election, 500 telegrams from Democratic Party operatives ended up in the editorial office of the New York Tribune, which had now returned to the Republican fold. Congress subpoenaed these telegrams as part of its investigation of voting irregularities during the 1876 presidential election, after which they were supposed to have been destroyed. The telegrams implicated several prominent Democrats, including Samuel J. Tilden's nephew, in a scheme to tip the electoral vote to the Democrats in three highly contested states. That Tilden had been unaware of these behind-the-scenes machinations seemed inconceivable: Tilden's nephew had been living under the same roof with Tilden at the time the fraud occurred. Although the telegrams were supposed to remain confidential, they were leaked to the New York Tribune, which decoded them and in 1878 printed them in its columns. The publication of the "cipher" dispatches, as these telegrams came to be known, caused a public uproar that seriously tarnished Tilden's reputation. Republican Party operatives had almost certainly sent similar telegrams; none, however, ever found their way to the press.[103]

The most serious challenge that Orton confronted in his ongoing campaign to protect the inviolability of telegrams came not from dishonest

Western Union operators, but from Congress. As a courtesy to its users, Western Union retained a copy of every telegram for at least six months. Judges occasionally subpoenaed a particular telegram to settle a disputed point in court, and Western Union leaders thought it best to provide them with the information they desired. Congress was less discriminating. Twice during Orton's tenure at Western Union—first during the impeachment trial of Andrew Johnson, and again in the months following the disputed election of 1876—Congress issued a "dragnet subpoena" ordering Western Union to turn over large numbers of telegrams. The 1876 subpoena was especially broad. Although Orton professed to deplore this violation of his customer's privacy, he ultimately agreed to transfer to Congress no fewer than 27,000 telegrams. If he did not, he was warned, Congress would jail Orton's entire executive board for noncompliance.[104]

The alacrity with which Congress relied on its subpoena power to commandeer telegrams was, for Orton, a compelling argument against the establishment of a government telegraph. "What would be the result," Orton asked a journalist rhetorically in 1868, if every telegraph office in the country were in the charge of men who "held their places by the favor of those who desire to use them for the accomplishment of personal and selfish ends?"[105] Under proper management, a private corporation was a far better guardian of personal information than a government agency. To make his point, Orton reminded lawmakers of the notorious informational blockade that Postmaster General Amos Kendall had established at the behest of the slaveholding states in 1835 to prevent the circulation of information on the slavery question. "It was a gross outrage," Orton exploded to a Kentucky lawmaker, "to rifle the mail in search of what was deemed incendiary newspapers in the days of Amos Kendall."[106]

Orton's most reliable ally in his long political struggle against hostile federal intervention was the press. Journalists had clamored for cheap postage in the 1840s. Yet with the notable exception of the *New York Herald,* no major New York City newspaper consistently backed federal telegraph legislation until after Jay Gould took control of Western Union in 1881. Journalists opposed federal telegraph legislation for various reasons. If the Post Office Department operated the telegraph, the size of the civil service would be significantly increased, creating a huge new "army" of officeholders that the party in power could enlist to support the reelection of party-backed candidates. If Congress chartered a federal telegraph corporation to contract with the Post Office Department to transmit messages over certain routes at specific rates, it would lavish special privileges on the new entrant while unfairly burdening Western Union. Each of these arguments had rejoinders, but few journalists gave them much play largely because of an additional consideration that few journalists were willing to broach. If the press endorsed legislation strengthening Western Union's rivals, it would antagonize Western Union, the corporation on which many of the nation's largest and most influential newspapers relied for the news reports that their subscribers demanded.

Western Union lavished a variety of special privileges on journalists. In accordance with a long-standing convention, it permitted the NYAP to gather, bundle, and transmit news reports to its members over its lines at extremely low rates. The magnitude of this special privilege was considerable. Nonpress users in 1870 paid Western Union $5.7 million to transmit 8 million messages, for an average cost of 71 cents per message. Newsbrokers, in contrast, paid a mere $1 million for 15 million messages, for an average cost of a mere 6.6 cents per message.[107] This differential understated the price break for the newspaper press, given the high cost of the various specialized services journalists demanded. To complicate matters even further, newspaper dispatches were, on average, more labor-intensive than ordinary telegrams. In addition to being unusually long, they had to be transmitted to multiple locations at night and on an extremely tight schedule.

Orton was proud of the special privileges that Western Union provided the press. No other government in the world, Orton boasted to a colleague, used the telegraph more extensively to "promote the education and the general well-being of the people," a feature "peculiar to this republican government."[108] Few Americans would have questioned the merits of Orton's policy had he extended these special privileges to every newsbroker: the Post Office Department had subsidized the press since the 1790s, and almost no one complained. Not even Western Union's most bitter critic proposed that Western Union raise rates for newsbrokers in order to lower rates for everyone else. Special privilege had long been a cornerstone of the American press. Just as the Post Office Department subsidized the circulation of news reports, so, too, did Western Union. The problem, rather, lay in Western Union's unwillingness to provide identical privileges to every newsbroker, regardless of its size.

The largest and most powerful newsbroker in the post–Civil War era was the NYAP. In Orton's day the NYAP was operated by seven New York City newspapers: the *Herald*, the *Sun*, the *Tribune*, the *Journal of Commerce*, the *Times*, the *World*, and the *Express*. Although the NYAP circulated news reports to newspapers throughout the country, it remained closely identified with New York City, a circumstance that contributed to its collapse in the 1890s. Unlike the present-day Associated Press, which is descended from a Chicago-based rival of the NYAP that was known originally as the Western Associated Press, the NYAP retained the right to restrict its membership, and, therefore, to determine which newspapers could obtain its news reports. Of the 971 daily newspapers published in the United States in 1880, the NYAP served only 355.[109] The NYAP was a "great mutual benefit co-operative association," explained its general agent in 1879, and, like all organizations of this kind, retained the right to pick its members, a right no less sacred than the right that men and women enjoyed to choose whom they would marry.[110] The presumption of NYAP critics that Congress should require it to provide every newspaper with news reports on equal terms struck its general agent as tantamount to contending that anyone who wished to publish a newspaper had a "God-given mission" to enter the business. This was precisely what the NYAP critics sought and precisely why the NYAP agent found their proposal so objectionable.[111]

The exclusivity of the NYAP predictably outraged journalists at newspapers the NYAP excluded. The young Henry George bitterly objected to Western Union's refusal to permit a San Francisco newspaper for which he worked to obtain news reports at preferential rates from the NYAP. A San Francisco–based press association allied with the NYAP had blackballed George's newspaper, and Orton declined to intervene. To get his revenge, George published a pamphlet detailing his unsuccessful attempt to break the Western Union–NYAP alliance; the *New York Herald* ran it in its entirety.[112] George soon turned his attention to the evils of private land ownership, another government-sanctioned monopoly that furnished the theme for George's classic antimonopoly tract, *Progress and Poverty* (1879). Yet it was a monopoly over the circulation of information, and not over the ownership of land, that first alerted George to the danger that government-sanctioned special privilege posed for equal rights.

Leadership in the fight against the Western Union–NYAP alliance devolved in the 1870s upon James H. Goodsell. Goodsell was the editor of the New York *Daily Graphic* and the president of the American Press Association, a newsbroker founded by the publishers of newspapers excluded from the NYAP. Goodsell was no more successful in breaking the Western Union–NYAP alliance than George had been. It was not for want of trying: Goodsell pilloried the "twin monopolies" in numerous editorials and cartoons that urged the establishment of "free trade" in news.[113]

Although Orton disapproved of the NYAP's exclusivity, he denied that as Western Union president he could do anything about it. The NYAP's exclusive control over its news reports was a point of "constant antagonism" between Western Union and the NYAP, Orton informed Congress in 1875. If the NYAP sold its news reports to every newspaper that requested it, Western Union would increase its telegraphic business and profits. Unfortunately, the NYAP refused to admit any newspaper "except on their own terms," and Orton knew of "no way to compel them."[114]

Orton's disclaimer fell on deaf ears, in large part because it was disingenuous. Western Union's refusal to interfere with the NYAP's internal affairs owed less to Orton's deference to NYAP bylaws than to his reliance on the NYAP to deflect political criticism of Western Union that might otherwise have led to hostile legislation. Orton could, in theory, have sold news reports to individual newspapers on advantageous terms. If he had, he would have risked offending the NYAP, and this Orton refused to do.

Orton's solicitude toward the NYAP was rooted in his conviction that the NYAP had the power to launch an editorial blitz that could hasten the enactment of legislation disadvantageous to Western Union. Not prying into the NYAP's internal affairs was a small price to pay to protect Western Union's operational autonomy. The "earnest" editorial support that several New York City–based NYAP newspapers had given Western Union during the recent congressional debate over possible telegraph legislation, Orton informed a colleague in 1869, had been "largely due" to the impending expiration of the NYAP's contract with Western Union, which made it "important for the press to stand by us."[115] The "substantially unanimous" voice of the press exercised a "powerful influence on Congress."[116]

Rival newsbrokers had two basic responses to the Western Union–NYAP alliance: advocate federal legislation to end it, or try to persuade Western Union to give them the same privileges the NYAP enjoyed. Goodsell endorsed legislation; Horace White of the *Chicago Tribune* urged accommodation. The *Chicago Tribune*'s refusal to run any editorials critical of

JUPITER AMMONOPOLY ORTON AND HIS VICTIM THE PRESS.

To minimize hostile newspaper coverage of Western Union, William Orton offered special privileges to the nation's most influential newsbroker, the New York Associated Press (NYAP). Orton's conduct outraged non-NYAP newspapers like the *Daily Graphic,* which found it impossible to obtain timely access to NYAP news reports. To publicize its outrage, this 1875 *Daily Graphic* cartoon depicted Orton as a classical deity who used his power over the "lightning" to trample on the press. "Jupiter Ammonopoly Orton and His Victim the Press," *Daily Graphic* 7 (March 24, 1875): front cover.

Western Union was unfortunate, conceded White in 1868. Yet the *Tribune* had no choice if it wished to obtain favorable rates from Western Union. "The fact is," White confessed, that the rival press association to which the *Tribune* belonged—the Western Associated Press—had been bound by a "written contract" with Western Union "not to advocate measures hostile to the interests of said telegraph company."[117] At least one of the various legislative proposals to transfer the telegraph to the Post Office Department that had been "strongly advocated" in Congress would undoubtedly have succeeded, Medill reminded his fellow journalists a few years later, had not the "powerful influence" of the press been "actively exerted" on Western Union's behalf.[118]

The telegraph business was more vulnerable to competition than any other business of comparable importance, Orton lectured investors in 1873.[119] Journalists could prove fickle, and exclusive right-of-way contracts could be broken. Rate-cutting rivals posed an even more immediate threat. If rights-of-way could be obtained, upstart rivals could parallel Western Union's lines for between $100 and $150 per mile, a tiny sum compared with the thousands of dollars it cost to build a single mile of railroad track.[120] Rate wars were endemic on highly trafficked routes, such as the routes between Washington and New York City and New York City and Chicago, and on several occasions Orton found it prudent to eliminate the competition by buying out the rival.

Orton's most determined rival was Jay Gould. In 1875 Gould commandeered a rival telegraph corporation—the Atlantic & Pacific—to launch a rate war against Western Union. He remained a rival until Orton bought him out in 1877. Orton's buyout only encouraged the financier, who organized a second telegraph corporation—American Union—to challenge Western Union for a second time after Orton's death. Gould's second challenge culminated in his takeover of Western Union in 1881.

To preempt rivals, Orton relied not only on tactical rate cuts and targeted buyouts, but also on technical advances. Although Orton himself had never been a telegraph operator, he was keenly aware of Western Union's vulnerability to technological obsolescence. If a rival promoter obtained broadly framed patents for inventions that reduced costs or improved performance standards, the promoter could offset the competitive advantage that Western Union had obtained from its exclusive right-of-way contracts and underbid it on highly trafficked routes.

Orton's commitment to technical advance led him to obtain a major stake in Gray and Barton, a Cleveland-based electrical equipment manufacturer founded by Elisha Gray and Enos Barton. Gray and Barton was one of the most technically advanced electrical equipment manufacturers of its day. By purchasing a major stake in the company, Orton hoped to obtain a steady supply of state-of-the-art telegraph equipment at a reasonable cost. To facilitate coordination between Gray and Barton and Western Union, Orton renamed it Western Electric and moved it to Chicago, Western Union's regional headquarters. Western Electric quickly became a major supplier of telegraph equipment for Western Union, as well as a major catalyst for technical innovation in the telegraph business.[121]

One technical advance in which Orton invested was the ticker, the first user-friendly electrical broadcast medium.[122] The ticker printed on paper tape time-sensitive price information about corporate securities and precious metals that bankers and brokers could read in their offices. No longer did telegraph users have to rely on a human intermediary, such as a telegraph operator or a newspaper editor, to obtain telegraphically transmitted information. "The merchant, manufacturer, editor, or politician," rhapsodized one ticker enthusiast in 1872, "may thus sit, spider-like, in the midst of his web of elaborate communications . . . catching with the sensitive quickness of light every shade of their variation or influence, and reacting in turn on each and all with a directness which a few decades ago would have seemed incredible."[123] To improve his position in the ticker business, Orton purchased the patent rights to a fast and reliable ticker invented by Thomas A. Edison and obtained a large financial stake in Gold & Stock, the largest ticker company in the country.[124]

The ticker was and would always remain a specialty service for an exclusive clientele. By 1876, only 700 had been installed in New York City, mostly in the offices of bankers and brokers.[125] A few nervous journalists warned that their installation might decrease the demand for newspapers by providing users with financial information in advance of the press. Orton demurred. The "little bits of information" that Gold & Stock transmitted merely whetted their users' appetite for newspapers, Orton explained. Indeed, Orton doubted whether a single newspaper had lost even one subscriber on account of Gold & Stock's financial reports.[126]

Orton also invested in the quadruplex, a device that enabled telegraph operators to send four messages simultaneously over a single wire. The quadruplex had the potential to significantly lower capital costs because it reduced the need to string additional telegraph wires to increase carrying capacity. Orton's interest in increasing a telegraph wire's carrying capacity dated back to 1868, when Gardiner G. Hubbard told him about the existence of the duplex, an invention that enabled operators to transmit two messages simultaneously. Orton initially ridiculed Hubbard's temerity in trying to tell Orton how to run his telegraph company. Shortly thereafter, Orton swallowed his pride and obtained the patent rights to the invention. To capitalize on the expertise of Elisha Gray, Enos Barton, and their colleagues at Western Electric, Orton offered financial incentives for the patent rights to inventions that Western Union might find useful or that might prove disadvantageous if they fell into a rival's hands. To keep abreast of developments along the Atlantic seaboard, Orton put the inventor Thomas A. Edison on a hefty annual retainer to invent patentable devices. Orton's contract with Edison failed to specify precisely that Western Union would acquire Edison's patent rights, an omission that would soon cause Orton a great many problems. From Orton's perspective, his intention was plain. Edison had been hired to "anticipate other inventors" by inventing devices as "insurance" for Western Union.[127]

The best known of the technical advances whose commercialization Orton helped to foster was the telephone. The earliest telephones were capable of transmitting sounds, such as musical tones, but not the human voice; their refinement had been a favorite pastime since the 1850s for inventors in Europe and the United States. The word "telephone" itself was first popularized around that time; it was long associated exclusively with the transmission of music by electrical current.[128]

The first telephones invented in the United States that were capable of transmitting the human voice were patented almost simultaneously by Elisha Gray, Alexander Graham Bell, and Thomas A. Edison. For all three inventors, the telephone was a by-product of their quest to patent the rights to a multiplex telegraph that they could sell to Orton to fortify Western Union in its contest with Gould.[129]

Orton's refusal to purchase the patent rights to Bell's telephone has been derided by chroniclers of American business and technology as one of the worst business decisions in American history. It is more aptly characterized as a prudent response to a highly fluid situation. Orton had a well-established business relationship with Gray and Edison, each of whom invented a telephone that Orton believed to be superior to Bell's. Had the subsequent legal maneuvering between Western Union and the owners of Bell's patent rights taken a different turn, Orton might well have been vindicated. To credit Bell alone with the invention of the telephone says more about the exigencies of patent litigation than it does about the process of invention. "It is futile," observed one distinguished historian of technology, "for an inventor, a historian of invention, or even the courts to attempt to prove who invented a machine, device, or process such as the steam engine, the telephone, or the transformer. . . . Alexander Graham Bell did not invent the telephone: he put together a telephone system that embodied a particular application of the principles of variable resistance and induction."[130]

The fact that Bell's principal financial backer was Orton's nemesis, Gardiner G. Hubbard, reinforced Orton's determination not to buy Bell's patent rights to his invention. Orton had acquired the patent rights to Gray's telephone, and he was understandably loath to pay off a promoter who had been lobbying Congress for years to enact legislation hostile to Western Union. Should Bell's patent rights become the nexus of a rival combine, Orton plausibly assumed that he had the requisite legal, technical, and financial resources to destroy it. For Orton to dismiss the telephone in the winter of 1876 as an "electrical toy," as he purportedly did, may well have reflected his genuine conviction.[131] Elisha Gray reached a similar conclusion at more or less the same time. Yet it may also have been a deliberate ploy to keep low the potential future price of the patent rights to an invention that Orton did not yet own.

Whatever misgivings Orton may have had about the commercial potential of the telephone in the winter of 1876, they had been overcome by February 1878. In that month, Orton confided to a colleague that, if the various telephone patents could be pooled, their owner would possess one of the "most valuable rights" in the country.[132] Had Orton lived only a few years longer, Western Union might have bested Hubbard and Bell and remained a major player in the telephone business. At the time of his death, Orton was rapidly building for Western Union an archipelago of telephone exchanges in cities and towns throughout the United States.

Orton's ambiguous relationship with the telephone was characteristic of his business strategy. If Western Union outperformed its rivals, lawmakers raised the specter of monopoly; if it did not, it was vulnerable to new entrants. Orton's dilemma was pithily summarized by James D. Reid in a history of the telegraph business that Reid dedicated to Orton and published shortly after Orton's death. Western Union, Reid declared, was simultaneously a "purely private enterprise" and a "recognized national means of intercourse."[133] It was never easy, and, in some instances, impossible, for Orton to strike a balance between the obligations Western Union owed to the nation and its shareholders. The management of an organization that was simultaneously a powerful institution and a major channel of communication posed an enormous challenge, and it was one that not even a manager as capable as Orton was always able to meet.

Reid's choice of words is revealing in a further regard. Western Union in the 1870s was indeed a "national" institution: though its wire network linked every major city in the United States, it had a minimal presence overseas. The major exception was the U.S.-Cuban telegraph line that Orton acquired in 1873. In the all-important Atlantic market, Western Union relied on the cable giant Anglo-American. Though Anglo-American's name implied that it was a joint U.S.-British venture, it was actually funded with British capital, operated by British engineers, and supplied by British equipment manufacturers.

To underscore the power of the network over which Western Union presided, Orton oversaw the construction of a huge and imposing new headquarters building in downtown New York City. This building was located on a choice piece of real estate on Broadway, the city's principal north-south thoroughfare, just north of the financial district, and within a few blocks of the city hall, the new main city post office, and the headquarters of several of the city's leading newspapers, including the *Herald*, the *Tribune*, and the *Times*. Completed in 1875, the building rivaled in its sheer massiveness the new city post office, an equally outsized structure that was rapidly rising a few blocks to its north. The Western Union headquarters building was an eloquent tribute to Orton's determination to ensure that Western Union would be no less enduring than the Post Office Department, the organization with which Western Union had been so often invidiously compared by its critics. The main facade included niches for huge sculptures of Franklin and Morse, though it is uncertain if these niches were ever filled. The building remained Western Union's headquarters until 1913, when it was torn down to make way for a joint headquarters building for Western Union and the American Telephone and Telegraph Corporation, which had acquired Western Union in 1909.

The pairing of Franklin and Morse was conventional, though not without political import. Each man was a celebrated inventor well known for a major technical advance in electrical science: the lightning rod for Franklin, the telegraph for Morse. Each buttressed Western Union's legitimacy as a private corporation that dominated an essential channel of commerce. Orton lionized Morse in the final years of Morse's life in a publicity campaign that successfully transformed the onetime proponent of a government telegraph into a corporate icon. The embrace of Franklin complicated the inventor's common association with the Post Office Department. Just as the Post Office Department claimed Franklin as its founder, so, too, did Western Union.

The Western Union building was a stunning visual icon. Ten and a half stories high, with each story of double height, it was four times taller than a typical five-story commercial structure.[134] Nothing better symbolized the rapid ascendancy of Western Union following its consolidation in 1866 as one of the largest and most powerful corporations in the nation. Only the spire of Trinity Church and the towers of the still-to-be-completed Brooklyn Bridge reached further into the sky. When the English scientist and agnostic Thomas Huxley learned, upon his arrival in New York City in the late 1870s, that its two tallest buildings were the headquarters buildings for Western Union and the *New York Tribune,* he did not fail to draw the moral. "Ah," he was reported to have said, "that is interesting; this is American. In the Old World the first things you see as you approach a great city are the steeples; here you see, first, centers of intelligence."[135]

Ostentatious, massive, and expensive, the Western Union building exuded what one real estate insider termed an "unbounded confidence" in the future potential of the telegraph business that was untroubled by its present cost.[136] Western Union spent several million dollars on its construction, a huge sum that obliged Orton to obtain funding in London. The lot itself cost $840,000, making it the single largest commercial real estate transaction in the history of New York City.[137]

Overtopping the building was a clock tower that loomed 226 feet above the sidewalk—six feet higher than the Bunker Hill Monument, one journalist duly noted—and almost as high as the west façade of Strasbourg Cathedral.[138] No one hailed the Western Union headquarters building in 1875 as a "skyscraper," since this word had not yet been applied to structures other than ships. Yet it would soon come to be hailed by architectural critics as one of the first skyscrapers in the world.[139]

The most unusual feature of the Western Union building was the elaborate time-keeping device atop its clock tower that was known as a time ball. To help mariners calibrate the chronometers they relied on to calculate the longitude, as well as anyone else who wished to know the time, this ball was automatically released every day precisely at noon on a signal from the United States Naval Observatory in Washington, which maintained a highly accurate clock. "Thousands of people depended upon the daily dropping of the old ball for the regulation of their time-pieces," reminisced one New Yorker in 1892, "and it was especially valuable to mariners, with whom accuracy of time is a matter of great moment."[140] The custom continued until the construction of even taller buildings in the vicinity blocked the view.[141] Its spirit lingers today with the ceremonial release at midnight on New Year's Eve of a brightly lit orb in New York's Times Square.

The Western Union time ball symbolized Orton's determination to burnish Western Union's reputation as a solid, reliable, and permanent institution. Time balls had previously been associated primarily with government agencies. The Royal Observatory at Greenwich, England, for example, had installed one of the earliest in 1833. Western Union was among the first corporations to follow its lead.

Ironically, the completion of the Western Union building coincided with the first of two challenges to Western Union by financier Jay Gould. Gould's takeover of Western Union in 1881 curtailed the operational autonomy that Orton had worked so doggedly to attain. Although Gould was an innovative business strategist, he did little to enhance Western Union's reputation and showed scant interest in furthering Orton's ambitious research and development program. Orton rejected as impractical Hubbard's "new postalic dispensation," yet he endorsed Hubbard's conviction that the operation of the telegraph network was a public trust that was best coordinated by its managers. Unfortunately for Orton, managerial control proved elusive. Following Gould's takeover in 1881, it ceased even to be an ideal.

5

RICH MAN'S MAIL

The fact that Mr. Jay Gould was the principal owner of the telegraph company was another circumstance which led the people generally to side with the strikers. . . . He cares nothing for the public: why should the public care anything for him? For years he has been defying law, and his entire business career is a terrible disgrace to the country.

Banker's Magazine, 1883

The Western Union building was a soaring monument to the dogged determination of Western Union's president, William Orton, to transform the corporation into an enduring institution. Unfortunately for Orton, it offered a highly visible temptation to Western Union's would-be rivals. None of these rivals proved more persistent, or more successful, than the financier Jay Gould.

Gould challenged Western Union twice, first in 1875 and again in 1879. His first raid targeted Western Union's patent portfolio; his second, its exclusive railroad right-of-way contracts. Gould's first raid ended in August 1877 when Orton bought Gould out. Gould's second raid ended in January 1881 with his installation as Western Union's de facto chief executive officer. Gould retained an office in Western Union's headquarters building from 1881 until his death in 1892. Although he had investments in many ventures, Western Union was, in the words of an early biographer, his "greatest enterprise."[1]

Gould's two raids on Western Union were but one chapter in a remarkable business career that was unparalleled in the annals of American business. Long before he set his sights on Western Union, Gould had acquired a formidable reputation as a speculator in railroad securities and gold. During the same years that he raided Western Union, he mounted a related, even more elaborate campaign to reorganize several of the nation's largest railroads. For a brief moment in 1881, Gould owned a controlling stake in both Western Union and the largest railroad network in the world. He soon relinquished part of his railroad empire, but he retained Western Union. No other chapter in Gould's life— not his raid on the Erie Railroad, not his attempt to corner the gold market, not even his takeover of the Union Pacific—did more to ensure his notoriety. Gould's takeover of Western Union, reminisced one chronicler, was the "most fantastic piece of financial piracy" during the "'robber baron'" age.[2]

When historians in the 1920s began to disparage the post–Civil War decades as a "gilded age," they singled out Gould as its most infamous financier. Few Americans have been more reviled—or more successful— in leaving their mark on an age. No individual better epitomized the combination of audacity and guile that prompted historians to term an entire generation of business leaders "robber barons." The cultural critic Matthew Josephson popularized the "robber baron" metaphor in a muckraking critique of the late-nineteenth-century business elite published in the depths of the Great Depression. Josephson dated the metaphor to 1880 and attributed to it to an antimonopoly pamphlet published by the "embattled farmers of Kansas." He was apparently unaware that it had been widely used and very possibly coined several decades earlier by the patrician bluebloods Charles Francis Adams Jr. and Josiah Quincy Jr.[3] In so doing, Josephson fostered the mistaken presumption that the antimonopoly movement originated in the hinterland, that it appealed primarily to farmers, and that it would only later be embraced by the urban middle class.[4]

Gould's takeover of Western Union was one of the many unanticipated consequences of the antimonopoly tilt in American law. Ironically, a self-proclaimed antimonopolist now presided over a corporation that controlled 90 percent of the telegraph market in the United States. To explain this puzzling, unexpected, and widely deplored development, a rising generation of social scientists popularized a new economic theory. This theory repudiated antimonopoly as a civic ideal by characterizing large and powerful corporations like Western Union as "natural monopolies."

The term "natural monopoly" went back at least as far as 1848, when it had been casually invoked by the English political economist John Stuart Mill in the first edition of his celebrated *Principles of Political Economy*. Mill used the term primarily to denote personal attributes that gave an individual a competitive advantage, such as talent or integrity. Mill reserved the related term, "practical monopoly," for certain capital-intensive organizations, such as a gas plant or water works, that were, in theory, vulnerable to competition but that, in reality, were not, making them even "more irresponsible" than the government.[5] Mill's more expansive definition appealed to the American political economist Richard T. Ely, who used the term "natural monopoly" to characterize Western Union in 1888. Implicit in Ely's definition was the then-novel presumption that the market power of corporations like Western Union owed more to technological imperatives and economic incentives than to government-granted special privilege. Ironically, Ely floated this new definition not to liberate Western Union from the political economy, but to bring it under more effective federal government control.

Gould's two raids on Western Union had several features in common. In each raid, he mounted a political campaign to whittle away Western Union's legal prerogatives, triggered wild swings in the market price of Western Union shares by floating rumors intentionally designed to mislead investors, netted large profits by buying and selling Western Union shares in which he took advantage of advance information on market trends, and built up a rival telegraph corporation—Atlantic & Pacific in 1874, American Union in 1879—that Western Union found it expedient to buy out. Largely by happenstance, each raid also had major consequences for American telecommunications.

Gould launched his first raid in January 1875 by challenging Western Union's patent rights to two recent inventions: the induction coil patented by the late Patent Office examiner Charles G. Page and the quadruplex patented by Thomas A. Edison. To challenge Page's patent, Gould instructed Washington lobbyist William E. Chandler to find out if Congress might be induced to void it.[6] Most patents were issued by the Patent Office. The Page patent, however, had been issued by Congress, raising the possibility that Congress might change its mind.[7] Gould stood to profit even if Congress stood pat. By floating rumors about the legality of the Page patent, Gould sent the market price of Western Union shares sharply downward, minimizing the risk that Gould had assumed by selling Western Union short. Short selling was a risky maneuver in which traders made money if the market price of securities that they sold dropped so that they could cover their sale price by purchasing these securities at a lower price. If the price of the securities rose instead, the short sellers' losses could be ruinous. Gould had the financial resources to buy or sell short large blocs of Western Union shares. If he correctly predicted the direction in which its share price was likely to trend, he would make money if it went either up or down.

The kerfuffle over the Page patent was the opening salvo in Gould's raid on Western Union. To further weaken the telegraph giant, Gould scaled up the Atlantic & Pacific, a modest telegraph line that he had recently acquired. To lure users from Western Union, Gould slashed rates on the highly trafficked New York City–Chicago route. Gould's rate war weakened Western Union in two ways. First, it reduced its revenue; and, second, it created anxiety in financial markets. Given the fickleness of Western Union's investors, either outcome could be expected to lower its share price. Gould's New York City–Chicago line had been established for "no other purpose," fumed Western Union president William Orton, than to depress Western Union's share price by slashing rates to an extent that was not only unremunerative but also "ruinous"; or, alternatively, to "put up" Western Union's share price by floating rumors in newspapers that Gould owned or could influence that the Atlantic & Pacific was about to sell out to Western Union.[8]

The masterstroke of Gould's first raid was his acquisition of the patent rights to Thomas A. Edison's quadruplex. Whether or not Gould actually intended to install the quadruplex on the Atlantic & Pacific was a mere detail. The reason for its acquisition, Gould informed Chandler, was to "settle" his "prestige" as a rival to Western Union.[9]

The quadruplex was an ingenious invention that significantly reduced the cost of maintaining a telegraph network by doubling its carrying capacity. The duplex had permitted telegraph operators to transmit two messages simultaneously on a single wire; the quadruplex permitted them to transmit four messages on a single wire simultaneously, two in each direction. Edison had invented his quadruplex while on a retainer from Western Union, and Orton assumed that Western Union owned the patent rights, even though Edison was not a Western Union employee and had not conducted his research at a Western Union–owned facility. Edison had other ideas. In his view, he, and not Western Union, owned the patent rights to his invention, and he found Gould's offer sufficiently attractive that he sold them to him.[10]

Orton considered Edison's conduct deplorable. Edison had a "vacuum" where his "conscience ought to be," huffed Orton to an English colleague, and the famous inventor should be reviled throughout the country as the "Professor of Duplicity."[11]

Spoiling for a fight, Orton took the offensive. To retaliate against Gould, Orton made it known throughout the technical community that Western Union would pay handsomely for the patent rights to any multiplex that did not infringe on the patent rights to Edison's quadruplex. The ownership of Edison's quadruplex was likely to be tied up in court for some time, and Orton was hoping to secure a competitive advantage that was not contingent on whatever the courts might decide. Orton's offer created an entrepreneurial hothouse that inspired a legion of inventors—including Elisha Gray and Alexander Graham Bell—to invent a multiplex that Orton would buy.

The rivalry between Gould and Orton ended in August 1877 when Orton bought out Gould's Atlantic & Pacific on terms that were highly advantageous to Gould. Western Union's buyout was a minor event in the history of communications and was soon forgotten. Since Atlantic & Pacific continued to operate under its own name, telegraph users unfamiliar with Wall Street finance may well have assumed that it remained a separate concern. The rivalry between Edison, Gray, and Bell was more consequential. Edison invested the money he obtained for the quadruplex in a research laboratory in Menlo Park, New Jersey. There he devised his two most celebrated inventions: the phonograph and the electric power station.[12] Gray and Bell invented—largely by accident and as a by-product of their efforts to design a superior multiplex to sell to Orton or Gould—a device that was capable of transmitting the human voice by varying the electrical current in a wire and that would soon become known as the telephone.

Bell, Gray, and Edison each had access to state-of-the-art electrical equipment and up-to-date technical knowledge. Yet the entrepreneurial gale of creative destruction that swept through the telegraph business in the 1870s would have been far milder in the absence of a specific constellation of governmental institutions and civic ideals. The circumstances that led to the almost simultaneous invention of the quadruplex, the phonograph, the telephone, and the electric power station had been nurtured by the theoretically illogical, yet practically robust, combination of a competitive state-oriented political economy that encouraged the chartering of telegraph corporations and a centralized, federally oriented political economy that offered a panoply of legal safeguards for the owners of patent rights.[13] Corporate law fostered antimonopoly;

patent law encouraged monopoly. Had corporate law been less accommodating to new entrants, Gould would have found it harder to raid Western Union. And had patent law not transformed inventions into tradable assets, he might never have tried.

Gray and Bell had very different goals, and their telephones had very different futures. Gray's telephone was a by-product of an ongoing research project that Orton had instituted several years earlier at Western Union to increase the carrying capacity of a telegraph wire. Gray resigned from Western Electric in 1874 to devote his full attention to this project unencumbered by any constraints that he might have faced had he remained a Western Electric employee. The ownership of Edison's patent rights remained disputed, whereas Gray's patent rights were his alone. Gray's mind-set as a professional inventor explained his priorities. Gray doubted that the telephone he invented had any commercial applications; to drive this point home, he derided it as a mere "scientific toy." His multiplex, however, solved the most pressing technical challenge that Western Union confronted. This made the multiplex not only a superior invention, but also the invention that was most likely to net Gray a substantial financial reward.[14]

Bell's telephone was initially a disappointment to his financial backer, Gardiner G. Hubbard. Hubbard had hired Bell to invent a multiplex telegraph that Bell could sell to either Orton or Gould. Like Gray, Hubbard initially doubted the commercial value of the telephone. Edison had made a small fortune from his quadruplex; if Bell invented a superior multiplex, he might too.

Hubbard obtained Bell's first telephone patent in March 1876. This patent covered the theory of transmitting sound by varying the resistance in an electrical current. Although the courts later interpreted Bell's patent to embrace the electrical transmission of the human voice, the patent itself said little about speech communications. It did not even refer to Bell's invention as a telephone, conceivably to meet Gray's objection that it was a mere "scientific toy." The vagueness of Bell's patent was not surprising. Hubbard had applied for it several weeks before Bell had demonstrated that he could in fact transmit the human voice.

Hubbard had encouraged Bell to patent his telephone in the assumption that Hubbard might be able to sell his patent rights to Western Union. Hubbard offered Bell's patent rights to Orton in the winter of 1876–1877, and Orton turned him down.[15]

Hubbard's failure to sell Bell's patent rights led Hubbard to wonder whether they might become the nucleus of a new kind of municipal franchise corporation. If properly configured, Hubbard now predicted, the telephone could provide a service to the inhabitants of a locality, in a manner analogous to a water works or gas plant.

Hubbard's analogy was built on his extensive familiarity with municipal franchise corporations. Hubbard had long invested in water works, gas plants, and horse-car lines, making it almost inevitable that he would regard the municipal franchise corporation as a suitable organizational form for the telephone. At this time Hubbard does not appear to have envisioned the interconnection of telephones into a multiple-user network in which a large number of users could communicate with each other. The telephone exchange would not be invented until the following year, and it would take several years before users would regard intercommunication as a major benefit.[16] Rather, Hubbard seems to have conceived of the telephone as an improvement on the district telegraphs that well-to-do city dwellers had for some time installed in their homes in order to send a one-way message to a central office. City dwellers used district telegraphs to order a cab, hire a messenger, or call the police. The telephone was in Hubbard's view its logical successor.[17]

To hasten the commercialization of the telephone, Hubbard obtained a second patent for Bell that included the specifications for a rudimentary telephone apparatus. Bell's apparatus did not differentiate the telephone transmitter from the telephone receiver; this was a relatively minor concern for a device that had been intended primarily for one-way communication.

Whatever initial misgivings Orton may have had about the commercial potential of Bell's invention did not last long. In early 1878, an unnamed official at Western Union offered Hubbard a $500,000 stake in a Western Union–backed telephone start-up in return for Bell's patent rights. Hubbard rejected this offer. In its place, he proposed to trade Bell's patent rights for a $1 annual royalty on every telephone that Western Union rented and $1 million in Western Union shares. The official rejected Hubbard's counteroffer, ending Hubbard's campaign to unload Bell's patent rights on Western Union.[18]

Whether or not Hubbard offered Bell's patent rights to Gould is unknown. That Hubbard and Gould were business associates is a matter of record. Gould had paid Hubbard a retainer as recently as 1875 for legal work presumably related to Gould's first raid on Western Union.[19]

Hubbard urged Bell to negotiate with Gould's Atlantic & Pacific; whether Bell did so is unclear.[20] Yet it is a matter of record that Gould's agent Benjamin F. Butler offered Hubbard's "company" $75,000 for something of value in June 1877, and that Hubbard declined.[21] What Butler wanted is unclear. It might have been the patent rights to Bell's telephone, or it might have been the patent rights to another one of Bell's inventions. If Hubbard had offered the patent rights for Bell's telephone to Gould, it would not have been particularly surprising. Hubbard was known to have tried to sell Bell's patent rights not only to Orton, but also to the manufacturer Peter Cooper and the geologist Clarence King.[22]

The most formidable challenge confronting early telephone promoters was neither technological nor economic, but political. The bruising telegraph patent fight between Morse and his rivals in the 1850s remained a living memory, and no one wanted to go down that path again. Cooper had been willing to invest $200,000 in the telephone to obtain the telephone patent rights granted to Bell, Gray, and Edison. Cooper desisted when King persuaded him that the likely patent litigation would significantly increase the cost of its commercialization.[23]

In the absence of a patent pool to preempt litigation, Orton shared King's concern that a "protracted fight" over patent rights might slow the commercialization of the telephone and "destroy" its value for its investors.[24] If the future litigation over the telephone was as extensive as the past litigation over the telegraph had been, the results would be disastrous, warned Western Union vice president Norvin Green in 1879. Green remembered the telegraph patent fights of the 1850s. Once the courts began to compare competing inventions, the public would be surprised to discover how easy it was to invent "the great thing," whether a telegraph or a telephone.[25]

In the end, Hubbard's failure to sell Bell's patent rights proved to be highly fortunate for both Hubbard and Bell. Bell's patent rights became the legal foundation of an extremely lucrative corporation that generated a sizable income for Bell for the rest of his life. As for Hubbard, he too profited handsomely from Bell's telephone. Indeed, the money Hubbard obtained from telephone stock became, in a way, a substitute for the financial windfall he had failed to obtain from Congress for his federally chartered Postal Telegraph Company.

Hubbard's relationship with Bell highlights the subtle way in which governmental institutions shaped technical progress. Bell had emigrated from Canada to the United States in 1871 at the invitation of the Boston

Board of Education, which had recruited him to teach a special class for the deaf in a public school. Had Boston's municipal government not deemed the instruction of the deaf a priority, Bell would have lacked an incentive to relocate and might well have lived his life in relative obscurity in Canada as what we would today call a special education teacher. Bell's research on the telephone was a by-product of his quest to better understand the physical properties of acoustics, a subject in which he had long been engaged as a teacher of the deaf.

Hubbard himself had long been interested in government funding for the physically disabled. Hubbard's daughter Mabel had lost her hearing following a bout of scarlet fever, and Hubbard hoped to find a way to enable her to overcome her disability. When Hubbard learned of Bell's experimental research in acoustics, he hired Bell to invent a multiplex. The Bell–Hubbard relationship became even stronger when Alexander and Mabel fell in love. In fact, it was largely to curry favor with his potential future father-in-law that Alexander accepted Hubbard's offer to bankroll the research on the multiplex telegraph that led to the invention of his telephone. Alexander and Mabel were married in Hubbard's front parlor shortly after Hubbard obtained Bell's first telephone patent. Patent commissioner Henry L. Ellsworth may or may not have regarded Morse's telegraph patent rights as a dowry for his daughter Anne, yet Hubbard unquestionably conceived of Bell's telephone patent rights as a wedding gift for his daughter Mabel.

Gould's first raid hastened the invention of the telephone; his second raid ensured that the market for electrical communications would be segmented between the telephone and the telegraph. The turning point in Gould's second raid came in June 1879 when Congress enacted a law known as the Butler Amendment, named after its sponsor, Massachusetts congressman and former Civil War general Benjamin F. Butler. The Butler Amendment took the form of a brief and seemingly innocuous amendment to the army appropriations bill that granted any railroad corporation that gave its written assent to the National Telegraph Act the authority to own and operate a telegraph line for the public along its rights-of-way even if the railroad had not been granted this privilege in its corporate charter.[26] In so doing, it overturned a legal convention that had long been a mainstay of the political economy: henceforth, railroad corporations that signed on to the National Telegraph Act were no longer constrained by the fear that, if they operated their own telegraph line, they might be sued by their owners for undertaking a business that had not been authorized by a state legislature.

Like the National Telegraph Act, the Butler Amendment was intended to foster rivalry in the telegraph business. By overriding the statutory limitations in the railroad's state charter, it challenged a legal convention that Western Union executives took for granted in negotiating exclusive railroad right-of-way contracts.[27] The law was a great victory for the "cheap transmission of intelligence," explained Butler in a newspaper interview shortly after its enactment.[28] By authorizing railroads to operate their own telegraph lines, it empowered them to compete directly with Western Union.

Although the Butler Amendment was seemingly arcane, lawmakers familiar with right-of-way law recognized it at once as a "jewel in a toad's head." With the stroke of a pen, declared one lawmaker, it "revolutionizes" the telegraph business in the United States.[29] Among its critics was Gardiner G. Hubbard. Hubbard had long opposed competition in the telegraph business and thus understandably regarded the Butler Amendment as a step in the wrong direction. Now that the telephone was opening up a "new field" for the telegraph business, why, at the very moment when there had emerged a "boundless prospect" for popularizing the "whole telegraph system," should Congress enact law that, by fostering competition among telegraph network providers, was certain to "increase rates, retard business, and multiply errors"?[30]

The Butler Amendment was part of a trap that Butler had laid for Western Union in 1875. During an investigation in that year of Western Union's relationship with the New York Associated Press (NYAP), Butler championed an expansive federal rationale for the regulation of the telegraph network. "It will not be denied," Butler declared, "that every civilized government, ancient or modern, has taken in charge and under its exclusive control the transmission of its own communications to its officers and of general intelligence among its people."[31]

In other circumstances Butler's declaration might easily have been forgotten. Butler worked diligently behind the scenes to ensure that it was not. Butler's lobbying paid off in October 1877, when, in *Pensacola v. Western Union*, Chief Justice Morrison Waite affirmed the constitutionality of the National Telegraph Act in a sweeping ruling that drew in part on Butler's 1875 report, a fact that Butler was too vainglorious not to publicize.[32] The telegraph was one of the "necessities" of commerce, Waite ruled, and the mandate of the Post Office Department to facilitate the "transmission of intelligence" extended to novel means of communication—like the telegraph—that were unknown when the Constitution had been ratified.[33] *Pensacola* was ostensibly a victory for Western Union because it overrode a state law that had blocked Western Union's ability to obtain a right-of-way in Florida. By affirming the constitutionality of the National Telegraph Act, however, it established a legal precedent that Gould was quick to exploit.

Among the Butler Amendment's supporters were the many journalists unable to obtain low-cost news reports from the NYAP. By encouraging the establishment of a rival telegraph network, the Butler Amendment opened the way for "free trade in news," explained James H. Goodsell of the New York *Daily Graphic*. Goodsell was in a position to know. His newspaper had been denied membership in the NYAP, and Goodsell was the president of a rival newsbroker eager to negotiate with the rival network providers the Butler Amendment was supposed to encourage.[34]

The Butler Amendment helped Gould to scale up a modest upstate New York telegraph line into a nation-spanning telegraph network that he called American Union. Gould owned several railroads that had negotiated exclusive right-of-way agreements with Western Union; the Butler Amendment freed them to also negotiate with American Union. In so doing, explained one of Gould's publicists, American Union would "emancipate the public" from the "exactions of a monopoly."[35]

Gould's artful deployment of the Butler Amendment raises the question of whether he might have been responsible for its enactment. No paper trail exists linking Gould to the law, though Gould had worked closely with Butler on several related matters in the past and was in close contact with him in the months preceding the law's enactment. Although it might seem odd for a principled antimonopolist like Butler to ally himself with an amoral financier like Gould, the two shared a common political agenda: the destruction of monopolies that limited access to the channels of trade.

Gould's machinations infuriated Norvin Green, who was now Western Union's president following Orton's death in 1878. Green denied Gould's right to build telegraph lines on railroads with which Western Union had negotiated exclusive right-of-way contracts. Gould rejected Green's interpretation of these contracts, however, and defeated him in the courts. The test case involved an American Union telegraph line on the Wabash Railroad, which Gould controlled. The Wabash had assented to the National Telegraph Act. As a consequence, ruled Supreme Court Justice John Marshall Harlan, Western Union could not block it from permitting American Union to string a telegraph wire along its right-of-way, even if Western Union had previously negotiated an exclusive right-of-way agreement with the Wabash.[36] Harlan's ruling enabled Gould to parallel Western Union's telegraph lines on railroads throughout the country. By brandishing Harlan's decision, Green fumed, Gould was "bull-dozing" railroads into breaking their exclusive right-of-way contracts with Western Union.[37] If Gould had actually intended to rival Western Union on a permanent basis, this would have been a cause for concern. Instead it was an occasion for outrage, since Gould had gone into business merely to orchestrate a "Wall Street drive" to manipulate the price of Western Union shares. If Gould succeeded with his second raid on Western Union, as he "most emphatically had" with his first, Western Union could expect that he would raid it a third time in the immediate future, forcing Western Union to once again buy him out.[38]

The disruptions accelerated by the Butler Amendment were heightened by a financial transaction that occurred a few weeks before its enactment. Not content with their annual dividend, Western Union's board of directors threw onto the market $15 million in Western Union shares that Orton had sequestered, a transaction that financial insiders euphemistically called "cutting the melon." The melon-cutting reversed the previous decision of Western Union investor Cornelius Vanderbilt to take Western Union shares off the market. Following Vanderbilt's death, his Western Union shares devolved on his son, William. William second-guessed his father and endorsed their return to the corporation's investors.[39]

The release of such a large number of Western Union shares furnished Gould with an impetus for his second raid. Once again, Gould relied on his connections with the press, newsbrokers, and the telegraph business to manipulate the market price of Western Union shares. And once again, he drove down Western Union's share price and made money by selling it short.[40]

Among the unanticipated consequences of Gould's second raid was the segmentation of the market for electrical communications between the telegraph and the telephone. In 1879 the telephone business consisted of a scattering of stand-alone telephone exchanges that had signed licensing agreements with either Western Union or National Bell. Western Union

GETTING READY TO CUT THE MELON.

To increase Western Union's operational autonomy, Orton bought up thousands of Western Union shares. Orton's purchase created a "melon" that, in this 1878 cartoon, financier William H. Vanderbilt had yet to cut. Seated on the table to Vanderbilt's right was financier Jay Gould. Gould was plainly impressed by the recent rise in the market price of Western Union shares; shortly thereafter, Gould would mastermind an even more audacious raid on the telegraph giant. "Getting Ready to Cut the Melon," *Daily Graphic* 17 (October 30, 1878): front cover.

entered the telephone business in a major way in 1878; its exchanges were equipped with telephones patented by Elisha Gray and Thomas A. Edison. National Bell was the holding company that financier William H. Forbes chartered to commercialize Bell's patents.

Gould's second raid convinced Green that Western Union had a vested interest in propping up National Bell. If Gould obtained control of the most important National Bell exchanges, which was a plausible scenario in the summer of 1879, he could gain a competitive advantage over Western Union by using them as local feeders for his long-distance telegraph network. Had Gould not raided Western Union a second time, Western Union would in all likelihood have remained in the telephone business and, very conceivably, would have bested Bell. Although Forbes represented a wealthy clique of Massachusetts-based investors, he was hard pressed to compete with Western Union. By the middle of 1879, National Bell was expanding at a slower pace than Western Union in both New York City and Chicago.

To stymie Gould, Green segmented the market for electrical communications between the telegraph and the telephone. The settlement between Green and Forbes was signed in November 1879. It transferred from Western Union to National Bell Western Union's telephone patent portfolio as well as its eighty-five telephone exchanges. National Bell, for its part, agreed to pay Western Union a 20 percent royalty on every telephone it rented during the remaining years of Bell's patents.[41] Although the value of this royalty was unknown, it turned out to be quite substantial: In the period between 1881 and 1895, it netted Western Union over $6 million, a sum that the telephone users who footed the bill understandably resented.[42]

The Western Union–National Bell settlement ceded to National Bell the telephone business in return for National Bell's promise to stay out of the telegraph business. The long-distance telephone business, however, remained with National Bell. For Western Union leaders, this was a minor concession. Telephone exchanges remained localized in individual cities or towns and thus could not possibly rival the telegraph in the long-distance market.[43]

Whether Gould intended to consolidate American Union with National Bell was anyone's guess. To keep his options open, Gould purchased several financially distressed Bell exchanges, including the Bell exchange in New Haven, Connecticut, the first to be open to the public in the world. Had Gould wished, he could easily have purchased more exchanges, since National Bell faced stiff competition from Western Union.[44] Green, for one, was not taking any chances. "I beg to call your attention" to the provision of the proposed Western Union–National Bell settlement that required Bell to make "exclusive connection" with Western Union, Green wrote a Bell lawyer in July 1879. This arrangement was a sine qua non of any settlement, since Western Union could not risk the possibility that the "united telephone interests" might consolidate their "local exchange machinery" with American Union's long-distance network to enable Gould to launch a third raid on Western Union.[45] Causes "outside the strength of our patents" had operated in Bell's favor in its contest with Western Union, reflected Forbes shortly after the Western Union–National Bell settlement had gone into effect: "The presence of Gould in the field and the existence of a considerable public opinion against the Western Union Telegraph Company without question added much to the anxiety of that company for a settlement."[46]

Gould never launched a third raid on Western Union because he did not have to. His second raid, after all, had culminated in his takeover of the telegraph giant in January 1881. By challenging Western Union, he had segmented the market for electrical communications between rival corporations. This outcome set apart the electrical communications sector in the United States from its counterparts in Great Britain and France.

The 1880s marked the culmination of the long struggle for comprehensive federal telegraph legislation that stretched all the way back to Morse's initial attempt to obtain federal funding for a demonstration project in 1838. On numerous occasions in this decade, lawmakers debated proposals that, collectively, came to be lumped under the rubric of "postal telegraphy." Although the term "postal telegraphy" dated back to the 1860s, it did not become part of the popular lexicon until the 1880s. Proponents of federal telegraph legislation elaborated on arguments that Hubbard pioneered and in several instances repeated claims that went back as far as the congressional debate that preceded the enactment of the National Telegraph Act in 1866. Once again, critics accused Western Union of overcharging users, squelching innovation, and discriminating in favor of the NYAP.

Nothing angered Western Union critics more than Gould's doubling of Western Union's capitalization from $40 million to $80 million immediately following his takeover of the telegraph giant in January 1881. Many telegraph insiders regarded $40 million as unduly high, but almost everyone other than Gould regarded $80 million as unconscionable. By doubling Western Union's capitalization, he doubled the number of shares on which Western Union paid dividends. Since Gould was the largest shareholder, and shareholders received new issues on the basis of their existing holdings, he had, in effect, paid a huge dividend to himself.

Gould's takeover of Western Union transformed the public debate over federal telegraph legislation. Few Americans used the telegraph, yet many reviled Gould, and this made all the difference. No longer could Western Union's leaders dismiss their critics as a tiny, self-interested cabal, as they had so often, by no means implausibly, before 1881. The hostility toward Gould during election campaigns was so intense that it was common to allege that a candidate for office had endorsed federal telegraph legislation in order to curry favor with the electorate. Federal telegraph legislation lodged itself squarely on the national political agenda within less than a week of Gould's takeover, where it would remain for the rest of the decade. Among the first to deride Gould's takeover was Henry Demarest Lloyd, a crusading journalist who would soon gain nationwide renown as the author of *Wealth against Commonwealth* (1894), a hard-hitting exposé of John D. Rockefeller's Standard Oil. Lloyd's indictment of Gould's Western Union in the *Chicago Tribune* helped him refine the rhetorical conventions that made *Wealth against Commonwealth* an instant classic.[47]

In the 1880s postal telegraphy jostled for attention with a galaxy of other public issues, including tariff reform, bimetallism, and railroad regulation. Almost never did it dominate the national political agenda. The closest it came was probably in 1887, when the editors of a magazine that specialized in the monitoring of popular trends judged it to have emerged as one of the leading public issues of the day.[48]

The popular furor over Gould failed to translate into a single major piece of federal telegraph legislation. In a decade that witnessed the enactment of two landmark pieces of legislation in the history of government–business relations—the Interstate Commerce Act in 1887 and the Sherman Antitrust Act in 1890—this failure was a source of intense frustration for Gould's critics. In no other decade did so many journalists, law-makers, and telegraph users invest such high hopes in the establishment of a government telegraph. And in no other decade did they come away more disappointed.

The only piece of federal telegraph legislation to find its way into law in the 1880s was the Anderson Act, which Congress enacted in 1888. Like the National Telegraph Act and the Butler Amendment, the Anderson Act was intended to discipline Western Union by fostering competition. Although the Anderson Act was by no means inconsequential, it was far from the comprehensive overhauling of federal telegraph legislation that Western Union critics had hoped for and for which so many had editorialized, petitioned, and lobbied.

The Anderson Act was named after its sponsor, the Presbyterian minister-turned-Kansas congressman John A. Anderson. It required railroads like the Union Pacific that had obtained land grants from the federal government to operate their own public telegraph lines, as their charters specified, rather than merely to contract with an existing network provider, as they typically had. If railroads operated their own telegraphs, it was assumed that they would compete with Western Union, lowering rates and raising performance standards.[49]

The closest Congress came to enacting a comprehensive telegraph law was probably in 1884, when Colorado senator Nathaniel Hill sponsored a postal telegraph bill loosely modeled on one of Hubbard's proposals. The history of Hill's bill highlights the magnitude of the challenge that postal telegraphers confronted in their contest with Gould. Its enactment seemed certain, recounted business leader and veteran Gould hater Charles Francis Adams Jr., until Vermont senator George F. Edmunds introduced a rival anti-Western Union bill at the last moment. Edmunds's rival bill was so radical that it distracted lawmakers from Hill's bill, which never came up for a vote.

For Adams, Edmunds's last-minute intervention was hardly accidental; it was, rather, a "neat" trick engineered by Gould to derail Hill. This was a remarkable claim, since Edmunds was the leading constitutional lawyer in the Senate. Edmunds had recently turned down a vacant seat on the Supreme Court and was briefly a contender for the Republican presidential nomination in 1884. Even so, Adams was convinced that Edmunds had deliberately sabotaged Hills's bill. Adams based his inference on his chance perusal of an entry in one of Gould's ledger books at the Western Union headquarters building in New York City. The smoking gun for Adams was his discovery that Gould was paying Edmunds a retainer. Adams inferred from this discovery that, bizarre as it might seem, Edmunds had introduced his anti-Gould bill at Gould's behest. Edmunds burned his personal papers shortly before his death, complicating the task of reconstructing his motives. The fact that Gould had permitted Adams access to one of his ledger books was itself suggestive. If Edmunds had defied Gould, it would have been out of character for Gould to apprise a longtime rival of the fact.[50]

The complexity of the legislative maneuvering over federal telegraph legislation prompted caution even among lawmakers who might in other circumstances have been expected to be numbered among its supporters. Ohio senator John Sherman was a case in point. Sherman opposed the enactment of federal telegraph legislation in 1884, despite—or perhaps because of—the major role that he himself had played many years earlier in the enactment of the National Telegraph Act.[51]

Support for federal legislation among telegraph users was widespread. Railroad leader John Murray Forbes praised New York Times editor George Jones for publicizing Gould's "Western Union irregularities." Jones had once helped destroy the politico Boss Tweed; now Forbes looked to Jones to marginalize the robber baron Gould. Forbes lamented that Jones's coverage was not likely to land Gould in jail, yet he hoped that Jones would forever after be remembered as the journalist who had "gibbeted" Gould on the bar of public opinion.[52]

The Philadelphia-based National Board of Trade endorsed federal telegraph legislation for the first time in December 1880, fearful of the havoc that would ensue if Gould took over Western Union. The board had debated the merits of federal legislation at almost every one of its annual meetings since 1868. Prior to 1880, however, it had refused to endorse federal telegraph legislation. Gould's raid tipped the balance.[53]

The New York Board of Trade and Transportation endorsed a postal telegraph at roughly the same time and for a similar reason. The board justified its decision in a long and impassioned report that almost certainly was authored by wholesale grocer Francis B. Thurber. Thurber had endorsed federal telegraph legislation since 1875; now, for the first time, he stood with the majority.[54] The Board of Trade and Transportation report pilloried Gould as a "freebooter" who "plundered" the public by operating under the "shield of laws" that Gould himself had "purchased." The potential disadvantages of a government telegraph were outweighed by the present danger of permitting Gould to control such a formidable instrument for "unduly taxing the people."[55]

Thurber has not left much of an impression on history. Yet in the years immediately following Gould's takeover of Western Union, he was one of the leading antimonopolists in the country. Thurber's anti-monopolism was, in part, a matter of self-interest. As a wholesale grocer, he dealt in perishable products and was thus highly dependent on the telegraph for time-sensitive information on market trends. Thurber's antimonopolism also had a civic dimension, however. He genuinely re-garded Gould as a menace to the republic. To publicize his views, Thurber founded *Justice,* a newspaper dedicated to the protection of the "rights of all" against the "privileges of the few" through the enactment of legislation ensuring that corporations would be "controlled" by the states in which they had been chartered.[56]

Thurber's antimonopolism made him an attractive Democratic candi-date for governor of New York. Antimonopolism was a popular issue not only in New York City, but also in the string of commercial cities and towns in upstate New York that stretched along the Erie Canal from Al-bany to Buffalo. The establishment of the Anti-Monopoly League in Utica in 1881, an organization in which Thurber was actively involved, gave not only antimonopoly, but also Thurber, a good deal of visibility among New York voters. For a fleeting moment it appeared that Thurber might throw his hat into the ring. When Thurber declined, the prize went to Grover Cleveland, an equally obscure antimonopolist who ultimately parlayed his victory in the gubernatorial election into the presidency of the United States.[57]

Gould's takeover also aroused the ire of the august New York Cham-ber of Commerce, which was the single most respected business associa-tion in the country. In a motion Thurber introduced in 1881, the Cham-ber of Commerce resolved that it was time for Congress to decide whether the Post Office Department might build and operate a telegraph net-work with "greater economy" and "better results" than the "present system."[58] Hubbard had lobbied the chamber to make the case for fed-eral telegraph legislation since 1868. Prior to 1881, he had always been refused. Following Gould's takeover, the chamber relented. In 1890, Hubbard finally delivered the brief for federal telegraph legislation that he had tried unsuccessfully to deliver to the chamber for over twenty years.[59]

The presumption among telegraph users that Gould's takeover made federal legislation imperative was not confined to the major commercial centers along the Atlantic seaboard. Business associations throughout the country flooded Congress with petitions begging for relief. The federal government had an obligation to build a cheap and efficient telegraph network "open to all" and without "discrimination," declared the Peoria Board of Trade, in a typical appeal.[60] If Congress did nothing, warned Henry Demarest Lloyd in the *Chicago Tribune,* it would be impossible to check the half-dozen speculators who had the necessary resources to drive up and down the market price of Western Union shares, and, in the process, "fleece and plunder" the "credulous people" who speculated in telegraph stocks.[61] "In the midst of the cotton season," warned the editor of the Mobile, Alabama, *Register and Journal,* the telegraph gave the "money kings" of New York City the power to manipulate market trends in the price of agricultural staples in ways that in an hour could "sweep away" the "hard-earned means of businessmen all over the South."[62]

The postal telegraph movement is sometimes remembered as a radical agrarian protest against the emerging corporate order that looked forward to the business-related regulatory legislation enacted during the Progressive era and the New Deal.[63] In reality, the enactment of federal telegraph legislation would not become a priority for farm groups until after it had been embraced by the National Board of Trade, the New York Board of Trade and Transportation, and the New York Chamber of Commerce. Few of the legislative proposals that farm groups endorsed after 1888 were more radical than the proposals that business associations floated beginning around 1881.[64] The nation's largest farm group, the National Grange, would not throw its support behind federal telegraph legislation until 1886, at a moment when the issue had broad support throughout the country. Moreover, the Grange would not unambiguously endorse a British-style government telegraph until 1912, one year after William Howard Taft's postmaster general had endorsed a congressional buyout.[65]

The farmer-backed Populist Party did include a government-ownership plank in its party platforms in 1892 and 1896. To justify telegraph nationalization, the Populists reiterated the familiar critique that the existing telegraph corporations had failed to guarantee the impartial transmission of news. The fact that the Populists had endorsed federal telegraph legislation was significant: with the exception of the Prohibition Reform Party in 1876 and the Union Labor Party in 1888, it was the first national party to include a telegraph plank in its party platform. Even so, the Populists' rationale for federal legislation was resolutely traditional. President Ulysses S. Grant had endorsed a congressional buyout on similar grounds in 1871, and Hubbard had articulated an even more expansive rationale for federal legislation as early as 1869.[66]

Labor support for federal telegraph legislation peaked in 1888. In that year, over 500,000 artisans and factory workers signed petitions circulated by the Knights of Labor urging the establishment of a postal telegraph under the control of the Post Office Department.[67] The Knights were a loose confederation of workers that championed the rights of labor. Knights leader Terence V. Powderly had been at odds with Gould ever since Gould had bested a Knights-backed telegraph operators' strike in 1883; Powderly calculated that an anti-Gould petition drive would improve the Knights' public image by identifying the organization with a popular cause.[68]

Although the Knights agreed that Congress had to do something, they remained uncertain about how best to proceed. Powderly endorsed the chartering of a federal telegraph corporation to rival Western Union; certain Knights assemblies favored a congressional buyout of Western Union and the establishment of a consolidated telegraph network under federal control.[69]

Skeptics questioned the Knights' familiarity with the fine points of political economy. Only a tiny number of the petitioners had ever sent a telegram in the past, they sneered, and would not be likely to do so in the future, whatever the cost.[70] This criticism failed to impress the well-respected, reform-minded minister and journalist Lyman Abbott. Abbott published a widely read regular column in one of the nation's most influential religious newspapers and was widely regarded as an opinion leader for the northern churchgoing middle class. Now that the masses had spoken, Congress could be expected to act: "The movement has ceased to be that of a few prophetic spirits; it has a rapidly increasing democratic sentiment behind it, giving it impulse and momentum." The issue had become sufficiently popular that, if lawmakers failed to respond, they could expect to be punished at the polls; after all, a workingman's vote counted for as much as the vote of a telegraph expert, a professor of political economy, or "even an editor of a metropolitan newspaper."[71]

Proposals for federal telegraph legislation fell into three categories: government ownership; antimonopoly; and regulation. Government ownership advocates confronted the formidable objection that a congressional buyout of Western Union would provide a huge financial windfall for Western Union's largest shareholder, Jay Gould. "Any suggestion that our government should buy that bloated monstrosity, the Western Union, with its dropsical weight of water," warned one journalist in 1883, "would be met with a storm of indignation from everybody except the monopolists themselves."[72]

Among the most thoughtful critics of government ownership was Franklin H. Giddings, a journalist who would later become an influential professor of sociology at Columbia University. As a sociologist, Giddings explored the social-theoretical implications of market competition; as a journalist, he championed the superiority of antimonopoly to government ownership. As long as Western Union remained privately owned, Giddings reasoned in 1881, the possibility remained that it might "kill itself of gluttony" or that a rival might emerge in "some unexpected way" to "strangle it." If Congress bought out Gould, these promising scenarios would be foreclosed. Government ownership was incompatible with the "broadest and freest development of industry." No matter how one might disguise it, it was certain to lead "like a 'broad road'" to the "bottomless pit" of the "socialism of Karl Marx."[73]

Critics who endorsed Giddings's critique of government ownership were left with two legislative options: antimonopoly and regulation. Antimonopoly was the time-honored remedy for corporate consolidation. Yet the advantages of a nationwide telegraph network were widely appreciated. No one endorsed the atomization of the telegraph business into regional units; nor, for that matter, did anyone want a return of the "methodless enthusiasm" of the 1850s. Many, however, favored the establishment of a rival, government-owned telegraph to keep rates low and performance standards high.

Western Union supporters decried a government rival as unfair. Western Union was an investor-owned corporation that had to cover its costs. In contrast, any government rival would have at its disposal all of the legal, financial, and administrative resources of the federal government, including the power to levy taxes to pay for its support. Had Western Union supporters been more familiar with the postal telegraph in Great Britain, they might have emphasized that it had long been heavily subsidized by the British post office, an advantage unavailable to them as a private corporation.[74]

To meet this objection, antimonopolists ventured an elaborate analogy. The Post Office Department's mandate had recently been expanded to embrace the conveyance of packages weighing up to 4 pounds. Package carriers derided this legislation as discriminatory because it forced them to slash rates in certain markets to compete with their government-backed rival. Shippers hailed it as a public good, as did an influential segment of the press. Supporters of a government telegraph pointed to the Post Office Department to make their case. Just as the Post Office Department had entered into the "expressage business," editorialized the *Chicago Tribune,* so, too, it could rival Western Union.[75] In "business circles," the *Tribune* opined, there was now a "universal expression" of support for establishing a government telegraph, and the press was considering the issue from "much the same point of view."[76]

The prospect of federal antimonopoly legislation intrigued a number of would-be telegraph magnates, of whom the most successful was John W. Mackay. Mackay was a fabulously wealthy silver miner who had struck it rich in Nevada's Comstock Lode. Unimpressed by Gould's speculative jugglery and convinced that a well-funded rival could underbid him and still make a tidy profit, Mackay joined together in 1883 with *New York Herald* editor James Gordon Bennett Jr. to lay an Atlantic cable. Gould himself had recently laid a cable of his own, and Mackay figured that he could too. To channel traffic to his cable company, Mackay purchased the Postal Telegraph Company, a financially troubled start-up that had coalesced around a large bundle of patents that a New York financier had purchased from Elisha Gray.[77] The name "Postal Telegraph" had no relationship to the federally chartered corporation that Hubbard had long touted. Rather, it was the name its promoters chose for a corporation chartered under the New York Telegraph Act of 1848. The name expressed the hope that Congress would favor it with the privileges necessary to permit it to rival Western Union.[78] Should Congress enact a favorable postal telegraph law, Mackay predicted to a Chicago reporter in 1883, he could make a fortune sending telegrams at one-half cent per word. The rate Mackay proposed was extremely low; at 5 cents for a ten-word telegram, it was only 3 cents more than a posted letter. All Mackay needed was federal legislation empowering the Post Office Department to link his corporation to the nation's big-city post offices. "By combining the postal telegraph with the post offices in the large cities,"

Mackay promised to give the public the "cheapest system" for the area of the country it covered in the world.[79]

Of all the rivals to challenge Gould in the 1880s, only Postal Telegraph endured. Postal Telegraph remained a small yet vigorous rival to Western Union from the 1880s until the Second World War, when it was finally merged with Western Union. Unlike Gould's other rivals, Postal Telegraph was privately held, and, thus, impossible to raid. Mackay's enormous personal wealth freed him from having to go to the capital markets. If Mackay ever ran low on money, Gould was reputed to have quipped, he could simply go back to Nevada and dig up some more.[80]

Mackay never obtained the federal legislation that he had predicted would permit him to lower telegraph rates to one-half cent per word. Even so, he remained convinced that the much-discussed potential of electrical communications was still to be tapped. "I think the time is drawing near," Mackay predicted around 1883, when "capitalists" like Gould would no longer find it necessary to "war" on the public to make money. The largest profits in the telegraph business were not made by charging telegraph users high rates for limited facilities so that investors could obtain dividends on an inflated capitalization. Rather, they were to be made by expanding facilities and lowering rates: "Instead of watering the stock and salting down profits, extend your business and cheapen your rates: That is the true principle."[81]

Mackay practiced what he preached. Although he had made his fortune in one of the riskiest businesses in the world, he shunned speculation, financed his investments conservatively, and never borrowed a dollar.[82] The miner-turned-telegraph magnate never issued watered stock, boasted an early biographer; he never floated any "fancy bonds" of dubious value; and he never plotted any "financial quagmires" to "ensnare and ruin innocent investors."[83]

Mackay's financial conservatism echoed the business strategy of steel baron Andrew Carnegie. For Mackay and Carnegie, speculation was a means to an end. Each made his fortune in a risky venture: Mackay in mining; Carnegie by using inside information to buy and sell the securities of railroad contractors, telegraph lines, and package carriers. Once they had made their fortunes, they reinvented themselves as proprietary capitalists. Their beau ideal was not the amoral financier Jay Gould, but the civic-minded industrialist Peter Cooper.

Antimonopoly was the most conventional of the legislative remedies that lawmakers considered in the 1880s. If it were possible to encourage competition in the telegraph business, few lawmakers doubted that the experiment should be tried. A large and growing number of lawmakers, however, had become convinced that even the most carefully drafted antimonopoly legislation was likely to lead to outcomes more or less precisely the opposite of what they had intended. An analogous logic had furnished a major rationale for telegraph legislation at both the federal and state level since 1848, and it had led to the domination of the telegraph business by Jay Gould. That Gould himself had taken advantage of antimonopoly legislation was a further objection, since his takeover of Western Union was precisely the eventuality that antimonopoly legislation had been supposed to prevent.

The presumed impracticality of government ownership and the demonstrated perversity of antimonopoly left regulation as the only viable legislative solution to the evils that lawmakers feared would follow Gould's takeover of Western Union. Regulation need not entail either rate caps or a ban on the special privileges that Western Union lavished on the NYAP. Rather, regulation might be limited to legislation designed to prevent the recurrence of the unprecedented shutdown of much of the telegraph network that followed the telegraph operators' strike of 1883.

The prospect of a work stoppage haunted E. L. Godkin. As the editor of *Nation*, Godkin was one of the most influential journalists in the country. In his view the telegraph had become so essential to commerce that Congress had an obligation to prevent telegraph operators from blocking the channels of commerce by going out on strike. The evils that would result from even a brief suspension of the telegraph were comparable to a "hostile invasion" of the United States by a foreign power.[84] To prevent telegraphers from striking, Godkin proposed that Congress enact legislation putting them under the jurisdiction of federal law. Soldiers who left their posts were prosecuted as deserters; telegraphers should be too: "The ten thousand to forty thousand men which some of our modern corporations now employ in telegraphic or railroad service are an army, and have to be governed on the same principles as an army."[85]

Godkin's military analogy offended Carl Schurz, a statesman-turned-journalist with whom Godkin had recently entered into an editorial partnership. Western Union was not an army, Schurz retorted: telegraphers had not enlisted, and Congress had no right to ban telegraphers from taking collective action to improve their lot. Yet Schurz, too, dreaded the prospect of any disruption to the telegraph. To minimize its likelihood, he recommended the enactment of federal legislation mandating binding arbitration to resolve labor disputes.[86]

The disagreement between Godkin and Schurz over the telegraphers' strike ended their short-lived partnership. Schurz never forgave Godkin for his indifference toward Western Union's telegraph operators, and Godkin resented Schurz's imputation that he was an unwitting accomplice of Gould's.[87]

Although the differences between Schurz and Godkin were considerable, so too were their similarities. Each regarded a telegraph strike as unacceptable; neither looked to market competition to prevent its recurrence; and both assumed that some kind of federal legislation was imperative. The contretemps between Jay Gould and Western Union telegraphers was not a mere private dispute between capital and labor. The telegraphers' strike had thrown the spotlight on the power of the network that Western Union operated. No longer was it plausible to assume that competition would solve the problems that consolidation had posed. Western Union had become too essential to commerce and public life for lawmakers to permit it to suspend its operations. The only question that remained was the form that legislative intervention would take. With antimonopoly rejected, and government ownership problematic, only regulation remained.

The rejection of the long-standing assumption that the telegraph was no different from any other business revived the perennial issue of why lawmakers had permitted the telegraph to remain a specialty service for an exclusive clientele. "Postal telegraphy is only the old question in a new form," proclaimed Lyman Abbott in 1888, at a moment when it seemed likely some kind of federal telegraph legislation might be forthcoming. "Are the great conveniences of modern civilization the luxury of the few or the instrument of the many?" For Abbott, the answer was obvious. The federal government had a moral obligation to make the telegraph accessible to the entire population. Whether Western Union could be induced to popularize the telegraph Abbott did not say. In the absence of federal legislation Abbott felt certain that the experiment would never be tried.[88]

Abbott's plea for popularization fell on deaf ears at Western Union. Gould recognized that he could make high profits by keeping Western Union rates at roughly the same level at which they had been when he took it over in 1881. Although these rates were higher than the rates Mackay envisioned, they were substantially lower than the rates that had prevailed when Orton took the helm in 1867. Even so, Gould never questioned the long-standing conviction of telegraph managers like Orton that the telegraph would always remain a specialty service for an exclusive clientele. His skepticism about the likely demand for a low-cost telegraph was echoed by Western Union president Norvin Green. There were thousands of "businesses of private enterprise," Green stated in 1890, in which the "people at large" were more interested, and in which, therefore, lawmakers had more cause to intervene if they wished to "lighten the burdens of the people."[89] The telegram would never supplant the posted letter, elaborated a Western Union publicist. The posted letter linked the sender and recipient in an intimate bond: the letter itself was a token of the sender's presence and contained a message written in a familiar hand. In contrast, a telegraph blank was coldly impersonal, with the "names wrongly spelled," making it "about as well adapted" for "chirography" as a "buckwheat pancake."[90]

The emerging consensus that the telegraph had become too essential to escape some kind of permanent federal regulation revived the time-honored debate over the relative merits of government administration and corporate management. Little had changed since 1848, when the English political economist John Stuart Mill had famously maintained that it was hard to know which kind of administrative coordination was worse. "Government management" was "proverbially jobbing, careless, and ineffective," Mill reflected, yet so too was "joint-stock management." If a government agency posed problems, so too did a private corporation: "The defects, therefore, of government management, do not seem to be necessarily much greater, if necessarily greater at all, than those of management by joint-stock."[91]

Critics of government administration had long warned that a government telegraph would foster political centralization and increase the political patronage at the disposal of the party in the power. The enactment of a strict new civil service law in 1883 partly addressed this criticism, as did the oft-publicized achievements of the Post Office Department.

The Post Office Department's achievements rebutted the stock objections that government administration was inflexible and unimaginative. Gould's indifference toward the sponsorship of technical advance actually emboldened commentators to praise it—surprising as this might seem—as a superior engine of innovation. Western Union's failure to sponsor technical research contrasted unfavorably with the "constant improvement" in the Post Office Department, editorialized the *Electrician and Electrical Engineer*. The "general management" of the Post Office Department had won the "substantial approval of the people"; Gould's management of Western Union had not.[92] The superiority of government administration to corporation administration seemed equally evident to the *Princeton Review*. No "great industry" in the United States was managed more "economically" than the Post Office Department, the *Review* opined.[93] "Administration is everywhere putting its hands to new undertakings," remarked the political scientist and future U.S. president Woodrow Wilson in 1887: "The utility, cheapness, and success of the government's postal service, for instance, point towards the early establishment of governmental control of the telegraph system."[94]

One of the relatively few business analysts to question the widespread disparagement of Western Union was Alfred D. Chandler, a Brookline, Massachusetts, corporate lawyer whose grandson and namesake would become a prominent business historian. In an 1889 pamphlet opposing government ownership, Chandler posited that Western Union was no less effective in operating the telegraph in the United States than the government telegraph ministries in Great Britain and Germany.[95]

Chandler's conclusion outraged Henry Willard Austin, a journalist who championed the political program of the influential utopian socialist Edward Bellamy. "The most audacious thing in Mr. Chandler's defense of our present rotting industrial system," Austin retorted, was his "claim of superiority for our blundering Western Union Telegraph over the superb nationalized systems of Germany and England."[96]

Austin's anger owed much to the cheery optimism of Bellamy's forecast of an age in which the fruits of invention would render poverty obsolete and material abundance widespread. In the future, Bellamy predicted, private corporations would be regarded as anachronistic vestiges of a failed economic order that had been superseded because they could not match the efficiency of a benevolent state staffed by an "industrial army" of able-bodied citizens. The nationalization of the telegraph was a harbinger of the coming age: the government would buy out its owners early and at a very good price. In short, the critical shortcoming of the private corporation was not the huge profits its owners accumulated, but the inherent weakness of corporate management in comparison to government administration.[97]

Chandler and Bellamy focused primarily on Western Union's organizational capabilities. The broader political and cultural implications of Gould's takeover furnished the theme for a much-discussed public letter by Minnesota senator William Windom, a figure much admired by antimonopolists for his endorsement of government-backed competition as a solution to the problem posed by railroad consolidation. In his public letter, Windom approached Gould's takeover in a similar spirit. Windom deplored not only Gould's doubling of Western Union's capitalization, but also his determination to lay an Atlantic cable to extend his telegraph empire overseas. "Look at it a moment," Windom warned: "One man, who controls more miles of railroad than any other in the world, and who is almost daily adding new lines to his colossal combination, now also controls the telegraphic system of the United States and Canada, and is reaching under the sea to grasp that of Europe." Most ominous of all was the potential threat that Gould posed to the press. Gould was already rumored to have gained control of three of the seven newspapers that controlled the NYAP: the *Tribune,* the *World,* and the *Mail and Express.* Should Gould obtain just one additional newspaper, he would possess "absolute control" over the news because the NYAP was the "agency" that distributed news not only within New York City, but also throughout the country: "When that takes place what will be our condition? What chance will the people then have to resist the encroachments of corporate power? How shall they even communicate with each other on the subject?"[98]

The significance of Windom's public letter was enhanced by the circumstances surrounding its composition. When Windom wrote it, the incoming president, James A. Garfield, had already tapped him for treasury secretary. Windom's host was a New York City–based antimonopoly lobby organized by Francis B. Thurber. Windom's letter was read at a public meeting at New York City's Cooper Union, an institution named for and bankrolled by Peter Cooper, a business leader widely praised for his moral rectitude—a trait widely presumed to have been conspicuously lacking in Gould.

Gould's takeover proved too much even for Connecticut senator Orville H. Platt. Platt was an unlikely foe. A reliable champion of business interests, he had often opposed legislation intended to restrain corporate excess, including the Sherman Act, which he deplored as inexpedient and very possibly unconstitutional.[99] Yet Platt had no qualms about the enactment of federal telegraph legislation to restrain Gould. The telegraph was nothing but a "rich man's mail," Platt complained to his fellow lawmakers in 1883: "If an individual in common life now received a telegraphic dispatch he fears that it means death or disaster." Would it not be better for the country if the telegraph became instead a "common means of communication" for the "common people" of the United States?[100]

Platt did not coin the phrase "rich man's mail." In fact, a Washington journalist had hurled an identical epithet over forty years earlier at a high-speed horse express established by Postmaster General Amos Kendall. The "rich man" the Washington journalist referred to was the user of Kendall's express; the "rich man" for Platt was not only the user of the telegraph but also the financier into whose hands the ownership of the dominant network had devolved.[101]

Nowhere were Gould's exploits dissected with greater brio than in the influential and widely circulated New York City–based weekly satirical magazines *Puck* and *Judge*. The circulation of *Puck* often topped 80,000, and *Judge* was not far behind. These were large totals for the day, especially given the avidity with which they were read. During times of great political excitement, such as the run-up to the 1884 presidential campaign, these magazines exerted an influence on national politics that, according to one seasoned political observer, was probably greater than that of "all the daily press combined."[102]

Political satire had long enjoyed a modest vogue; *Puck* and *Judge* transformed it into a political force. Earlier political cartoonists worked exclusively in black-and-white, and, with the exception of Thomas Nast, rarely translated political issues into a compelling visual form. *Puck* and *Judge* took advantage of recent technical advances in chromolithography to feature elaborate multicolor topical cartoons on the issues of the day. Gould's financial maneuvering was a subject of intense public interest to the readers of both magazines, and his frequent presence on their covers presumably boosted sales. Prior to the 1880s, a "robber baron" had been little more than an arcane literary metaphor tossed about by certain learned Easterners familiar with medieval German history. Henceforth, he became a visual icon.

Party politics had little influence on the cartoonists' editorial stance on Gould. *Puck* editor H. C. Bunner was more sympathetic to Democratic presidential contender Grover Cleveland in 1884 than *Judge* editor James

A. Wales. Both magazines ridiculed Gould with nonpartisan zeal. In image after image, cartoonists skewered Gould as a grasping monopolist who harassed his workforce, blocked commerce, manipulated financial markets, subverted the press, and perverted the political process. Gould had become more powerful than the "Czar of all the Russias," warned Bunner in explaining one of *Puck*'s many anti-Gould cartoons. "No country" could be "called free" in which a private individual could own as his personal property all of its "means of communication."[103]

Sometimes Gould acted alone; at other times he schemed with his fellow robber barons William H. Vanderbilt and Cyrus Field. Strangulation was a recurrent theme in the cartoons attacking these business moguls. In one anti-Gould *Puck* cartoon by Joseph Keppler, Gould was depicted as a devilish child on a swing held up by telegraph wires who was seemingly unaware that the wires were garroting statues representing "commerce" and the "press." In another, Gould and Vanderbilt impaled Uncle Sam on a telegraph pole that resembled the cross on which Jesus had been crucified.[104]

The visual counterpoint to Gould was often the Post Office Department—the deus ex machina that solved the problems Gould had caused. Some things were "born to be monopolized," reflected Wales, while others were impartially distributed: "Among the latter are mosquitoes, spring and fall influenzas, and profanity; among the former are the best seats in the cars, the second-hand clothes business, and the telegraphs." And if the telegraph was a monopoly, then the Post Office Department should operate it, so that everyone could "have a finger in the pie."[105] The Post Office Department, ran the caption of a representative anti-Gould cartoon in *Judge,* was the "Best Monopolist": "Let the people control the people's information."[106] Interestingly, no anti-Gould cartoonist derided the Post Office Department as a sinkhole of corruption. This was a surprising omission: in the 1880s the Post Office Department was reeling under the revelation that government officials had funneled kickbacks from contractors to fund the 1880 Republican presidential campaign. The kickbacks had mostly come from contractors who had bid on the so-called star routes in thinly settled regions over which contractors exercised a great deal of discretion. Unfazed by these revelations, cartoonists in both magazines depicted postal administrators in a highly admiring way. In October 1881, for example, *Puck* ran a flattering and emphatically nonsatirical engraving of Postmaster General

Gould's takeover of Western Union in January 1881 outraged the financial world. In this pointed cartoon, Gould was cast as a satanic scamp whose financial legerdemain threatened both commerce and the press. Gould's challenge to the press rested not only on his control over the nation's most important telegraph network, but also on his holdings in two major New York City newspapers: the *Tribune* and the *World*. Joseph Keppler, "Consolidated," *Puck* 8 (January 26, 1881): 352–353.

Thomas L. James as "The Man Who Stamped Out the Star Route Swindle."[107]

Had Gould wished to become Western Union's president, he could almost certainly have installed himself in office. He was, after all, its largest single shareholder, and he exercised considerable influence over the company's executive committee. Yet like many financiers, Gould preferred to delegate routine day-to-day operations to a trusted lieutenant. Gould's lieutenant was Norvin Green, a veteran telegraph manager who had been active in the business since the 1850s and who had become Western Union's president following Orton's unexpected death in 1878.

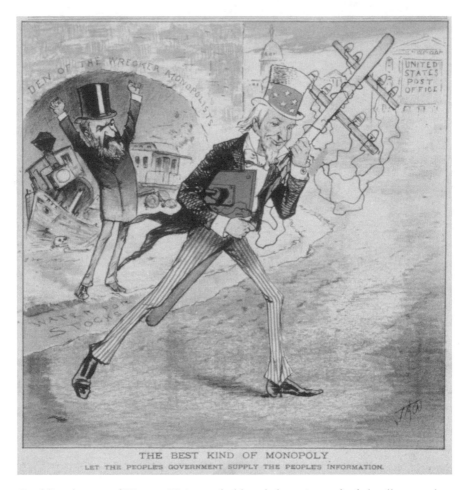

THE BEST KIND OF MONOPOLY
LET THE PEOPLE'S GOVERNMENT SUPPLY THE PEOPLE'S INFORMATION.

Gould's takeover of Western Union emboldened champions of a federally owned and operated "postal telegraph" to push for federal legislation to limit his power. To hasten this much-touted reform, this 1882 cartoon depicted the Post Office Department as the "best kind of monopoly." Should Congress empower it to operate the telegraph network, the "people's information" would be free from "wrecker monopolists" like Gould. James A. Wales, "The Best Kind of Monopoly," *Judge* 2 (October 7, 1882): front cover.

Green was a genial Kentuckian who combined a passion for horse racing with the calm of a stoic philosopher. Never vexed or hot-tempered, he denied himself "none of the indulgences" of the "gentleman of leisure," reminisced a journalist who knew him well.[108] As Western Union's president, Green wrote hundreds of business letters. Many dealt with

Western Union's enormous array of exclusive right-of-way contracts, an arcane subject that Green had mastered and for which he was often praised.[109] Others concerned Green's large personal investment portfolio. Almost never did these letters touch on research and development or operational autonomy, topics that had been of considerable interest to William Orton. One of Green's few innovations was his publication of signed essays in the popular press opposing federal telegraph legislation. To appeal directly to the public in a popular magazine was a new departure for a corporate leader; Green's arguments were not. To make the case against federal intervention, Green reiterated the hoary contention that a congressional buyout of Western Union was unconstitutional, a position even strict constructionists rejected. To disparage the Post Office Department, Green revived pre-Civil War shibboleths about political corruption that harked back to the intemperate screeds of Jacksonians like Duff Green. These echoes were by no means coincidental; Green considered himself a Jackson Democrat and was proud to number Duff Green among his distant relations.[110]

Western Union in the 1880s remained the loosely structured horizontal combine that Hiram Sibley had cobbled together before the Civil War. Although Western Union was sometimes dignified as a "system," it lacked the esprit de corps of government agencies like the Railway Mail Service (RMS). The RMS routinely sponsored conferences at which division managers discussed organizational protocols and operational routines; Western Union did not. In recognition of its disjointedness, journalists customarily referred to it as a collectivity—that is, as "the Western Union," rather than simply as "Western Union." At its core, reported one sympathetic observer in 1887, it remained an "enormous aggregation of contracts" cobbled together with railroads, newsbrokers, telephone companies, mercantile exchanges, and a large number of other concerns.[111]

Green was ostensibly Western Union's president, yet Gould remained the power behind the throne. Indeed, in many ways, the influence Gould exerted on Western Union during the eleven years that he remained its largest single investor (1881–1892) was no less far-reaching than the influence that Orton had exerted during his presidency (1867–1878). Industrious, detail-oriented, and daring in the realms of publicity and corporate finance, Gould shared Orton's keen appreciation of the power of the telegraph network. Like Orton, Gould regarded Western Union's huge size as an asset rather than a liability; and like Orton, he preferred to buy up rivals rather than compete with them directly.[112] One of Gould's acquisitions was Mutual Union, a telegraph start-up organized by New York banker George F. Baker; another was the Baltimore & Ohio, a large network operated by the Baltimore & Ohio Railroad. Had Mackay's cable-telegraph network been for sale, Gould might well have bought it too. Critics routinely charged Gould with keeping rates high; only rarely, however, did he raise them above the levels they had attained in 1881. In the hotly contested Atlantic cable market, rates actually declined.[113]

The similarities between Gould and Orton were impressive, but so, too, were their differences. Orton championed managers, Gould investors. Orton purchased Western Union shares from investors to limit the revenue that he had to earmark for shareholder dividends. Gould doubled Western Union's capitalization to $80 million, hugely increasing the number of shares on which dividends were paid. To limit insider trading on market trends, Orton permitted only the NYAP to lease an intercity line; untroubled by Orton's scruples, Gould leased private lines to whoever would foot the bill. Within the first two years of Gould's takeover, Western Union leased 12,000 miles of private lines. While this worked out to a mere 3 percent of the 425,000 miles of lines that Western Union's operated, it was a huge increase over the mileage that Western Union had leased prior to Gould's takeover in 1881.[114]

In few realms was the contrast between Gould and Orton more pointed than in their attitude toward technical advance. Orton put Edison on a retainer and invested heavily in the Chicago-based electrical equipment manufacturer Western Electric. Gould stopped subsidizing inventors and sold off Western Electric. Gould took no pride in "building up an enterprise," Edison later reminisced, but "was after money and money only." Edison's assessment was colored by his personal pique at losing his retainer, yet his disparagement of Gould underscored a basic truth. Gould's takeover had signaled the end of the entrepreneurial hothouse in telegraph-related inventions that had briefly flourished in the 1870s: "When Gould got the Western Union, I knew that no further progress in telegraphy was possible and I went into other lines."[115]

The most fundamental difference between Orton and Gould lay in their different conception of the proper relationship between a corporation and its investors. Orton regarded investors as potential antagonists in his quest for the operational autonomy that he regarded as a prerequisite for maintaining high performance standards; for Gould, maximization of the return on the investor's capital was the corporation's primary rationale. Orton tried valiantly to separate management from ownership; Gould put the owners back in charge. Gould harked back to the owner-operator proprietary capitalist; Orton looked forward to the salaried manager for whom the investors' return had become subordinated to the managers' autonomy.

Gould's most controversial decision as Western Union's largest shareholder was his doubling of its capitalization, a maneuver similar to one engineered by Hiram Sibley in 1866. To justify it, however, Gould articulated a rationale for the valuation of corporate assets that even Sibley rejected. The size of Western Union's capitalization, in Gould's view, should be based not on the physical assets it had acquired in the past, but on the "net earning power" that it could be expected to generate in the future.[116]

Gould's theory of valuation is conventional today. The value of a corporation's shares is determined by whatever its investors are willing to pay in the expectation of the earnings these shares will yield in the future, rather than by the money their investors contributed in the past or the cost of replacing the corporation's physical plant. In the 1880s, however, this actuarial convention was novel and would remain controversial for several decades.[117] Only a smattering of journalists openly defended Gould's doubling of Western Union's capitalization. Among them was Murat Halstead. By linking Western Union's capitalization with the "growth and prosperity of the country," Gould deserved not condemnation but praise: though he was a gambler, at least he had been "betting on the United States."[118] Far more typical was the accusation that Gould's "watering" of Western Union's stock had forced him to keep rates high, facilities limited, and operators' salaries low. By "net earning power," editorialized the *New York Herald,* Gould meant merely the maximum amount that he, as the owner of a corporation that monopolized one of the "great necessaries of life," could "screw out of the public."[119]

Gould's willingness to openly discuss his controversial theory of corporate valuation was characteristic of his adversarial relationship with the press. Orton maintained close ties with the NYAP to block hostile legislation that might threaten his operational autonomy. Gould negotiated with NYAP rivals like the Chicago-based Western Associated Press to limit NYAP prerogatives, a stratagem that may help explain why newspapers associated with the NYAP condemned him with such ferocity.[120] Orton feared the press; Gould manipulated it to shape public perceptions that would enable him to profit on market trends. No nineteenth-century financier was more adept at staging what a later generation of journalists would call a media event.

It will never be known precisely how many rumors Gould floated or how many stories he planted. It was, however, a matter of record that for several years Gould owned a major financial stake in the *New York World* and had a close relationship with the *New York Tribune*.[121] The precise nature of Gould's involvement with other newspapers is harder to document. Yet William Windom was by no means the only contemporary to warn that Gould had designs on the NYAP. Windom was mistaken. Gould was less beholden to the NYAP than Orton and more willing to negotiate with rival newsbrokers like the Western Associated Press. To raise such a caveat, however, missed the point. Gould flaunted not only his personal power, but also the power of Western Union's telegraph network, exhibiting a brazenness that outraged business leaders, lawmakers, and journalists alike throughout the United States.

The audacity of Gould's press strategy is highlighted by a remarkable pamphlet that a pro-Gould publicist published for the benefit of potential Western Union investors shortly after Gould's takeover of Western Union. To convince investors that Western Union could, in fact, pay a steady dividend on its huge capitalization, the publicist highlighted the "perfection of system" that Western Union had attained. With the exception of the Post Office Department, Western Union had become the most important means of communication in the country. Like an "army of occupation," it dominated the territory it had seized. No "competing company" could supplant it, even if it gained control of technical contrivances Western Union lacked: "New inventions of an experimental character, such as automatic systems and postal telegraph devices, and the extension of telephonic facilities, may threaten the completeness of the grasp which the Western Union has upon the power of instantaneous communication in this country, but until there is some better evidence of ability to compete with profit, with the perfection of system attained by this company, no fear need be entertained but that it will retain its capacity to earn in larger proportion than almost any other enterprise in the country."[122] By ostentatiously flaunting the power of Western Union's network, this pamphlet did little to calm the fears of Western Union's critics that the corporation was a dangerous monopoly that lawmakers should not permit to remain independent of federal control.

Among the most notorious of all of Gould's public pronouncements was the testimony he delivered in 1883 before a congressional committee on the present state of "labor and capital" in the United States. In this testimony Gould defended his conduct during the recent telegraph operators' strike. If Congress disapproved of the way he operated the telegraph network, it could buy him out. To simplify matters, Gould named his price. If Congress would pay Western Union's investors $80 million, he would guarantee that the sale would occur.[123]

The likelihood that lawmakers would vote Gould this sum was exceedingly small. Even so, Gould's candor was bracing and documented the resolutely nonideological character of the early government ownership movement. The lawmakers' reservations concerning a congressional buyout owed less to any abstract fear of creeping socialism than to their practical realization that if Congress bought Western Union out, Gould would be the largest benefactor.

The widespread conviction that Gould covertly exerted a major influence over the press reached a fever pitch during the days leading up to the presidential election of 1884. According to widely circulated newspaper accounts that probably had little basis in fact, Gould had used his control over the telegraph network to deliberately delay the nationwide distribution of the election returns from upstate New York. In so doing, it was alleged, he hoped to depress voter turnout for Grover Cleveland and throw the election to James G. Blaine. Cleveland, it was widely presumed, would win far more Democratic votes in upstate New York than was customary for a Democrat, since Cleveland had many ties with the region and had recently served as the mayor of Buffalo, the region's largest city.[124]

Gould's supposed gambit infuriated New York City Democrats. Shortly after the polls closed, an irate crowd that was reputed to number 5,000 assembled in front of Western Union's headquarters building, where Gould had reputedly camped out. Had circumstances been only slightly different, Green wrote a colleague, an "incendiary mob" might well have torched the building.[125] Newspaper accounts of this episode differed widely. Yet few denied that Gould had somehow been involved in a convoluted scheme to throw the election.

The presumption that Gould had manipulated the election by holding back news reports struck Green as ridiculous. "The absurdity of the idea," Green wrote a fellow Democrat just after the election, "that the will of one large investor controlled the politics of this company is shown by the fact that three-fourths of the men on the executive floor supported and voted for Cleveland, whilst the treasurer, who has always voted the Republican ticket, also voted for Cleveland."[126] Unconvinced, the *New York Times* did not fail to draw the moral. "Mr. Gould's performance during the past forty-eight hours," the *Times* editorialized the day after the election, "has made a government postal telegraph a necessity in this country."[127]

The furor over Gould's alleged manipulation of the 1884 presidential returns and his handling of the previous year's telegraph operators' strike left a deep and enduring impression on the rising generation of university-trained social scientists. No longer could the federal government rely on antimonopoly legislation to regulate Western Union. The prophetic warning of Samuel F. B. Morse had come true: corporate ownership had delivered the telegraph into the hands of one of the most notorious speculators in the land.

This new consensus found expression in a celebrated essay that political economist Henry C. Adams delivered at the inaugural meeting of the American Economic Association in 1887. "Industrial action," Adams posited, fell into one of three categories. In the first category were businesses whose average costs rose as the scale of their operations increased; in the second category were businesses whose costs remained the same; and in the third category were businesses whose average costs declined. Adams dubbed this third kind of business a "natural monopoly." A natural monopoly could be expected to dominate the market for whatever good or service it provided, even if it obtained no special privileges from the state. Adams made no specific reference in his essay to the telegraph. Yet it resembled a "natural monopoly" in several respects. It had come under "centralized control"; it was no longer effectively regulated by competition; and it could no longer be "safely consigned" to "private financiering."[128]

The designation of a business as a natural monopoly presupposed that it should be controlled by the state, since it was inconceivable that lawmakers would permit such a powerful entity to remain unconstrained. Two kinds of control suggested themselves: government ownership and government regulation.

Among the most enthusiastic popularizers of government ownership was Adams's colleague Richard T. Ely. Less cautious than Adams, Ely flatly proclaimed in 1888 that the telegraph was a "natural monopoly" from which the "steady, constant pressure of competition" had been excluded. For a miller to remain in business he had no choice but to meet his competitor's price; if he did not, his customers would abandon him, since entry to the milling business remained open. However, if a telegraph corporation raised its prices, the corporation retained its customers, since they had nowhere else to go. The fact that a mere 3 percent of the population used the telegraph did nothing to alter this fact. The critical issue was not the inclusiveness of telegraph facilities for its users, but the openness of entry into the telegraph business for its providers. Even if the telegraph were only used by the few, its effects were felt by the many. Telegraph users passed onto customers the high fees Western Union charged, and, thus, their cost was "felt by everybody."[129]

Ely conceded that economic theory had no definitive answer to the question of whether the federal government should own and operate the telegraph, or whether it should merely regulate the rates that private corporations like Western Union charged. The example of the Post Office Department led him to favor ownership and operation. The mail was a public monopoly and a national blessing; the telegraph a private monopoly and "nothing less" than a "national calamity."[130] Ely took pains to stress that he was by no means an across-the-board supporter of federal spending. He regarded it as deplorable, for example, that Congress appropriated large sums to lavish "indiscriminate" pensions on Civil War veterans. The congressional buyout of the telegraph, however, was one kind of federal spending that Ely endorsed. Instead of lavishing money on Civil War veterans, Congress should buy out Western Union and establish a telegraph network under the jurisdiction of the Post Office Department.[131]

For Congress to buy out Western Union, it would have to negotiate with Gould. Well aware of this fact, Ely challenged the financial orthodoxy that lawmakers should limit the value of Western Union's assets to the cost of its wires, poles, and equipment. The "fair value" of Western Union, rather, should include the money its management had expended to scale up its network. This total was significantly higher than the cost of replicating Western Union's physical assets because it included the large sums that the corporation had paid out to buy up rivals whose entry into the telegraph business had been encouraged by the "false social policy" of antimonopoly.[132]

Ely's rationale for government ownership was controversial. A "natural monopoly," sneered one unsympathetic journalist in 1895, was a favorite expression of populists and socialists for any business that they wanted to bring under the "direct control" of the national, state, or municipal government.[133]

Ely had little patience with critics who labeled any regulatory scheme socialistic. Though Ely called himself a Christian socialist, he remained a firm believer in competition in those businesses in which competition remained a realistic option. He simply did not believe that the telegraph was among them. In no sense, in Ely's view, did his endorsement of government ownership of the telegraph challenge the long-standing Anglo-American presumption in favor of individual initiative. The distinction between private enterprise and public enterprise had long been enshrined in "Anglo-Saxon" law and would in no way be subverted should Congress buy out Western Union. In fact, a congressional buyout would create more business opportunities than it foreclosed and was thus an "extension" of the "principle of individualism" and "not socialism at all." If telegraph rates were reduced and the telegraph network extended, many individuals who had never before been able to avail themselves of its facilities would find them within reach. Ely had "never thought it worthwhile" to "spoil pen and paper and waste ink" in exposing the socialists' errors: "the only dangerous socialism in America is monopoly controlled by private greed."[134]

Ely's endorsement of government ownership troubled Adams. Adams recognized that Ely had based his conclusions partly on Adams's essay on "industrial action," yet drew from his own analysis of the telegraph business a different moral. Federal regulation of the telegraph was a policy Adams supported; government ownership was not.[135] If Congress ran a budget surplus, lawmakers were best advised to spend this surplus on a tax cut rather than on a buyout of Western Union.[136] Even so, Adams regarded a congressional buyout as highly likely and presumed that, as a specialist in public finance, he had an obligation to figure out how the federal government would cover the cost.[137]

Whereas government ownership remained controversial, federal regulation was not. A case in point was its endorsement by Arthur T. Hadley, a specialist in railroad regulation who taught at Yale for many years. Much less controversial than Ely and better known among nonacademics than Adams, Hadley was one of the most respected social scientists of his age. Hadley's investigation of the railroad business had convinced him that certain forms of competition were counterproductive, and he had long urged the legalization of rate-fixing schemes, known as pools, to keep rates at acceptable levels. Hadley viewed the telegraph business through a similar lens. He conceded that Western Union had made many mistakes that it ought to have avoided. Even so, he did not regard government ownership as a solution. To demonstrate its shortcomings, Hadley compared the corporately managed telegraph network in the United States with the government-administered telegraph network in Germany. It seemed irrefutable that government administration at its best was little better than "corporation management at its worst."[138]

If Hadley had stopped here, his conclusion would have been more or less identical to the conclusion that Alfred D. Chandler, the corporate lawyer who had incurred the wrath of the Bellamyites, reached at around the same time. Yet Hadley took the argument one step further. Like most well-educated Americans, he despised Gould and had no intention of giving him the last word. The "radical evil" in Gould's career, Hadley observed shortly after the financier's death, was his arrogant belief that business was a game rather than a public service. This belief was wrong-headed and immoral, Hadley said, and had done more than anything else to embolden the socialists, since it had obscured the timeless truth that wealth was a public trust.[139] American socialists were democrats first and socialists second. "Modern socialism" was less of a misguided attempt to extend the realm of the state than an understandable protest against the "uncontrolled power" of financiers like Gould. To marginalize the influence of Gould and his ilk, Hadley endorsed legislation that would encourage corporate leaders to substitute "cooperation" between producers and consumers for competition between rival promoters. Capitalism worked best, in his view, if the ability of maverick promoters to disrupt existing institutional arrangements was tightly circumscribed.[140]

Hadley's anti-investor bias hastened the transformation of morally engaged political economists into morally neutral economists. No longer was the unit of analysis the political economy in which proprietors competed; henceforth, it became the economy in which corporations matched supply and demand.[141] Hadley quarreled with Adams and Ely about many things. Yet he endorsed their presumption that a corporation could acquire special privileges in the absence of a government grant, as well as the related presumption that certain businesses had become too essential for lawmakers to permit them to suspend operations. In so doing, he shifted the public debate over giant corporations like Western Union from the glorification of equal rights and the vilification of special privilege to the idealization of public utility and disparagement of unnecessary waste.

The popularization of natural monopoly theory by Adams, Ely, and Hadley was part of a deliberate campaign by the first generation of academically trained social scientists to marginalize investor-managers like Gould by transforming giant corporations like Western Union into functional systems driven by technical imperatives and economic incentives. To attain this goal, they proposed various schemes to insulate the telegraph business from the competitive maelstrom occasioned by antimonopoly legislation. Antimonopoly legislation emboldened financiers like Gould while saddling the corporations that they controlled with huge dividend payments that limited their ability to improve performance standards, raise employee salaries, and fund research and development. To marginalize Gould, academic social scientists minimized the influence of governmental institutions and civic ideals on business strategy and emphasized the power of technological imperatives and economic incentives.

Shortly after Jay Gould's death in 1892, *Puck* editor H. L. Bunner paused to reflect on the anxiety that Gould's takeover of Western Union had caused. That Gould had used his control over the telegraph to manipulate market trends seemed likely to Bunner; that he had misused Western Union's wires for political purposes during the election of 1884 Bunner had no doubt. Indeed, for a time there had been a "very general feeling" that the federal government ought to take charge of the telegraph business. Yet this fear had since been "removed" by the enormous growth in the facilities for electrical communication, which had by now become a "machine too huge" to be "readily perverted" from its "proper working" by any one man. Even so, it could not be said that Gould had ever inspired the people with confidence or endeavored to justify himself before the bar of public opinion.[142]

Bunner's postmortem on Gould's tenure at Western Union highlighted a marked change in conventional assumptions about cause and effect. Habits of causal attribution change slowly, and when they do, the implications can be profound.[143] One major transformation in these habits occurred in the 1880s, when social scientists began for the first time to emphasize the instrumentality of corporations as agents of change. In so doing, they invested corporations with the kind of agency that they had formerly reserved for the state and the market. While the anti-Gould hysteria was overblown, it underscored a basic truth. By demonizing Gould, critics challenged the legitimacy not only of an individual, but also of an institution. Gould's legacy haunted business leaders in the telegraph and the telephone business long after his death in 1892. Not until the First World War would the management of the American Telephone and Telegraph Company exorcise his ghost by championing technical progressiveness and financial orthodoxy. In so doing, a later generation of corporate leaders laid to rest, as Gould himself had not, the lingering presumption that the nation's communications networks were best operated by a government agency rather than a private corporation.

6

THE TALKING TELEGRAPH

> The day is coming when telegraph wire will be laid on to houses just like water or gas—and friends converse with each other without leaving home.
>
> *Alexander Graham Bell, 1876*

No "literary genius" has immortalized the telephone, lamented the English telephone engineer J. E. Kingsbury in 1915. Nor had a statistical enthusiast quantified the economic effects of the "electrical extension of human converse."[1] A few writers like Mark Twain found the telephone sufficiently intriguing to explore its literary possibilities.[2] But Twain was unusual. The telephone inspired less commentary than the telegraph, and its social consequences were often overlooked. With the exception of trade journals and chronicles of notable inventions, the telephone rarely received more than a passing mention in the press. Characteristic was the journalistic silence that greeted the exhibition of Alexander Graham Bell's telephone at the Philadelphia Centennial Exposition in 1876. In a magazine essay on the exposition in the *Atlantic Monthly,* William Dean Howells did not even list Bell's telephone in his catalogue of the fair's attractions.[3] Few hailed the telephone as a harbinger of world peace or an indispensable agent of the nation's "manifest destiny"; no one in the 1870s urged Congress to buy out its owners because of the evils that were likely to transpire should it be commercialized as a private enterprise. The telephone found its way into print for more prosaic reasons. Subscribers objected to the rates that operating companies charged, the performance standards they maintained, and the hazards that the tangle of overhead wires posed.

The telephone prompted less reflection than the telegraph, yet it was more highly regulated. Patent law loomed large, as it had for the

200

telegraph; so too did municipal franchise law, a body of law that affected only the relatively small part of the telegraph business that operated inside city boundaries. Patent law and municipal franchise law had different implications for business strategy. Whereas patent law spurred the construction of a long-distance network, municipal franchise law encouraged the frequent upgrading of telephone switchboards in the nation's largest cities.

For several decades the telephone was a specialty service for an exclusive clientele. Although the first exchange opened in 1878, only around 1900 would it be reconfigured as a mass service in San Francisco, Chicago, New York City, and the many others cities and towns that followed their lead. Its early history is in many ways surprising, since it was filled with challenges that later would not only be met but also forgotten. Some of these challenges were confronted in the boardroom of American Bell, the holding company that owned the largest and most valuable portfolio of telephone patents. Others were encountered in the switching centers of big-city telephone companies. Still others spilled over into city councils and state legislatures and became a subject of political contestation. From the moment Alexander Graham Bell obtained his first telephone patent in 1876, the telephone has been a creature not only of technology and economics but also of politics and culture.

The telephone business in the United States evolved out of the patent portfolio that William H. Forbes acquired in November 1879 as part of a market-segmenting agreement between Western Union and National Bell. National Bell was reorganized in 1880 as American Bell, which remained the holding company until 1899, when American Bell transferred its assets to American Telephone and Telegraph. American Bell did not provide telephone service. Rather, it was a holding company that managed a patent portfolio, collected licensing fees from telephone operating companies, and received dividends on its holdings of telephone operating companies and telephone equipment manufacturers. For the small number of individuals who were fortunate enough to own its shares, it was a lucrative investment. The average annual profit rate of American Bell in the 1880s hovered around 46 percent, an impressive showing.[4] Some of these profits were plowed back into the business; the rest were distributed to shareholders in the form of a generous dividend. Most American Bell investors regarded their holdings as a permanent investment. Only rarely did large blocs of shares find their way to the market; in part for this reason, their market price never displayed the wild fluctuations that made Western Union shares notorious.

The president of American Bell during its early years was William H. Forbes. Forbes joined together with a group of Boston investors who had grown intrigued by the commercial potential of the telephone and who were willing to invest in the fledgling venture spawned by Bell's patent rights. In March 1879, these investors elected Forbes president of National Bell.

Forbes was 39 in 1879 and exuded a youthful energy that concealed the tuberculosis that would kill him in 1897, at the age of 57. As a Union officer in the Civil War, Forbes had contracted tuberculosis as a prisoner-of-war. The son of the railroad magnate John Murray Forbes, William inherited from his father a modest personal fortune as well as the confidence of a tight-knit circle of well-to-do investors known colloquially as the "Forbes group." William attended Harvard, and while he did not distinguish himself as a student, he mingled with members of the region's elite. Like many men of his station, he married well. His wife, Edith, was the daughter of philosopher Ralph Waldo Emerson—who greatly admired his father.[5]

The original investors in American Bell, like the original investors in Western Union, were members of a commercial elite bound together by ties of family and friendship. Western Union originated in Rochester, New York; American Bell in Boston, Massachusetts. To help put the telephone business on a sound financial footing, Forbes obtained capital from some of the wealthiest and most socially prominent people in the city. Forbes's hand was strengthened in April 1879 when eighteen of his principal investors agreed not to sell their shares. This impressive display of solidarity strengthened Forbes's hand in his negotiation with Western Union and discouraged a speculative raid that might have swept him from power.[6]

Well born, well bred, and well connected, Forbes was a capable steward of the money with which he had been entrusted. His financial orthodoxy was nicely summarized by an offhand remark his father made to a colleague concerning a dubious investment scheme. Forbes's father had declined to invest on account of what "Boston might think."[7] William brought to American Bell a similar frame of mind: no matter what happened, no one would mistake him for Jay Gould.

Forbes's reputation for financial probity was one of the reasons that he had been originally encouraged to invest in the telephone. Forbes first learned about the telephone from Theodore N. Vail, the first general manager of National Bell. Vail had learned about Forbes during Vail's years at the Railway Mail Service. Vail had worked for a time as a railway mail clerk of the Chicago, Burlington & Quincy Railroad (CB&Q), a much-admired railroad owned by William's father. Vail was impressed by the CB&Q, which had a well-deserved reputation as one of the best-operated railroads in the country. Vail assumed—correctly, as it turned out—that William, like his father John, possessed not only the financial resources, but also the moral integrity, to oversee a large and complex organization.[8]

The November 1879 Western Union–National Bell settlement left National Bell in sole possession of two valuable assets: a patent portfolio that included the patents granted to Alexander Graham Bell, Thomas Edison, and Francis Blake, and an archipelago of telephone exchanges. This portfolio included the eighty five exchanges that Western Union had operated during the brief period it had competed head-on with National Bell. This was a valuable acquisition, since the Western Union exchanges had gained a decisive advantage over their rivals in several cities, including New York City and Chicago.

The brief, pre-1879 rivalry between Western Union and National Bell did much to accelerate the rise of the telephone business. In dozens of cities and towns, rival, nonconnecting exchanges sprang up almost overnight, spurring a telephone boom that had no parallel in Great Britain or France. By "accustoming" the public to the new medium, observed one American Bell staffer a few years later, this brief competitive interlude had performed a function that "no other agency" could have matched.[9]

American Bell's telephone patent portfolio was strong yet by no means invincible. To defend it, Forbes hired a crack legal team. In the fifteen-year period between 1879 and 1894, American Bell lawyers initiated around 600 patent infringement suits; they won every contest involving Bell's patents.[10]

Although patent litigation was complex, it hinged on a deceptively simple question. Who had been the first individual to demonstrate a workable invention? The rightful inventor was not, as in Great Britain, the first individual to file a patent; rather, it was the first individual to demonstrate a working model of the invention, whether or not this individual had obtained a patent. Claimants included, in addition to Bell, the Chicago electrician Elisha Gray, the Wisconsin doctor Sylvanus D. Cushman, and the Pennsylvania mechanic Daniel Drawbaugh. Foreign inventors also had their defenders, including the German scientist Johann Philipp Reis and the Italian stagehand Antonio Meucci.[11]

To settle the question, American Bell and its rivals squared off in court. These legal proceedings culminated in 1888 when, in a 4–3 decision, the Supreme Court affirmed Alexander Graham Bell's intellectual priority as the inventor of a particular method of transmitting sound, a method American Bell lawyers dubbed "undulatory current." Writing for the court, Chief Justice Morrison Waite credited Bell with the invention of the telephone, which Waite defined as a method of "transmitting speech telegraphically" in a closed electrical circuit in a manner "exactly analogous" to the "undulatory motion" of the human voice.[12] The "telephonic fraternity" should revere Waite's memory, declared one telephone manager, for the late chief justice had placed the "seal of judicial authority" upon the "scroll of fame" that bore the name of Alexander Graham Bell as the inventor of the telephone.[13]

To reach this conclusion, Waite and his colleagues evaluated a huge mass of evidence. In sheer bulk, this evidence was more voluminous than any that had previously been generated by any legal proceeding in the history of the Court. The final decision filled an entire volume of the Supreme Court's published reports, a unique event in the history of the judiciary. Waite's opinion was his last. He died a mere four days after having vindicated Bell; it was rumored that Waite died a victim of the strain that the litigation had caused.[14]

Among the dissenters was Joseph Bradley, the court's leading expert on patent law. Long before Bell had begun his research, Daniel Drawbaugh claimed to have demonstrated a working telephone capable of transmitting the human voice. Dozens of individuals had witnessed Drawbaugh's demonstration, and their depositions had been entered as evidence.[15] The existence of this "cloud of witnesses" led Bradley to conclude that Bell was not the first to demonstrate a workable telephone, and thus that his patents were void.[16]

Under other circumstances, American Bell might have capitalized on the enhanced prestige it obtained from its court victory to buy out Western Union. American Bell was flush with cash and had at its disposal the formidable financial resources of Boston's financial elite. Western Union remained a potential rival, and its telegraph network was a low-cost alternative to the long-distance telephone network that American Bell had recently begun. Yet simple prudence dictated that American Bell lie low. The "prevailing opinion," Forbes reminded American Bell shareholders, was that it was against the "public interest" for the telephone in the United States to remain "substantially under one control."[17] The establishment of a joint telegraph–telephone combine might be politically feasible, Forbes conceded, if it could be accomplished in such a way as to avoid arousing a "serious excess of wrath" against "monopolies." Yet an American Bell buyout of Western Union was out of the question: it was virtually guaranteed to hasten such an "uproar and attack" in the electorate that Congress might well enact legislation to buy out both Western Union and American Bell "by acclamation." Should Congress buy out American Bell after American Bell had acquired Western Union, Western Union would prove to be an albatross, for Congress would never match the high price "covering water" that American Bell had paid for it. Rather, Congress would demand a much lower price that reflected more closely the replacement cost of the physical assets on which Western Union's share price was ostensibly based.[18]

The large profits that American Bell generated for its shareholders in the 1880s made the telephone business an attractive opportunity for investors. Gould had profited handsomely by twice raiding Western Union. That Gould might enter the telephone business seemed entirely plausible; if he did not, someone else assuredly would.

Among the would-be telephone moguls was J. Webb Rogers, a Tennessee-born promoter who had settled in Washington, D.C. Rogers had watched Gardiner G. Hubbard dangle Alexander Graham Bell's patent rights before a parade of investors in the 1870s, and Rogers saw no reason why he could not emulate Hubbard's example.

Rogers's gambit hinged on the ingenuity of his son, James Henry ("Harry") Rogers. Harry was a talented inventor of electrical devices who had studied with Joseph Henry at Princeton before obtaining an appointment as the electrician of the Capitol in Washington. Bell netted Hubbard a fortune by inventing on demand; Rogers figured that his son Harry could too. Eager to please, Harry invented for his father both an improved telephone and a high-speed telegraph. The most plausible purchaser of the patent rights to Harry's improved telephone was American Bell: Vail was reputed to have been willing to buy them, and named a price, which Rogers deemed too low. Among the possible buyers of the patent rights to Harry's high-speed telegraph was the recently chartered Postal Telegraph Company; Postal Telegraph's investors were reputed to have offered $1 million for these rights. Once again, Rogers declined.[19]

To enhance the credibility of his scheme, Rogers obtained a charter for a corporation—the Pan-Electric Company—whose expansive name matched the scope of his ambition. Pan-Electric was a highly speculative venture that had been chartered primarily to raise capital from gullible investors. Its promoters included several politically prominent Southerners who had held major positions in the Confederacy during the Civil War. Pan-Electric's president was the ex-Confederate general Joseph E. Johnston. Backers included the ex-Confederate governor of Tennessee Isham G. Harris, now a Tennessee senator, and an ex-Confederate lieutenant colonel H. Casey Young, who was now a Tennessee representative.

To obtain favorable federal legislation, Rogers counted on Young to win over his congressional colleagues. Just as Hubbard had tried to obtain a federal charter for his Postal Telegraph Company, so Young would obtain a federal charter for Pan-Electric. "Political influence" would secure the charter for Pan-Electric, Rogers boasted; charter in hand, Pan-Electric would control the *grandest monopoly in the world.*[20]

Rogers's scheme presumed a congressional buyout of Western Union. Once Congress bought out Western Union, Rogers predicted that Jay Gould—Western Union's largest investor—would invest his windfall in the telephone business, a scenario that, bizarre as it might seem, was regarded as plausible at the time. For Gould to go head-to-head against American Bell, he would need patented inventions and Rogers felt certain that his son Harry could meet the demand. "If Harry can by any possibility invent any kind of a telephone system that will not be a palpable infringement of any existing patent," Young explained, "we can start it on a small scale and dictate terms to Gould."[21]

Congress's refusal to buy out Western Union left Rogers unfazed. Thinking quickly, he embarked on an even more convoluted scheme. To boost the value of Pan-Electric shares, Rogers joined forces with a New Orleans streetcar magnate to mobilize the federal Justice Department to annul Bell's telephone patents on the grounds that Bell had obtained them through fraud. It had long been hinted that a Patent Office examiner had improperly helped Bell to obtain his first patent in 1876 and that Bell might even have been tipped off regarding certain features of a rival telephone invented by Gray. Whether or not Bell had done anything improper remains an open question. If Bell had borrowed certain ideas from Gray, he soon changed his mind. As it happens, the telephone as it would come to be commercialized did not incorporate any of the ideas that Bell had purportedly stolen.[22]

For Rogers, however, the actual history of Bell's relationship with Gray was irrelevant. Win or lose, the lawsuit could be expected to generate a great deal of publicity that would boost the sale of Pan-Electric stock. No less importantly, it would prevent American Bell from prosecuting Pan-Electric for patent infringement. Lawsuits instituted by the federal government had priority over lawsuits instituted by private corporations. As long as the fraud investigation remained undecided, Pan-Electric would be spared the negative publicity that was certain to follow its legal defeat in a patent infringement suit.

For a time, it appeared that the fraud investigation might succeed. American Bell had few allies in the press and had earned the special enmity of the influential *New York Times*. *Times* editor George Jones had no doubt that Bell's patents were fraudulent and said so repeatedly on his editorial page. Jones rejoiced at the Pan-Electric lawsuit and went so far as to accuse Joseph Pulitzer of the *New York World* of accepting a bribe from American Bell to run stories critical of Pan-Electric in his newspaper in an attempt to derail its lawsuit against American Bell.[23]

The Pan-Electric lawsuit was obviously a scam. Even so, Forbes regarded it as a sufficiently worrisome scam that he arranged a one-on-one interview with President Grover Cleveland to apprise the president of the situation. Forbes found Cleveland's reaction reassuring. The president had little patience with "bogus concerns"—though he conceded that, until Alexander Graham Bell's patent rights expired, rivals would continue to "fire" away at American Bell in order to entice gullible "gudgeons" to invest in rival concerns.[24]

The Pan-Electric lawsuit collapsed in a huge public scandal when Pulitzer's *World* revealed that Cleveland's attorney general, Augustus H. Garland, owned thousands of Pan-Electric shares that were likely to skyrocket in value if the Justice Department won its lawsuit against American Bell. Although the fraud investigation would not be closed for several years, this journalistic revelation broke its momentum. The case never came to trial, the fraud charge was forgotten, and American Bell once again had a clear field to prosecute its would-be rivals for patent infringement in the courts.

The fact that the Pan-Electric lawsuit had proceeded as far as it had was a testament to the magnitude of popular outrage not only at American

Bell, but also at Gould, who, as Western Union's largest shareholder, received a royalty on every telephone licensed by American Bell. In the mind of one Chicago journalist, this made Gould the "autocrat" behind both Western Union and American Bell. Should Pan-Electric prevail, its victory would "destroy" the "most rapacious corporate alliance" ever devised by the "wizard of Wall Street"—that is, Gould.[25] To most people, conceded humorist H. L. Bunner, the Pan-Electric scandal was a "wild muddle and mystery." Even so, Bunner hoped that American Bell would take a "more retired seat in the rear." When it did, the country would be relieved: "The Bell Telephone Company is an unpopular monopoly, an ally of the Western Union Telegraph Company, and the public has very little use for it."[26]

The precariousness of American Bell's patent rights convinced Forbes to adopt a business strategy that relied less on politics and more on technology. This alternative technological strategy had two pillars: the upgrading of switchboard facilities in telephone exchanges, and the interconnection of these exchanges into a single network.

Interconnection was slow and expensive and only gradually covered its cost. Milestones included the opening of long-distance telephone service between New York City and Philadelphia in 1887; New York City and Chicago in 1893; and New York City and San Francisco in 1915. The construction of a long-distance telephone network did not ensure that American Bell would become a first mover in the telephone business because the bulk of the business was highly localistic. Far more consequential was the upgrading of switchboard facilities in the big-city operating companies.

Although the long-distance network earned American Bell high praise from engineers, it long remained peripheral to Bell's federation of big-city exchanges. Early on, in fact, it was a drain on revenue that might otherwise have been used to improve performance standards and lower rates. Yet with the exception of rival telephone providers and their allies in the trade press, few doubted its epochal significance. Its construction demonstrated Forbes's determination to build an enduring institution that would outlast the expiration of Alexander Graham Bell's patents. Amos Kendall had relied on patent law to retain control of the telegraph business; though he won in the courts, he failed in the market. Forbes used his patent monopoly as a springboard for technical advances that would create a corporation that would dominate the American telephone business for the next 100 years.

Forbes had originally assumed that American Bell would own and operate the long-distance network directly. He changed his mind when the Massachusetts state legislature refused to increase American Bell's capitalization. As an alternative, Forbes chartered the American Telephone and Telegraph Company in New York in 1885. New York had a more permissive attitude toward corporate capitalization than Massachusetts, and the New York Telegraph Act of 1848 had eliminated the need to obtain a special charter, an advantage for a corporation in a business whose future potential remained unknown. Western Union, the American Telegraph Company, and the Postal Telegraph Company had each found the New York Telegraph Act convenient. So, too, had American Telephone and Telegraph. The inclusion of the word "telegraph" in its corporate name anticipated the objection that it could not be chartered under the New York Telegraph Act since it was not in fact a telegraph corporation.

Among the technical challenges that interconnection posed was the standardization of telephone equipment. Telephone instruments were mass produced. To guarantee a steady supply at a reasonable price, Forbes obtained a large financial stake in Western Electric. Western Electric quickly became a major supplier of telephone instruments for the Bell operating companies, hastening its rise as one of the largest electrical equipment manufacturers in the country.[27]

The standardization of telephone equipment was facilitated by a decision that Gardiner G. Hubbard made at the very beginning of the telephone business. To maintain control over the operating companies, Hubbard insisted that they lease telephone instruments rather than purchase them outright. Telephone subscribers did not own their instruments, even if the instruments had been installed in their own residence. Leasing hastened the interconnection of the Bell operating companies while providing American Bell with yet another revenue stream. It long remained a pillar of telephone policy and would not be abandoned by the Bell operating companies until the breakup of the Bell System in 1984.[28]

Few Americans who were neither American Bell employees nor American Bell investors understood why a single corporation should enjoy a monopoly over the telephone business in the entire United States. Interconnection transformed a patent monopoly into a nationwide network that could credibly be claimed to promote the public good. Had Forbes not invested in the long-distance network, he would have been hard pressed to explain why lawmakers should permit American Bell to retain its monopoly. Monopoly control was necessary to standardize equipment, and standardized equipment was a prerequisite for interconnection, Forbes explained to American Bell's investors in 1885.[29] No one, declared Connecticut operating company manager Morris F. Tyler in 1895, should have to travel more than one hour by horse to reach a telephone pay station that was capable of linking the caller with any other telephone in the region.[30]

American Telephone and Telegraph remained a wholly owned subsidiary of American Bell until 1899. In that year, American Bell transferred its assets to American Telephone and Telegraph in a bit of legal legerdemain that transformed the former subsidiary into the corporate parent. Henceforth, American Telephone and Telegraph became both a long-distance network provider and a holding company for the federation of operating companies that held licenses from American Bell. In the twentieth century American Telephone and Telegraph would come to be known by its acronym, AT&T. It retained its dual identity as a holding company and network provider until 1984 when a federal judge forced it to sell off its operating companies, ending a financial relationship that in many localities was over a century old.

Early boosters of long-distance telephone service included Theodore N. Vail, Edward J. Hall, and Angus Hibbard. Vail entered the telephone business in 1878, having been recruited by Gardiner G. Hubbard to manage the Bell patent portfolio. Hubbard admired Vail's work as superintendent of the Railway Mail Service; Vail was intrigued by the operational autonomy of a private corporation, as well as by the money that he presumed he could make as an early investor in a high-tech start-up. Vail had a weakness for speculative ventures and relished the opportunities that he assumed the telephone would afford for insider trading. Among the positions in the telephone business that he held in the 1880s was president of the Bell operating company in New York City and president of American Telephone and Telegraph.

Vail left the telephone business in 1889 with few regrets. Like most first-generation telephone managers, he had assumed that the business had reached a technological plateau and that it was time to move on to more promising ventures. To recoup the fortune he had lost in a steam-heating plant, Vail moved to Argentina in the 1890s, where he built electric power stations and electric street railways. Following an eighteen-year hiatus, Vail returned to the presidency of American Telephone and

Telephone in 1907.[31] The telephone business had been utterly transformed in the intervening years, and upon his return Vail envisioned possibilities for its future expansion that no one in 1889 could have realistically foreseen.

Hall was a Yale-educated engineer who began his telephone career as the manager of the Bell operating company in Buffalo, New York. Hall's industriousness impressed Vail and led to his appointment as the first general manager of American Telephone and Telegraph. More analytical than most of his colleagues, Hall used his berth at American Telephone and Telegraph to standardize operating company procedures by devising the first telephone operating company organizational charts. An organization chart might appear to be a relatively prosaic management tool. In fact, it played a major role in the popularization of telephone service that began around 1900. By increasing the autonomy of operating company managers, it emboldened them to embark on experiments that their superiors might otherwise have blocked.

Hibbard made a name for himself by stringing wire for a Bell operating company in Wisconsin. Although Hibbard lacked Hall's formal engineering training, he too had a logical and disciplined mind. In 1886 Vail convinced him to become the first general superintendent of American Telephone and Telegraph. To facilitate interconnection, Hibbard and two colleagues published a technical manifesto for telephone engineers in 1889. In the "new era" that would follow the expiration of the two fundamental Bell patents, this manifesto declared, the Bell operating companies would dominate their respective territories through a combination of high technical standards and the rigorous training of telephone engineers.[32] To advertise the possibilities of long distance, Hibbard designed a distinctive logo for American Telephone and Telegraph. This logo—a blue bell, honoring Alexander Graham Bell—would long be one of the most widely recognized corporate symbols in the United States.[33]

The huge surpluses that American Telephone and Telegraph generated in the mid-twentieth century from it long-distance network became such a cornerstone of its business strategy that it is hard to envision a time when the long-distance network failed to generate a profit. Early on, however, no one knew for certain if it would ever cover its cost. It took courage, Vail later recalled, to even embark on its construction.[34] The long-distance network had been "fondly regarded" by certain American Bell executives as a source of great profits, reported Morris F. Tyler in his annual report to the shareholders of the Southern New England Telephone Company in 1886. In practice, however, it had always been a source of "actual loss" to his company. One line in which Tyler invested had been patronized during one three-month period a mere nineteen times—which generated far too little revenue to justify the expense of its operation.[35]

The artfulness with which telephone accountants obscured internal fund transfers complicated the task of determining how much money the long-distance network cost—a perennial problem for investors—as did the intractable challenge of apportioning the cost of long-distance telephone service between the long-distance provider and the operating companies. Had telephone accountants generated cost data that could be conveniently manipulated by economists, it would have been easier to determine when the long-distance network ceased to be a drain on the operating companies, as it most assuredly was in its opening years. Yet they did not. The failure of American Telephone and Telegraph to make cost data accessible, complained one sympathetic economist in 1925, made it impossible to reach an informed conclusion with regard not only to the magnitude of the fund transfers between the operating companies and the long-distance provider, but also to their direction.[36]

The losses that American Bell sustained early on with its long-distance network reinforced the long-standing skepticism of Western Union president Norvin Green regarding the telephone's potential. Green's doubts were self-serving: Green had negotiated the sale of Western Union's telephone business to Forbes in 1879. Yet it had a solid basis in fact. To compensate for the lack of telephone traffic, American Bell had leased its telephone wires to telegraph users, a practice Green pointedly derided as a violation of the market-sharing agreement that he had negotiated with Forbes in 1879. "The fact is," Green explained to an investor in 1889, "their long distance telephone is a failure as a commercial enterprise, and they have had to resort to leasing their wires."[37] American Bell insiders concurred. Citing an American Bell official as his source, American Bell agent Frank R. Colvin reported in 1899 that American Bell had made $900,000 by leasing long-distance telephone lines to telegraph users. "Without this [telegraph leasing] business," Colvin recounted the American Bell official observing, "you can see we would not be in it."[38]

The financial limitations of American Bell's long-distance network were a subject of concern to Gardiner G. Hubbard. Hubbard ceased to play a major role in the telephone business after 1879, yet he retained an abiding interest in its development and, as one of the largest shareholders in American Bell, had a voice in its affairs. Hubbard had built up a formidable grasp of telegraph and mail usage patterns as a Western Union critic and presumed that this knowledge could help him forecast likely usage patterns for the telephone. The primary long-distance market for the telephone, Hubbard informed American Bell president John E. Hudson in 1889, using telegraph and mail data as a proxy, was not nationwide but regional, while most telephone calls for the foreseeable future would remain confined to a radius of no more than 100 miles.[39]

Hubbard's conservative estimate of the potential demand for long-distance telephone service reinforced his nagging concern that operating company managers were insufficiently attentive to the needs of telephone subscribers. Telephone rates were too high, Hubbard complained, and performance standards too low. The telephone was a "quasi-public corporation" that had obligations to the public as well as its shareholders. "For many years," Hubbard reminded Forbes in 1885, he had been "largely interested" in horse-drawn streetcar lines, gas plants, and water works, bringing him into "more immediate contact" with the public than had "fallen to the lot" of the executive committee of American Bell.[40]

Hubbard's misgivings led him to endorse a plan for a hybrid telephone-telegraph network floated by Postmaster General John Wanamaker in 1889. In Wanamaker's plan big-city post offices and small-town telephone exchanges would become feeders for the long-distance telegraph network. If American Bell signed on, Hubbard assured Hudson, it would "ensure our success for many years to come."[41] For thirty years Hubbard had tried to convince lawmakers to link the long-distance telegraph network with the local pick-up and drop-off facilities operated by the Post Office Department. Wanamaker's plan, for which Hubbard had served as a technical adviser, was its logical successor. Not only would it be less expensive than the construction of a long-distance telephone network, but it would also be more likely to meet the needs of most telephone subscribers, since long-distance telephone service was likely to remain far too expensive to be anything more than a specialty service for an exclusive clientele. To Hubbard's chagrin, Wanamaker's plan was shelved. It would not be revived until 1909, when Vail briefly championed it in a somewhat different form.

The organizational forms that telephone managers relied on in building the telephone network owed something to the telegraph. The telephone, like the telegraph, was a form of electrical communication, and telephone and telegraph managers confronted similar challenges in obtaining rights-of-way, stringing wire, and linking the network to its users. The terms "operator," "switchboard," and "exchange" all had telegraphic counterparts, and telegraph inventor Elisha Gray was by no means the only contemporary to refer to the telephone as a "talking telegraph."[42] The telephone exchange, reminisced New York Telephone general manager Howard F. Thurber in 1910, was originally intended to supplant the "district telegraphs" that Western Union and its rivals operated in the 1870s. District telegraphs transmitted electrical signals to a central office from a business or residence to facilitate the completion of a limited number of prearranged tasks, such as the hiring of a messenger to perform an errand. Given the highly specialized tasks for which the district telegraph had been designed, no one envisioned that it might permit patrons to connect with each other, much less that it might expand beyond the boundaries of a city or town.[43]

One of the first telephone executives to envision the establishment of a long-distance telephone network was Theodore N. Vail. Curiously enough, the organizational form Vail relied on for inspiration was not the telegraph but the Post Office Department.

In the 1870s the Post Office Department was a vast, sprawling organization that had entered into an uneasy alliance with the nation's railroads to speed the circulation of the mail. To coordinate mail–rail logistics, postal administrators established the Railway Mail Service (RMS). The RMS enjoyed an enviable reputation as one of the most technically advanced and administratively complex organizations in the country. Few other organizations outside of the military displayed a comparable commitment to systemwide integration. RMS superintendents regularly convened conferences at which regional superintendents refined organizational protocols with a deliberateness that far exceeded any comparable forum sponsored by Western Union.[44] One outcome of these deliberations was the "Fast Mail," a high-speed mail–rail link between New York City and Chicago that was capable of transmitting information from one city to the other in a mere twenty-six hours. This impressive feat garnered the Post Office Department a great deal of favorable coverage in the press.[45]

Vail's tenure at the RMS gave him a lifelong appreciation for the inherent power of huge, spatially extensive communications networks. The value of the RMS network could not be calculated in purely monetary terms; following Vail's return to American Telephone and Telegraph as its president in 1907, he would come to view the telephone business through a similar lens.

The Post Office Department had aspired to circulate information with great rapidity ever since Postmaster General John McLean had first enunciated his gospel of speed in 1825. Yet no pre–Civil War postal initiative was as ambitious as the "Fast Mail." Railroad owners demanded additional compensation for meeting the Post Office Department's exacting performance standards; RMS superintendents defended the Fast Mail as a public good that the railroads had a civic obligation to sustain. During his tenure as RMS superintendent, Vail had become involved in a pointed dispute with New York Central Railroad president William K. Vanderbilt over the fees that Vanderbilt demanded to keep the Fast Mail in operation. When negotiations broke down, Vanderbilt actually threw the mail off his train. This provocative act left Vail with an abiding distrust of business ventures that focused narrowly on the bottom line.[46] When a reporter asked Vanderbilt several years later why he had defied the public by suspending the fast-mail train between New York City and Chicago, Vanderbilt sardonically replied, "the public be damned! I am working for my stockholders."[47] Vail deplored Vanderbilt's single-minded solicitude for his investors and was determined to invest the telephone business with a rationale that transcended mere money-making.

Vail was one of several RMS veterans recruited by American Bell. C. J. French came to American Bell after having served for several years as a regional RMS superintendent; so too did Alonzo Burt. French became general manager of American Bell, and Burt the president of Bell operating companies in Missouri and Wisconsin. Nathan C. Kingsbury also entered the telephone business after having worked in the RMS; following a stint as vice president of the Bell operating company in Michigan, Kingsbury became vice president of American Telephone and Telegraph.

The RMS was by no means the only government agency that left its mark on American Bell. Forbes might not have bested Green in 1879 had he not already acquired the patent rights to a transmitter invented by Francis Blake, a government scientist who had recently retired from the U.S. Coast Survey. The technical knowledge that Blake acquired in the federal government proved indispensable to his invention, as did the timely intervention of his government supervisor who brought Bell's invention to Blake's attention after he himself had learned about it as a judge at the Philadelphia Centennial.[48]

Other notable early telephone managers with federal government experience included Marshall Jewell, David B. Parker, and Union N. Bethell. Jewell served as postmaster general before, at Vail's suggestion, investing in some early telephone companies. When the telephone business took off, Jewell became the first president of the telephone operating company managers' trade association, the National Telephone Exchange Association (NTEA). Had Jewell not died unexpectedly in 1883, he might well have become a key figure in the commercialization of the long-distance telephone network. Parker distinguished himself as superintendent of the Post Office Department's inspection service before signing on with American Bell. As a postal inspector, Parker had gleaned many insights that he would draw on during his long and distinguished telephone career. Bethell cultivated a talent for public relations during a stint in the 1880s as a special agent for the federal pension office. Bethell put these skills to good use as president of several Bell operating companies, including New York Telephone.

At the center of the telephone business in its formative era was the federation of operating companies that had obtained licenses from American Bell. The largest and most lucrative of these operating companies were organized in, and for a time largely confined to, the central business districts of the nation's largest cities. It was here, in the hustle-and-bustle of the big-city telephone exchange—and not in the Olympian calm of Forbes's boardroom at American Bell—that telephone managers solved the technical challenges that made the telephone a commercial success.

The telephone operating companies that held licenses from American Bell were customarily referred to as "Bell" companies, even though the word "Bell" was only rarely included in their corporate name. Before 1896, for example, the American Bell licensee in New York City was known as the Metropolitan Telephone Company and after 1896 as the New York Telephone Company. Until 1920 the American Bell licensee in Chicago was known as the Chicago Telephone Company. Under other circumstances, the word "Bell" might have been quietly forgotten. The parent company, after all, did not even have the word "Bell" in its name after 1899. Hubbard lobbied to retain the word "Bell" as a tribute to his famous son-in-law.[49] Vail followed his lead when he trumpeted the existence of a "Bell System" that linked together the Bell-licensed operating companies in a single network in his annual report for 1908.

Telephone operating companies flourished in a densely layered political economy that embroiled them in almost constant negotiation with governmental institutions ranging from the Patent Office and the courts to state legislatures and city councils.[50] Municipal franchises were negotiated one-by-one, and, in contrast to telegraph charters, they were often quite detailed. Some mandated rate caps and performance standards; many obliged the operating company to provide certain facilities for the city government free of charge; a few had expiration dates. The franchise that the Chicago Telephone Company obtained in 1889, for example, expired in 1909.

A municipal franchise was a special privilege that a city council conferred on an individual or a corporation. This privilege, one expert explained, did not belong by "common right" to the "citizens of a country generally."[51] Although the franchise—"or right" to use the streets of a city was "derived from the state acting through the legislature," elaborated a standard legal treatise, "the *consent of the municipality* when required by constitution or by statute must be obtained before the right to exercise the franchise is complete."[52] The capitalization of franchises was controversial because it smacked of corruption to monetize a special privilege. Yet it was taken for granted that, if a franchise were monetized, its value would be considerable. The "value" of a "public service corporation," explained one telephone investment adviser in 1905, depended "largely" on the "terms of its franchise."[53]

Municipal franchises shaped the business strategy of operating companies in various ways. Incumbents relied on them to forestall competition, whereas insurgents used them to enter the market. Once an operating company had strung its wires in a particular locality, it could hardly ignore municipal politics. Manufacturers confronted with burdensome municipal ordinances could plausibly threaten to shut their plants and relocate in a more hospitable locality. But the Chicago Telephone Company could not move to Milwaukee.

The two largest operating companies were headquartered in New York City and Chicago, New York City being the nation's biggest city and

Chicago the fastest growing and after 1890 its second largest. For many years New York City and Chicago housed the two largest telephone companies not only in the United States but also in the world (see Table 2).[54]

The centrality of New York City and Chicago to the early telephone business was evident to Vail and Hubbard. The establishment of an operating company in Chicago would give owners of Bell's patent rights a "hold" on the entire Northwest, predicted Vail in October 1878.[55] Chicago was of greater importance than even New York City, Hubbard confided to Vail one week later. As long as Bell retained an office in New York City, it would be easy to keep watch on the New York City–based licensee, while the Chicago company might do many things that were "opposed to our interests" of which the investors would remain oblivious until the "evil was done."[56]

The first users of the telephone were businessmen and professionals. Merchants used the telephone to complete transactions, doctors to fill prescriptions. Chicago businessmen were addicted to labor-saving " 'short cuts,' " reported one chronicler in 1893: "But the telephone is the thing that has found more favor in the eyes of the businessmen of this city than any other invention." The ability to talk to a colleague without leaving one's office was a huge boon that was "eagerly seized" upon by every man who could afford the "extortionate prices" demanded by a "grasping monopoly." The telephone doubled the working time of the one-tenth of the population that was most active in business by saving the time that it had formerly "wasted" in traveling from one part of the city to another.[57] To speed the movement of lumber inside Chicago, wholesalers hired spotters to coordinate its transshipment from its arrival on barges in the city's harbor to its departure in railroad cars parked on sidings

Table 2. The five largest telephone exchanges in the world, 1882, 1895, 1910, and 1920.

1882		1895		1910		1920	
New York	3,125	Berlin	25,000	New York	361,302	New York	845,890
Chicago	2,610	Paris	12,500	Chicago	239,083	Chicago	575,840
Philadelphia	1,804	Stockholm	11,536	Berlin	174,572	Berlin	310,660
Paris	1,400	Chicago	11,680	London	172,000	London	310,000
London	1,338	New York	9,627	Boston	120,769	Boston	272,244

Source: All cities besides Chicago: *Telecom History* 1 (1994): 84; *Telecom History* 2 (1996): 96; *Telecom History* 3 (2002): 30; Chicago: Homer Hoyt, *One Hundred Years of Land Values in Chicago* (Chicago: University of Chicago Press, 1933), p. 490.

adjoining the vast lumberyards that stretched for 12 miles along the Chicago River.[58] The average subscriber in New York City used his telephone sixteen times a day, reported a journalist in 1894, while the heaviest users used it as many as 200 times; on an average business day, operators made between 80,000 and 90,000 connections.[59] One Chicago businessman informed a reporter in 1901 that he was at his desk every day by 7:00 A.M. and had completed fifty transactions by telephone by lunch.[60]

One of the most important performance standards for telephone subscribers was the call-connection delay. If it took ten minutes for an operator to make a connection, a circumstance that was by no means unusual in the early 1880s, wholesalers might well wonder why they did not hire an errand boy instead. A Wall Street trader might well grow impatient if it took 60 seconds to make a connection, observed a journalist in 1886, even if it took a messenger 90 minutes to perform an identical task.[61]

The telephone had not been designed to sustain sociability, and it would only gradually be reimagined to encourage the maintenance of social bonds. Only a small fraction of the residential telephones in Chicago in 1895, for example, were used for incoming calls. Householders installed the telephone primarily to help their servants perform routine errands. To permit a total stranger to cross the threshold by ringing a bell was an invasion of privacy, and telephone managers saw little reason to promote a service that few desired.[62]

The most serious limitation of the telephone for business subscribers was its inability to leave a written record. Stockbrokers, observed one journalist in 1887, were not likely to issue a directive by telephone that might be "indistinct" when they could be certain that it would be accurately transmitted by telegraph.[63]

The impermanence of telephone conversations inspired Thomas A. Edison to devise in the late 1870s what is sometimes regarded as his single most remarkable invention: the "phonograph." The phonograph was a machine for recording sound. The telephone would remain confined to mere "conversational chit chat," Edison explained, as long as the information sent over its wires remained ephemeral. But if it could record conversation, it would quickly become a "conscientious and infallible scribe." For many telephone users, the absence of a transcript would later become an asset because it fostered open discussion. For Edison, however—as for Morse before him—an electrical communications medium was of limited value if it failed to generate a permanent record. Businessmen who had begun a conversation face to face, Edison predicted, would agree to hive off into separate rooms in which phonograph-equipped telephones had been installed so that they might obtain a verbatim record, or "phonogram," of what had been said: "In fact, all correspondence will be greatly simplified and widely abbreviated by the use of phonograms. A telephone subscriber can place at his telephone a phonogram which will announce to the exchange, whenever he is called up, that he has left the office and will return at a certain time."[64]

By 1915 it was theoretically possible to talk by telephone between New York City and San Francisco. Bell publicists trumpeted this fact in countless public relations advertisements and did their best to underscore its significance by linking it with earlier triumphs of long-distance communications such as the French optical telegraph and the Pony Express. For most telephone subscribers, however, long-distance service remained too expensive to be practicable until after the Second World War.[65]

Even if long-distance telephone service had been cheap, skeptics doubted it would have been popular. A "new economy" was coming, predicted the utopian socialist Laurence Gronlund in 1898, one that would be profoundly shaped by recent technical advances in science and technology. Even so, Gronlund did not believe that the day would ever come when a man living in Seattle would have any need to converse by telephone with a man in Boston, even if it were possible to do so at a reasonable cost, if he could "cheaply" send a telegram instead.[66]

The telephone business in its formative era was more heterogeneous, confusing, and even chaotic than it would later be remembered by Bell publicists and the many scholars who followed their lead. The relationship between American Bell and the operating companies was rarely harmonious: Had Hall not been permitted to implement his planned decentralization of the operating companies, it is conceivable that the federation might have collapsed. American Bell regarded the operating companies in more or less the same spirit that a wealthy landlord did his impecunious tenants. The operating companies, for their part, resented the licensing fee that American Bell charged and bridled at the cost of the telephone equipment that American Bell required them to buy. Operating company resentment at American Bell hastened the formation in 1880 of the NTEA. Like so many trade groups, the NTEA had been established to meet a political challenge: the continuing subordination of telephone operating companies to a holding company whose power derived from a federally authorized monopoly grant.[67]

American Bell had its own technical staff, yet it took little part in NTEA deliberations. In large part, this was because NTEA members viewed American Bell staffers as agents of the American Bell–owned telephone equipment manufacturer Western Electric, which they regarded with suspicion. As a consequence, the NTEA, and not American Bell, served as the primary forum for the circulation of technical information. The absence of central direction was a major advantage in the view of British telephone engineer J. E. Kingsbury: a more "dogmatic authority" would have slowed innovation.[68]

The possession of a municipal franchise did not authorize a telephone company to string wire indiscriminately. Streets were public property; even after an operating company had obtained a citywide franchise, it still had to secure a license for a specific right-of-way. If it did not, the city council retained the authority to condemn its poles and wires as nuisances and to order their removal.

Wire stringing required wire pulling: the granting of right-of-way licenses furnished venal lawmakers with lucrative opportunities for graft. The telephone gave unscrupulous aldermen an opportunity for "countless commercial transactions," noted one Chicago editorialist sardonically in 1883. Aldermen could solicit kickbacks to grant operating companies' permission to string telephone wire overhead and even to delay their compliance with the city ordinance that required their burial underground.[69] No more than eighteen of Chicago's sixty-eight aldermen were honest, estimated one Chicago newspaper around 1894. In an average year, a crooked alderman could make as much as $20,000 in kickbacks, a huge sum that dwarfed the salary of most business executives.[70] Telephone operating companies were hardly the only victims of aldermanic cupidity. Yet the operating companies were wealthy and entrenched, making them especially vulnerable to extortion.[71]

To combat unwelcome political intervention, operating companies defined their obligations narrowly. The operating company resembled a men's club more than a common carrier, declared one telephone manager in 1882. Even though it was dependent on a municipal body for permission to install poles and string wire, it served a "well-defined" number of subscribers with whom it had entered into a "more or less permanent contract" and retained the right to maintain "some control" over its "membership."[72] The "one competitor" to the telephone, explained a business journalist, was the "small boy" hired as a messenger at $3 a week. If employers could not afford $1 a week for telephone service, they were best advised not to subscribe.[73]

Telephone wires were initially mounted on overhead poles installed alongside city streets. Overhead installation was cheaper than underground burial and posed fewer technical challenges. Before long, telephone wires jostled not only with telegraph wires, but also with electric light wires and streetcar wires. Major thoroughfares like lower Broadway in New York City or South La Salle Street in Chicago quickly became blanketed with a dense network of wires, cables, and poles. "The sky," reported one English visitor to New York City in 1881, had become "obscured by the countless threads of wire."[74] Thirty-two different companies had been granted permission to string wires overhead, reported one electrical expert four years later.[75] One pole held 100 wires and reached 96 feet up into the sky.[76]

Overhead wires were not only unsightly, but also dangerous. Telegraph and telephone companies relied on low-voltage current, but electric light and streetcar companies did not. If a telephone wire crossed an electric light or a streetcar wire, any person who came into contact with the telephone wire, or who picked up a telephone to which it had been connected, risked serious injury or even death. Lawsuits were common and much feared by telephone operating companies, since the damage awards were unpredictable and potentially huge. The Buffalo operating company was held partly liable in 1888 for the death of a man who had been electrocuted by a low-voltage telephone wire that had inadvertently crossed a high-voltage electrical power line. In the opinion of the jury, overhead telephone wires were "secret and deadly traps to human life."[77]

As the number of overhead wires increased, so too did public pressure to require franchise corporations to bury them underground. The first major city in the United States to enact an underground wire ordinance was Chicago. Every franchise corporation that had strung wires in the city's central business district had two years to bury its overhead wires, decreed the city council in May 1881.[78] Shortly thereafter, a jury declared certain telephone poles in New York City a nuisance under common law, rendering the operating companies vulnerable to lawsuits.[79] To clarify the legal situation, in 1884 the New York state legislature enacted a comprehensive underground wire law that mandated the burial of thousands of miles of telephone wire.[80] Three years later, the state legislature established a board of electrical control to coordinate their burial.[81] Underground interment accelerated following a horrific accident in 1889; the body of a Western Union lineman who had been accidentally electrocuted by a crossed wire was left dangling on a telegraph pole for several hours within sight of New York's city hall.[82] Shortly thereafter, New York mayor Hugh J. Grant ordered work crews of city employees equipped with axes and nippers to cut down the remaining telegraph poles at Union Square.[83] In short order, Grant's work crews toppled 800 poles and 1 million feet of wire.[84]

Telephone operating companies routinely failed to meet the original deadlines that lawmakers mandated. Yet lawmakers remained insistent, and the companies begrudgingly complied. In hundreds of cities and towns throughout the country, thousands of miles of overhead wires were removed from poles in the 1880s and 1890s and reinstalled in underground conduits.

Operating companies reacted to underground wire legislation with alarm. The Chicago wire ordinance, warned Connecticut operating company president Morris F. Tyler, was the "severest attack" that the operating companies had yet to confront. Tyler considered the law unenforceable, since he doubted that its provisions could be met. If the operating companies could demonstrate that by burying their wires the business would be "buried with them," the law was inoperative: it was an "elementary principle" of jurisprudence that any law that required something "physically impossible" was void.[85] Chicago Telephone Company general manager Charles N. Fay shared Tyler's skepticism about the practicality of the underground wire ordinances. To prevent the city from fining his company for noncompliance, Fay secured an injunction stipulating that, as long as his company spent $10,000 a year putting wires underground, it was presumed to have complied with the law.[86] The solution to the "'overhead wire nuisance,'" Vail informed the shareholders of a New England operating company in 1884, should be left to telephone companies rather than state legislatures because it involved various technical and economic puzzles that telephone engineers had yet to solve, especially with regard to long-distance service.[87]

The skepticism of operating company managers resonated with officials at American Bell. In no sense was the movement to bury overhead wires "truly" popular, observed American Bell electrician Thomas D. Lockwood in 1883. On the contrary, its main supporters were "special interests," including, in particular, the "professional inventors" who stood to reap a financial windfall from the sale of the cables, pipes, and wire-laying machinery that threatened to keep city thoroughfares in a state of "volcanic eruption."[88]

The suspicion among American Bell executives that the self-interest of equipment manufacturers had spurred lawmakers to action was reinforced by a discovery that Chicago Telephone counsel Norman Williams made in 1883. In that year, it came to Williams's attention that Western Electric president Enos Barton and Western Electric engineer Milo Kellogg were lobbying the Chicago city council to force the Chicago Telephone Company to hasten the burial of a large number of its wires in Chicago's central business district. In a "business way," Williams conceded, what Barton and Kellogg had done was "entirely proper." Yet in their "anxiety" to sell wire-laying equipment to the telephone company, they had adopted a course of action that was likely to cost the Chicago Telephone Company a large sum of money. American Bell owned a large stake in Western Electric, and Vail was an officer of American Bell. Might not Vail undertake some "missionary work" and encourage Barton and Kellogg to be more discreet in their future public statements about the "practicality" of these cables, and, in particular, their suitability for telephone service over long distances? "The slightest comfort in the way of the use of these cables will be seized upon by the city, and by the newspapers, and therefore it becomes necessary to be very careful in their statements to the public."[89]

One of the first publications to champion underground-wire legislation was *Manufacturer and Builder,* a trade journal for general contractors. That the "nuisance" of overhead wires was tolerated, and even defended, huffed its editor in 1881, was yet "another illustration" of the "many that could be named" of the "unaccountable willingness" with which the "average American citizen" allowed himself to be "kicked, cuffed, pilfered, and generally abused" by "soulless corporations."[90] The willingness of *Manufacturer and Builder* to take the lead in this issue was not surprising: if lawmakers forced the wires underground, it would generate business for its subscribers.

The electrical trade press was more sympathetic to the telephone operating companies and echoed the skepticism of telephone executives like Vail. The burial of overhead wires was a formidable technical challenge, and it took telephone engineers several years of experimentation to devise cables that could maintain the performance standards to which their subscribers had become accustomed. "The Telephone Wires Cannot be Sunk," ran one headline in the *Electrical Review* in 1884. In the absence of solid evidence that underground-wire legislation was technically feasible and economically sound, not even the political influence of the "scheming band of monopolists" who owned the rights-of-way to the "subways" in which the operating companies were supposed to lay their wires could force the operating companies to bury them underground.[91] Few trusted the operating companies to take the lead. Journalistic pressure to bury the wires grew rapidly, especially in general-circulation magazines like *Harper's Weekly*. Even telephone inventor Alexander Graham Bell supported legislative intervention. Only lawmakers could force telephone operating companies to bury their wires underground, Bell candidly predicted in a newspaper interview in 1884: "The corporations will never do it, I fear, until they are required by law to do so."[92]

The recalcitrance of telephone and telegraph operating companies furnished cartoonists with a host of opportunities to illustrate how cities and municipal franchise corporations had quite literally become entangled. "What the Telegraph Companies Will Do Next" ran the caption for one cartoon in which a telegraph company had strung telegraph wires over a piano inside a middle-class parlor. "Whoa, There! What Are We Coming To?" ran a caption for another cartoon in which overhead wires tripped up Santa Claus's sleigh. "A Peep into the Future" ran the caption for a third cartoon in which telegraph and telephone companies draped overhead wires around the outstretched arm of the Statue of Liberty.[93]

Goaded by lawmakers and ridiculed in the press, operating companies responded. Vail had questioned the efficacy of underground-wire legislation as late as 1885; yet as the president of the Metropolitan Telephone Company, he buried thousands of miles of telephone wire in New York City.[94] Vail's leadership role in the burial of overhead telephone wires was often featured in later journalistic accounts of his telephone career. For most of New York City's telephone subscribers, it was of far greater practical significance than his brief stint between 1885 and 1887 as the first president of American Telephone and Telegraph.[95] The last overhead wires in Manhattan were buried in 1896. In the previous nine years, reported the mayor of New York City in that year, municipal franchise corporations had removed 20,337 poles and 29,802 miles of wire at no cost to the taxpayer. This claim was not entirely true, for several of the affected corporations, including Metropolitan, passed the cost on to their subscribers in the form of higher rates.[96]

The underground burial of telephone wires eliminated the environmental hazard posed by wind and ice. The "archenemy" of the telephone, declared one early telephone manager, was the weather. Especially damaging was the blizzard of 1888: the storm brought down thousands of miles of overhead telephone wires throughout the Northeast and wreaked havoc in New York City, which was blanketed under about four feet of snow.[97]

The hazards posed by the weather were outside of human control; other hazards were not. Telephones operated on a low-voltage direct current that was easily distorted by the more powerful alternate current generated by electric power stations, a problem known as induction. Induction could render unintelligible even a conversation that spanned a mere two blocks. The distortion was so serious that, for a few years around 1890, telephone managers warned that, if the problem was not solved quickly, the telephone was doomed.[98] To complicate matters even more, judges typically ruled against telephone companies when they sued electric streetcar companies for interference on the grounds that transportation and not communication was the primary function of the streets.[99]

To eliminate induction, operating companies replaced one-wire "grounded circuits" with two-wire "metallic circuits." Grounded circuits were vulnerable to induction; metallic circuits were not. This technical fix was effective, but it was expensive, especially in the big-city exchanges in which the problem was the most serious. Metallic circuits used twice the wire of grounded circuits and were not compatible with existing switchboards. To cover the cost of making the change, operating companies in New York City, Chicago, and several other cities raised subscribers' rates. To justify the rate increases, operating companies downplayed the benefits of metallic circuits for local service and emphasized their necessity in making long-distance connections. If the company focused merely on local service, it was vulnerable to the objection that it had no right to raise the rates because it was technically not a service upgrade, but merely a stopgap to maintain a performance standard that it had previously provided. Operating companies lacked the operational autonomy to raise rates unilaterally. In the absence of a compelling rationale, they were vulnerable to challenges not only from lawmakers, but also from their own subscribers. Unfortunately for the company, neither lawmakers nor subscribers found its rationale for a rate increase convincing. Few subscribers had any desire to make long-distance calls, and they resented the long-distance option as nothing but a ruse to jack up the rates.[100]

The most controversial of the many operational issues that operating companies confronted concerned the pricing of telephone service. The most common calling plans provided subscribers with unlimited access to telephone service inside a spatially delimited zone in return for the payment of a fixed monthly fee. This calling plan was known as "flat rate" to distinguish it from "measured service," a calling plan that linked the cost of telephone service to the number of calls a subscriber made. The boundaries of the unlimited access zone varied over time and from company to company. Early on, this zone often coincided with the boundaries of the exchange in which the subscriber's telephone had been installed. This territory was sometimes as small as a few square miles. In Chicago, for example, it was 16.3 square miles in 1889.[101] As the exchange grew more spatially extensive, so too did the unlimited access zone—sometimes as a result of the voluntary decision of operating companies and sometimes as a result of legislation.

Although calling plans differed from company to company, they had certain common features. First, and most obviously, they presupposed that the location of the telephone was fixed. Journalists occasionally speculated that it might one day be possible to carry around a wireless telephone in one's pocket, yet this remained a visionary dream.[102] Second, subscribers who wanted to reach a telephone that was connected to the exchange but outside of the unlimited access zone had to pay an additional fee known as a toll. Third, the calling plans permitted subscribers to make an unlimited number of calls at no additional charge from any telephone located inside the unlimited access zone. This feature was intended to appeal to subscribers who frequented drugstores and other public places in which proprietors had installed telephones for the convenience of nonsubscribers. To notify the storekeeper that an individual was a subscriber, the Chicago Telephone Company printed up special cards that subscribers were supposed to present if they wished to make a call. To the "free use of public telephone as designated"—"for city connections only"—declared one subscriber's card that expired in December 1888: "*If presented* by any other than the person within named, it will be taken up, cancelled and returned to the company."[103]

Flat rates advertised the potential of the telephone by permitting subscribers to experiment with its possibilities without having to reflect that every call was, as one contemporary put it, a "definite expense."[104] Subscribers concurred. Just as flat rates had familiarized householders with the intercom—or "speaking tube," as the intercom was then called—reflected one group of Chicago telephone subscribers in 1884, so too would they create a market for the telephone.[105]

Flat rates appealed to subscribers but posed challenges for operating companies. Most obviously, they increased operating costs as the exchange expanded. Subscribers had no incentive to limit the number of outgoing calls, and, as the number of subscribers in the unlimited access zone expanded, they had more people to call. Each call had to be connected manually by a telephone operator; as traffic increased, costs did too. Even if the operating company increased its workforce to meet the demand, a problem remained: if a line were engaged, it could not be reached. Caller notification devices like the now ubiquitous "call waiting" signal had yet to be devised. In major cities such as Chicago, it was not uncommon for wholesalers and commission merchants to make dozens and in some instances hundreds of calls per day. If the telephones they wanted to reach were in use, as they often were, their calls would prove unavailing.

To minimize congestion, operating companies tried to discourage subscribers from making frequent calls. Some threatened to cancel the contracts of subscribers who permitted their telephone to be used by nonsubscribers. "Allowing non-subscribers the use of the telephone," warned the Bell operating company at Terre Haute, Indiana, "authorizes the company to cancel and remove the instrument."[106] Others relied on moral suasion. "The use of subscribers' telephones by transient customers," observed Metropolitan, was a "violation of the contract and a detriment to business."[107]

Neither threats nor moral suasion had much practical effect. Subscribers presumed that they had a right to use the telephone in any way they saw fit, and nonsubscribers felt no inhibition about using telephones that had been leased by neighbors or friends. The Chicago Telephone Company's repeated attempt to prevent nonsubscribers from using subscribers' telephones, reported one journalist in 1893, had had "no effect worth mentioning."[108]

Far different in his approach to the congestion problem was Edward J. Hall. Instead of damping down demand, Hall conceptualized measured service as a way to link price to cost. By 1881, Hall had instituted measured service at the Buffalo, New York, exchange. Instead of requiring subscribers to pay a fixed monthly rate, Hall charged a small rental fee, to which he added a 10-cent charge for every telephone call, with a minimum of 500 calls per year. Hall's rationale for measured service was straightforward: the most appropriate unit of service was not the telephone instrument, but the telephone call.[109] Hall recognized that measured service was a hard sell for telephone subscribers accustomed to flat rates. Yet he remained convinced that the "true system" was to "get money" for "every service" and "in proportion to the service."[110]

With measured service, the operating company had an incentive to promote telephone usage and the subscriber had a way to economize. With flat rates, the situation was reversed.[111] Operating companies, Hall believed, had a social obligation not only to subscribers, but also to the public. To meet this obligation, its management should do whatever it could to make telephone service "open and free"—provided it was paid for.[112] To encourage telephone use among nonsubscribers, Hall sold prepaid tickets that permitted the bearer to make a certain number of telephone calls. These tickets, mused one journalist in 1885, solved the "Telephone Dead Head Evil" while increasing popular awareness of the telephone as a "great convenience."[113] One further, and by no means incidental, advantage of measured service might be best described as political. As long as operating companies charged every subscriber an identical monthly fee, subscribers had an obvious rallying cry: keep the rate low. Measured service made it harder for subscribers to mobilize: it "spoilt the unanimity," Hall sardonically observed, with which telephone subscribers lobbied lawmakers to lower the rates.[114]

Measured service solved one of the most perplexing problems in the telephone business: namely, the unusual relationship between operating costs and network expansion. In most businesses, the cost of providing a unit of a good or service decreased as volume increased. In the telephone business, the relationship between costs and volume was reversed. As the network expanded, it became more rather than less expensive for the operating company to complete a telephone call. If an exchange doubled in size, the number of possible connections increased fourfold. To make these additional connections was expensive, entailing the upgrading of telephone switchboards and the retraining of telephone operators. The average subscriber, Hall had learned from "bitter experience," found the relationship of operating costs and network expansion incomprehensible. By linking prices to costs, measured service encouraged network expansion. If operating companies stuck with flat rates, they would find it necessary to raise rates to such a "stiff" level that subscribers would abandon the service.[115]

Measured service had the further advantage of transforming telephone-using nonsubscribers from liabilities into assets. The percentage of telephone calls that nonsubscribers made in a flat-rate exchange fluctuated, according to Hall's estimates, from 25 to 35 percent. Flat rates encouraged nonsubscribers to freely borrow subscribers' telephones, a practice that increased costs. As long as storekeepers paid a flat rate regardless of how many calls they made, they had little incentive to monitor the telephone usage of nonsubscribers, and nonsubscribers were "not apt to pay except with thanks."[116] To reduce the "dead-head business," Hall recommended that operating companies require users to pay a small fee for every single call. If they did, storekeepers would be less likely to permit nonsubscribers to use their telephone, since the storekeepers would have to foot the bill.[117]

Hall's experiment with measured service was a response to the complications occasioned in many cities by the consolidation of the previously rival and nonconnected telephone exchanges that had been operated by Western Union and National Bell. The "peculiar and unfortunate conditions" under which telephone service had been initially established had rendered most operating companies unprofitable, leaving little time for "deliberation or study" with regard to rates. Chicago operating company manager Charles N. Fay raised the rates; Hall shifted to measured service.[118]

Flat rates had the virtue of simplicity. They required minimal bookkeeping and no measurement equipment more sophisticated than a calendar. Measured service presupposed a more elaborate administrative apparatus. To determine what a subscriber owed, the company had to keep track of every single telephone call. To shift from flat rates to measured service would be a "nightmare," warned St. Louis operating company manager George F. Durant. In St. Louis, Durant had eliminated recordkeeping altogether: "We never have, and so far as we can see now, never will use a piece of paper in the office. That is what we are trying to avoid . . . we don't keep a record of anything."[119] If Hall wished to minimize the frustration that subscribers experienced when they failed to complete a connection, why not raise the rates? A rate increase was the best way to prevent the exchange from being congested, since it would keep the size of the exchange small and the service quality high for the subscribers who remained.[120]

Hall rejected Durant's logic. In lieu of limiting the size of the telephone exchange, Hall preferred to improve the ability of telephone operators to cope with the increased traffic that accompanied network expansion. District telegraph companies had long maintained a "post office system" of boxes in which operators deposited a ticket every time a subscriber requested that a task be performed. Telephone operating companies could establish an analogous "system" to keep track of outgoing calls. "If you have ever been in a post office and seen them distribute letters you will be able to imagine how rapidly an operator will distribute these tickets after becoming accustomed to it."[121]

Hall was proud of his success in Buffalo. The only subscribers to object to measured service were twenty lumber wholesalers who, in a fit of pique, temporarily ordered their telephones removed.[122] In other exchanges, opposition was more intense. Subscriber boycotts followed the switchover to measured service in many cities, including Rochester, New York, an exchange that fell within Hall's territory. Not until the 1890s would opposition to measured service diminish. And when it did, it was less because existing subscribers changed their minds than because operating companies cultivated a previously untapped market of small telephone users who had neither the desire—nor, in many instances, the means—to pay a high monthly fee.

The most important piece of equipment in a telephone exchange was not the telephone instrument, but the switchboard that operators used to complete connections. The switchboard was a large, expensive, and intricate machine that often cost more than the building in which it was located. In all but the smallest exchanges, it was custom-built. Few producer goods demanded greater technical skill or were more often upgraded.

Although a switchboard might seem to be a mere technical contrivance, in fact, it was a social innovation that had far-ranging implications for user-provider relations. The installation of large and complex switchboards in a big-city operating company gave it a first-mover advantage that new entrants ordinarily found impossible to match.

Every operating company operated at least one switchboard; the larger ones operated several. To speed the connection of calls inside an exchange, big-city operating companies "trunked" together switchboards located in switching centers scattered throughout the city. The Chicago exchange, for example, operated twelve different switching centers in 1899.[123] Subexchange switching centers were, confusingly, sometimes also called exchanges, even though telephone engineers regarded them as components of a single interactive system. This distinction was significant because telephone subscribers were highly sensitive to the speed with which operators connected calls that originated inside the exchange and the transfer of calls from one switching center to another slowed their completion.

Many operating companies operated more than one exchange. The Chicago Telephone Company operated exchanges not only in Chicago, but also in many cities and towns in the Chicago metropolitan area. In 1897, for example, the company operated exchanges in 109 cities and towns located in eight counties in Illinois and two counties in Indiana.[124] To place a call from one exchange to another required the payment of a toll. The completion of an interexchange connection was almost always slower, and sometimes much slower, than the completion of an intraexchange connection; this delay troubled few subscribers, since interexchange calls were comparatively rare.

Telephone switchboards were custom-made in industrial districts located in close proximity to big-city telephone operating companies. Most were manufactured in New York City and Chicago. Independent inventors located outside of these two industrial districts rarely had the necessary know-how to advance the state of the art. Not surprisingly, virtually every major telephone inventor lived in or near one of these two cities. The Chicago industrial district was a spawning ground for innovation. It was here that originated many, if not most, of the 900 patented inventions that American Bell owned in 1894, the year in which the second of Bell's fundamental telephone patents expired.[125]

Correspondence preserved in the archives of the law firm retained by the Chicago Telephone Company documents the intimate relationship between the operating company and its equipment supplier. A number of Chicago Telephone Company employees, including its general manager Angus Hibbard, had standing arrangements with American Bell to purchase any telephone-related inventions that they had devised. These arrangements had the effect of creating a thriving market in patentable inventions. For each invention that American Bell purchased, the Chicago Telephone Company employee obtained a modest honorarium, usually $50.[126] By 1903, one Chicago Telephone Company employee had submitted no fewer than sixty-five different patented inventions to headquarters.[127]

Switchboards fell into two broad groups: operator assisted and electromechanical. Operator-assisted switchboards required the intervention of at least one operator to complete a connection; for this reason, they were often called "manual." Electromechanical switchboards did not rely on operators, leading their enthusiasts to dub them "automatic." Electromechanical switchboards became commercially viable around 1900; they were soon installed in dozens of non-Bell, or independent, exchanges, large and small. To make a connection in an electromechanical exchange, callers had to know the number of the telephone with which they wished to connect; to make a call in a manual exchange, the caller simply rang up the operator with a verbal request. Bell operating companies sometimes operated electromechanical switchboards that they had acquired as a result of mergers with non-Bell operating companies. Yet in big cities like New York City and Chicago, they would not install electromechanical switchboards until after 1920.

Prior to 1920, every single telephone call that was completed in the New York City and Chicago Bell exchanges involved the real-time cooperation of at least three different people: the caller, the operator, and whoever picked up the telephone that the operator had connected. To complete a connection in the early 1880s sometimes required the cooperation of as many as five different people. Telephone operators communicated with each other by word-of-mouth or by circulating paper slips known as "tickets," in a manner reminiscent of the sorting methods devised for big-city post offices. The process was so clumsy and time-consuming that one journalist derided the telephone as old-fashioned. The telephone would never supplant the telegraph, since the telephone was labor-intensive and the age demanded machinery rather than men.[128]

The first telephone operators were young boys. They proved unsatisfactory and were soon replaced with unmarried women. Female telephone operators were less likely than young boys to loiter, curse, or bully telephone subscribers, most of whom were men. Carrie Meeber, the fictional heroine of Theodore Dreiser's novel, *Sister Carrie*, dreamed of a career as an actress. Yet for the many women like Carrie who flocked to the country's big cities in search of a better life, a position as a telephone operator was one of the best jobs to which they could realistically aspire.[129]

To reduce the call-connection delay, telephone engineers invented an ingenious machine known as the "multiple" switchboard. The first multiple switchboard was built by Western Electric in Chicago for the Metropolitan Telephone Company in New York City.[130] It was installed in 1884, at a time when the company had 4,600 subscribers.[131] The multiple switchboard was a manual switchboard. Its "fundamental idea," explained one telephone manager, was the minimization of the physical exertion necessary to complete a call. No longer would operators repeat instructions by tickets or word of mouth.[132] Henceforth, they would complete a connection without leaving their stools. In practice, the maximum size of a multiple switchboard was around 10,000 lines, since this was the largest number of lines that a seated operator could connect by stretching her arms.[133] If an exchange operated more than 10,000 lines, operators would "trunk" from one multiple switchboard to the next. This procedure required the intervention of at least one additional operator to complete the connection.

For a multiple switchboard to work effectively, operators needed a quick and easy way to ensure that the telephone a caller wished to reach was not already in use. To minimize the call-connection delay, telephone engineers devised a feedback mechanism that was known as the "click test," "busy test," or "busy signal." A high percentage of early telephones were in almost continuous use, making the busy signal an especially vital refinement. "On its efficiency," declared telephone engineer Kempster Miller in 1899, depended to a "great extent" the "operativeness" of the multiple switchboard.[134]

The multiple switchboard reduced the call-connection delay in every operating company in which it had been installed. Prior to its installation, the delay could be considerable. In Chicago, the call-connection delay for a local connection was five minutes in 1882; it remained forty-five seconds as late as 1887.[135] The delay remained high in certain exchanges even after multiple switchboards had been installed: in New York City, for example, it remained around forty seconds as late as 1896.[136] By 1900, the delay in Chicago had been reduced to a mere 6.2 seconds. Telephone engineers claimed that no electromechanical switchboard could match this time if one factored in the time it took to dial up the number.[137]

Like so many technical advances in telephone equipment, the multiple switchboard was the product of a fruitful collaboration between Western Electric and the big-city Bell operating companies. The Chicago Telephone Company played a pivotal role in this collaboration. Engineers at the Chicago Telephone Company and Western Electric worked together to introduce a variety of technical refinements that included the multiple switchboard, electric signal lights, and the busy signal.[138] Operating company–equipment manufacturer links, reflected Vail in 1909, had been essential to the "thousand and one little patents" that Bell owned for the "valuable auxiliary apparatus" that had made the telephone a commercial success.[139]

That Chicago did not have the first multiple switchboard was in a sense surprising. The multiple switchboard that Western Electric installed for Metropolitan's switchboard had been designed in Chicago in consultation with Chicago Telephone Company engineers. Western Electric had tried to sell a multiple switchboard to Chicago Telephone but had been rebuffed by its general manager, Charles N. Fay. Fay preferred a non-multiple switchboard of his own design, and so the Chicago Telephone Company would not install its first multiple switchboard until after Fay's resignation in 1887. Why Fay rejected the multiple switchboard is a matter of speculation. He may well have regarded it as overly complicated and unduly expensive: Fay saw little reason to increase the number of telephones in his exchange to serve the larger and more heterogeneous market for which the multiple switchboard had been designed.

American Bell often purchased inventions patented by outside inventors. The steady stream of inventions generated by the Chicago Telephone Company underscored the existence of an in-house engineering tradition that a later generation of telephone managers would mistakenly credit to Theodore N. Vail following his appointment as president of American Telephone and Telegraph in 1907.[140]

Patent rights, observed telephone expert Herbert Laws Webb in 1892, had been the "nucleus" of the telephone business, but they were not the "key-stone" of the "telephonic arch." The keystone, rather, was the multiple switchboard, an intricate machine that was being constantly upgraded to meet the demand for higher performance standards. For the Bell operating companies, switchboard upgrades became a functional substitute for the patent protection that they lost following the expiration of Alexander Graham Bell's telephone patents in 1894. "No other public service" was "liable" to the "upheavals" occasioned by switchboard upgrades; none was the object of such "constant modification."[141]

The multiple switchboard protected the single greatest asset that an incumbent operating company possessed: its subscriber list. The value of telephone service increased as the size of its exchange expanded, explained American Bell critic Grosvenor P. Lowrey in 1893. If an additional user was hooked up to a gas plant or water works, the value of the service to existing users remained the same. If an additional subscriber contracted with a telephone exchange for telephone service, the value of the service for existing subscribers increased. As a consequence, incumbents were extremely hard to dislodge: first on the scene, they had typically signed up the most coveted subscribers. "Telephone service" was in this way "essentially different" from any other municipal franchise corporation with which it might be compared: "Forty gas, water, or electric-light companies may lay pipes in my street," Lowrey elaborated, "and I may be equally well served with gas or water or electric light by any of them. The value of a telephone in my house is based on the subscription list of the company. The instrument of a company with 1,000 subscribers is twice as valuable to me as that of a company with only 500 subscribers. An instrument becomes less valuable according to the inability to connect with some one that I want to reach."[142]

The Bell operating companies enjoyed a formidable position following the expiration of Bell's second patent in 1894 for two main reasons. The first was the construction of a long-distance telephone network linking the various Bell telephone exchanges into an interconnected network; the second was the entrenchment of Bell operating companies in the nation's largest cites. Politics had artifacts: patent law fostered the construction of a long-distance telephone network, and municipal franchise law promoted the construction of consolidated telephone exchanges. American Bell's cultivation of an ongoing relationship between operating companies and equipment manufacturers distinguished it from the loose federation of telegraph operating companies that Amos Kendall had coordinated for Samuel F. B. Morse and helps explain why Bell became a first mover and Morse did not.

Consolidation was well underway by the time the second of Alexander Graham Bell's patents expired in 1894. It would accelerate beginning around 1900, when, in response to the threat of new entrants and the specter of municipal ownership, big-city operating companies transformed the telephone from a specialty service for an exclusive clientele into a mass service for the entire population. The anticompetitive logic of the consolidationist political economy would not be seriously challenged until Congress abolished telephone franchise monopolies in the Telecommunications Act of 1996, ending a relationship between city and corporation that went all the way back to the opening of the first telephone exchange in 1878.

7

TELEPHOMANIA

The greedy and extortionate nature of the telephone monopoly
is notorious. Controlling a means of communication which has
now become indispensable to the business and social life of the
country, the company takes advantage of the public's need to
force from it every year an extortionate tribute.

New York Times, 1886

The hostility of telephone subscribers toward telephone operating companies in the 1880s was pervasive. Telephone subscribers boycotted telephone service in several cities, lawmakers introduced bills to institute
telephone rate caps in many states, and journalists derided telephone
corporations as unprincipled monopolists in every part of the country in
which operating companies had been established. The "wave" of popular
hostility toward Bell and its operating companies had become a "tele-
phomania," complained Chicago Telephone Company general manager
Charles N. Fay in 1886.[1] Part of the problem, in Fay's view, originated
with lawmakers and journalists. Yet the main culprit was the telephone
subscriber. The "ordinary businessman" who subscribed to telephone
service was a "'telephomaniac'"—the "only fit word" to describe an individual so lacking in gratitude toward the telephone corporation that
he had the temerity to complain about the rates it charged and the performance standards it maintained.[2]

The nadir in Bell's corporate reputation came in 1888. In that year,
Supreme Court Chief Justice Morrison Waite affirmed the legality of
Alexander Graham Bell's telephone patent rights. Waite's ruling guaranteed that Bell would retain its legal monopoly of the telephone business until January 1894, when the second of Bell's telephone patents
expired.

Journalists greeted Waite's ruling with contempt. The prevailing senti- ment in New York City and Chicago was aptly summarized in the cap- tion of a pointed cartoon by Grant E. Hamilton that ran in the New York City–based satirical magazine *Judge:* "In the Clutch of a Grasping Monopoly." Hamilton's cartoonist depicted the "Bell Telephone Mo- nopoly" as a wily spider that had entrapped the city's telephone subscrib- ers in tentacles labeled "trickery," "undue influence," "extortion," "brib- ery," and "bribed official." Although telephone service was local, Bell's political influence was nationwide: With Waite's ruling, the spider's shadow extended all the way to the Capitol in Washington, D.C. The victims of the monopoly were not the many but the few. In fact, every one of the subscribers whom Hamilton depicted was a businessman: a banker, a broker, a manufacturer, a grocer, a dry goods merchant, a druggist, a doctor, a produce merchant, a liveryman, an importer, and a hotelkeeper.[3]

Telephone subscribers were not as powerless as Hamilton's cartoon implied. In addition to organizing subscriber boycotts, they backed rival network providers, lobbied for legislatively mandated rate caps, and endorsed the establishment of permanent regulatory commissions. The cumulative impact of these initiatives was substantial. By demon- strating the vulnerability of operating companies to legislative interven- tion, they goaded a new generation of telephone managers into provid- ing telephone service to thousands of potential telephone users whom their predecessors had ignored. The popularization of the telephone was the result.

The popularization of the telephone was an outcome that neither op- erating companies nor telephone subscribers intended. Operating com- panies feared its economic cost and technical challenge. Telephone sub- scribers warned that popularization would degrade the performance standards to which they had become accustomed. A small percentage of subscribers had come to recognize the advantages of network expan- sion. Yet few were willing to pay for the privilege.

The single most contentious issue dividing telephone subscribers and telephone operating companies in the 1880s concerned the rates oper- ating companies charged. Telephone subscribers recognized that Bell was raking in huge profits and resented having to pay the high prices that operating companies demanded. A frequent catalyst for subscriber

IN THE CLUTCH OF A GRASPING MONOPOLY.

The high rates that Bell telephone companies charged big-city subscribers in the 1880s sparked public outrage in large cities throughout the United States. In this ominous cartoon, Bell was depicted as a grasping spider that had manipulated the political process to victimize telephone users. Grant E. Hamilton, "In the Clutch of a Grasping Monopoly," *Judge* 14 (April 7, 1888): 16.

discontent was the determination of operating companies to shift their calling plans from flat rates to measured service. Flat-rate calling plans charged subscribers a single "flat" annual fee for an unlimited number of calls in a spatially delimited zone, whereas measured service calling plans charged subscribers for every single call. The flashpoint was not the shift from flat rates to measured service. If measured service had been a focal point for subscriber discontent, it would be hard to explain why, in the following decades, thousands of big-city telephone subscribers made this shift from flat rates to measured service without complaint. The crux of the controversy, rather, lay in the presumption that the shift to measured service would increase the subscribers' telephone bill. Subscribers resented the sum that operating companies demanded for flat-rate service, but what they feared even more was the seemingly unlimited potential for rate hikes concealed by measured service.

In the 1880s, several big-city operating companies experimented with measured service. Among them were the Bell licensees in Boston, San Francisco, Buffalo, Pittsburgh, Indianapolis, Washington, D.C., and Rochester, New York. Measured service succeeded in Buffalo and San Francisco but failed in every other major city in which it was attempted. Not until the 1890s would measured service gain widespread acceptance. For operating companies, measured service fended off legislatively mandated rate caps; for city dwellers, it extended the market for telephone service to the large number of individuals who were unable or unwilling to pay the hefty flat-rate fee.

The opposition of telephone subscribers to rate hikes led to subscriber boycotts that were commonly referred to as "strikes." The term "strike" has come to be associated primarily with a work stoppage; in the 1880s, its meaning was broader. A corporation could be struck not only by workers, but also by consumers and even lawmakers. A consumers' strike was a boycott; a lawmakers' strike was extortion.

The first well-publicized subscriber boycott began in Washington, D.C., in April 1881 when 300 of the city's 700 telephone subscribers organized a "Telephone Subscribers' Protective Association" to contest the recent switchover to measured service. Like most organizations of telephone subscribers, the subscribers' association was an ad hoc advocacy group rather than a self-perpetuating organization. Since every subscriber paid an identical rate, it was relatively easy to rally support. The boycott lasted twelve days; it ended when the company abandoned measured service and restored flat rates.[4] Similar boycotts followed soon thereafter in Pittsburgh and Indianapolis. Each had the same denoue-ment: the operating company abandoned measured service.[5]

The longest and most bitterly contested subscribers' boycott occurred in Rochester, New York. The boycott lasted nineteen months: it began in November 1886 and was not resolved until May 1888. Of the city's 950 telephone subscribers, over 700 signed a pledge to "hang up" their tele-phones. At the peak of the boycott in October 1887, 800 subscribers had signed on. Hiram Sibley had obtained pledges from the merchants of Rochester in the 1850s to help him build up Western Union. The tele-phone boycotters in the 1880s relied once again on collective action—this time to obtain a rate cut. Almost no one violated the pledge, render-ing telephone service "practically useless" for well over a year.[6]

The organizers of the Rochester boycott styled themselves the "People's Telephone Association." Despite its expansive name, the As-sociation had no interest in popularizing telephone service. Its goals were instead to reduce rates and improve performance standards for existing subscribers, who consisted primarily of the city's business elite. Toward this end, it negotiated on behalf of Rochester telephone sub-scribers with the Bell Telephone Company of Buffalo, the operating company whose jurisdiction included the Rochester exchange.

The boycotters' frustration with the operating company was visceral. "We don't want the useless thing around," exploded one boycotter in a letter to a company official in which he requested the removal of its tele-phone from his office: "Anything connected with the Bell Telephone Co. is undesirable and an eye-sore." Please do not reply, the boycotter added: "Get out of town as soon as you possibly can, give us a rest."[7] To test the boycotters' resolve, one newspaper editor made an experimental tele-phone call. When the boycotters learned about the test, they warned the editor that, should he persist, they would prevail upon local merchants to stop advertising in his newspaper.[8]

The irony of a boycott led by wealthy businessmen was not lost on one Rochester laborer. Had the boycott been organized by telephone operators, the laborer sardonically observed, the same men who had "plugged" their telephones to keep them from being used would have felt no hesitation in calling out the militia to break the strike.[9]

The catalyst for the boycott was the determination of operating com-pany manager Edward J. Hall to switch Rochester telephone subscribers from flat rates to measured service. Hall had successfully introduced measured service in Buffalo and assumed that he could duplicate his success in Rochester. Measured service had the endorsement of many Bell insiders, including telephone inventor Alexander Graham Bell. "I see no other equitable plan," Bell informed a journalist, when asked about the situation in Rochester, "than to charge so much per message."[10] Many of the conversations that flat rates encouraged were "useless and unnecessary": "Servants gossip over it to their friends; people call up their neighbors many times when they would not do so if they were charged a certain sum every time they did so."[11]

The elimination of measured service troubled Rochester telephone subscribers in part because of the extent to which they had come to regard the telephone as a social medium. For the boycotters, measured service was an unwarranted intrusion by the telephone company into the household. As long as flat rates prevailed, one boycotter saw nothing wrong with permitting his children to use his telephone to call their friends. Yet if he had to pay 10 cents for every outgoing call, he would stop this practice immediately. It was outlandish, the boycotter explained, for the company to presume that it could deny him the right to permit his neighbors to use his telephone whenever he wished. "I am glad to accommodate my neighbor in this as in any other way, and it is none of the company's business."[12]

Measured service was the catalyst for the boycott, but it was by no means the subscribers' only grievance. Subscribers also objected to the threatened alternative: an increase in the basic flat rate. Other grievances included the presence of overhead wires on their city's boulevards, which subscribers deplored as unsightly and dangerous, and the absence of local control. The headquarters of the Rochester operating company was located not in Rochester, but in Buffalo. How could this be, Rochesterians wondered, in a city that had not only attained an impressive reputation as a "scientific center," but that had given birth to Western Union? Should not the businessmen of Rochester band together once again to build up a communications corporation of "national importance"?[13]

The operating company's position worsened when the Rochester city council denied it the right-of-way licenses it needed to expand and hinted that it might even pull down its wires as a nuisance under common law. "There was a strong popular impression," Hall informed Bell vice president John E. Hudson, that Bell's Rochester company had no legal rights.[14] To complicate matters, a rival group of telephone promoters was actively lobbying city officials to grant it a franchise.[15] These promoters had purchased the rights to a telephone that had been purportedly invented in Wisconsin by Sylvanus D. Cushman in 1851. It was "perfectly evident," Hall told Hudson, that the Rochester telephone subscribers were "simply being 'worked'" by promoters intent on developing "some opposition scheme."[16]

To end the impasse, Bell President William H. Forbes delegated David B. Parker to negotiate with the boycotters. Parker succeeded where Hall failed. Although Parker did not guarantee the boycotters a permanent rate cap, he did promise the speedy burial of overhead wires, a five-year moratorium on measured service, and the appointment of at least one Rochesterian to the operating company's board.[17]

Parker charmed everyone he met and was praised by a Rochester journalist as the "shrewdest and sharpest man in the telephone company."[18] Parker's effectiveness owed something to his personal background. Hailing as he did from nearby Jamestown, New York, he well understood the moralism of Rochester's business elite. An additional resource was his previous work experience. Before Parker had signed on with Bell, he had worked for many years as a high-level administrator in the Post Office Department, an experience that gave him many opportunities to hone his skills in resolving arcane and seemingly intractable disputes.

Metropolitan president Theodore N. Vail greeted the settlement of the Rochester boycott with relief. Troubled by the boycott, the New York legislature had decided to hold hearings on the telephone business that Vail feared might result in the enactment of a statewide rate cap. The Indiana State Supreme Court had recently declared a legislatively mandated rate cap to be constitutional; the New York courts might too. New York City telephone subscribers paid a flat rate of $150 a year. If the New York legislature followed Indiana's lead, it could destroy the exchange.

Vail found it particularly exasperating that a Bell official in Boston had clumsily intervened by suing Cushman for patent infringement. At the very moment that it seemed as if the dispute might be resolved, the Bell official had "created an excitement" that inflamed public opinion and ended the possibility of the "truce" that had been "pending."[19]

No user boycott occurred in New York City or Chicago, which then were the country's two largest telephone exchanges. Yet frustration at Bell in both cities was intense. Chicago telephone subscribers had been angered by high rates and poor service ever since Chicago Telephone's general manager Charles N. Fay had raised the annual flat rate to $125 a year following the consolidation of the Western Union and Bell exchanges in 1881. Only in New York City did subscribers pay more. Subscribers in both cities regarded telephone rates as extortionate and blamed not only the local operating company, but also its absentee owner, American Bell.

Chicago Telephone was run like a proprietorship. Fay regarded his operational autonomy as absolute: he assumed, for example, that he could charge whatever he pleased. If his subscribers disapproved, they could cancel their service. The fact that the Chicago market was uncontested made no difference. The city council had the authority to license a rival; if it did not, this was not the company's fault. "What we make," explained Fay in a tart interview with a reporter in December 1887, was "nobody's business but ourselves." Fay's indifference to subscriber discontent was paralleled by his rejection of the still novel idea that the value of telephone service for telephone subscribers increased as the size of its network expanded. Fay demurred: If he reduced the size of his subscription list from 5,000 to 1,000 by quadrupling its rates from $125 to $500, he presumed that he could still make a profit while maintaining a performance standard "absolutely satisfactory" to the subscribers the company retained. No one told department store magnate Marshall Field what prices he should charge his customers; what gave anyone the right to propose a rate cap for the telephone business?[20]

Fay's insistence on his company's right to set its own rates struck the reporter who recorded his interview as outrageous. To drive the point home, the reporter compared Fay to the railroad magnate William H. Vanderbilt. When Vanderbilt had recently been asked by a Chicago reporter if he had an obligation to the public to operate a high-speed express train for the Post Office Department, Vanderbilt curtly replied, "the public be damned." Fay viewed Chicago Telephone through a parallel lens. That "settles the question," explained the reporter, paraphrasing Fay: "'The public be ——!' We will tax the business all it will bear and you can go to thunder!"[21]

Fay's remarks prompted the *Chicago Tribune* to investigate telephone conditions in Chicago. The *Tribune* polled 500 businesses; over 350 replied, a very high response rate for a user survey. Ninety-eight percent of the respondents found telephone rates to be too high; over 90 percent expressed dissatisfaction with the company's performance standards; and 70 percent believed that the maximum rate should be no more than

$60 per year. To lend credibility to its survey, the *Tribune* reprinted verbatim a large number of detailed subscriber complaints. Fay had no right to contend, the *Tribune* editorialized, that Chicago Telephone could charge whatever it pleased. Marshall Field had rivals; Chicago Telephone did not.[22]

Emboldened by subscriber discontent, the city council enacted an ordinance banning Chicago Telephone from stringing additional telephone wires either overhead or underground.[23] The city council ban prevented the company not only from soliciting new business, but also from continuing service for existing subscribers who had changed their address. Subscriber dissatisfaction mounted when Chicagoans learned that Chief Justice Waite had upheld the validity of Alexander Graham Bell's telephone patents. Shortly thereafter—and almost certainly in a direct response to the court's ruling—the council granted a franchise to Cushman, the first credible rival that it had permitted to enter Chicago since the Western Union–Bell settlement in 1879.[24] Cushman was a telephone equipment manufacturer headquartered in Chicago. Like many Chicago businesses, it enjoyed a close relationship with city officials: among its investors was the city treasurer.[25] The Cushman franchise granted the company rights-of-way in return for the stipulation that it would provide subscribers with unlimited local telephone service for $75 a year, which was $50 less than the $125 charged by Chicago Telephone.

The Cushman franchise strengthened the resolve of Chicago Telephone subscribers to lower telephone rates. The St. Louis city council had recently mandated that the St. Louis telephone company reduce its rates 50 percent, from $100 to $50.[26] Although this mandate would soon be countermanded by the state legislature, no one knew this outcome at the time. Fortified with the news from St. Louis and emboldened by the willingness of a credible rival to provide flat-rate telephone service for no more than $75, 3,000 telephone subscribers—almost half the subscribers in the city—petitioned the city council to institute an identical rate cap for Chicago Telephone.[27]

To capitalize on the situation, the city council proposed a new franchise for Chicago Telephone to replace the franchise that it had earlier granted American Bell. One provision of the proposed new franchise was a $75 rate cap modeled on the rate cap in the Cushman franchise.[28] Had Chicago Telephone accepted this proposed franchise, its assent would have significantly altered the balance of power between the city, the company, and the company's subscribers. Yet the company refused. The city lacked the authority to set a rate cap, concluded Chicago Telephone's president George L. Phillips, after consulting with one of the city's lawyers. In place of the proposed franchise that the city council enacted, Phillips drafted a proposed franchise of his own—which, predictably—was more advantageous to the company.[29]

Phillips's refusal to accept the city council's proposal infuriated the city's telephone subscribers. In response, they organized yet another petition drive. Over 5,500 Chicagoans signed on. This was an extraordinary total, given the fact that at the time the telephone company had only 5,000 subscribers.[30] No crisis that telephone executives confronted in the twentieth century—not the takeover of the telephone network by the federal executive during the First World War; not the telephone operator strikes of 1919; and not even the court-ordered breakup of the Bell System in 1984—occurred in a political economy that was more resolutely adversarial than the crisis that Chicago Telephone confronted in 1888.

Just as the company confronted angry subscribers, so too did the city council. At more or less precisely the same time that the 5,500 Chicagoans protested Phillips's recalcitrance, 400 telephone subscribers petitioned the city to repeal its ban on wire stringing. The subscribers had recently relocated, and the ban prevented them from obtaining telephone service.[31]

The telephone subscribers' protest was led by William Bodemann, a retail druggist who leased a telephone in his store. Druggists were among the heaviest telephone users in the city. Of the 5,000 telephones in Chicago, druggists rented 500. If the city found it impossible to negotiate a franchise more favorable to telephone subscribers than the "monstrously unjust" one that Phillips proposed, Bodemann urged his fellow druggists to boycott the company and "order out" their telephones.[32] The threatened boycott was not to be confined to druggists or even telephone subscribers. Rather, Bodemann proposed that it extend to every property owner affronted by the "defacement and dangers" of the company's overhead wires, the "vandalism" of the contractors hired by the company to bury its wires underground, and the "grasping and unscrupulous" attempt of its president to overawe the city council through "persuasion, influence, and intimidation."[33]

The franchise fight ended in January 1889, with the signing by Chicago Telephone of a compromise franchise. Chicago Telephone could not hold out forever. It had made a huge investment in its physical plant, and the city council had declared it illegal to transfer to Chicago Telephone the original franchise that the city council had granted to American Bell. The city council also feared a continuation of the standoff. Chicagoans had adapted to the telephone more readily than Rochesterians. Bodemann's threatened boycott would have been enormously disruptive. Even a weeklong boycott would have caused a major disruption to lumber wholesalers and other heavy users for whom the telephone had become second nature. The city council ban on wire stringing had proved controversial; a boycott would prove equally divisive.

The new franchise included concessions for each contending party. To mollify the city council, the franchise required the company to pay 3 percent of its gross earnings to the city. To appease telephone users, it limited the length of the franchise to twenty years. To earn the company's approval, it did not mandate a rate cap. Instead, it stipulated that the company would not increase the "rates for telephone service now established" for its "present or future subscribers." This phrase had been carefully crafted to be deliberately ambiguous. Telephone company lawyers interpreted the qualifier "now established" to modify "telephone service," and, thus, to deny that the city council had capped rates, since it left the company free to charge a higher rate if it made a service upgrade. In contrast, telephone subscribers contended that the qualifier "now established" modified "rates" and, thus, that the company had no right to charge more than the $125 it currently charged for flat-rate service, no matter what upgrades it might make. The ambiguity remained unresolved until 1902, when an Illinois judge defied Bell and sided with the subscribers.[34]

The specter of a state-mandated rate cap haunted the managers of the Bell operating companies in the 1880s. Among the states in which rate caps found their way onto the legislative agenda were Massachusetts, New York, Ohio, Indiana, Illinois, Iowa, and Missouri. The only state that actually enacted a rate cap was Indiana, though no one could predict what the future might bring.

The conduct of the Massachusetts legislature was revealing of trends nationwide. If any state should have been solicitous to Bell, it should have been Massachusetts. American Bell held a Massachusetts charter, and a majority of Bell shareholders hailed from the state. Yet Massachusetts had a long tradition of regulatory activism, and, in the end, it was this tradition that prevailed. Massachusetts had established the first state railroad commission in 1869 and the first state commission to regulate municipal gas works in 1885. And once the state undertook the regulation of gas works, it seemed to many that the regulation of telephone exchanges could not be far behind. Both gas works and telephone exchanges were municipal franchise corporations, and neither faced much competition. A short-lived user group—the Telephone Subscriber's Union—endorsed commission regulation as early as 1885; their proposal was a "polite way," as one journalist put it, "of saying 'reduce.' "[35] The Massachusetts legislature's "constant interference" in the company's affairs, brooded Bell president William H. Forbes in 1886, in conjunction with a threatened court challenge to Bell's patents, had prompted him to sell his own holdings in the operating company that did business in the state.[36]

Bell executives found the Massachusetts legislature's conduct so troubling that they hired Walter S. Allen to monitor government–business relations. Allen was a protegé of Charles Francis Adams Jr., a business leader well known as the father of the Massachusetts railroad commission. Trained as an engineer at MIT, Allen served as secretary of the Massachusetts gas commission in the 1880s. Allen brought to the telephone business a vast knowledge not only of municipal franchise law, but also of the history of regulatory activism dating back to the founding of the republic. The "great mass" of the people, Allen observed candidly in 1914, believed that municipal franchise corporations were "desirous only" of "squeezing as much money as possible out of their patrons" and had only a "slight regard for the wishes of the users in regard to the service given." This belief was unfortunate, since no other kind of business touched the lives of the people more directly. In addition, it complicated the task of resolving the inherent conflict between the doctrine of "individual freedom" that legitimated the competitive political economy that had emerged in the mid-nineteenth-century and the even older doctrine that lawmakers should regulate every business in accordance with the will of a sovereign power.[37]

Proponents of legislative intervention received a boost with the publication in 1888 of Edward Bellamy's immensely popular utopian novel *Looking Backward*. Bellamy endorsed the nationalization not only of the telegraph, but also of the telephone, as did the many "Nationalist Clubs" that sprang up to champion his ideas.[38] Nationalism appealed even to telephone insiders: among its enthusiasts was Thomas A. Watson, Alexander Graham Bell's partner in his early telephone experiments.[39]

The expiration of the second of Bell's two telephone patents in January 1894 further emboldened Massachusetts lawmakers who were critical of Bell. In the absence of government ownership, warned a joint resolution of the Massachusetts House and Senate, the telephone was likely to remain a monopoly no less burdensome than the telegraph.[40] To endure a patent monopoly was bad enough; to perpetuate a monopoly after its patent rights had expired was intolerable. Although the Massachusetts legislature permitted American Bell to increase its capitalization to $50 million, it required it to sell new shares at the same price at which existing shares were trading, rather than at their much lower par value. If any shared remained unsold, American Bell had to sell them at auction. In so doing, lawmakers guarded against the possibility that insiders might emulate Gould and obtain windfall profits.[41] As a further slap to American Bell, a Massachusetts court had previously voided a valuable microphone patent that Bell had acquired from Emile Berliner. The Berliner decision was soon overturned on appeal. Even so, it sent an unambiguous signal to would-be telephone equipment manufacturers that the courts would not permit American Bell to rely on patent law to thwart its rivals.[42] The Massachusetts legislature finally asserted its control over telephone rates in 1906, when it augmented the jurisdiction of the state highway commission to all corporations that were engaged in the "transmission of intelligence by electricity."[43] The reconstitution of the railroad commission as a "public service commission" followed in 1913.[44]

The first and only statewide rate cap to be enacted before the twentieth century was instituted by the Indiana state legislature in April 1885. Henceforth, the legislature decreed, no Indiana-based telephone operating company could charge more than $3 per month for a telephone rental or 15 cents for the first five minutes of a toll call within the state.[45] The rate cap was the brainchild of Samuel Wardell Williams, a lawmaker popularly known as "Telephone Sam."[46] Whether Williams intended the bill to pass is uncertain. Fay insinuated that Williams had intended it to fail, as was common with bills of this kind, but had changed his mind when telephone lobbyists refused to pay him off to let the matter drop.[47] Whatever Williams's motives, his bill became law. The Bell operating company for Indiana, Central Union, challenged the law's constitutionality, and the case found its way to the Indiana Supreme Court, which upheld it.

The test case involved a telephone subscriber who lived four and a half miles from Central Union's Indianapolis telephone exchange. Prior to the rate cap, the subscriber paid $33.50 per quarter to be connected to the exchange, a rate higher than the rate paid by subscribers living closer to the city center. The company justified the rate by pointing to the additional cost of maintaining the line. Following the rate cap, the subscriber briefly agreed to pay the premium. Three months later, the subscriber changed his mind and sued the company for charging him more than the legislatively mandated maximum of $12 per quarter.[48] The court sided with the subscriber and ordered the company to lower its rate. The telephone, it ruled, was a "common carrier of news," making it a legitimate object of regulation.[49]

The Indiana rate cap met with a withering attack from Forbes. The federal government had granted American Bell patent rights, and the Indiana legislature had no authority to contest them. The "peculiar value" of American Bell "wholly depends" on its patents, and the courts should not permit a state government to destroy property that the patent system had created.[50] Rate caps were not only illegal, but also inexpedient, because they slowed the construction of a "complete working system" of telephone exchanges throughout the United States.[51] The fact that Bell enjoyed a de facto monopoly over the telephone business was beside the point. Monopoly was the "very essence" and "lifeblood" of patent law, elaborated a like-minded business journalist; to contend that a patent holder was a monopolist was "simply to say that he is exactly what the law intended he should be."[52]

To discourage other states from following Indiana's example, American Bell teamed up with Central Union to punish Indianans for the temerity of challenging its prerogatives. When Central Union's executive committee learned that the rate cap would not be overturned, it voted unanimously to close every exchange in the state, with the exception of those exchanges that could be operated with profit on measured service, or what it termed the "toll plan."[53] In the next few months, Central Union closed two-thirds of its Indiana exchanges, including almost every exchange in towns and cities along the Ohio River. Overall, the number of telephones in Indiana declined by half.[54] When 500 subscribers in Indianapolis banded together and refused to pay the new rates, Central Union threatened to remove the telephones of the "striking" subscribers.[55]

When Central Union departed, Cushman moved in. The first Cushman exchanges were installed in small towns and moderately sized cities. This was a prudent decision, since the rate cap had rendered the provisioning of telephone service in the larger cities unremunerative.

To simplify the task of collecting damages while discouraging Indianans from signing up, American Bell collaborated with Central Union to sue individual Cushman subscribers for patent infringement. In Elkhart, Indiana, for example, Bell sued fifty-one Cushman subscribers for illegally using telephones that relied on equipment to which American Bell held the patent rights without paying licensing fees to American Bell. American Bell instituted similar lawsuits in La Porte, a town in which Cushman had not only established an exchange, but had also supplanted an operating company once operated by Central Union.[56]

Despite this legal harassment, Cushman persisted. Cushman lawyers contended that Bell had vacated the territory and, therefore, that Cushman had a right to provide telephone service even if its equipment infringed on American Bell's patent rights. The possibility that Cushman might become a credible rival to Central Union would not be dashed until a judge ruled that Cushman's infringement on American Bell's patent rights could not be excused even if Bell had withdrawn from the locality in which the infringement had occurred.[57] All in all, Cushman was said to have withstood 200 lawsuits until it finally succumbed.[58] To leave no doubt as to the illegality of Cushman's conduct, a judge was reputed to have ordered the burning of the Cushman switchboard in the La Porte, Indiana, town square.[59]

Bell may have won in the courts, but it lost in the court of public opinion: telephone subscribers throughout Indiana condemned Bell's conduct. In Indianapolis, telephone subscribers boycotted the Central Union exchange. The revulsion toward Bell was so great that its lawyers warned against appealing the Indiana Supreme Court ruling that had legalized the rate cap. The Indianapolis boycott was in "such energetic and competent hands," explained two Chicago lawyers close to the scene, that Bell was best advised to stand pat. If it challenged the rate cap, the Indianapolis city council might well rescind the franchise that it had granted the Bell operating company in Indianapolis, and lead to the "breaking up" of the exchange, the largest in the state.[60]

Although the Indiana pullout was controversial, it had the desired effect. No other state legislature instituted a rate cap, and lawmakers in several states, including New York, cited the failure of the Indiana rate cap as a warning of what might happen in their state if they did.[61] The rate cap had proved disastrous, gloated one operating company manager, and would serve as a warning to other states not to emulate Indiana's example.[62] It was "mischievous," observed Forbes dryly in his 1886 annual report, since it had stopped the "steady improvement" of telephone service in Indiana and aroused a strong popular sentiment for its repeal.[63] Even journalists unsympathetic to Bell agreed that it had failed. The Bell "boycott" had defeated the Indiana rate cap, reported one Chicago journalist, though it was hardly a "gratifying state of affairs" when a state legislature did nothing to forestall a "corporate monopoly" from suspending a "public service" unless it was permitted to exact the "most exorbitant rates."[64]

The Indiana legislature repealed its rate cap in 1889. When it did, Central Union agreed to reinstitute flat rates and "do away with" the "obnoxious toll system" that it had instituted in several exchanges.[65] The failure of the Indiana rate cap would put to an end the "injudicious" and "often malicious" rate legislation that was currently under consideration in many states, predicted one pro-Bell journalist.[66] The journalist was mistaken. In fact, a major push for a rate cap was just getting underway in New York. To take advantage of Bell's withdrawal from La Porte, Cushman installed an electromechanical switchboard, the world's first. Not until after 1920 would Bell install electromechanical switchboards in New York City or Chicago. Yet the La Porte exchange pointed the way toward the future.[67]

Few Bell staffers in the 1880s commented publicly on pending legislation. Forbes summarized the political situation in his annual reports for American Bell and Vail gave occasional interviews to reporters. Yet neither published essays under his own name in general-circulation magazines like the *North American Review*—as had, for example, Western Union president Norvin Green. Neither Metropolitan nor Chicago Telephone published annual reports, and the few operating companies that did were cautious in their pronouncements.

A notable exception was Charles N. Fay. The best way to protect telephone operating companies from legislative intervention, Fay maintained, was not to ignore it, but to give it the widest possible publicity. Long before the muckraking journalist Lincoln Steffens documented the "shame of the cities," Fay cast a spotlight on the extortionate practices of city councils and state legislatures. Telephone operating companies should no longer "sneak and dodge behind trees." The most serious challenge that they confronted came not from self-professed radicals, but from greedy—and resolutely nonideological—lawmakers who floated punitive "strike" bills in the expectation that they would be paid off by corporate lobbyists to ensure that they failed.[68] In 1871 the Illinois state legislature had enacted a law capping the rates that grain warehouses could charge; several years later the Supreme Court upheld the rate cap in a landmark case known as *Munn v. Illinois*. That the Illinois state legislature might institute an analogous rate cap for telephone operating companies seemed entirely possible. The time-honored method of defeating unwelcome legislation was to pay off the lawmakers. Only if this failed would the press expose their corruption.

The corruptibility of lawmakers posed a special problem for telephone operating companies. Although every corporation was a potential target of legislative intervention, telephone companies were especially vulnerable. The looming presence in every large city of a tangle of overhead wires made operating companies the "most visible and tangible" of all the "monopolies," Fay warned. Operating companies were "everywhere localized": no matter what they did, they could never escape this basic fact.[69]

That politics corrupted business was one of the most venerable clichés of American statecraft. To minimize the baleful effects of special privilege, lawmakers enacted general incorporation laws. The telegraph business had been organized to frustrate would-be monopolists, even though it was widely assumed that, like the mail, it was best operated under unified control. In the case of the telephone, antimonopoly was irrelevant. Telephone operating companies were municipal franchise corporations, and special privilege was unavoidable. As a consequence, the specter of corruption haunted even seemingly innocent transactions. It was a "delicate" matter, Fay explained to Vail, to prevent city officials from overtaxing his corporation, since it was hard to ensure a fair valuation for his company without being accused of "bribing the assessors."[70]

The profitability of telephone operating companies only increased their vulnerability to extortion. Although there were no telephone millionaires to compare with telegraph magnates Jay Gould and William H.

Vanderbilt, certain "manipulators" of telephone securities had learned how to make large profits from the business. These fortunate few, along with their counterparts in railroad, mining, and manufacturing, were a source of resentment, while the "unlucky telephone man"—by which Fay meant operating company managers like himself—became the "scapegoat for the whole."[71]

Fay never wavered in his conviction that rate caps were unjust. Just as department stores charged what they pleased, so too should operating companies. He regarded as farcical the contention that rate caps might hasten the popularization of telephone service. The 160,000 telephones that operating companies had installed in the United States in 1887 served an exclusive clientele that consisted of no more than one-quarter of 1 percent of the population. The "great mass of the people" did not care whether rates were high or low because in the "nature of things," they had "nothing whatever" to do with the telephone. Telephone subscribers were confined "almost entirely" to the "plutocrats of the country": merchants, bankers, professionals, and corporation executives.[72] "In our wildest dreams," Fay exclaimed, the telephone would never be used by more than one-half of one percent of the population, while telephone use would forever remain confined "most emphatically" and in "every way, shape and manner" to the "rich capitalist class."[73] And this class had more than enough money to pay whatever fee the telephone company charged:

> Telephone users are men whose business is so extended and whose time is so valuable as to demand rapid and universal local communication. A laborer who goes to work with his dinner basket has no occasion to telephone home that he will be late to dinner; the small householder, whose grocer lives just around corner, would not pay one cent for a telephone wherewith to reach him; the villager, whose deliberate pace is never hurried, will walk every time the few steps necessary to see his neighbor in order to save a nickel. The telephone, like the telegraph, post office and the railroad, is only upon extraordinary occasions used or needed by the poor. It is demanded, and daily depended upon, and should be liberally paid for by the capitalist, mercantile and manufacturing classes.[74]

The phony populism of telephone users prompted Fay to lump them together with labor agitators as menaces to the republic. To make his point, Fay delivered an incendiary address before the NTEA in October

1887. Fay opened his address with a startling disclosure. In every locality in which a telephone operating company had been established, he observed, nine subscribers out of ten were hostile to its operations and subscriber discontent was the "most conspicuous weakness" of the business and a "serious menace" to its "very existence." Subscriber outrage fostered a political climate that encouraged unfavorable legislation and the "vague feeling" that operating company franchises should be given over to a "vast third party" called the state, a sentiment that Fay derided as "un-American, unnatural, and nothing short of socialism pure and simple."[75]

To underscore his disgust with telephone subscribers, Fay dubbed them "Knights of Labor." The Knights of Labor was a workers' federation that endorsed collective action to limit the operational autonomy of corporations. Telephone subscribers who were intent on circumscribing the prerogatives of telephone operating companies had an identical goal. Subscriber boycotts were particularly insidious. A "great and intelligent people" should not assail institutions that had become the foundation of the country's existence, even if, like Chicago Telephone, their facilities were patronized by a tiny fraction of the population. Like all corporations, telephone operating companies had "transcendent powers for good"; for the wealthy to deride them as the "natural enemies" of the people was absurd. If the wealthy did not concede their greatness, they might well fall victim to confiscatory legislation, leaving their "sorrowing patrons" to compose their epitaph: "Here lies the telephone, the greatest and most benevolent of all the monopolies."[76]

Fay's screed was provocative, confrontational, and shrill. Yet it ably articulated the uncompromising procorporate, antigovernment mindset that was characteristic of telephone operating company managers in the 1880s. Fay was the operating company managers' collective voice. In addition to being himself the manager of a big-city operating company, he was the president of the operating company managers' trade association, the National Telephone Exchange Association (NTEA). More candid than his peers, Fay expressed sentiments that they endorsed but left unrecorded: every telephone manager in the 1880s echoed Fay's suspicion of state legislatures. Not until after 1900 would the managers of Bell operating companies begin to conceive of the state legislatures as potential allies, and then only because lawmakers delegated rate setting to regulatory commissions that ruled on individual cases that the operating companies had a right to appeal. Not even Edward J. Hall envisioned in the 1880s that the telephone might one day become a mass service for the entire population. If Forbes or Hall had addressed telephone managers with comparable candor, there is little reason to suppose their assessment of the political situation or their explanation of its cause would have been any different.

Fay valued publicity; his colleagues did not. The NTEA published two sets of proceedings in 1887, a unique event in its history. Only one set included Fay's "Knights of Labor" address. The set that excluded the speech seems to have been the one that was more widely distributed. It is the only edition, for example, preserved at the AT&T corporate archive in Warren, New Jersey.[77] Business journalists proved equally reluctant to publicize Fay's address. The three leading trade journals—*Western Electrician*, *Electrical Review*, and *Electrical World*—all reported that Fay had given a speech, but none revealed its contents. *Electrical World* went so far as to title Fay's address incorrectly as "Telephone Users *versus* Knights of Labor," a mistake that rendered innocuous Fay's provocative analogy between telephone users and labor agitators.[78]

Although Fay spent most of his business career in Chicago, he never considered himself a Chicagoan. Raised in a pious household in Burlington, Vermont, he retained throughout his life the earnest moralism of a New England minister's son. Fay obtained his position at Chicago Telephone shortly after his graduation from Harvard through the influence of a cousin who was one of the original incorporators of American Bell. Fay's father railed against selfishness from the pulpit; Fay harangued Chicago's plutocrats as class traitors.

Fay was a capable operating company manager. He held several important positions following his departure from Chicago Telephone in late 1887 and was briefly president of the Chicago Gas Trust, after which, for a longer period, he was the president of the typewriter manufacturer Remington-Sholes. A lifelong bachelor, Fay moved to Cambridge, Massachusetts following his retirement, and lived for many years at Harvard University's Faculty Club, where he regaled faculty members with tall tales of his wild days in Chicago. Fay died in 1944, shortly after he attended his sixty-fourth Harvard reunion; he was 96.[79]

Fay never regarded network building with the evangelical exuberance of Hiram Sibley, the moral fervor of William Orton, or the intellectual rigor of Edward J. Hall. Instead, Fay's most enduring monument was a cultural institution. Passionate about classical music, he was instrumental in founding the Chicago Symphony Orchestra and was one of its principal benefactors.

In looking back on his Chicago years, Fay repeatedly emphasized the pervasiveness of political corruption. No muckraker was more pitiless in his denunciation of the cupidity of lawmakers. In a biting essay, "Is Democracy a Failure," Fay recounted a conversation that he once had with an Illinois state legislator who had recently built for himself an imposing estate. When the legislator was asked how he had been able to afford such a grand edifice, the legislator dryly replied that there were "lots of Ayes and Noes in *that* house."[80] Fay always denied that he had ever tried to obtain special legislation for Chicago Telephone from the Chicago city council or the Illinois state legislature, and the legislative record bore him out. If he had, it would have proved expensive because it was impossible to get any bill through the city council or the legislature without "paying toll to the boys."[81]

To obtain special legislation was one thing, but to pay off lawmakers to bury confiscatory legislation was another. Fay bribed lawmakers to retract bills that he had good reason to assume they had floated to extort Chicago Telephone with a clear conscience. Corruption was part of the price of doing business: lawmakers routinely crafted bills that were intended to go down to defeat. To expose how the process worked, Fay published a series of tart essays following his retirement that he later collected in a book.

To explain to the uninitiated how lawmakers extorted municipal franchise corporations, Fay conjured up a hypothetical state legislator, whom he called O'Brien. The name Fay chose was revealing. O'Brien was an Irish name, and the Irish were an ethnic group often linked with shady political dealings. To shake down Chicago Telephone, O'Brien drafted a bill to cap telephone rates in any Illinois city with a population of over 500,000. Since Chicago was the only city in the state that fell into this category, the bill had been intended to catch Fay's attention. O'Brien next sent a friend to Chicago Telephone, offering to kill the bill in return for a payoff. When the company refused, O'Brien leaked a story to the press that charged the telephone company with trying to bribe a lawmaker. During the many years that he had worked for corporations holding right-of-way franchises in Chicago, first as general manager of Chicago Telephone and then as president of the Chicago Gas Trust, Fay declared that he had never paid off a lawmaker for any legislation other than a bill of this kind.[82]

The threat of a legislatively mandated rate cap troubled telephone managers throughout the country. Yet in no state did it prompt more concern than in New York. New York City's Metropolitan Telephone Company was the largest in the world, and Brooklyn's New York and New Jersey Telephone Company was not far behind. In the years between 1888 and 1895, rate cap bills were debated in the New York state legislature on numerous occasions. At the height of the protest no fewer than forty-two different commercial groups lobbied the state legislature in favor of legislation.[83]

None of these groups had any interest in transforming the telephone into a mass service for the entire population. Instead they sought to lower rates and improve performance standards for their members. Prominent among their grievances was the rate hike Metropolitan had instituted to cover the cost of upgrading the New York City exchange. Flat-rate telephone service in 1888 cost subscribers $150; in October 1894 it jumped to $240.[84] Metropolitan justified the rate hike as a prudent response to the city council ordinance requiring it to bury its wires underground. Grounded lines worked poorly underground; the more expensive metallic circuits worked well. Whether or not Metropolitan could justify metallic circuits as an upgrade was hotly contested. Metropolitan considered them an upgrade because they made it possible to make a long-distance call on an ordinary telephone. Subscribers objected that they were not an upgrade because they had been installed not to facilitate long-distance telephone service but to prevent interference from streetcar and electric power wires inside the city.

The simmering quarrel between Metropolitan and its subscribers prompted the New York state legislature to mount an investigation of the telephone business. This investigation was headed up by Danforth E. Ainsworth, a lawmaker from Oswego, a tiny town hundreds of miles from New York City. Ainsworth had little first-hand knowledge of telephone conditions in New York City. Even so, in the report he issued in 1888 he did his best to be evenhanded. To mollify telephone subscribers, the Ainsworth report endorsed a state-mandated rate cap; to accommodate Metropolitan, it advocated a gradual switchover to measured service. If operating companies received a "fair minimum" as a rental fee, as well as a reasonable price for individual connections, the "toll system"—that is, measured service—was "decidedly" the "most equitable" calling plan for both the customer and the company. Even so, the report conceded—with the Rochester subscribers' boycott very much in mind—that, thus far, measured service did not seem to "meet with favor" by the people of the state.[85]

Among the legislative options the report rejected was the encouragement of new entrants. Lawmakers had long regarded antimonopoly as the solution to the problems that market power caused. The telephone business was an exception. The telephone exchange was, like a gas plant, a monopoly in the "very nature of things"—even though it was a "universally accepted theory" that in the telephone business, unlike virtually any other business, the cost of providing a unit of telephone service increased as the business expanded, with the possible exception of the very largest exchanges.[86] This "theory" had yet to be accepted by everyone. The *New York Times,* for example, questioned it as late as 1901.[87] Even so, it echoed the conviction of telephone managers, who took for granted the geometrical relationship between network expansion and unit cost.

Heading up the legislative campaign against Metropolitan was Simon Sterne. A largely forgotten figure today, in the late nineteenth century he was well known as a principled champion of municipal reform. Sterne's influence stemmed in part from the breadth of his intellectual interests. He published a well-regarded three-volume history of the Constitution, corresponded with John Stuart Mill, and briefly edited one of the first social science journals in the country. As counsel for the New York Board of Trade and Transportation, Sterne frequently lobbied against Metropolitan in the New York state legislature between 1888 and 1895. Sterne never endorsed telephone popularization, yet he remained unwavering in his conviction that telephone operating companies were inherently monopolistic. Never did he doubt that lawmakers had an obligation to regulate them to protect the rights of their existing subscribers.

Sterne was no stranger to controversy. In the 1870s, he had played a major role in bringing to justice William Marcy Tweed, the notoriously corrupt political boss who had gained control of city government. Shortly thereafter, he won a national reputation for a comprehensive report on railroad rate setting that he prepared for the New York legislature. Sterne built on his expertise in railroad rate setting to help draft the Interstate Commerce Act, the first federal law to establish a permanent federal regulatory commission.[88] Having jousted with the political machine and the railroad, Sterne entered the lists against the municipal franchise corporation.

Sterne criticized Metropolitan on three counts: its rates were exorbitant, its profits too large, and its performance standards too exacting. Sterne had no quarrel with the "message-rate" measured service calling plan that Metropolitan instituted in 1894, as long as it was optional and its charges were low.[89] His primary target was the business flat rate, which he hoped to reduce. Sterne deemed it contemptible for Bell to contend that telephone operating companies were exempt from state legislation because they enjoyed certain rights under federal patent law: "Are our legislators wholly under the domination of the great corporations?"[90] Every year between 1880 and 1887, Sterne calculated, Metropolitan had made an average of $72 per year on each telephone it rented, for a total profit of 473 percent.[91]

Sterne found particularly provocative the newspaper accounts that telephone inventor Alexander Graham Bell had earned $10 million from his telephone patents. If Congress legally limited to $10 million the amount of money that anyone could obtain from a patent, Sterne did not believe that it would either suppress invention or cause anyone an injustice.[92]

To dramatize his opposition to Metropolitan's rate hike, Sterne staged a flamboyant publicity stunt. Unwilling to pay the higher fee that Metropolitan demanded for a metallic circuit, he obtained a court injunction to block the company from removing his telephone. Sterne considered it fatuous that Metropolitan had justified this rate increase by calling it a service upgrade. He had neither the need nor the desire to use Bell's long-distance network, and he did not see why he should have to help pay for its cost. A grounded line was good enough for him.[93]

Sterne intended his injunction to force the courts to clarify the social obligations of the telephone operating company. In Sterne's view, the telephone operating company was not a "private concern" that should be permitted to charge whatever it wished. Rather, it was a "public service" that should be regulated by law. "I propose to fight this matter out if it takes ten years," Sterne declared in 1895: "I won't be bulldozed into paying arbitrary rates by anybody simply because there happens to be a monopoly in control of the telephone service. If the company was a private concern it would be a different matter. People could pay their price or leave it alone. But here we have a concern which has a public service to perform, and it cannot demand any rate it chooses."[94] Sterne's case never came to trial. Had he not died unexpectedly in 1901, he might have had his day in court.[95]

Sterne's characterization of the telephone operating company as a "public service" built on his empirical observation that it had become impossible in New York City for a new entrant to dislodge the incumbent. The incumbent's subscriber list gave it such an "immense advantage" over a would-be rival that, even if the rival offered lower rates, it would find it impossible to "render like facilities."[96] And if no new entrant could contest the market, then lawmakers had a choice between regulation and government ownership. Mill had reached an identical conclusion in the first edition of his *Principles of Political Economy*. Sterne's innovation was to identify the subscriber list as the source of the "practical monopoly" that the operating company enjoyed.

Sterne's admiration for Metropolitan's subscriber list notwithstanding, he opposed network expansion if it increased the cost of his telephone bill. Nothing exasperated Sterne more than the repeated contention of Metropolitan officials that the recent expansion in the size of the New York City exchange justified a rate increase. He believed that the value of telephone service for its subscribers did not necessarily bear a relationship to the size of its exchange. Just because he had the theoretical ability to talk to any one of the city's million-and-a half inhabitants did not mean that he—or any "sane man"—would. To make his point, Sterne compared a telephone exchange to a busy city street. Every day he passed by thousands of people as he strolled down Broadway in New York City, without feeling the slightest compunction to greet any of them in person. In theory, Sterne could converse with anyone whose telephone had been hooked up to the network; in practice, his "intercourse" was limited to those individuals with whom he had "business or social relations" and was typically brief and to the point. The lengthy telephone conversations that sometimes occurred in small towns in which the pace of life was slower were "almost wholly unknown" in the big cities. City dwellers were simply too busy to waste their time on the telephone.[97]

To rebut Sterne, Metropolitan enlisted Benjamin Tracy, a respected lawyer and native New Yorker who had served as the secretary of the navy during the Benjamin Harrison administration. Tracy derided as unrealistic the rate cap Sterne proposed, and justified the rate increase to

$240 as necessary to cover the cost of installing metallic circuits. This upgrade had not only brought Metropolitan into compliance with the state-mandated ban on overhead wires, but it had also permitted subscribers to make long-distance calls from their own telephones. No one would want to see Manhattan again disfigured by the unsightly poles that Metropolitan had pulled down or the hundreds of miles of telephone wires that it had buried.[98]

Sterne is often dismissed as a reactionary snob, a charge rooted in his principled critique of the dubious methods political bosses used to finance civic improvements.[99] He is more aptly characterized as one of the nation's first consumer advocates. The term "consumer" was not widely used in the 1890s to characterize individuals who purchased goods and services. Yet it was often used in a more specialized sense to describe the collectivity that licensed franchise corporations, such as gas plants, water works, and telephone exchanges. City government, declared a prominent sociologist in 1902, was an "organization of consumers."[100] It was this kind of consumer interest that Sterne championed, making him a nineteenth-century incarnation of the twentieth-century public interest lawyer Ralph Nader.

Neither Sterne nor anyone else in the 1880s envisioned the huge expansion in the installed base that would accompany the switchover to measured service. Had the New York legislature enacted Simon Sterne's maximum rate law, reflected one trade press editor in 1900, it would have "killed" Metropolitan's experiment with measured service and forced it to retain a calling plan that was unsuited to the "mass" of the public.[101] Yet Sterne was prescient in his conviction that operating companies had an obligation to match price to cost. Sterne died in 1901, nine years before the New York legislature put the telephone under the jurisdiction of a regulatory commission. Among his most enduring legacies was the intellectual rationale for telephone rate regulation. In pamphlets, newspaper interviews, and government hearings, Sterne articulated a rationale for government regulation of the telephone that would soon become so conventional that it was easy to forget that it was not coeval with the beginning of the business.

Sterne favored regulation to rein in telephone operating companies; others endorsed municipal ownership. If a municipality owned a telephone exchange, it could operate it as a government agency or lease it to a private corporation. Either way, the exchange would no longer generate the huge profits that Sterne had deplored.

Municipal ownership was a favorite cause of Albert Shaw. Shaw was the recipient of one of the nation's first Ph.D.'s in history and political science, which he obtained from Johns Hopkins University in 1884. Shaw's mentor at Hopkins was Richard T. Ely. Shaw's dissertation analyzed a socialistic experiment in Iowa, a topic of considerable contemporary interest, given the popular fascination with Edward Bellamy's *Looking Backward*. Following a brief stint as a newspaper editorialist, Shaw traveled to Europe to study the administration of its principal cities; in 1895, he published two well-regarded books that sympathetically documented recent European experiments with the municipal ownership of gas plants, water works, electric power stations, streetcar lines, and telephone systems.[102] Shaw denied that he was an "advocate" of municipal ownership, yet remained convinced that it was "always advantageous" for municipalities to have the option to shift from one organizational form to another.[103] Even so, no one who read his books or editorials in the 1890s could doubt that Shaw—like his mentor, Richard T. Ely—regarded municipal ownership as one solution to the seemingly intractable problems posed by municipal franchise corporations.

Municipal ownership of telephone operating companies remained on the political agenda in many cities—including San Francisco and Chicago—from the 1890s until the First World War. The San Francisco city charter of 1900 endorsed the municipal ownership of telephone service, and in 1908 the San Francisco board of supervisors acquired the authority to set local telephone rates.[104] Among its champions in Chicago was the city's longtime mayor Carter Harrison Jr.: "I am for municipal ownership of telephones," Harrison declared in 1903: "It would be an exceedingly simple matter for the city to operate a telephone system."[105]

Municipal ownership gained a modest foothold in gas and electric power. Twenty of the nation's 981 gas plants were publicly owned in 1900, as were 193 of the nation's 1,471 electric power systems.[106] In the telephone business, however, public ownership was much less common. The largest municipal telephone exchange was located in tiny Brookings, South Dakota. The city government purchased a failing operating company for $18,000 in 1903 and paid off the cost of its purchase in ten years. The municipal system offered the same rates as the private company it had supplanted: $30 a year for business, $18 for residence, and $12 for party lines.[107]

The municipal ownership movement is sometimes characterized as the entering wedge for a more thoroughgoing collectivization of the economy. For this reason, it is sometimes termed "municipal socialism" or even "civic populism."[108] The movement might be more aptly characterized as "municipal capitalism"; for political economists from John Stuart Mill to Richard T. Ely, it was less an alternative to capitalism than its complement.[109] Reducing the cost of a vital service fostered individual opportunity. If the government owned a small number of businesses, the rest of the economy could remain market-based.

In devising a criterion for municipalization, Ely relied on a distinction that went back to Mill. Did entry into the business remain open for promoters, or did the incumbent enjoy advantages that were so insurmountable that no rival could contest it? If the answer was the latter, then government ownership was the remedy. Any "class of business" in which it had become necessary to "abandon" the "principle of freedom" in the establishment of new enterprises, Ely explained in 1889, should be "entirely turned over" to either the municipal, state, or national government, depending on the scale of its operations.[110]

The constant negotiation demanded by franchise politics, Ely contended, had long been the single "most potent cause" of political corruption.[111] If a municipality bought out its municipal franchise corporations, the corruption would cease. For a municipality to own a "natural monopoly"—such as a big-city telephone exchange—would benefit city and consumer alike: "Natural monopolies owned and controlled by cities always work well, and you may search the world over for an exception."[112]

Ely's faith in the theory of municipal ownership coexisted uneasily with his skepticism regarding the day-to-day administration of the nation's cities: "The men now in our municipal councils are not the kind of men to whom we would gladly turn over vast business interests," Ely conceded in 1903: "The very thought repels us." Even so, Ely held out high hopes for the future. The municipal government's acquisition of municipal franchise corporations would encourage a higher class of city dweller to run for office. Once in power, they would eliminate the endemic corruption that had made municipal franchise politics so notorious.[113]

Municipal ownership made for strange bedfellows. Among its most fervent champions was the legal academic Christopher G. Tiedeman, who was well known as a principled critic of government intervention and an apostle of what historians have come to call laissez-faire constitutionalism. Tiedeman's anti-interventionism presupposed that new entrants had the opportunity to challenge incumbents. If they did, then it guaranteed equal rights; if they did not, then the remedy was not regulation but government ownership. Every business that was dependent on special privilege should be administered not as a "private monopoly," but as a state or municipal monopoly, depending on the scale of the business.[114] Among the businesses that fell into this category were telephone operating companies. It was impossible to string wires along a city street in the absence of a special privilege. As a consequence, telephone companies by their very nature violated the "constitutional guaranty" of "equal privileges and immunities," and should be owned and operated by the municipality in which they were located.[115]

Government ownership was essential to Tiedeman both to counter special privilege and to coordinate the flow of information. The likelihood that a communications channel might be interrupted—as, for example, the telegraph had been during the telegraph operators' strike in 1883—made it imperative that lawmakers put the channel under federal control: "No private corporation or syndicate of capitalists should be vested with the ownership and control of any of the means of intercourse or communication of people with each other."[116]

The linkage of special privilege with municipal ownership seemed equally self evident to Supreme Court justice Henry B. Brown. "If our municipalities may supply us with water," Brown queried a prominent group of lawyers in 1893, may they then not also "supply us with gas, electricity, telephones, and street cars?": "They are all based upon the same principle of a public ownership of the streets and highways, and a power to grant franchises to third persons, which the municipality, if it chooses, may reserve to itself."[117]

The special privilege–government ownership syllogism prompted contemporaries wary of government expansion to speculate on whether some criteria other than special privilege distinguished the public works that cities should own and operate from those that they should not. One criterion was the civic ideal of inclusivity. The "sound natural law," posited one editorialist in the New York Times in 1899, was for a city to own and operate all of the systems, works, and plants that met the "needs of the entire people." Such a criterion included water and gas, but excluded those public works that, like the telephone, were of "public utility," though not a "universal necessity," since they were consumed not by the entire population but by an exclusive clientele. It would "abuse the taxing power" and be an "act of flagrant misgovernment" for city officials to tax the 3 million New Yorkers who never used the telephone to pay the cost of operating it for the half million who did make use of it.[118]

To highlight the emerging conflation of municipal ownership with inclusivity, municipal ownership enthusiasts floated a new collective noun: "public utility."[119] The term "public utility" first regularly appeared as a stand-alone noun in the *Chicago Tribune* in 1898. In no sense was it a neutral descriptor: municipal ownership advocates used the term self-consciously to make the case for a municipal buyout. The idea that a franchise corporation might be "of public utility" had a venerable pedigree; the related, yet distinct, idea that it might be "a public utility" was not. The public utility concept would soon be widely used to characterize investor-owned franchise corporations. Initially, however, it was a rallying cry for critics of corporate management.

There had recently been a "craze" for the municipal ownership and operation of "'public utilities,'" observed one unsympathetic editorialist in 1899. To underscore his disdain, he put the collective noun "public utilities" in quotation marks.[120] Under the circumstances, it was perhaps not surprising that critics of municipal ownership were reluctant to characterize franchise corporations as public utilities. In its place, they preferred clumsy circumlocutions such as "quasi-public works" and even "quasi-public utilities."[121]

The presumption that a telephone operating company had a social obligation to provide facilities for the entire population would have seemed strange to William H. Forbes, was anathema to Charles N. Fay, and had little appeal for Simon Sterne. Not until after 1900 would this presumption be wholeheartedly embraced by a rising generation of political economists who endorsed the then-novel principle that the telephone should be accessible to the entire population as a matter not of privilege, but of right.

This new, broader understanding of the social obligation of telephone operating corporations was endorsed by the authors of an influential collection of essays on municipal public utilities edited by the University of Pennsylvania professor of political science Clyde Lyndon King and published in 1912. These essays summarized an emerging academic consensus regarding regulatory commissions that has come to be called progressive. The primary "regulative factor" in the nineteenth century was competition, King observed. In the case of municipal franchise corporations, however, competition could not safeguard the public interest. The corporation's franchise was "licensed inequality," making its regulation imperative. As a consequence, lawmakers had an obligation to ensure that telephone corporations promoted not only their own self-interest, but also the "social welfare." In so doing, they hastened the emergence of a future "social democracy" in which the "latent powers and possibilities" of every individual would have an opportunity for expression: "Without adequate and competent regulation of the most vital necessities of the citizens and the city, served to-day by quasi-public corporations, no such equality of opportunity is even thinkable."[122]

King's faith in the democratic promise of municipal franchise corporations would have astonished Forbes, Fay, and Sterne. By 1912, it had become the conventional wisdom not only for progressive reformers, but also for the telephone managers Union N. Bethell and Angus Hibbard. Beginning around 1900, Bethell, Hibbard, and a generation of like-minded managers transformed the telephone operating company from a specialty service for an exclusive clientele into a mass service for the entire population. In so doing, they tilted the public debate on the telephone from the rights of network providers to the utility of network users and from the vilification of privilege to the disparagement of waste.

8

SECOND NATURE

It seems to me that the brains and the imagination of America shone superlatively in the conception and ordering of its vast organizations of human beings, and of machinery, and of the two combined.

Arnold Bennett, 1912

"What strikes and frightens the backward European almost as much as anything in the United States," remarked English visitor Arnold Bennett in 1912, was the "fearful universality" of the telephone. Vast numbers of telephones had been installed in big cities like Chicago not only in businesses and residences, but even in hotels. The millions of "live filaments" that big-city telephone companies had threaded under streets, over roofs, and between the floors, ceilings, and walls of buildings, had transformed the "privacies" of the city's inhabitants into "one immense publicity." Nowhere in Europe were hotel guests confronted, as Bennett had been in Chicago, with the "dreadful curse" of a telephone in every single guest room. Unwilling to risk the possibility that a total stranger might interrupt his repose, Bennett unhooked his telephone. When he did, a member of the hotel staff politely but firmly requested that he restore it to its receiver. Bennett recognized that Chicago was not the only city to have embraced the telephone. Yet he felt certain that no European nation had adopted it as avidly as the United States: "The European telephone is a toy, and a somewhat clumsy one, compared with the inexorable seriousness of the American telephone."[1]

The "fearful universality" of the telephone that so impressed Bennett was a recent development. The popularization of the telephone began around 1900. At its core, it consisted of reenvisioning the telephone as a mass service for the entire population rather than a specialty service for an exclusive clientele. The popularization of the telephone was not syn-onymous with the installation of telephones in a majority of the nation's residences. This latter development would not occur until many decades later. Rather, it consisted of the telephone operating companies' accep-tance of the novel idea that they had an obligation to provide the entire population with some kind of access to the telephone network.

The popularization of telephone service began at different times in different localities and took a different form in big cities than in small towns. This was to be expected, given the diversity of the country, the magnitude of the project, and the large number of corporations it in-volved. In small towns and middle-sized cities, popularization entailed the construction of modest-sized switchboards of no more than 10,000 lines that in many ways resembled the switchboards that Bell operating companies had installed in the 1880s in the nation's big cities. Predomi-nantly rural states, such as Iowa, took to the telephone with alacrity. Hundreds of mostly small operating companies had been established by 1907, giving the state one of the lowest ratios of inhabitants per tele-phone in the country.[2]

The popularization of telephone service proceeded the furthest in the nation's largest cities, and, in particular, in New York City and Chicago. The ratio of inhabitants to telephone was often higher in a big city than in a small town. As a consequence, historians have sometimes inferred that cities lagged in adapting the telephone. This inference is mistaken. A typical big-city telephone was used more intensively and by a larger number of people. It was in the big cities, observed political scientist Delos F. Wilcox in 1914, that the telephone had become, like the electric streetcar and electric lighting, such a fixture of the "artificial natural environment" that it had become "second nature."[3] If a powerful hand could reach down from above and take hold of all the wires that entered the central telephone exchange of a great American city, every store, ev-ery factory, every public building, every office building, most of the fine residences, and many of the humble ones, would all "dangle in the air together." In short, the whole city had become "caught" in a "network of sound-conductors" through which human voices were "ceaselessly" speaking to human ears.[4]

The popularization of the telephone was the product neither of the high standard of living that Americans enjoyed nor of the rivalry be-tween nonconnecting telephone operating companies to cover the ground. Although Americans in the nineteenth century enjoyed one of the highest standards of living in the world, no telegraph corporation had popularized the telegraph, while the rivalry of noninterconnecting operating companies was rarely a major factor in the nation's largest cities. The decisive factor in popularizing the telephone lay, rather, in the impetus to network expansion that had been fostered by the political economy: federal, state, and municipal governments limited the contractual freedom of telephone operating companies and empowered state and municipal governments to retain authority over their regulation. Government intervention, and even the threat of government intervention, was an engine of innovation. The influence of the political economy on business strategy is well illustrated by the popularization of the telephone in Chicago in the opening years of the twentieth century. In this period Chicago boasted not only the second largest population of any city in the United States but also the second largest telephone exchange in the world.

The operating companies that popularized telephone service fell into two main groups. The oldest group was the relatively small federation of operating companies that were owned in whole or in part by American Telephone and Telegraph (AT&T), the holding company that had acquired the assets of American Bell in 1899. This federation consisted of thirty-two operating companies in 1905, of which American Telephone and Telegraph owned a majority stake in twenty-three.[5]

The president of Bell in 1905 was Frederick P. Fish, a prominent patent lawyer chosen by the Boston investors who had long dominated Bell's board of directors. Succeeding Fish was Theodore N. Vail, a public utilities promoter who had held various positions at American Bell and its operating companies during the early years of the telephone business. Vail remained president of Bell from 1907 until 1919. As it happens, Vail had been briefly the first president of American Telephone and Telegraph when it had been organized as the long-distance network provider for Bell in 1885. Like so many first-generation telephone managers, Vail was discouraged by the enormous challenge posed by network expansion, and so he left the business in 1889. Vail returned to the telephone business around 1900 at the behest of Postal Telegraph president John W. Mackay; Mackay had recruited Vail as part of an abortive scheme to combine Bell with Postal Telegraph. Vail owed his appointment as Bell president in 1907 to a combination of factors, including his base of support among a group of mostly Bell directors who remembered his industriousness in the 1880s.

American Telephone and Telegraph's financial relationship to its operating companies often puzzled contemporaries. Shortly after Vail's appointment as American Telephone and Telegraph president in 1907, for example, Vail was surprised to learn that a prominent banker in Denver, Colorado, had no idea that American Telephone and Telegraph had a large financial stake in Colorado Telephone.[6] Exacerbating the confusion was the absence of a common nomenclature. Only five of the thirty-two Bell operating companies in 1905 had the word "Bell" in their corporate names. To highlight the relationship of American Telephone and Telegraph to its operating companies, Vail popularized the notion that every Bell operating company was a component of a "Bell System." This catchphrase had appeared in an American Telephone and Telegraph shareholders' report as early as 1904 and was featured in American Telephone and Telegraph public relations announcements beginning in 1908.[7] Although American Telephone and Telegraph was occasionally abbreviated in financial circles as "AT&T," it was popularly known as "Bell" and its operating companies were called the "Bell companies." To facilitate the interconnection of its operating companies, Bell operated a long-distance network known as the "long lines."

The Bell operating companies commercialized many of the technical and organizational innovations that facilitated the popularization of telephone service. The principal exception was electromechanical switching. Electromechanical switching—including the rotary or dial-up telephone—was commercialized by non-Bell operating companies. It remained unknown in the Bell exchanges in New York City or Chicago until after 1920.

The second group of operating companies had no financial relationship with Bell. Far more numerous than the Bell companies, they were also more variegated. Non-Bell operating companies numbered in the thousands, ranging from big-city operating companies to tiny farmers' cooperatives, with everything in between. Although the non-Bell companies had far less in common than the Bell companies, they were known collectively as the "independents," an umbrella term that exaggerated their cohesiveness. The independents had their own equipment manufacturers, trade associations, and trade press. Emboldened to enter the telephone business by the expiration of Alexander Graham Bell's telephone patents in 1894, they proliferated beginning around 1900.

The independents hastened the remarkable expansion in telephone service that one business journalist in 1902 dubbed the "telephone invasion."[8] One index of their rise was the number of telephones that they had installed. By 1907, independents operated almost as many telephones as Bell: the independents had 2.4 million and Bell 3.1 million.[9] Another index was the number of localities in which they operated. Of the 1,002 cities with a population over 4,000 in 1902 in which a telephone operating company had been established, 41 percent had a Bell exchange; 14 percent an independent exchange; and 45 percent rival Bell and independent exchanges.[10] Of the 19,093 localities of all sizes in 1914 in which a telephone operating company had been established, only 23 percent had operating companies owned in whole or in part by Bell. And in 1,864 of the localities in which a Bell exchange had been established, so too had an independent.[11]

By 1907 independent operating companies had established a major presence in several of the nation's largest cities, including Philadelphia, St. Louis, Baltimore, and Buffalo.[12] Yet their primary stronghold was in middle-sized cities and small towns. Independents wielded great influence in state legislatures and, in part for this reason, thrived in state capitals.[13] State capitals that boasted independent operating companies in the 1900s included Lincoln, Madison, Indianapolis, and Columbus. Independents also flourished in rural districts, where they were sometimes organized not as corporations, but as co-ops known as mutuals.[14]

The apparent parity between Bell and the independents in 1907 was misleading. Bell operating companies dominated the nation's largest cities, the source of the bulk of the profits in the telephone business; the independents' numbers were swelled by many companies that were overextended and would soon collapse. Even so, the rapid expansion of the independents beginning around 1900 was a fact that not even the most self-satisfied Bell apologist could deny.

Most independent operating companies relied on switching equipment similar to the switching equipment that Bell companies had installed before 1900. A few of the more ambitious replaced operator-assisted switchboards with electromechanical switchboards. Independents had installed electromechanical switchboards in 26 cities by 1904 and in 131 cities by 1910.[15] Large cities with independent electromechanical exchanges included Chicago, Buffalo, San Francisco, Los Angeles, and Columbus, Ohio.

Bell and independent operating companies competed vigorously in cities and towns throughout the United States. The Bell–independent rivalry was intensified by the fact that, in many localities, Bell and independent operating companies did not interconnect. Non-interconnection frustrated businessmen, who often found it necessary to install two telephones in their office: one for the Bell company and one for the independent. "The public usually shies at the term," reflected onetime independent telephone promoter and future U.S. president Warren G. Harding in 1907, "but the telephone is and ought to remain a natural monopoly regulated by some competent authority." Although "dual service" in the Marion, Ohio, independent in which Harding had invested held the promise of lower rates, the cost to the city's businessmen outweighed the benefits: "In short, what seemed a beautiful dream in promotion was very much a nightmare in realization."[16] Harding's caveat notwithstanding, dual service did hasten the proliferation of telephones; promoters recognized that the first entrant in a new market enjoyed major advantages over its rivals, a process that economists call "access competition."[17] Bell staffers downplayed the achievements of the independents in their public pronouncements but were more forthright in their private correspondence. That the independents had spurred the improvement of telephone service was undeniable, observed Bell staffer Walter S. Allen in a confidential memorandum to Frederick P. Fish in 1906, as was the fact that the rapid increase in the installation of telephones had been a direct result of the "stimulus of competition."[18]

Bell operating companies provided their subscribers with access to a larger network and, beginning around 1900, to a wider variety of calling plans. Independents typically offered lower rates for local service and a smaller number of toll-line connections. In certain localities, Bell permitted independent operating companies to interconnect with their toll lines, but in many others they refused. Interconnection was least likely in those localities in which Bell and independent companies competed head-on, since Bell regarded interconnection as a competitive weapon.

Bell built a nation-spanning long-distance network, but the independents did not.[19] The technical sophistication of Bell's long-distance network received a good deal of favorable press, much of which was generated by Bell's formidable publicity machine. These press accounts, in turn, have influenced the subsequent interpretations of historians and sociologists, many of which mistakenly credit Bell's long-distance network with a pivotal role in the ascendancy of Bell operating companies over their independent rivals.[20] In fact, Bell's long-distance network was of limited significance in the Bell–independent rivalry. Few telephone users were willing to pay the high rates for a long-distance call, and those who were willing almost always had access to a public telephone that was hooked into Bell's long-distance network. The toll lines operated by Bell operating companies generated more revenue, yet even they were rarely decisive in tipping the balance in favor of Bell. The independents operated their own toll-line networks, and Bell encouraged interconnection with noncompeting independents beginning around 1900 and accelerating after 1907.[21] On those rare occasions when an individual wished to make a toll call, in every city and many towns there was always a public telephone nearby that interconnected with Bell's long-distance network.

Telephone popularization was a product neither of technological imperatives nor of economic incentives. Network expansion increased switching costs, and operating companies had long made large profits by serving an exclusive clientele. The catalyst, rather, was political. In the telephone business, unbridled competition never existed; regulation was inescapable, and competition was always contrived.

The expiration of Alexander Graham Bell's second telephone patent in January 1894 symbolized the end of the original Bell patent monopoly. Yet the long-term import of this event remained uncertain, for no one could guess how broadly the courts would construe the scope of the 900 patents that Bell retained. Far more important was the voiding in the following December of a patent that Bell had obtained in 1891 for a microphone invented by Emile Berliner.[22] By voiding the Berliner patent, the courts signaled that the Bell patent portfolio would no longer preclude rival equipment manufacturers from entering the field. Although the Supreme Court would overturn the Berliner ruling in 1897, the Court limited the patent's scope, to the enormous relief of the independents.[23] Henceforth, not only Bell, but also Bell's rivals, found it advantageous to build large patent portfolios.

Bell looked to the Berliner patent to perpetuate the patent monopoly it had enjoyed since 1879; the voiding of the patent in 1894 was a rude awakening. In public, Bell insiders maintained the "golden silence" with which they customarily greeted bad news, a tactic that has misled historians into overlooking its significance.[24] In private, they recognized that they would have to change course. The monopoly that Bell had been granted by the courts, reflected one Bell lawyer in 1891, had been more profitable, more "controlling," and "more generally hated" than any other monopoly that had crystallized around the protection of patent rights: "Patents which would stand ordinary litigation have been known to give way under great strain, if they turn on questions when it is humanly possible to take an adverse view."[25] The lawyer was prescient: the "strain" proved too great, and the patent was voided.

The Berliner ruling had an immediate impact on Bell investors: upon its announcement, the share price of American Bell dropped a full 10 percent. This was an ominous sign in an age in which investors presumed the market price of a corporation's shares to be closely related to the value of its assets.[26]

Bell's defeat in the courts was counterbalanced by the legal advantages it enjoyed in the nation's largest cities. Big-city Bell operating companies all held municipal franchises, and municipal franchises were hard to obtain. It was, for example, far more difficult for a potential new entrant in the telephone business to obtain a municipal franchise than it had been for a potential new entrant in the telegraph business to obtain a state charter. Telegraph corporations were incorporated under general incorporation laws that encouraged open entry, whereas big-city telephone corporations needed a municipal franchise to go into business, which were negotiated one by one.

Bell's legal advantages in the big cities were checked by the independents' political clout in the states. The independents recognized that their collective prosperity hinged on a favorable political economy and did their best to turn it to their advantage. Twenty-seven states and territories had enacted laws to prevent or destroy trusts and monopolies by 1890, and in their political contest with Bell the independents found these laws to be an effective tool.[27] Antimonopoly remained a compelling civic ideal, and it was relatively easy for lawmakers to prosecute Bell for restraining trade. In the period between 1894 and 1907, when the Bell–independent rivalry was most intense, state legislators, state attorneys general, and state judges handed down a welter of laws, court rulings, and administrative decisions that benefited the independents in their contest with Bell. City officials and federal judges often came to the independents' aid as well, especially in instances when Bell had tried to expand its position in toll-line provision or telephone equipment manufacturing by acquiring independent properties. The acquisitions that lawmakers disallowed all had the approval of buyer and seller. For state and municipal governments, however, contractual freedom was a less worthy civic ideal than the enforcement of competition and the prevention of monopoly.

In the period before 1900, independents typically supported and Bell typically opposed state legislation mandating a Bell–independent interconnection. In the period between 1900 and 1907, however, many independents also opposed interconnection in the conviction that interconnection eliminated a necessary incentive for the construction of an independent-only toll network.

The most ambitious independent toll network was the Cleveland-based United States Telephone, which was owned by two Cleveland streetcar magnates intent on interconnecting the many independent operating companies that had recently sprung up in Ohio. Its most valuable asset was the portfolio of exclusive ninety-nine-year interconnection contracts that it had entered into with 300 Ohio independents. The financial condition of United States Telephone was always precarious. Following an adverse court ruling in May 1909, it was sold to a bank that acted as a proxy for the New York investment banker J. P. Morgan & Co. Shortly thereafter, J. P. Morgan & Co. acquired its assets.

United States Telephone owed its brief existence less to its commercial success than to a panoply of special privileges that it had obtained under state law. Ohio was hostile to out-of-state corporations, and Ohio courts were reluctant to permit operating companies that had signed up with United States from switching their toll connections to its Bell rival, Central Union. United States Telephone had negotiated its ninety-nine-year interconnection contracts with independent operating companies at a time when Central Union refused to interconnect. The courts regarded these contracts as sacrosanct, even if their enforcement proved costly to the operating company with which they had been negotiated. Ninety-nine-year exclusive contracts were not a restraint of trade, ruled an Ohio judge in 1908, since the independents did not intend to monopolize the telephone business. The judge's ruling was narrowed in May 1909 in a decision that accelerated United States Telephone's demise, and was overturned in February 1913 by a judge who was outwardly sympathetic to the independents. Despite his pro-independent predilections, this second judge found it impossible to deny what many suspected— namely, that the ninety-nine-year exclusive interconnection contracts were a restraint of trade.[28]

Operating companies received a major setback in 1899 in their contest with municipal governments when the Supreme Court ruled in *Richmond v. Southern Bell* that the Bell operating company in Richmond, Virginia was not exempt from municipal regulations even if it had signed on to the National Telegraph Act. Congress had not intended the National Telegraph Act to embrace every conceivable form of electrical communications, the Court ruled. The National Telegraph Act, for example, included a clause providing for the low-cost transmission of "governmental communications" to distant points. This clause was irrelevant to the telephone, for the telephone was limited to "oral communications," and government communications to distant places were almost invariably sent in writing.[29]

Had Bell won *Richmond,* city councils would have found it more challenging to regulate telephone rates and performance standards. Richmond did not settle the question of whether a city council had the authority to buy out a telephone company and operate it as a government agency. It did, however, preclude Bell from relying on federal law to prevent city councils from regulating telephone rates and performance standards. If a big-city city council wanted to franchise a new entrant, Bell had no way to block it.

It is impossible to know how a Bell victory in *Richmond* might have reshaped the telephone business. In Chicago, it might conceivably have slowed its popularization. Network expansion required a substantial investment in new telephone equipment, and no one knew for certain if it would cover its cost. Equipment upgrades were easier to justify to investors if they could be characterized as a preemptive strike against new entrants and unwelcome regulations.

The influence of the political economy on network expansion is highlighted by a comparison of the telephone business in Chicago and Toronto. Although Chicago was considerably larger than Toronto, the two cities had much in common. Both were bustling commercial centers; both were rapidly expanding; and both had Bell operating companies. The decisive difference was political. The Toronto city council lost its authority over the regulation of its telephone operating companies in 1904. Henceforth, rate setting, performance standards, and the licensing of new entrants devolved on the Canadian federal government.[30] In Chicago, in contrast, *Richmond* ensured that the city council would reign supreme. This political divergence between the United States and Canada had economic consequences. The Toronto operating company, having nothing to fear from municipal authorities, opposed network expansion as unduly expensive. The Chicago operating company, however, feared municipal interference with its prerogatives and embraced network expansion, regardless of the cost. In so doing, it preempted rivals and curried favor with the large segment of the electorate that had previously ignored it.[31] Early twentieth-century business leaders routinely complained that the adversarial relationship between government and business slowed innovation, and later historians have followed their lead. In Chicago, the opposite pattern prevailed. The very fractiousness of the political economy—including, in particular, the unpredictability, capriciousness, and cupidity of its city council—was an engine of innovation.

The popularization of the telephone in Chicago can be dated to 1900, the year in which Chicago Telephone general manager Angus Hibbard instituted a new calling plan that was destined to hasten an unprecedented expansion of the telephone network inside the city. When Angus Hibbard arrived in Chicago in 1893 to become general manager of Chicago Telephone, the company's Chicago exchange had only 11,400 subscribers. When Hibbard left in 1911, it boasted over 250,000 telephones, a phenomenal increase. In the same period, the company's capital investment increased from $3 million to $30 million.[32] No operating company in the country made a larger number of daily connections.[33] There were more telephones in Chicago than in London, even though Chicago's population was smaller, and its operators made connections at a much faster speed.[34] In fact, there were almost as many telephones in Chicago in 1909 as there were in France.[35]

The telephone business in Chicago provides a vantage point from which to survey the popularization of the telephone in the United States. In no sense was Chicago representative. Rather, it is its very atypicality that makes its history so revealing. Chicago in 1900 was the second largest city in the country and, after New York City, home to its second largest telephone exchange. Chicago was also the country's largest supplier of telephone equipment and, after New York City, its most important telephone trade press publishing center. Historians have long characterized late nineteenth-century Chicago as a processor of agricultural staples.[36] But Chicago also had a thriving manufacturing sector that included the world's largest industrial district for the manufacture of telephone equipment.

The presence of a thriving trade press in Chicago ensured that innovations originating in the city were widely reported. City boosters were notorious for inflating Chicago's achievements, yet there is much truth in the boast of the Chicago chronicler who in 1918 called Chicago the "telephone capital of the world" and "the Mecca toward which telephone experts in all lands look for inspiration and guidance."[37] Illinois factories, of which the vast majority were located in the Chicago metropolitan area, were reputed by a Chicago trade press editor in 1926 to have manufactured 80 percent of all the telephones in the country.[38]

Chicago Telephone was large and profitable, paying its shareholders an annual dividend of 10 to 12 percent, a rate of return that compared favorably with most corporations, including Western Union.[39] Over half of Chicago Telephone's dividend went to its corporate parent, American Telephone and Telegraph; this dividend, in turn, accounted for a substantial percentage of American Telephone and Telegraph's annual revenue. American Telephone and Telegraph obtained annual dividends from thirty-two operating companies in 1905. Of this revenue, it received 35 percent of its income from just two: New York Telephone and Chicago Telephone.[40] "Our experience has proven," declared one operating company manager in 1902, "that pretty much all the money which is to be made out of the telephone business will come from the larger cities, and about in proportion to the population and business activity."[41]

The largest Chicago telephone equipment manufacturer was Western Electric, whose factory complex anchored Chicago's west side industrial district. Western Electric sold non-telephonic electrical equipment to many companies; prior to April 1908, however, Bell proscribed it from selling telephone equipment to its independent rivals.[42] Western Electric's annual sales in 1914 were around $77 million, making it one of the largest manufacturers in the nation.[43] It broke ground in 1904 on the Hawthorne Works, a huge new factory complex just outside of Chicago's city's limits. For much of the twentieth century, Hawthorne remained the largest telephone-equipment-manufacturing complex in the nation.[44]

Western Electric invented much of the equipment that made possible the popularization of the telephone. The most seminal telephonic invention to originate in its Chicago factory was the multiple switchboard, one of the most complex producer goods of the age.

Among the switchboard refinements that Western Electric pioneered were three feedback mechanisms: the electric signal lamp, the "howler," and the busy signal. The electric signal lamp was located on the switchboard at the telephone exchange and informed the operator that a caller wished to make a call and that a call had ended. The howler was an attention-getting buzz that reminded a subscriber when the telephone had not been properly hung up and remained "off the hook."[45] The busy signal was a constant beep that signaled to the caller that a line was unavailable because it was already engaged.

The howler and the busy signal provided users with information that telephone operators had previously transmitted orally. The electric signal lamp replaced the electromagnetic "annunciator" whose release had announced to the operator that a caller wished to make a connection. Telephone operators had been previously obliged to reset the annunciator by hand, a time-consuming task; the electric signal lamp switched itself off automatically, simplifying the operator's work.

Western Electric engineers benefited from their spatial proximity to Chicago Telephone. In refining the multiple switchboard, for example, Western Electric engineer Charles E. Scribner worked closely with Chicago Telephone engineers; among the switchboard refinements that he helped design was the busy signal.[46] The electric signal lamp, the howler, and the busy signal were all invented at Western Electric and first put into commercial operation at the Chicago exchange. Each was the result of a creative collaboration between Western Electric and Chicago Telephone. Hibbard knew this well, even though, many years later, he could not resist the opportunity to joke that he himself had invented the busy signal.[47]

The multiple switchboard solved the first "technical crisis" that had threatened to "overwhelm" the telephone business, explained one twentieth-century telephone historian. In addition, it gave Western Electric a formidable competitive advantage. Western Electric's patent portfolio was so large and so variegated that it covered virtually every facet of operator-assisted switching. To avoid litigation, the German electrical equipment manufacturer Siemens licensed Western Electric's multiple switchboard patents; to run its Berlin telephone equipment factory, it hired an engineer who had been trained at Western Electric in Chicago.[48]

No Western Electric engineer was better known in his day—or more swiftly forgotten by posterity—than Charles E. Scribner. Praised by Thomas A. Edison as the "most industrious inventor" he had ever known, Scribner had 441 patents to his credit, a total that contemporaries believed to have been exceeded only by Edison himself.[49]

Historians of industrial research often underplay the creative achievements of Scribner and his colleagues by contending that Bell did little in-house research and development prior to Theodore N. Vail's return to the presidency of American Telephone and Telegraph in 1907. These accounts credit Vail with recruiting a team of university-trained scientists to push back the frontiers of knowledge, rather than merely to upgrade switchboards, cables, and telephone instruments, as had Western Electric engineers like Scribner. One of the first notable achievements of this research team was the three-element high-vacuum tube. The high-vacuum tube was the first invention to amplify electrical signals, rather than merely to slow their attenuation, making its invention coeval with the birth of electronics.

The high-vacuum tube provided the necessary amplification to transmit the human voice across the continent, making possible the New York–San Francisco hookup. It would also prove indispensable in the commercialization of radio broadcasting that began in 1920. To build on this post-1907 legacy, Bell publicists contend, Vail's successors established the fabled Bell Telephone Laboratories in 1925.

Bell-centric historians of technology have long regarded the invention of the high-vacuum tube as marking a fundamentally new departure in the history of industrial research. Bell scientist Frank B. Jewett saw things somewhat differently. Although Jewett played a major role in shifting Bell toward basic research, he heaped praise on Scribner and his colleagues for laying the foundation for Bell's later achievements in industrial research. "That the engineering structure which is our glory today exists at the very heart of a great industry," Jewett declared in 1919, "is due to Charles E. Scribner and the men with whom he has surrounded himself." Without this foundation, "no such organization as we have today could hope to exist."[50] The steady stream of inventions that Scribner and his colleagues had patented has been the "acorn" out of which emerged the "sturdy oak" of Bell Laboratories.[51]

Western Electric's Chicago factory anchored an industrial district that spawned several of the nation's most important independent telephone equipment manufacturers. Eventually the independents would follow Western Electric out of the city for more spacious green field sites in the Chicago metropolitan area. As late as 1902, however, Chicago factories manufactured over 90 percent of all the equipment installed by independent telephone operating companies in the United States.[52]

The largest and most ambitious of the independents—Kellogg, Stromberg-Carlson, and Automatic Electric—built their factories in close proximity to Western Electric. Milo Kellogg and James E. Keelyn had designed telephone equipment for Western Electric before establishing their own factories. Alfred Stromberg and Androv Carlson worked at Chicago Telephone as switchboard technicians before they founded the independent telephone manufacturer that bore their names.[53]

The most technically innovative of the Chicago independent manufacturers was Automatic Electric. Most independents were staffed by ex-Western Electric engineers and built equipment modeled on Western Electric's. Automatic Electric broke the mold. It recruited engineers from throughout the Midwest to manufacture electromechanical switchboards and dial-up telephones.[54] The technical expertise that Automatic Electric marshaled and the patent portfolio that it owned made it a world leader for several decades.[55]

The telephone in the 1900s remained a local medium. A few telephone users—mostly wholesalers, manufacturers, brokers, and bankers—used it to maintain connections between the city and the wider world. The rest used it to run errands, summon a doctor, or catch up with family and friends. Most telephone calls were highly localized. The average distance of a telephone call originating in Chicago in 1900 was 3.4 miles. This distance may well seem small today, but at the time Chicago Telephone's president hailed it as proof that the city's telephone users had begun to place calls that reached out beyond the narrowly bounded neighborhoods in which they lived.[56] The significance of this advance in intra-urban electrical communications is easily overlooked. Yet it was not lost on the Chicago Telephone publicist who reflected in 1906 on the "awesome thought" that Chicago's telephone users could "project" themselves "into the presence" of any of the many thousands of Chicagoans who could be reached by telephone.[57]

Nonlocal calls remained rare; the long-distance calls made possible by the new high-vacuum tube were almost unknown. A mere 2.4 percent of Chicago's telephone users regarded the ability to make a long-distance call a major benefit, reported one internal Bell survey in 1904.[58] Only one out of every 100 Chicago telephone users made even one telephone call a year that reached over 100 miles, estimated a public utility expert in 1914. It was, therefore, of greater import for operating companies to upgrade equipment that would facilitate the interconnection of telephones located no more than 100 miles away. This conclusion was a pointed critique of the large sums Bell was lavishing on its long-distance network.[59]

Telephone subscribers who wished to reach a telephone located outside of the flat-rate zone had two options. If the telephone they wished to reach was located in an exchange operated by Chicago Telephone, they placed a toll call. Alternatively, if the telephone was located in the territory of another operating company, they made a long-distance call. Toll and long-distance calls were paid for individually; both were expensive. Few calls of any kind reached out beyond the Chicago metropolitan area. Only 10 percent of the toll calls handled by the Chicago exchange in 1900 reached beyond a 100-mile radius of the city. Fully 50 percent of the revenue that Chicago Telephone obtained for toll calls in 1906 was for toll calls *inside* the city.[60]

In Chicago's hinterland, the story was much the same. Toll-line connections were a luxury for the few, while local connections were a necessity for the many. Every city and town within a 100-mile radius of Chicago had been linked to the Chicago exchange by 1906. Yet there is little evidence that the inhabitants of these localities placed a high priority on the high-speed connections afforded by a direct line to the Chicago exchange; if they needed to reach the city, they could always place a call from a public telephone. The Business Man's Association in Naperville, Illinois, then a tiny market town located 40 miles west of Chicago, voted in 1906 not to switch to Bell from an independent, even though the two companies offered identical business rates and only Bell offered direct connections to Chicago. The independent offered lower residential rates. For the businessmen of Naperville, this feature seems to have tipped the balance.[61] The demand for a direct Chicago connection among independent operating companies was equally limited. The recently completed St. Louis–Chicago toll line was a money-loser, testified the general manager of a St. Louis independent toll-line company in 1915. Had he known in advance how little business it would generate, he would never have authorized its construction.[62]

Angus Hibbard's first assignment as general manager of Chicago Telephone was to hook up every telephone in Chicago with the long-distance network that Bell had extended in 1892 to Chicago from New York City. The linkage of New York City with Chicago was the brainchild of

Bell president John E. Hudson. By linking New York City and Chicago, Hudson hoped to ensure that Bell would retain the high profits and operational autonomy in the post-patent monopoly era that it had enjoyed before 1894.

The official opening of the New York City–Chicago line was timed to coincide with the Columbian Exposition, a lavish world's fair certain to draw a multitude of visitors to Chicago. Hudson hoped that the hookup might generate some favorable publicity for a corporation that had come to be regarded as one of the most reviled in the land. Unfortunately for Hudson, the New York City–Chicago hookup failed to capture the imagination of the Chicago journalists who covered the exposition.

Far more celebrated was Elisha Gray's teleautograph. The commercialization of the telephone had created a demand for a "better and different class of service," Gray explained in an 1893 magazine article describing his invention. In the coming "revolution" in the "means of communication," no invention would be more important. By transmitting an "exact fac-simile"—or "tele"-"autograph"—of a written text, it would "do what a letter does in matters of business, and can be sent as quick as a telegram."[63] For a reporter from the *Chicago Tribune*, Gray's teleautograph was an impressive debut. The teleautograph, the reporter gushed, was in many ways superior to both the telephone and the telegraph, since messages could neither be heard nor interrupted, while their accuracy was guaranteed.[64]

The New York City–Chicago hookup proved more technically complicated than Hudson assumed.[65] Most telephones in Chicago had yet to be outfitted with the metallic circuits necessary for long-distance service, and their upgrading was time-consuming and expensive. In fact, the line would not be commercially practical until after it was outfitted around 1900 with loading coils to limit the attenuation of electrical impulses over long distances.[66]

Even if Hibbard surmounted these technical challenges, a problem remained. For most Chicagoans, long distance was less of a priority than the improvement of performance standards inside Chicago. The subscriber protests that had dogged the tenure of Hibbard's predecessor, Charles N. Fay, remained a living memory, and Hibbard was determined to prevent their recurrence.

The most pressing operational problem confronting Chicago's telephone subscribers was congestion. The call-connection delay was unacceptably long, and a large percentage of calls were unavailing because the line was already in use. If a telephone line were in use, it could not be interrupted, and, thus, the operator had no alternative to reporting that it was "busy."[67] It was not uncommon, Hibbard later reminisced, for a lumber wholesaler on a flat-rate line to instruct an operator to connect him with twenty different dealers in succession. If a large number of similar calls came in at the same time, they could "almost paralyze the exchange."[68]

Of all the upgrades Hibbard installed, the most far-reaching in its implications for the average telephone user was the common battery. The common battery was a centralized power source that replaced the local batteries that had generated the current necessary to translate the human voice into electrical current. Its adoption created the steady electrical current that was necessary for three feedback mechanisms: the electric signal lamp, the howler, and the busy signal. In addition, it rendered superfluous the hand-powered cranks known colloquially as "coffee grinders" that telephone subscribers had turned when they wanted to get the operator's attention. Henceforth, if callers wished to get the operator's attention, they merely had to take their telephone receiver off its hook.

The common battery significantly simplified the maintenance of the subscriber's telephone. Local batteries were temperamental and required frequent adjustments to remain in proper working order. Some required servicing as often as once a week. Local batteries were unsightly, messy, and bulky. With their elimination there came a subtle shift in telephone nomenclature. It now became increasingly common to refer to the subscriber's telephone not as a station but as an instrument.

Hibbard attributed the chronic congestion at the Chicago exchange to two main factors: the call-connection delay and the high percentage of unavailing calls. To minimize the call-connection delay, Hibbard analyzed calling patterns by charting daily telephone usage. On a typical business day, the number of calls spiked upward after 9:00 A.M., declined around lunch, and increased again for a second time in the afternoon. Hibbard believed the second spike was unique to Chicago and a tribute to the industriousness of its businessmen.[69] Calling patterns varied little from day to day, making it possible to forecast with reasonable accuracy the number of operators that would be necessary to minimize the duration between the moment a caller signaled that he wanted to make a call and the moment the call was connected. To forecast his staffing needs, Hibbard compiled daily usage charts. Hibbard's charts enabled him to hire the optimal number of operators for every hour of the day: not too many, which would unnecessarily increase his labor costs; and not too few, which would increase the call-connection delay.

To conceptualize usage patterns, Hibbard made analogies with the railroad and the electric power station. The railroad gave Hibbard the evocative "traffic" metaphor, along with the related concept of a "deadhead." For a railroad manager, a "deadhead" was an empty car that generated no revenue; for Hibbard, it was a call for which the company received no payment. The electric power plant gave Hibbard the "load" metaphor. In an electric power station, the "load" quantified the demand for electricity at a given point in time; in a telephone exchange, it modeled usage patterns. Chicago electric power magnate Samuel Insull had demonstrated how pricing schemes intended to minimize sudden spikes in demand for electrical power could improve the efficiency of an electric power station. Hibbard looked to measured service to "level" the "load."[70]

Hibbard's usage charts disclosed a surprising fact. The effectiveness of an exchange depended to a large extent on the cooperation of its subscribers. "The record of telephone traffic upon the subscribers' lines," Hibbard explained in 1894, "is showing clearly every day that the final completion of a telephone call depends not wholly upon the telephone company or its agents, but very largely, and in many cases, almost wholly, upon the intelligent use of the telephone by the subscriber." To minimize congestion, the subscriber must become "part of the 'system'"; indeed, the subscriber was one of the system's "most vital parts." A telephone exchange was in this respect qualitatively different from every other municipal franchise corporation with which it might be plausibly compared. Unlike a gas plant or a water works, it was intrinsically collaborative: its effectiveness depended on the ongoing cooperation of the company and its customers. If a subscriber failed to speak properly into his telephone, left it unhooked, or clogged the line with pointless chatter, everyone's service was impaired.[71] Storekeepers lost customers if they neglected to keep their entry free from obstruction; telephone subscribers cost themselves money if they permitted the blockage of their "telephone door."[72]

Hibbard's obsession with unnecessary waste was so pronounced that he forbade operators from using the word "hello" when callers requested that they make a connection. The salutation was superfluous, he insisted. In its place, Hibbard required operators to answer with the

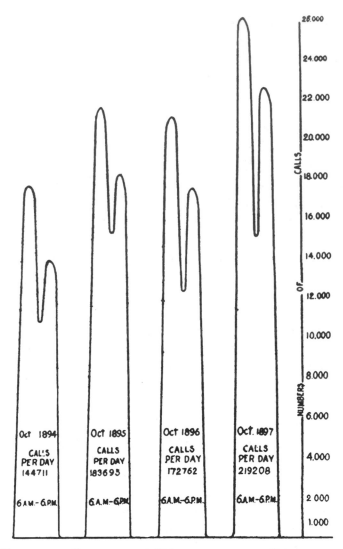

26.000

24.000

22.000

20.000

18.000

16.000

14.000

12.000

10.000

8.000

6.000

4.000

2.000

1.000

CALLS

OF

NUMBERS

Oct 1894
CALLS
PER DAY
144711
6A.M.-6P.M.

Oct 1895
CALLS
PER DAY
183695
6A.M.-6P.M.

Oct 1896
CALLS
PER DAY
172762
6A.M.-6P.M.

Oct. 1897
CALLS
PER DAY
219208
6A.M.-6P.M.

CURVES SHOWING ORIGINATING CALLS IN
THE CHICAGO TELEPHONE EXCHANGE,
FROM 6 A.M. TO 6 P.M., ON OCTOBER
10, 1894, 1895, 1896, 1897.

In the 1890s, Chicago Telephone Company general manager Angus Hibbard
pioneered the hour-by-hour analysis of telephone usage. The data that Hibbard
generated, and which this 1897 chart depicted, provides a rare glimpse of usage
patterns in a large American city in the early years of the telephone business.
"Telephone Traffic in Chicago," *Electrical Review* 31 (November 17, 1897): 236.

utilitarian "number please." Hibbard even tried to discourage subscribers from saying "hello" when they picked up their receiver; how successful he was, it is impossible to say. In the place of "hello," Hibbard recommended that callers state their last name clearly and distinctly.[73] There were, after all, only so many operators, switches, and lines.

Hibbard occasionally poked fun at women for gossiping on the telephone. Yet he remained convinced that the unnecessary waste occasioned by telephone sociability had been caused primarily by men. The "especial stumbling block" was the "'deadly office boy'" who clogged the flat-rate business subscriber's line to gamble, check out the latest baseball scores, or catch up with his chums.[74] "Investigation shows," declared Chicago Telephone's telephone directory for 1906, "that in the absence of a proprietor, or indeed in his presence, the flat rate telephone is used by neighbors, office boys, clerks and other employees all day long, without limit, for frivolous and useless conversation."[75]

Even after women began to use the telephone in large numbers, female sociability was for Hibbard of little concern. The reason was simple. Business telephones generated the bulk of the congestion, and women rarely used business telephones. Residential telephones posed less of an operational challenge because they were used less intensively. Like the district telegraphs that they superseded, these telephones had been intended to facilitate a relatively limited number of household chores. Residential subscribers used their telephones to order groceries or perform errands and did not wish to be called at home. In many well-to-do households in which servants were employed, the only telephone was located in the kitchen, where it was used primarily by the staff.[76]

Hibbard's gendered presumptions reflected a common view among telephone experts. Although women used the telephone with increasing frequency after 1900, early twentieth-century telephone experts ordinarily blamed telephone congestion on men. "General, frivolous, and senseless messages over the 'phone will cease," declared the authors of a special report on telephone rates issued by the Chicago city council in 1903, if it must "necessarily be paid for." At the same time, the unnecessary waste occasioned by use of the telephone by clerks, stenographers, and office boys to discuss their personal, social, and "usually insignificant affairs" would be "greatly lessened." With measured service, the telephone would be confined to those important conversations for which it had been "primarily designed."[77] Many an office boy, reflected one telephone analyst, would never dream of filching a postage stamp from his employer's desk to mail a personal letter to a friend. Yet the very same office boy thought nothing of tying up his employer's telephone for hours with a "vast amount" of talk on non-work-related topics that served "no useful purpose" whatsoever. It was a "public delusion," the analyst fumed, to assume that the cost of telephone service was proportional to the number of telephones rather than to the number and duration of telephone calls. As long as rates and costs were unrelated, this misunderstanding would persist, and subscribers would use their telephones "almost as freely as the air."[78]

The congestion caused by business subscribers led Hibbard to lobby for the abolition of the business flat rate. Hibbard's campaign failed. Business subscribers were easily mobilized, and they recognized the benefits of unlimited access inside the flat-rate zone. Telephone experts would later conclude that the business flat rate was regressive: the per-call cost of telephone service for business subscribers was substantially less than the per-call cost for residential subscribers.[79] Hibbard never wavered in his conviction that it was the primary cause of congestion in the Chicago exchange. Chicago's 9,300 flat-rate telephones, Hibbard complained in 1907, caused more "bad service" than "perhaps all other causes combined"—even though these lines accounted for a mere 8 percent of all telephones in the city.[80]

Hibbard's crusade to eliminate unnecessary waste led him to reengineer the specially designated telephones that his company had installed for public use. These telephones had been installed in stores, railroad stations, and other public places, and for this reason were known as "public telephones." As late as 1900, the public telephone remained the only kind of telephone accessible to most Chicagoans. Thousands of Chicagoans made their first telephone call not in an office or a residence, but in a store. Like radio and television, the telephone was first encountered by most city dwellers in an emphatically public setting and would only later be domesticated. Public telephones proved especially popular with druggists. Inviting and well lit, drugstores became a logical place for Chicagoans who had yet to lease a telephone in their office or residence to make a call.[81]

Chicago Telephone occasionally permitted the installation of public telephones even before it obtained its 1889 franchise. Yet it was not until after 1889 that public telephones began to proliferate. Public telephones cost storekeepers $150 per year: $125 for flat-rate telephone service, and $25 for the privilege of charging nonsubscribers a 10-cent fee for every local call. The 10-cent fee was to be collected by the storekeeper. It was intended not only to cover the cost of the $25 surcharge, but also to discourage the congestion that Hibbard feared would be occasioned by its frivolous use.[82] The storekeepers' self-interest would limit usage, or so Hibbard hoped. Few storekeepers maintained a second telephone for their personal use: if customers kept the line constantly in use, the storekeeper would not be able either to make outgoing calls or to receive calls from customers, family, and friends.

To Hibbard's exasperation, storekeepers refused to keep their part of the bargain. To increase foot traffic, they routinely waived the 10-cent fee. The public telephone was "one of the greatest advertisements" he had, one druggist explained. Customers lured into a drugstore to make a free telephone call were likely to buy something on the way out. Every business day, he estimated, it generated $1 in sales, which more than balanced its cost.[83]

Hibbard found the popularity of the public telephone heartening, yet he remained troubled by his company's inability to obtain more than the $25 surcharge from it. Hibbard had no objection to the extension of telephone service to nonsubscribers, yet he did not see why they should obtain telephone service free of charge. Just as storekeepers benefited from the "transient business" the public telephone generated, so too should the telephone company.[84] "Deadheadism" raised labor costs, discouraged the installation of private lines, and increased congestion by encouraging thousands of "frivolous, and entirely useless conversations." And for Hibbard, this was not only wasteful, but also unfair: "every consideration of personal comfort and social and business advantage suggests allowing the public to do with this as with every other kind of service received—pay for what it gets."[85]

To align the public's desire for telephone service with the cost of providing it, Hibbard lobbied storekeepers to permit the company to mount on their telephones a locked coin box into which users had to insert a coin before the operator completed their call. To encourage storekeepers to make the switch, Hibbard waived the rental fee and permitted shopkeepers to make a certain number of free calls per month; the company, in turn, would pocket the proceeds of the coin box.[86] The first coin-box telephones in Chicago were installed in 1894; by 1900 there were 1,950, of which 775 had been installed in drugstores.[87] To make a five-minute call, the caller deposited 10 cents.[88] No longer, predicted one newspaper reporter, would the druggists' telephone be clogged for twenty minutes at a time by giggling girls gossiping with their friends.[89] Before long, the "old free-lunch telephone system" faded from memory, and Chicagoans forgot that it had ever been possible to make a call from a public telephone without depositing a coin.[90]

The coin-box telephone found favor with thousands of Chicagoans who had neither the means nor the desire to pay the high monthly fee the company charged for a flat-rate subscription. Small tradesmen found even low-cost flat-rate service exorbitant, one journalist explained. Yet they would gladly pay 10 cents to make a telephone call, even if, at the end of the year, they had spent more for coin-box service than they would have paid out in rental fees, since they could not "bring themselves to the point of deliberately incurring such an obligation in bulk."[91]

The legal status of the coin-box telephone remained uncertain until 1900. In that year, the counsel for the city of Chicago endorsed Hibbard's position that it was a permissible variant on the public telephone that the company had been permitted to install in its 1889 franchise. A public telephone, the counsel ruled, was any telephone that had been "set up and operated and controlled" by a telephone company for the "use and convenience of the entire public." Anyone could use this telephone without the "permission, interference, or control of any other person," provided the caller had complied with the regulations that the company had prescribed.[92]

The replacement of non-coin-box public telephones with coin-box public telephones enabled Chicago Telephone to increase its revenue from nonsubscribers, but it did nothing to expand its installed base. To further popularize the telephone, Hibbard introduced a variety of calling plans that calibrated the price of telephone service to the cost of completing the call. Measured service had long been anathema to telephone subscribers. Yet if Hibbard wished to popularize telephone service, he had no alternative. For technical reasons familiar to business analysts, though mysterious to everyone else, the per-unit cost of telephone service was higher in a large city than in a small town. If Hibbard had not experimented with measured service, he would have found it impossible to expand telephone service beyond the business elite.

Measured service linked the cost of telephone service to the number of connections that users made rather than to the duration for which they had rented their telephone. If the connection were the basic unit, then the rates for telephone service should be measured rather than flat.

Toll and long-distance calls had always been measured. Hibbard's innovation—which had been anticipated by Hall in Buffalo, John I. Sabin in San Francisco, and Union N. Bethell in New York City—was to extend the pay-as-you-go principle to local service.

Hibbard's calling plans differed in several respects from the calling plans that Hall had tried with limited success to introduce in the 1880s. Hall's experiment had occurred at a relatively early stage in the technical evolution of the telephone switchboard; Hibbard's followed the introduction of the common battery. Hall conceived of measured service primarily as a cost-saving measure and only secondarily as a marketing tool; Hibbard regarded it primarily as a marketing tool that would cover its cost in the long term, even if it initially proved expensive to implement.[93] Perhaps most importantly, Hibbard did not force subscribers to make the switch. Not until 1906 would Hibbard try to abolish outright the business flat rate, and when he did, he failed. Chicago Telephone stopped offering the business flat rate to new subscribers by 1914. Existing flat-rate users, however, were unaffected until 1919, when it was eliminated by an executive order of the postmaster general.[94]

Measured service significantly decreased the cost of telephone service for the occasional user. The only calling plan that the company had offered Chicagoans in 1893 was a flat-rate charge for unlimited usage inside the spatially delimited flat-rate zone, which, in that year, covered 16.3 square miles.[95] Although business subscribers appreciated unlimited service, the annual charge was high: $125 for a grounded circuit and $175 for a metallic circuit wired for long-distance connections. Measured service was much cheaper, particularly for the small user. Following its introduction, the average cost of telephone service in Chicago dropped to $35 per year, a substantial savings from the $125 that subscribers had paid in 1893.[96] "There is no other so-called 'public utility' in Chicago," declared a business journalist, "in which the amount of service given in return for a dollar received has increased so rapidly of late, as in the telephone service."[97]

Hibbard introduced three different calling plans for three different classes of potential telephone users. For residential users who sought high performance standards at a modest cost, he installed multiple party lines; for residential users for whom low cost was more important than high quality, he established neighborhood exchanges; and for residential or business users for whom low cost was the overriding consideration, he rolled out a low-cost pay-as-you-go option known as the nickel-in-the-slot.

Multiple party lines increased the number of subscribers while minimizing the increase in operating costs. Four hundred had been installed in Chicago by 1896.[98] To economize on switchboard space, each multiple party line used only one switchboard plug at the exchange.

Multiple party lines introduced telephone service to many middle-class households. Face-to-face social calls had long been a tradition among well-to-do women. Now, for the first time, Chicago's society matrons began to make their calls by telephone. "Morning telephone calls" had become "quite the thing" in all the "residence portions" of the city, reported one journalist shortly after the first multiple party lines were installed.[99]

Multiple party lines worked best if subscribers could determine in advance for which party an incoming call was intended. To differentiate one multiple party line from another, Hibbard patented an invention called "selective ringing." This innovation was not without its problems. In Chicago, for example, it was adversely affected by the induction caused by electric street railways. At the same time, it was a major technical advance and would eventually be adopted nationwide.[100]

Measured service hastened a minor revolution in telephone accounting. To charge callers by the call, operators had to record the number and duration of every single call that originated on a measured service line. The duration of a call varied from three to five minutes, depending on the calling plan. Although operators did not customarily interrupt callers to inform them of how long they had been connected, the operator was the timekeeper; and after each call, she recorded its duration by hand.[101]

Measured service subscribers often complained that operators overcharged them by making educated guesses as to the duration of their call.[102] To eliminate operator discretion, they lobbied the telephone company to install meters that would automatically measure telephone usage.[103]

The invention of an automatic telephone meter might appear to be relatively straightforward, but in practice it took many years to perfect a machine that could simultaneously record the number and duration of successful calls that had been made on a particular telephone. The first meter of this kind would not be installed in Chicago until after the First World War.[104] Unsuccessful calls were a particular stumbling block because it was hard to design a meter that could differentiate calls that went through from calls that did not.[105]

The installation of multiple party lines provided subscribers with the same high performance standards that business subscribers had come to expect. For subscribers who preferred low cost to high quality, Hibbard established neighborhood exchanges, which were well suited for residential districts that happened to be located inside the city's borders. In Chicago, these included Pullman, Roger's Park, and Austin. From an operational standpoint, a neighborhood exchange was a suburban exchange that happened to be located inside the city. Subscribers to the neighborhood exchange could make an unlimited number of calls for an annual flat rate inside an unlimited access zone that typically stretched no further than a few city blocks. If subscribers wished to make a call outside of their "neighborhood," they paid by the call.[106]

To keep operating costs low, the neighborhood exchange employed fewer operators per connection than was customary for the Chicago exchange. This cost-cutting measure increased the call-connection delay, especially for calls to neighborhoods located outside of the unlimited access zone. Had subscribers desired the higher performance standards that business subscribers demanded, they could pay a premium to connect their telephone to the Chicago exchange. Yet few did.[107] Residential users of "modest means," explained one telephone expert, had "no interest in or care for the remarkable speed and accuracy which characterizes the telephone service of many American cities."[108]

Multiple party lines and neighborhood exchanges expanded the network without providing the pay-as-you-go convenience of the public telephone. To tap this market, in 1900 Hibbard rolled out a new kind of coin-box telephone for residential users that became known as the "nickel-in-the-slot." This telephone had certain features in common with the public telephone. Like the public telephone, it was intended for multiple users, and it required the deposit of a coin to complete a connection. Unlike the public telephone, it was wired for a multiple party line and was intended not for the customers of a store, but for the residents of boardinghouses, apartment buildings, and bungalows.[109]

The nickel-in-the-slots for the first time put the telephone within easy reach of a broad cross-section of Chicago's middle class. No longer was it necessary to journey to a corner drugstore to make a telephone call. Almost 40,000 ten-party nickel-in-the-slots had been installed by 1906—fully one-third of all the telephones in the city (see Table 3).[110]

Table 3. The popularization of the telephone in Chicago, 1899–1906.

Year	Total	Flat-rate business	Measured service (excluding ten-party line nickel-in-the-slots)	Nickel-in-the-slot (ten-party line only)	Other*
			Telephones		
1899	18,013	—	—	—	—
1900	23,187	—	—	—	—
1901	32,728	6,769	10,564	3,848	11,547
1902	50,118	7,440	12,556	13,989	16,133
1903	68,508	7,291	18,220	20,167	22,830
1904	82,217	7,596	22,950	23,568	28,103
1905	96,260	8,183	27,216	27,959	32,902
1906	115,427	9,163	30,657	38,461	37,146

Source: Dugald C. Jackson, William H. Crumb, and George W. Wilder, *Report on the Telephone Situation in the City of Chicago* (Chicago: Gunthrop-Warren, 1907), pp. 92, 96.

Note: Totals are for August.

* Private branch exchange, flat-rate residence, and extension.

Nickel-in-the-slots had become "part of the paraphernalia" of the "regulation boarding house" as well as the "private flat," observed one journalist shortly thereafter.[111]

The term "nickel-in-the-slot" antedated the rollout; it had been in use for some time as a generic term for any machine that provided a good or service in return for the payment of a coin or token. Nickel-in-the-slot phonographs had for several years been popular in train stations and other public places. The reengineered coin-box public telephone that was commonly located in a drugstore was sometimes called a "nickel-in-the-slot" even though it originally cost a dime.

The nickel-in-the-slot was cheap and convenient. Users paid no installation fee, no monthly charge, and no advance deposit. The only expense was the cost of placing a call: 5 cents, or a nickel, for a call in the unlimited access zone, which, after November 1907, embraced the entire city, a vast 191-square-mile territory. The only obligation was to guarantee that they would make a minimum number of calls per month: initially two per day and soon thereafter one per day. At a nickel a day, this worked out to $1.50 a month, or $18.25 a year, far less than the $175 the company long charged a flat-rate subscriber for a dedicated line on a metallic circuit. Although nickel-in-the-slots had been wired for long-distance service, few Chicagoans used them to place calls outside of the 5-cent zone. Toll calls were expensive, and it took a lot of nickels to call Joliet, let alone St. Louis.

The lowest grade of nickel-in-the-slots linked as many as ten telephones on a single line. This experiment proved controversial and was quickly abandoned. Yet it had a plausible rationale. Switchboard space was expensive and a ten-party line required only a single plug on the operator's switchboard. Ten-line nickel-in-the-slots had the further advantage of shifting from the operator to the user the perennial challenge of coping with congestion. Nickel-in-the-slots permitted users to make only one call at a time; to keep the line free, users limited the duration of each other's calls, simplifying the work of the operator. The ten-line nickel-in-the-slots were "telephone educators," one journalist observed. Even if their performance standards proved unsatisfactory, they familiarized Chicagoans with the possibilities of the telephone and encouraged them to trade-up to a higher grade of service for which the cost had "hitherto been a bar."[112]

The nickel it cost to make a telephone call was hardly a trivial expense. A nickel in 1900 was the price of a package of cigarettes, a streetcar ride, or a Coca-Cola.[113] Even so, there is little evidence that many Chicagoans objected to the cost. Although the occasional gadfly lobbied for a "penny" telephone, no popular movement emerged to agitate for lower rates.[114] Hibbard guessed that the 5-cent-per-day rate would be sufficiently low to appeal to a substantial percentage of the city's inhabitants, and he was right. No one objected to paying by the call, especially since there was "no such thing" as a telephone bill.[115] Prior to the rollout of the nickel-in-the-slots, Chicago's North Side residents had found "private telephones" to be too expensive, observed Hibbard in October 1900, in explaining the rationale for the new calling plan.[116] The nickel-in-the-slot laid this objection to rest.

To use a nickel-in-the-slot, a caller picked up the receiver to determine whether the line was in use. If the line was open, the caller requested a connection from the operator, which the operator completed. If the line that the caller wished to reach was also open, the caller put a nickel in the coin box and waited to be connected. Calls were supposedly limited to five minutes: it was up to the operator to measure their duration and to inform callers when their time was up.[117] To limit congestion, most nickel-in-the-slots linked together no more than four telephones, the legal maximum in Chicago after 1907.

Hibbard's rollout of the nickel-in-the-slot was a testament to the financial clout of Chicago Telephone and the organizational capabilities of Western Electric. The initial rollout was rumored to have cost $1.5 million, a substantial sum for a company whose total capitalization in 1900 was $5 million.[118] No independent operating company had the financial resources or organizational capabilities to match Chicago Telephone's investment. Not surprisingly, no big-city independent reached out in a comparable way to the masses.

While nickel-in-the-slots were expensive to roll out, they were easy to service. Once a month, the telephone company sent out collectors with a key to the coin box. If the box contained 30 nickels, the service had been paid for; if not, the subscribers made up the difference.[119]

To market the nickel-in-the-slot, Hibbard hired a small army of canvassers. On at least one occasion, Hibbard himself went door-to-door in the city's populous North Side residential district. "Our sales talk was brief," Hibbard explained: "Do you want our telephone service and why? Is it worth five cents to you?" The installation of hundreds of thousands of nickel-in-the-slots during the next few years—in boarding houses, apartments, and private residences—was a convincing reply. In this way, Hibbard reminisced, thousands of Chicagoans acquired the "telephone habit," and once they did, they would "never get over it."[120]

The popularization of the telephone in Chicago would have been impossible in the absence of technical advances in switchboard design. Yet it would never have been attempted had no one championed the cause. Technical advance created new possibilities; organizational innovation transformed these possibilities into reality. Samuel Insull had increased the profitability of his electric power company by promoting an energy-intensive lifestyle; Hibbard improved his company's bottom line by commodifying conversation. Neither Insull nor Hibbard was motivated exclusively or even primarily by short-term considerations of profit and loss. Hibbard had an almost irrational desire to meet the diverse demand for telephone service inside Chicago. The popularization of the telephone was one element in a cultural agenda launched by a rising generation of business leaders to broaden the ambit of corporations that dominated the channels of communication. Henceforth, Chicago Telephone was no longer a mere "private enterprise" like a textile mill or a department store. Rather, it was now a socially responsible "public utility" that had a social obligation to provide access to the facilities for telephone service to the entire population.

During the years that Hibbard popularized telephone service in Chicago, a new, resolutely ethnographic tradition of sociological inquiry originated in the city. This tradition, later known as the Chicago School of Sociology, analyzed social relationships that had been recently transformed not only by electric power and the electric streetcar, but also by electrical communications. The telephone helped create the social circumstances that the sociologists explored and the moral philosophers who followed their lead would celebrate.[121]

The popularization of the telephone accommodated the consolidationist political economy in which the telephone business emerged. Network expansion in New York City followed, and was in part a response to, the threat of a state-mandated rate cap, whereas network expansion in Chicago was hastened by the city council's recent franchising of an independent operating company to compete head-on with Bell. Chicago Telephone depended on the city council not only for its franchise, but also for the right-of-way licenses to use the streets to string or bury wire. By enmeshing the telephone in the everyday lives of a substantial percentage of the city's inhabitants, Hibbard improved the company's bargaining position in its ongoing contest with the city council. If Hibbard had been less preoccupied with operational efficiency, he might not have envisioned the long-term potential of network expansion. And if his relationship with the city council had been less adversarial, he might never have translated his vision into reality.

The likelihood Chicago Telephone would soon have a rival in the Chicago market prompted Hibbard's official superior, Chicago Telephone president John M. Clark, to articulate a rationale in 1898 for telephone service in Chicago. Clark's report was the first sustained attempt by a Chicago Telephone executive to publicly justify to shareholders the expansive business strategy Hibbard had pioneered. Chicago Telephone held a municipal franchise from the Chicago city council, Clark reminded his shareholders, and, as a consequence, had a social obligation that transcended the rate of return that it generated for its investors. To meet this social obligation, Clark endorsed network expansion.[122] Clark's report was one of the first public acknowledgments by a Chicago Telephone executive that the company had a social obligation to the people of Chicago; it was also the first report of the company's to be printed in a pamphlet form that facilitated its circulation.[123]

Clark's report built on his firsthand knowledge of Chicago business and politics. Clark had long been active in various city-based public works projects, including streetcars and sidewalk improvements. He also had extensive experience in Chicago politics, having served as an alderman, run for mayor, and held the office of collector of the port of Chicago. To meet the objection of business subscribers that network expansion might increase congestion, Clark reassured them that his company would maintain the high performance standards that they had come to enjoy.[124] To appease the city council, Clark underscored the dependence of the telephone exchange on the city. If Chicago Telephone were to retain the special privileges that the council had the power to revoke, the company had an obligation to meet the needs of the people.

Clark did his best to mediate between the telephone company, its subscribers, and the city council. Clark's successor, John I. Sabin, was less politic. Sabin lacked Clark's familiarity with Chicago's business elite and, perhaps for this reason, was less sensitive to its fear of congestion. To make the case for network expansion, Sabin ventured an analogy between the telephone and the mail. The "sole purpose" of the mail, he said, was to enable people to communicate with each other. The same was true for the telephone: the bigger the network, the greater its value. Businesses routinely dispatched through the mail thousands of letters every day to customers who might not send one letter a week. Yet no one contended that the Post Office Department should exclude small users from the postal network on account of the modest amount of postage that they paid. Indeed, had the Post Office Department excluded small users, they would probably have been less inconvenienced than the businesses that would no longer be able to reach them in such a cheap and convenient way. The postal-telephonic analogy was also an argument in favor of measured service. No country had ever instituted a fixed monthly charge for the mail. Telephone rates, by analogy, should be based on a "fair average charge," a principle that, if implemented consistently, would eliminate the flat-rate option Chicago business subscribers had long enjoyed.[125]

Sabin's hypothesis is a truism today. Economists routinely contend that the value of a communications network increases as it becomes more extensive and interconnected and that the pricing of network access should be linked to its cost. Yet when Sabin issued his report, it was vulnerable to several plausible objections. Sabin's official superiors worried about the point at which the cost of network expansion exceeded its benefits. Network expansion was expensive, and no one could be certain that the extension of telephone service to thousands of Chicagoans who had never made a telephone call would cover its cost. Business subscribers remained fearful that network expansion would degrade the performance standards that they currently enjoyed and hasten the elimination of the business flat rate.

The expansive rationale for telephone service championed by Hibbard, Clark, and Sabin won the approval of the city council. If the company wished to enter into measured-service contracts to place telephone facilities at the "disposal of the small user," the city council would not object.[126] To require small users to pay flat rates obliged them to pay for more telephone service than they needed.[127] City council approval was important because it had the power to disallow novel calling plans as a violation of the company's 1889 charter. Although the great majority of business subscribers with whom he had spoken regarded the flat rate to be essential, reported one Chicago lawyer in 1907, even they freely conceded that measured service was a "more equitable way" of charging for telephone service.[128]

Hibbard's novel calling plans did not go unopposed. Among his adversaries were three groups that he ignored at his peril: druggists, business subscribers, and high-ranking Bell officials.

Druggists objected to the nickel-in-the-slots because they reduced foot traffic. Customers who had formerly spent a dime to place a call in a drugstore telephone now preferred to save 5 cents by making the same call from a boardinghouse, bungalow, or flat. The higher performance standard of the druggist's dedicated line did not overbalance the low cost and convenience of the nickel-in-the-slots.[129]

Business subscribers complained that the nickel-in-the-slots degraded performance standards by increasing congestion.[130] Chicago Telephone's general manager was unimpressed. Business subscribers had anointed themselves the "telephone aristocracy," the general manager stated: they suffered in the same way that a newspaper publisher would if its readership was doubled or a retail store would if "increased multitudes" entered its doors every day.[131]

The business subscribers' complaints found a receptive audience among Hibbard's official superiors. The nickel-in-the-slots were a "most radical departure" from "proper standards," huffed Bell's chief engineer John J. Carty, and posed a particular problem for business subscribers who paid for the "higher forms of service." In addition to increasing the call-connection delay, they ensured that a much higher percentage of calls would prove unavailing: the failure rate for the Chicago nickel-in-the-slots, he was reliably informed, could be as high as 70 percent.[132]

Hibbard so "dominated" Chicago Telephone, fumed Western Electric president Harry B. Thayer, that he should be held directly accountable for all the changes in the Chicago exchange—"good and bad"—and "there is much that is bad."[133] The nickel-in-the-slots were "abnormal": their rates were too low, and they were certain to cost the company more in operating costs than they generated in revenue.[134] Bell president Theodore N. Vail concurred. The business flat rate remained a good measure of the value of telephone service for its subscribers and should not be abandoned.[135] "The pay-as-you-go principle is bad enough," Vail complained to Sabin's successor Bernard E. Sunny, in opposing a proposed refinement to the nickel-in-the-slots, "but let us . . . stick to that, or at least not adopt anything else until it has been thoroughly threshed out."[136]

Vail's disdain for the nickel-in-the-slots underscored his limited grasp of the full significance of the popularization of telephone service that had occurred in the years since he had resigned the presidency of Metropolitan in 1889. Like so many first-generation big-city telephone managers, Vail remained fixated on business subscribers even though they were becoming an increasingly small percentage of the installed base. Vail did not object to telephone popularization in the abstract, but in practice he lacked Hibbard's ability to translate it into a reality.

Had Bell been rigid and autocratic, Hibbard's superiors might have ordered his dismissal. Its organizational structure discouraged such a draconian measure. The planned decentralization of the Bell operating companies that Edward J. Hall institutionalized in the 1880s gave Hibbard the operational autonomy he needed to strike out on his own. The business strategy that Hibbard adopted in Chicago was different from, and in certain respects antithetical to, the business strategy that Hudson sent him to Chicago to implement. That Hibbard had the operational autonomy to go his own way was a tribute to the organizational form that Hall had devised and that Hudson and his successors chose not to countermand.

Organization charts are sometimes associated with the squelching of initiative. For Hibbard they had the opposite effect. By clarifying the lines of authority, organization charts emboldened him to innovate, even if his innovations seemed wrongheaded to higher-ups in the organization.

Hall intended his organization charts to overcome a seemingly crippling disadvantage of the corporation as an organizational form. Unlike a proprietorship, a corporation lacked the "soul" essential to the "perfection" of the "natural person." In the absence of an organization chart, employees had trouble figuring out whom they reported to, who reported to them, and what tasks they had a specific responsibility to perform. To solve this problem, Hall provided them with a mental map of their location within the organization that would encourage them to challenge the informal "'rule of thumb'" methods they had relied on in the past.[137] The keynote of all successful organizations could be found in the biblical injunction: "'no man can serve two masters.'"[138] Hibbard later reminisced that the sheaf of organization charts that he brought with him to Chicago were the first that had ever been devised for a telephone operating company in the United States.[139] Hibbard himself had had a hand in their creation, having been delegated by Hall to restructure the Bell-associated operating companies in New York City and Philadelphia.[140]

If Carty, Thayer, and Vail had paid closer attention to the rapidly changing conditions in the nation's big-city telephone exchanges, they would have learned that Hibbard was hardly alone. In big cities throughout the country around 1900, operating companies began to supplement flat-rate calling plans with a menu of measured-service calling plans similar to those that Hibbard had introduced in Chicago. Measured service popularized the telephone by meeting the needs of the many city dwellers for whom low cost was more important than high quality, and the pay-as-you-go principle a convenience rather than a burden.

The rapid adoption of measured service calling plans in big-city telephone exchanges was incontrovertible. Measured service calling plans had been instituted in eighteen of twenty large U.S. cities, observed Chicago city electrician Edward B. Ellicott in 1902. In addition to Chicago, these cities included New York City, Philadelphia, Baltimore, Boston, St. Louis, Cleveland, Cincinnati, and Denver. Measured service was popular with "small users" and economical if callers made fewer than nine or ten calls a day.[141] The switchover to measured service in New York City began in 1894. By 1897, 10,700 of the city's 18,000 subscribers had abandoned the flat rate.[142] By 1901, a mere 1,200 of the city's 60,000 subscribers remained on a flat rate, with three-quarters, noted one business journalist approvingly, paying the "exact amount of goods delivered."[143] By 1906, 99 percent of all the telephones in Manhattan, and 90 percent in Brooklyn, were on measured service.[144]

Nickel-in-the-slots were rolled out in several cities other than Chicago. San Francisco, St. Louis, Cleveland, Milwaukee, and Baltimore all tried the experiment. Ten-party-line nickel-in-the-slots were briefly installed in San Francisco and Baltimore. Although they had served as "telephone educators," they caused so much congestion that they were quietly abandoned, mostly for four-party-line nickel-in-the-slots, the most common variant in Chicago after 1907.[145]

The popularization of the telephone service was coordinated in New York City by Union N. Bethell; in San Francisco by John I. Sabin; and in Nashville, Tennessee, by James E. Caldwell. Like Hibbard, Bethell, Sabin, and Caldwell belonged to a generation of operating company managers whose formative business experience postdated the Bell patent monopoly. It was this second generation of telephone managers—rather than the generation of Vail, Edward J. Hall, and Charles N. Fay—that invented telephone sociability. The "greatest factor" in our success, reflected one operating company manager in 1900, was the still largely untapped market of women and the poor. If operating companies could find some "means" to provide them with cheap and convenient telephone service, their success would be assured.[146]

Bethell was a lawyer from southern Indiana who combined a persuasive speaking style with a faith in the power of newspaper advertising. He was the first big-city operating company manager to advertise widely, the first to introduce measured service following the expiration of the Bell patent monopoly in 1894, and the first to break the informal ban against public speaking before legislative bodies and civic groups. The advantages of measured service in New York City, reminisced Bethell's colleague and brother in a public hearing in 1914, led swiftly and for the first time to the establishment of a "real selling department" with advertising, trained canvassers, and "all that sort of thing."[147]

Sabin was well known for his rollout of the nickel-in-the-slots in San Francisco. The nickel-in-the-slots, Sabin explained to his colleagues in 1900, had popularized the telephone in San Francisco by making it accessible to the "little fellow." Prepayment proved to be a particular boon with middle-class women, for they no longer had to inveigle their husbands to pay for a flat-rate subscription.[148] Hibbard himself learned about the nickel-in-the-slots during a visit to Sabin's San Francisco exchange in the late 1890s. Sabin, Hibbard later reminisced, had installed telephones in cigar stores, saloons, Chinese laundries, newsstands, hotels, restaurants, boarding houses, private residences, and many other places where telephones had "never been seen before."[149]

Sabin's faith in network expansion had a political logic. San Francisco in the 1890s was a hotbed of the municipal ownership movement, and the new city charter that went into effect in 1900 explicitly authorized the city council to buy out any telephone operating company that did business in the city. San Francisco city officials obtained the authority to set telephone rates in 1908; they lowered rates in every year between 1908 and 1915. Had Sabin not popularized telephone service, his successors might have lacked the political capital to block the city government from buying out his exchange.[150]

Less flamboyant than Sabin, yet equally successful in popularizing the telephone, was James E. Caldwell, a Nashville banker and longtime president of Cumberland Telephone, the most progressive operating company in the South. Caldwell's territory was enormous: it was centered in Kentucky and Tennessee, stretched northward to Evansville, Indiana, and southward to New Orleans. Caldwell was the first operating company president to publish a company magazine and one of the first to publicly defend telephone popularization as a social obligation. "In various forms of party-line and measured service," Caldwell informed his shareholders in 1901, "rates have been made to put the telephone in the reach of the masses." In endorsing telephone popularization, Caldwell addressed the perennial objection of business subscribers that network expansion would cause congestion. Nothing that his company did, Caldwell promised, would impair the "higher class service" that business subscribers enjoyed.[151]

Caldwell prided himself on his operational autonomy and missed few opportunities to heap ridicule on his ostensible superiors at Bell. Although Bell had long touted the legal support it provided the operating companies, Caldwell was unimpressed. At no point had he relied on "patent protection" to institute lawsuits to fend off rivals, Caldwell proudly reported in his memoir. Instead, Caldwell cultivated the enormous market for telephone service that had yet to be tapped. Caldwell was particularly contemptuous of Vail, whom Caldwell derided as a self-aggrandizing publicity seeker intent on rewriting telephone history to exaggerate his role in popularizing telephone service. The adulation heaped on Vail in the popular press struck Caldwell as ridiculous: Vail had not even been living in the United States during the critical years of "real strain" when operating company managers like Caldwell himself had labored tirelessly to bring telephone service for the first time to the "masses of people."[152]

The upward spike in telephone usage in the nation's largest cities that began around 1900 would have been inconceivable had operating companies failed to launch a sustained advertising campaign to popularize telephone service. Electric power magnate Samuel Insull had orchestrated an advertising campaign to promote an energy-intensive lifestyle, and telephone operating company managers sold city dwellers on the wonders of electrical communication. Operating company managers looked back on this campaign with pride. Carefully preserved among the records of the Milwaukee-based Bell company, for example, was a scrapbook that featured page after page of flyers, return postcards, and handbills, that the company's publicity department prepared around 1900 to popularize telephone service inside Milwaukee.[153]

The first big-city advertising campaign began in New York City in 1894. Bethell launched it to accompany the introduction of measured service. The campaign featured the simple yet memorable catchphrase— "Don't Travel—Telephone." The slogan was the brainchild of Herbert L. Webb, a British telegraph engineer-turned-business journalist who trumpeted the marvels of the big-city telephone operating company in numerous articles for trade journals and the popular press. Among Webb's other contributions to telephone advertising was the first widely used advertising jingle for long-distance telephone service: "The mail is quick, the telegraph is quicker, but long distance telephone is instantaneous, and you don't have to wait for an answer."[154]

No big-city operating company appears to have featured the phrase "universal service" as an advertising slogan, though the concept was implicit in Hibbard's campaign to instill the "telephone habit" in every class of Chicagoans. Even so, and like so many other early twentieth-century innovations, universal service was born in the city. In fact, telephone publicity departments may have borrowed the phrase "universal service" from big-city department store advertisements, which had begun around 1900 to boast that the goods that they sold provided "universal service" all year round.[155]

Generic catchphrases such as "Don't Travel—Telephone" were long a staple of operating company advertisements. Yet operating company publicists soon grew adept at devising more specialized appeals. Newspaper advertisements for telephone service began to appear with regularity in the *Chicago Tribune* in 1900. "It is the purpose of the management of the Chicago Telephone Company," declared one typical advertisement, "to place a telephone at the most reasonable rates, within easy and immediate reach of every person whose income is sufficient to permit him to ride in street cars"—which was, at the time, a substantial percentage of the adult population of the city.[156] Several advertisements were aimed specifically at women, a group Hibbard worked assiduously to cultivate. The telephone offered "The Way Out of a Social Dilemma," hinted one. No longer need women exert themselves to organize a friendly game of cards: "Getting a fourth hand for 'bridge' is only one of a thousand social uses of the telephone, and telephone service promotes sociability and good-fellowship because it brings neighbors closer together. Your friends all live within talking distance."[157]

A recurrent feature of early twentieth-century telephone advertising was the utility of the telephone in fostering sociability. "Telephone your happiness," announced an advertisement in New York Telephone's company magazine in 1911.[158] "I Called up to Ask You Over this Evening," remarked one farmer's wife in an advertisement run by the Bell Telephone Company of Pennsylvania.[159]

The possibilities of the telephone as a social medium were explored in a series of alluring color lithographs that New York Telephone ran on the cover of its company magazine. This series featured a succession of attractive young women who used the telephone to thank a beau for a bouquet of flowers, to receive words of encouragement while convalescing, and to stay in touch with a friend when her sweetheart was overseas serving his country in the First World War.[160]

The Bell operating companies' advertising campaigns preceded and were intended for a more diverse audience than the better-known public relations campaign that Theodore N. Vail instituted in 1908. Vail's public relations campaign had been intended not to increase the market for telephone service, but to associate the "Bell System" with cherished civic ideals. Like many public relations campaigns, it had an emphatically upper-middle-class tone. The public relations firm that Vail hired took it for granted that the well-to-do exerted a disproportionate influence in

The Telephone Brings Companionship

BOOKS, piano, needlework—these are sometimes divert-
ing, but a woman craves real companionship. She longs
to hear a living, laughing, human voice—longs for
someone to talk to about the little, intimate, personal things.

Then the telephone bell rings.

"Oh, Edith," she exclaims, "you don't know how glad
I am you called me up. * * * * * * No, George isn't home
yet. I'm *so* lonesome and——"

She talks and listens to the voice that talks to her about
the things she likes best. The telephone has banished her
loneliness.

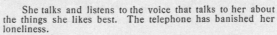

Have you a telephone in your home?

NEW YORK TELEPHONE COMPANY.

Telephone sociability was a recurrent theme in big-city operating company
advertisements beginning around 1900. In this 1911 New York Telephone Company advertisement, the telephone is hailed for banishing loneliness and enabling
women to talk with their friends about the "little, intimate, personal things." The
sales pitch was subtle, yet direct: "Have *you* a telephone in *your* home?" "The
Telephone Brings Companionship," *Telephone Review* 2 (February 1911): back
cover.

shaping public opinion and pitched their appeals accordingly.[161] Operating company advertising campaigns were less pretentious. To sell telephone service, operating company publicity departments realized that they had to reach out to the many as well as the few.

The popularization of the telephone in the United States was accelerated by the multitude of non-Bell, or independent, operating companies that sprang to life following a succession of court rulings in the 1890s that had been intended to foster competition. The consequences of telephone competition were substantial and enduring. Yet competition cannot fully explain the popularization of telephone service in the nation's largest cities. In Chicago, as well as in New York City and several other large cities, the incumbent preempted rivals by providing telephone facilities to a large, diverse, and previously untapped urban market.

The first generation of big-city telephone managers—Theodore N. Vail in New York City and Charles N. Fay in Chicago—conceived of the telephone as a specialty service for an exclusive clientele. Beginning in the 1890s and reaching a crescendo around 1900, a second generation of telephone managers—Union N. Bethell in New York City, John I. Sabin in San Francisco, James E. Caldwell in Nashville, and Angus Hibbard in Chicago—popularized the telephone as a mass service for the entire population. Bethell, Sabin, Caldwell, and Hibbard each had an intuitive grasp of the interconnectedness of urban life and made it a cornerstone of their business strategy. By combining technical advances in switchboard design with innovative calling plans, they made the fruits of invention accessible to the many as well as the few. Many people, of course, remained excluded. No network is ever seamless, and every network has gaps. Yet by 1907 it had become inconceivable for a telephone manager to contend, as Fay had as recently as 1887, that the day would never come when more than one-half of 1 percent of the population would ever have occasion to make a telephone call.

All the world was not Chicago. Yet innovations that originated in Chicago—as well as in New York City, San Francisco, and Nashville, Tennessee—had enduring implications for telephone service throughout the nation. In the telephone business, as in many other realms, cities were the seedbeds of innovation. Only after operating companies had become entrenched in their urban strongholds would they reach out to the hinterland. For the majority of Chicago telephone users, the failure of electromechanical switching was less newsworthy than the success of the nickel-in-the-slot, and the long-distance hookup was a less essential upgrade than the busy signal. The telephone was not only the first electrical communications medium to be marketed as a mass service; it was also the first to be popularized. Henceforth, the telephone became second nature not only for business, but also for the business of everyday life.

9

GRAY WOLVES

Our inquiries show that "telephone free trade" is plainly not
desired by the people of responsibility related to either the Bell
or the independent companies.

Dugald C. Jackson, 1907

One of the "greatest obstacles" Bell's independent rivals confronted,
reflected public relations expert Ivy L. Lee in 1906, was their inability
to secure a beachhead in New York City or Chicago: "So long as the Bell
company stands safely fortified within these two great citadels, with
New England still in the hands of the Bell army, there will be many
people who feel that independent telephone securities, especially of long
distance lines, are not the most attractive investments."[1]

Lee's assessment casts a spotlight on the single most difficult challenge
that the independents faced in their attempt to supplant Bell. By 1906
independent operating companies had built exchanges in several of the
nation's largest cities, including Philadelphia, St. Louis, Baltimore, and
Buffalo. Yet they faced stiff competition in each of these cities from
older and better-established Bell rivals. Big-city Bell operating companies had made a large investment in switching equipment, wires, and
telephones. In addition, and no less importantly, they had entered into
informal—and, typically, collusive—relationships with city councils that
blocked new entrants from contesting the market. The independents
tried repeatedly, and without success, to establish a rival operating company in New York City. The only independent to contest the Chicago
market—Illinois Telephone and Telegraph—fared poorly and was a
major embarrassment for the independents, since Chicago was the epicenter of the independent movement and the company's failure was
widely reported in the press.

311

The campaign to supplant Bell met with two crippling setbacks in 1907. The first was the collapse in February of the United States Independent Telephone Company; the second came in November with the rechartering of Chicago Telephone. For many decades after November 1907 the independents would remain a major presence in the telephone business; never again, however, could they realistically aspire to supplant Bell.

The independents' setbacks were a logical consequence of the divergent organizational responses of Bell and independent operating companies to the consolidationist political economy that had been fostered by municipal franchise law. This political economy was very different from the competitive political economy in which Western Union had bested its rivals following the enactment of the New York Telegraph Act of 1848.

Among the factors that were not responsible for the independents' setbacks was the supposed collusion between Bell and the New York investment bank of J. P. Morgan & Co. J. P. Morgan's alleged influence on the early twentieth-century telephone business has subtly biased historical writing on this topic since the 1930s. Like a mustachioed villain in a silent movie, J. P. Morgan himself is blamed for blocking the independents from obtaining venture capital by gaining control of Bell in 1907 and appointing Vail as its president.

None of these claims holds up under close scrutiny. The independents had little trouble obtaining investment capital before the collapse of United States Independent in 1907; J. P. Morgan & Co. exerted, at best, a marginal influence on Bell business strategy; and Vail's appointment had the backing not only of J. P. Morgan, but also of Clarence Mackay—who at the time owned the largest single bloc of Bell shares—as well as a still-influential cadre of longtime Bell directors who remembered Vail's leadership role in the fledgling telephone business of the 1880s.[2] Bell in 1907 was not Western Union in 1881. The telephone business in the 1900s had become far too large and variegated to be dominated by a single investor, as Jay Gould had dominated Western Union. Thus it was not anomalous that one of the best-documented instances of Bell's relationship with J. P. Morgan & Co. was adversarial. In 1909, J. P. Morgan & Co. bought a bundle of failed Ohio independents in the expectation that it would soon unload them on Bell. When political circumstances made this impossible, Bell saddled J. P. Morgan & Co. with the loss.[3]

If any investment bank could claim credit for shaping Bell policy, it was Kidder, Peabody & Co. No other financial institution enjoyed as long a relationship with Bell or played a more central role in the all-important financing of its big-city operating companies. Kidder, Peabody & Co. financed the takeover of a would-be Bell rival in 1901 and sold nearly $70 million in bonds for New York Telephone between 1909 and 1912.[4] Had Kidder, Peabody not been greatly weakened during the Great Depression—the decade in which the J. P. Morgan legend first gained prominence—a counter mythology might have emerged in which Kidder, Peabody and not J. P. Morgan became the deus ex machina that explained why Bell and not the independents prevailed.

The independents would never interconnect with Bell, predicted independent spokesman James M. Thomas in 1901. Even so, Thomas fully expected that the independents would soon form a single combine that would be more or less analogous to Bell's: there would be "two great companies" in the telephone business—one Bell and one independent—just as there were in the telegraph business.[5] Had unbridled competition prevailed, independents would presumably have found it advantageous to compete with each other. Yet they did not: independents often competed with Bell, but almost never with other independents. It would be "suicidal" for an independent to challenge another independent, warned one independent booster in 1907. Indeed, it would be the "death of the movement," since it would make it impossible for either company to obtain the necessary capital to expand: "It does not require a prophet of finance to foresee that such a policy as this would do more to check independent telephone development than all the diplomacy, trickery, slander and bluster of the allied Bell companies."[6] Once an independent had built a toll line, declared an independent investor, other independents should grant it "vested rights" to the route.[7]

Although the independents hoped to take Bell's place, they refused to adopt certain network-building innovations that Bell operating companies had pioneered. Among the most notable of these innovations were multiple party lines, measured service, and nickel-in-the-slots. Multiple party lines were inconvenient, insecure, and a breeding ground for gossip, warned an advertising brochure issued by one Cleveland-based independent around 1900: "Your 'phone may not be a party line, but how about the other fellow's? Ever think of that? Dangerous, isn't it?"[8]

Unlike its Bell rival, the Cleveland independent promised "Unlimited, Individual, Full Metallic Service to Every Subscriber." The performance standards that the Cleveland independent advertised had been designed for, and were presumably appreciated by, the business subscribers for whom they had been intended. Yet the Cleveland independent's refusal to offer as wide a menu of low-cost calling plans as its Bell rival limited its appeal to the rest of the city's population. If the Cleveland independent wished to expand, Bell staffer Frank R. Colvin confided to an official superior at Bell, its management would have no choice but to emulate Bell and introduce multiple party lines and measured service; its low flat rate had already secured it all of the business subscribers it could realistically hope to attain.[9]

The refusal of independent operating companies to expand their menu of calling plans limited their ability to compete head-to-head with Bell. Not until 1902 would a single independent operating company acknowledge the limitations of the flat-rate principle and shift to measured service, observed one business journalist, even though the Bell operating companies had "so actively developed" measured service for several years as a result of their "experience."[10] The independents' predicament was underscored by the dilemma that a St. Louis independent operating company experienced when it tried to match the low prices that its Bell rival offered its residential customers. The pay-as-you-go nickel-in-the-slots that his Bell rival had recently installed in the city's residential districts were a "nuisance" for which he had no good remedy, explained the independent operating company manager. Their company only offered flat rates, and many preferred the "inferior" service that Bell offered at the cheaper pay-as-you-go rates to the higher-quality, though more expensive, service that they provided.[11] The nub of the problem was that his company required subscribers to sign a year-long contract, with three months paid up in advance, whereas his Bell rival did not. Moreover, the subscribers preferred to pay "equally as much" for Bell coin-slot telephones as they would pay him for "unlimited service." The convenience of paying by the call, rather than the year, balanced out the benefit of unlimited local service, even if, in the end, the cost was the same.[12] Bell's principal advantage over the independents was not its long-distance network—a feature irrelevant to most telephone users—but the array of low-cost calling plans it offered users inside the city. Multiple party lines were more complicated to operate in the city than in the countryside, conceded one independent journalist in 1905. Yet this was no reason for independents not to make the investment to install them.[13] Unfortunately for the independents, few independent operating companies heeded the journalist's advice.

The independents' reluctance to expand their menu of low-cost calling plans can be partly explained by their fixation on business subscribers. Business subscribers preferred flat rates and disliked multiple party lines, and the independents followed their lead. Independent spokesman James M. Thomas repeatedly urged his colleagues to think more creatively about calling plans, but he had only limited success. Measured service, Thomas declared in 1900, gave the "greatest number of advantages to all classes of people" and was the "only fair way" to charge for telephone service in large cities where "extremes of service are demanded."[14] Yet even Thomas drew the line at multiple party lines and nickel-in-the-slots. The recent introduction of these innovations by big-city Bell operating companies, Thomas predicted, would work to the benefit of the independents, since it advertised Bell's poor-quality service.[15] Missing from Thomas's analysis was any recognition of the fact that for many, if not most, telephone users, high quality was of less moment than low cost.

Left unspoken by Thomas was an even more basic issue: it was expensive to make the large financial outlays necessary to implement the calling plans that big-city Bell-associated operating companies had pioneered, and few independents had the resources to make the investment. Paradoxically, it cost more to meet the diverse demand for cheap and convenient telephone service inside a big city than to satisfy the dispersed demand for toll-line service within a metropolitan region. Independents underinvested in switching equipment and overinvested in toll lines. In so doing, they missed the opportunity to tap the huge urban market that their Bell rivals had begun to exploit.

Among the most ambitious of the early independents was the Chicago-based telephone equipment manufacturer James E. Keelyn. Keelyn acquired in the 1890s a national reputation as the organizer of an independent trade group that would come to be known as the National Independent Telephone Association (NITA). He had been active in the telephone business since 1892, when he obtained several municipal franchises in anticipation of the expiration of Alexander Graham Bell's patents. To Keelyn's surprise, he could not find a manufacturer who was willing to supply him with necessary equipment. To meet this demand, Keelyn went into the telephone equipment manufacturing business himself.[16]

The NITA was originally a legal defense fund for independent equipment manufacturers. For many years Bell had successfully sued would-be rivals for patent infringement, and independent telephone equipment manufacturers were determined to fight back. NITA's first members were forty equipment manufacturers, many of which were headquartered in Chicago.[17] The NITA was originally known as the Telephone Protective Association; Keelyn founded it to thwart a would-be monopolist from wielding patent rights that the federal government had certified. In short, the catalyst for its establishment was not the weakness of the federal government—the time-honored Tocquevillian explanation for the proliferation of voluntary associations in the United States—but its power. Just as the New York Associated Press had been established in the 1840s to defend New York newspapers against a telegraph corporation that brandished patent rights granted by the federal government to Samuel F. B. Morse, so the NITA had been established in the 1890s to protect Chicago telephone equipment manufacturers from a corporation that had coalesced around a federal monopoly grant. Although Alexander Graham Bell's patents had expired in 1894, Bell was determined to perpetuate its monopoly by flaunting the patent rights to Emile Berliner's microphone, an invention to which Bell had obtained the patent rights in 1891.

Keelyn recognized that would-be operating company promoters might hesitate to enter the telephone business if they had a reasonable expectation that the equipment they purchased might land them in court for patent infringement. To stay abreast of the latest developments in patent law, Keelyn hired Kempster Miller, a college-educated engineer who had previously worked as an examiner in the Patent Office. There Miller had been responsible for judging the merits of new telephone inventions.[18] To fortify the timid, Keelyn promised to pay the legal expenses of any operating company sued by Bell for using telephone equipment that his company manufactured.[19] Taking the offensive, he even briefly investigated the possibility in 1895 of prosecuting Bell under the Sherman Act for restraining trade.[20]

Keelyn scored his greatest legal triumph in 1897 when he prevailed on the courts to void a patent Bell held for a device known as a switch hook. A switch hook closed a circuit when a caller picked up a telephone receiver to make a call. The courts rejected all eight of the reasons that Bell advanced to justify its legality, handing Keelyn a huge victory. Three years earlier the independents had convinced a judge to void the Berliner microphone patent, yet this ruling was soon overturned. The switch hook patent was the first to be permanently voided, a major psychological boost.[21]

High on Keelyn's wish list was the construction of an independent long-distance network. The commercial value of Bell's long-distance network was limited; in fact, its construction was a major financial drain. Yet Keelyn recognized its symbolic import. If the independents were to prevail in their contest with Bell, he believed it imperative that they offer their users something equally grand.

The easiest way for the independents to replicate Bell's long-distance network would be to persuade state lawmakers to mandate the interconnection of Bell and independent operating companies. The independents unsuccessfully sponsored several interconnection bills in the 1890s. Bell opposed them all: Bell–independent interconnection, Bell lawyers contended, was technically demanding and morally wrong, because it would give a rival access to facilities for which it had not paid.

Next, a small but determined group of independents decided to build their own long-distance network. To create an incentive for operating companies to sign on, these independents reversed the independents' traditional position on mandatory interconnection. In Ohio, for example, independent promoters opposed mandatory interconnection laws as late as 1908. If the state legislature permitted independent operating companies to sign on with Bell, the most compelling rationale for the construction of an independent long-distance network would disappear.[22]

The enormity of the challenge of building a rival long-distance network led Keelyn to propose that Congress enact legislation mandating the construction by the federal government of a long-distance network that was open to all. If the federal government built a long-distance network that was open to the independents—or alternatively, if it bought out Bell's long-distance telephone network—the problem was solved. Keelyn was convinced that it was more important for the federal government to own and operate a long-distance telephone network than to deliver the mail. The federal government—and only the federal government—had the organizational capabilities to satisfy the "public needs" for "inter-communication between cities of the United States."[23]

Keelyn was but one of several independents to endorse federal ownership of the telephone. "Were it practical," and "our admirable, economical and effective mail system" indicated that it was, reflected an independent business journalist in 1903, "it would evidently be an ideal thing for Uncle Sam to own and operate every telephone box (private lines excepted) in our vast country." The federal government would match price to cost, hastening a "colossal curtailment" in the rates Bell charged for the "indispensable telephone luxury." To highlight the superiority of consolidation to competition, the journalist ventured a postal-telephonic analogy: "Were Uncle Sam out of the mail business and there were as many limited companies to transport letters as there are to transport sound, how much do you think it would cost to send a letter from New York City to San Francisco? Certainly more than two cents. Let us have a telephone merger, if it merges into the hands of the government."[24]

Hundreds of independent operating companies were prudently financed and well run. Many endured for decades. Indeed, over 1,300 remained in existence as recently as 1989. In that year, the independents provided telephone service to 20 percent of American people and two-thirds of the land area occupied by the United States.[25] Yet it would be myopic to deny that in the period between 1894 and 1907 many independent equipment manufacturers ventured overly optimistic forecasts about the likely market for telephone service or that many independents were financed in a highly risky way. Equipment manufacturers assured would-be independent promoters that Bell operating companies were vulnerable on account of their economic subordination to Bell. In their view, operating companies kept rates high and performance standards low because Bell required each company to pay it not only a dividend on its holdings in operating company stock, but also a licensing fee of 4.5 percent of its annual revenue.[26] Independent operating companies bore neither burden; as a consequence, they should have little trouble providing superior facilities at a lower cost.

To lure potential investors, independent equipment manufacturers advertised heavily in the trade press. It was not surprising that the editors of these publications "paint the situation as rosy as the imagination may permit," reflected one Bell publicist in 1903.[27] Independent telephone equipment manufacturers profited even if the operating companies that they supplied did not. "Fortunes have been made in the BUILDING of competing telephone plants," declared one unusually candid business analyst in 1908, "and fortunes have been lost in OPERATING them."[28]

The prospectuses issued by the first Texas independents, reminisced one Texas telephone promoter in 1914, "read like the literature composed by the dream department of some transportation company."[29]

The overoptimism of the independents led to many financial debacles. In dozens of cities and towns, independents negotiated franchises with local officials that obliged them to furnish telephone service at extremely low rates. Next they purchased equipment, solicited subscriptions, and went into business. When their bonds came due, they defaulted. Eighty-five independent operating companies went into receivership between 1903 and 1906. In percentage terms, this total was quite small; independents, after all, numbered in the thousands. Even so, by casting a spotlight on the precariousness of independent finance, this information scared off more than a few potential investors.[30]

The most spectacular independent financial debacle was the collapse of Telephone, Telegraph, and Cable in 1901. Few independents had gone into business with brighter prospects. Its manager was W. J. Latta, a former divisional superintendent on the Pennsylvania Railroad, and its backers were headed up by a wealthy clique of New York City investors that included George Gould, William C. Whitney, P. A. B. Widener, and John Jacob Astor.[31]

The idea of a vast independent combine went back at least as far as 1899. In that year, Postal Telegraph president John W. Mackay met with independents in Chicago in the hope that they might join together in an anti-Bell combine. Had Mackay not died in 1902, he may well have become a major force in the telephone business, just as he had become a major player in the telegraph business following Jay Gould's takeover of Western Union in 1881.[32]

Among the most prized possessions of Telephone, Telegraph, and Cable was Erie, a holding company for operating companies in Texas, Minnesota, North and South Dakota, Michigan, Wisconsin, and Cleveland, Ohio. At its peak in 1900, Erie controlled 15 percent of all the telephone lines operated by Bell companies.[33] Erie was controlled by Charles Glidden, a well-regarded member of the first generation of Bell operating company managers. Among Bell insiders, Glidden was best remembered for building a toll line between Boston and Lowell, one of the first such toll lines in the country.

Another telephone company allied with Telephone, Telegraph, and Cable was People's Telephone, a would-be rival to Bell. In 1900 it was headed up by Darwin R. James, a former congressman who had long been active in the New York Board of Trade and Transportation. Its expansive name notwithstanding, People's Telephone had not been intended to extend access to telephone service to underserved groups. Rather, it complemented Simon Sterne's political campaign to lower telephone rates for New York City's business elite.

Under other circumstances, Telephone, Telegraph, and Cable might have established a federation of operating companies that could have held their own against Bell. Unfortunately for its promoters, it made two serious miscalculations that ensured its demise. The first miscalculation was its acquisition of Erie at a ridiculously inflated price. Had Glidden not been such a "hog," confided Bell staffer Frank R. Colvin, Telephone, Telegraph, and Cable might well have succeeded in becoming a permanent rival to Bell. Yet Glidden had sold a group of gullible investors a worthless "gold brick," and the opportunity was lost.[34] To salvage at least part of the investment, Telephone, Telegraph, and Cable was quietly sold Erie to Kidder, Peabody & Co.; never again would a Bell licensee stray from the Bell fold.[35]

The second unfortunate decision was the independents' underestimation of the likelihood of gaining entry to the lucrative New York City market. Although People's Telephone owned a franchise to build a telephone operating company in New York City, it found it impossible to gain access to the underground conduits necessary to build a network. The owner of these conduits—the Empire Subway Company—was controlled by New York Telephone; not surprisingly, it found a way to keep its would-be rival, People's, at bay.[36]

The most notorious of all the independent collapses was that of United States Independent in 1907. Like Telephone, Telegraph, and Cable, United States Independent was a holding company for independent operating companies. Capitalized at a hefty $50 million, it had been organized in 1905 by a well-heeled group of investors based in Rochester, New York. Among its backers were camera magnate George Eastman and Hiram Sibley, Jr., the son of the by-now-legendary telegraph magnate Hiram Sibley.[37] Eastman and Sibley, remembering the huge profits that an earlier generation of Rochester investors had made from the telegraph, hoped to repeat their success with the telephone. Sibley's father had successfully challenged the telegraph monopoly that had grown up around patent rights granted to Samuel F. B. Morse. Sibley Jr. envisioned United States Independent supplanting the telephone monopoly spawned by the patent rights owned by Alexander Graham Bell.

United States Independent was modeled on Bell. Like Bell, it combined an independent equipment manufacturer, an independent long-distance provider, and a portfolio of independent operating companies. To increase its credibility, United States Independent convinced a leading telephone equipment manufacturer—Stromberg-Carlson—to relocate from Chicago to Rochester. If the independents were going to rival Bell, they needed a manufacturing district independent of Western Electric. Like Telephone, Telegraph, and Cable, United States Independent had also acquired a franchise to build a telephone operating company in New York City and hoped to obtain the underground rights-of-way necessary to get underway.

Unfortunately for Eastman and Sibley, United States Independent was no Western Union. None of its operating companies generated enough revenue to cover interest payments on its debt, and its backers found it impossible to raise additional revenue by selling stock. The inevitable collapse came in February 1907. To salvage at least part of their investment, bondholders agreed to accept 35 cents on the dollar, a humiliating end for a venture whose promoters had dreamed of building a first mover in the telephone business to match Western Union.[38]

The collapse of United States Independent occasioned a flurry of newspaper articles on the precariousness of independent securities. To raise capital so that an "opposition" telephone operating company might challenge an incumbent that was already "in possession of the field" would henceforth be "almost impossible," editorialized the *Wall Street Journal*.[39] The cumulative effect of this negative publicity was far-reaching. Never again would an independent seriously contemplate overmatching Bell as the nation's dominant network provider. Not until the 1910s would the independents once again find it possible to raise the capital necessary for network expansion as a by-product of a favorable legal ruling by the U.S. Department of Justice. To protect their collective interests, the independents increasingly turned to the federal government: Having failed in the market, they looked to the state. Henceforth the independents' political agenda focused less on encouraging competition than on preserving competitors, including, in particular, those competitors engaged in a head-on contest with Bell.[40]

The collapse of United States Independent had a devastating impact on the independent investor. These investors—often small-town bankers, merchants, and well-to-do farmers—had believed the lurid tales spun by independent publicists about the financial vulnerability of the

Bell "octopus" and so had invested in independent companies in the expectation that they would soon be as lucrative as Bell. The most elaborate anti-Bell polemic ran not in *McClure's*, a general interest magazine renowned for its hard-hitting exposés of business corruption, but in *Success*, a self-help magazine that ran a steady diet of stories on how its readers could get rich quick. Shortly thereafter, its author started up a tip sheet for would-be independent investors entitled *Telephone Securities Weekly*.[41]

"Our greatest success in raising capital," reminisced one ex-independent stock canvasser in 1907, "was among the farmers who had read about enormous profits in the Bell companies and were ready to lend their influence and capital to down them, for what reason they knew not." The canvasser promised the farmers an 8 percent dividend and, to sweeten the pot, handed out free passes for telephone service that were almost equal to the farmers' investment. The canvasser himself received a generous $20 commission on every $100 in shares that he sold, netting him several hundred dollars a day. In due course, independent operating companies installed switchboards made of "inferior material" bought at exorbitant prices from opportunistic independent manufacturers. As long as stock sales continued, so too did the 8 percent dividend, with the new stock sales covering the old investors' dividend. When no one remained to be gulled, the operating company tried to sell out to Bell, frequently without success. The failed exchanges were often located in territory Bell already occupied, rendering their acquisition redundant. In several instances in which Bell was willing to buy independents out, the courts blocked the sale as a restraint of trade. Under the circumstances, it was only a matter of time before the independent movement would implode, and, confessed the canvasser, "I have had enough."[42]

The shaky finances of independent operating companies did not go unnoticed at Bell. If the independents wished to remain in business over the long haul, Bell President Frederick P. Fish lectured a reporter in 1903, they would have no choice but to emulate the most prudently financed Bell operating companies and set aside 10 percent of their annual revenue for a replacement fund. Yet if they did, this would destroy every single independent operating company in the country.[43] "All this hue and cry about 'Bell monopoly' and 'Bell extortion' is used for the purpose of getting the good money of the public into the hands of the promoters and the franchise vendors," fumed Bell president Theodore N. Vail in 1908. Vail found it particularly troubling that independents paid out dividends on the basis of revenue they had generated from the sale of securities: "This proposition to guarantee the payment of interest on bonds and dividends on capital, by the bonds or stock so guaranteed, is one of the oldest and most fallacious methods in financial history. It is good only so long as you can sell the securities, and no longer."[44]

For Bell loyalists, the moral was plain. The independents played fast and loose with the rules of financial propriety to make a quick killing; Bell looked to the future. Long time horizons were a defining feature of Bell's emerging managerial ideology. The esprit de corps of Bell staffers, reflected Bell staffer Frank R. Colvin in 1899, had its origins in their dedication to the "cause" of building a network that would endure long after they were gone. Colvin himself had once been an independent telephone equipment manufacturer, and like many converts, he was zealous in his newfound faith. The principled refusal of two high-level Bell engineers to jump ship to an independent that offered them the unheard-of annual salary of $20,000 was for Colvin a special point of pride.[45] Independents might give the telephone business a try, yet, when the going got tough, they would take a flier on a gold mine or "God knows what." Bell true believers knew better: "We youngsters in the Great Cause all have a good long time to live yet; and my belief is that the best capital we can have, in addition to our ability and efficiency, is a reputation for loyalty of the kind that money can't buy—a loyalty that our presidents and directors can absolutely bank on."[46]

No single venture promised to do more to raise the independents' visibility than the establishment of an independent operating company in Chicago. For Keelyn, the establishment of a Chicago independent was an obsession. Keelyn got his wish in 1898, when the city council awarded a franchise to the Illinois Telephone and Telegraph Company. No one knew it at the time, but Illinois Telephone and Telegraph would be the only independent operating company to ever build a rival telephone network in Chicago's downtown business district.

Illinois Telephone and Telegraph obtained its franchise under suspicious circumstances that were almost certainly tainted with fraud. Chicago aldermen routinely obtained kickbacks from municipal franchise corporations that needed special privileges from the city, and Illinois Telephone and Telegraph was no exception. To secure its franchise, Illinois Telephone and Telegraph was rumored to have paid out $100,000 to twenty-one aldermen.[47] Funding for Illinois Telephone and Telegraph was easily obtained. Inside Chicago, it had the backing of Chicago independent telephone equipment manufacturers Milo Kellogg, James E. Keelyn, Alfred Stromberg, and Androv Carlson.[48] Among its largest non-Chicago investors was the wealthy St. Louis brewer Adolphus Busch. One of the lawmakers to cry foul was John Peter Altgeld, a former Illinois governor well known as a fearless critic of corporate malfeasance. The backers of the Illinois Telephone and Telegraph franchise, Altgeld charged, were venal speculators who had backed it so that they could unload it on the highest bidder. Altgeld's suspicions were vindicated when the backers sold the franchise to an investors' consortium headed up by Albert G. Wheeler, a promoter who had once helped Jay Gould battle Western Union. Now Wheeler would take on Bell.[49]

Illinois Telephone and Telegraph never posed a credible threat to Chicago Telephone. Its exchange remained confined to Chicago's central business district, a part of the city already well served by Chicago Telephone. At no point in its brief history did its subscription list top 20,000, a tiny fraction of the several hundred thousand telephones that its Bell rival operated in 1907.[50] Particularly telling was the inability of the Illinois Telephone and Telegraph sales department to obtain the permission of downtown Chicago druggists to install public telephones in their stores. The potential future advantage of contracting with the new entrant, the druggists calculated, failed to outweigh the current benefits they obtained from Chicago Telephone.[51]

Illinois Telephone and Telegraph's poor showing prompted speculation that its owners had brokered a deal with Bell to limit its expansion. Whether or not Illinois Telephone and Telegraph had entered into a noncompete agreement with Bell is a matter of speculation: If it had, it was one of the best-kept business secrets of the day. What is known is that an Illinois Telephone and Telegraph lawyer approached Bell president Frederick P. Fish several years after Illinois Telephone and Telegraph went into operation with an offer to enter into a noncompete agreement. In return for a cash payment, Illinois Telephone and Telegraph would cap its Chicago exchange at 20,000 telephones, the minimum number it needed to avoid forfeiting its franchise. "If we were to do anything"—Fish reported to a Bell shareholder—"I should suppose

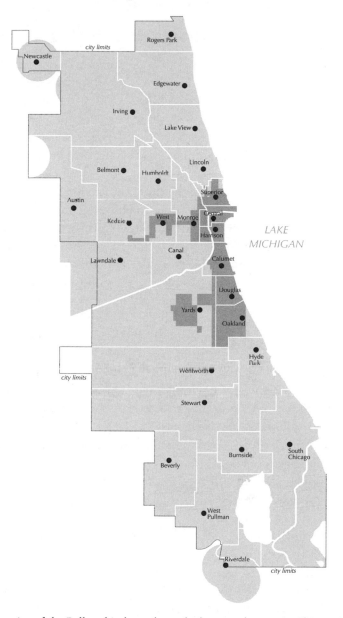

The relative size of the Bell and independent telephone exchanges in Chicago in 1915. By 1915, the Chicago Telephone Company operated a spatially extensive exchange in Chicago that was more or less congruent with the city's limits. Its territory is the light gray area on the map, with dots for the individual switching centers. Its rival, Illinois Telephone and Telegraph, served a much smaller territory—the dark gray area on the map—that was mostly confined to the central business district, the stockyards, and certain well-to-do residential districts to the west and the south. Kempster B. Miller, *Report on the Automatic Telephone Situation in the City of Chicago* (Chicago: n.p., 1915), p. 32.

that it would be better to give a spot cash sum or annual payment, with the understanding that they would limit their development to 20,000 telephones, the number that they are obliged to have in order to comply with their ordinance."[52] If Fish accepted the Illinois Telephone and Telegraph offer, there is no record of it. Given Chicago Telephone's strong position in the Chicago market, it would not have been surprising if he had refused.

The Illinois Telephone and Telegraph franchise stipulated that the company was to leave the city's pavement undisturbed. Undaunted, Wheeler built an elaborate maze of tunnels underneath Chicago's streets. The tunnels originated in an alley located directly behind the saloon of the notoriously corrupt Chicago alderman Johnny Powers. Powers was the ringleader of the "gray wolves," a group of aldermen who had long supplemented their modest salaries by shaking down municipal franchise corporations (the name alluded not only to the color of the aldermens' hair but also to their cunning). The gray wolves had profited handsomely from the negotiations that culminated in granting the Illinois Telephone and Telegraph franchise, and Powers saw no reason why he could not also profit from the construction of its network.[53] The proximity of the tunnel entrance to Powers's saloon told a tale that no reform-minded Chicagoan could miss: Chicago Telephone's challengers were not visionary promoters but venal speculators backed by a notoriously corrupt city official.

Illinois Telephone and Telegraph went into receivership in 1909. Following its reorganization, it limped along until 1913, when Bell quietly bought it out. The purchase hinged on the approval of the Chicago city council, which was not forthcoming.[54] Three years later, following a long and rancorous city council debate, it changed its mind. The final purchase price was deemed excessive by public utility expert Edward W. Bemis, fueling rumors that its owners had been paid off.[55] Chicago alderman Charles E. Merriam shared Bemis's concern. In reflecting on the city council vote, Merriam declared that he had a "strong feeling" that "many members" of the council had been bought.[56] Thus ended the brief career of the only operating company to go head-to-head against Chicago Telephone in Chicago.

For telephone analysts, Illinois Telephone and Telegraph's failure was an object lesson in the futility of competition. Another lesson that they took away was the unsuitability of electromechanical switching in big-city exchanges like Chicago's. Illinois Telephone and Telegraph had originally installed a manual switchboard; by the time it went into receivership in 1909, it had replaced its manual switchboard with an electromechanical switchboard manufactured by Automatic Electric. Electromechanical switching had failed in Chicago, and everyone knew it. "No one to my knowledge," declared Chicago's city statistician Hugo S. Grosser, "will state that the existence of the Illinois Telephone Company, with its automatic phones, has been of any special advantage to our business world."[57] For Automatic Electric, the poor performance of its Chicago switchboard was a public relations fiasco. Although Automatic Electric had an enviable reputation for technical virtuosity, it remained dogged in the United States by the presumption that electromagnetic switching was best suited to small and middle-sized cities and that it could not meet the unusually heavy demand for telephone service in Chicago, the very city in which Automatic Electric was headquartered. "The fact that the automatic was installed here a few years ago and has not worked out successfully," conceded one well-informed insider, "has been a strong point against the development of the automatic outside of Chicago."[58] Its installation, concluded independent telephone engineer Kempster Miller, had been a "flat failure."[59]

Illinois Telephone and Telegraph failed as a telephone operating company, but it succeeded as a freight hauler. Shortly after Wheeler began digging his tunnels, he negotiated an agreement with a consortium of coal magnates based on Scranton, Pennsylvania, to expand these tunnels into a right-of-way for an electric railroad underneath the city's crowded streets that could carry coal and other bulky commodities. The railroad soon eclipsed the telephone, and the telephone became, as one insider informed Fish, the "tail of the kite."[60] The underground freight service remained in operation until 1959. The now empty tunnels lay forgotten until 1992 when, in a bizarre accident, a construction crew repairing a bridge pier on the Chicago River accidentally punctured one of their walls, flooding hundreds of basements in the city's downtown.

Chicago Telephone's most formidable challenge in the early twentieth century came not from a rival operating company but from a segment of its subscribers. The most dissatisfied segment of telephone subscribers in Chicago hailed from the upper ranks of its business elite. When Chicago Telephone raised the annual rate for flat-rate business service from $125 to $175 in the 1890s, this group mobilized. To rescind the rate increase, it enlisted the Illinois Manufacturers' Association (IMA) to make its case before the Chicago city council.

The IMA was a well-funded business lobby whose membership included factory owners, wholesalers, and retailers. Though perhaps best known for its hostility to organized labor, it agitated on a wide range of business-related issues. High on its list was the reduction of the $175 annual fee for business subscribers.

To fight the rate increase, the IMA enlisted the prominent Chicago lawyer Levy Mayer. To make the case for a rate reduction, Mayer charged the company with violating its 1889 franchise. According to Mayer, this franchise limited the company to no more than $125 for flat-rate service. In fact, the relevant phrase of the agreement was deliberately ambiguous: the company agreed not to increase the "rates for telephone service now established." The company contended that the phrase "now established" modified "telephone service"; Mayer countered that it modified "rates."[61]

To sweeten the pot for the aldermen, Mayer contended that Chicago Telephone owed thousands of dollars in back taxes. Chicago Telephone lawyers responded that, under its 1889 agreement, the corporation only had to pay taxes on those assets that were located inside the city of Chicago at the time its franchise had been approved. Since 1889, however, the city had annexed over 125 square miles of territory: the company's tax bill, in Mayer's view, should be based on the city's current boundaries rather than on its boundaries in 1889.

One of Mayer's most ingenious arguments concerned the company's rationale for a rate increase. Chicago Telephone lawyers defended the $50 rate increase as a service upgrade that had been necessitated by the hookup of the subscribers' telephones to Bell's long-distance network, a service that it had not offered in 1889. Long-distance service required two-wire metallic circuits, yet many Chicago telephones remained on single-wire grounded lines.[62] Mayer responded that the company had installed metallic circuits not to facilitate long-distance service—an upgrade few subscribers valued—but to maintain preexisting performance standards inside Chicago. Metallic circuits eliminated the hazard posed by induction, a serious problem following the construction of electric streetcar lines and electric power stations. Company lawyers ruefully conceded that, in the main, Mayer was right: "I suppose it is one of the weak points in our case that as a matter of fact, a very strong motive in the change from grounded to metallic circuit service was the necessity of overcoming the disturbance arising from strong currents."[63] Yet if the company had installed metallic circuits merely to maintain a preexisting performance standard rather than to provide a service upgrade, this reinforced Mayer's argument that its 1889 franchise did not entitle it to raise its rates.[64] Ironically, the only permissible upgrade was for a service for which few subscribers were willing to pay.

Mayer's willingness to challenge Chicago Telephone owed something to his personal background. Like the Boston lawyer Louis Brandeis, Mayer was a German Jew in an age in which anti-Jewish sentiment was pervasive. By championing a reduction in the business flat rate, Mayer could plausibly claim to be fighting a powerful corporation, even though the only subscribers for whom this calling plan was of any practical concern were themselves a business elite. The fact that many members of the IMA were proprietors—and not corporate managers—made their cause seem all the more worthwhile. Brandeis, too, had championed proprietors against corporations. Yet unlike Brandeis, Mayer lacked a squeaky-clean reputation. Among his previous clients had been the notorious Chicago streetcar magnate Charles Yerkes. Mayer declined to emulate Brandeis's innovative legal strategy of recruiting efficiency experts such as Frederick W. Taylor to take corporations to task for overcharging the public through unnecessarily wasteful business methods. Even if he had, he would have found it hard to enlist a single reputable electrical engineer who was willing to defend the business flat rate in Chicago.

Mayer won a major victory in 1902 when he convinced the courts that Chicago Telephone lacked the authority under its 1889 ordinance to charge subscribers more than $125 a year.[65] Chicago Telephone suffered a second setback when, shortly thereafter, Mayer persuaded the courts to require Chicago Telephone to pay the city thousands of dollars in back taxes. The company appealed both rulings, but in February 1906 the Illinois Supreme Court rejected its appeals.[66] Lacking legal recourse, the company restored the $125 flat-rate fee and agreed to pay the city comptroller $260,000 in back taxes and flat-rate subscribers $85,000 in overcharges.[67]

Flush with success, Mayer looked to the city council to institute a rate cap. Chicago Telephone's 1889 franchise expired in 1909. Its reauthorization was certain to prompt a prolonged contest between the city, the company, and the city's telephone users that Mayer hoped to turn to his client's advantage.

The impending expiration of Chicago Telephone's franchise presented the city council with four options: renew the company's franchise; award the franchise to a different operating company; give a franchise to both Chicago Telephone and a rival operating company; or buy out Chicago Telephone's assets and operate its plant as a government agency. All but one of these options received careful consideration in the more than 100 meetings the city council convened to discuss the telephone situation in Chicago.[68]

The only option that the city council rejected out of hand was the franchising of a new entrant to compete directly with Chicago Telephone. This alternative had been effectively foreclosed by the Illinois Telephone and Telegraph debacle. With the possible exception of speculators interested in obtaining a lucrative franchise, no one could be enlisted to commend a "duplicate or triplicate system anywhere," declared the city statistician in 1906.[69] Competition was roundly denounced not only by telephone experts but also by telephone subscribers. Should the city council encourage the establishment of two competing telephone systems in Chicago, declared the secretary of the Telephone Users' Protective League, Chicago's telephone subscribers would be subjected to the "greatest possible inconvenience and unnecessary expense." The Telephone Users' Protective League was a hastily organized federation of twenty-eight business associations headed up by the Chicago Board of Trade. It had two main goals: keep telephone rates inside Chicago low and block the city council from granting a franchise to a rival operating company.[70]

One option that the city council debated was a municipal buyout. Among its champions was Chicago mayor Edward F. Dunne and a smattering of civic groups that included the Woman's City Club.[71] Dunne spoke for many when he predicted that municipal ownership would hasten the emergence of an operating company that combined high performance standards with low rates: "Such is the history of our waterworks and our post office."[72]

Others regarded municipal ownership as a trap. Just as corporate management was open to various objections, so too was government administration. The fear that the city might municipalize the telephone was one of the "chief weapons" the company had at its disposal in its contest with the city, editorialized the *Chicago Tribune* in 1907: the advent of a "political telephone service" would inspire such revulsion among the people that they would, as an alternative, have consented to almost anything.[73]

No matter how popular municipal ownership might be with the electorate, aldermen had a vested interest in voting it down. The "real enemies" of the independents in Chicago were neither the telephone user nor Bell, opined an independent commentator in 1906, but the corrupt aldermen who opposed new entrants in return for a steady stream of financial payouts from Bell.[74] If the city municipalized its telephone business, the opportunities for extortion would disappear.

The discrediting of municipal ownership left two options: the renewal of the Chicago Telephone franchise or the transfer of the Chicago Telephone's franchise to a new operating company. The IMA preferred the latter. To increase its plausibility, Mayer conjured up a would-be successor to Chicago Telephone that he called Manufacturers' Telephone. To make the case for Manufacturers' Telephone, Mayer credited it with two advantages over Chicago Telephone. The first was technical. To reduce the call-connection delay, it would install a new kind of "semiautomatic" switchboard. The second was economic. To mollify users—including, in particular, the elite businessmen who dominated the IMA—it would offer business subscribers a low flat rate.

Mayer provided few details as to how the new switchboard would work. He promised only that it would speed connections and that it would not be entirely electromechanical. Mayer's concession was prudent, given the sorry history of electromechanical switching in Chicago. Mayer's reluctance to endorse the establishment of an operator-assisted switchboard underscored the unwillingness of even one of Chicago Telephone's most unrelenting critics to challenge the consensus that an electromechanical switchboard suitable for a city as large as Chicago had yet to be invented.

Chicago Telephone general manager Angus Hibbard challenged Mayer's proposal point by point. In numerous appearances before the city council, Hibbard impugned Mayer's credibility, defended his company, and fought "inch by inch" to sustain its "right" to retain its Chicago franchise.[75] "I know nothing about the telephone business," Mayer was reputed to have confessed at one point during a council debate, an admission that Hibbard put to good use.[76] Particularly objectionable to Hibbard was Mayer's endorsement of the business flat rate. Reiterating arguments that he had made for over a decade, Hibbard blamed the business flat rate for congestion. Hibbard ordinarily blamed congestion on men. In his critique of Mayer, however, Hibbard singled out women and children, presumably to mollify the male business elite that Mayer represented: "Traffic, which is the basis of an efficient telephone system, would be tied up and the exchanges would be swamped by free, un-limited conversations of nursemaids, servants, and children."[77]

The franchise fight culminated in a marathon all-night city council meeting in November 1907. When it ended, Chicago Telephone had secured a new twenty-year franchise. The meeting was presumably a lucrative one for the many aldermen well versed in the art of extorting kickbacks from municipal franchise corporations. Particularly suspi-cious was the last-minute elimination of a clause that would have lim-ited the company's dividend to 7 percent, instead of the current 10 percent. Why this clause was scrapped was a mystery; had company of-ficials paid off a few aldermen to strike it out, no one would have been surprised.[78]

The new Chicago Telephone franchise was a compromise between the company, the city, and the consumers of telephone service. The company obtained its franchise, though with terms less advantageous than Hib-bard had wished. The city reserved to itself the right to set telephone rates and to buy out the company for a mutually agreed upon price. Con-sumers obtained a rate cut on calls inside the city. Henceforth, no in-city telephone call would cost more than 5 cents. This was a major victory for small users with measured service calling plans: the city in 1907 stretched over 192 square miles. The extension of the no-toll zone was a major concession by the company: as recently as 1905, the no-toll zone had been only 82 square miles.[79] Prior to 1907, the company had obtained over half of its toll revenue from in-city calls.[80] When business subscrib-ers retained the $125 flat rate, Mayer and the IMA scored a victory and Hibbard suffered a humiliating defeat.

The continuation of the business flat rate was a testament to the power of a well-organized lobby to retain a special privilege that was of scant concern to most telephone users. The privileged status of flat-rate users was highlighted by an engineering study of telephone costs that was completed in 1910. The study showed that flat-rate users made 30 percent of the calls in the Chicago exchange, but generated a mere 15 percent of the revenue.[81] Chicago Telephone had spent $500,000 in the months before the council vote on a lavish public relations cam-paign to abolish the flat rate. The campaign had emphasized that flat rates lowered performance standards and that measured service would reduce the telephone bill for 95 percent of Chicago's telephone users.[82] The city council was unconvinced, not because of its solicitude for the many, but because of its deference to the few.

Hibbard's critique of the business flat rate received a ringing endorsement from Dugald C. Jackson, a university-trained electrical engineer who had recently obtained a prestigious appointment at the Massachusetts Institute of Technology. The city council had hired Jackson to compare the facilities Chicago Telephone provided with the facilities promised by Manufacturers' Telephone. To complete this assignment, he prepared a remarkably thorough analysis of the big-city telephone exchange. No state regulatory commission would prepare a more thorough analysis of the telephone business in a large American city until 1910, when the New York state legislature commissioned an exhaustive analysis of telephone service in New York.

Jackson conceded that flat rates remained the norm in many cities and towns in the United States. Yet he derided the proposed retention of the business flat rate by Manufacturers' Telephone as outmoded, unfair to small users, and impractical for an exchange as large as Chicago's. The single largest factor in the popularization of telephone service inside Chicago was the pay-as-you-go nickel-in-the-slots, an innovation that would have been impossible had the city council not permitted the company to experiment with measured service. Flat rates caused congestion and slowed the reconfiguration of telephone service from a specialty service for an exclusive clientele into a mass service for the entire population. This calling plan had been almost entirely abandoned in New York City and had fallen out of favor with the best-informed telephone experts in London. To compare Chicago with small-town exchanges in which flat rates remained the norm was farcical. The only telephone exchange in the United States comparable with the Chicago exchange was in New York City, and the only European exchange was in London. Certain commentators praised the Stockholm exchange, but Jackson ignored it, presumably because he regarded it as too small to furnish a useful point of comparison.[83]

Jackson's arguments echoed Hibbard's and rebutted Mayer's. Yet it would be a mistake to assume that Jackson was doing Chicago Telephone's bidding. Jackson's critique of the business flat rate, for example, reiterated arguments that every big-city telephone expert in the country had advanced. "I believe in the measured service plan for large places," declared the veteran public utility watchdog Frank Parsons during the Chicago franchise fight, though he conceded that the "double flat rate" that charged businesses more than residences was "simpler and better" for small exchanges. The proliferation of calling plans had been highly beneficial to city dwellers, and nothing would be gained by reverting to the simple, flat-rate calling plans that had once prevailed: "There can be no such thing as a standard telephone rate."[84]

In retrospect, it is perhaps unsurprising that Chicago Telephone prevailed upon the city council to renew its franchise. It is rarely easy to topple a wealthy, thriving, and, quite literally, entrenched corporation that is willing to spend liberally to defend its prerogatives. Close observers of the political scene took it for granted that Chicago Telephone had paid off the gray wolves to obtain its new franchise. Chicago politics was no less corrupt in 1907 than it had been in 1889, and the city's aldermen recognized in the impending expiration of Chicago Telephone's franchise a rare opportunity to extort a wealthy corporation. Kickbacks, or "soap," as the bribery of city officials was euphemistically called, were a Chicago political tradition.[85] One-third of the city council was up for sale, estimated the University of Chicago political scientist-turned-alderman Charles E. Merriam; one-third was not; and the remaining third kept an eye on public opinion.[86]

The pervasiveness of political corruption inspired a revealing political cartoon in the *Chicago Tribune*. This cartoon depicted Chicago's aldermen as a parade of nervous Bell-shaped toadies lined up outside the council chamber door. Its caption read: "I Hope Our Bell Boy Hurries with That Ordinance—I'm Getting Nervous." Readers familiar with franchise politics would have immediately gotten the joke: the aldermen were terrified of being jailed for accepting illegal payouts from Bell. To explain their anxiety to the uninitiated, the wall of the council chamber door was hung with the picture of a jailed San Francisco politico who had been convicted a few years earlier of accepting a bribe from a Bell official in return for a favorable city council vote.[87]

For Chicago Telephone, publicity became an antidote for corruption. No longer could lawmakers assume that graft would go unexposed or extortionate bills unreported. The power of publicity for municipal franchise corporations was a constant refrain in *Public Service*, a Chicago magazine founded in 1906 by H. J. Gondon. The magazine sought mainly to help municipal franchise corporations burnish their public image and improve their bargaining position in state legislatures and

How Will You Vote Today, Mr. Alderman?

?	For the People		?
	For the Telephone Company		

The rechartering of the Chicago Telephone Company in 1907 involved extensive political negotiations, and corruption was rampant. To draw attention to the venality of the city council, this cartoon depicted Chicago's aldermen as corporate toadies. To drive the point home, the aldermen wore suits patterned on Bell's ubiquitous bell-shaped advertising logo while glancing anxiously at a mug shot of a San Francisco city official who had been arrested for accepting a bribe from Bell's San Francisco licensee. "I Hope Our Bell Boy Hurries with That Ordinance—I'm Getting Nervous," *Chicago Tribune*, September 12, 1907.

city councils. Several years before Bell president Theodore N. Vail launched his celebrated public relations campaign in 1908, Gondon had been coaching corporate managers in the fine art of persuasion.

Telephone managers like Charles N. Fay had been complaining about the shady dealings of city officials since the 1880s. Now, for the first time, these complaints captivated the nation. The publication of Lincoln Steffens's *Shame of the Cities* in 1904 documented in vivid detail the political payoffs made by municipal franchise corporations like Chicago Telephone. It was Steffens who popularized the characterization of Powers and his allies as "gray wolves." Paradoxically, Steffens's tract strengthened the position of incumbent municipal franchise corporations such as Chicago Telephone in their ongoing contests with city government. Perceptive readers learned not only, or even primarily, about how business corrupted politics. Now they also discovered how the political economy of municipal franchise politics made corruption pervasive, systemic, and inescapable. The arch villain in Steffens's exposé—and in the many muckraking publications that it inspired—was not the franchise corporation, but the corrupt city officials who shook it down with the connivance of bogus new entrants like Johnny Powers.[88]

While the power of publicity helped Chicago Telephone, it hurt the IMA. Outside of the IMA, few Chicagoans relished the possibility of an IMA-backed telephone operating company. The IMA proposal received an especially frosty reception from the city's labor organizers; this is not surprising, given the IMA's endorsement of the anti-union open shop. Labor organizers had no "kick against the charges" proposed by Chicago Telephone, reported one journalist in 1906. Instead, their primary grievance against the company was its retention of a nonunion printing company to publish its telephone directory.[89] In 1887–1889, Chicago Telephone earned the enmity of virtually every telephone user in the city. In 1906–1907, the company won at least begrudging support from every class of telephone users except for the small percentage of flat-rate business subscribers who refused to give up the special privileges to which they had become accustomed. No longer were business subscribers the only or even the most important voice in the public debate. No fewer than 250,000 Chicagoans signed a petition in 1906 urging the city council to renew the company's franchise. This petition had been circulated by Chicago Telephone's telephone operators and was proudly displayed in its headquarters building. Although it was well known that the company had sponsored the petition drive, even the unsympathetic *Chi-*

cago Record-Herald conceded that it expressed the "honest conviction" of the great majority of the city's telephone users.[90]

Extortion was a constant in Chicago municipal franchise negotiations; the business strategy of municipal franchise corporations was not. Whereas the aldermen had changed little in the two decades between 1887 and 1907, Chicago Telephone had changed a good deal, with its network becoming more extensive, its equipment more advanced, and its public relations more sophisticated. No longer did Chicago Telephone officials boast, as Charles N. Fay had in 1887, that the company had the right to charge whatever rates it pleased, even if its rates were so exorbitant that a majority of subscribers abandoned the service.

By 1907 telephone popularization was no longer controversial. Even the most hidebound operating company manager disparaged unnecessary waste, idealized public utility, and presumed that telephone service should be a mass service for the entire population. The only question was how best to attain that agreed-upon goal. Few contemporaries were more eloquent in endorsing popularization than municipal franchise expert Delos F. Wilcox. In making the case for the telephone as a "democratic instrument," Wilcox invoked the time-honored duality of special privilege and equal rights, rather than the emerging duality of public utility and unnecessary waste. The special privileges city councils conferred on telephone companies required them to provide facilities at reasonable rates for the entire population.[91] Even so, the equal rights Wilcox championed were the rights not of network providers but of network users: "The immediate requirement is for adequate service at reasonable rates, so adjusted that the telephone shall not become a factor in the strengthening of the privileged classes of the community, but rather shall be a democratic instrument of development helping to equalize conditions and to open to all citizens alike the advantages of intercommunication."[92] Hibbard himself could not have put it any better.

It is impossible to know for certain whether Hibbard originally conceived of popularization as a political strategy. His primary goal may well have been merely to expand the market for telephone service. What is certain is that popularization transformed the relationship of the company and the city. In 1906–1907, a large percentage of the Chicago electorate had a vested interest in cheap and convenient telephone service. No such group had existed in 1887–1889. Even if the "telephone aristocracy" of flat-rate business subscribers represented by Levy Mayer remained discontented, their dissatisfaction was easier to discount because they were now but a small percentage of the total user base. In a newspaper interview early in the francise fight, Hibbard stressed the importance of the telephone to nonsubscribers: "Good service was of just as much interest to the man or woman who has to use the druggist's phone as to the comparatively few who had phones of their own."[93] The absence in 1906–1907 of a sustained public opposition to the rechartering of Chicago Telephone was a tribute not only to Hibbard's business strategy, but also to the political benefit for the company of its indispensability.

The most significant event in the American telephone business in 1907 was neither the return of Theodore N. Vail as Bell president, nor the supposed takeover of Bell by the New York City investment banking house of J. P. Morgan & Co., nor even the decision of the Wisconsin legislature to expand the jurisdiction of its state regulatory commission to embrace the telephone. Far more consequential were the collapse of United States Independent and the rechartering of Chicago Telephone. These two events marked the end of the brief period during which it seemed conceivable that the independents might build a telephone network to rival Bell. The collapse of United States Independent was a cautionary tale for investors, and the rechartering of Chicago Telephone signaled the demise of antimonopoly in the telephone business as a civic ideal. Not until the federal government intervened in the 1910s to stabilize the market for telephone securities would investors again regard independent properties as a sound investment. No longer was competition the solution; henceforth it became a source of the unnecessary waste that only government could eliminate. Special privilege in the telephone business had become inevitable, and the unnecessary waste fostered by competition a bane. In the political economy of antimonopoly, opinion leaders hailed antimonopolists as high-minded scourges of special privilege; in the political economy of progressivism, opinion leaders derided antimonopolists as parasitic breeders of unnecessary waste.

The equanimity with which Chicagoans viewed the renewal of Chicago Telephone's franchise in 1907 stood in marked contrast to the popular furor that accompanied the franchise fight of 1887–1889. In 1889, government–business relations in the Chicago telephone business were genuinely adversarial. By 1907 this adversarial relationship had given way to a spirit of mutual accommodation that rested not only in the popular consensus that competition was wrongheaded, but also in the remarkable expansion in the telephone business that had occurred in the intervening years. In large cities like Chicago, telephone companies embraced popularization as a business strategy to preempt rivals, neutralize lawmakers, and marginalize investors in league with potential new entrants. Network expansion eventually became an ostensibly value-neutral economic truism; in 1907, it remained a civic ideal.

10

UNIVERSAL SERVICE

Mr. Vail, president of the American Telephone & Telegraph Co., has said, "There is a road to every man's house, and there ought to be a telephone inside." That is, I think, a correct ideal, and the parallel is indisputable, but he neglects to observe that it was society, with its public-service motive, that built those roads and not a privately financed monopoly.

David J. Lewis, 1914

The time was coming, predicted Bell president Theodore N. Vail in his annual shareholders' report for 1910, when the telephone and the telegraph would be linked in a *"universal wire system"* for the *"electrical transmission of intelligence"* that was as extensive as the "highway system" that reached from "every man's door" to "every other man's door."[1] Vail had recently purchased for Bell a large financial stake in Western Union and had grand plans for consolidating its telegraph network with Bell's telephone network. If the Republicans had won the 1912 presidential election, Vail might have translated his forecast into reality. The victory of the Democratic candidate, Woodrow Wilson, spoiled Vail's plans. Wilson's attorney general, James C. McReynolds, accused Bell of violating the Sherman Act. To avoid prosecution, Bell agreed in December 1913 to divest Western Union, restoring the boundary between the telephone and the telegraph that had been established with the Western Union–National Bell settlement of 1879.

Vail's "universal wire system" was a calculated response to a legislative juggernaut. In June 1910, Congress put the telephone and the telegraph under the jurisdiction of the Interstate Commerce Commission (ICC). One week later, the New York state legislature put the telephone and the telegraph under the jurisdiction of the state's Public Service

Commission. Commission regulation encouraged consolidation, and Vail was determined to ensure that it worked to Bell's advantage.

Competition in the telephone business was always contrived. Would-be telegraph promoters could go into business in most states by merely filling out a form. Telephone promoters, in contrast, had to negotiate with city officials for a municipal franchise. Before 1907, competition in the telephone business remained a plausible alternative to commission regulation or government ownership. Two events in that year signaled its eclipse: the collapse of the United States Independent Telephone Company in Rochester, New York, and the rechartering of the Chicago Telephone Company by the Chicago city council. The New York legislature would not put the telephone and the telegraph under commission regulation until 1910. Yet few doubted in 1907 that it was only a matter of time before it did. Commission regulation had the enthusiastic support of New York governor Charles Evans Hughes and was actively debated by the National Civic Federation, a New York City–based business lobby that aspired to speak for the nation.[2]

Commission regulation received a major boost from a series of widely publicized political scandals involving corporate malfeasance. Hughes's disclosure in 1905 of a tangle of collusive relationships between the New York legislature and New York–chartered insurance corporations inspired a hard-hitting exposé by the muckraking journalist Burton J. Hendrick. Hendrick's exposé appeared first in *McClure's Magazine* and was published shortly thereafter as a book; it augured a sea change in public attitudes toward government regulation.[3]

Commission regulation had the endorsement of two Republican presidents—Theodore Roosevelt (1901–1909) and William Howard Taft (1909–1913). Roosevelt endorsed federal legislation to regulate the telephone and the telegraph as "common carriers" in 1908; Taft endorsed the inclusion of the telephone and the telegraph under the jurisdiction of the ICC in 1910.[4] Taft's attorney general, George W. Wickersham, drafted an early version of the bill that put both networks under the ICC's jurisdiction. Wickersham also endorsed a related proposal that, had it been enacted, would have permitted the chartering of telephone and telegraph corporations by the federal government. For Taft and Wickersham either option was preferable to the prosecution of Bell under the Sherman Act, which, at the time, was the federal lawmakers'

primary tool to prevent restraints of trade. As attorney general, Wickersham had instituted Sherman Act prosecutions against both Standard Oil
and American Tobacco. As a result of this experience, Wickersham had
become convinced that the federal government needed a better way to
regulate vast corporate combines like Bell.

Twenty-seven states had put the telephone and the telegraph under
commission regulation by 1912.[5] Among the first to take this step was
Massachusetts, which in 1906 authorized its highway commission to
regulate every company operating within its borders that was "engaged
in the transmission of intelligence by electricity." In the following year,
Wisconsin added the telephone and the telegraph to its railroad commission.[6] New York followed in 1910, and Illinois in 1913.[7] Illinois
presumably held out as long as it did because of the state lawmakers'
propensity to defer to the Chicago city council, which had been actively
regulating the telephone business in Chicago for over thirty years. Four
days before it put the telephone under the jurisdiction of a regulatory
commission, it had extended the jurisdiction of every municipality in the
state to embrace the ownership and operation of any "public utility,"
including a telephone operating company.[8]

Commission regulation proscribed intercorporate rivalry. By 1910 this
proscription had met with the approval not only of Bell, but also of most
telephone users and many of Bell's one-time independent rivals. The consolidation of once-rival telephone operating companies, opined one well-
informed independent lawyer in 1915, had the support not only of "substantially all" of the state regulatory commissions, but also of a "very
substantial majority of the public affected."[9] No longer would independents attack Bell as an evil "octopus" intent on strangling its rivals, reflected one independent journalist. Commission regulation had become
the norm, and "commission law is monopoly."[10]

Commission regulation met with the approval even of journalists hostile toward government intervention. If the only rationale for putting the
telephone under the jurisdiction of a state regulatory commission had
been to improve telephone performance standards, editorialized the
Wall Street Journal in 1909, it would have opposed it. Yet it was not. By
shifting the jurisdiction over the franchising of new telephone corporations from the municipality to the state, commission regulation would
prevent "crooked franchise 'magnates' " from extorting large sums from
operating companies for bogus telephone franchises. The savings on this

item alone would exceed the $1.3 million cost of the commission.[11] If the state legislature put the telephone business under the jurisdiction of the regulatory commission, editorialized the *New York Times* approvingly in 1907, it would be more difficult for the notoriously corrupt Atlantic Telephone Company to obtain a telephone franchise in New York City: its promoters would now have to make their case for a franchise before a state commission.[12]

The federal law that put the telephone and the telegraph under the ICC's jurisdiction was popularly known as the Mann-Elkins Act, after its cosponsors, James R. Mann of Illinois and Stephen B. Elkins of West Virginia. Enacted in June 1910, Mann-Elkins classified the telegraph, telephone, and cable as "common carriers" and placed them under the ICC's jurisdiction.[13] The "common carrier" designation was controversial; telegraph and telephone lawyers had long opposed it, and they had often prevailed in the courts. Mann-Elkins also established a new judicial body—the commerce court—to adjudicate disputes that came before the ICC. Had the commerce court worked as Wickersham had intended, it might have provided an orderly forum for the solution of the myriad legal conundrums posed by economic consolidation. Unfortunately for Wickersham, it proved impractical and was abolished in December 1913.

The Mann-Elkins Act was one of several major pieces of business legislation enacted by Congress in the opening years of the twentieth century to regulate the emerging corporate order. In transportation, its counterpart was the Hepburn Act (1906); in banking, the Federal Reserve Act (1913); and in commerce, the Federal Trade Commission Act (1914). Each of these laws had been intended to preserve capitalism from its worst excesses by constraining the passions that innovation had unleashed.[14]

Wickersham regarded the regulation of the telephone business by the ICC as inevitable and desirable. As attorney general, Bell's rivals had repeatedly urged him to prosecute Bell under the Sherman Act. Although he did consider doing so, in the end he demurred. The telephone business was best regulated not by competition, Wickersham lectured independent investor Samuel Hill in January 1913, but as "one system" under "proper and effective governmental control."[15] If the federal government wished to restructure the telephone business, it should first enlist the ICC to conduct a full-scale investigation.

If Wickersham rather than McReynolds had been attorney general in 1913, the Bell–Western Union merger might well have met with the approval of the Justice Department. Wickersham had been highly critical of the zeal with which McReynolds had lobbied for the atomization of American Tobacco and shelved a pending lawsuit against Bell for its alleged violation of the Sherman Act.[16] Wickersham's solicitude for corporate consolidation irritated McReynolds and helps explain why McReynolds was so eager to reopen the Sherman Act lawsuit against Bell that Wickersham had shelved following McReynolds's appointment as Wilson's attorney general in March 1913.

The extension of ICC jurisdiction to the telephone and telegraph business met with the approval of Bell president Theodore N. Vail. By 1910 Commission regulation had become unavoidable, and for Vail it was preferable to regulation by state legislatures and city councils. The possibility that a state legislature might enact a rate cap remained a concern. Vail remembered the Indiana rate cap law of 1885 and he did not want to go down that road again. The New York legislature had debated a rate cap law on numerous occasions in the 1890s, as had the legislatures in several other states. It would be unfortunate, Vail thought in 1909, if an increasing number of municipalities obtained legal authority to fix telephone rates as, for example, they had in Chicago and San Francisco. It would be positively calamitous if this rate-setting authority devolved onto state legislatures. Once a state legislature had mandated a rate structure for telephone operating companies, it would be "almost impossible" to "secure any subsequent revision" in their favor.[17]

Vail remained adamantly opposed to legislatively mandated rate caps. Yet by 1910 he had made his peace with state regulatory commissions. Regulatory commissions staffed by highly respected jurists could resolve thorny technical issues such as the establishment of interconnection protocols. Although these issues could be complex, Vail saw no reason why federal judges could not resolve them. Federal judges routinely determined the scope of patents for inventions they did not understand. So why should they not be able to render sound verdicts on technical issues pertaining to electrical communication?[18]

The rapid extension of commission regulation to the telephone business gave Vail a platform to formulate a business strategy that would increase Bell's operational autonomy. The business strategy that Vail articulated in his 1910 annual report would shape the Bell System's corporate identity for the next seventy years.

The centerpiece of Vail's business strategy was his declaration that Bell had a social obligation to provide "universal service." Vail had alluded to this theme in the shareholders' report that he had authored following his return to Bell in 1907.[19] Yet it was not until both Congress and the New York legislature had put the telephone business under the jurisdiction of a regulatory commission that he deemed it expedient to make this social obligation a corporate goal in an annual report.

Universal service for Vail had several dimensions. At its most basic, it obliged Bell to provide telephone service to the country's sprawling hinterland. "Some sort of a connection" with the "telephone system," Vail declared, should be "within reach of all."[20] The extension of telephone service to thinly settled regions could be expensive, and Vail was reluctant to commit Bell to huge outlays for which there might be no commensurate financial return. Even so, he endorsed the continuing popularization of local telephone service, if lawmakers permitted Bell to transfer revenue from the city to the countryside.

The popularization of telephone service in the nation's cities as well as in countless towns and rural hamlets was well underway by 1910. Popularization had begun around 1900, seven years prior to Vail's appointment as Bell president and at a time when he had had no official connection to the telephone business for eleven years. It was at this time—several years prior to Vail's return to Bell in 1907—that Bell operating company managers first justified telephone popularization in their annual reports. Vail's distinctive contribution was to link this already existing business strategy with a catchphrase sufficiently capacious to maximize Bell's operational autonomy.

Universal service presupposed the establishment of a single, interconnected nationwide network. For Vail, interconnection was an obsession. The Bell network in 1910 consisted of two noninterconnected clusters: one cluster linked the principal cities east of the Mississippi River and reached as far west as Denver, Colorado, and the other linked the principal cities on the Pacific Coast.

The interconnection of these two clusters posed a daunting technical challenge. Technical constraints limited the distance over which the human voice could be transmitted electrically to around 2,000 miles. Using existing technology, Bell engineers had successfully introduced telephone service between New York City and Denver in 1911 (a distance of 1,800 miles). The linkage of New York City and San Francisco, however, remained out of reach.

To meet this challenge Vail enlisted Bell's chief engineer John J. Carty to embark on a sustained program of basic research, the first in Bell history. Carty publicly committed Bell in 1909 to spanning the continent. This was an audacious goal because at the time no one knew how such a linkage could be accomplished.[21] Carty's gamble paid off, and Bell successfully linked New York City and San Francisco in 1915. This remarkable event was made possible by a team of Bell scientists led by Harold D. Arnold, who refined a device to amplify electrical signals. This device— the three-element high-vacuum tube—was the culminating achievement of the research program Carty had coordinated under Vail's supervision beginning in 1909. Although the high-vacuum tube was invented at Bell, it was, in fact, less of a technical breakthrough than an incremental improvement of a low-vacuum tube that had previously been patented by the independent inventor, Lee de Forest, and to which Bell had acquired the rights in 1913.

The high cost of a New York City–San Francisco telephone call would long confine the service to businessmen, government officials, and the affluent. Even so, transcontinental telephone service provided a service that was "universal" in the sense that every telephone in Bell's nationwide network could now interconnect.

Interconnection involved not only Bell but also the independents. The piecemeal interconnection of certain independents with the Bell telephone network had been well advanced by 1910. Now that Congress had put the telephone business under the ICC's jurisdiction, Vail envisioned a more permanent integration of the once-rival networks. To bring this about, Vail proposed consolidating every major telephone operating company in the country—Bell and independent—into a single vast combine. He laid out his plan at a secret meeting at Chicago's newly completed Blackstone Hotel in December 1910. In attendance were Vail, J. P. Morgan & Co. partner H. P. Davison, and a committee representing seven of the nation's largest and most successful independent operating companies, which became known as the "group of seven."[22] Vail fixed the capitalization of the Bell–independent combine at $1.3 billion, which would have made it one of the largest corporations in the world. When Vail was asked how he would justify such an enormous capitalization, he conceded that it exceeded by a large margin the physical value of properties being merged and had been necessitated by the enormous "waste" caused by a decade of wrongheaded Bell–independent competition encouraged by myopic lawmakers in league with shortsighted promoters.[23]

The Blackstone Hotel meeting was the brainchild of Chicago banker Charles G. Dawes. Having invested heavily in the independents, Dawes was determined to prevent their financial collapse. To establish a relationship between the independents and the New York investment bank J. P. Morgan & Co., Dawes introduced Morgan partner H. P. Davison to independent leader Frank H. Woods. Woods next invited six of his independent colleagues to meet with Davison and Vail.[24]

Woods was the president of a thriving independent in Lincoln, Nebraska. Although his own company was financially sound, he recognized that many of his independent colleagues were in a parlous financial condition. The independents' failure to supplant Bell had complicated the task of raising capital, and many independents had become tempted to sell out to Bell at an advantageous price. One independent financial adviser put it this way: had he himself been the owner of a bundle of independent securities, he would be inclined to sell them at a good price—no matter who might be its purchaser. This was especially the case if he had become convinced that the purchaser (by which he presumably meant either J. P. Morgan & Co. or Bell) had the power to boost their value at the right "psychological moment" by playing "'ducks and drakes'" with the financial markets not only of the United States, but also the world.[25]

Vail's Bell–independent combine went nowhere. The independents favored "consolidation," Woods explained, but not a "Telephone Trust."[26] More acceptable to the independents was Vail's promise to slow Bell's acquisition of independent operating companies. Vail reneged on his promise, or so contended several independents, when, two years later, he entered into negotiations with the owners of an independent operating company in Kansas City, Missouri, who were eager to sell. Vail's negotiation angered Woods, and the truce was broken. Vail's negotiation with the Kansas City independent epitomized the independents' dilemma: to remain united, they had to deprive their fellow independents from reaping a financial windfall by selling out to Bell.[27]

Among the most pointed critics of Vail's proposed Bell–independent combine was John H. Wright, the president of a modest independent operating company in Jamestown, New York. Wright was also a minority shareholder in a number of other operating companies in upstate New York and western Pennsylvania. The interests of large and small independents often diverged, and Wright championed the small independents. He was proud of his operating company and regarded it and the hundreds of operating companies like it as an indispensable agent in popularizing local telephone service in the United States. "There was no policy of universal service," Wright protested to Wickersham in November 1911, "until the independent companies forced its adoption."[28]

For Wright the proposed Bell–independent combine was unnecessary, pernicious, and illegal. Bell's much advertised catchphrase "one universal service" was a "chimera" that was as undesirable as it was impractical, Wright complained to Wickersham in November 1911: "Localism is an inherent and controlling factor in ninety percent of the telephone business."[29] When Bell bought out an independent toll-line provider, it sometimes cut the independent's toll-line connections.[30] If the Justice Department failed to block Bell from buying up its rivals, the larger independents would be "entirely annihilated" and the smaller ones would be left to the "tender mercies" of the "great telephone trust." Independents would never have entered the telephone business had they not been confident that the "strong arm of the government" would preserve "reasonable competition under the law" and the federal government had an obligation to keep up its part of the bargain.[31] Wright had invested almost everything he owned in independent telephone properties for which there existed no plausible buyer other than his arch-nemesis Bell. If Bell continued its aggressive program of network expansion, it might well render his investments worthless.[32] For Wright, like most independents by 1910, "reasonable competition" meant not the dynamism of market rivalry—a dynamism that independents often denounced as "predatory pricing"—but the preservation of competitors.[33] Should competition hasten economic consolidation, and, therefore, reduce the number of competitors, Wright opposed it.

Vail may never have heard of the word "telecommunications." Even so, the consolidation of the telephone with the telegraph that this word had been coined to describe had been a priority for him ever since he had first entered the telephone business in 1878. Vail's acquisition of Western Union in 1909 extended his communication network overseas. Bell's telephone network had been confined to the United States and Canada; Western Union had partial control over several Atlantic cables, as well as a direct line to Cuba.[34] Vail had no intention of using the overseas cables for voice communications, and if he had, he would soon have discovered that it was technically impossible. Yet he relished the opportunity to become a major player in international diplomacy and global commerce. To elevate the mental horizons of his staff, Vail installed a thirty-six inch globe in the Bell headquarters building in New York City featuring the principal cable lines of the world.[35]

The benefits of telephone–telegraph consolidation were not only international but also domestic. Now that Vail controlled both a telephone network and a telegraph network, he hoped to realize the long-deferred dream of providing the entire population with the facilities for low-cost, long-distance electrical communications. The popularization of local telephone service had occurred in the years preceding Vail's return to Bell in 1907; the popularization of the telegraph had yet to begin. Now that Bell owned Western Union, Vail hoped to reconfigure the telegraph as a mass medium, a goal Western Union always opposed. The "universal service" of the future would combine cheap and convenient local telephone service with cheap and convenient long-distance telegraph service. Long-distance telephone service remained out of reach for the masses, yet the telegraph could easily be made accessible to the entire population. "Strictly speaking," explained one Bell publicist, the telephone was the "ideal method" for "short haul communications," and the telegraph for the "very long haul business."[36]

Vail's first experiment with popularizing the telegraph was the "night letter"—a telegram that, unlike a regular telegram, was sent not in the order in which it was received, but, rather, at night, when the telegraph network was underutilized. Although it cost as much as a regular ten-word telegram, it could include up to fifty words, a feature that was designed to encourage its adoption as a social medium. Vail deplored the underutilization of the telegraph network as waste; the night letter improved its efficiency. During its brief existence, the night letter gave thousands of Americans their first opportunity to experience firsthand the possibilities of point-to-point, long-distance electrical communications. Western Union had experimented with cheap night rates in the 1870s, yet it had never championed cheap telegraphy as a social obligation. Vail took this additional step, and it made all the difference. Henceforth, boasted a Bell publicist, the telegraph would be utilized not only for business messages but also for "social correspondence." If a telephone subscriber wished to send a night telegram, all that the subscriber needed to do was to contact a telephone operator and say the word "telegram"; Western Union did the rest.[37]

The night letter had the potential to help Bell cover the cost of its long-distance telephone network. The long-distance network was expensive to build and maintain, and the demand for long-distance telephone service was limited owing to the prices Bell charged. The soon-to-be completed transcontinental telephone line between New York City and San Francisco would not be "commercially practicable" as a telephone line for many years, explained Vail to a reporter in 1911. Yet if it were configured to transmit telegraph messages as well as telephone calls, it might well break even, or at least lose less money.[38]

Vail's night letter realized a major goal of the post–Civil War postal telegraph movement. As early as 1868, Gardiner G. Hubbard had lobbied lawmakers to make the telegraph accessible to the entire population; Vail realized Hubbard's dream in 1910. Its most immediate precursor was the never-implemented "limited" postal telegraph that Postmaster General John Wanamaker had advocated in 1889. Wanamaker's limited postal telegraph was supposed to combine the telegraph, the telephone, and the mail in a single interconnected network that would permit not only "wealthy business people" but also "plain people" to send "electrical letters" over vast distances. In those cities in which the Post Office Department had established free home delivery, the mail would provide the local hookup; in those cities in which it had not been established, the telephone would provide the local hookup. By combining the telegraph, mail, and telephone, Wanamaker hoped to bring "electrical communication" to "every man's door."[39]

Wanamaker's use of the phrase "every man's door" was revealing. Francis Wayland had used an identical phrase in the first edition of *Elements of Political Economy* in 1837 to characterize the mandate of the Post Office Department. That Vail also used the phrase "every man's door" in his 1910 report was suggestive. Vail had served in the Post Office Department, admired its civic mandate, and aspired to align Bell's business strategy with its time-honored civic ideal of equal access for all.

Vail's telephone–telegraph hybrid won plaudits from contemporaries all across the political spectrum. Its "economies of joint operation" impressed Charles Van Hise, a political economist who would serve as a major adviser to Theodore Roosevelt during his 1912 presidential campaign.[40] The consolidation of the telephone and the telegraph provided users with an "ideal service," elaborated business journalist and former Chicago Telephone general manager Charles N. Fay: "The telephone was used as a feeder and distributor of telegraph service, to the great convenience of the public."[41] The cost savings were considerable and rendered the cost of the telephone calls "actually free."[42] The Bell–

Western Union merger had been a step in the right direction, editorialized social critic Lyman Abbott. To realize its potential, Abbott urged Congress to buy out at "satisfactory prices" both the telephone and the telegraph. Now that Bell had taken over Western Union, Congress should awaken itself to the "desirability" of providing the American people with the same low-cost facilities for electrical communications that had long been enjoyed by the inhabitants of other countries.[43]

The Bell–Western Union merger seemed so advantageous that several journalists mourned its demise. With the divestiture, lamented one business journalist, the country had lost a "system of communication" that would have "revolutionized letter-writing."[44] That the divestiture was ill-advised seemed self-evident to Arthur Brisbane, a respected journalist who wrote an influential column for the newspaper chain owned by William Randolph Hearst: "Thus a combination NOT IN RESTRAINT OF TRADE, but made to give cheaper and better service in order to extend trade, will be destroyed. The price of stock will rise. The price of service will rise. The people . . . will pay the price."[45]

Vail's telephone–telegraph hybrid was not without its detractors. It was "too intricate and rigid," complained operating company president James E. Caldwell. To make his point, Caldwell compared it with the notoriously convoluted French government-operated telephone–telegraph hybrid that had prompted the French postal administrator Edouard Estaunié to coin the neologism "telecommunications" in 1904.[46] Even if Vail's hybrid proved to be a technical success, Caldwell doubted that it would meet with public approval. The American people would probably not object to a "straight telephone system throughout the country," as long as it accommodated "incidental and local competition." Yet they would never countenance the consolidation of the telephone and the telegraph. "As far as we have a record," such a "unification" was certain to offend the "Anglo-Saxon type of man," who resented and was "ready to make any sacrifice" to destroy "every semblance" of monopoly.[47]

A Taft victory in 1912 would probably have enabled Bell to retain the "universal wire system" that Vail forecast in his 1910 annual report. Taft's defeat set in motion a sequence of events that would rapidly lead to its dismantling in 1913. Taft's successor Woodrow Wilson, being far more skeptical than Taft of sprawling corporate combines like Bell, appointed a raft of administrators who shared his views.[48] Wilson's political manifesto, the "New Freedom," excoriated big business for impeding innovation and promised to "release" the entrepreneurial energy that big business had suppressed. Among the big businesses that Wilson berated for their technical conservatism was Bell, which Wilson faulted for refusing to innovate on account of its sunk costs and outmoded equipment.[49]

To eliminate the inefficiency that Wilson regarded as intrinsic to huge corporate combines, his administration pursued two seemingly antithetical strategies: market segmentation and government ownership. Market segmentation was the remedy favored by Wilson's attorney general, James C. McReynolds; Wilson's postmaster general, Albert S. Burleson, preferred government ownership.

Missing from the Wilson administration's policy repertoire was antimonopoly. Neither Wilson nor any member of his cabinet publicly expressed any interest in encouraging new entrants in the telephone or telegraph business or in atomizing the telephone business by forcing Bell to divest its holdings in its operating companies, long-distance network, or equipment manufacturer. Had McReynolds not brokered an agreement with Bell that ended the government's lawsuit, it is conceivable that he would have broken up Bell's telephone network into regional units. Atomization, after all, had been McReynolds's favored remedy for the Sherman Act violations committed by American Tobacco. Yet McReynolds brokered an agreement before the lawsuit went to trial, and so Bell's telephone network remained intact.

The Sherman Act was a federal law that prohibited the restraint of trade. Enacted in 1890, it had been named in honor of Senator John Sherman, the same Ohio lawmaker who had sponsored the National Telegraph Act in 1866. In theory, the Sherman Act was intended to prevent corporations from restraining trade by forming combines known as "trusts." For this reason, Sherman Act prosecutions were often called "antitrust" lawsuits. In practice, the Sherman Act empowered federal prosecutors to challenge any merger, contract, or business practice that lawmakers deemed anticompetitive.

The prevention of anticompetitive behavior was quite different from the promotion of the equal rights of independent promoters to enter a business. Open entry had been a rationale for general incorporation, a pillar of the antimonopoly political economy in which the telegraph business had evolved. In the telephone business, however, open entry was no longer a realistic remedy for the evils of economic consolidation. The political economy that emerged following its discrediting supplanted antimonopoly with progress as a civic ideal. In particular, it presumed that economic consolidation hastened technical advance and that technical advance guaranteed the economic abundance that was a harbinger of moral progress.

McReynolds's reopening of the lawsuit that Wickersham had shelved caught Vail by surprise. Bell operating companies had long been subject to prosecution under state antimonopoly laws, as had Bell's equipment manufacturer, Western Electric. Yet Vail was firmly convinced—as was his immediate predecessor, Frederick P. Fish—that Bell's long-distance network was a "natural monopoly" that was exempt from Sherman Act prosecution because it was impervious to competition. How, Vail wondered, could the federal government enforce competition in a business in which competition was impossible?[50]

Vail's incredulity was self-serving. Even lawmakers like Wickersham who were generally sympathetic to corporate consolidation warned that certain Bell business practices might run afoul of the law. The test case for Wickersham was Bell's long-awaited purchase of United States Telephone, a financially troubled Ohio independent holding company that J. P. Morgan & Co. had acquired for Bell in 1909 in the expectation that Bell would purchase it once any legal complications surrounding its acquisition had been resolved. Should Bell buy United States Telephone from J. P. Morgan & Co., Wickersham warned Bell vice president Nathan C. Kingsbury in 1913, Wickersam "very strongly" believed that it would violate the Sherman Act.[51]

United States Telephone was one of several ambitious independent ventures that had fallen on hard times. Its assets included a modest toll-line network, as well as independent operating companies in Cleveland, Columbus, Toledo, and Dayton. Taken together, these properties remained the "cream" of the independent business, as one financial journalist termed them.[52] It had gone into receivership in 1909 following a court ruling that challenged the legality of the ninety-nine year exclusive contracts that it had negotiated with several hundred Ohio independents. In 1913, it was still owned by J. P. Morgan & Co.[53]

Kingsbury took Wickersham's hint and decided against purchasing United States Telephone from J. P. Morgan & Co. To eliminate any legal objections inside Ohio, J. P. Morgan & Co. had obtained an exemption from the state's strict antimonopoly law that would have permitted Bell to take it over. Wickersham's warning occasioned a further delay, much to the exasperation of J. P. Morgan & Co. The investment bank had already lost money on United States Telephone, which, of course, it had purchased not on its own account, but on Bell's. Understandably, the investment bank feared that, if it held the properties much longer, they might become utterly worthless.[54]

McReynolds's lawsuit met with a mixed response from the independents. Among its critics was Frank H. Woods, the chair of the "committee of seven" that had met with Vail at the Blackstone Hotel in 1910. Now that the ICC had gained jurisdiction over the telephone business, Woods looked to the ICC rather than the Justice Department to safeguard the independents' collective interests. In Woods's view, the independent movement had more to gain from cooperating with Bell than by antagonizing it by throwing its support behind a lawsuit that might not produce any tangible gains. Such a lawsuit, he feared, would impede Bell's purchase of independent properties whose owners would be financially ruined if the sale were disallowed.[55]

McReynolds's lawsuit proved more congenial to small independents such as John H. Wright. Like most small independents, Wright dreaded Bell's legal and financial clout and cast a wary eye at its repeated incursions into the independents' financially precarious toll-line business. Since 1911 Wright had lobbied the Justice Department to prosecute Bell and was delighted when McReynolds reopened the Sherman Act lawsuit that Wickersham had shelved.[56]

To build a case against Bell, McReynolds arranged for public hearings on the telephone situation in Chicago and Portland, Oregon. The Chicago hearings focused on Bell's recent acquisition of the failed Chicago independent operating company that operated under a franchise that the city council had granted to Illinois Telephone and Telegraph. If Bell had purchased United States Telephone, this transaction would presumably also have been on the agenda. Yet it had not, and so the Justice Department found itself in the awkward position of rummaging around for something else to pin on Bell. The Portland hearings focused on Bell's recent acquisition of Northwestern, a cash-strapped independent toll-line provider in the Pacific Northwest.

The Chicago independent was itself of little concern: everyone agreed that it had failed. Of greater consequence was its ownership of a controlling stake in Automatic Electric, a major independent equipment manufacturer.[57] Independent equipment manufacturers had relied on the courts to segment the telephone equipment market ever since the Berliner ruling in 1894. McReynolds's lawsuit was yet another variation on a theme. Bell's acquisition of the Chicago independent was subject to the approval of the Chicago city council, which had granted the independent its municipal franchise. McReynolds's antitrust suit complicated the purchase, for it created the presumption that Bell had to obtain the approval not only of the city council, but also of the attorney general.

Among the witnesses to testify against Bell was Bert G. Hubbell, an independent telephone equipment manufacturer who had invested heavily in an independent telephone operating company in Buffalo, New York. Hubbell was also one of the "committee of seven" who had met with Vail at the Blackstone Hotel in December 1910. His participation in the committee of seven was of considerable significance because he was the only representative of a large independent to break rank and testify against Bell. Hubbell had recently outfitted his own Buffalo, New York, independent with Automatic Electric electromechanical switching equipment. If the city council approved the purchase of Automatic Electric, he feared that it would destroy his investment.[58]

According to Hubbell, Bell coveted Automatic Electric not to advance the art of electromechanical switching, but to stifle it. Bell had made a $300 million investment in operator-assisted switching, which electromechanical switching now threatened to render obsolete. Hubbell himself had been an independent telephone equipment manufacturer in Chicago in the 1890s and well understood the vulnerability of even the largest independent equipment manufacturers to a hostile takeover. Automatic Electric owned a formidable portfolio of patents for electromechanical switching equipment. If Bell gained control of this portfolio, it would have the power to extort every electromechanical exchange in the country, or, at the very least, to slow the diffusion of the new technology by refusing to defend Automatic Electric's patent rights in court.[59]

Hubbell faulted Bell not only for its technical backwardness, but also for pricing practices that he labeled predatory. In particular, Hubbell objected to the adoption of statewide rate averaging by New York Telephone. It had long been New York Telephone's "defined policy," Hubbell testified, to transfer revenue that it generated in its big-city exchanges—such as its exchange in New York City—to subsidize the many smaller exchanges located in the less populous parts of the state: "It is so argued, that the burden of the expenses of telephone operation should be borne by the large communities, to sustain the losses incident to operation under the plan in the small communities."[60]

Hubbell warned that rate averaging imperiled the future not only of his own Buffalo independent, but also of the many independent operating companies that had long flourished in upstate New York. Hubbell was no government ownership enthusiast. Yet if Bell continued to expand, he was convinced that the country would be best served if the telephone network were operated by a government agency accountable to the American people rather than by a private corporation that—while ostensibly owned by its shareholders—was actually controlled by a tiny, self-perpetuating managerial elite: "Morally and economically, it would be wrong for one set of men to control the transmission of thought of 50,000,000 people."[61]

The Chicago hearings proved less damning to Bell than McReynolds had hoped. Bell's acquisition of Automatic Electric had yet to take place and, as it turned out, would never be consummated. The Portland hearings had been more successful. No one denied that Bell had acquired Northwestern, or that its acquisition had the potential to restrain trade, making Bell vulnerable to prosecution under the Sherman Act.

Heading up the Portland hearings was Nebraska lawyer Constantine Smyth. Smyth was a fervent admirer of the Populist and three-time Democratic presidential contender William Jennings Bryan. Like Bryan, Smyth was hostile toward vast corporate combines and had confidence in government ownership as a remedy for corporate malfeasance. When a reporter asked Smyth why he was prosecuting a "natural monopoly," his response was blunt. Bell might well be a natural monopoly, but that would not exempt it from liability under the Sherman Act, and, in fact, would "furnish an excellent argument" for government ownership.[62]

In building a case against Bell, Smyth found a ready ally in Samuel Hill. Hill was a wealthy and eccentric public utilities promoter who had filed the original complaint against Bell that had prompted McReynolds to reopen the lawsuit shelved by Wickersham. Hill owned a Portland independent, Home Telephone of Portland, as well as a stake in the toll-line provider Northwestern. Both were in trouble: Home Telephone had a mere 17,000 subscribers in 1913, roughly half the number its Bell rival had, while Northwestern had recently been acquired by Bell.[63]

Having failed in the marketplace, Hill turned to the courts. Hill condemned Bell's acquisition of Northwestern as a restraint of trade. By imperiling the toll-line connections that had formerly linked Home Telephone with its fellow independents in Seattle, Tacoma, and Bellingham, the acquisition threatened to destroy Hill's investment in Home Telephone. The Pacific Northwest, Hill announced to the press, was the "last place where a fight can be made against the great monopoly."[64]

Hill's lawsuit was one element in a larger, highly speculative scheme to build a long-distance telephone network to rival Bell's. The best way to prevent monopoly in the telephone business, Hill explained to his shareholders in 1912, was to consolidate the independents with Postal Telegraph. Postal Telegraph president Clarence Mackay had recently embarked on an ambitious scheme to build a long-distance network to rival Bell's. To help Mackay—while making some money on the side— Hill had invested in Northwestern. Bell's acquisition of Northwestern spoiled Hill's plans.[65]

The credibility of Hill's antimonopoly crusade was undermined by his own dubious business practices. Northwestern had been "grossly over-capitalized" and "ridiculously mismanaged," reported a lawyer at the Portland hearings who compiled the evidence against Bell. According to one plausible journalistic account, Hill had intentionally overstated its value in the expectation that Mackay might buy it at an inflated price, netting Hill a financial windfall.[66] Interestingly, the lawyer did not regard these circumstances as a reason to abandon the lawsuit. If Bell had restrained trade, Bell was liable to be prosecuted under the Sherman Act, even if the telephone business were, as Vail had contended, a natural monopoly and, thus, properly exempt from the Sherman Act. If the telephone business were to be exempted from the Sherman Act, the exemption should be written into law.[67]

The Portland lawsuit rested on shaky foundations, and everyone knew it. By 1913, competition in the telephone business had been rejected not only by telephone users, but also by most of the country's independent operating companies. East of Oregon, predicted the *Wall Street Journal* in 1913, it would have been hard to find an operating company willing to prosecute Bell.[68] Had McReynolds or Smyth located a more incriminating smoking gun, they would never have pinned their hopes on Bell's takeover of Northwestern. Yet they had little choice: the failure of the Chicago hearings to turn up anything more damning left them with no alternative.

Hill's willingness to challenge Bell owed much to circumstances that had little to do with the telephone business. Born in North Carolina of

Quaker ancestry, Hill was educated at Harvard; following his graduation, he moved to Minneapolis to seek his fortune. There he met railroad magnate James J. Hill (who was no relation), for whom he worked for several years, and whose daughter he married. Samuel Hill enjoyed being regarded as an empire builder in the mold of his famous father-in-law and, on account of their identical last name, was sometimes mistaken for his son. Samuel Hill plowed his wife's dowry into public utilities. In addition to the Portland operating company and the toll-line provider, his investments included a gas plant and an electric power station.

Samuel Hill's lawsuit was, in part, a by-product of his own oversized personality. Wealthy, ambitious, and imperious, he had no qualms about taking on one of the largest and most powerful corporations in the country. Even sympathetic press accounts duly noted his "colossal egotism." He was "almost a maniac on the subject of himself," reported one generally sympathetic journalist, and his personal conversation invariably took the form of a "never-ceasing flow of entrancing stories of which he is the star and hero."[69] Among Hill's personal acquaintances were Queen Marie of Romania and the mistress of the French sculptor Auguste Rodin. To house the art works that he had collected on various European trips, he built an imposing mansion that he called "Maryhill" on a desolate bluff overlooking Mount Hood on the Columbia River 75 miles east of the city. Hill filled Maryhill with gifts from Queen Marie, as well as several sculptures by Rodin. Ever eager to make a grand gesture, he erected on its grounds a life-size replica of Stonehenge as a memorial to the First World War. Dubbed "Castle Nowhere" by his biographer, Maryhill is today a tourist attraction and has the distinction of being one of the most geographically isolated art museums in the world.[70]

Hill's education, marriage, and lifestyle set him apart from the stolid midwesterners who dominated the independent telephone business. Although Hill was listed, along with John H. Wright, as a director of the short-lived anti–National Independent Telephone Association, pro-antitrust Independent Telephone Association that Hubbell organized in 1912, there is no record of him actually attending a meeting.[71] Not surprisingly, he was rarely mentioned in the independent trade press and was ignored in the standard histories of the independent movement.

Hill's lawsuit heartened Postal Telegraph president Clarence Mackay. Mackay yearned to supplant Vail as "Ruler of the Wires"—as one journalist dubbed Mackay in 1910—though, unlike Vail, he lacked the resources to fuel his ambitions.[72] As a consolation, Mackay dreamed of building a long-distance telephone network for the independents to rival Bell's. Mackay's long-distance network would relieve the independents of one of the "chief handicaps" under which they had labored, observed one journalist in 1911. In particular, it would counterbalance the "universal service" that Vail declared he would provide the Bell companies by completing his Bell-only long-distance network.[73]

When Mackay's project fizzled, he too turned to the courts. Complaints about the "Telephone Trust" had flooded the Justice Department immediately after Vail's acquisition of Western Union in 1909.[74] Yet only after Vail announced his "universal service" scheme did Mackay enter the fray. Particularly distressing to Mackay was the automatic connection to Western Union of every telephone caller who informed an operator that he wished to send a telegram.[75] If this policy were not countermanded, it would put Postal Telegraph at a competitive disadvantage. If the Justice Department did not restrain Bell, Mackay warned, public revulsion at Vail's reckless empire building might well force Congress to buy out the entire telephone and telegraph business—including Mackay's Postal Telegraph—an outcome Mackay deplored.[76] The single "greatest force" hastening government ownership of the telephone and the telegraph, Mackay warned, was the aggressively expansionist business strategy on which Vail had embarked.[77]

McReynolds's lawsuit ended unexpectedly in December 1913 with the brokering of an agreement between the Justice Department and Bell. This agreement settled the antitrust suit before it went to trial. This settlement is conventionally known as the Kingsbury Commitment, in reference to Nathan C. Kingsbury, the Bell vice president who approved it on behalf of Bell. It is more aptly called the McReynolds settlement because it was, in fact, a major defeat for Bell.

The McReynolds settlement had four provisions. The first provision was a promise by the Justice Department to suspend its lawsuit if Bell met certain conditions. The remaining three provisions were the conditions that McReynolds expected Bell to meet. The first of these three conditions concerned the relationship of Bell and Western Union. McReynolds disapproved of Bell's takeover of Western Union and ordered Bell to divest its holdings in the company. Bell complied, restoring the boundary between the telephone and the telegraph that had existed between 1879 and 1909. The second condition concerned the future financial relationship between Bell and the independents. McReynolds disapproved between Bell's attempted monopolization of the telephone business and ordered Bell to desist from making any future acquisitions of independent operating companies. The third condition concerned the operational relationship of Bell and the independents. McReynolds endorsed the interconnection of Bell and noncompeting independent operating companies and ordered Bell to devise protocols necessary to give these noncompeting independents access to Bell's long-distance network.[78]

The McReynolds settlement segmented the market for electrical communications. Wickersham had opposed the prosecution of Bell under the Sherman Act in the conviction that the ICC had the authority to segment the market in a more orderly way. McReynolds created a cartel. The first application of its principles came the following March, when a federal court in Portland ordered Bell to divest Northwestern, the toll line whose acquisition had been the catalyst for McReynolds's lawsuit. Bell's acquisition of Northwestern, the court ruled, had been a restraint of trade in violation of the Sherman Act.[79] Shortly thereafter Bell sold its shares of Western Union. In the next few years, it moved cautiously to facilitate interconnection with those independents that remained outside of its network.

The McReynolds settlement was by no means a total defeat for Bell. Had McReynolds proceeded with his lawsuit, the consequences would have been hard to predict. McReynolds's endorsement of market segmentation gave the federal Justice Department's imprimatur to Vail's contention that the telephone network was, in fact, a natural monopoly. It also legitimated Bell's dominant position in the telephone business, a position it retained until 1984, when a neo-McReynoldsian team of Justice Department lawyers dismantled the Bell System. The restriction on the acquisition of independents was lifted in 1921, largely at the behest of the independents eager to sell out to Bell.

For Vail the most unfortunate feature of the McReynolds settlement was the divestiture of Western Union. No longer could Vail promise, as he had in 1910, to provide telephone users cheap and convenient facilities for long-distance communications. In public, Vail acquiesced, following a venerable Bell tradition of remaining silent when the news was bad; in private he was crushed.[80]

The Bell–Western Union divestiture was also a disappointment for Chicago Telephone general manager Angus Hibbard. Hibbard had left his position in Chicago to coordinate the consolidation of Bell and Western Union. To learn how the British had acquired the "telegraph habit," Hibbard traveled to Great Britain, where he studied the recent consolidation of the telephone and the telegraph. Hibbard had popularized local telephone service inside Chicago; now he would popularize long-distance telegraph service throughout the nation. After the divestiture wrecked his plans, Hibbard never worked in the telephone business again.

The Western Union divestiture met with a more favorable reception from Bell's rivals. The McReynolds settlement might just as plausibly be called "Mackay's Revenge" or even "Wright's Vindication," since its primary beneficiaries were Mackay's Postal Telegraph and the large number of small independents that had rallied around Wright. The antitrust suit was an "utter rout and complete surrender" for Bell, crowed one Postal Telegraph insider, in a congratulatory letter to Postal Telegraph lawyer William W. Cook.[81] We have gained all we hoped for, Wright gloated to Cook, and Postal Telegraph has won a "most signal victory."[82] Automatic Electric president Joseph Harris was equally pleased. The settlement was proof that the Wilson administration would deal fairly with large corporations, a stance that "promises much for industrial prosperity, particularly in the telephone business."[83]

Why Bell had capitulated, independent trade press editor Harry B. MacMeal could not say. Yet MacMeal found the settlement "very generous" and "the greatest boon the independents could desire." He guessed that Bell's willingness to compromise might have had something to do with the "strong agitation" to enlist Congress to buy out Bell's long-distance network: "Perhaps it was a case of 'Your long-distance lines or your life,' but, anyway, the fight for recognition of independent telephony has been won." Had the settlement failed, a congressional buyout of Bell's long-distance network might well have been the result.[84]

For many independents, the most important feature of the antitrust settlement was what MacMeal had called "recognition." The cartelization of the telephone business made it easier for the independents to convince skeptical creditors that they would make good on their loans and retain their existing user base. The independents had had a difficult time raising capital since the collapse of United States Independent in

1907, and Bell's aggressive merger policy made it hard to keep creditors at bay. Independent discontent with Bell persisted; for many, however, the survival of the independents was victory enough. Recognition entailed not only Bell's acknowledgment of the specific grievance that had sparked the lawsuit, but also the promise that Bell would respect the territorial division of the telephone business between Bell and the independents that existed in 1913, a territorial division that, with a few notable exceptions, remained intact for the next seventy years.

Wright himself regarded the settlement as a personal triumph whose significance was undiminished by the passage of time. The "adjustment" that McReynolds had negotiated with Bell in 1913, Wright reminded a Justice Department official four years later, had been of "inestimable value" to the "independent telephone interests" in the United States and had "permitted their continued existence."[85] Wright's assessment was revealing, for by 1917 many independents had found the interconnection provision to be less advantageous than they had hoped.[86] In a fitting gesture of reconciliation, Bell obtained Justice Department approval for a complicated swap that transferred to Wright his Bell rival in Jamestown, New York, and to the Rochester independent its Bell rival, in return for the transfer to Bell of Hubbell's Buffalo independent.[87]

Another independent who benefited from the settlement was Frank H. Woods. Flush with cash, Woods joined with Missouri independent Theodore Gary in 1919 to buy Automatic Electric, ensuring a steady supply of electromechanical switching equipment for his Lincoln, Nebraska, independent.[88]

The biggest loser in the antitrust settlement was Samuel Hill. Hill's Portland independent went into receivership in 1917, following a referendum in which Hill failed to persuade Portland voters to require the interconnection of Hill's Portland-based operating company with its Bell rival. A "yes" vote would have given subscribers to Hill's exchange legal access to the local, toll-line, and long-distance network operated by Bell. To Hill's chagrin, Portland voters voted "no" to interconnection, and when the results became known, Hill's creditors put his exchange into receivership.[89] Two years later, Hill sold out. Although Hill's operating company had been appraised at $2.1 million, it was snapped up for a mere $500,000 by an investors' consortium connected with Automatic Electric.[90] If Bell had bought Hill out—as, for example, Bell had bought out Hubbell in Buffalo—Hill would almost certainly have obtained a better price. Yet Bell did not. It was one thing for Hubbell to criticize Bell in a public hearing but quite another for Hill to institute a lawsuit accusing Bell of violating the Sherman Act. After all, remarked one Bell staffer sardonically, Hill had tried to get Vail indicted.[91]

The cartelization of the telephone business completed a transition that had begun in 1907 with the collapse of United States Independent and the rechartering of Chicago Telephone. No longer could lawmakers rely on competition as a plausible remedy for the problems posed by economic consolidation. Henceforth, the only remedies that remained were government regulation and government ownership. Under the circumstances, many preferred government ownership. In cities like Chicago, government regulation had proved to be a sinkhole of corruption that invariably led at the very least to collusion between the regulatory agency and the corporations it was ostensibly regulating, and at the worst to what economists would soon call the "capture" of the regulatory agency by the corporations it was supposed to oversee.

Government ownership of the telephone had widespread support among the nation's leading social scientists. A majority of the country's "theoretical" economists favored it, reported Bell staffer Walter S. Allen in 1909.[92] Richard T. Ely had endorsed government ownership as early as 1888, and the respected Columbia University political economist Edwin Seligman followed suit in 1899.[93]

Among the most influential champions of government ownership was Arthur H. Holcombe, a professor of government at Harvard who had completed a dissertation on the ownership and operation of the telephone in Europe. Government ownership, he contended, fulfilled the "direct purpose of production" more "economically" than corporate management. Had "free competition" existed in Europe, lawmakers could rely on the market as an "automatic governor." In Europe, however, competition was proscribed. Technical advance might be less rapid under government administration than under corporate management, yet rates would be lower because operating companies would no longer have to "reward" investors for risking their capital by purchasing telephone stock.[94]

While Holcombe endorsed government ownership, he remained skeptical of government operation and seems to have preferred a commission-regulated managerial corporation that in its internal organization resembled the Bell System that emerged after the First World War. On one point he was adamant. Neither government administrators nor corporate managers possessed—or in the foreseeable future were likely to possess—the organizational capabilities to install a telephone in "every man's home."[95]

Holcombe's case study of the telephone business informed his theory of American politics. His investigation of municipal franchise politics had convinced him that classes and not regions were the most powerful interest group. By classes, Holcombe did not mean groups whose interests originated in their relationship to the means of production; rather, he meant groups whose common interests originated in their relationship to the state.

Holcombe was but one of several early twentieth-century social scientists to discern in municipal franchise politics a microcosm of the interest-group politics that political economists were beginning to regard as the engine of American political development. Also among these social scientists was Charles Beard. Today Beard is best known as a historian, but in the 1900s he was a leading authority on municipal reform and a firsthand witness to the bruising municipal franchise fights in New York City over gas plants, electric streetcar lines, electric power stations, and telephone exchanges. The interpretative framework that underlay Beard's *Economic Interpretation of the Constitution* (1913) drew on his personal experience. Beard's *Economic Interpretation* was not only or even primarily a muckraking exposé of the influence of economic interests in the drafting of the federal Constitution. More significantly, it was a lucid analysis of how economic classes were shaped by the structuring presence of the state.[96]

Arthur M. Schlesinger Jr.'s father, Arthur M. Schlesinger Sr., was in the early twentieth century the nation's foremost historian of the modern American city and a pioneering student of the role of social classes in the American past. Like father, like son: in his celebrated *Age of Jackson* (1945), Schlesinger Jr. relied on a class-based interpretative framework to analyze American national politics. The interpretative framework Schlesinger employed drew not only on his father's scholarship, but also on Holcombe's lectures on American politics that Schlesinger had attended in college. Like Holcombe, Schlesinger treated class rather than region as the mainspring of American national politics.[97]

The desirability of government ownership of the telephone was not in any obvious way a partisan issue. Although its most prominent supporters were Democrats, it also appealed to many progressive-minded Republicans. Theodore Roosevelt regarded a buyout of the telephone with relative equanimity, whereas William Howard Taft's postmaster general had anticipated Burleson by endorsing a congressional buyout of the telegraph in 1911.[98] The debate over government ownership revolved around waste and utility rather than privileges and rights. It was "a mere matter of expediency" whether a "given thing" should be operated by "private individuals or by the government," reflected Roosevelt in a letter to a Kansas editor in 1914. The limited facilities and low performance standards of the government telephone in Great Britain led Roosevelt to embrace private ownership under "wise regulation." If government ownership in Great Britain had worked better, Roosevelt might well have urged the United States to follow its lead.[99]

Among the Republican true believers was department store magnate and former postmaster general John Wanamaker. The government had an obligation to own "all methods of written or spoken communication between people," including the telegraph and the telephone, Wanamaker declared in a magazine interview in 1906.[100] No longer was he content to accept a "limited" postal telegraph, as he had been as postmaster general. Now only a congressional buyout of the entire telephone and telegraph network would meet the needs of the day.

The leading congressional champion of government ownership was David J. Lewis. This Maryland Democrat represented the mountainous far western corner of the state, where as a boy he had toiled as a coal miner. A firm believer in activist government, Lewis played an instrumental role in expanding the Post Office Department's mandate to embrace the conveyance of packages weighing more than four pounds, an innovation known as parcel post. In Lewis's view, the Post Office Department was the "best institution of our government." For over a century it had provided the American people with a panoply of services—including, most recently, parcel post—that had "meant so much to all of us as plain human beings."[101] The "postalization" of the telephone—by which Lewis meant its ownership by the federal government and its operation by the Post Office Department—was an event of such momentous significance that he found it "difficult to describe or even to exaggerate."[102]

To make the case for government ownership, Lewis appealed to the "science" of political economy.[103] Political economists had long contended that private corporations were qualitatively different from government agencies, and Lewis agreed. The "normal rule" of "private financiering" led private corporations to heap up huge profits in big cities while neglecting the countryside. "Public financiering" transferred the surplus generated in the cities to the countryside, ensuring equal access for all: "The Post Office makes the profit from Chicago and New York pay for the non-profitable rural and other services, while the private telephone and telegraph investor naturally restricts his activities to the particular points which promise a satisfactory profit."[104] Mere government regulation could accomplish some of the "postal objects" of "universal and cheap communication," yet corporations had no right to "take chances" with "other people's property."[105]

Nothing angered Lewis more than Vail's public assertion in 1911 that the federal government should not buy out the telegraph because it remained a "luxury."[106] Vail's argument was carefully nuanced. Unlike previous generations of telegraph managers, he had not contended that the telegraph would always remain confined to an exclusive clientele. On the contrary, he wholeheartedly embraced its popularization as a complement to the telephone. Rather, he meant merely that the medium was not yet a necessity, and therefore that it was best left under corporate control. To clarify his position, Vail explained two years later that, although the telephone and the telegraph had each become a convenience of the "highest importance," neither was—like potable water— indispensable to human life.[107] Lewis found Vail's caveat insulting: like so many progressives, Lewis had come to regard material abundance as a civic ideal, and he yearned to make the fruits of invention accessible to all. "This is bold language," Lewis stated, in responding to Vail's 1913 report: "We are virtually told that of the three great agencies of communication only one, the letter post, may be used by all the people, and that the other two, the phone and the telegraph, are conveniences or luxuries, not popular necessities, and for that reason should be at the cost of the few, that is, of the business office and the rich, to which class largely the present rates confine the service. But this is not a justification. It is a confession. These long-distance rates are endured because the service is known only to those in easy circumstances, who overlook the rates in the glamour of the marvelous character of the process of communication."[108]

Lewis's bill never came up for a vote. If it had, it might well have garnered a respectable number of votes because government ownership had a solid base of support in both the Senate and the House.[109] Though Lewis's bill was unrelated to McReynolds's lawsuit, it had been introduced on the same day that McReynolds negotiated his agreement with Bell. That Bell had reached a settlement in order to preempt a congressional buyout seemed to Lewis incontrovertible. The McReynolds settlement, as Lewis explained it, was a "coup d'état" to forestall "postalization."[110]

Joining Lewis in his endorsement of government ownership was Postmaster General Burleson. Burleson considered himself a "conservative" Democrat. He opposed, for example, government ownership of the railroad. Yet he made an exception for the telephone and the telegraph. "However strict a constructionist" one might be, Burleson found it inconceivable that anyone would object to the Post Office Department's ownership of the "electrical means of communication."[111] The Post Office Department should have control over "all means of the communication of intelligence," Burleson declared rather grandly in his 1914 annual report. Government ownership would hasten the practical realization of the "universal service" ideal that Vail had championed, but that only the government could attain. Universal service for Burleson meant far more than the interconnection of every telephone in the country, or even the interconnection of the telephone and the telegraph. In addition, and more importantly, it embraced the "equalization of rates," a mandate to which the Post Office Department, as a government agency, had been long committed. For private corporations "equalization" was impossible, given their dependence on profit-seeking investors. In contrast, government agencies had a civic mandate to serve even the "poorest self-sustaining individual."[112]

To buttress the case for government ownership, Burleson reminded lawmakers that the federal government had owned and operated the first public telegraph line in the country. When Congress funded Samuel F. B. Morse's Washington–Baltimore demonstration project in 1843, it was "universally admitted" and "acquiesced in by everybody" that the telegraph would become part of the Post Office Department. Government ownership in the 1840s had failed because of a "false idea of economy." The "small deficiency" run-up by the Washington–Baltimore line under President James K. Polk prompted a timid Congress to authorize its sale, despite the eloquent appeals of Polk's postmaster general to retain it under government control.[113]

To document the divergent motives of government agencies and private corporations, Burleson commissioned an elaborate report on "Government Ownership of the Electrical Means of Communication." This report was prepared under the supervision of first assistant postmaster general Daniel C. Roper and released in 1914.

The Roper report used the progressive dichotomy between public utility and unnecessary waste to make the case for a congressional buyout of the telephone. Government administration would end the "economic waste" of corporation management and restore the efficiency gains that had been lost with the court-ordered breakup of Western Union and Bell. Vail was correct to affirm the "economic doctrine" that the telephone was a natural monopoly. Yet self-interest blinded him from the "inevitable conclusion" of "practically all the economists" who had compared government administration and corporate management: namely, that government administration was superior. The Post Office Department already reached "every man's door"; when the government owned and operated the "wire system," it would too. "Universal service" presupposed not only interconnection but also the "equalization" of rates.[114] The Roper report closed with the recommendation that Congress buy out every commercial telephone operating company in the country— local, toll line, and long distance—and that it issue revocable licenses to telegraph companies and the many small, noncommercial telephone operating companies that were known as "farmers' lines." The cost of the buyout was estimated to be around $900 million: $700 million for the operating companies and $200 million for the toll-line and long-distance companies.[115] Although the much-touted congressional buyout never occurred, the seriousness with which the authors of the Roper report made the case for government ownership was a testament to the high expectations with which it had come to be invested.

The federal government's civic mandate to coordinate the circulation of information was a theme to which Roper returned in a thoughtful book on the Post Office Department that he published in 1917. The critical issue for lawmakers was neither government ownership nor government regulation, Roper now believed. Rather, it was the "motive" of the institution to which the means of communication had been entrusted. Corporate management was "soulless" and "selfish"; the "soul" of government administration, in contrast, was "unselfish" and rooted in the sacred "spirit of '76." The "highest ideal" of any means of communication was the "annihilation" of distance that followed its "elimination" as a "barrier to intercourse": "The telegraph and the telephone networks of the country now constitute wonderfully efficient institutions, receiving and disbursing more money than the entire Postal Service, and affording, for ordinary uses of modern business and society, important means of communication. These electrical mail services have realized the highest ideal of postal service, which is the elimination of distance as a barrier to intercourse among men."[116] If properly harnessed by the state, they could realize the progressive dream of making the fruits of invention accessible to all.

Government ownership would emerge as a major public issue in the months immediately following the McReynolds settlement in December 1913. Its endorsement not only by lawmakers, but also by a substantial segment of the public, testified to the continuing uneasiness with which many Americans regarded huge corporate combines like Bell.

11

ONE GREAT MEDIUM?

The time may come when the telephone will be a walking companion, will be carried in the pocket like a note book, and while walking the crowded avenue or by the shaded brook, or lying on the sands of the sea, one may be able to communicate with princes or command the work of multitudes thousands of miles away.

Wall Street Journal, 1907

It was an "embarrassing fact," observed the editor of a Texas telephone trade journal in March 1914, that the American people supported government ownership of the telephone to "quite a large extent." It was even more unfortunate that this sentiment had been "fostered and developed" by the policies of Bell president Theodore N. Vail and other "men of his kind." The editor deplored government ownership, yet he was convinced that the "only practicable method" of rebutting its supporters was to "offer something in its place." By this "something" the editor did not mean the regulation of telephone operating companies by state regulatory commissions and the Interstate Commerce Commission (ICC). Regulatory commissions worked "beautifully" for the "monopolists" by keeping competition out of their territory. Rather, the only remedy was to restore competition: the "best regulator ever known." And if competition failed, the only alternative was government ownership.[1]

The Texas editor's faith in competition as a remedy for the problems posed by corporate consolidation set him apart from most telephone experts not only in the United States, but also in the rest of the world. In Great Britain, France, and many other countries, the telephone in 1914 was owned and operated by a government agency in a configuration that has been aptly dubbed the "postal-industrial complex."[2] In the United States, however, private ownership remained the norm. This contrast proved remarkably enduring. Outside of the United States, the privatization of the telephone would not begin until the 1980s, reversing a trend that dated back to the late nineteenth century.

Popular support for government ownership of the telephone peaked during the administration of Woodrow Wilson (1913–1919). Government ownership had the endorsement of a cohort of lawmakers led by Maryland congressman David J. Lewis, who introduced a government ownership bill in December 1913. The government ownership movement was sufficiently powerful that Wilson met with little opposition when in July 1918 he issued an executive order transferring control of both the telephone and the telegraph to the Post Office Department as a military necessity. In the following November, Wilson expanded the Post Office Department's jurisdiction to include any overseas cable that had been landed on American soil. Although Wilson never publicly endorsed government ownership of the telephone, the telegraph, or the cable, the control his administration exerted over these media gave the public a vivid impression of what it might expect should government ownership become the law of the land.

The Wilson administration's experiment in government control was an abject failure. Paradoxically, the operation of the telephone and the telegraph by a government agency had legitimated their operation by private corporations. In so doing, the Wilsonians unwittingly laid the groundwork for the ascendancy of the managerial corporation as a central institution of the twentieth-century political economy in the United States.

Wilson was more skeptical of corporate consolidation than his predecessors Theodore Roosevelt and William Howard Taft. Yet neither Wilson nor any member of his cabinet contemplated legislation to encourage new entrants in either the telephone or the telegraph business. More plausible was a congressional buyout of the telephone and the telegraph and their operation by a government agency. Government ownership had the endorsement of Wilson's secretary of state, William Jennings Bryan; his postmaster general, Albert S. Burleson; and his navy secretary, Josephus Daniels.

The 1912 Democratic platform had not included a government ownership plank, nor had Wilson campaigned on the issue. Yet government ownership of the telegraph was no longer particularly controversial.

"For a long time," Wilson wrote Burleson shortly after he took office, "I have thought that the government ought to own the telegraph lines of the country and combine the telegraph with the post office. How have you been thinking in this matter?"[3]

Government ownership of the telephone was more problematic. Wilson found troubling Bell's supposed technical conservatism and alluded to it in a political manifesto that he published during the election campaign.[4] Yet Wilson never publicly endorsed government ownership of the telephone as a remedy for corporate consolidation. In an interview with a Boston banker in 1914, Wilson was reputed to have privately disclosed that he was "strongly opposed" to a congressional buyout of Bell's long-distance network.[5] Whether Wilson would have endorsed municipal ownership of individual operating companies is a matter of speculation. Two things are certain. First, Wilson did nothing to block Burleson from vigorously championing the "postalization" of the telephone during Burleson's eight-year tenure as postmaster general. Second, in 1918 Wilson himself seriously contemplated including in his annual message a rousing pro-government ownership peroration that Burleson had penned. For some reason Wilson changed his mind, and the peroration was dropped. Even so, it remains suggestive that Wilson was willing to consider it at all.[6]

Government ownership of the telephone appealed to two very different segments of the electorate: neo-Populists and city dwellers. Among the neo-Populists were Burleson, Bryan, and Daniels. Among the city dwellers were the city councils of many cities, including San Francisco, Los Angeles, Portland, Salt Lake City, Minneapolis, Milwaukee, Cleveland, and Cincinnati.[7] Proposals varied as to precisely how the buyout should be structured. Burleson favored a congressional buyout of the entire telephone network; Bryan, in contrast, endorsed a congressional buyout of the long-distance telephone network and a municipal buyout of individual telephone operating companies. "I am glad to note that the local telephone exchanges will be interfered with as little as possible," Bryan wrote Postmaster General Burleson shortly after Burleson took control of the wires: "There is no reason why a city cannot attend to the telephone for its own citizens."[8]

Support for government ownership was particularly widespread in the Midwest. To monitor the public pulse, a Bell staffer compiled an analysis of the editorial position on the government ownership question in 160 newspapers in Ohio, Indiana, Illinois, Wisconsin, and Michigan.

His study revealed that forty-four newspapers with a circulation of 2.4 million endorsed government ownership of the telephone, sixty-five newspapers with a circulation of 2.3 million opposed it, and fifty-one newspapers with a circulation of 900,000 remained neutral.[9]

Among the newspapers that endorsed government ownership was the large-circulation chain owned by William Randolph Hearst. The federal government had built the Panama Canal as well as the "fleetest" battleships, editorialized Hearst columnist Arthur Brisbane in December 1913. Who then could possibly contend that the government lacked the organizational capabilities to operate the telephone? If the government needed to recruit high-powered executive talent to operate the network, it could easily "train up" another Vail or Bethell.[10] Hearst himself, Brisbane reminded his readers, had introduced a bill to nationalize both the telegraph and the telephone when he had been a member of Congress in 1905. In point of fact, Brisbane erred. The bill that Hearst had introduced said nothing about the telephone, though it did call for government ownership of the telegraph.[11] Yet it was a pardonable exaggeration for Brisbane to credit Hearst with having supported government ownership of the telephone in 1905. Hearst had championed municipal ownership of streetcar lines and electric plants, and, had he considered government ownership of the telephone a winning public issue, he would doubtless have endorsed it too.[12]

Support for government ownership was, in the main, resolutely traditional. Although the issue appealed to doctrinaire socialists, socialist newspapers were by no means the only ones to take up the cause. In a judicious overview of the government ownership issue, a British journalist concluded that the "chief cause and stimulus" for government ownership of municipal franchise corporations came not from socialists, but from the overly generous dividends that corporations paid their shareholders and the "waterlogged condition" of their securities.[13] There was nothing socialistic about government ownership of the telephone and the telegraph, editorialized the *Wall Street Journal* in 1918: it was merely stupid.[14]

The rationale for government ownership could be frankly conservative. "When the government takes over the telegraph and telephone, it will simply be extending its old work of facilitating communication between the people," editorialized the Lincoln, Nebraska, *Daily Star* in December 1913: "The telegraph and telephone are but better methods of communication than the letter and the newspaper." Far more radical was the recent augmentation of the Post Office Department's mandate to embrace the conveyance of parcels weighing more than four pounds. Parcel post "invaded" the field of commerce and might logically culminate in government ownership of the railroad. In contrast, government ownership of the telephone and the telegraph was merely an incremental augmentation of the federal government's time-honored mandate to promote communication by facilitating the circulation of "intelligence."[15]

That a congressional buyout would succeed seemed likely to business journalists Elbert Hubbard and E. J. Edwards. Hubbard urged President Wilson to appoint Vail the "general commissioner" of the board that Congress would establish when it took over the telephone, an event that Hubbard considered inevitable.[16] Edwards felt certain that Vail would sell out if the price were right. Jay Gould, too, would have sold Western Union to the federal government in the 1880s if Congress had been willing to come to terms, Edwards reminded his readers, citing as his source a confidential conversation that he had had with Western Union president Norvin Green. Vail would too.[17]

The possibility that Congress might buy at least certain parts of the telephone network spurred a good deal of sober reflection among senior Bell staffers. If the American people wanted to buy out the telephone business, Vail wrote a colleague in 1914, there was nothing he or anyone else could do to stop them. "Whenever the sentiment of the people as a whole is in favor of government ownership, we must expect that it will be accomplished."[18]

The future looked sufficiently bleak that in October 1913 Vail hinted in a newspaper interview that, under certain circumstances, he might be willing to sell Congress Bell's vaunted long-distance network. Bell made most of its profits on short-distance traffic, and in some parts of the country less than 1 percent of telephone calls crossed state lines: "We would not be adverse to any government action which would result in reducing the expense of operating our long-distance service."[19] The rate of return on long distance was probably no more than 2.5 percent, editorialized the *Wall Street Journal* the following day, making it "relatively the least profitable portion of the Bell System." In the railroad business, carriers made money on the long-haul business and lost money on the branch lines. In the telephone business, the opposite was true: "Telephones lose money on a large percentage of long-distance traffic and make net profits on the 'branch or exchange' business, as it is called."[20]

The rate of return that the business journalist reported was markedly lower than the rate of return that would many years later be publicized by Bell statisticians: 2.5 percent versus 11.5 percent. It is hard to determine which figure was the more accurate, inasmuch as Bell was notoriously reluctant to compile data about its long-distance network in a straightforward way. Even so, given the limited demand for long-distance service, it would seem probable that the lower figure was closer to the truth.[21]

Vail's interview displayed a fatalism characteristic of the public pronouncements of Bell executives during the Wilson administration. "The people, through their state commissions and city commissions, are closing in on the Bell companies," declared signal corps officer Charles M. Saltzman in a December 1913 letter to postal administrator Daniel C. Roper, "and before their attorneys are through with a hearing at 'A,' they are rushed to 'B' to attend another hearing." Saltzman added that he had recently spoken with a Bell executive who confidently expected that the federal government would soon take over both the operating companies and the long-distance network. The executive added that he believed the government would "make a success" of this "great undertaking," provided that it was "so arranged that politics would not embarrass the department in appointments."[22] Bell was "taking desperate chances," brooded Chicago Telephone Company president Bernard E. Sunny in surveying the political landscape in the Midwest. The Illinois legislature would soon enact a law permitting any municipality to buy out its telephone exchange, and the prospects seemed good that municipal governments throughout the Midwest would buy up the lucrative big-city telephone operating companies one by one—beginning, perhaps, with Indianapolis—saddling Bell with the less lucrative territory in between.[23] Public utilities like the telephone were uniquely vulnerable to government interference, reflected Bell staffer Walter S. Allen. No other business touched the individual "so personally and directly." Moreover, because the "nature of the service" demanded that it had to be performed by large units for a large number of small users, the users' "small irritations and petty grievances" inevitably became "concentrated" on the corporation that supplied the service.[24]

The pessimism of Bell staffers was exacerbated by the complexity of the political economy. The "people generally" had become convinced that the telephone was a natural monopoly, explained Bell vice president

Charles G. DuBois in a letter to Vail. Yet there was no "general disposition" to confine its regulation to the state regulatory commissions and the ICC. As a consequence, Bell simultaneously confronted regulatory challenges from a variety of governmental institutions: state legislatures, state attorney generals, city councils, the federal Justice Department, and the courts.[25]

In DuBois's nightmare scenario, government-mandated rate caps would make it impossible for Bell operating companies to obtain the necessary capital to maintain performance standards, which would decline, while user discontent mounted, ratcheting up the "general public sentiment" against "private monopoly." The only exit from this labyrinth might well be government ownership, unless public opinion could be "crystallized" in opposition to the enormous public debt that a congressional buyout would create.[26]

If a congressional buyout occurred, DuBois envisioned a "compromise scheme" between Bell and the federal government. In this scenario, Bell would transfer the operation of its telephone and telegraph network to a "National Telephone and Telegraph Board" that would operate them under the "direct and permanent control and administrative responsibility of the federal government."[27] DuBois preferred the greater operational autonomy that Bell would retain if the telephone and the telegraph were under corporate management. Yet he conceded that his "compromise scheme" might be the best that Bell could expect.

Echoing the pessimism of Bell staffers were the bankers Bell relied on for the marketing of its bonds. "I am wondering how our friends in the telephone company are going to provide for theirs, especially if these attacks or threatened attacks of the government continue," remarked London banker Gaspard Farrer in 1913, after learning of McReynolds's lawsuit: "Frankly I do not see how the company can find fresh buyers for some £20,000,000 a year of securities, which I understand is the minimum they need, if the present conditions are maintained. The government ought frankly and speedily to announce whether they intend to continue their prosecution or endorse the company's past actions and future policy; unless they do I cannot see any other end but government ownership."[28]

Government ownership was inconceivable in the absence of an agreed-upon criterion for the valuation of telephone assets. The intricacies of corporate valuation could be arcane. Yet it was predicated on two more-or-less coherent methods of corporate accounting: valuation could be based on the likely profits that a corporation would generate in the future or on the fixed costs that it had incurred in the past. Jay Gould had pioneered the future-oriented method to value Western Union in the 1880s. Most early twentieth-century public utility accountants favored the past-oriented method, which was called physical valuation.[29] It was this method—rather than Gould's—that Vail endorsed in the first annual report that he issued following his return to Bell in 1907. Vail's decision was of "extraordinary interest," editorialized the *Wall Street Journal,* and a major step forward for a corporation that, as recently as 1902, had opposed even the most rudimentary kinds of financial disclosure.[30]

Vail was not entirely consistent in his embrace of physical valuation. In his secret negotiation with the independents at Chicago's Blackstone Hotel in 1910, for example, he was reputed to have proposed a capitalization that included a generous allowance for costs that were unrelated to physical assets, such as the "waste" occasioned by competition. Yet in his public pronouncements Vail was more restrained. Bell, he promised, would assign no monetary value to any of the special privileges it had obtained from the government, whether these privileges took the form of municipal franchises or patent rights.

Vail's embrace of financial orthodoxy projected into a distinctively new, progressive idiom his long-standing conviction that Bell shared little with, and, indeed, had long opposed, "big business" interests like Jay Gould's Western Union.[31] Western Union under Gould had been financially progressive and technically orthodox. The Bell System under Vail was—or, at least, was supposed to be—financially orthodox and technically progressive. "One thing" that probably had as much influence on the telephone business as anything else, Vail observed, was the decision of the first generation of telephone managers to make Bell a "great utility" rather than a "mere money-making proposition."[32]

Financial orthodoxy gave Vail a powerful weapon in his contest with the independents. The widespread establishment of state regulatory commissions, he declared in 1911, had been spurred by the "popular odium" that originated in the manipulation of gullible investors by "professional speculative promoters" and "swindling security vendors."[33] Vail's analysis was self-serving. Lawmakers had many reasons to support regulatory commissions that had nothing to do with the dubious financial methods of certain independent operating companies. Even so, it was telling that Vail aligned Bell against the venal speculator and with the passive rentier. By marginalizing the investor, Vail enhanced the operational autonomy of managers like himself.

The recent valuation of Bell assets by the ICC, Bell vice president Nathan C. Kingsbury noted approvingly in 1914, had been undertaken not by financiers but by engineers. "We are not now in the position of cutting melons," Kingsbury elaborated, in a pointed reference to the notorious late-nineteenth-century "stock watering" schemes made infamous by Gould—and "never have been." The current capitalization of the Bell operating companies was $61 million less than their "actual physical property." In reaching this total, the ICC had taken "no account whatever" of intangible assets—such as goodwill, patents, franchises, research and development—or "going concern values"—even though each might plausibly have been regarded as part of the cost of reproducing its physical plant.[34]

Bell's financial orthodoxy was conceded even by some of its fiercest critics. "Be it said for the Bell System," declared Maryland congressman David J. Lewis, "that it is the one great corporation in our country that has not issued tons of counterfeit capital." The soundness of Bell accounting was for Lewis no small matter, for it eliminated a roadblock that might otherwise have impeded a congressional buyout: "Its stock and bonds today represent the actual contributions of its shareholders in money to a great common enterprise, and we have not that unfortunate circumstance, overcapitalization, to deal with in the valuation of their properties."[35]

Bell's financial orthodoxy simplified the negotiations that would inevitably precede a congressional buyout. Yet it did nothing to mollify critics convinced that even the most exemplary private corporation lacked the economic incentives to provide a mass service for the entire population. To challenge this premise, Bell publicists became increasingly forthright in their defense of the deliberate subsidization of certain groups of telephone users, a practice known as rate averaging. The term "rate averaging" could refer to a variety of revenue transfers: the transfers could shift revenue from the city to the countryside; from operating companies to long-distance network providers; or from business users to residential users.

Rate averaging could be a powerful competitive weapon. The earning power of Bell's New York City operating company, Vail informed one of its largest shareholders in 1907, was so "conspicuous" that it rendered the company vulnerable to interference by lawmakers, rivals, or both. As a consequence, it was expedient to conceal the profits generated in New York City by spreading them around the state. Rate averaging had the further benefit of mollifying upstate investors who feared that rate increases in upstate operating companies might encourage new entrants. If the profits were judiciously distributed, rate averaging would keep rates at an acceptably low level for those operating companies most vulnerable to competition—and, in so doing, "practically settle the independent situation" throughout the state.[36]

Had Vail's justification for rate averaging become widely known, it might well have been condemned. Regional cross-subsidies raised the specter of predatory pricing, a practice opposed by both courts and regulatory commissions.[37] To avoid unwelcome political scrutiny, Bell staffers downplayed the magnitude of the cross-subsidies in the Bell System. Unlike the Post Office Department, explained Bell staffer Walter S. Allen in 1914, Bell provided few services at less than cost, in keeping with the strictures of the courts and the regulatory commissions regarding the setting of "rates below cost" regardless of the potential "advantages to the community."[38]

Allen's allusion to the Post Office Department highlighted a feature of rate averaging that was obvious to contemporaries but is often forgotten today. Rate averaging was linked in the public mind with the Post Office Department, an organization that had been balancing regions and classes for over 100 years. Pricing practices that Bell critics derided as predatory impressed political economists as a laudatory application of the "post office principle." The pervasiveness of rate averaging was one reason the Post Office Department became known as a system. It may also explain why Vail chose the system metaphor to characterize the relationship of the Bell operating companies. Like the "postal system," the "Bell System" promoted the public good by balancing the interests of different regions and classes, in a manner analogous to the "American System" that the statesman Henry Clay had championed following the War of 1812.

Rate averaging did not match cost to price; rather, it guaranteed equal access to the network. It was predicated on the assumption that the Post Office Department had an obligation to provide inclusive facilities for the entire population. Not yet an economic truism, it remained a civic ideal. The "post office principle," explained political economist

Henry C. Adams in 1918, guaranteed that every citizen should have use of the mail on "equal terms" and that the profits made in those parts of the country in which the traffic was dense should be transferred to "make good the loss" in those parts of the country in which the traffic was sparse.[39]

The similarities between rate averaging in telephone operating companies and rate averaging in the Post Office Department became a favorite theme of Bell managers beginning around 1900. The first Bell manager to endorse the postal principle was probably Chicago Telephone Company president John I. Sabin. To build support for rate averaging inside Chicago, Sabin ventured a postal-telephonic analogy. Sabin's unqualified endorsement of network expansion was controversial, with business subscribers fearing that network expansion might degrade the performance standards they currently enjoyed.[40]

Sabin's successors were more politic. The extension of telephone facilities to thinly settled districts was essential, posited New York Telephone Company president Union N. Bethell in 1906, even if it was not "apparently" remunerative: "As with the postal service and most other public utilities, so with the telephone service, some branches or routes must be conducted apparently at the expense of the other branches or routes."[41] As commission regulation became entrenched, the rationale for rate averaging became increasingly explicit. "Our business" resembled the Post Office Department in a "considerable degree," explained the president of a Colorado-based operating company in 1910: "One post office serving a single community, without reference to or exchanging letters with other post offices serving other communities, would be of little value; it is the relationships between post offices, the exchange of information between communities, that makes the service valuable."[42]

Bell publicists sometimes invoked the postal principle to justify network expansion. The rate structure that the Colorado state public utilities commission had approved, explained Bell staffer Chester I. Barnard in 1918, had been designed not only to ensure a reasonable return on the existing level of telephone service, but also to encourage its extension into Colorado's thinly settled hinterland: "The principle largely resembled that governing the federal postal rates and the record and decision by this committee is recommended to the careful perusal of all state commissions, as being one of the most recent decisions based upon a careful and scientific investigation and probably being less discriminatory than any other rates covering so large a territory."[43]

Rate averaging significantly narrowed the gap between the business strategy of the Bell operating companies and the civic mandate of the Post Office Department, as did the repeated declarations by Bell staffers that operating companies owed their primary obligation not to their shareholders but to the public. Here, too, Bell insiders parried the objection of corporate critics that private corporations lacked the economic incentives to provide inclusive facilities for the entire population. The telephone business was not a "private business," declared Bell vice president Nathan C. Kingsbury in December 1913: the "public is our master."[44] The most challenging problem confronting the telephone business, Kingsbury elaborated, was the "problem of giving service to the public." It was to uphold this "high civic duty"—and for "this alone"—that the telephone business existed.[45] The public had the "exclusive right" of conducting the telephone business, affirmed another Bell staffer at around the same time: "We are only in here by permission."[46]

The Bell managers' deference toward the public was in no sense entirely altruistic. The declaration that the public was one's "master" buttressed two pillars of Bell's emerging managerialism and met the objection that government ownership was necessary for government control. In particular, it marginalized investors by rejecting the presumption that maximizing the shareholders' rate of return was Bell's primary obligation. In addition, it enhanced the autonomy of Bell's managers by identifying their business strategy with a civic ideal. If Bell had a social obligation to the nation, it was up to Bell's managers—and only Bell's managers—to ensure that this obligation was met. For Vail and his like-minded colleagues, managers—and only managers—could simultaneously maximize efficiency and economy, promote public utility, and eliminate unnecessary waste. Neither "efficiency" nor "economy" was value-neutral, and neither was "utility." Unlike "equal rights," each presumed an outcome rather than an opportunity, and each could be attained only through deliberate design. These designers came to be known as managers. Just as governments required administrators, so corporations demanded managers.

The United States' declaration of war against Germany in April 1917 gave Bell an opportunity to demonstrate to the nation the seriousness with which it took its social obligations. To assist the war effort, Bell built and maintained a battlefield telephone network in France; to provide logistical support for the navy, Bell conducted research on wireless telegraphy.[47]

Wireless telegraphy posed a major challenge for Bell. If a rival found a practical way to operate a telephone business without wires, Bell's largest single investment, its wire network, would be imperiled. In 1910 the wireless telegraph remained confined to coded signals, almost all of which were transmitted in Morse code. Yet its future seemed unlimited. The most important wireless network in the United States in 1910 was operated by Marconi, a British-owned corporation whose assets included a portfolio of wireless patents. Marconi assiduously cultivated American investors, as seen in its advertisements, which often featured testimonials from prominent Americans like Thomas A. Edison and Andrew Carnegie.[48] To entice investors, Marconi advertisements compared the potential yield of "Marconi System" securities in the future to the actual yield of "Bell System" securities in the past. Bell shares that had originally been sold for $1.00 a share now commanded $1,000 a share. Who knew how much Marconi shares might one day be worth?[49]

The possibility that Marconi's wireless network might supersede Bell's wire network was a topic of frequent discussion in the press.[50] Wireless telephony would take the place of wired telephony in a mere ten years, predicted the *Literary Digest,* rendering worthless Bell's huge investment in wires and poles.[51] If the federal government were to buy Bell's long-distance network, it might be "backing the wrong horse," editorialized the *New York Times* in 1913, for wireless telephony might soon make it obsolete. The federal government should instead remain neutral in order to facilitate the "free competition" between wire and wireless.[52] Although one Texas telephone promoter in 1915 reported that he had supported government ownership of the telephone for twenty-five years, he had recently changed his mind, having discovered that new inventions—including, in particular, the wireless telegraph—might well render the existing telephone properties "practically worthless within a few weeks." Such an eventuality would leave the government behind the "march of progress" by saddling it with an investment that would "soon be consigned to the scrap pile."[53]

To remain abreast of the latest technical developments in wireless, Bell accumulated a portfolio of wireless patents. Yet it had no interest in commercializing the wireless telephone itself. Having spent millions of dollars building a wire network, it did not want this investment to go to waste. Yet if the wireless telephone proved to be practical, Bell did not want anyone else commercializing it either. Thus wireless research was partly defensive. The goal was less to commercialize a wireless telephone than to assemble a patent portfolio so formidable that it would discourage anyone else from entering the field.[54]

Another realm in which Bell feared that technical advance might threaten its capital investment was switchboard design. Prior to 1920, most telephone calls made on Bell equipment—local as well as long distance—required the assistance of one or more telephone operators. Vail's faith in operator-assisted telephone service was unwavering. "We are not building up our [financial] reserves with the idea that we may be compelled to abandon the manual system for the automatic," Vail informed a *Wall Street Journal* reporter in 1912. In the "great majority of cases," the operator was now and would remain in the future an "essential part of the system." There must always be "intelligence" in the line should something go wrong, while operator-assisted service was in fact "automatic" from the moment a caller informed the operator which telephone the caller wished to reach.[55] The superiority of the operator-assisted telephone over the electromechanical telephone would remain an article of faith for Chester I. Barnard for the next thirty years.[56] Not until 1947 would Bell publicly showcase the percentage of telephones that it had converted from operator-assisted switching to electromechanical switching, as opposed to, say, the percentage of the world's telephones located in the United States.[57]

The almost exclusive reliance of Bell operating companies on operator-assisted switching distinguished them from the small but influential group of independents that had shifted to electromechanical switching beginning around 1900. Non-Bell operating companies operated by far the largest number of electromagnetic switchboards in the period before 1920. Although a few Bell operating companies operated electromechanical switchboards, Western Electric engineers failed to develop a patent portfolio comparable to Automatic Electric's. Angus Hibbard claimed that he had tried to convince Bell president John E. Hudson to invest in some electromechanical switching patents in the 1890s, but Hudson declined.[58] As a consequence, Bell was at a competitive disadvantage in this branch of the telephone equipment manufacturing business. Not until after 1920 would Western Electric begin to manufacture electromechanical switchboards in large quantities for Bell.[59]

The Bell operating companies' reliance on operator-assisted switching posed a thorny problem for Bell publicists. Electromechanical switching had come into widespread use by 1910, and consumer surveys consistently revealed that a majority of telephone users preferred the dial-up telephone to the operator-assisted telephone. The superiority of the dial-up telephone lay neither in its privacy nor even in its alleged reduction of the call-connection delay. Rather, explained a group of telephone users in Dayton, Ohio, in 1904, it lay in its impersonality. The "vocal transmission of numbers" caused mistakes, and callers had grown weary of the unpleasant relations between caller and operator that sprang up on the "slightest provocation."[60] The telephone operator's "exasperating indifference" and her "parrot-like response of "'busy'" left telephone users feeling that they wanted to smash their telephone, reported public utility expert Delos F. Wilcox in 1910, since they had no idea where the problem lay. Busy signals generated by an electromechanical switchboard occasioned little concern because users could take comfort in the fact that they were not being singled out for discrimination.[61] To solve these problems, Automatic Electric advertisements urged operating companies to shift from operator-assisted switching to electromechanical switching: only the "girlless, cussless, out-of-order-less" telephone could provide "secret service."[62]

Bell's reluctance to adopt electromechanical switching occasioned a great deal of speculation. Why was Bell so slow to make the transition? critics demanded. Electromechanical switching had not worked out well in large cities, Bell engineers replied, citing the failure of Illinois Telephone and Telegraph in Chicago as a case in point. A further constraint was user-based: If Bell upgraded certain parts of its network, but not others, those users who had yet to be switched over might complain that their equipment was not up to date.[63] Bell critics contended that Bell's reluctance to innovate could be traced to its disinclination to risk its huge investment in operator-assisted switching. Electromechanical switching worked fine in Los Angeles and Lincoln, Nebraska, Bert G. Hubbell reminded President Wilson in July 1913. In fact, Hubbell himself had recently switched to electromechanical switching in his Buffalo exchange. Yet Hubbell doubted Bell would ever make the transition because it would then face a $300 million "shrinkage" in its investment in operator-assisted switching equipment. It was a familiar story of monopoly stifling innovation—precisely the theme Wilson himself had recently elaborated on in his magazine article on the "New Freedom."[64]

To rebut the presumption that Bell operating companies were wedded to an obsolete technology, Bell publicists lauded the female telephone operator as a faithful servant. The "excellence" of telephone service was attributable to the "skill and faithfulness" of its telephone operators, Bell publicists proclaimed.[65] The telephone operator was the "most economical 'servant' "—the only flesh-and-blood servant many telephone users could afford.[66] The idealization of the female telephone operator drew on conventional gender stereotypes of women as eager-to-please helpmeets. It also kept alive the waning association of the telephone with high social status. Just as the well-to-do relied on servants to run errands, so too they could enlist a telephone operator to complete a connection. The telephone operator was the "Invisible Servant," rhapsodized traffic supervisor J. L. Turner in March 1918. "Unseen but ever-present," she labored mightily amidst the "wild tumult" of the telephone exchange to personify the "strong and lasting spirit of service."[67]

The idealization of the female telephone operator had a special allure for union organizers intent on protecting telephone operators from technological obsolescence. Electromechanical switching had not worked as advertised in Chicago, testified a labor organizer in 1940, echoing an argument that had been widely rehearsed during the past thirty years. It was "inanimate," "unresponsive," and "stupid," and did "none of the things which machinery is supposed to do in industry"—making it a "perfect example of a wasteful, expensive, inefficient, clumsy, anti-social device."[68]

The almost ritualistic paeans of Bell executives to the power of public opinion took inspiration from the elaborate public relations campaign that Vail launched in 1908. The novelty of Vail's campaign lay in its transparency. Bell publicists had long recognized the power of public opinion. Yet prior to Vail's return, they had worked almost exclusively behind the scenes, placing articles surreptitiously in publications such as the *Boston News Bureau* and the *Electrical Review*. One way or another, it is probably safe to assume that Bell publicists had a hand in many, if not most, of the newspaper and magazine articles sympathetic to Bell that appeared in mass-circulation publications before 1908. In 1906 alone, Bell publicists took credit for placing no fewer than 1,700 telephone-related articles in newspapers and magazines.[69]

The defining feature of pre-1908 Bell public relations was stealth. While Bell publicists labored mightily to improve Bell's public image, they almost never informed readers that Bell was footing the bill. The "golden silence" of Bell insiders extended even to the publication by its engineers of articles dealing with technical issues.[70] If Bell started up its own technical journal, Vail explained to an operating company president in 1907, "we would have to cease discouragement of publication by our own people."[71] Even the phrase "Bell System" was taboo, and in its place, Bell publicists substituted "Bell Companies." As Bell publicist James D. Ellsworth later reminisced, it "seemed injudicious to use the term Bell System which suggested a trust."[72] To a "substantial part of the public," elaborated another Bell publicist, the phrase had a "sinister meaning."[73]

All this changed beginning in 1908. Henceforth, Bell not only paid for its publicity, but took credit for the message. The results were far more positive than Bell's advertising agency F. W. Ayer had anticipated. Ayer had warned Vail not to characterize Bell as a "system," lest its market power become a campaign issue in the 1908 presidential election.[74] Vail ignored the advice and nothing happened. Although Theodore Roosevelt had drawn attention to the financial relationship of telephone, telegraph, and cable corporations in a major address one month before the election, neither he nor anyone else who was not an independent promoter seems to have regarded Bell's market power as a campaign issue.[75] Like the "postal system," the "Bell system" by 1908 had come to be regarded not only as a powerful institution, but also as a channel of communications.

Vail's public relations campaign had four themes: the education of telephone users; the superiority of the telephone monopoly to competition; the superiority of corporate management to government administration; and the identification of corporate management with technical progressiveness. The centerpiece of the campaign was the regular monthly placement of handsomely designed "public service" announcements in mass-circulation magazines. These announcements were not an "invitation" to "purchase telephone service," explained a Bell staffer. They had been intended to increase neither Bell's market share nor its shareholders' dividend. Rather, they were supposed to sell the Bell System.[76]

The first theme that Vail hit upon in his campaign was the "peculiar character" of telephone service. If a caller experienced an undue delay in obtaining a connection, or if a call proved unavailing, the problem originated with telephone subscribers, and not with the operating company making the connection.[77]

Following a consultation with James D. Ellsworth, Vail scrapped this theme. Ellsworth was a journalist-turned-publicity agent who for several years had coordinated the surreptitious placement of favorable news items for Bell. Ellsworth had a better intuitive understanding of public sentiment than Vail and questioned the efficacy of a public relations campaign that blamed telephone users for the problems they experienced with telephone service. Under Ellsworth's tutelage, Bell's public relations campaign shifted from the shortcomings of telephone subscribers to the benefits of the Bell System. In so doing, it aspired to impress on the public the still-controversial idea that Bell was a socially responsible corporation that was performing a public service that deserved the special privileges it had been granted.

The first public relations announcement set the tone. The facilities Bell provided should not be criticized as monopolistic; rather, they should be praised as a "universal service." Hostility toward Bell, the announcement predicted, would diminish once the public realized that the "legitimate" scope of the telephone network was equivalent with the nation, and public hostility toward Bell should disappear once the public grasped the "necessity" of "universal service."[78] To fault Bell for dominating the telephone business ignored the extent to which the telephone, like the mail, had become a mass service for the entire population. To attack Bell for enjoying a monopoly overlooked its rationale: "The postmaster does, too, for the same reason." The postal-telephone analogy elided a major difference between the Post Office Department and Bell: the Post Office Department circulated information throughout the country at a uniform cost, but Bell did not. Even so, by tapping into the century-old identification of network with nation, Bell's public relations campaign linked Bell with the beguiling conceit that communications annihilated distance and created community.

The frequent repetition in Bell's public service announcements of phrases such as "public utility," "public service," and "universal service" linked Bell's business strategy with venerable civic ideals. The elusiveness of this language exasperated New York City banker Emerson McMillan, who derided it as evasive, and in the main, he was right. By articulating a business strategy that was broad and open-ended, Vail enhanced the operational autonomy of the managers responsible for carrying it out and limited the options of those investors who might be inclined to call them to account.[79]

To personalize the Bell System, Vail granted numerous interviews, testified freely and without equivocation at several government hearings, and published many essays and speeches. Every single telegram that

Western Union delivered during the years when it was under Bell control bore Vail's signature, a fact that disgusted one Vail detractor, who sneered that Vail had become as shameless a self-promoter as Theodore Roosevelt.[80] Vail also encouraged the publication of numerous accounts of his life. One theme of these accounts was the formative influence of his tenure in the Railway Mail Service.[81] The challenge of administering a network that was as spatially extensive as the Railway Mail Service, remarked one journalist, had "lifted" Vail up to a "higher point of view."[82] It has "always been surmised," observed another journalist, that Vail "fixed upon" the commercialization not merely of the telephone, but of "electricity," as a consequence of his very competent work at the Railway Mail Service and "by reason of this service."[83]

The ingenuity of Bell's public relations campaign impressed oil baron John D. Rockefeller Jr. Rockefeller's father had founded Standard Oil, one of the trusts that Attorney General George W. Wickersham had prosecuted in 1911. The secret of Vail's success in Rockefeller's view lay in publicity. Through public lectures, the planting of sympathetic articles in newspapers and magazines, and in "other ways," Vail had "constantly and persistently" kept up a "campaign of education." The very fact that the Justice Department had permitted Bell—one of the greatest, if not the greatest, monopoly in the country—to continue "unmolested" and, in particular, that it had obtained for its monopoly the approval not only of the "people at large" but also of the courts, was "indication enough of his success."[84]

Even the construction of a new headquarters building became an occasion to advertise Bell. Following his acquisition of Western Union in 1909, Vail decided to replace Western Union's headquarters building in New York City with a new joint headquarters building for both corporations. While this building was originally known as the "Western Union Building," it was intended to project the expansive corporate vision that Vail envisioned for Bell.[85]

The new headquarters building did not flaunt its height, as the old building had. Even so, it was no less effective an advertisement for the corporation. Just as Christian churches appropriated sites formerly occupied by pagan temples, so the new Bell–Western Union building commanded the location formerly occupied by Western Union alone. Atop its tower—in the same place in which, in decades past, New Yorkers gazed upward to watch the daily descent of the Western Union time ball—Bell mounted a massive bronze statue: the "Genius of Electricity."

The statue had been sculpted by Evelyn B. Longman, a talented young artist who had won a competition sponsored by Western Union. The "requirement," explained a contemporary art critic, was for a "sitting figure representing telegraphy."[86] The building's architect himself had explained to Longman that he envisioned a seated figure holding a thunder-bolt that was "somewhat allied to the electricity utilized by the tele-phone and telegraph company."[87] Longman modified the architects' in-structions and proposed a standing male nude that was loosely modeled on an ancient Greek god. The nude held a lightning bolt in one hand and an electric cable in the other. The iconography was deliberately vague, not unlike Vail's open-ended vision for Bell.

The theme of Bell's public relations campaign shifted dramatically in 1913. The gravest threat that the telephone business confronted, Bell's public relations announcements now proclaimed, originated neither with Bell's users nor with its rivals, but with lawmakers advocating govern-ment ownership. To target specialized audiences, Bell publicists prepared "Five-Minute Talks" on various topics, including "Government Own-ership and the Farmer" and "Government Ownership and Taxation: The High Cost of Governing."[88]

In the course of the public debate over government ownership, Bell publicists discovered that Bell's long-distance network had great popu-lar appeal. The opening of telephone service between New York City and Denver was a "godsend to us in the publicity field," reminisced Bell publicity agent James D. Ellsworth.[89] The opening of telephone service between New York City and San Francisco occasioned an even more favorable public reaction. In conjunction with the wireless telegraph, it had a "profound effect" in shaping the public's view of the telephone business, observed one Bell staffer. These two triumphs of "private initia-tive" furnished the "best argument" in favor of the "continuance" of pri-vate ownership and operation.[90] One of the most significant facts about this "famous achievement," observed one journalist, was the extent to which it had been "turned to account by the publicity departments of the telephone companies." We "venture to guess" that the "advertising value of the ocean-to-ocean line is quite as great so far as the actual value de-rived from it."[91]

The transcontinental telephone was a tribute not only to Bell but also to the American government, explained Bell lawyer A. Lincoln Lavine in a history of Bell's wartime military service. To make his point, Lavine contrasted the American government with the German government. The

American government was a democracy that encouraged private corporations like Bell to promote uniformity from the bottom up, whereas the German government was an autocracy that dragooned government agencies like the German army to enforce uniformity from the top down. For Lavine, this political contrast explained not only the superiority of telephone service in the United States, but also the victory of the allies over the Germans in the First World War. "Two events, apparently unrelated, occurred on one and the same day," Lavine pontificated: "On July 29, 1914, Austria invaded Serbia, and fired the opening guns of the great war of autocracy against democracy. On July 29, 1914, Vail, sitting in his office in New York City, sent his voice 3,400 miles across the country, and quietly conversed with the president of the Pacific Telephone and Telegraph Company, sitting in his office in San Francisco. . . . Unification in Germany from the top down had been virtually consummated, and was ready to work its purpose. Unification of America from the bottom up had also been virtually consummated, and it, too, was ready to work its purpose."[92]

The iconography that Bell publicists devised to visualize the transcontinental telephone harked back to late nineteenth-century paintings such as John Gast's "American Progress." To symbolize the transcontinental telegraph, Gast envisioned a female goddess spanning the continent; to symbolize the transcontinental telephone, Bell publicists recast the goddess as a telephone operator. Gast saw the transcontinental telegraph, in part, as a political project; the goddess, for example, bore on her forehead the star of empire. Bell also linked network and nation. "Making a Neighborhood of a Nation," proclaimed a public relations announcement that heralded the completion of the New York City–San Francisco line. Yet the word emblazoned on the operator's headband made no reference to any social collectivity: it was neither "nation," nor "neighborhood," nor even "empire," but "science."[93]

For one Texas independent telephone promoter, transcontinental telephone service was nothing to brag about. In contrast to Bell, this promoter observed, the Post Office Department did not herald its achievements in the press. Instead of purchasing space for a "page ad'" in a magazine "telling of the wonderful flight of sound," it preferred to invest its facilities to better meet the "diverse demands" of the people.[94] It was a testament to the artfulness of Bell's public relations campaign that the Texas promoter was one of the few Americans to hint that the money Bell spent perfecting the transcontinental telephone might have been

While the opening of transcontinental telephone service between New York City and San Francisco in 1915 had little commercial significance, it emboldened American Telephone and Telegraph to link its business strategy with the "triumph of science." To symbolize this event, Bell publicists cast the telephone operator as a classical goddess who held the country together in her embrace. "The Triumph of Science," *Southwestern Telephone News* 1 (February 1915): back cover.

better spent on technical refinements that were more likely to meet the "diverse demands" of the people. Long-distance telephone service, after all, was, and would long remain, a specialty service for an exclusive clientele.

It has become so commonplace today for corporations to flaunt their technical wizardry that it is easy to forget that the linkage of corporate management and technical progressiveness is relatively new. Critics routinely criticized Bell for holding back inventions so that it could maximize profits or limit competition. The sober-minded and eminently respectable political economist Arthur T. Hadley faulted Bell for its technical conservatism as early as 1888.[95] Some of the "most glorious and useful inventions of the nineteenth century" were "lying under lock and key" as the "fruit of 'free competition,'" complained one particularly indignant Bell critic in 1891.[96] Critics honed in on Bell's reluctance to adopt electromechanical switching and invest in wireless telegraphy. In both instances, critics charged, Bell had slowed the pace of innovation to block business rivals from gaining a competitive advantage that might imperil Bell's enormous investment in its physical plant.

To rebut these critics, Bell publicists touted the superiority of giant organizations like Bell as agents of change. In so doing, they raised an awkward question about the relationship of Bell's organization to heroic inventors such as Bell's eponymous founder, Alexander Graham Bell. The relationship between Bell the organization and Bell the inventor had caused confusion since the 1880s. Many people, reported one business journalist in 1887, assumed that the word "Bell" referred not to the inventor, but, rather, to the metal cups mounted on the telephone that jingled to alert the subscriber that a caller was on the line.[97] To capitalize on this happy coincidence, Angus Hibbard incorporated a bell into the logo that Bell used to advertise long-distance service.[98]

Few events threw the ambiguous relationship between the organization and the inventor into sharper relief than the elaborate public ceremony that Bell staged in 1915 to commemorate the beginning of transcontinental telephone service between New York City and San Francisco. The ceremony featured two famous telephone inventors: Alexander Graham Bell and his assistant Thomas A. Watson. Bell and Watson linked the telephone giant with the independent inventor of yore. Yet neither had had anything to do with the invention and refinement of the three-element high-vacuum tube—the technical breakthrough that had made transcontinental telephone service possible.

Had Bell publicists wished to enroll an individual in the pantheon of heroic inventors, the transcontinental telephone provided them with a tailor-made opportunity. After all, the development of the high-vacuum tube by Bell scientist Harold D. Arnold had not only made transcontinental telephone service possible, but had also marked the advent of a new branch of science that would come to be known as electronics. Yet Bell publicists neither attributed the high-vacuum tube to a single inventor nor trumpeted its historical significance. Instead of lionizing heroic inventors and chronicling blockbuster inventions, as had been the custom in the nineteenth century, they lauded the organization that had translated the invention into an innovation. The decision to give Bell and Watson the honor of making the first transcontinental telephone call was purely symbolic: neither had played any role whatsoever in the refinement of the vacuum tube. The implicit devaluation of the individual in relationship to the organization troubled President Wilson, as was clear in his congratulatory message commemorating the opening of the line. In his message, he took care to distinguish between the organization that had made the invention practical and the "inventive genius and scientific knowledge" that the organization had mobilized. Transcontinental telephone service was the product not of many individuals, Wilson emphasized, but of one individual—telephone inventor Alexander Graham Bell.[99]

To equip Bell staffers with the information they needed to win the public debate on government ownership, Vail assembled what he claimed to be the "best library in existence" on the relative merits of government administration and corporate management.[100] Particularly useful for Bell publicists was a massive three-volume *Brief of Arguments against Public Ownership*—with twenty-five supplements—compiled by Bell staffer Chester I. Barnard.[101]

Barnard's brief included a vast amount of comparative data on the telephone in the United States and in Europe that was intended to furnish Bell publicists with the ammunition needed to make the case against government ownership. In Barnard's view, public education, in the form of speeches, informational pamphlets, press releases, and congressional lobbying, was the first line of defense against government takeovers.[102]

Bell staffers mined this library for the information they relied on in the dozens of pamphlets, essays, and magazine articles that Bell published in the 1910s to document the superiority of corporate management to government administration. If Bell could prevail in the court of public opinion, Vail believed it would have a better chance of persuading Congress not to buy it out. Almost none of these position papers were overtly polemical. Conspicuously absent, for example, were blanket pronouncements about the perils of socialism or the slippery slope that led from government ownership to the horrors of the Russian Bolshevists. Rather, these documents piled fact upon fact to make their case. The title of a position paper prepared by Bell staffer Walter S. Allen was characteristic of their tone: "Twenty Five Reasons Why a Privately Owned Telephone System Is Better for the Users than a System Owned and Operated by the United States Government."[103]

The exception that proved the rule was a histrionic editorial signed by Bell engineer John J. Carty that appeared in *Public Service* in January 1917. The government ownership movement was a conspiracy launched by subversives to "Russianize America," Carty warned: "They forget that there is more government ownership in Russia than anywhere in the world, and that it is just because government interferes so much in business in Russia, and does not let the people attend to their own affairs, that so many people have fled from Russia to a land where freedom and opportunity prevails." That a Bell staffer would characterize the government ownership movement in this way was not surprising. The Russian Revolution was brewing, and anticommunist sentiment was running high. More revealing was the disclaimer that ran in the very next issue: "John J. Carty Not the Author": "Mr. Carty, well known as chief engineer of the American Telephone and Telegraph Company, was not the author and had nothing to do with the preparation or publication of the article."[104] For some time it had been permissible for Bell staffers to explore the operational consequences of government ownership in print; even so, it had been judged best—almost certainly by Vail himself—for them to avoid discussing the broader political ramifications of government ownership.

One unanticipated consequence of Vail's public relations campaign was the boost it gave to social science research. The data that Bell compiled was useful not only to make the case against government ownership, but also to forecast future demand for telephone service, rebut the contention that Bell made excessive profits, and value the assets that Bell might wish to acquire. In an effort to systematize this research, Bell staffer Malcolm R. Rorty approached Dean Edwin F. Gay of the recently established Harvard Business School to fund a study of national income. Gay responded that Rorty's projected study would be best coordinated by a quasi-public agency. Taking the hint, Rorty raised funds from several private foundations to found the National Bureau of Economic Research (NBER) in 1920. The NBER would soon become one of the nation's leading sponsors of social scientific research.[105]

The insights into organizational dynamics that Barnard gleaned during the government ownership campaign would later inform his magnum opus, *Functions of the Executive* (1938). *Functions* was a pioneering analysis of the internal dynamics of corporate organization. A recurrent theme was the extent to which corporate managers had replaced government administrators in coordinating vast organizations. The operational autonomy that enabled corporate managers to perform this "function" was one of the legacies of the antigovernment ownership campaign in which Barnard had participated two decades before.

In July 1918 President Wilson issued an executive order transferring control of both the telephone and the telegraph to the Post Office Department. The ostensible rationale for the takeover was military necessity. The United States was at war with Germany, and lawmakers regarded the uninterrupted flow of information as essential to the military. The Wilson administration had justified the takeover of the railroad the previous December as a military necessity to ensure the uninterrupted flow of matériel: an analogous logic justified the takeover of the telephone and the telegraph.[106] Although military necessity was the justification for the takeover, the looming threat of a union-backed telegraph operators' strike in the summer of 1918 was the catalyst. The vulnerability of the telegraph network to disruption had troubled lawmakers ever since the telegraph operators' strike of 1883. To avert a possible work stoppage, Postal Telegraph president Clarence Mackay negotiated directly with the telegraphers' union, implicitly conceding its right to engage in collective bargaining. Western Union president Newcomb Carlton refused to follow Mackay's lead, preferring a government takeover to recognizing the union. Carlton's intransigence put Western Union and its operators on a collision course, and left the Wilson administration with no option but to intervene.[107]

The takeover of the telephone was harder to justify. The telephone network had not been overloaded, and no work stoppage loomed on the horizon. The previous year, a federally appointed management–labor mediator had opined that any disruption to the telephone network "hampered the country's effectiveness at war." Yet no disruption seemed imminent.[108] Even so, no lawmaker expressed surprise when the Wilson administration lumped together the telephone with the telegraph. The world-historical significance of Bell's long-distance network had been a recurrent theme of Bell's monthly public relations announcements for almost a decade. Had the Wilson administration declined to nationalize the telephone, Bell publicists would have had a hard time explaining why, in time of war, the federal government had deemed the telegraph but not the telephone indispensable to the nation.

The Post Office Department retained control of the telephone and the telegraph for the duration of the war and did not return them to their prewar owners until July 1919. The Post Office Department also briefly assumed control of those segments of the global cable network that touched the United States. Federal control of the cables began on November 16, five days after the armistice that ended the war.[109]

Military necessity was the ostensible rationale for the government takeover of the telephone, telegraph, and cable, yet it was but a partial explanation for the Wilson administration's conduct. In fact, several members of Wilson's inner circle had additional reasons to endorse a federal buyout that had nothing to do with the war. The superiority of government administration to corporate management had been a favorite theory of Postmaster General Burleson ever since his appointment in March 1913. The First World War gave him the opportunity to translate theory into practice. Burleson handed down forty-six directives during the year in which he controlled the wire network; of these, only ten were issued during the war.[110]

Government control had a remarkably varied base of public support. Wilson's private secretary, Joseph R. Tumulty, had endorsed government ownership of all of the "instrumentalities" connected with the "basic needs of our life" in January 1918, long before the telegraph strike. Wall Street banker and J. P. Morgan & Co. partner Thomas Lamont predicted that government control would be good for investors. Labor organizer Sylvester Konenkamp endorsed it in the expectation that it would be good for telegraphers; so too did the American Federation of Labor. Konenkamp had witnessed firsthand how a government-appointed labor mediator had averted a strike by obtaining a favorable settlement for telegraph operators. He anticipated that a federal government takeover of the telegraph would improve organized labor's bargaining position.[111]

The postalization of the telephone empowered Burleson to institute a number of innovations that Bell endorsed but had found it inexpedient to implement. Among them were rate increases for several classes of service. To limit the diversion of revenue from the operating companies to the long-distance network, Burleson increased long-distance rates between 18 and 20 percent. To keep up with the rate of inflation, Burleson increased rates for local service. To eliminate the subsidy long enjoyed by Chicago's business elite, he abolished the business flat rate, achieving with the stroke of a pen a goal that had eluded Hibbard for many years.[112] Each of these innovations was controversial. Yet with the possible exception of the long-distance rate hike, none would have ruffled feathers at Bell.

Vail regarded the government takeover as both a challenge and an opportunity. The challenge was to limit government interference with the operational autonomy of Bell. The opportunity was to transform the three main forms of electrical communications—telephone, telegraph, and cable—into "one great medium" that would strengthen Bell's position as the dominant network provider and hasten the ascendancy of the United States as a world power. To grasp the nettle, Vail recast Bell's antigovernment ownership campaign as a campaign to accommodate Bell to the new reality of federal government control. Government worked best, Vail explained, if it eschewed "direct operation" in favor of "private operation," since only private operation fully mobilized the "initiative and interests" of the "subject." Even so, government remained indispensable. The "potency of the sovereign" was a formidable instrumentality for raising revenue, ensuring uniformity, and negotiating with foreign rivals.[113] Vail's enthusiasm for media consolidation was so marked that Bell staffers found it necessary to reassure lawmakers that Vail had not, in fact, been instrumental in persuading the Wilson administration to issue the executive order that gave it control of the telephone and the telegraph.[114]

Vail's relationship with Burleson was a marriage of convenience. Vail enjoyed the opportunity to play the role of senior adviser in a time of national emergency, and Burleson was flattered to have at his beck and call a business executive who was widely hailed in the press (in large part because of Bell's own formidable publicity machine) as the world's greatest authority on electrical communications.

In no realm was the "potency of the sovereign" more indispensable than in restructuring the cable network. Burleson gained control of all cables lines that landed on American soil on November 16, 1918, five days after the armistice ending the First World War. The timing proved awkward for the Wilson administration. Although the transfer had been in the planning stages for the several months, the war ended more quickly than the administration had anticipated, leaving it in the embarrassing position of justifying a takeover as a military necessity after the military necessity had passed. For Vail, this accident of timing was a mere detail. Vail had long yearned to control the cable network, and now that he had reinvented himself as one of Burleson's most trusted advisers, this goal was finally within reach. In explaining why the Wilson administration had proceeded with the transfer after the war had come to an end, one journalist went so far as to contend that it had acted at Vail's behest.[115]

The "wire system" that Vail envisioned was not a global telephone network, which at the time was technically impossible. Cables lacked the repeaters necessary to amplify telephone signals: in fact, Bell's first transatlantic telephone cable—TAT-1—would not go into operation until 1956. Rather, the network would link the telephone, telegraph, and cable into "one coordinated operating system" that would take advantage of their complementarity. Vail's goal was not only interconnection, but also the efficient utilization of the physical plant. "The wire system of the future" would facilitate the circulation of "every kind of electrical transmission of intelligence" from every person in "any one place" to every person "in every other place" with the consolidated plant "utilized to the greatest possible extent."[116]

The federal government's establishment of a government-owned cable network impressed Vail as vital to national security. Every cable linking the United States and Europe in the First World War was under British control.[117] If the United States government owned its own cable network, its military would no longer have to depend on a foreign power. Commerce would also benefit. The United States was at present at the "side" of the "world system"; if the government took charge, it could rival Great Britain as one of its centers.[118] "Commerce," Vail elaborated, "follows the development of facilities of communication." If the United States wished to rival Great Britain as a center of the "world system" for "electrical intercommunication," it needed to obtain control of a cable network, and the only way to do this would be under the "aegis" of "governmental authority" and "thorough specially shaped legislation."[119]

The transformation of the United States into a major player in the cable business was no easy feat. To challenge the British corporations that dominated the cable network would require vigorous government action. To leave the cable business to "private initiative" and "foreign enterprise" would be a huge mistake.[120] On the contrary, Vail urged the federal government to move swiftly to establish a government-owned, corporately operated "United States system" that would put the country's diplomats and businessmen in direct communication with every country with which the United States had, or hoped to have, commercial relations. Vail respected private property; yet he did not believe that Congress should defer to the existing corporations, most of which were British owned. Only a "unified service" in which government ownership was combined with corporate operation could promote the public good.[121] To obtain the optimal result, lawmakers should enact legislation that would combine the "admitted advantages of private operations" with the "prestige" of government ownership.[122]

Vail's proposal for a U.S. government–owned, Bell-operated cable network intrigued lawmakers as late as 1922.[123] Yet it was never implemented. Like so many wartime initiatives, it was a casualty of the revulsion against government activism that gripped lawmakers in the aftermath of the First World War. The cable business would remain dominated by British corporations until the mid-twentieth century, when it was supplanted by radio, in which the United States enjoyed a far stronger position.

In radio, too, political factors loomed large. The rise of the American radio business owed much to the stubborn determination of Wilson's navy secretary Josephus Daniels to transfer Marconi's patent rights from a British to an American corporation. Daniels regarded government ownership as preferable to either; yet U.S. corporate ownership of radio was plainly preferable to its ownership by a foreign corporation. The Marconi network became the nucleus of the Radio Corporation of America (RCA), a leading manufacturer of radio equipment after the war.[124]

Although Vail favored a government-owned cable network, he remained opposed to government ownership of the telephone and the telegraph. This provoked an awkward question. How could Vail justify government ownership in one realm and not another? To answer this question, Vail set forth what he regarded to be the essential differences between government administration and corporate management.

Government ownership in Vail's view could be as efficient as corporate management, but not as economical. Government administrators lacked the incentives—primarily in the form of higher salaries—to embolden corporate managers to economize. To combine efficiency and economy was the special task of corporate management. It demanded not only high salaries, but also operational autonomy, and for Vail this combination was possible only in a private corporation.

The primary difference between government administration and corporate management was organizational. The federal government had yet to emulate Bell and institute meritocratic personnel policies to encourage ambitious men to rise through the ranks: "The fact is that average ability and inherent initiative of the minor government employee is at least equal to that of the best private industrial." Once the federal government found a way to ensure their professional advancement inside it, then "all objections" to government administration would "disappear."[125] Vail himself had served in the federal government and may well have assumed that these conditions would never be met. In public, however, he consistently downplayed the contrasts between government administration and corporate management.

In comparing government administration and corporate management, Vail pointedly avoided criticizing government administrators. In no instance did he disparage the federal civil service as lazy or deride the Post Office Department as inefficient. To the contrary, Vail's characterization of the civil service was highly admiring: Government administrators had the same "enthusiasm and energy" as the managers of our "best industrial organizations." Their industriousness was all the more remarkable because their salaries were lower, their operational autonomy more limited, and their opportunities for personal advancement stunted by bureaucratic inertia and party politics.

Vail's proposal to combine the telephone, the telegraph, and the cable into "one great medium" met with a good deal of criticism. For Bell manager James E. Caldwell, the "one system idea" was yet more proof that Vail was a megalomaniacal empire-builder who yearned to be "wire king of the world."[126] For Postal Telegraph president Clarence Mackay, it was a thinly disguised power grab to build a "world-encircling wire monopoly."[127] For Illinois senator Lawrence Y. Sherman, it revealed Vail as a subversive "Bolshevist in disguise" who, like the Russian revolutionaries, was determined to commandeer the means of communication to consolidate the power of the state.[128] Vail himself conceded to a Boston banker that the "one system idea" had long been "unpopular both inside and outside telephone circles." Even so, Vail remained committed to "centralization."[129]

The opprobrium that contemporaries heaped on Vail was mild in comparison to the abuse they hurled at Burleson. The telephone rate hikes that Burleson ordered aroused the ire not only of telephone users but also state public utility commissioners, who resented his encroachment in a regulatory arena in which they had come to regard themselves as the final arbiter.[130] Burleson's unwillingness to treat Postal Telegraph president Clarence Mackay as Vail's equal outraged Mackay, who redoubled his staunch opposition to government control. Burleson's refusal to permit collective bargaining among telephone and telegraph workers antagonized union organizers, who had mistakenly assumed that they would fare better under government administration than corporation management. One Boston telephone operator went so far as to term Burleson's administration a "reign of terror." This characterization was based on the Post Office Department's refusal to accord unions the same privileges they had enjoyed when the telephone operating company had been under corporate management.[131]

Bell publicists tactfully refrained from issuing public statements critical of Burleson's conduct during the period in which the telephone network had been under his control. It was more prudent—and in the end, more effective—to let Burleson hang from his own rope. Independents were less restrained. Burleson's administration of the telephone had proved to be so disastrous, exploded independent operating company manager-turned Democratic congressman Henry A. Barnhart in February 1919, that Barnhart threatened to give a speech criticizing his own party for its incompetence. The ultimate consequence of postalization, Barnhart predicted, had been to instill in the American people the realization that government ownership meant "most unsatisfactory management and conditions."[132]

No other event could have transformed public opinion so swiftly and decisively with regard to the relative merits of government administration and corporate management. Prior to Burleson's takeover of the telephone and the telegraph, state socialism retained many admirers; by July 1919, its prestige had suffered an irrevocable blow from which it would never recover. To only a minor extent was this remarkable transformation a result of the censorship of antiwar newspapers, the arrest of prominent socialists, or the overheated rhetoric with which American commentators responded to the Russian Revolution. Far more consequential was the actual experience of government administration. Few events did more to legitimate the managerial corporation or to limit the ambit of the federal government in the postwar world.

The final blow to Burleson's administration of the "wire system" came in April 1919 when telephone operators staged a five-day walkout in New England that was coordinated by the Boston Telephone Operators' Union. Hundreds of operators put down their headsets, crippling telephone service in all five of the states in which New England Telephone operated exchanges: Massachusetts, Rhode Island, New Hampshire, Vermont, and Maine. The Telephone Operators' Union was a female-dominated union that had successfully organized telephone operators, a key component of the Bell System. The telephone operators' strike received lavish coverage in the press, almost all of which was sympathetic to the "hello girls" and hostile to the government. Boston newspapers vied with each other to depict the strikers in the most favorable light. Readers might be forgiven if they confused the strike with a beauty pageant: the strike occurred during Holy Week, and newspapers featured page after page of pictures of attractive telephone operators in their Easter bonnets.[133] To bring the strike to an end, Burleson sent a subordinate to Boston to negotiate with the telegraphers' union; the agreement that emerged conceded every one of the striking operators' major demands, including a wage increase. In a year in which thousands of strikes disrupted businesses throughout the United States—the vast majority of which failed, with many turning violent—the strikers' victory was as remarkable as it was rare.

The New England telephone operators' strike was a public relations bonanza for Bell. Since it occurred at a moment when the telephone was under the control of the Post Office Department, public opprobrium was directed toward the government rather than the corporation.[134] It is impossible to know for certain whether New England Telephone was deliberately colluding with the press to embarrass Burleson. Its refusal to call in permanent replacement for the striking operators—as it had, for example, in a strike in 1913—was suggestive: if it had been covertly hoping the strikers would prevail, few insiders familiar with the sophistication of Bell's formidable publicity machine would have been surprised.[135]

The New England telegraph operators' strike crystallized the hostility toward government administration that had been steadily mounting in the months since Burleson had taken control of the telephone in July 1918. No comparable labor disturbance had occurred when the telephone had been under Bell control, inverting the long-standing presumption that the nation's communications networks would be less likely to be disrupted if they were under government control. Even the pro-Wilson *New York World* urged Burleson to resign.[136] "No one," predicted an editorialist in the *Cleveland Plain Dealer* shortly after the end of the strike, "is likely to ride into an important office this year or next on a public ownership plank."[137]

Wilson's private secretary Joseph R. Tumulty agreed. Although Tumulty had been an enthusiastic supporter of government ownership, the events of the past few months had led him to change his mind. The federal government's continuing control of the telephone and the telegraph, Tumulty now wrote Wilson, had become the administration's single greatest source of irritation and popular discontent. Moreover, Tumulty added, the Republican Party leaders' endorsement of the immediate return of these "instrumentalities" to private control had given them a "tremendous advantage" at the polls: "Frankly, the people are sick of all kinds of controls and war restrictions."[138]

The Republican takeover of both the House and the Senate in the 1918 congressional elections ensured that the conduct of the Wilson administration in operating the telephone and the telegraph would be the subject of detailed scrutiny. The Wilson administration's refusal to relinquish the wires immediately after the end of the war mystified Charles Evans Hughes, Wilson's unsuccessful opponent in the 1916 presidential election. The entire subject received detailed attention in a lengthy series of congressional hearings in 1919.[139]

Few Americans found the experiment in government control more unsettling than the labor leaders who had witnessed its unfolding firsthand. The takeover of the telephone and the telegraph had been endorsed by many labor unions, including the American Federation of Labor. Now that the experiment had been tried, almost everyone had second thoughts. The American Federation of Labor officially dropped its call for the nationalization of the telephone and the telegraph in June 1919.[140] Post–Civil War labor leaders had been conspicuously reluctant to endorse government ownership as a panacea: the experiment with government control in the First World War confirmed their fears.

President Wilson endorsed the return of the telephone and the telegraph to their former owners in a special message to Congress in May

1919. In his message, Wilson put the best face he could on the experiment in government control. In a sentence that could have been written by Vail, Wilson urged Congress to enact legislation that would ensure that the corporations operating the electrical communications networks that had become "indispensable instrumentalities" of "modern life" would be organized as a "uniform and coordinated system." In particular, Wilson hoped that lawmakers would ensure that Bell, Western Union, and the nation's other communications corporations would provide the American people with facilities for local and long-distance communications that would be as comprehensive and as certain as the facilities they had obtained for many years from the Post Office Department—"and at rates as uniform and intelligible."[141]

The theoretical distinction that Burleson and his subordinates had made before the war between government administration and corporate management proved to have few practical consequences. This was largely because the business strategy of the Bell operating companies had already been reshaped to accommodate a political economy in which the utility of network users had supplanted the rights of network providers as a civic ideal.

The actual transfer of the telephone from the Post Office Department back to Bell was uneventful. In large part, this was because government control had had little impact on the day-to-day management of the Bell operating companies. "Let me make myself clear," explained Post Office Department solicitor William H. Lamar in 1919, in explaining how the government takeover had worked: "The government has taken over the wires; it has taken control of the operations; it has taken control of the revenues they produce; but it has not taken control of the corporations themselves."[142] In explaining how government control worked, Bell staffer Nathan C. Kingsbury emphasized the bright line that Bell staffers drew between government administration and corporate management, and the limited impact of government control on the level of service that the operating companies provided. "I lost my job as the manager of the long-distance lines," Kingsbury explained in a Senate hearing shortly after the war, "but that has not hurt the service a particle": "I have not gone with the government. I have no connection with government administration whatever. My work is all with the corporation."[143]

For Bell executives, the return of the telephone was an enormous relief. Military necessity may have been the ostensible rationale for the government takeover, reflected Vail's successor Harry B. Thayer in 1922. Yet he had assumed it was a mere cover for the Wilson administration's neo-Populism, and that, once the federal government got control of the telephone it would never give it up. In explaining why Bell had prevailed, Thayer pointed to Vail's public relations campaign. The relentless flood of pamphlets, magazine articles, and public relations advertisements had made the case for corporate management far more effectively than any single decision by a Bell manager to lower rates or increase performance standards. Of special significance had been Vail's public persona. By cooperating fully with Burleson, Vail had achieved far more for Bell than would have been possible had he pursued a less conciliatory course. During the entire period Burleson had been in control of the telephone, Burleson had neither appointed nor dismissed a single telephone employee. In fact, during the year that it controlled the telephone, the federal government had taken no action whatever that had been a cause for complaint.[144]

Burleson's failure to prevent the New England telephone operators' strike—as well as several other telephone operators' strikes during the period of government control—demolished the venerable argument that government administration provided a better guarantee of uninterrupted service than corporate management.[145] The 1883 telegraph operators' strike hastened the ascendancy of natural monopoly over competition as an economic theory; the 1919 telephone operators' strike demonstrated the superiority of Vail's managerial capitalism over Burleson's democratic statism as a civic ideal.

The failure of "postalization" legitimated the ownership and operation of the telephone, telegraph, and cable by private corporations that would become a hallmark of managerial capitalism and a defining feature of the twentieth-century American political economy. Never again in the twentieth century would government ownership of the telephone and the telegraph occupy so prominent a place on the national political agenda. Government ownership of the electrical means of communication had appealed to a galaxy of corporate critics ever since Samuel F. B. Morse had first broached the issue in 1838. Yet no prominent lawmaker would champion nationalization of the telegraph or telephone during the Second World War. Government regulation had precluded new entrants from entering the business, yet for most Americans this was preferable to government ownership, so long as Bell, Western Union, and other network providers took care not only to provide users with a basic level of service, but also to persuade the public that they remained mindful of their social obligation to make the fruits of invention accessible to all.

EPILOGUE:
THE TECHNICAL MILLENNIUM

If we were to look forward and try to picture the technical millennium, it might be something like this: You would be able to pick up a telephone and talk to anybody anywhere just as quickly as you can talk to anyone across the street by telephone today, and do it for a very reasonable cost.

Walter S. Gifford, 1928

The Bell System that Theodore N. Vail envisioned in 1910 was a curious mix. Technically progressive yet financially orthodox, it was the organizational response to a progressive political economy that rejected antimonopoly, but that remained uneasy with regulation. The antimonopoly political economy promised equal access to the fruits of invention for network providers; the progressive political economy guaranteed equal access to the fruits of invention for network users. Bell's financial orthodoxy shielded it from the moral opprobrium that had haunted Western Union following its takeover in 1881 by the financier Jay Gould. Its technological progressiveness would be institutionalized with the establishment of Bell Laboratories in 1925.

The antimonopoly political economy encouraged network builders to devise a business strategy that minimized their social obligations. The social consequences of the telegraph for commerce and public life were far more direct—and, for many, far more troubling—than the social consequences of the telephone for patterns of urban sociability. Yet Western Union network builders such as Hiram Sibley and William Orton characterized Western Union as private enterprise, whereas Bell network builders such as Vail and Angus Hibbard did not. The contrasting business strategies of network builders at Western Union and Bell had less to do with the intrinsic nature of the medium, or even with its economic ramifications, than with the cultural norms fostered by the political economy in which it evolved.

The Bell System emerged in the years following Vail's death in 1920 as an exemplar of an organizational form that historians call the managerial corporation. The managerial corporation was the organizational response to a political economy in which lawmakers permitted—and, indeed, encouraged—a self-perpetuating managerial elite to operate major corporations with minimal interference from the investors who were these corporations' ostensible owners. Politics had artifacts: the markets in which these corporations operated were politically defined, further enhancing their managers' operational autonomy. The marginalization of investors and the elevation of managers were interrelated. Had investors been less marginalized, managers would have been more constrained.

To keep local telephone rates low, by the 1970s the Bell System began to transfer revenue to the local operating companies that had been generated by its long-distance network. To maintain good relations with state regulators, operating company managers set local rates in accordance with what telecommunications lawyers would wryly call the "pizza test": under no circumstances was the monthly fee for basic residential service to exceed the price of a pizza—medium size—with two toppings.[1]

The direction of this transfer was new. Before 1910, the transfers had gone in the opposite direction—that is, from the operating companies to the long-distance network provider. What had not changed was the presumption that rate averaging promoted the public good. Rate averaging antedated the telephone. The Post Office Department had been using the method since the 1790s, a precedent that telephone managers often alluded to when they sought to justify telephone rate averaging to shareholders, lawmakers, and users.

The regulatory compromises on which the Bell System was built unraveled after 1970. New entrants like MCI, which had invested in wireless networks, challenged Bell in the long-distance market, and big users lobbied for lower rates. This alliance goaded the Department of Justice to once again accuse Bell of violating the Sherman Act. The Justice Department's lawsuit culminated with the court-ordered breakup of the Bell System in 1984. The settlement permitted Bell—now called simply AT&T—to retain its holdings in Western Electric and Bell Labs, but it required it to divest its holdings in its federation of telephone operating companies, ending a relationship that in localities such as New York City and Chicago dated back over 100 years.

The Bell breakup was a notable example of the post–1970 revival of antimonopoly as a remedy for the social, political, and economic challenges posed by vast corporate combines. The Bell System had provided the entire population with low-cost access to local telephone service. Bell's post–1970 rivals aspired to provide the entire population with low-cost access to a rapidly evolving electrical communications network that stretched throughout the nation and around the world. Although the Bell System had kept local telephone rates low—in keeping with the "pizza test"—it had never provided the low-cost, long-distance telephone service that post–1970 users came to demand. The low-cost long-distance communications facilities that Vail envisioned in 1910 were telegraphic—that is, Vail saw Bell providing the entire population with low-cost local telephone service and low-cost long-distance telegraph service. The court-ordered divestiture of Western Union in 1913 spoiled Vail's plans. Never again would Bell offer users a "universal service" that linked the telephone and the telegraph as one "great medium."

Had Bell wanted to provide the entire population with low-cost long-distance telephone service, it could have. The problem was neither technological nor economic. Nor was it cultural. The "technical millennium," predicted Bell President Walter S. Gifford in 1928, would be reached when Bell had provided everyone with low-cost telephone service not only in a specific locality, but around the world.[2] The problem, rather, was political. The Bell System was most emphatically not, as its apologists loudly proclaimed, the one best way to coordinate the technical imperatives and economic incentives of voice communication. Instead, it was the organizational response to a political economy that idealized public utility and deprecated waste. And only slowly would this political economy adjust itself to the new post–1970 reality of low-cost long-distance telephone service, to say nothing of the panoply of tasks that the telephone has since come to perform.

The breakup of the Bell System prompted AT&T executives to rethink the history of the telephone business. This project was necessarily revisionist: AT&T had been shorn of its operating companies. Predictably, the scholarship on telephone history that AT&T sponsored focused on those components of the telephone business that AT&T retained—namely, Bell Labs and Western Electric—while slighting those elements that it had divested—namely, the operating companies.[3]

The historian of technology Thomas P. Hughes has posited that, in the period after 1870, the United States was transformed by a technologically based "material constitution" that was no less far-reaching in its social consequences than the political constitution that had transformed the United States in the early republic.[4] In the telephone business, however, technology and politics were inseparable. In myriad ways, governmental institutions and civic ideals shaped the telephone business from the moment of its inception. Nothing has more distorted our understanding of the formative era of American telecommunications than the presumption that telephone regulation began around 1907 with the enactment of legislation putting telephone operating companies under the jurisdiction of state regulatory commissions. Politics always mattered. To praise Theodore N. Vail for his prescience in embracing government regulation after 1907 is to miss the larger point: Vail was accommodating a political economy that he had neither created nor condoned and that he could not control. The relevant historical issue is not whether the telephone business would remain unregulated, or, for that matter, whether competition would remain "unbridled." For the telephone business had *always* been regulated, and competition had never been unbridled. Open entry had never been the rule, and municipal franchises had always been negotiated. The relevant historical question was, rather, how would the telephone business be regulated, by whom, and to what end? In the telephone business, competition was always contrived.[5]

Politics always mattered in the telegraph business too. Yet its implications for business strategy were very different. Had telegraph corporations come under the jurisdiction of regulatory commissions before 1910, it is conceivable that they would have moved more swiftly to provide a mass service for the entire population. The antimonopoly political economy in which telegraph corporations operated fostered innovation: among its by-products were the telephone and phonograph. Yet it was not Western Union, but its critics, that articulated the most expansive vision of the new medium's political, social, and cultural possibilities.

The Bell System flourished in a political economy in which lawmakers regarded market segmentation as a solution to the problem that monopoly posed. Notable examples of market segmentation included the court-ordered divestiture of Western Union in 1913. Later market-segmenting agreements restricted Bell's involvement in the radio business, the computer business, and, eventually, the local telephone operating company business. Market segmentation received a legal imprimatur in the Radio Act of 1927 and the Federal Communications Act of 1934. Both of these laws limited Bell's options, while solidifying even further its position in the voice-communication business. Politics had artifacts: what Europeans called cartels, Americans called industries. And in telecommunications, the boundaries dividing industries were politically defined.

The Radio Act of 1927 segmented the market for electrical communications in several ways. In addition to upholding existing antimonopoly laws designed to foster competition in the manufacture of radio equipment, it barred radio stations from owning telegraph, telephone, or cable networks, and rejected the presumption that the electromagnetic spectrum was a form of property that—like land—could be bought or sold.[6] The operation of a radio station required a federal license, just as the operation of a telephone operating company required a municipal franchise. The electromagnetic spectrum, much like the right-of-way to a city's streets, could be leased, but never owned.

The Federal Communications Act of 1934 transferred government control of electrical communications from the Interstate Commerce Commission to the Federal Communications Commission (FCC). The FCC's jurisdiction was broad: it embraced the telephone, the telegraph, cable, radio, and—eventually—television.

The chair of the committee that drafted the legislation authorizing the establishment of the Federal Communications Commission was Daniel C. Roper, Franklin D. Roosevelt's commerce secretary. Twenty years earlier, as an administrator in the Post Office Department, he had headed up the committee that generated a notable report on the "postalization" of the telephone and telegraph. In 1914, Roper had endorsed media consolidation; by 1934, he had changed his mind, no longer championing the nationalization of the telephone and telegraph as the best solution to the problem of monopoly. Now he instead endorsed market segmentation.[7]

Roper was almost certainly the first federal government administrator to use the word "telecommunications" in a published report. The consolidation of the telephone, cable, and radio, Roper warned in 1934, might "retard the development or expansion" of "any phase" of the "art of telecommunications."[8] The word "telecommunications" had been coined by a French postal administrator in 1904 to facilitate the consolidation of the telephone and telegraph. Roper used the word in a different, and in some ways, opposite way: For Roper, telecommunications was an "art" whose future might be imperiled should the federal government condone the consolidation of the telephone, telegraph, radio, and cable.

Market segmentation in the telephone business survived until 1996. In that year, Congress enacted a sweeping new telecommunications act that rejected the market-segmenting logic of the Radio Act of 1927 and the Federal Communications Act of 1934. For more than a century, municipalities had had the authority to restrict entrants in the telephone business. With the enactment of the Telecommunications Act of 1996, all this changed. Rivalry in the local telephone business had been anathema to lawmakers since 1907, when the Chicago city council rechartered the Chicago Telephone Company. Now it had been rehabilitated, and, with it, the long-dormant political economy of antimonopoly was revived.

Of all the market-segmenting arrangements to be codified in the period between 1907 and 1996, few had more far-reaching consequences than the segmentation between network providers and content providers of radio and television. "Toll broadcasting"—or, simply, broadcasting, as it would come to be known—grew directly out of the leasing of telephone lines to radio stations. Beginning in the 1920s, and continuing for many decades, Bell provided the country's principal radio broadcasters—NBC, CBS, and ABC—with the transmission facilities to broadcast programming nationwide. After the Second World War, it provided comparable facilities for television broadcasters. For millions of Americans for much of the twentieth century, the programming on radio and television networks transmitted over Bell's long-distance network defined what it meant to live in a networked nation.

The breakup of the Bell System in 1984 was a harrowing experience for the many Bell executives who had come to link their social obligations as network providers with the civic ideal of equal access.[9] Yet the meaning of equal access had never remained static. In the nineteenth-century telegraph business, equal access referred primarily to the promotion of open entry for network providers. In the twentieth-century telephone business, it referred primarily to the provisioning of inclusive facilities for network users. Open entry promised opportunities; inclusive facilities guaranteed outcomes. Open entry was compatible with an antimonopoly political economy that glorified equal rights and vilified special privilege; inclusive facilities were compatible with a progressive political economy that idealized public utility and deprecated waste.

Opportunity was the province of lawmakers, whereas outcomes were the responsibility of managers. The Bell System was sustained in a corporate culture that had been nurtured by a distinctive configuration of governmental institutions and civic ideals. This corporate culture was not free-floating: rather, it was the organizational response to the structuring presence of a progressive political economy. The waning of this political economy brought with it an uncertainty about the relationship of technology and politics. Lawmakers in the early twentieth century regarded technical advance as a harbinger of moral progress. So, too, did network providers. The only real debate concerned the means that would best bring about the agreed-upon end: Postmaster General Burleson championed government administration, whereas Bell president Vail advocated corporate management. For both, organizational capabilities held the key. If contemporaries continue to frame the debate in this way, progressivism will hold sway. If they do not, then it may be time to remember not only the limitations but also the possibilities of antimonopoly as a civic ideal.

CHRONOLOGY OF AMERICAN
TELECOMMUNICATIONS

1792   Congress enacts the Post Office Act of 1792. This law facilitates the circulation of information on public affairs over long distances by admitting newspapers into the mail at low rates and by transferring control over the designation of new post routes from the Post Office Department to Congress.

1794   The French government establishes an optical telegraph between Paris and Lille; access is restricted to the French government.

1825   Postmaster General John McLean issues a circular that expands the mandate of the Post Office Department to embrace the outpacing of private carriers in the circulation of information on market trends.

1836   War hero and optical telegrapher Samuel C. Reid urges Congress to build and operate an optical telegraph between New York City and New Orleans as a branch of the Post Office Department; Reid's telegraph is never built.

1836–1839   Postmaster General Amos Kendall operates a horse express to outpace private carriers in the circulation of information on market trends.

1838   Maine congressman Francis O. J. Smith hails Samuel F. B. Morse's electric telegraph in a government report as one of the greatest inventions of the age. Prior to his report, Smith signs an agreement with Morse giving him a financial stake in Morse's invention.

1840 Morse obtains a patent for an electromagnetic recording telegraph.

1843 Congress appropriates $30,000 to enable Morse to build a demonstration project of his telegraph between Washington and Baltimore.

May 1844 Morse completes his demonstration project. Morse gives Anne Ellsworth the privilege of choosing the text of the first official message to be sent over the Washington–Baltimore line; Anne's mother chooses the text: "What Hath God Wrought."

May 1844– March 1847 Morse lobbies Congress to buy his patent rights and build a countywide telegraph network under the jurisdiction of the Post Office Department.

March 1845 Congress enacts the Post Office Act of 1845. This law transfers jurisdiction over Morse's demonstration project to the Post Office Department and expands the mandate of the Post Office Department to embrace the low-cost circulation of information on personal matters.

The Post Office Department opens the Washington–Baltimore line to the public on a fee-for-service basis.

Morse hires Amos Kendall to manage his patent rights; Kendall endorses Morse's federally oriented business strategy.

1846 Morse obtains a patent for an electromagnetic relay.

1848 The New York state legislature enacts the New York Telegraph Act of 1848. This law establishes the legal foundation for the state-oriented political economy that will hasten the rise of Western Union.

1849 Telegraph promoter Henry O'Rielly proposes the construction of a Pacific telegraph to link the eastern seaboard with California.

1850 Smith tries unsuccessfully to sue telegraph inventor Royal House for infringing on Morse's patent rights. Supreme Court Justice Levi Woodbury sustains House's patent rights; they become a legal cornerstone of the telegraph corporation that Hiram Sibley will soon call Western Union.

1854   Supreme Court Chief Justice Roger Taney narrows the scope of Morse's patent rights by denying that Morse can patent a principle; to mollify Morse, he anoints him the inventor of the telegraph.

1856   Following a series of mergers, Hiram Sibley renames his telegraph corporation Western Union.

Aug. 1857   Hiram Sibley establishes a cartel that includes six of the countries' most important telegraph companies; the cartel agreement is known as the Treaty of Six Nations. The only major telegraph companies that are excluded are those controlled directly by Morse and Smith.

1858   Cyrus Field lays and briefly operates an Atlantic cable; almost immediately, the line goes dead.

1859   Morse and Smith sell their companies to American Telegraph.

American Telegraph and the New York Associated Press (NYAP) agree on an entente to facilitate the low-cost circulation of information on public affairs.

1861   Sibley completes the Pacific telegraph; shortly thereafter, he commences an even more ambitious project to link the United States and Europe by way of a mostly overland route that stretches from Alaska to Siberia by way of the Bering Strait.

1861–1865   The Civil War expands the market for the telegraph; American Telegraph cooperates with the Lincoln administration and the NYAP to control the flow of war news.

1864   United States Telegraph is chartered; William Orton is appointed president shortly thereafter.

1866   Western Union acquires American Telegraph and United States Telegraph, its two principal rivals.

July 1866   Congress enacts the National Telegraph Act. This law is intended to encourage new entrants in the telegraph business; it grants consenting telegraph companies access to certain rights-of-way; empowers the postmaster general to set telegraph rates for government departments; and establishes a mechanism to enable Congress to buy out consenting telegraph corporations at any point five years after its enactment.

Aug. 1866   A British consortium spans the Atlantic by cable, dooming Sibley's trans-Siberian telegraph.

June 1867   Western Union assents to the National Telegraph Act.

1868   Municipal franchise corporation promoter Gardiner G. Hubbard lobbies Congress to charter a telegraph corporation; Hubbard lobbies Congress in almost every session between 1868 and 1874.

1870   Control of Western Union passes from its original Rochester investors to a New York City-based clique of financiers that journalists dubbed the "Vanderbilt interest." The clique includes railroad magnate Cornelius Vanderbilt and his son-in-law, Horace C. Clark.

Dec. 1871   President Ulysses S. Grant endorses a congressional buyout of Western Union in the first annual message following the five-year window specified in the National Telegraph Act.

1875   The Western Union Headquarters Building in New York City is completed.

1875–1877   Jay Gould makes his first raid on Western Union; he targets Western Union's patent rights.

March 1876   Alexander Graham Bell obtains a patent for the electrical transmission of sound. Bell receives legal assistance from his future father-in-law Gardiner G. Hubbard; Hubbard had enlisted Bell to invent a multiple telegraph for sale to Jay Gould or Western Union.

Jan. 1877   Bell obtains a patent for a telephone instrument.

Oct. 1877   The Supreme Court affirms the constitutionality of the National Telegraph Act in *Pensacola v. Western Union*.

1878–1879   Western Union and National Bell establish rival telephone exchanges in many cities and towns; these exchanges are organized as municipal franchise corporations.

Feb.–March 1879   National Bell is formed to commercialize Bell's patents; William H. Forbes is elected president.

May 1879   Gould makes his second raid on Western Union; he targets Western Union's rights-of-way.

June 1879   Congress enacts the Butler amendment, which authorizes railroads to operate telegraph lines if they consent to be bound by the provisions of the National Telegraph Act.

Nov. 1879   Western Union signs an agreement with National Bell that cedes to National Bell the telephone business; this agreement segments the electrical communications business between the telephone and the telegraph.

March 1880   American Bell succeeds National Bell.

1881–1888   The National Telephone Exchange Association formulates procedures for telephone operating companies.

Jan. 1881   Gould's second raid culminates in his takeover of Western Union.

1883–1884   Congress debates several bills to regulate Western Union; none is enacted.

July 19–Aug.   Telegraph operators strike Western Union; the strikers are
28, 1883   viewed sympathetically by the many newspapers hostile to Jay Gould.

1885   The Indiana state legislature establishes a rate cap for telephone rates; the Bell operating company in Indiana begins to pull out of the state.

American Bell establishes American Telephone and Telegraph as the long-distance network provider for its federation of operating companies.

Nov. 1886–   Rochester telephone subscribers boycott the Rochester
May 1888   Telephonic Exchange, the Bell operating company in Rochester, New York.

1888   Political economist Richard T. Ely popularizes the idea that Western Union is a natural monopoly.

Edward J. Hall devises an organizational chart for telephone operating companies that empowers operating company managers to experiment with novel methods and services.

1888–1895   Telephone operating companies in every state other than Indiana successfully prevent the enactment of laws instituting rate caps; hostility between users and operating companies mounts.

March 1888   Chief Justice Morrison Waite affirms Alexander Bell's priority as the inventor of the telephone.

Jan. 1889   Chicago Telephone obtains a twenty-year franchise after a long and contentious struggle in the Chicago city council.

March 1889   The Indiana legislature repeals its telephone rate cap.

1892   Bell establishes telephone service between New York City and Chicago.

1893–1894   Metropolitan (in New York City) and Chicago Telephone increase telephone rates for flat-rate business service. The increase in New York City is from $150 to $240, and in Chicago from $125 to $175. The rate hike is justified as necessary to equip subscribers' telephones for long-distance service.

March 1893   Bell's patent for the electrical transmission of sound expires.

Jan. 1894   Bell's telephone instrument patent expires.

June 1894   Union N. Bethell introduces measured service in New York City.

Dec. 1894   Angus Hibbard proclaims traffic management to be the central challenge for operating company managers.

A Massachusetts court voids a microphone patent granted to Emile Berliner and owned by American Bell. Non-Bell or independent telephone equipment manufacturers regard this decision as a major victory that opens the way for the establishment of independent telephone exchanges.

1897   Independent manufacturer James E. Keelyn leads a successful court fight to void American Bell's switch hook patent.

ca. 1898   Advocates of municipal ownership begin to refer to telephone operating companies as "public utilities."

1899   Illinois Telephone and Telegraph obtains a license from the Chicago city council to build an exchange in Chicago to rival Chicago Telephone.

May 1899   The Supreme Court excludes the telephone from the National Telegraph Act in *Richmond v. Southern Bell;* this ruling expands the jurisdiction of municipalities over telephone operating companies.

Dec. 1899   American Bell transfers its assets to American Telegraph and Telephone, which is popularly known as Bell.

1900   Hibbard introduces the pay-as-you-go "nickel-in-the-slots" in Chicago, hastening the popularization of telephone service in the city.

May 1906   The Massachusetts state legislature puts all corporations that transmit "intelligence" by electricity under the jurisdiction of the state highway commission.

1907   New York Governor Charles Evans Hughes supports the inclusion of the telephone and telegraph under the jurisdiction of the state public service commission; the telephone and the telegraph are omitted from the final version of the law.

Feb. 1907   United States Independent collapses; its collapse makes it almost impossible for independents to obtain capital for equipment upgrades.

July 1907   The Wisconsin legislature puts the telephone and telegraph under the jurisdiction of the state railroad commission.

Nov. 1907   Chicago Telephone obtains a new franchise; the franchise preserves the business flat-rate while lowering telephone rates for most users and limiting the cost of a telephone call inside Chicago to 5 cents.

Oct. 1908   President Theodore Roosevelt supports federal legislation designating telephone and telegraph corporations as common carriers.

Dec. 1908   Bell president Theodore N. Vail publicizes the existence of a "Bell System" that interconnects the Bell operating companies.

1909   Bell acquires a large financial stake in Western Union.

June 18, 1910   Congress enacts the Mann-Elkins Act. This act classifies the telegraph and telephone as common carriers and puts them under the jurisdiction of the Interstate Commerce Commission.

June 25, 1910   The New York legislature puts the telephone and telegraph under the jurisdiction of the state public service commission.

Dec. 1910   Theodore N. Vail commits the Bell System to establishing a "universal wire system" that will combine the telephone and telegraph in a single interactive network.

1913   Attorney General James McReynolds charges Bell with violating the Sherman Act.

Dec. 1913   Attorney General McReynolds brokers an agreement with Bell vice president Nathan C. Kingsbury that ends McReynolds's lawsuit. McReynolds orders Bell to divest its holdings in Western Union; to stop acquiring independents; and to create protocols to facilitate the interconnection of Bell and noncompeting independent operating companies.

Maryland Congressman David J. Lewis introduces a bill calling for government ownership of the telephone.

1914   Bell divests its holdings in Western Union.

1915   Bell begins long-distance telephone service between New York City and San Francisco, a distance of 2,900 miles; the spanning of such a distance is made possible by the invention of the three-element high-vacuum tube, the invention that marks the birth of electronics.

April 1917   The United States declares war on Germany.

July 1918   President Woodrow Wilson transfers control of the telephone and telegraph to the Post Office Department as a military necessity.

Nov. 11, 1918   The First World War ends.

Nov. 16, 1918   President Wilson transfers control of cable lines that touch U.S. soil to the Post Office Department as a military necessity.

1919   Vail proclaims all forms of electrical communication "one great medium" and endorses the establishment of an interconnected combine linking the telephone, the telegraph, and cable.

April 15–19, 1919   The Boston Telegraph Operators' Union calls a strike that disrupts telephone service in Massachusetts, New Hampshire, Vermont, Maine, and Rhode Island; telephone operators force the Post Office Department to negotiate and obtain a wage increase.

May 1919   Congress restores control of the cable lines to their owners.

July 1919   Congress restores control of the telephone and telegraph to their owners.

1920   Commercial radio broadcasting begins.

1927   Congress institutionalizes the segmentation of the market between telephone, telegraph, and radio by enacting the Radio Act of 1927.

1934 Congress shifts the jurisdiction of the telephone and telegraph from the Interstate Commerce Commission to the Federal Communications Commission (FCC).

1976 The U.S. Justice Department charges Bell with monopolizing the telephone business.

1984 Bell divests itself of its operating companies to settle the Justice Department's antitrust suit, ending the Bell System.

1996 Congress enacts the Telecommunications Act of 1996; among its provisions is the abolition of municipal franchise monopolies.

NOTES

Abbreviations

ABTC	American Bell Telephone Company
AT&T	American Telephone and Telegraph Company
AT&T-NJ	AT&T Archives and History Center, Warren, New Jersey
AT&T-TX	AT&T Archives and History Center, San Antonio, Texas
CCC-NEIU	Chicago City Council Records, Northeastern Illinois University
C-CU	Ezra Cornell Papers, Cornell University
CTC	Chicago Telephone Company
CTCR	Chicago Telephone Company Records
DOJ-NA	U.S. Department of Justice, RG 60, National Archives
FHS	Filson Historical Society, Louisville, Kentucky
HP-NA	House Committee on the Post Office and Post Roads, RG 233, National Archives
HSP	Historical Society of Pennsylvania
JH	*The Papers of Joseph Henry*, ed. Nathan Reingold et al. (Washington, D.C.: Smithsonian Institution Press, 1972–2007)
LC	Library of Congress
MHS	Massachusetts Historical Society
MIT	Massachusetts Institute of Technology
M-LC	Samuel F. B. Morse Papers, Library of Congress
NA	National Archives

NA-GL   National Archives, Great Lakes Region

NTEA   National Telephone Exchange Association

NYHS   New-York Historical Society

NYPL   New York Public Library

O-RHS   Henry O'Rielly Papers, Rochester Historical Society

PL   president's letterbook

POD-NA   Post Office Department Records, RG 28, National Archives

RG   record group

SA-C   Chicago Telephone Company files, Sidley Austin Brown & Wood
           Archives, Chicago

SI   Smithsonian Institution

S-MeHS   Francis O. J. Smith Papers, Maine Historical Society

SP-NA   Senate Committee on Post Offices and Post Roads, RG 46,
           National Archives

S-UR   Hiram Sibley Papers, University of Rochester

WU-SI   Western Union Collection, Archives Center, National Museum of
           American History, Smithsonian Institution

W-WRHS   Jeptha H. Wade Family Papers, Western Reserve Historical Society

Introduction

1. Lewis Mumford, *Technics and Civilization* (1934; New York: Harcourt, Brace, Jovanovich, 1963), pp. 221, 239; Edward Tenner, "'Information Age' at the National Museum of American History," *Technology and Culture* 33 (October 1992): 780–787.

2. Brooke Hindle, *Emulation and Invention* (New York: New York University Press, 1981), p. 85.

1. Making a Neighborhood of a Nation

1. Henry Adams, *The Education of Henry Adams,* ed. Ernest Samuels (1906; Boston: Houghton Mifflin, 1974), p. 5.

2. John Bach McMaster, *History of the People of the United States, from the Revolution to the Civil War,* vol. 7: *1841–1850* (New York: D. Appleton & Co., 1910), pp. 106–120, 124–134.

3. Thomas J. Schlereth, *Victorian America: Transformations in Everyday Life, 1876–1915* (New York: HarperCollins, 1991), p. xii.

4. Norvin Green to Henry H. Bingham, December 11, 1890, president's letterbook, Western Union Collection, Archives Center, Smithsonian Institution, Washington, D.C.

5. Albert-László Barabási, *Linked: The New Science of Networks* (Cambridge, Mass.: Perseus Publishing, 2002).

6. Manuel Castells, *The Rise of the Network Society* (Oxford: Blackwell, 1996), pp. 171, 198.

7. Carl Shapiro and Hal R. Varian, *Information Rules: A Strategic Guide to the Network Economy* (Boston: Harvard Business School Press, 1999), chap. 7.

8. "The Magnetic Telegraph—Some of Its Results," *New York Daily Tribune*, July 8, 1845.

9. Orin Fowler, *Remarks of Mr. Orin Fowler, of Mass. . . . on a Motion to Reduce Postage on All Letters to Two Cents* (Washington, D.C.: Buell & Blanchard, 1851), p. 5.

10. Cromwell Childe, "Social Uses of the Telephone," *Telephone Review* 4 (September 1913): 236–237.

11. Stephen Graham and Simon Marvin, *Splintered Urbanism: Networked Infrastructures, Technological Mobilities, and the Urban Condition* (London: Routledge, 2001), pp. 186–194; Bruno Latour, *We Have Never Been Modern* (Cambridge, Mass.: Harvard University Press, 1993), pp. 117–122.

12. Marshall McLuhan and Bruce R. Powers, *The Global Village: Transformations in World Life and Media in the Twenty-First Century* (New York: Oxford University Press, 1989), frontispiece.

13. William Ellery Channing, "The Union," *Christian Examiner* 6 (May 1829): 160.

14. Morse to Francis O. J. Smith, February 15, 1838, in *Electro-Magnetic Telegraphs*, 25th Cong., 2nd sess., 1838, H. Rpt. 753 (serial 335), p. 9.

15. Herbert N. Casson, "The Telephone and National Efficiency," *Telephone Review* 1 (June 1910): 2.

16. "Making a Neighborhood of a Nation," *Telephone Review* 6 (January 1915, supplement): inside front cover.

17. David F. Weiman, "Building 'Universal Service' in the Early Bell System: The Co-Evolution of Regional Urban Systems and Long-Distance Telephone Networks," in Timothy W. Guinnane et al., eds., *History Matters: Essays on Economic Growth, Technology, and Demographic Change* (Stanford, Calif.: Stanford University Press, 2004), p. 351.

18. Leo Marx, *The Machine in the Garden: Technology and the Pastoral Ideal in America* (New York: Oxford University Press, 1964), p. 194.

19. "Letter Writing; in Its Effects on National Character," *Ladies' Magazine and Literary Gazette* 4 (1831): 242.

20. *National Intelligencer* (Washington, D.C.), April 13, 1837.

21. "Amos Kendall," *United States Magazine* 1 (March 1838): 411.

22. Edouard Estaunié, *Traité Pratique de Telecommunication Électrique (Télégraphie-Téléphonie)* (Paris: Charles Dunod, 1904).

23. Daniel R. Headrick, *When Information Came of Age: Technologies of Knowledge in the Age of Reason and Revolution, 1700–1850* (Oxford: Oxford University Press, 2000), pp. 193–197.

24. Gerald C. Gross, "The World's First Telecommunication Convention," *Radio News* 16 (September 1934): 136.

25. "Secretary Roper's Report on Communications Study," *Wall Street Journal,* January 30, 1934; "World Radio Code Links 75 Nations," *New York Times,* May 6, 1934. A keyword search of the machine-readable version of the *Wall Street Journal* and the *New York Times* turned up only scattered occurrences of the word "telecommunications" for the period before 1940.

26. James M. Herring and Gerald C. Gross, *Telecommunications: Economics and Regulation* (New York: McGraw-Hill, 1936).

27. Thaddeus M. Harris, *The Minor Encyclopedia, or Cabinet of General Knowledge,* vol. 4 (Boston: West & Greenleaf, 1803), p. 219.

28. Gerard J. Holzmann and Björn Pehrson, "The First Data Networks," *Scientific American* 270 (January 1994): 128–129.

29. Richard R. John, *Spreading the News: The American Postal System from Franklin to Morse* (Cambridge, Mass.: Harvard University Press, 1995), pp. 86–87.

30. "A New Era in Civilization—the Electric Telegraph," *New York Herald,* August 5, 1844.

31. "Napoleon's Visual Telegraph: The First Long Distance System," box 2061, AT&T Archives and History Center, Warren, N.J.

32. John Pickering, *A Lecture on Telegraphic Language, Delivered before the Boston Marine Society* (Boston: Boston, Hilliard, Gray and Co., 1833), pp. 9–11, 28.

33. "Magnetic Telegraph," *Niles's Register* 71 (December 19, 1846): 243.

34. *National Intelligencer,* December 28, 1807.

35. Cited in Mary Orne Pickering, *Life of John Pickering* (Boston: John Wilson and Son, 1887), p. 405.

36. William Thornton, "Outlines of a Constitution for United North and South Columbia," in N. Andrew et al., eds., "Thornton's Outline of a Constitution for United North and South Columbia," *Hispanic American Historical Review* 12 (May 1932): 214.

37. Samuel C. Reid to Levi Woodbury, April 1837, in *Telegraphs for the United States,* 25th Cong., 2nd sess., 1837, H. Doc. 15 (serial 322), p. 9.

38. Samuel C. Reid, *Petition . . . Praying for the Establishment of a Line of Telegraphs from New York to New Orleans,* 24th Cong., 2nd sess., 1837, S. Doc. 107 (serial 298), p. 2.

39. Geoffrey Wilson, *The Old Telegraphs* (London: Phillimore & Co., 1976), pp. 210–217; William Upham Swan, "Early Visual Telegraphs in Massachusetts," *Proceedings of the Bostonian Society* 10 (1929–1933): 30–47.

40. I. N. Phelps Stokes, *The Iconography of Manhattan Island, 1498–1909,* vol. 5 (New York: Robert T. Dodd, 1926), p. 1564.

41. John R. Parker, *A Treatise upon the Telegraphic Science* (Boston: Dutton and Wentworth, 1835), p. 16.

42. John R. Parker, *The United States Telegraph Vocabulary: Being an Appendix to Elford's Marine Telegraph Signal Book* (Boston: W. L. Lewis, 1832).

43. Andrew T. Goodrich, *The Picture of New York, and Stranger's Guide to the Commercial Metropolis* (New York: A. T. Goodrich, 1828), p. 208.

44. Henry O'Rielly to Samuel F. B. Morse, February 6, 1846, letterbook, Henry O'Rielly Papers, New-York Historical Society, New York.

45. *American Telegraph System Semaphoric as Well as Magnetic* (n.p., [1845]).

46. William F. Friedman, *International Radiotelegraph Conference of Washington: 1927* (Washington, D.C.: U.S. Government Printing Office, 1928), p. 7.

47. John Archibald Wheeler, *Geons, Black Holes, and Quantum Foam: A Life in Physics* (New York: W. W. Norton & Co., 2000), pp. 63–64.

48. Theodore M. Porter, "Information, Power, and the View from Nowhere," in Lisa Bud-Frierman, ed., *Information Acumen: The Understanding and Use of Knowledge in Modern Business* (London: Routledge, 1994), pp. 217–230.

49. Geoffrey Parker, *The Grand Strategy of Phillip II* (New Haven, Conn.: Yale University Press, 1998), p. 74.

50. "Simplifying radically," the French historian Robert Darnton observed, "I would insist on a basic point: information about the inner workings of the power system was not supposed to circulate under the Old Regime in France." Robert Darnton, "An Early Information Society: News and the Media in Eighteenth-Century Paris," *American Historical Review* 105 (February 2000): 4.

51. Cited in Julian P. Bretz, "Some Aspects of Postal Extension into the West," *American Historical Association Annual Report* 5 (1909): 145.

52. Francis Wayland, *The Elements of Political Economy* (New York: Leavitt, Lord & Co., 1837), p. 200.

53. Douglas's postal-telegraphic analogy has been misattributed to Delaware senator James A. Bayard for over a century. In fact, Bayard opposed federal funding for the Atlantic cable. *Congressional Globe,* 34th Cong., 3rd sess., January 22, 1857, p. 421; Henry Martyn Field, *The Story of the Atlantic Telegraph* (New York: Charles Scribner's Sons, 1898), p. 100.

54. *Congressional Record,* 43rd Cong., 2nd sess., June 19, 1875, pp. 5210–5211.

55. C. C. Nott, "The Defects of the Postal Service," *Nation* 17 (September 4, 1873): 157–158.

56. H. T. Newcomb, *The Postal Deficit* (Washington, D.C.: William Ballantine & Sons, 1900), p. 9.

57. Henry C. Adams, *Description of Industry: An Introduction to Economics* (New York: Henry Holt and Co., 1918), p. 258.

58. John McLean, "Circular," May 27, 1825, in *National Intelligencer,* May 26, 1826.

59. John McLean, "The Express Mail" [1827], McLean Papers, Library of Congress, Washington, D.C.

60. George B. Prescott, *History, Theory, and Practice of the Electric Telegraph* (Boston: Ticknor and Fields, 1860), pp. 7, 431.

61. Harrison G. Dyar, deposition, in *French v. Rogers,* E. D. Pa. 104 (1851), 15.

62. Senate Committee on Post Offices and Post Roads, *Condition and Proceedings of the Post Office Department,* 23rd Cong., 2nd sess., 1835, S. Doc. 86 (serial 268), p. 113.

63. *Laws and Regulation for the Government of the Post Office Department* (Washington, D.C.: Alexander and Barnard, 1843), p. 21.

64. Jeremiah Libbey to Josiah Bartlett, July 25, 1792, in *The Papers of Josiah Bartlett,* ed. Frank C. Meyers (Hanover: University Press of New Hampshire, 1979), p. 381.

65. Leonard Bacon, "The Post Office System as an Element of Modern Civilization," *New Englander* 1 (January 1843): 15–16.

66. George Sauer, *The Telegraph in Europe: A Complete Statement of the Rise and Progress of Telegraphy in Europe* (Paris: Printed for Private Circulation, 1869), p. 144.

67. "Our Postal System," *Republic* 2 (July 1874): 28.

68. Edward Everett Hale, "A Public Telegraph," *Cosmopolitan Magazine* 12 (December 1891): 249, 251.

2. Professor Morse's Lightning

1. *Telegraphs for the United States,* 25th Cong., 2nd sess., 1837, H. Doc. 15 (serial 322), pp. 1–3.

2. Alfred Vail, January 15, 1848, "Miscellaneous Telegraph Papers," box 5, Vail Telegraph Collection, Archives, Smithsonian Institution, Washington, D.C. (hereafter SI).

3. Eben Norton Horsford, "Recording Telegraph," in Samuel Irenaeus Prime, *The Life of Samuel F. B. Morse. LL.D., Inventor of the Electro-Magnetic Recording Telegraph* (New York: D. Appleton and Co., 1875), p. 295; David Paul Hochfelder, "Taming the Lightning: American Telegraphy as a Revolutionary Technology, 1832–1860" (Ph.D. diss., Case Western University, 1999), pp. 112–113.

4. *Memorial of E. Gonon,* 27th Cong., 1st sess., 1841, Sen. Doc. 77 (serial 390), pp. 1–2; *Mr. Gonon,* 27th Cong., 2nd sess., 1842, H. Rpt. 325 (serial 408), pp. 1–2.

5. Morse to Woodbury, September 27, 1837, in *Telegraphs for the United States*, p. 30.

6. Kenneth Silverman, *Lightning Man: The Accursed Life of Samuel F. B. Morse* (New York: Random House, 2003), p. 194.

7. Samuel F. B. Morse, *Foreign Conspiracy against the Liberties of the United States* (New York: Leavitt, Lord & Co., 1835); Morse, *Foreign Conspiracy against the United States* (n.p., 1861); Morse, *An Argument on the Ethical Position of Slavery in the Social System* (New York: Society for the Diffusion of Political Knowledge, 1863).

8. John R. Parker, *The United States Telegraph Vocabulary: Being an Appendix to Elford's Marine Telegraph Signal Book* (Boston: W. L. Lewis, 1832), p. 3.

9. J. Cummings Vail, *Early History of the Electro-Magnetic Telegraph* (New York: Hine Brothers, 1914), p. 8.

10. William Baxter, "The Real Birth of the Electric Telegraph [c. 1880]," Historic Speedwell, Morristown, N.J.; Vail to George Vail, February 20, 1838, cited in Silverman, *Lightning Man*, p. 168.

11. James M. Elford to John R. Parker, 1830, Parker Papers, University of Pennsylvania, Philadelphia.

12. Volker Ashoff, "Die Synthematographik des Johann Andreas Benignus Bergsträsser (1785–1788)," *Technikgeschichte* 42 (1975): 203–212.

13. Werner von Siemens, *Inventor and Entrepreneur: Recollections of Werner von Siemens* (1847; New York: Augustus M. Kelley, 1968), p. 82.

14. Morse to Woodbury, September 27, 1837, in *Telegraphs for the United States*, p. 28.

15. Gerard J. Holzmann and Björn Pehrson, "The First Data Networks," *Scientific American* 270 (January 1994): 128–129.

16. Prime, *Life of Samuel F. B. Morse*, p. 284.

17. George B. Prescott, "The Progress of the Atlantic Telegraph," *Atlantic Monthly* 5 (March 1860): 297.

18. Morse to Charles G. Ferris, December 6, 1842, in *Electro-Magnetic Telegraphs*, 27th Cong., 3rd sess., 1842, H. Rpt. 17 (serial 426), p. 9.

19. Morse to Woodbury, September 27, 1837, in *Telegraphs for the United States*, pp. 30, 31.

20. Morse to Smith, February 15, 1838, in *Electro-Magnetic Telegraphs*, 25th Cong., 2nd sess., 1838, H. Rpt. 753 (serial 335), p. 8.

21. Ibid., pp. 8–9.

22. Morse to William W. Boardman, August 10, 1842, in Prime, *Life of Samuel F. B. Morse*, p. 434.

23. Morse to Smith, February 15, 1838, in *Electro-Magnetic Telegraphs* (1838), p. 8.

24. Ibid., pp. 8–9.

25. Samuel C. Reid, *Petition ... Praying for the Establishment of a Line of Telegraphs from New York to New Orleans,* 24th Cong., 2nd sess., 1837, S. Doc. 107 (serial 298), p. 1.

26. *Globe* (Washington, D.C.), February 15, 1837.

27. *Report of the Committee on Naval Affairs, on the Petition of Captain Samuel C. Reid,* 15th Cong., 1st sess., 1818, H. Doc. 135 (serial 10), p. 2; *A Collection of Sundry Publications and Other Documents, in Relation to the Attack Made during the Late War upon the Private Armed Brig General Armstrong, of New-York, Commanded by S. C. Reid ...* (New York: John Gray, 1833), pp. iii–iv.

28. William Rea Furlong, *So Proudly We Hail: The History of the United States Flag* (Washington, D.C.: Smithsonian Institution Press, 1981), p. 183.

29. John W. Kirk, "Historic Moments: The First News Message by Telegraph," *Scribner's Magazine* 11 (May 1892): 652–653.

30. Edward Lind Morse, ed., *Samuel F. B. Morse: His Letters and Journals,* vol. 2 (Boston: Houghton Mifflin Co., 1914), p. 83.

31. Iwan Rhys Morus, *Frankenstein's Children: Electricity, Exhibition, and Experiment in Nineteenth-Century London* (Princeton, N.J.: Princeton University Press, 1998), p. 221.

32. Smith, "Report," in *Electro-Magnetic Telegraphs* (1838), p. 2.

33. Steven Lubar, "The Transformation of Antebellum Patent Law," *Technology and Culture* 32 (October 1991): 932–959.

34. Smith, "Report," in *Electro-Magnetic Telegraphs* (1838), p. 2.

35. Morse to Smith, February 2, 1839, Francis O. J. Smith Papers, Maine Historical Society, Portland (hereafter S-MeHS).

36. Alonzo Cornell, *"True and Firm": Biography of Ezra Cornell* (New York: A. S. Barnes & Co., 1884), pp. 85–86.

37. Ibid., p. 82.

38. Morse to Smith, December 3, 1841, in Prime, *Life of Samuel F. B. Morse,* p. 418.

39. Smith to Cornell, April 15, 25, 1844, March 10, 1845, Ezra Cornell Papers, Cornell University, Ithaca, N.Y. (hereafter C-CU).

40. Frederick Merk, *Fruits of Propaganda in the Tyler Administration* (Cambridge, Mass.: Harvard University Press, 1971), pp. 63–69.

41. Smith to Cornell, April 15, 1844, C-CU.

42. Willie P. Mangum reminiscence, May 29, 1844, in Charles Warren, *The Supreme Court in the United States,* vol. 2: *1836–1918* (Boston: Little, Brown, and Co., 1937), p. 135; Vail to Morse, June 3, 1844, Samuel F. B. Morse Papers, Library of Congress, Washington, D.C. (hereafter M-LC).

43. "A Bill for the Purchase and Construction of Morse's Electro Magnetic Telegraph from Washington City, to New York City," S. 190, 28th Cong., 1st sess., 1844, Sen. 28A-B2, RG 46, National Archives, Washington, D.C.

44. Smith to Morse, June 1, 1844, S-MeHS.

45. Cornell to Mary Ann Cornell, June 10, 1844, C-CU.

46. Ibid.

47. Smith to Morse, June 10, 1844; Smith to Rufus Choate, June 11, 1844; both in S-MeHS.

48. Carolyn C. Cooper, *Shaping Invention: Thomas Blanchard's Machinery and Patent Management in Nineteenth-Century America* (New York: Columbia University Press, 1991), chap. 3; Naomi R. Lamoreaux and Kenneth L. Sokoloff, "Intermediaries in the U.S. Market for Technology, 1870–1920," in Stanley L. Engerman et al., eds., *Finance, Intermediaries, and Economic Development* (Cambridge: Cambridge University Press, 2003), p. 223.

49. Cornell to Mary Ann Cornell, June 10, 1844, C-CU.

50. Post Office Department, *Annual Report* (1845), p. 860.

51. Orrin Wood to Cornell, March 1, 1845, C-CU.

52. Smith to Johnson, March 12, 24, 1845, Office of the Electro-Magnetic Telegraph, Post Office Department Records, RG 28, National Archives, Washington, D.C. (hereafter POD-NA).

53. Smith to Cornell, March 1, 1845, C-CU.

54. Smith to Johnson, March 12, 24, 1845, Office of the Electro-Magnetic Telegraph, POD-NA.

55. Morse to Smith, December 20, 1844, S-MeHS.

56. Francis O. J. Smith, *The Secret Corresponding Vocabulary: Adapted for Use to Morse's Electro-Magnetic Telegraph: And Also in Conducting Written Correspondence, Transmitted by the Mails, or Otherwise* (Portland, Maine: Thurston, Ilsley & Co., 1845), preface.

57. Smith, "The Post Office Department: Considered with Reference to Its Condition, Policy, Prospects, and Remedies," *Hunt's Merchants' Magazine* 11–12 (December 1844–February 1845): 151.

58. Smith, "Post Office Department," pp. 538, 147, 148.

59. Christine MacLeod, *Heroes of Invention: Technology, Liberalism, and British Identity, 1750–1914* (Cambridge: Cambridge University Press, 2007), pp. 220, 245.

60. Joseph Henry, "Extracts from the Proceedings of the Board of Regents of the Smithsonian Institution, in Relation to the Electro-Magnetic Telegraph," in *Smithsonian Miscellaneous Collections,* vol. 2, pt. 2 (Washington, D.C.: Smithsonian Institution, 1856), p. 39.

61. Steven W. Usselman, *Regulating Railroad Innovation: Business, Technology, and Politics in America, 1840–1920* (Cambridge: Cambridge University Press, 2002), chap. 3.

62. B. Zorina Khan, *The Democratization of Invention: Patents and Copyrights in American Economic Development, 1790–1920* (Cambridge: Cambridge University Press, 2005), chap. 2.

63. Abraham Lincoln, "Second Lecture on Discoveries and Inventions," February 11, 1859, in *Collected Works of Abraham Lincoln,* vol. 3, ed. Roy P. Basler (New Brunswick, N.J.: Rutgers University Press, 1953), p. 363.

64. W. H. Preece, "American Telegraph System," *Journal of the Society of Telegraph Engineers* 7 (1878): 49–50.

65. Geof Bowker, "What's in a Patent?" in Wiebe E. Bijker and John Law, eds., *Shaping Technology/Building Society: Studies in Sociotechnical Change* (Cambridge, Mass.: MIT Press, 1992), pp. 53–74.

66. Samuel F. B. Morse, "Telegraph Signs," patent 1,647, June 20, 1840.

67. James Delbourgo, *A Most Amazing Scene of Wonders: Electricity and Enlightenment in Early America* (Cambridge, Mass.: Harvard University Press, 2006), chaps. 1–2.

68. Smith, *Secret Corresponding Vocabulary,* preface.

69. George B. Prescott, *History, Theory, and Practice of the Electric Telegraph* (Boston: Ticknor and Fields, 1860), p. 425.

70. W. James King, "The Development of Electrical Technology in the Nineteenth Century: The Electrochemical Cell and the Electromagnet," *Contributions from the Museum of History and Technology* 28 (1962): 233–271.

71. Prescott, *History, Theory, and Practice of the Electric Telegraph,* pp. 7, 431.

72. Baxter, "Electric Telegraph."

73. Henry to Wheatstone, February 27, 1846, in *The Papers of Joseph Henry,* vol. 6, ed. Nathan Reingold et al. (Washington, D.C.: Smithsonian Institution Press, 1972–2007), p. 385.

74. Henry, "Extracts," p. 35.

75. Patent Office, *Annual Report* (1843), pp. 5–6.

76. Douglas E. Bowers, "Department of Agriculture," in *Historical Guide to the U.S. Government,* ed. George T. Kurian (New York: Oxford University Press, 1998), p. 24.

77. Patent Office, *Annual Report* (1844), p. 5.

78. Morse received his patent (no. 1,647) on June 20, 1840; Wheatstone and Cooke received their patent (no. 1,622) on June 10, 1840. The latter patent was incorrectly dated 1842.

79. Patent Office, *Annual Report* (1844), p. 5.

80. *Electro-Magnetic Telegraphs* (1842), p. 1.

81. Robert C. Post, *Physics, Patents, and Politics: A Biography of Charles Grafton Page* (New York: Science History Publications, 1976), pp. 40–51.

82. J. Thomas Scharf, *History of Baltimore City and County* (Philadelphia: Louis H. Everts, 1881), p. 502.

83. Morse, *Letters and Journals,* vol. 1, p. 112.

84. Morse to Ellsworth, February 7, 1844, in Morse, *Letters and Journals,* vol. 2, pp. 217–218.

85. Alfred Vail to George Vail, August 13, 1845, Vail Telegraph Collection, Archives, SI.

86. Susan Morse to Morse, June 7, 1845, cited in Silverman, *Lightning Man,* p. 256.

87. Julia G. Webster correspondence, box 4, folders 44–48, Goodrich Family Papers, Yale University, New Haven, Conn.

88. Morse addressed his poem to "Miss A. G. E."—that is, Anne Goodrich Ellsworth; it included the following stanza:

> So when I review all the scenes that have past
> Between me and thee, be they dark, be they light,
> I forget what was dark, the light I hold fast,
> "I note not the hours except they be bright."

Morse, "The Sun Dial," *Scribner's Monthly* 11 (March 1876): 757.

89. Harriet White, "Who Informed Morse of the Passage of the Telegraph Bill?" *Western Electrician* 9 (November 21, 1891): 303.

90. *Rover,* August 31, 1844, p. 393.

91. Benson Lossing, "Professor Morse and the Telegraph," *Scribner's Monthly* 5 (March 1873): 579–589.

92. The telegraphic tape is preserved among Morse's personal papers in the Library of Congress, which might lead one to guess that Morse retained it as a keepsake. In fact, it had been kept by Anne herself and would not get to the Library of Congress until after her death. Telegraphic dispatch, May 24, 1844, M-LC.

93. Prime, *Life of Samuel F. B. Morse,* pp. 492, 494.

94. John Bach McMaster, *History of the People of the United States, from the Revolution to the Civil War,* vol. 7: *1841–1850* (New York: D. Appleton & Co., 1910), pp. 129–130; Morse to Smith, March 3, 1844, in Morse, *Letters and Journals,* vol. 2, p. 201; Morse to Vail, March 3, 1844, Vail Telegraph Collection, Archives, SI; Horatio Greenough to Henry Greenough, March 3, 1844, in *Letters of Horatio Greenough to His Brother, Henry Greenough* (Boston: Ticknor and Co., 1887), p. 146.

95. Morse's infatuation with Anne was part of a broader pattern. Several years earlier, Morse had fallen in love with Susan Cooper. As a token of his affection, Morse painted her into the "Gallery of the Louvre," one of his most ambitious compositions. What Susan thought of Morse's suit is unknown. Susan's father, the novelist James Fenimore Cooper, doubted that Morse could captivate a woman half his age; according to one recent Morse biographer, this did not stop Morse from trying. Silverman, *Lightning Man,* pp. 113–114.

96. "The Magnetic Telegraph," *National Intelligencer* (Washington, D.C.), October 25, 1845.

97. Petition of Baltimore merchants, January 11, 1847, House Committee on the Post Office and Post Roads, RG 233, National Archives, Washington, D.C.

98. Alexander Jones, *Historical Sketch of the Electric Telegraph* (New York: G. P. Putnam, 1852), p. 135.

99. "The Private Signal Telegraph," *Burlington* [New Jersey] *Gazette,* reprinted in *Public Ledger* (Philadelphia), January 7, 1846.

100. "The Telegraph," *American Republican and Baltimore Daily Clipper,* December 3, 1846.

101. This generalization is based on a day-by-day inspection of over thirty newspapers from throughout the United States for the period between 1843 and 1847.

102. "Magnetic Telegraphs," *Niles's Register* 71 (September 26, 1846): 60–61. Like most nineteenth-century newspaper editorials, Hughes's was unsigned, making their attribution a matter of speculation. In keeping with convention, I attribute unsigned editorials to the senior editor of the newspaper in which they appeared.

103. "Electric Telegraph," *New York Herald,* April 22, 1845.

104. "The Magnetic Telegraph," *New York Sun,* February 13, 1846.

105. "The Telegraph," *Utica Daily Gazette,* February 12, 1846.

106. "The Magnetic Telegraph," *New York Evening Express,* June 25, 1846.

107. Ibid.

108. *Bank of Augusta v. Earle,* 38 U.S. 519 (1839).

109. "The Magnetic Telegraph," *New York Evening Express,* June 25, 1846.

110. Richard B. Kielbowicz, "Newsgathering by Printers' Exchanges before the Telegraph," *Journalism History* 9 (Summer 1982): 42–48.

111. "The Magnetic Telegraph," *Baltimore Patriot and Commercial Gazette,* November 14, 1845.

112. "The Telegraph Office in Washington," *Baltimore Patriot and Commercial Gazette,* May 21, 1846.

113. Crawford Livingston to Erastus Corning, August 4, 1845, cited in Diane De Blois and Robert Dalton Harris, "1845: Cultural Nexus in Transportation and Communication," *Congress Book* 74 (2008): 31.

114. Benjamin Sidney Michael Schwantes, "Fallible Guardian: The Ambiguous Utility of Telegraphy for Railroad Operations in Nineteenth-Century America" (Ph.D. diss., University of Delaware, 2008), chap. 3.

115. "The Postal Telegraph System," *Independent,* February 15, 1872.

116. Lot Clark to Charles Wickliffe, April 28, 1842, U.S. Postal Service Library, Washington, D.C.

117. Henry Clay to Alfred Vail, September 10, 1844, Vail Telegraph Collection, Archives, SI.

118. Robert C. Post, "The Page Locomotive: Federal Sponsorship of Invention in Mid-Nineteenth-Century America," *Technology and Culture* 13 (April 1972): 144; Robert C. Bruce, *The Launching of American Science, 1846–1876* (New York: Alfred A. Knopf, 1987), p. 166.

119. "For the Union," *Daily Union* (Washington, D.C.), December 24, 1846.

120. F. W. Ritter to Henry O'Rielly, June 6, 1846, O'Rielly Papers, New-York Historical Society, New York.

121. Ibid.

122. *Congressional Globe,* February 21, 1843, 27th Cong., 3rd sess., 323.

123. Post Office Department, *Annual Report* (1845), p. 861.

124. Ibid.

125. *Boston Daily Advertiser,* January 1, 1869.

126. Smith to O'Rielly, January 29, 1873, O'Rielly Papers, Rochester Historical Society, Rochester, N.Y.

127. Morse, *Letters and Journals,* vol. 2, p. 86.

128. Nathaniel P. Hill, *Speech of N. P. Hill, of Colorado, Delivered in the Senate of the United States, January 14, 1884* (Washington, D.C.: n.p., 1884), p. 9.

129. Walter Clark, "The Telegraph and the Telephone Properly Parts of the Post Office System," *Arena* 5 (March 1892): 465; Clark, "The Telegraph in England," *Arena* 13 (August 1895): 374.

130. *Electrical Review* 21 (November 19, 1892): 155.

131. Frank G. Carpenter, "Henry Clay on Nationalizing the Telegraph," *North American Review* 154 (March 1892): 382.

132. David A. Wells, *The Relation of the Government to the Telegraph: Or, a Review of the Two Propositions Now Pending before Congress for Changing the Telegraphic Service of the Country* (New York: n.p., 1873), p. 12.

133. Green to Walter Q. Gresham, October 29, 1883, president's letterbook, Western Union Collection, Archives Center, National Museum of American History, Smithsonian Institution, Washington, D.C. (hereafter WU-SI).

134. George B. Prescott, *The Proposed Union of the Telegraph and Postal Systems: Statement of the Western Union Company* (Cambridge, Mass.: Welch, Bigelow, and Co., 1869), pp. 1–2, 33. For the attribution to Prescott, see Western Union executive committee, minutes, January 9, 1869, WU-SI.

135. Prescott and Smith's wife, Junia Loretta Bartlett, were both descended from members of the Bartlett family in Kingston, New Hampshire.

136. "The Morse Banquet," *New York Herald,* December 30, 1868.

137. Horace Greeley et al., eds., *The Great Industries of the United States: Being an Historical Summary of the Origin, Growth, and Perfection of the Chief Industrial Arts of the Country* (Hartford, Conn.: J. B. Burr & Hyde, 1872), pp. 1239–1240, 1247.

3. Antimonopoly

1. Amos Kendall, "Magnetic Telegraph," *Daily Union* (Washington, D.C.), September 22, 1847.

2. Morse to James Gordon Bennett, December 28, 1847, in Kendall, *Morse's Telegraph and the O'Reilly Contract: The Violations of the Contract*

Exposed, and the Conduct of the Patentees Vindicated (Louisville, Ky.: Prentice and Weissinger, 1848), p. 34.

3. Donald B. Cole, *A Jackson Man: Amos Kendall and the Rise of American Democracy* (Baton Rouge: Louisiana State University Press, 2004), chaps. 17–18.

4. *Globe* (Washington, D.C.), February 15, 1837; "Amos Kendall," *United States Magazine* 1 (March 1838): 410.

5. Robert C. Post, "'Liberalizers' versus 'Scientific Men' in the Antebellum Patent Office," *Technology and Culture* 17 (January 1976): 24–54.

6. "Government," *Kendall's Expositor* (Washington, D.C.) 3 (July 25, 1843): 242–243.

7. Kendall to Morse, February 25, 1845, Morse Papers, Library of Congress, Washington, D.C. (hereafter M-LC).

8. Ibid.

9. Marvin Meyers, *The Jacksonian Persuasion: Politics and Belief* (1957; Stanford, Calif.: Stanford University Press, 1960), chap. 2.

10. Kendall to George W. Hopkins, February 24, 1838, in *Letter Postage*, 25th Cong., 2nd sess., 1838, H. Rpt. 909 (serial 336), pp. 8–9.

11. Kendall to Lewis Linn, February 16, 1837, Postmasters General letterbooks, Post Office Department Records, RG 28, National Archives, Washington, D.C. (hereafter POD-NA).

12. Kendall to Hopkins, in *Letter Postage*, pp. 8–9.

13. Ibid., p. 9.

14. Ibid.

15. Richard A. Schwartzlose, *The Nation's Newsbrokers: The Formative Years* (Evanston, Ill.: Northwestern University Press, 1989), p. 41; Brooke Hindle, *Emulation and Invention* (New York: W. W. Norton & Co., 1981), p. 85.

16. Henry O'Rielly, *American Telegraph System: Great Central Range between the Atlantic and Mississippi, Including the Ohio Valley and the Lake Country* (n.p., [1845]).

17. Frederick W. Seward, *Reminiscences of a War-Time Statesman and Diplomat, 1830–1915* (New York: G. P. Putnam's Sons, 1916), p. 91.

18. Amos Kendall to John Marron, April 8, 1845, Records of the Office of the Electro-Magnetic Telegraph, POD-NA.

19. Kendall to Smith, August 12, 1845, Smith Papers, Maine Historical Society, Portland (hereafter S-MeHS).

20. Kendall to Smith, August 31, 1845, S-MeHS.

21. Kendall to Smith, August 12, 1845, S-MeHS.

22. Kendall to Smith, September 1, 1845, S-MeHS.

23. Kendall to Smith, May 10, 1847, S-MeHS.

24. Benjamin B. French to James D. Reid, January 19, 1869, Robert Dalton Harris Collection, Wynantskill, N.Y.; James D. Reid, *The Telegraph in America:*

Its Founders, Promoters, and Noted Men (New York: Derby Brothers, 1879), p. 112.

25. "Mercator," *Morning Courier* (New York), April 25, 1845.

26. Frederic Hudson, *Journalism in the United States from 1690 to 1872* (New York: Harper & Brothers, 1873), pp. 604–605.

27. *New York Evening Express*, April 26, 29, 1845; Kendall to Morse, April 16, 1845, M-LC.

28. "Magnetic Telegraph," *Public Ledger* (Philadelphia), May 13, 1845.

29. Reid, *Telegraph in America*, p. 143.

30. James W. Milgram, *The Express Mail of 1836–1839* (Chicago: Collector's Club of Chicago, 1977), chap. 4.

31. Kendall to _____, September 18, 1846, in Reid, *Telegraph in America*, p. 143.

32. "The Telegraphic Communication between Baltimore and New York," *Baltimore Sun*, May 27, 1845.

33. Hudson, *Journalism*, p. 447.

34. Richard B. Kielbowicz, "Newsgathering by Printers' Exchanges before the Telegraph," *Journalism History* 9 (Summer 1982): 42–48.

35. Kendall to _____, September 18, 1846, in Reid, *Telegraph in America*, p. 143.

36. Reid, *Telegraph in America*, p. 353.

37. Kendall to Robert Gorman, November 1, 1845, S-MeHS.

38. Post Office Department, *Annual Report* (1836), p. 512.

39. Amos Kendall, "Post Office Circular," *Kendall's Expositor* 3 (October 17, 1843): 342–344.

40. *Articles of Association, and Charter from the State of Maryland, of the Magnetic Telegraph Company . . .* (New York: Chatterton & Crist, 1847), pp. 3–4.

41. *Baltimore Patriot and Commercial Gazette*, June 20, 1845.

42. Amos Kendall, "The Magnetic Telegraph," *New York Morning Express*, March 10, 1846.

43. Menahem Blondheim, *News over the Wires: The Telegraph and the Flow of Public Information in America, 1844–1897* (Cambridge, Mass.: Harvard University Press, 1994), chap. 6; Edward C. Mack, *Peter Cooper: Citizen of New York* (New York: Duell, Sloan & Pearce, 1949), pp. 238–242.

44. Horace Greeley et al., eds., *The Great Industries of the United States: Being an Historical Summary of the Origin, Growth, and Perfection of the Chief Industrial Arts of the Country* (Hartford, Conn.: J. B. Burr & Hyde, 1872), pp. 1239–1240, 1247.

45. Taliaferro P. Shaffner, *The Telegraph Manual: A Complete History and Description of the Semaphoric, Electric, and Magnetic Telegraphs* (New York: Pudney and Russell, 1859), pp. 745, 747.

46. Reid, *Telegraph in America,* pp. 301, 320–321.

47. Morse and Smith to Colt, May 8, 1845, Colt Papers, Connecticut Historical Society, Hartford (hereafter Colt Papers).

48. "Morse's New York and Offing Magnetic Telegraph," *New York Evening Express,* November 25, 1845; William B. Edwards, *The Colt's Revolver: The Biography of Colonel Samuel Colt* (Harrisburg, Pa.: Stackpole, 1953), pp. 177–199.

49. Samuel Colt and William Robinson, *New York and Offing Line of Magnetic Telegraph* (n.p., 1845), Colt Papers.

50. Robinson to Colt, November 20, 1845, Colt Papers.

51. Philip K. Lundeberg, *Samuel Colt's Submarine Battery: The Secret and the Enigma* (Washington, D.C.: Smithsonian Institution Press, 1974), p. 31.

52. Colt and Robinson, *Magnetic Telegraph.*

53. Edwards, *Colt's Revolver,* p. 199.

54. "Morse's New York and Offing Electro Magnetic Telegraph," *Evening Post* (New York), November 25, 1845.

55. "The Magnetic Telegraph—Some of Its Results," *New York Daily Tribune,* July 8, 1845.

56. Menahem Blondheim, "The Click: Telegraphic Technology, Journalism, and the Transformations of the New York Associated Press," *American Journalism* 17 (Fall 2000): 27–52.

57. Schwarzlose, *Nation's Newsbrokers,* chap. 2 ("Technological Imperatives and the First Newsbrokerage"); Blondheim, *News over the Wires,* chap. 3 ("'A Better-Organized System': Establishing the New York Associated Press").

58. Reid, *Telegraph in America,* p. 153. O'Rielly originally spelled his last name "O'Reilly"; at some point in the 1840s he changed it to "O'Rielly," a preference that was not always honored by his critics, but which I have adopted, with the exception of instances in which it might impede the retrieval of documents.

59. Alexander Jones, *Historical Sketch of the Electric Telegraph: Including Its Rise and Progress in the United States* (New York: G. P. Putnam, 1852), p. 78.

60. O'Rielly to M. B. Bateham, January 23, 1847, O'Reilly Papers, New-York Historical Society, New York (hereafter NYHS).

61. Reid, *Telegraph in America,* pp. 122–123, 156–159, 198; William Bender Wilson, "The Early Telegraph," *Historical Papers and Addresses of the Lancaster County Historical Society* 1, no. 6 (1896–1897): 236–239.

62. James D. Reid, Pittsburgh, Cincinnati, and Louisville Telegraph Company, "Annual Report," 1849, vol. 1126, Ohio Historical Society, Columbus.

63. John J. S. Lee to Jeptha Wade, January 20, 1851, Jeptha H. Wade Family Papers, Western Reserve Historical Society, Cleveland (hereafter W-WRHS).

64. David Paul Hochfelder, "Taming the Lightning: American Telegraphy as a Revolutionary Technology, 1832–1860" (Ph.D. diss., Case Western University, 1999), chap. 3.

65. Kendall to editors, April 27, 1848, *Journal of Commerce* (New York), April 29, 1848.

66. *Louisville Courier,* c. 1848, cited in Alvin Harlow, *Old Wires and New Waves* (New York: D. Appleton-Century Co., 1936), p. 163.

67. Kendall, *Morse's Telegraph,* pp. 13–14.

68. Henry O'Rielly, "Open Letter," *Journal of Commerce,* September 22, 1848; O'Rielly to James S. Wallace, September 6, 1848, O'Reilly Papers, NYHS.

69. O'Rielly to Josiah Quincy Jr., January 16, 1848, O'Reilly Papers, NYHS.

70. Hindle, *Emulation and Invention,* p. 99.

71. James R. Cameron, *The Public Service of Josiah Quincy, Jr., 1802–1882* (Quincy, Mass.: Quincy Cooperative Bank, 1964), pp. 12–13; Arthur P. Dudden, "Antimonopolism, 1865–1890: The Historical Background and Intellectual Origins of the Antitrust Movement in the United States" (Ph.D. diss., University of Michigan, 1950), pp. 201–208.

72. *New York Times,* February 9, 1859; Charles Francis Adams Jr. to David A. Wells, January 14, 1869, Wells Papers, Library of Congress, Washington, D.C. (hereafter LC); Joseph Dorfman, *The Economic Mind in American Civilization,* vol. 3: *1865–1918* (New York: Viking Press, 1949), p. 23.

73. Gardiner G. Hubbard, *The Postal Telegraph: The Only Means by Which the Telegraph Can Be Made the Ordinary Method of Communication—An Address . . . Before the Board of Trade and Commercial Exchange, Philadelphia* (Boston: Rand, Avery, & Frye, 1869), p. 7; "The Freight Convention," *New York Times,* May 8, 1873.

74. *Scientific American* 4 (December 9, 1848): 3; Robert Charles Post, *Physics, Patents, and Politics: A Biography of Charles Grafton Page* (New York: Science History Publications, 1976), p. 70.

75. *O'Reilly v. Morse,* 56 U.S. 62 (1853); Carl B. Swisher, *History of the Supreme Court of the United States,* vol. 5: *The Taney Period, 1836–64* (New York: Macmillan, 1974), chap. 20.

76. Kendall, *Morse's Telegraph,* p. 8.

77. Kendall to Jeptha H. Wade, November 14, 1853, in Russell H. Anderson, "Jeptha H. Wade and the Cleveland and Cincinnati Telegraph Company," *Ohio State Archaeological and Historical Quarterly* 58 (January 1949): 91.

78. Benjamin B. French, "Address," *American Telegraph Magazine* 1 (July 1, 1853): 283–284.

79. Ezra Cornell to Mary Anne Cornell, April 24, 1853, Ezra Cornell Papers, Cornell University, Ithaca, N.Y.

80. "An Act to Incorporate the New York and Offing Magnetic Telegraph Association," in *Laws of the State of New York,* chap. 335 (Albany, N.Y.: C. Van Bentheusen, 1846), pp. 474–475.

81. "Mercator," *Morning Courier* (New York), April 21, 1845.

82. George H. Miller, *Railroads and the Granger Laws* (Madison: University of Wisconsin Press, 1971), pp. 177–178; Rush Welter, *The Mind of America, 1820–1860* (New York: Columbia University Press, 1975), chap. 6.

83. Ronald E. Seavoy, "Laissez-Faire: Business Policy, Corporations, and Capital Investment in the Early National Period," in Jack P. Greene, ed., *Encyclopedia of American Political History,* vol. 2 (New York: Scribner's, 1984), pp. 728–737.

84. Joseph Whitworth, "Electric Telegraphs," in *The American System of Manufactures,* ed. Nathan Rosenberg (1854; Edinburgh: Edinburgh University Press, 1969), p. 369.

85. "An Act to Provide for the Incorporation and Regulation of Telegraph Companies," in *Laws of the State of New York,* chap. 265 (Albany, N.Y.: C. Van Bentheusen, 1848), p. 395.

86. Ronald E. Seavoy, *The Origins of the American Business Corporation, 1784–1855: Broadening the Concept of Public Service during Industrialization* (Westport, Conn.: Greenwood Press, 1982), pp. 196–199.

87. Howard Bodenhorn, "Bank Chartering and Political Corruption in Antebellum New York," in Edward L. Glaeser and Claudia Goldin, eds., *Corruption and Reform: Lessons from America's Economic History* (Chicago: University of Chicago Press, 2006), pp. 231–257.

88. "Purchase of the Magnetic Telegraph by the Government," *Albany Evening Journal,* December 14, 1846; "Memorial of Henry O'Rielly" [1848], Blatchford, Seward, and Griswold Records, MIT, Cambridge, Mass.; "Memorial against Telegraph Monopolies," January 25, 1853, O'Rielly Papers, Rochester Historical Society, Rochester, N.Y. (hereafter O-RHS).

89. "The Magnetic Telegraph Companies," *New York Evening Express,* February 13, 1847.

90. Ibid.

91. *Albany Evening Journal,* January 18, 19, 1848.

92. New York state law, chap. 265 (1848), p. 395.

93. *Smith v. Downing,* 22 F. Cas. 511.

94. Royal E. House, "To the American People: The Telegraph System—And the Attempt to Monopolize It," *Nashville Union,* November 3, 1847.

95. Reid, *Telegraph in America,* p. 530.

96. "Telegraph History," *Evening Post,* February 27, 1885.

97. Ibid.

98. Ibid.

99. Whitworth, "Electric Telegraphs," p. 369.

100. "Telegraph History," *Evening Post.*

101. Reid, *Telegraph in America,* pp. 468–469.

102. Ibid., p. 479.

103. Stager to Sibley, January 1, 1854, Sibley Papers, University of Rochester, Rochester, N.Y. (hereafter S-UR).

104. *Electric Age* 8 (June 7, 1890): 9.

105. Sibley to John Dean Caton, January 8, 1860, Caton Papers, LC.

106. Julius Grodinsky, *Jay Gould: His Business Career, 1867–1892* (Philadelphia: University of Pennsylvania Press, 1957), p. 148.

107. Jeptha H. Wade, memoir, 1889, W-WRHS.

108. Kendall to Smith, December 26, 1857, Smith Papers, New York Public Library.

109. Kendall to Morse, October 3, 1857, in Frank Luther Thompson, *Wiring a Continent: The History of the Telegraph Industry in the United States* (Princeton, N.J.: Princeton University Press, 1947), p. 317.

110. North American Telegraph Association, *Proceedings* (1861), p. 27.

111. *Biographical Sketch of Dr. Norvin Green, from Encyclopedia of Contemporary Biography of New York* (New York: Atlantic Publishing and Engraving, 1887), p. 9.

112. Henry O'Rielly, *A Few Suggestions Respectfully Submitted Concerning the Senate Bill Now Pending in the House of Representatives* (n.p., 1860), O-RHS.

113. Matthew Fontaine Maury, *The Physical Geography of the Sea*, ed. John Leighly (1855; Cambridge, Mass.: Harvard University Press, 1963), p. 37; Frances Leigh Williams, *Matthew Fontaine Maury: Scientist of the Sea* (New Brunswick, N.J.: Rutgers University Press, 1963), p. 230.

114. Reid, *Telegraph in America*, p. 496.

115. J. Loughborough, *The Pacific Telegraph and Railway* (St. Louis: Charles & Hammond, 1849), p. 64; "The 'People's Highway' between the Atlantic and the Pacific States," *American Telegraph Magazine* 1 (October 1852): 23; R. S. Cotterill, "The National Railroad Convention in St. Louis, 1849," *Missouri Historical Review* 12 (July 1918): 211.

116. Asa Whitney, *A Project for a Railroad to the Pacific* (New York: George W. Wood, 1849).

117. John J. Speed to Sibley, August 20, 1857, S-UR.

118. *Congressional Globe*, April 12, 1860, 36th Cong., 1st sess., 1696–1697.

119. George B. Prescott, "The Progress of the Electric Telegraph," *Atlantic Monthly* 5 (March 1860): 292.

120. Sibley to Field, October 10, 1861, S-UR; Charles Vevier, "The Collins Overland Line and American Continentalism," *Pacific Historical Review* 28 (August 1959): 237–253.

121. Orton to Manton Marble, Marble Papers, February 3, 1868, Marble Papers, LC.

122. Henry Martyn Bannister journal, undated, in James Alton James, *The First Scientific Exploration of Russian America and the Purchase of Alaska*

(Evanston, Ill: Northwestern University Press, 1942), p. 45; Arthur Power Dudden, *The American Pacific from the Old China Trade to the Present* (New York: Oxford University Press, 1992), p. 32.

123. Rebecca Robbins Raines, *Getting the Message Through: A Branch History of the U.S. Army Signal Corps* (Washington, D.C.: Center of Military History, 1996), pp. 16–17.

124. Stager to Stanton, November 1, 1863, in *War of the Rebellion: A Compilation of the Official Records of the Union and Confederate Armies,* series 3, vol. 3 (Washington, D.C.: U.S. Government Printing Office, 1899), p. 970.

125. William Bender Wilson, *A Few Acts and Actors in the Tragedy of the Civil War in the United States* (Philadelphia: Published by the Author, 1892), p. 99.

126. William R. Plum, *The Military Telegraph during the Civil War in the United States,* vol. 2 (Chicago: Jansen, McClurg & Co., 1882), p. 339.

127. Thompson, *Wiring a Continent,* p. 394.

128. Menahem Blondheim, "'Public Sentiment Is Everything': The Union's Public Communications Strategy and the Bogus Proclamation of 1864," *Journal of American History* 89 (December 2002): 869–899.

129. "Telegraph History," *Evening Post.*

130. Green to Pinckney Green, October 29, 1865, Green Family Papers, University of Kentucky, Lexington, Ky.

131. "Telegraph History," *Evening Post.*

132. Shaffner, *Telegraph Manual,* p. 745.

133. Oliver H. Palmer to Hubbard, December 26, 1868, Hubbard Papers, LC.

134. *Union and Advertiser* (Rochester, N.Y.), January 22, 1881.

135. Shaffner, *Telegraph Manual,* p. 745.

136. "In the Midst of a Revolution," *New York Herald,* June 6, 1844.

137. "A New Era in Civilization—The Electric Telegraph," *New York Herald,* August 5, 1844.

138. "The Telegraph," *Harper's New Monthly Magazine* 47 (August 1873): 334.

139. Reid, *Telegraph in America,* p. 181.

140. "Electricity as a Factor in Happiness," *Appleton's Journal* 11 (November 1881): 467.

141. "The Magnetic Telegraph as a Means of Defense in War," *New York Evening Express,* June 9, 1846.

142. "The Importance of the Magnetic Telegraph," *Public Ledger,* June 11, 1846.

143. George Templeton Strong, *The Diary of George Templeton Strong: The Turbulent Fifties, 1850–1859,* ed. Allan Nevins and Milton Hasley Thomas (New York: Macmillan, 1952), pp. 409–410.

144. "The Telegraph," *Harper's New Monthly Magazine,* p. 359.

145. New York Postal Reform Committee, *Proceedings of a Public Meeting and Address of the New York Postal Reform Committee* (New York: Baker & Godwin, 1856), p. 15.

146. John W. Post to Congress, March 25, 1856, HR 34A-G14.6, House Committee on the Post Office and Post Roads, RG 233, National Archives, Washington, D.C.

147. Henry David Thoreau, *Walden,* ed. J. Lyndon Shanley (1854; Princeton, N.J.: Princeton University Press, 1971), p. 52.

148. Abraham Lincoln, "Second Lecture on Discoveries and Inventions," February 11, 1859, in *Collected Works of Abraham Lincoln,* vol. 3, ed. Roy P. Basler (New Brunswick, N.J.: Rutgers University Press, 1953), p. 357; Stephen W. Usselman, *Regulating Railroad Innovation: Business, Technology, and Politics in America, 1840–1929* (Cambridge: Cambridge University Press, 2002), pp. 47–51.

149. Albert Gallatin, *Report of the Secretary of the Treasury, on the Subject of Public Roads and Canals* (Washington, D.C.: R. C. Weightman, 1808), pp. 5, 8.

150. "The Magnetic Telegraph," *New York Herald,* June 15, 1844.

151. "Ocean Steam Navigation and the Magnetic Telegraphs," *New York Herald,* July 12, 1846.

152. "The Magnetic Telegraph and the Press," *Daily Union,* August 12, 1847.

153. Julius W. Pratt, "The Origin of 'Manifest Destiny,'" *American Historical Review* 32 (July 1927): 795–798; John L. O'Sullivan, "Annexation," *United States Magazine* 17 (July 1845): 9.

154. "In the Midst of a Revolution," *New York Herald,* June 6, 1844.

155. "Morse's Electro-Magnetic Telegraph," *De Bow's Review* 1 (February 1846): 132–141; George Fitzhugh, "The Atlantic Telegraph, Ancient Art, and Modern Progress," *De Bow's Review* 25 (November 1858): 507–511; Fitzhugh, "Uniform Postages, Railroads, Telegraphs, Fashions, Etc.," *De Bow's Review* 26 (June 1859): 657–664.

156. Samuel F. B. Morse, *An Argument on the Ethical Position of Slavery in the Social System* (New York: Society for the Diffusion of Political Knowledge, 1863).

157. William H. Seward, "To the Pacific Railroad Convention at St. Louis," in *The Works of William H. Seward,* vol. 3, ed. George E. Baker (Boston: Houghton, Mifflin and Co., 1887), p. 424.

158. Millard Fillmore to O'Rielly, February 16, 1853, O-RHS; *American Telegraph Magazine* 1 (October 1852): 23.

159. Thomas C. Leonard, *The Power of the Press: The Birth of American Political Reporting* (New York: Oxford University Press, 1986), pp. 92–93.

160. Buchanan to James Gordon Bennett, December 20, 1860, in *The Works of James Buchanan: Comprising His Speeches, State Papers, and Private*

Correspondence, vol. 10, ed. John Bassett Moore (London: J. Lippincott Co., 1910), pp. 69–70.

161. "The President's Policy," *North American Review* 98 (January 1864): 236.

162. Field to Lincoln, October 24, 1861, in Thompson, *Wiring a Continent,* p. 368.

163. "The First Telegraphic Message from California," *Harper's Weekly* 5 (November 23, 1861): 752.

164. F. P. Stanton, "The Press in the United States," *Galaxy* 2 (November 1862): 606–607.

165. Lincoln, "Annual Message to Congress," December 1, 1862, in Basler, *Collected Works,* vol. 5, p. 527.

166. Casper Thomas Hopkins, *Manual of American Ideas* (San Francisco: Printed for the Author, 1872), pp. 106–107.

167. Charles A. Young, "Practical Uses of Electricity," *Princeton Review* 1 (May 1881): 296.

168. Patricia Hills, "Picturing Progress in the Era of Westward Expansion," in William H. Truettner, ed., *The West as America: Reinterpreting Images of the Frontier, 1820–1920* (Washington, D.C.: Smithsonian Institution Press, 1991), pp. 97–147.

169. Albert D. Richardson, *Beyond the Mississippi: From the Great River to the Great Ocean* (Hartford, Conn.: American Publishing Co., 1867), frontispiece.

170. J. Valerie Fifer, *American Progress: The Growth of the Transport, Tourist, and Information Industries in the Nineteenth-Century West* (Chester, Conn.: Globe Pequot Press, 1989), pp. 202–205.

171. George A. Crofutt, *Crofutt's New Overland Tourist and Pacific Coast Guide* (Chicago: Overland Publishing Company, 1878), frontispiece.

172. Ibid., p. 157.

4. The New Postalic Dispensation

1. William Orton to Anson Stager, January 24, 1871, president's letter-book, Western Union Collection, Archives Center, National Museum of American History, Smithsonian Institution, Washington, D.C. (hereafter PL, WU-SI).

2. The National Telegraph Act is sometimes called the Post Roads Act of 1866, a convention that originated around 1900. For an early occurrence (the "so-called Post Roads Act"), see A. H. McMillan, *Telephone Law* (New York: McGraw Publishing Co., 1908), p. 47.

3. "An Act to Aid in the Construction of Telegraph Lines, and to Secure to the Government the Use of the Same for Postal, Military, and Other Purposes,"

in *Statutes at Large of the United States of America, 1789–1873,* vol. 14, chap. 230 (Boston: Little, Brown, 1866), p. 221.

4. John Wanamaker, *An Argument in Support of the Limited Post and Telegraph* (Washington, D.C.: U.S. Government Printing Office, 1890), app. H.

5. Western Union, *Annual Report* (1869), p. 40.

6. Norvin Green to Martha Green, January 30, 1869, Norvin Green Family Papers, University of Kentucky, Lexington, Ky.

7. William Letwin, *Law and Economic Policy in America: The Evolution of the Sherman Antitrust Act* (Chicago: University of Chicago Press, 1954), pp. 87–95; George F. Edmunds, "The Interstate Trust and Commerce Act of 1890," *North American Review* 194 (December 1911): 801–817.

8. Sherman to Cooke, July 30, 1866, Cooke Papers, Historical Society of Pennsylvania.

9. *Chicago Tribune,* June 15, 1866.

10. "An Act to Attach Certain Conditions to the Construction of Future Railways," *Statutes of the Realm,* 7–8 Vict., c. lxxxv, August 9, 1844.

11. John Stuart Mill, *Principles of Political Economy,* vol. 2 (Boston: Charles C. Little & James Brown, 1848), p. 540.

12. Josiah Quincy Jr., *Figures of the Past: From the Leaves of Old Journals* (Boston: Roberts Brothers, 1883), pp. 338–340.

13. Josiah Quincy Jr., *The Railway System of Massachusetts: An Address Delivered before the Boston Board of Trade* (Boston: Mudge & Son, 1866), p. 21.

14. Isaac F. Redfield, *The Law of Railways* (Boston: Little, Brown, and Co., 1867), p. 239.

15. William L. Scott and Milton P. Jarnigan, *A Treatise on the Law of Telegraphs* (Boston: Little, Brown, and Co., 1868), p. iii.

16. Frank Luther Thompson, *Wiring a Continent: The History of the Telegraph Industry in the United States, 1832–1866* (Princeton, N.J.: Princeton University Press, 1947), pp. 407–408.

17. Ibid.

18. *Congressional Globe,* June 27, 1866, 39th Cong., 1st sess., 3428.

19. Cooke to Sherman, April 20, June 22, 1866, vol. 99, 103, Sherman Papers, Library of Congress (hereafter LC).

20. *Congressional Globe,* February 23, 1866, 39th Cong., 1st sess., 979–980.

21. Ibid.

22. Orton to Edwin D. Morgan, June 8, 12, 1866; Orton to Gardiner G. Hubbard, October 20, 1873; both in PL, WU-SI.

23. Sibley to _____, June 5, 1867, Post Office Department Records, RG 28, National Archives, Washington, D.C.

24. William Orton, *Government Telegraphs* (New York: Russells' American Steam Printing House, 1870), p. 28.

25. "An Act to Facilitate Communication between the Atlantic and Pacific States by Electric Telegraph," *Statutes at Large of the United States of America, 1789–1873,* vol. 12, chap. 137 (Boston: Little, Brown, 1860), pp. 41–42.

26. Eric D. Craft, "The Value of Weather Information Services for Nineteenth-Century Great Lakes Shipping," *American Economic Review* 88 (December 1998): 1074–1075.

27. Rebecca Robbins Raines, *Getting the Message Through: A Branch History of the U.S. Army Signal Corps* (Washington, D.C.: Center of Military History, 1996), chap. 2; James Rodger Fleming, *Meteorology in America, 1800–1870* (Baltimore, Md.: Johns Hopkins University Press, 1990), chap. 7.

28. *Electro-Magnetic Telegraph—Astronomical Observations,* 30th Cong., 2nd sess., 1849, H. Ex. Doc. 21 (serial 540); Hugh Richard Slotten, *Patronage, Practice, and the Culture of American Science: Alexander Dallas Bache and the U.S. Coast Survey* (Cambridge: Cambridge University Press, 1994), pp. 141–143; Raines, *Getting the Message Through,* p. 45.

29. Cited in James Rodgers Fleming, "Storms, Strikes, and Surveillance: The U.S. Army Signal Office, 1861–1891," *Historical Studies in the Physical and Biological Sciences* 30 (2000): 316.

30. *Postal Telegraph in the United States,* 41st Cong., 2nd sess., 1870, H. Rpt. 114 (serial 1438).

31. Lucile M. Kane, *The Falls of St. Anthony: The Waterfall that Built Minneapolis* (St. Paul: Minnesota Historical Society Press, 1987), pp. 75–77, 92–94.

32. Ulysses S. Grant, "Annual Message," December 4, 1871, in *Papers of Ulysses S. Grant,* vol. 22, ed. John Y. Simon (Carbondale: Southern Illinois University Press, 1998), p. 259.

33. *Congressional Globe,* January 21, 1862, 37th Cong., 2nd sess., 424.

34. "Republican Mass Meeting—Speech of Mr. Creswell," *Baltimore American,* October 18, 1873.

35. Ezra Cornell, diary, September 3, 1850, Cornell Papers, Cornell University, Ithaca, N.Y.; "An Act to Incorporate the New England Telegraph Company," in *Acts and Resolves Passed by the General Court of Massachusetts,* chap. 97, April 30, 1851, p. 607; Robert V. Bruce, *Bell: Alexander Graham Bell and the Conquest of Solitude* (1973; Ithaca, N.Y.: Cornell University Press, 1990), pp. 83–84.

36. W. Bernard Carlson, "The Telephone as Political Instrument: Gardiner Hubbard and the Political Construction of the Telephone, 1875–1880," in Michael Thad Allen and Gabrielle Hecht, eds., *Technologies of Power: Essays in Honor of Thomas Parke Hughes and Agatha Chipley Hughes* (Cambridge, Mass.: MIT Press, 2001), pp. 25–55.

37. *Minutes of a Hearing Before the Committee on Railroads . . . January 28, 1879,* p. 82.

38. Hubbard, "The Proposed Changes in the Telegraphic System," *North American Review* 117 (July 1873): 106.

39. Gardiner G. Hubbard, *Commerce by Railroad: Memorial,* 43rd Cong., 1st sess., 1874, H. Misc. Doc. 140 (serial 1619), pp. 3–4; Hubbard, *Memorial,* 41st Cong., 3rd sess., 1871, H. Misc. Doc. 39 (serial 1462), p. 13.

40. Hubbard, "Proposed Changes," pp. 82, 104.

41. Orton to Thomas Orton, February 23, 1870; Orton to George Walker, February 28, 1870; both in PL, WU-SI.

42. Orton to Hubbard, October 20, 1873, PL, WU-SI.

43. *Chicago Times* [c. 1871], in scrapbook, folder 5, box 35, PL, WU-SI.

44. "The Telegraph," *Harper's New Monthly Magazine* 46 (February 1873): 472; Joseph Medill to Elihu B. Washburne, November 25, 1868; E. D. L. Sweet to Washburne, December 9, 1868; both in Washburne Papers, LC; Resolution of Providence Board of Trade, 1868, Sen. 40A-H18.1; Resolution of San Francisco Chamber of Commerce, 1869, Sen. 41A-H117.4; both in committee papers, Senate Committee on Post Offices and Post Roads, RG 46, National Archives, Washington, D.C. (hereafter SP-NA).

45. Resolution of New York Chamber of Commerce, 1870, Sen. 41A-H17.4, committee papers, SP-NA; Boston Board of Trade, *Annual Report* (1868), p. 106; National Board of Trade, *Proceedings* (1868), pp. 62–63.

46. National Board of Trade, *Proceedings* (1868), pp. 62–63.

47. J. L. Kieve, *The Electric Telegraph in the U.K.: A Social and Economic History* (Newton Abbott, U.K.: David & Charles, 1973), pp. 125–126.

48. Medill to Orton, December 17, 1872, in David A. Wells, *The Relation of the Government to the Telegraph* (New York: n.p., 1873), pp. 155–158.

49. George W. Curtis, "A Government Telegraph," *Harper's Weekly* 17 (August 23, 1873): 738.

50. Hubbard to Gertrude Hubbard, February 27, 1872, Hubbard Papers, LC.

51. "The Postal Telegraph System," *Independent,* February 15, 1872.

52. "The Postal Telegraph System," *Chicago Tribune,* June 9, 1867.

53. Resolution of National Typographical Union, 1870, Sen. 41A-H17.4, committee papers, SP-NA.

54. Osbourne Ward, *A Labor Catechism of Political Economy: A Study for the People* (New York: n.p., 1878), pp. 8, 34, 100–102.

55. A. C. Cameron, "A Popular Fallacy," *Workingman's Advocate,* February 11, 1871.

56. Robert V. Bruce, *1877: Year of Violence* (Indianapolis, Ind.: Bobbs-Merrill Co., 1959), pp. 212–222.

57. "The Government and the Telegraphs," *Telegrapher* 4 (May 9, 1868): 302; "Telegraphic Competition: A General System of Competing Lines Needed," *Telegrapher* 5 (May 15, 1869): 304; "A Government Telegraph," *Operator,*

January 15, 1884, p. 19; "Postal Telegraphy Objectionable to Operators," *Operator,* February 1, 1884, p. 37.

58. This generalization is based on a box-by-box inspection of the petition files of the post office committees of both the House and the Senate in the period between 1840 and 1920.

59. Gertrude Hubbard to Hubbard, January 23, 1877, Hubbard Papers, LC.

60. *Minutes of a Hearing before the Committee on Railroads . . . January 29, 1879,* p. 29; *Telegrapher* 11 (January 30, 1875): 26.

61. Citizens of Adams County, Ohio, *Petition for Cheap Telegraphy,* January 23, 1877, HR 44A-H12.1, House Committee on the Post Office and Post Roads, RG 233, National Archives, Washington, D.C.

62. Henry O'Rielly, *A Few Suggestions Respectfully Submitted Concerning the Senate Bill Now Pending in the House of Representatives* (n.p., 1860), Henry O'Rielly Papers, Rochester Historical Society.

63. John Niven, *Salmon P. Chase: A Biography* (New York: Oxford University Press, 1995), pp. 345, 358–359.

64. "Mr. Orton's Salary and Life-Insurance," *Chicago Tribune,* April 29, 1878.

65. Ibid.

66. Richard A. Easterlin, "Interregional Differences in Per Capita Income, Population, and Total Income, 1840–1950," in National Bureau of Economic Research, *Trends in the American Economy in the Nineteenth Century* (Princeton, N.J.: Princeton University Press, 1960), p. 102.

67. Frank D. Y. Carpenter, "The Remuneration of Public Servants," *North American Review* 135 (August 1882): 185.

68. Maury Klein, *The Life and Legend of Jay Gould* (1986; Baltimore, Md.: Johns Hopkins University Press, 1997), p. 196; *Report of the Committee of the Senate upon the Relations between Labor and Capital,* 1885, vol. 1, p. 949; T. J. Stiles, *The First Tycoon: The Epic Life of Cornelius Vanderbilt* (New York: Alfred A. Knopf, 2009), pp. 510–511, 541–542.

69. Julius Grodinsky, *Jay Gould: His Business Career, 1867–1892* (Philadelphia: University of Pennsylvania Press, 1957), pp. 150–153; Western Union, *Annual Report* (1873), p. 3; Orton to Vanderbilt, November 19, 1875, PL, WU-SI.

70. Orton to Samuel Kepler, February 23, 1870, PL, WU-SI.

71. Orton to George Ladd, January 10, 1878, PL, WU-SI.

72. "Congress and the Telegraph," *Telegrapher* 8 (December 9, 1871): 122.

73. "The Future of the Telegraph in the United States," *Telegrapher* 8 (September 23, 1871): 36.

74. "The Hatchet Buried—Horace Greeley at the White House—The President Lectured," *New York Herald,* January 4, 1871.

75. "Combination the Only Safety," *Telegrapher* 7 (January 14, 1871): 164.

76. *Congressional Globe,* December 5, 1871, 42nd Cong., 2nd sess., 17; *Commercial Advertiser* (New York), December 5, 1871.

77. *New York Sun,* December 9, 1871.

78. "The Western Union Telegraph Company—A Card," *New York Times,* February 7, 1868.

79. Orton, *Government Telegraphs,* p. 28.

80. *Telegrapher* 2 (August 1, 1866): 169; George B. Prescott, *The Proposed Union of the Telegraph and Postal Systems: Statement of the Western Union Company* (Cambridge, Mass.: Welsh, Bigelow, and Co., 1869); Orton to Prescott, December 12, 1868, PL, WU SI.

81. James A. Garfield, *Diary:* vol. 2, *1872–1874* (East Lansing: Michigan State University Press, 1967), p. 45.

82. Jorma Ahvenainen, *The History of the Caribbean Telegraphs before the First World War* (Helsinki: Suomalainen Tiedeakatemia, 1996), p. 50.

83. "Telegraphic Progress in America in 1874–5," *Telegraphic Journal* 3 (November 15, 1875): 268.

84. Orton to Stager, February 15, 1870, PL, WU-SI.

85. Orton to James D. Reid, November 21, 1869, PL, WU-SI.

86. "The Situation," *Operator* 3 (August 15, 1875): 6.

87. James Anderson, "Statistics of Telegraphy," *Journal of the Statistical Society of London* 35 (September 1872): 309, 312.

88. Ibid., pp. 275, 284.

89. "Would a Postal Telegraph Be Cheap?" *Nation* 15 (December 19, 1872): 403; Hubbard, "Proposed Changes," p. 95.

90. Orton to Prescott, September 21, 1876, PL, WU-SI.

91. Green to Charles H. Haskins, October 28, 1881, PL, WU-SI.

92. W. C. Rogers, "Liability of Telegraph Company for Mental Suffering," *American Law Review* 29 (March–April 1895): 209–226.

93. "Telegraph-Buying," *New York Tribune,* December 12, 1871.

94. Orton to D. W. Patterson, January 20, 1868, PL, WU-SI.

95. *Postal-Telegraph Bill,* May 27, 1874, pp. 17, 21.

96. *Argument of William Orton on the Postal Telegraph Bill . . . January 20, 21, 22, and 23* (New York: n.p., 1874), p. 61.

97. House Judiciary Committee, "In the Matter of the Western Union Telegraph Company," 43rd Cong., 1875, pp. 22–23, HJ-TI, RG 233, National Archives.

98. House Judiciary Committee, "Western Union," p. 24.

99. Menahem Blondheim, "Rehearsal for Media Regulation: Congress versus the Telegraph-News Monopoly, 1866–1900," *Federal Communications Law Journal* 56 (March 2004): 299–327.

100. William Henry Smith to Rutherford B. Hayes, September 6, 1876, Hayes Presidential Center, Fremont, Ohio.

101. Henry Watterson, "*Marse Henry*": *An Autobiography,* vol. 1 (New York: G. H. Doran, 1919), p. 296; Isaac F. Marcosson, "*Marse Henry*": *A Biography of Henry Watterson* (1951; Westport, Conn.: Greenwood Press, 1971), p. 118.

102. Orton to Edwin D. Morgan, July 18, 1872, Morgan Papers, New York State Library, Albany, N.Y.

103. Charles Richard Williams, *The Life of Rutherford Birchard Hayes: Nineteenth President of the United States,* vol. 2 (Boston: Houghton Mifflin Co., 1914), pp. 142–169.

104. Green to Shelby Cullom, February 24, 1888, PL, WU-SI; David J. Seipp, *The Right to Privacy in American History* (Cambridge, Mass.: Program on Information Resources Policy, 1978), pp. 31–38.

105. Orton to Manton Marble, May 29, 1868, vol. 18, Marble Papers, LC.

106. Orton to James B. Beck, February 3, 1872, PL, WU-SI.

107. *Postal Telegraph System,* 41st Cong., 2nd sess., 1870, H. Rpt. 115 (serial 1438), p. 2.

108. Orton to Prescott, December 12, 1868, PL, WU-SI.

109. S. N. D. North, *History and Present Condition of the Newspaper and Periodical Press of the United States* (Washington, D.C.: U.S. Government Printing Office, 1881), p. 107.

110. *Report to Accompany Amendment to H. R. 6471,* 45th Cong., 3rd sess, 1879, S. Rpt. 805 (serial 1838), pp. 38–40.

111. *Minutes of a Hearing before the Committee on Railroads . . . January 28, 1879,* p. 100.

112. Henry George, "The Western Union Telegraph Company and the California Press," *New York Herald,* April 25, 1869; Charles Albro Barker, *Henry George* (New York: Oxford University Press, 1955), pp. 112–119.

113. "The Telegraph Monopoly," *Daily Graphic* (New York), September 15, 1874; "Free Trade in News," *Daily Graphic,* November 7, 1874.

114. House Judiciary Committee, "Western Union," pp. 28–29.

115. Orton to Stager, February 26, 1869, PL, WU-SI.

116. Orton to Stager, May 31, 1873, PL, WU-SI.

117. White to Washburne, June 4, 1868, Washburne Papers, LC.

118. Western Associated Press, *Proceedings* (1873), p. 10.

119. Western Union, *Annual Report* (1873), p. 21.

120. W. H. Preece, "American Telegraph System," *Journal of the Society of Telegraph Engineers* 7 (1878): 35.

121. Stephen B. Adams and Orville R. Butler, *Manufacturing the Future: A History of Western Electric* (Cambridge: Cambridge University Press, 1999), chap. 1.

122. David Hochfelder, "'Where the Common People Could Speculate': The Ticker, Bucket Shops, and the Origins of Popular Participation in Financial

Markets, 1880–1920," *Journal of American History* 93 (September 2006): 335–358.

123. "Nebulae," *Galaxy* 14 (December 1872): 871.

124. Paul Israel, *From Machine Shop to Industrial Laboratory: Telegraphy and the Changing Context of American Invention, 1830–1920* (Baltimore, Md.: Johns Hopkins University Press, 1992), pp. 125–127, 210–211n16.

125. Orton to Henry Weaver, February 11, 1876, PL, WU-SI.

126. Orton to R. M. Pulsiver, December 12, 1876, PL, WU-SI.

127. Cited in Israel, *Machine Shop to Industrial Laboratory,* p. 138.

128. "The Telephone," *Journal of the Telegraph* 2 (June 1, 1869): 1.

129. David A. Hounshell, "Elisha Gray and the Telephone: On the Disadvantages of Being an Expert," *Technology and Culture* 16 (April 1975): 138–152.

130. Thomas P. Hughes, *Networks of Power: Electrification in Western Society, 1880–1930* (Baltimore, Md.: Johns Hopkins University Press, 1983), pp. 94–95.

131. Hounshell, "Elisha Gray," p. 157.

132. Orton to James Gamble, February 23, 1878, PL, WU-SI.

133. James D. Reid, *The Telegraph in America: Its Founders, Promoters, and Noted Men* (New York: Derby Brothers, 1879), p. 531.

134. Sarah Bradford Landau and Carl W. Condit, *The Rise of the New York Skyscraper, 1865–1913* (New Haven, Conn.: Yale University Press, 1996), pp. 78–82.

135. Leonard Huxley, ed., *Life and Letters of Thomas Henry Huxley,* vol. 1 (New York: D. Appleton and Co., 1900), p. 494.

136. Cited in Thomas P. Van Leeuwen, *The Skyward Trend of Thought: The Metaphysics of the American Skyscraper* (Cambridge, Mass.: MIT Press, 1988), p. 36.

137. David M. Scobey, *Empire City: The Making and Meaning of the New York City Landscape* (Philadelphia: Temple University Press, 2002), p. 170.

138. "Color in Architecture," *Appleton's Journal* 13 (1875): 55–56.

139. Montgomery Schuyler, "The 'Sky-Scraper' Up to Date," *Architectural Record* 8 (January–March 1899): 232.

140. "Time-Ball Service Resumed," *Electrical Age* 10 (June 18, 1892): 335.

141. Alexis McCrossen, "Time Balls: Marking Modern Times in Urban America, 1877–1922," *Material History Review* 52 (Fall 2000): 11.

5. Rich Man's Mail

1. Murat Halstead and J. Frank Beale Jr., *Life of Jay Gould: How He Made His Millions* (Philadelphia: Edgewood Publishers, 1892), p. 299.

2. Trumball White, *The Wizard of Wall Street and His Wealth: Life and Deeds of Jay Gould* (n.p., 1892), p. 152; Victor Morris Tyler, *A Short History of*

Connecticut Telephony, 1878 to 1907 (New Haven, Conn.: Victor Morris Tyler, 1957), p. 9.

3. Matthew Josephson, *The Robber Barons: The Great American Capitalists, 1861–1901* (1934; New York: Harcourt, Brace & World, 1962), p. vi.

4. Daniel T. Rodgers, "In Search of Progressivism," *Reviews in American History* 10 (December 1982): 123–124.

5. John Stuart Mill, "Differences Arising from Natural Monopolies," and "Cases of Delegated Management," in *Principles of Political Economy* (Boston: Charles C. Little & James Brown, 1848), vol. 1, pp. 465–468, and vol. 2, p. 539.

6. Gould to William E. Chandler, January 10, 15, 16, 1875, Chandler Papers, Library of Congress, Washington, D.C. (hereafter LC); Margaret Susan Thompson, *The "Spider Web": Congress and Lobbyists in the Age of Grant* (Ithaca, N.Y.: Cornell University Press, 1985), pp. 264–265.

7. Robert Charles Post, *Physics, Patents, and Politics: A Biography of Charles Grafton Page* (New York: Science History Publications, 1976), pp. 173–181.

8. Orton to Joseph Medill, June 9, 1876, president's letterbook, Western Union Collection, Archives Center, National Museum of American History, Smithsonian Institution, Washington, D.C. (hereafter PL, WU-SI).

9. Gould to William E. Chandler, January 18, 1875, Chandler Papers, LC.

10. Paul Israel, *Edison: A Life of Invention* (New York: John Wiley & Sons, 1998), pp. 97–104; "The Dispute over the Quadruplex," in *The Papers of Thomas A. Edison,* vol. 2, ed. Reeve V. Jenkins et al. (Baltimore, Md.: Johns Hopkins University Press, 1991), pp. 794–815.

11. Cited in E. C. Baker, *Sir William Preece, F.R.S., Victorian Engineer Extraordinary* (London: Hutchinson, 1976), p. 157; Orton to J. B. Stearns, December 2, 1874; Orton to Thomas A. Edison and George B. Prescott, January 19, 1875; both in PL, WU-SI.

12. Paul Israel, "Telegraphy and Edison's Invention Factory," in William S. Pretzer, ed., *Working at Inventing: Thomas A. Edison and the Menlo Park Experience* (Baltimore, Md.: Johns Hopkins University Press, 2002), pp. 66–83.

13. Jesse W. Markham, "The Joint Effects of Antitrust and Patent Laws upon Innovation," *American Economic Review* 56 (March 1966): 291–300.

14. David A. Hounshell, "Elisha Gray and the Telephone: On the Disadvantages of Being an Expert," *Technology and Culture* 16 (April 1975): 133–161; Robert V. Bruce, *Bell: Alexander Graham Bell and the Conquest of Solitude* (1973; Ithaca, N.Y.: Cornell University Press, 1990), p. 210.

15. Bruce, *Bell,* pp. 141–142, 229–230; Catherine Mackenzie, *Alexander Graham Bell: The Man Who Conquered Space* (Boston: Houghton Mifflin, 1928), pp. 157–158.

16. Bruce, *Bell,* chaps. 16, 19.

17. Joel A. Tarr, with Thomas Finholt and David Goodman, "The City and the Telegraph: Urban Telecommunications in the Pre-Telephone Era," *Journal of Urban History* 14 (November 1987): 38–80.

18. Hubbard to Alexander Graham Bell, February 1, 5, 8, 22, 1878, family correspondence, Bell Family Papers, LC.

19. Gould to William E. Chandler, January 27, 1875, Chandler Papers, LC.

20. Bruce, *Bell*, p. 141.

21. Butler to James H. Goodsell, June 6, 20, 1877, Butler Papers, box 217, LC.

22. Edward C. Mack, *Peter Cooper: Citizen of New York* (New York: Duell, Sloan, and Pearce, 1949), pp. 308–309; Thurman Wilkins, *Clarence King: A Biography* (Albuquerque: University of New Mexico Press, 1988), p. 259.

23. Mack, *Peter Cooper*, pp. 308–309.

24. Orton to Samuel S. White, March 1, 1878, PL, WU-SI.

25. Green to William H. Forbes, July 2, 1879, PL, WU-SI.

26. "An Act Making Appropriations for the Support of the Army," in *Statutes at Large of the United States of America, 1789–1873*, vol. 21, chap. 35 (Boston: Little, Brown, 1879), p. 31.

27. *Minutes of a Hearing before the Committee on Railroads . . . January 28, 1879*, p. 12.

28. Typescript of newspaper interview, February 27, 1879, box 221, Butler Papers, LC.

29. *Congressional Record*, February 22, 1879, 45th Cong., 3rd sess., 1763.

30. *Minutes of a Hearing before the Committee on Railroads . . . January 28, 1879*, p. 84.

31. "Telegraph Lines," 43rd Cong., 2nd sess., H. Rpt. 125, 1875 (serial 1657), p. 1; *Telegrapher* 11 (January 30, 1875): 26.

32. *Minutes of a Hearing before the Committee on Railroads . . . January 28, 1879*, p. 35.

33. *Pensacola v. Western Union*, 96 U.S. 1 (1877) 9.

34. James H. Goodsell, "Two Powerful Monopolies," *Daily Graphic* (New York), February 19, 1879.

35. *American Union Telegraph Co.* (n.p., 1880), American Union Records, Western Union Collection, Archives Center, National Museum of American History, Smithsonian Institution, Washington, D.C. (hereafter WU-SI).

36. *Western Union v. American Union*, 29 Fed. Cas. 790 (1879); "Another Blow for Telegraph Monopoly," *Daily Graphic*, October 17, 1879.

37. Green to Edwin D. Morgan, February 27, 1880; Green to George S. Hale, August 28, 1880; both in PL, WU-SI.

38. Green to Hugh Allan, August 19, 1879, PL, WU-SI.

39. "Getting Ready to Cut the Melon," *Daily Graphic*, October 30, 1878.

40. "About the Telegraph," *Daily Graphic*, October 28, 1878; "Sliced Up at Last," *Daily Graphic*, June 12, 1879; Maury Klein, *The Life and Legend of Jay Gould* (Baltimore, Md.: Johns Hopkins University Press, 1986), p. 196.

41. Agreement between Western Union and National Bell, November 10, 1879, in Federal Communications Commission, *Accounting Department: Telephone*

Investigation, vol. 3 [Washington, D.C.: Federal Communications Commission], 1936–1937, app. 7.

42. "Royalties Paid the Western Union," *Electrical Review* 29 (September 30, 1896): 1; David Hochfelder, "Constructing an Industrial Divide: Western Union, AT&T, and the Federal Government, 1871–1971," *Business History Review* 76 (Winter 2002): 705–732.

43. "The Telephone on Top," *Electrical World* 54 (November 29, 1909): 1.

44. J. Leigh Walsh, *Connecticut Pioneers in Telephony: The Origin and Growth of the Telephone Industry in Connecticut* (New Haven, Conn.: Telephone Pioneers of America, 1950), pp. 76–90.

45. Green to George Gifford, July 8, 1879, PL, WU-SI.

46. Forbes to James Jackson Storrow, January 1880, in Arthur S. Pier, *Forbes: Telephone Pioneer* (New York: Dodd, Mead & Co., 1953), p. 133.

47. Charles McArthur Destler, *Henry Demarest Lloyd and the Empire of Reform* (Philadelphia: University of Pennsylvania Press, 1963), pp. 133–134.

48. "The Week," *Public Opinion* 4 (November 12, 1887): 97.

49. Lucius S. Merriam, "The Telegraphs of the Bond-Aided Pacific Railroads," *Political Science Quarterly* 9 (June 1894): 183–223.

50. Charles Francis Adams Jr., diary, February 1, 1889, Adams Papers, Massachusetts Historical Society.

51. Sherman to John Hay, February 10, 1884, Hay Papers, John Carter Brown Library, Brown University, Providence, R.I.

52. John Murray Forbes to George Jones, December 16, 1882, Chicago, Burlington, & Quincy Railroad Records, Newberry Library, Chicago, Ill.

53. National Board of Trade, *Proceedings* (1880), p. 167.

54. National Board of Trade, *Proceedings* (1875), pp. 70–71.

55. "Report" [1881], Board of Trade and Transportation Records, New York Historical Society, New York (hereafter NYHS).

56. "Our Principles," *Justice,* September 15, 1883.

57. New York Board of Trade and Transportation, board minutes, September 25, 1907, New York Board of Trade and Transportation Records, NYHS.

58. New York Chamber of Commerce, *Annual Report* (1881), pt. 1, p. 104.

59. Hubbard to Robert McCurdy, July 1, 1868, December 26, 1868, December 23, 1869, box 3, Hubbard Papers, LC; Hubbard, *Postal Telegraph: An Address Delivered by the Hon. Gardiner G. Hubbard, before the Chamber of Commerce of the State of New-York, April 3, 1890* (New York: Chamber of Commerce, 1890).

60. Resolution of the Peoria Board of Trade, 1888, HR 50A-H22.1, House Committee on the Post Office and Post Roads, RG 233, National Archives (hereafter HP-NA).

61. Henry Demarest Lloyd, "The Telegraph Consolidations," *Chicago Tribune,* January 14, 1881; Destler, *Henry Demarest Lloyd,* p. 546.

62. Cited in John Wanamaker, *An Argument in Support of the Limited Post and Telegraph* (Washington, D.C.: U.S. Government Printing Office, 1890), p. 191.

63. Dan Schiller, *Theorizing Communication* (New York: Oxford University Press, 1996), pp. 9–15.

64. This generalization is based on a reading of business, farm, and labor publications for the period between 1865 and 1892, and a keyword search of state party platforms for the period between 1877 and 1900.

65. National Grange, *Proceedings* (1886), p. 134; National Grange, *Proceedings* (1912), p. 148; Post Office Department, *Annual Report* (1911), p. 15.

66. "People's Party Platform," 1892; "People's Party Platform," 1896; both in Kirk H. Porter and Donald Bruce Johnson, eds., *National Party Platforms, 1840–1968* (Urbana: University of Illinois Press, 1970), pp. 52, 83, 91, 105.

67. Terence V. Powderly, *Thirty Years of Labor, 1859–1889* (1890; New York: Augustus M. Kelley, 1967), p. 200; Knights of Labor, *Proceedings* 11 (1888): 5–9.

68. Edward Topping James, "American Labor and Political Action, 1865–1896: The Knights of Labor and Its Predecessors" (Ph.D. diss., Harvard University, 1954), pp. 398–403.

69. Powderly, *Thirty Years of Labor, 1859–1889*, p. 200; petition from Knights of Labor in Benoitville, Wisconsin, January 9, 1888, HR50A-H22.1, House Committee on the Post Office and Post Roads, RG 233, HP-NA.

70. "A Great and Worthless Petition," *New York Times*, January 17, 1888; "The Postal-Telegraph Scheme," *New York Tribune*, January 28, 1888.

71. Lyman Abbott, "The Outlook," *Christian Union* 37 (January 26, 1888): 1.

72. Cited in *Statement of Mr. Gardiner G. Hubbard on Postal Telegraph . . . February 8, 1884*, p. 41.

73. Franklin H. Giddings, *Railroads and Telegraphs: Who Shall Control Them?* (Springfield, Mass.: Manufacturer and Industrial Gazette, 1881), pp. 7, 9; Giddings, "The Persistence of Competition," *Political Science Quarterly* 2 (March 1887): 62–78.

74. C. R. Perry, *The Victorian Post Office: The Growth of a Bureaucracy* (London: Royal Historical Society, 1992), chaps. 4–5; David Hochfelder, "A Comparison of the Postal Telegraph Movement in Great Britain and the United States, 1866–1900," *Enterprise and Society* 1 (December 2000): 743.

75. "The New Telegraph Monopoly," *Chicago Tribune*, January 6, 1881.

76. "The Movement for a Government Telegraph," *Chicago Tribune*, July 28, 1883.

77. "A New Telegraph Line," *New York Times*, July 29, 1881.

78. *Fortieth Anniversary of the Mackay System* (New York: Mackay Companies, 1924), pp. 14–15.

79. "Postal Telegraphy," *Electrical Review* 3 (November 22, 1883): 7.

80. William W. Cook, "John W. Mackay," in Sam P. Davis, ed., *History of Nevada*, vol. 2 (Reno: Elms Publishing Co., 1913), p. 1065.

81. *Appeal* (Carson, Nev.), [c. 1883], Scrapbook, 1883–1884, WU-SI.

82. William W. Cook, "John W. Mackay," *Postal Telegraph* (January 1914): 5–6.

83. "John William Mackay," in Henry Hall, ed., *America's Successful Men of Affairs: An Encyclopedia of Contemporaneous Biography*, vol. 1 (New York: New York Tribune, 1895), p. 423.

84. E. L. Godkin, "The Threatened Strike of the Telegraphers," *Nation* 37 (July 19, 1883): 47; Godkin to Schurz, July 24, 1883, in William M. Armstrong, ed., *The Gilded Age Letters of E. L. Godkin* (Albany: State University of New York Press, 1974), pp. 299–300;

85. "The Telegraph Strike," New York *Evening Post,* August 8, 1883; William M. Armstrong, *E. L. Godkin: A Biography* (Albany: State University of New York Press, 1978), p. 150.

86. Carl Schurz, "Corporations, Their Employés, and the Public," *North American Review* 138 (February 1884): 101–119.

87. William M. Armstrong, "The Godkin-Schurz Feud, 1881–1883, over Policy-Control of the *Evening Post,*" *New-York Historical Society Quarterly* 48 (January 1964): 19–20.

88. Lyman Abbott, "The Outlook," *Christian Union* 37 (February 2, 1888): 130.

89. Green to Henry H. Bingham, December 11, 1890, PL, WU-SI.

90. "Popularizing the Telegraph," *Journal of the Telegraph* 17 (June 20, 1884): 84; Frederick Leland Rhodes, *Beginnings of Telephony* (New York: Harper & Brothers, 1929), app. B ("Early Uses of the Word 'Telephone' ").

91. Mill, *Principles of Political Economy,* vol. 2, pp. 537–538.

92. "The Government and the Telegraph," *Electrician and Electrical Engineer* 3 (January 1884): 1.

93. David Bennett King, "The Telegraph Question," *Princeton Review* 7 (September 1884): 166–167.

94. Woodrow Wilson, "The Study of Administration," *Political Science Quarterly* 2 (June 1887): 201.

95. Alfred D. Chandler, *Municipal Control of Commercial Lighting: "Nationalism" Analyzed* (Boston: n.p., 1889), pp. 22–26.

96. Henry Willard Austin, "Reviews," *Nationalist* 1 (June 1889): 62.

97. Edward Bellamy, *Equality,* 2nd ed. (New York: D. Appleton and Co., 1897), pp. 376–377

98. William Windom, "Senator Windom's Letter," February 19, 1881, Windom Papers, Minnesota Historical Society.

99. Louis A. Coolidge, *An Old-Fashioned Senator: Orville H. Platt of Connecticut* (New York: G. P. Putnam's Sons, 1910), p. 442.

100. *Congressional Record,* January 19, 1883, 48th Cong., 1st sess., 1334–1335.

101. Francis P. Blair to Van Buren, July 14, 1836, Van Buren Papers, LC.

102. Joseph Bucklin Bishop, *Our Political Drama: Conventions, Campaigns, Candidates* (New York: Scott-Thaw, 1904), p. 156; Samuel J. Thomas, "The Tattooed Man Caricatures and the Presidential Campaign of 1884," *Journal of American Culture* 10 (Winter 1987): 1–20.

103. H. C. Bunner, "Cartoons and Comments," *Puck* 8 (January 26, 1881): 346.

104. Joseph Keppler, "Consolidated," *Puck* 8 (January 26, 1881): front cover.

105. James A. Wales, "The Best Monopolist," *Judge* 2 (October 7, 1882): 2.

106. James A. Wales, "The Best Kind of Monopoly," *Judge* 2 (October 7, 1882): front cover.

107. "Thomas L. James, "The Man Who Stamped Out the Star Route Swindle," *Puck* 10 supplement (October 19, 1881): 96.

108. Henry Watterson, "*Marse Henry*": *An Autobiography,* vol. 1 (New York: G. H. Doran, 1919), p. 201.

109. "Doctor Norvin Green," in *Encyclopedia of Contemporary Biography of New York,* vol. 5 (New York: Atlantic Publishing and Engraving Co., 1887), p. 332.

110. Green to Mrs. Benjamin Burton, November 23, 1887, Green letterbooks, Green Papers, Filson Historical Society, Louisville, Ky. (hereafter FHS).

111. "Doctor Norvin Green," in *Encyclopedia of Contemporary Biography,* vol. 5, p. 332.

112. "Is the Telegraph War to End?" *Electrical World* 8 (October 9, 1886): 174.

113. "John William Mackay," in Hall, *America's Successful Men of Affairs,* vol. 1, p. 423.

114. "Private Telegraph Wires," *Review of the Telegraph and Telephone* 2 (August 2, 1883): 7.

115. Thomas A. Edison, "Mr. Edison's Notes," in *The Papers of Thomas A. Edison,* vol. 2, ed. Reeve V. Jenkins et al. (Baltimore, Md.: Johns Hopkins University Press, 1991), p. 789.

116. *Report of the Committee of the Senate upon the Relations between Labor and Capital,* vol. 1 (Washington, D.C.: U.S. Government Printing Office, 1885), pp. 1074–1075.

117. Thomas R. Navin and Marian V. Sears, "The Rise of a Market for Industrial Securities, 1887–1902," *Business History Review* 29 (June 1955): 124–125; Sears, "The American Businessman at the Turn of the Century," *Business History Review* 30 (December 1956): 411–413, 442–443.

118. Murat Halstead, "Increase of the Standing Army," *North American Review* 146 (March 1888): 311.

119. *New York Herald,* September 6, 1883.

120. Gould to William Henry Smith, June 2, 1882, box 3, Smith Papers, Indiana Historical Society, Indianapolis, Ind.

121. Klein, *Jay Gould,* pp. 135–136, 394; Don C. Seitz, *Joseph Pulitzer: His Life and Letters* (New York: Simon & Schuster, 1924), pp. 126–131.

122. *A Talk on Telegraphic Topics: A Bid for Business* (New York: Francis Hart & Co., [1882]), pp. 32, 40.

123. *Labor and Capital,* vol. 1, p. 1071.

124. "A Dangerous Gamble," *New York World,* November 8, 1884; "A Postal Telegraph," *New York World,* November 9, 1884; "Jay Gould's Bluffing," *New York Times,* November 6, 1884; *New York Times,* November 7, 1884.

125. Green to Stephen B. French, November 6, 1884, PL, WU-SI.

126. Green to Abram Hewitt, December 8, 1888, Green Papers, FHS.

127. *New York Times,* November 7, 1884.

128. Henry C. Adams, "Relation of the State to Industrial Action," *Publications of the American Economic Association* 1 (January 1887): 52, 64.

129. Ely, *Problems of To-Day: A Discussion of Protective Tariffs, Taxation, and Monopolies,* 3rd ed. (New York: Thomas Y. Crowell & Co., 1890), pp. 117–118.

130. Ibid., p. 108.

131. Ely, "Social Studies: The Future of Corporations," *Harper's New Monthly Magazine* 75 (July 1887): 264n.

132. Richard T. Ely, "Natural Monopolies and the Workingman: A Programme of Social Reform," *North American Review* 158 (March 1894): 302.

133. *Western Electrician* 17 (October 19, 1895): 190.

134. Ely, *Problems of To-Day,* pp. 110, 272, 283.

135. A. W. Coats, "Henry Carter Adams: A Case Study in the Emergence of the Social Sciences in the United States, 1850–1900," *Journal of American Studies* 2 (October 1968): 191.

136. Henry C. Adams, "Surplus Financiering," in Albert Shaw, ed., *The National Revenues: A Collection of Papers by American Economists* (Chicago: A. C. McClurg & Co., 1888), pp. 49–50.

137. Henry C. Adams, *Public Debts: An Essay in the Science of Finance* (London: Longman, Green, and Co., 1888), p. 281.

138. Arthur T. Hadley, "Telegraph Charges in Germany and America," *Nation* 49 (August 1, 1889): 85.

139. Arthur T. Hadley, "Jay Gould and Socialism," *Forum* 14 (January 1893): 689.

140. Arthur T. Hadley, "Some Difficulties of Public Business Management," *Political Science Quarterly* 3 (December 1888): 572.

141. Ibid., p. 576.

142. Joseph Keppler, *J. Keppler: A Selection of Cartoons from Puck,* ed. H. C. Bunner (New York: Keppler & Schwarzmann, 1893), p. 10.

143. Thomas L. Haskell, *Objectivity Is Not Neutrality: Explanatory Schemes in History* (Baltimore, Md.: Johns Hopkins University Press, 1998), chap. 10.

6. The Talking Telegraph

1. J. E. Kingsbury, *The Telephone and Telephone Exchanges: Their Invention and Development* (London: Longmans, Green, & Co., 1915), pp. 497–498.

2. "Telephonic Novel," *Manufacturer and Builder* 10 (June 1878): 134.

3. William Dean Howells, "A Sennight of the Centennial," *Atlantic Monthly* 38 (July 1876): 92–107.

4. Gerald W. Brock, *The Telecommunications Industry: The Dynamics of Market Structure* (Cambridge, Mass.: Harvard University Press, 1981), pp. 107–108.

5. Ralph Waldo Emerson, *Works of Ralph Waldo Emerson,* vol. 8 (Cambridge, Mass.: Riverside Press, 1883), p. 101; Arthur S. Pier, *Forbes: Telephone Pioneer* (New York: Dodd, Mead & Co., 1953), p. 7.

6. N. R. Danielian, *AT&T: The Story of Industrial Conquest* (New York: Vanguard, 1939), p. 42.

7. Arthur M. Johnson and Barry E. Supple, *Boston Capitalists and Western Railroads: A Study in the Nineteenth-Century Railroad Investment Process* (Cambridge, Mass.: Harvard University Press, 1967), p. 337.

8. Pier, *Forbes,* p. 123.

9. Thomas D. Lockwood, "Ten Years of Progress in Practical Telephony," National Telephone Exchange Association (hereafter NTEA), *Proceedings* (September 1887): 66.

10. Danielian, *AT&T,* p. 94.

11. Christopher Beauchamp, "The Telephone Patents: Intellectual Property, Business and the Law in the United States and Britain, 1876–1900" (Ph.D. diss., University of Cambridge, 2006), chap. 4.

12. The Telephone Cases, 126 U.S. 1 (1888) 536.

13. NTEA, *Proceedings* (September 1888): 16.

14. Charles Fairman, *History of the Supreme Court of the United States,* vol. 7, pt. 2: *Reconstruction and Reunion, 1864–88* (New York: Macmillan, 1987), p. 127.

15. Warren J. Harder, *Daniel Drawbaugh: The Edison of the Cumberland Valley* (Philadelphia: University of Pennsylvania Press, 1960), chap. 2.

16. The Telephone Cases, 126 U.S. 1 (1888) 574.

17. American Bell, *Annual Report* (1884), p. 5.

18. Forbes to Howard Stockton, April 5, 1888, president's file, AT&T Archives and History Center, Warren, N.J. (hereafter AT&T-NJ).

19. Frank B. Williams, "The Pan-Electric Telephone Controversy," *Tennessee Historical Quarterly* 2 (June 1943): 144–162; Homer Cummings and Carl McFarland, *Federal Justice: Chapters in the History of Justice and the Federal Executive* (New York: Macmillan, 1937), pp. 296–305.

20. Cited in *Testimony Taken by the Committee Appointed by the House of Representatives to Investigate Charges Against Certain Public Officers Relating to the Pan-Electric Telephone Company, and to Suits by the United States to Annul the Bell Telephone Patents*, 49th Cong., 1st sess., 1886, H. Misc., Doc. 355 (serial 2424), p. 781.

21. H. Casey Young to J. Webb Rogers, August 21, 1883, in *Pan-Electric Telephone Company*, p. 208.

22. Bernard S. Finn, "Bell and Gray: Just a Coincidence," *Technology and Culture* 50 (January 2009): 193–201.

23. "The Government in the Telephone Suit," *New York Times,* September 26, 1885; "A Bluff Game," *New York Times,* March 4, 1886; "Mr. Hubbard's Company," *New York Times,* April 30, 1886; "The Telephone Reports," *New York Times,* June 30, 1886; "Copyright and Telephones," *New York Times,* January 29, 1890; Williams, "Pan-Electric Controversy," p. 158.

24. Cited in Pier, *Forbes,* p. 172.

25. "The Western Union and the Bell Company," *Chicago Tribune,* February 27, 1886.

26. *Puck* 18 (February 17, 1886): 386.

27. George David Smith, *The Anatomy of a Business Strategy: Bell, Western Electric, and the Origins of the American Telephone Industry* (Baltimore, Md.: Johns Hopkins University Press, 1985), chap. 4.

28. Robert W. Garnet, *The Telephone Enterprise: The Evolution of Bell's Horizontal Structure, 1876–1909* (Baltimore, Md.: Johns Hopkins University Press, 1985), chap. 2.

29. American Bell, *Annual Report* (1885), pp. 24–26.

30. Victor Morris Tyler, *A Short Review of Connecticut Telephony, 1878 to 1907* (New Haven, Conn.: Victor Morris Tyler, 1957), p. 65.

31. James E. Caldwell, *Recollections of a Life Time* (Nashville, Tenn.: Baird-Ward Press, 1923), pp. 194–195; Albert Bigelow Paine, *In One Man's Life: Being Chapters from the Personal and Business Career of Theodore N. Vail* (New York: Harper & Brothers, 1921), chap. 31.

32. Angus Hibbard, James J. Carty, and Frank A. Pickernell, "The New Era in Telephony," NTEA, *Proceedings* (September 1889): 34–43; Angus Hibbard, *Hello Goodbye: My Story of Telephone Pioneering* (Chicago: A. C. McClurg & Co., 1941), pp. 134–136.

33. Hibbard, *Hello Goodbye,* chap. 8.

34. American Telephone and Telegraph, *Annual Report* (1908), p. 22.

35. J. Leigh Walsh, *Connecticut Pioneers in Telephony: The Origin and Growth of the Telephone Industry in Connecticut* (New Haven, Conn.: Telephone Pioneers of America, 1950), p. 143.

36. J. Warren Stehman, *The Financial History of the American Telephone and Telegraph Company* (Boston: Houghton Mifflin Co., 1925), p. 217.

37. Norvin Green to Peters, Schneck & Co., July 27, 1889, personal letterbook, Green Papers, Filson Historical Society, Louisville, Ky.

38. Frank Colvin to Winfield S. Hutchinson, November 29, 1899, Colvin letterbook, AT&T-NJ.

39. Hubbard to Hudson, June 23, 1889, box 1264, AT&T-NJ.

40. Hubbard to Forbes, October 29, 1885, box 1115, AT&T-NJ.

41. Hubbard to Hudson, January 20, 1890, box 1264, AT&T-NJ.

42. David A. Hounshell, "Elisha Gray and the Telephone: On the Disadvantages of Being an Expert," *Technology and Culture* 16 (April 1975): 152; Hibbard, *Hello Goodbye*, p. 23.

43. *Investigation of the Telephone and Telegraph Companies in New York State*, 1910, S. Rpt. 37, p. 932; Gregory J. Downey, *Telegraph Messenger Boys: Labor, Technology, Geography* (New York: Routledge, 2002), chap 3.

44. Richard R. John, "Theodore N. Vail and the Civic Origins of Universal Service," *Business and Economic History* 28 (Winter 1999): 77–79.

45. "The Fast Mail," *Harper's Weekly* 19 (October 9, 1875): 814–818.

46. John, "Civic Origins," p. 78.

47. "Vanderbilt in the West," *New York Times*, October 9, 1882; Henry Clews, *Twenty-Eight Years in Wall Street* (New York: Irving Publishing Co., 1887), p. 370.

48. Elton W. Hall, *Francis Blake: An Inventor's Life, 1850–1913* (Boston: Northeastern University Press, 2003), pp. 71–74.

49. Robert V. Bruce, *Bell: Alexander Graham Bell and the Conquest of Solitude* (1973: Ithaca, N.Y.: Cornell University Press, 1990), p. 284.

50. George L. Priest, "The Origins of Utility Regulation and the 'Theories of Regulation' Debate," *Journal of Law and Economics* 36 (April 1993): 289–323.

51. A. H. McMillan, *Telephone Law* (New York: McGraw Publishing Co., 1908), pp. 45–46.

52. John F. Dillon, *Commentaries on the Law of Municipal Corporations*, vol. 3 (Boston: Little, Brown, and Co., 1911), p. 1942.

53. Frederick S. Dickson, *Telephone Investments and Others* (Cleveland: Cuyahoga Telephone Co., 1905), p. 28.

54. *Telecom History* 1 (1994): 84; *Telecom History* 2 (1996): 96; *Telecom History* 3 (2002): 30.

55. Vail to Executive Committee, October 2, 1878, Chicago Telephone Company Records (hereafter CTCR), AT&T Archives and History Center, San Antonio, TX (hereafter AT&T-TX).

56. Hubbard to Vail, October 9, 1878, CTCR, AT&T-TX.

57. *Moran's Dictionary of Chicago* (Chicago: n.p.,1893), p. 247.

58. "The Metropolis of the Prairies," *Harpers' New Monthly Magazine* 61 (October 1880): 729–730.

59. "New Telephone Central Office," *New York Times,* January 4, 1894.

60. Frederic Harrison, "Impressions of America," *Current Literature* 31 (August 1901): 135.

61. "The Telephone," *New York Times,* January 1, 1886.

62. "Only $5 per Month," *Chicago Tribune,* April 13, 1895.

63. *Electrical Review* 10 (August 6, 1887): 6.

64. Thomas A. Edison, "The Phonograph and Its Future," *North American Review* 126 (May 1878): 536; Edison, "The Perfected Phonograph," *North American Review* 146 (June 1888): 649.

65. David F. Weiman, "Building 'Universal Service' in the Early Bell System: The Co-Evolution of Regional Urban Systems and Long-Distance Telephone Networks," in Timothy W. Guinnane et al., eds., *History Matters: Essays on Economic Growth, Technology, and Demographic Change* (Stanford, Calif.: Stanford University Press, 2004), p. 331.

66. Laurence Gronlund, *The New Economy: A Peaceable Solution of the Social Problem* (Chicago: Herbert S. Stone & Co., 1898), p. 241.

67. George C. Maynard, "The History of the Telephone," *Electrical Review* 32 (January 5, 1898): 14–15.

68. Kingsbury, *Telephone and Telephone Exchanges,* pp. 306–307; Maynard, "History of the Telephone," pp. 14–15.

69. "Prices of Political Trustees," *Chicago Tribune,* October 28, 1883.

70. William T. Stead, *If Christ Came to Chicago,* ed. Harvey Wish (1894; New York: Living Books, 1964), p. 181.

71. Werner Troesken, *Why Regulate Utilities? The New Institutional Economics and the Chicago Gas Industry, 1849–1924* (Ann Arbor: University of Michigan Press. 1994), chap. 2.

72. Morris F. Tyler, "Report of the Committee on Legislation," NTEA, *Proceedings* (September 1882): 29.

73. "The Telephone's One Competitor," *Electrical Review* 4 (July 19, 1884): 4.

74. W. G. Marshall, *Through America: Or. Nine Months in the United States* (London: Sampson Low, Marston, Searle & Rivington, 1881), p. 8.

75. David Brooks, *Argument of Mr. David Brooks, before the Judiciary General Committee of the Senate of the State of Pennsylvania* (Philadelphia: Burk & M'Fetridge, 1885), p. 8.

76. W. H. Preece, "American Telegraph System," *Journal of the Society of Telegraph Engineers* 7 (February 13, 1878): 36.

77. *Democrat Chronicle* (Rochester, N.Y.), February 16, 1888, March 20, 1888.

78. NTEA, *Proceedings* (September 1881): 18.

79. NTEA, *Proceedings* (October 1883): 31.

80. "An Act in Relation to Telegraph and Electric Light Companies in Cities of This State," in *Laws of the State of New York,* chap. 534 (Albany: Banks & Brothers, 1884), p. 647.

81. I. N. Phelps Stokes, *The Iconography of Manhattan Island, 1498–1909,* vol. 5 (New York: Robert T. Dodd, 1926), pp. 1985, 2023.

82. "The Board of Electrical Control of New York City," *Electrical Review* 27 (July 31, 1895): 58.

83. "Putting the Wires Underground," *Harper's Weekly* 33 (April 27, 1889): 331.

84. William L. Strong, "Report," January 12, 1897, in Stokes, *Iconography,* vol. 5, p. 2023.

85. Morris F. Tyler, "Report of the Committee on Legislation," in NTEA, *Proceedings* (September 1882): 22.

86. William O. Kurtz, *The Telephone in Chicago: A Story of Communication Progress* (n.p., 1944), p. 74.

87. New England Telephone and Telegraph, *Report* (1884), pp. 13–14.

88. *Electrical Review* 3 (December 27, 1883): 6; "London Telephone Wires May Be Strung Overhead," *Electrical Review* 6 (May 23, 1885): 4.

89. Williams to Vail, March 6, 1883, CTCR, AT&T-TX.

90. "Underground Telegraphy," *Manufacturer and Builder* 13 (March 1881): 51.

91. "The Telephone Wires Cannot Be Sunk," *Electrical Review* 4 (March 6, 1884): 6.

92. "Future of the Telephone: A Talk with Professor Bell," *New York Tribune,* December 21, 1884.

93. "What the Telegraph Companies Will Do Next," *Harper's Weekly* 30 (January 9, 1886): 32; "Whoa, There! What Are We Coming To?" *Harper's Young People* 11 (December 24, 1889): 144; "A Peep in the Future," *Judge* 11 (October 30, 1886): 16.

94. Paine, *In One Man's Life,* chap. 30.

95. "Theodore N. Vail: The Commander of a $500,000,000 Service Organization," *Public Service* 4 (June 1908): 165; Edward Mott Wooley, "A $100,000 Imagination," *McClure's* 43 (May 1914): 128–129; Paine, *In One Man's Life,* chap. 30.

96. William L. Strong, "Report," January 12, 1897, in Stokes, *Iconography,* vol. 5, p. 2023.

97. Tyler, *Short Review,* p. 4; Southern New England Telephone, *Report* (1884), p. 2; Southern New England Telephone, *Report* (1908), p. 8.

98. Walsh, *Connecticut Pioneers,* p. 157; Caldwell, *Recollections,* p. 129.

99. *City of Richmond v. Southern Bell Telephone & Telegraph Co.,* 174 U.S. 761 (1899); Morton Keller, *Regulating a New Economy: Public Policy and*

Economic Change in America, 1900–1933 (Cambridge, Mass.: Harvard University Press, 1990), p. 78.

100. Frederick Leland Rhodes, *Beginnings of Telephony* (New York: Harper & Brothers, 1929), pp. 130, 151–153.

101. "Chicago Telephone Annual," *Economist* (Chicago) 35 (January 20, 1905): 203.

102. "A Mighty Revolution," *Wall Street Journal,* January 23, 1907.

103. "Subscriber's Ticket," c. 1888, CTCR, AT&T-TX.

104. Kingsbury, *Telephone and Telephone Exchanges,* pp. 470, 473; "The Telephones," *Chicago Tribune,* July 19, 1881; "Telephone Tolls," *New York Times,* November 9, 1885.

105. "Editorial Notes from Chicago," *Electrical Review* 5 (November 22, 1884): 4.

106. Cited in Stephen R. Shearer, *Hoosier Connections: The History of the Indiana Telephone Industry and the Indiana Telephone Association* (Indianapolis: Indiana Telephone Association, 1992), pp. 29–30.

107. Metropolitan Telephone Company, "Subscriber's List," 1884, Warshaw Collection, Archives Center, Smithsonian Institution, Washington, D.C.

108. "New-Fangled Telephone Aimed to Defeat Deadheadism," *Chicago Tribune,* December 30, 1893.

109. "The 'Buffalo System,'" *Electrical Review* 5 (October 18, 1884): 4–5.

110. NTEA, *Proceedings* (September 1880): 175.

111. Ibid., p. 176.

112. Ibid., pp. 180, 184.

113. "The Telephone Dead Head Evil," *Electrical Review* 5 (February 28, 1885): 5.

114. NTEA, *Proceedings* (April 1881): 128.

115. NTEA, *Proceedings* (September 1880): 175, 177; Milton L. Mueller, "The Switchboard Problem: Scale, Signaling, and Organization in Manual Telephone Switching, 1877–1897," *Technology and Culture* 30 (July 1989): 534–560.

116. "The Telephone Dead Head Evil," *Electrical Review* 5 (February 28, 1885): 5.

117. Hall to William M. Mallett, October 10, 1886, *Union and Advertiser* (Rochester, N.Y.), October 22, 1886.

118. NTEA, *Proceedings* (April 1881): 119; *Chicago Tribune,* July 19, 1881.

119. NTEA, *Proceedings* (September 1880): 182.

120. Ibid., p. 183.

121. NTEA, *Proceedings* (April 1881): 120.

122. Ibid., p. 128.

123. "Chicago Telephone Year," *Economist* (Chicago) 21 (January 21, 1899): 71.

124. "The Chicago Telephone Company," *Economist* (Chicago) 18 (December 31, 1897): 769.

125. Brock, *Telecommunications Industry,* p. 109.

126. A. A. Thomas to C. Jay French, November 25, 1892; Thomas to John E. Hudson, March 6, 1894; Thomas to Angus Hibbard, July 29, 1895; Holt, Wheeler & Sidley to Frederick Fish, September 12, 1901; all in Chicago Telephone files, Sidley Austin Archives, Chicago (hereafter SA-C).

127. Thomas D. Lockwood to Holt, Wheeler & Sidley, August 13, 1903, SA-C.

128. R. B. Borden, "The Telephone in Illinois," chap. 3, p. 19, AT&T-TX; Charles Barnard, "The Telegraph of To-Day," *Harper's New Monthly Magazine* 63 (October 1881): 713.

129. Stephen H. Norwood, *Labor's Flaming Youth: Telephone Operators and Worker Militancy, 1878–1923* (Urbana: University of Illinois Press, 1990), chap. 1; Kenneth J. Lipartito, "When Women Were Switches: Technology, Work, and Gender in the Telephone Industry, 1890–1920," *American Historical Review* 99 (October 1994): 1075–1111.

130. Hibbard, *Hello Goodbye,* p. 137.

131. "New Telephone Exchange," *Electrical Review,* p. 1.

132. "The New Telephone Exchange," *Electrical Review* 3 (February 7, 1884): 2.

133. S. J. Larned, "The Telephone Exchange," *World To-Day* 8 (July 1907): 690; Walsh, *Connecticut Pioneers,* p. 240.

134. Kempster B. Miller, *American Telephone Practice* (New York: American Electrician Co., 1899), p. 201.

135. Ralph L. Mahon, "The Telephone in Chicago, 1877–1940," typescript, pp. 6–7, AT&T-TX.

136. Martha Joanna Lamb, *History of the City of New York: Its Origin, Rise, and Progress,* vol. 2 (New York: A. S. Barnes & Co., 1896), p. 827.

137. *Western Electrician* 28 (March 23, 1901): 198; "Arguments for and against Automatic Telephony," *Electrical World* 35 (March 10, 1900): 366.

138. Stanley Swihart, "Early Automatic Telephone Systems," *Telecom History* 2 (Spring 1995): 7; M. D. Fagen, ed., *A History of Engineering and Science in the Bell System: The Early Years (1875–1925)* (New York: Bell Telephone Laboratories, 1975), p. 495; Hibbard, *Hello Goodbye,* pp. 185, 202, 242.

139. Theodore N. Vail testimony, in *Western Union Telegraph Company et al. v. American Bell Telephone Company,* vol. 1 (Boston: The Clerk, 1909), pp. 1542, 1544; Lilian Hoddeson, "The Emergence of Basic Research in the Bell Telephone System, 1875–1915," *Technology and Culture* 22 (July 1981): 512–544.

140. A. A. Thomas to John E. Hudson, January 25, 1893, Chicago Telephone letterbook, SA-C.

141. Herbert Laws Webb, "The Future of the Telephone Industry," *Engineering Magazine* 2 (March 1892): 754–755.

142. "Telephone Patents Expiring—But It Will Apparently Bring Little Benefit to the People," *New York Times*, January 22, 1893.

7. Telephomania

1. Fay, "Address of the President," National Telephone Exchange Association (hereafter NTEA), *Proceedings* (September 1886): 7.

2. Fay, "Telephone Subscribers as Knights of Labor," NTEA, *Proceedings* (September 1887): 33.

3. Grant E. Hamilton, "In the Clutch of a Grasping Monopoly," *Judge* 14 (April 7, 1888): 16.

4. Richard T. Loomis, "The Telephone Comes to Washington: George C. Maynard, 1839–1919," *Washington History* 12 (Fall/Winter 2000–2001): 38.

5. "Strike of Business Men," *National Labor Tribune* (Pittsburgh), January 29, 1887; Fay, "Telephone Subscribers as Knights of Labor," pp. 27, 30; Norman Williams and John Leverett Thompson to Theodore N. Vail, July 18, 1885, Chicago Telephone Company files, Sidley Austin Archives, Chicago (hereafter SA-C).

6. *Post-Express* (Rochester, N.Y.), November 20, 1886; *Union and Advertiser* (Rochester, N.Y.), November 20, 1886; *Democrat Chronicle* (Rochester, N.Y.), May 15, 1888; *Electrical Review* 10 (March 5, 1887): 5; "Rochester Telephone Business," *Electrical Review* 11 (October 29, 1887): 1; Blake McKelvey, *Rochester: The Flower City, 1855–1890* (Cambridge, Mass.: Harvard University Press, 1949), pp. 253–254.

7. F. J. Amsden to William M. Mallett, December 22, 1886, Rochester file, AT&T Archives and History Center, Warren, N.J. (hereafter AT&T-NJ).

8. Robert S. Boyd to American Bell, December 10, 1886, Rochester file, AT&T-NJ.

9. *Post-Express*, December 2, 1886.

10. "Interview with Alexander Graham Bell," *Electrical Review* 10 (April 2, 1887): 6.

11. "Professor Alexander Graham Bell," *Electrical Review* 21 (September 10, 1892): 28.

12. *Union and Advertiser*, November 2, 1886.

13. *Democrat Chronicle*, November 25, 1886.

14. Hall to John E. Hudson, December 15, 1886 Rochester file, AT&T-NJ.

15. *Democrat Chronicle*, December 2, 1886.

16. Hall to Hudson, December 15, 1886, AT&T-NJ.

17. Harry B. Macmeal, *The Story of Independent Telephony* (Chicago: Independent Pioneer Telephone Association, 1934), pp. 110–111.

18. *Democrat Chronicle,* November 15, 1887, February 25. 1888.

19. Vail to _____, December 1, 1887, Rochester file, AT&T-NJ.

20. "Bad Telephone Service," *Chicago Tribune,* December 30, 1887.

21. Ibid.

22. "Telephones a Nuisance," *Chicago Tribune,* January 1, 1888.

23. "The Telephone," *Western Electrician* 2 (February 25, 1888): 107; "Chicago Telephone Controversy," *Western Electrician* 3 (August 25, 1888): 97.

24. "The Chicago Cushman Telephone Company," *Western Electrician* 2 (April 14, 1888): 181.

25. "The Telephone," *Western Electrician* 2 (January 21, 1888): 35.

26. "St. Louis Telephone Troubles," *Western Electrician* 2 (June 23, 1888): 310, 313.

27. "Chicago Telephone Matters," *Western Electrician* 3 (September 22, 1888): 160.

28. Chicago City Council, *Proceedings,* October 15, 1888, p. 443.

29. *Western Electrician* 3 (November 17, 1888): 258; *Western Electrician* 3 (November 24, 1888): 270.

30. "'L' Roads and 'Phones," *Chicago Tribune,* December 22, 1888.

31. "Chicago Telephone Question," *Western Electrician* 3 (December 22, 1888): 313.

32. "A Boodle Ordinance," *Chicago Tribune,* October 10, 1888.

33. William Bodemann et al., *Let Us Have a Fair Telephone Ordinance* [December 1888], Chicago City Council records, January 4, 1889, Northeastern Illinois University, Chicago, Ill. (hereafter CCC-NEIU).

34. *Special Ordinances of Chicago,* vol. 11, January 4, 1889 (Chicago: W. B. Conkey Co., 1898), p. 1870; George L. Phillips to mayor and city council, November 10, 1888, January 4, 1889, CCC-NEIU; *Chicago Telephone Company v. Illinois Manufacturers' Association,* 106 IL app. 54 (1903); "Walker Wants Cheaper 'Phones," *Chicago Tribune,* July 21, 1901.

35. "Concerning Telephone Charges," *Electrical Review* 6 (March 7, 1885): 4.

36. Forbes to Higginson, March 18, 1886, in Arthur S. Pier, *Forbes: Telephone Pioneer* (New York: Dodd, Mead & Co., 1953), pp. 156–157.

37. Walter S. Allen, "Public Service Corporations and the Government," 1914, p. 1, box 1067, AT&T-NJ.

38. Edward Bellamy, "First Steps toward Nationalism," *Forum* 10 (October 1890): 174–180; Edward Bellamy, "'Looking Backward' Again," *North American Review* 150 (March 1890): 362–363.

39. H. M. Boettinger, *The Telephone Book: Bell, Watson, Vail, and American Life, 1876–1976* (Croton-on-Hudson, N.Y.: Riverwood, 1977), p. 120.

40. Massachusetts Senate, *Resolution Relative to the Establishment of a Government Telegraph and Telephone Service,* March 31, 1893.

41. "An Act to Authorize the American Bell Telephone Company to Increase Its Capital Stock," in *Acts and Resolves Passed by the General Court of Massachusetts,* chap. 544 (Boston: Wright & Potter, 1894), pp. 753–754.

42. "The Telephone Question: The Effect of the Berliner Decision on the Industry," *Electrical Review* 25 (December 26, 1894): 320.

43. "An Act Relative to the Supervision by the Massachusetts Highway Commission of All Companies Engaged in the Transmission of Intelligence by Electricity," in *Acts and Resolves Passed by the General Court of Massachusetts,* chap. 433 (Boston: Wright & Potter, 1906), pp. 448–451.

44. "An Act to Change the Name, Enlarge the Membership and Increase the Powers of the Board of Railroad Commissioners," in *Acts and Resolves Passed by the General Court of Massachusetts,* chap. 784 (Boston: Wright & Potter, 1913), pp. 815–833.

45. "An Act to Regulate the Rental Allowed for the Use of Telephones, and Fixing a Penalty for its Violation," in *Laws of the State of Indiana,* chap. 92 (Indianapolis: William Burford, 1885), pp. 227–228.

46. Stephen R. Shearer, *Hoosier Connections: The History of the Indiana Telephone Industry and the Indiana Telephone Association* (Indianapolis: Indiana Telephone Association, 1992), pp. 34–35.

47. Fay, "Telephone Subscribers as Knights of Labor," p. 26.

48. W. W. Thornton "Supreme Court of Indiana, Hockett v. State," *American Law Register* 34 (May 1886): 318–319.

49. Ibid., p. 322.

50. American Bell, *Annual Report* (1885), p. 20.

51. Ibid., pp. 24, 26.

52. "The Telephone 'Monopoly,' " *Electrical Review* 6 (April 5, 1885): 4.

53. Executive Committee Minutes, 1887, Central Union Telephone Company, AT&T Archives and History Center, San Antonio, Tex. (hereafter AT&T-TX).

54. "Telephone Litigation in Indiana," *Electrical Review* 14 (March 9, 1889): 1.

55. NTEA, *Proceedings* (September 1885): 95.

56. "Thirty-Seven Telephone Suits," *New York Times,* October 17, 1887.

57. *Electrical Review* 11 (October 22, 1887): 6; "The Bell Company's Victory over Cushman," *Electrical Review* 13 (November 10, 1888): 1, 13.

58. Walton Hamilton, "Patents and Free Enterprise," in *Investigation of Concentration of Economic Power* (Washington, D.C.: U.S. Government Printing Office, 1941), p. 89.

59. Stanley Swihart, "Early Automatic Telephone Systems," *Telecom History* 2 (Spring 1995): 8.

60. Norman Williams and John Leverett Thompson to Vail, July 18, 1885, SA-C.

61. *Report of the Committee to Investigate Telephone Charges,* New York State Assembly Rpt. 60, 1888, pp. 67–70.

62. H. L. Storke, "Report on Legislation," NTEA, *Proceedings* (September 1886): 77.

63. American Bell Telephone Company, *Annual Report* (1886), p. 7.

64. "Telephone Rates in Iowa," *Chicago Tribune,* March 18, 1886.

65. "Telephone Litigation in Indiana," *Electrical Review* 14 (March 9, 1889): 1.

66. "The Indiana Telephone Laws Repealed," *Electrical Review* 14 (March 9, 1889): 4.

67. Robert J. Chapuis, *One-Hundred Years of Telephone Switching (1878–1978)* (Amsterdam: North-Holland Publishing Co., 1982), pp. 61–62.

68. NTEA, *Proceedings* (September 1884): 40.

69. Fay, "Address of the President," p. 7.

70. Fay to Vail, June 5, 1885, Chicago Telephone Company Records, AT&T-TX.

71. Fay, "Address of the President," p. 7.

72. Fay, "Telephone Subscribers as Knights of Labor," p. 24.

73. Fay, "Address of the President," pp. 7–8.

74. Ibid., p. 8.

75. Fay, "Telephone Subscribers as Knights of Labor," pp. 22–23.

76. Ibid., pp. 33, 34.

77. Fay's address can be found in the edition of the NTEA proceedings at the Crerar Library at the University of Chicago. All quotations are from the Crerar Library edition.

78. "Ninth Annual Meeting of the National Telephone Exchange Association," *Electrical World* 10 (October 1, 1887): 178; *Western Electrician* 1 (October 1, 1887): 161; *Electrical Review* 11 (October 1, 1887): 9.

79. William O. Kurtz, *The Telephone in Chicago: A Story of Communication Progress* (n.p., 1944), p. 72.

80. Charles N. Fay, "Is Democracy a Failure: Another Plain Tale from Chicago," *Outlook* 97 (April 8, 1911): 775.

81. Charles N. Fay, *Big Business and Government* (New York: Moffat, Yard, and Co., 1912), p. 191.

82. Ibid.

83. "Power of Removal Bill," *New York Times,* February 6, 1895.

84. "Simon Sterne's Telephone Safe," *New York Times,* December 29, 1895.

85. *Report of the Committee to Investigate Telephone Charges,* pp. 10–12, 58, 61, 75.

86. Ibid., pp. 58, 61.

87. "Topics of the Times," *New York Times,* November 4, 1901.

88. "The Telephone Business," *New York Times,* December 14, 1901; "Growth of the Telephone Service," *New York Times,* December 3, 1901.

89. "Cost of the Telephone," *New York Times,* March 6, 1895.

90. New York Board of Trade and Transportation, *Oppressive Telephone Charges* (New York: n.p., 1889), p. 5, Baker Library, Harvard Business School, Boston.

91. "Metropolitan Telephone and Telegraph Company," appendix to New York Board of Trade and Transportation, *Oppressive Telephone Charges*.

92. Simon Sterne, *Speech of Simon Sterne, Esq., before the Assembly Committee on General Laws, January 30, 1889, in Favor of Bill Limiting Telephone Charges* (New York: George F. Nesbitt & Co., 1889), pp. 5, 19.

93. "Does a Telephone Company Control Its Own Instruments?" *Electrical Review* 26 (February 6, 1895): 66; "The Telephone Controversy in New York State," *Electrical Review* 26 (March 27, 1895): 166.

94. "Telephones Too Costly," *New York Times*, February 3, 1895.

95. John Foord, *The Life and Public Services of Simon Sterne* (London: Macmillan and Co., 1903), p. 332.

96. "Cost of the Telephone," *New York Times*, March 6, 1895.

97. Sterne, *Speech*, pp. 18–19.

98. Benjamin Tracy, *Argument of Gen. Benjamin F. Tracy, Counsel for the Metropolitan Telephone and Telegraph Company, of New York, Against the Gerst-Persons Telephone Bill* (n.p., 1895).

99. Sven Beckert, "Democracy in the Age of Capital: Contesting Suffrage Rights in Gilded Age New York," in Meg Jacobs, William J. Novak, and Julian E. Zelizer, eds., *The Democratic Experiment: New Directions in American Political History* (Princeton, N.J.: Princeton University Press, 2003), pp. 146–174.

100. Charles Zueblin, *American Municipal Progress* (1902: New York: Macmillan Co., 1919), p. 359.

101. "Telephone Service No Longer in Demand," *Electrical Review* 36 (April 4, 1900): 332.

102. Albert Shaw, *Municipal Government in Continental Europe* (New York: Century Co., 1895); Shaw, *Municipal Government in Great Britain* (New York: Century Co., 1895).

103. Shaw, "Municipal Ownership-Discussion," *Publications of the American Economic Association* 7 (February 1906): 154.

104. Meighan Jeanne Maguire, "The Local Dynamics of Telephone System Development: The San Francisco Exchange, 1893–1919" (Ph.D. diss., University of California at San Diego, 1990), chap. 1.

105. "To Get a 'Phone Ruling," *Chicago Tribune*, June 30, 1901; "Telephone Grab Avoids Council," *Chicago Tribune*, June 30, 1903; "Platforms and Candidates," *Chicago Tribune*, March 4, 1907.

106. Morton Keller, *Regulating a New Economy: Public Policy and Economic Change in America, 1900–1933* (Cambridge, Mass.: Harvard University Press, 1990), p. 56.

107. Zueblin, *American Municipal Progress,* p. 371; Floyd R. Simpson, "Public Ownership of Telephones in the U.S.: A Survey of the Brookings, S.D. Telephone System," *Journal of Land and Public Utility Economics* 19 (February 1943): 99–103.

108. Douglass Steeples, *Advocate for American Enterprise: William Buck Dana and the Commercial and Financial Chronicle, 1865–1910* (Westport, Conn.: Greenwood Press, 2002), p. 158 ("municipal socialism"); Christopher Armstrong and H. V. Nelles, *Monopoly's Moment: The Organization and Regulation of Canadian Utilities, 1830–1930* (1986; Toronto: University of Toronto Press, 1988), pp. 141–169 ("civic populism").

109. Bob Millward, "Emergence of Gas and Water Monopolies in Nineteenth-Century Britain: Contested Markets and Public Control," in James Foreman-Peck, ed., *New Perspectives on the Late Victorian Economy: Essays in Quantitative Economic History, 1860–1914* (Cambridge: Cambridge University Press, 1991), p. 96 ("municipal capitalism").

110. Richard T. Ely, *An Introduction to Political Economy* (New York: Chautauqua Press, 1889), p. 82.

111. Richard T. Ely, "Public Control of Private Corporations," *Cosmopolitan* 30 (February 1901): 432.

112. Richard T. Ely, *Problems of To Day: A Discussion of Protective Tariffs, Taxation, and Monopolies,* 3rd ed. (New York: Thomas Y. Crowell & Co., 1890), p. 260.

113. Richard T. Ely, *Studies in the Evolution of Industrial Society* (New York: Macmillan Co., 1903), pp. 227–228.

114. Christopher G. Tiedeman, *A Treatise on State and Federal Control of Persons and Property in the United States,* vol. 1 (St. Louis: F. H. Thomas Law Book Co., 1900), p. 592.

115. Christopher G. Tiedeman, "Government Ownership of Public Utilities: From the Standpoint of Constitutional Limitations," *Harvard Law Review* 16 (May 1903): 479, 488.

116. Tiedeman, *Treatise,* pp. 596–597.

117. Henry Brown, "The Distribution of Property," *Report of the Sixteenth Annual Meeting of the American Bar Association* 16 (1893): 236–237; Brown, "The Twentieth Century," *Forum* 19 (August 1895): 649.

118. "Municipal Ownership," *New York Times,* March 27, 1899.

119. This generalization is based on a keyword search of the *New York Times* and *Chicago Tribune.* Prior to the 1890s, the phrase "works of public utility" was relatively common; as a collective noun, however, "public utility" was virtually unknown.

120. "Public Money and Public Works," *New York Times,* December 9, 1899.

121. Allen R. Foote, *Municipal Ownership of Quasi-Public Utilities* (Washington, D.C.: Ramsey & Bisbee, 1891), pp. 12–13.

122. Clyde Lyndon King, "The Need for Regulation," "Franchise Essentials," and "In Conclusion," in King, ed., *The Regulation of Municipal Utilities* (New York: D. Appleton and Co., 1912), pp. 10, 75, 383.

8. Second Nature

1. Arnold Bennett, "Your United States," *Harper's Monthly Magazine* 125 (July 1912): 191–192, 198.

2. Ronald B. Kline, *Consumers in the Countrywide: Technology and Social Change in Rural America* (Baltimore, Md.: Johns Hopkins University Press, 2000), chap. 1; Roy Alden Atwood, "Telephony and Its Cultural Meaning in Southeastern Iowa" (Ph.D. diss., University of Iowa, 1984).

3. Delos F. Wilcox, "Effects of State Regulation upon the Municipal Ownership Movement," *Annals of the American Academy of Political and Social Science* 53 (May 1914): 71–72.

4. Delos F. Wilcox, *Municipal Franchises: A Description of the Terms and Conditions upon Which Private Corporations Enjoy Special Privileges in the Streets of American Cities,* vol. 1: *Pipe and Wire Franchises* (Rochester, N.Y.: Gervaise Press, 1910), p. 26.

5. American Telegraph and Telephone, *Annual Report* (1905), pp. 31–32.

6. James Drummond Ellsworth, "The Twisting Trail," p. 57, box 1066, AT&T Archives and History Center, Warren, N.J. (hereafter AT&T-NJ).

7. American Telephone and Telegraph, *Annual Report* (1904), p. 11.

8. "The Telephone Invasion," *Electrical Review* 40 (June 14, 1902): 777–778.

9. J. Warren Stehman, *The Financial History of the American Telephone and Telegraph Company* (Boston: Houghton Mifflin Co., 1925), p. 78.

10. Richard Gabel, "The Early Competitive Era in Telephone Communication, 1893–1920," *Law and Contemporary Problems* 34 (Spring 1969): 345.

11. Nathan C. Kingsbury, "An Address," *Telephone Review* 5 (April 1914): 92.

12. "Independent Telephones in Large Cities," *Public Service* 2 (March 1907): 68.

13. "Nothing Succeeds Like Success," *American Telephone Journal* 8 (November 21, 1903): 328.

14. Steven J. Keillor, *Cooperative Commonwealth: Co-Ops in Rural Minnesota, 1859–1939* (St. Paul: Minnesota Historical Society Press, 2000), chap. 11.

15. *Journal* (Chicago), April 20, 1904; New York Board of Estimate and Apportionment, *Result of Investigation of the Operation of a Dual System of Telephones in Various Cities* (n.p., 1906); Robert J. Chapuis, *One-Hundred*

Years of Telephone Switching (1878–1978) (Amsterdam: North-Holland Publishing Co., 1982), p. 67.

16. *Public Service* 2 (May 1907): 160.

17. Milton L. Mueller Jr., *Universal Service: Competition, Interconnection, and the Making of the American Telephone System* (Cambridge. Mass.: MIT Press, 1997).

18. Walter S. Allen to Frederick P. Fish, May 16, 1906, 46-07-02-05, AT&T-NJ.

19. The independents built several durable toll-line networks, which, somewhat confusingly, they called long-distance networks. In fact, however, these independent networks were comparable not to Bell's long-distance network, but to the toll-line networks operated by individual Bell operating companies. This distinction is explained by the fact that Bell operating companies typically covered much more territory than the independents: a long-distance network for an independent was a toll-line network for Bell.

20. Kenneth J. Lipartito, "Component Innovation: The Case of Automatic Telephone Switching, 1891–1920," *Industrial and Corporate Change* 3, no. 2 (1994): 341–342; Bruno Latour, *Science in Action: How to Follow Scientists and Engineers through Society* (Cambridge, Mass.: Harvard University Press, 1987), pp. 125, 127. "Can you imagine that?" Latour wrote: "A transcontinental line tying the United States together, and rendering Bell the indispensable go-between of a hundred million people, eliminating all the small companies. . . . Without building expensive laboratories that they could not afford in an attempt to attract physics and electrons back into their own camp, the small companies eliminated by Bell could not resist."

21. Robert W. Garnet, *The Telephone Enterprise: The Evolution of the Bell System's Horizontal Structure, 1876–1909* (Baltimore, Md.: Johns Hopkins University Press, 1985), chaps. 8–9.

22. *United States v. American Bell Telephone and Emile Berliner,* 65 F. 86 (1894).

23. *United States v. American Bell,* 167 U.S. 224 (1897).

24. "The Telephone Question: The Effect of the Berliner Decision on the Industry," *Electrical Review* 25 (December 26, 1894): 320.

25. James J. Storrow to John E. Hudson, November 17, 1891, in N. R. Danielan, *AT&T: The Story of Industrial Conquest* (New York: Vanguard Press, 1939), p. 97.

26. "Telephone Question," *Electrical Review,* pp. 311, 320.

27. Melvin I. Urofsky, "Proposed Federal Incorporation in the Progressive Era," *American Journal of Legal History* 26 (April 1982): 163; Naomi R. Lamoreaux, *The Great Merger Movement in American Business, 1896–1904* (Cambridge: Cambridge University Press, 1985), chap. 6.

28. *United States Telephone Company v. Delphos Home Telephone Company,* 19 Ohio Dec. 193 (1908); *Times-Democrat* (Lima, Ohio), July 28, 1908;

Harry B. MacMeal, *The Story of Independent Telephony* (Chicago: Independent Pioneer Telephone Association, 1934), pp. 174–177, 197.

29. *Richmond v. Southern Bell Telephone and Telegraph Company,* 174 U.S. 761 (1899).

30. Christopher Armstrong and H. V. Nelles, *Monopoly's Moment: The Organization and Regulation of Canadian Utilities, 1830–1930* (Philadelphia: Temple University Press, 1986), pp. 164–168.

31. Robert MacDougall, "The People's Telephone: The Politics of Telephony in the United States and Canada, 1876–1926" (Ph.D. dissertation, Harvard University, 2004), pp. 17–18, 48–51, 188–195.

32. Homer Hoyt, *One Hundred Years of Land Values in Chicago: The Relationship of the Growth of Chicago to the Rise in Its Land Values, 1830–1933* (Chicago: University of Chicago Press, 1933), p. 490; Angus Hibbard, *Hello Goodbye: My Story of Telephone Pioneering* (Chicago: A. C. McClurg & Co., 1941), p. 179.

33. Edward W. Bemis, *Report on the Investigation of the Chicago Telephone Company* (Chicago: n.p., 1912), p. 8.

34. Herbert N. Casson, *The History of the Telephone* (Chicago: A. C. McClurg & Co., 1910), pp. 186, 268; *Wall Street Journal,* November 27, 1906.

35. "Failure of Government Telephones," *Wall Street Journal,* October 26, 1909.

36. William Cronon, *Nature's Metropolis: Chicago and the Great West* (New York: W. W. Norton & Co., 1991).

37. J. Seymour Currey, *Manufacturing and Wholesale Industries of Chicago,* vol. 2 (Chicago: Thomas B. Poole, 1918), p. 311.

38. MacMeal, *Independent Telephony,* p. 252.

39. *Western Electrician* 21 (July 24, 1897): 21; *Western Electrician* 26 (March 24, 1900): 191; "Chicago Pays Tribute," *Chicago Tribune,* September 8, 1907; "Western Union," *Wall Street Journal,* January 28, 1896; *Wall Street Journal,* January 10, 1901.

40. David Gabel, "Federalism: An Historical Perspective," in Paul Teske, ed., *American Regulatory Federalism and Telecommunications Infrastructure* (Hillsdale, N.J.: Lawrence Erlbaum Associates, 1995), p. 23.

41. C. F. Cutler to Frederick P. Fish, December 22, 1902, in "The Central Union Telephone Company," AT&T-NJ.

42. Stehman, *Financial History,* p. 132.

43. Morton L. Johnson to Thomas W. Gregory, November 21, 1914, box 38, U.S. Department of Justice, RG 60, National Archives, Washington, D.C.

44. Stephen B. Adams and Orville R. Butler, *Manufacturing the Future: A History of Western Electric* (Cambridge: Cambridge University Press, 1999), chaps. 2–3.

45. Hibbard, *Hello Goodbye,* p. 203.

46. Ibid., pp. 185, 202, 242; M. D. Fagen, ed., *A History of Engineering and Science in the Bell System: The Early Years (1875–1925)* (New York: Bell Telephone Laboratories, 1975), p. 495.

47. Hibbard, *Hello Goodbye,* pp. 185, 197, 242.

48. George Siemens, *History of the House of Siemens,* vol. 1: *The Era of Free Enterprise* (Freiburg: Karl Kaber, 1957), pp. 131–135.

49. Edison to Sterling Patterson, July 12, 1926, box 1284, AT&T-NJ; Hibbard, *Hello Goodbye,* p. 150; Fagen, *Engineering and Science,* p. 44.

50. Charles E. Scribner, "History of the Engineering Department," *Western Electric News* 8 (November 1919): 10.

51. Hibbard, *Hello Goodbye,* p. 150; Lillian Hoddeson, "The Emergence of Basic Research in the Bell Telephone System, 1875–1915," *Technology and Culture* 22 (July 1981): 512–544.

52. *Western Electrician* 30 (January 25, 1902): 67.

53. Alfred Stromberg affidavit, January 28, 1895, *Western Telephone Construction Co. v. Alfred Stromberg,* U.S. Circuit Court, no. 23568, RG 21, National Archives, Great Lakes Branch, Chicago.

54. Emory Lindquist, "The Invention and Development of the Dial Telephone: The Contribution of Three Lindsborg Inventors," *Kansas Historical Quarterly* 23 (Spring 1957): 1–8.

55. Chapuis, *Telephone Switching,* p. 68; Thomas E. McCarthy, *The History of GTE: The Evolution of One of America's Great Corporations* (Stamford, Conn.: GTE, 1990), p. 39.

56. "Chicago Telephone Company," *Economist* (Chicago) 18 (December 18, 1897): 694; "Chicago Telephone Year," *Economist* (Chicago) 25 (January 19, 1901): 68.

57. *Chicago Telephone Directory* (1906), p. vi.

58. "Tests of the Strowger Automatic System in Chicago, Illinois," 1904, 11-07-01-02, AT&T-NJ.

59. Edward W. Bemis testimony, in *Regulation of Telephone Rates: Public Service Commission of the Commonwealth of Pennsylvania* (Harrisburg: n.p., 1914), p. 1667a.

60. Dugald C. Jackson, William H. Crumb, and George W. Wilder, *Report on the Telephone Situation in the City of Chicago* (n.p., 1907), pp. 50, 75, 90.

61. "Developments in Telephone-Franchise Negotiations in Chicago," *Western Electrician* 39 (November 24, 1906): 426.

62. H. Linton Reber testimony, docket 4235 (November–December 1915), Public Utilities Commission, Illinois State Archives, Springfield, Ill.

63. Elisha Gray, "A Revolution in the Means of Communication," *Cosmopolitan* 15 (May 1893): 124.

64. "Electricity Exhibit—Many Wonderful Inventions to Be Seen There," *Chicago Tribune*, August 6, 1893.

65. Hibbard, *Hello Goodbye*, chap. 11.

66. Fagen, *Engineering and Science*, p. 656.

67. Hibbard, *Hello Goodbye*, chap. 12.

68. Ibid., p. 181.

69. "Conference Held at Boston, January 23 and 24, 1900: Telephone Service and Charges," p. 146, box 185-02-03, AT&T-NJ; S. J. Larned, "Telephone Service," *Western Electrician* 32 (March 28, 1903): 247–248.

70. Hibbard, *Hello, Goodbye*, pp. 205, 210.

71. Hibbard, "The Telephone Door," *Electrical Engineering* 4 (December 1894): 262; Hibbard, *Hello Goodbye*, p. xii.

72. Hibbard, *Hello Goodbye*, p. 90.

73. Ibid., p. 190; *Western Electrician* 5 (December 7, 1889): 296.

74. Hibbard, "Telephone Door," p. 263; Howard S. Knowlton, "Aspects of Recent Telephone Development," *Electrical World* 49 (March 30, 1907): 639.

75. *Chicago Telephone Directory* (1906), p. 534.

76. Angus Hibbard, "The Telephone in Chicago: The Exchanges, the System, the Users," *Western Electrician* 40 (January 19, 1907): 65; "Electricity Exhibit," *Chicago Tribune*, April 13, 1895.

77. Linn H. Young, Francis D. Connery, and Edward B. Ellicott, "Special Committee on Telephone Rates," March 2, 1903, in Chicago City Council, *Proceedings* (1903), p. 2365.

78. Knowlton, "Recent Telephone Development," pp. 638–639.

79. "Chicago Telephone Rates," *Public Service* 9 (July 1910): 6.

80. Hibbard, "Telephone in Chicago," p. 66.

81. "Druggists' Public Telephones," *Western Electrician* 41 (December 7, 1907): 453.

82. "Slot Telephones in Chicago," *Western Electrician* 23 (October 15, 1898): 218.

83. "Telephones in Drug Stores," *Western Electrician* 17 (September 14, 1895): 125–126.

84. "Slot Telephones in Chicago," *Electrical Review* 24 (January 10, 1894): 14.

85. "New-Fangled Telephone Aimed to Defeat Deadheadism," *Chicago Tribune*, December 30, 1893; "Telephones in Drug Stores," *Western Electrician*, pp. 125–126; "Split on the Slot Phones," *Chicago Tribune*, May 23, 1896; Hibbard to Noble B. Judah, October 27, 1896, Chicago City Council Records, Northeastern Illinois University (hereafter CCC-NEIU).

86. "Telephones in Drug Stores," *Western Electrician*, pp. 125–126; "Split on the Slot Phones," *Chicago Tribune*; Hibbard to Noble B. Judah, October 27, 1896, CCC-NEIU.

87. Chicago Telephone Company, *Report* (1899), p. 9.

88. "Split on the Slot Phones," *Chicago Tribune; Chicago Telephone Directory* (1898), p. 5.

89. "Shuts off the Girls from Indulging in Gossip," *Chicago Tribune,* April 11, 1896.

90. William Bodemann, "The Chicago Telephone Trouble," *Druggists' Circular* 40 (December 1896): 308; Bodemann, "The Origin of the Slot Pay Telephone System," *Druggists' Circular* 51 (January 1907): 99; "Druggists' Public Telephones," *Western Electrician* 41 (December 7, 1907): 453.

91. "Shuts off the Girls from Indulging in Gossip," *Chicago Tribune.*

92. "A Public Telephone Defined," *Western Electrician* 26 (June 30, 1900): 424.

93. Hibbard, "A Phase of Telephone Engineering," *Electrical Engineering* 4 (March 1894): 83.

94. "The Two Chicago Systems," *Telephony* 67 (November 14, 1914): 17.

95. "Chicago Telephone Annual," *Economist* (Chicago) 35 (January 20, 1905): 203.

96. *Western Electrician* 29 (July 6, 1901): 8.

97. "Chicago Telephone Company," *Economist* (Chicago) 26 (December 31, 1901): 824.

98. "Chicago Telephone," *Economist* (Chicago) 15 (January 18, 1896): 72.

99. "Telephone Traffic in Chicago," *Electrical Review* 31 (November 17, 1897): 236.

100. "Chicago Telephone Company," *Economist* (Chicago) 43 (January 8, 1910): 124; Hibbard, *Hello Goodbye,* p. 208.

101. "What 'Measured Service' Means," *Chicago Tribune,* June 28, 1903; "Phone Meters," *Chicago Record-Herald,* April 20, 1909.

102. "Phone Company to Be Pilloried," *Chicago Tribune,* March 14, 1906.

103. "Reopens Battle on Phone Meter," *Chicago Tribune,* June 21, 1907; Hamilton Club of Chicago, "Report of the Special Telephone Franchise Committee," June 24, 1907, box 310, CCC-NEIU.

104. *Telephone Meter: How Telephone Service Is Measured* (Chicago: Chicago Telephone Co., 1919), Chicago Telephone Company Records, AT&T Archives and History Center, San Antonio, Tex. (hereafter CTC, AT&T-TX).

105. Wilcox, *Municipal Franchises,* vol. 1, pp. 227, 248–250; D. W. Bliss, "Telephone Meters versus the 'Measured Rate,'" *Electrical World* 46 (August 25, 1900), p. 286; Linn H. Young, "Report of the Committee on Gas, Oil, and Electric Light, to the City Council of Chicago," September 3, 1907, Chicago City Council, *Proceedings* (1907), p. 1166; "Phone Meters," *Chicago Record-Herald,* April 20, 1909; "Basis for Metering Service," *Telephony* 77 (November 15, 1919): 11.

106. "Telephone Rates," *Economist* (Chicago) 43 (June 18, 1910): 1142.

107. Ibid.

108. Dugald C. Jackson, "Is a Rational Basis Possible for Telephone Rates?" in Clyde Lyndon King, ed., *The Regulation of Municipal Utilities* (New York: D. Appleton and Co., 1912), p. 115.

109. Businesses had to guarantee two calls a day; residences one call. "Only $5 per Month," *Chicago Tribune*, April 13, 1895; "Five-Cent Telephone Service in Chicago," *Electrical World* 36 (November 3, 1900): 670.

110. Hibbard to John M. Clark, April 10, 1900, box 1134, AT&T-NJ; "Five-Cent Slot Telephones in Chicago," *Western Electrician* 27 (October 27, 1900): 273; Hibbard, "Telephone in Chicago," p. 65.

111. "Phone Meters," *Chicago Record-Herald*, April 20, 1909.

112. "Cut in Telephone Rates," *Chicago Tribune*, October 24, 1900.

113. Thomas J. Schlereth, *Victorian America: Transformations in Everyday Life, 1876–1915* (New York: Harper & Row, 1991), pp. 84–85.

114. "Wants City to Own Phones," *Chicago Tribune*, July 26, 1911; Dan Schiller, "Social Movements in Telecommunications: Rethinking the Public Service History of U.S. Telecommunications, 1894–1919," *Telecommunications Policy* 22 (1998): 397–408.

115. Hibbard to John M. Clark, April 10, 1900, box 1134, AT&T-NJ; "Five-Cent Slot Telephones in Chicago," *Western Electrician*, p. 273; Hibbard, "Telephone in Chicago," p. 65.

116. "'Phone Calls Cut to 5 Cents," *Chicago Tribune*, October 23, 1900.

117. Chicago Telephone Company, *Nickel Prepayment Service* (Chicago: Chicago Telephone Co., 1907), CTC, AT&T-TX.

118. "'Phone Calls Cut to 5 Cents," *Chicago Tribune*; "Chicago Telephone Statement," *Economist* (Chicago) 23 (January 20, 1900): 73–74.

119. Chicago City Council, *Proceedings* (1907), p. 1166; *Chicago Telephone Directory* (June 1908), p. 8.

120. Hibbard, *Hello Goodbye*, pp. 209–210.

121. Jean B. Quandt, *From the Small Town to the Great Community: The Social Thought of Progressive Intellectuals* (New Brunswick, N.J.: Rutgers University Press, 1970), part 1 ("The Uses of Communication").

122. Chicago Telephone Company, *Report* (1898), pp. 3–4.

123. "Chicago Telephone Year," *Economist* (Chicago) 25 (January 19, 1901): 68.

124. Chicago Telephone Company, *Report* (1898), pp. 3–4.

125. Chicago Telephone Company, *Report* (1901), pp. 7–8.

126. Chicago City Council, *Proceedings* (1899), p. 1529.

127. Young, Connery, and Ellicott, "Telephone Rates," pp. 2364–2365.

128. Hamilton Club of Chicago, "Report."

129. "Chicago Telephony," *Electrical World* 39 (February 8, 1902): 265; "Druggists Join Telephone War," *Chicago Tribune*, January 29, 1902.

130. "Chicago Phones Worst on Record," *Chicago Tribune,* November 1, 1901; "War on 10-Party 'Phones," *Chicago Tribune,* February 15, 1902.

131. Larned, "Telephone Service," p. 247.

132. John J. Carty to Harry B. Thayer, March 1, 1909, box 1357, AT&T-NJ.

133. Thayer to Vail, March 2, 1909, box 1357, AT&T-NJ.

134. Thayer to Bernard E. Sunny, March 17, 1914, box 1134, AT&T-NJ.

135. Vail to Arthur D. Wheeler, July 18, 1907, president's letterbook, AT&T-NJ.

136. Vail to Sunny, June 3, 1909, president's letterbook, AT&T-NJ.

137. Edward J. Hall, "Corporate Organization," National Telephone Exchange Association, *Proceedings* (1890), pp. 43, 49.

138. Ibid., p. 43.

139. Hibbard, *Hello Goodbye,* pp. 61–68, 175.

140. Ibid., pp. 62–67.

141. Edward B. Ellicott, Department of Electricity, "Report," January 7, 1902, Chicago City Council, *Proceedings* (1902), p. 1752; Young, Connery, and Ellicott, "Telephone Rates," p. 2366.

142. "Telephone Rates in New York," *Electrical Review* 30 (April 14, 1897): 179.

143. "Telephonic Intelligence," *Electrical World* 38 (October 26, 1901): 671.

144. Department of Commerce and Labor, *Special Reports: Telephones and Telegraphs* (Washington, D.C.: Government Printing Office, 1906), p. 57.

145. "May Need 60,000 'Phones," *Chicago Tribune,* October 24, 1900; "War on 10-Party Phones," *Chicago Tribune,* February 15, 1902.

146. "Conference Held at Boston," AT&T-NJ, p. 218.

147. Frank H. Bethell testimony, in *Regulation of Telephone Rates,* p. 1334a.

148. "Conference Held at Boston," AT&T-NJ, p. 220.

149. Hibbard, *Hello Goodbye,* pp. 205–206.

150. Meighan Jeanne Maguire, "The Local Dynamics of Telephone System Development: The San Francisco Exchange, 1893–1919" (Ph.D. diss., University of California at San Diego, 1990), chap. 1.

151. Cumberland Telephone Company, *Report* (1901).

152. James E. Caldwell, *Recollections of a Life Time* (Nashville, Tenn.: Baird-Ward Press, 1923), pp. 141, 197.

153. Wisconsin Telephone Company, scrapbook, c. 1900, Wisconsin Telephone Company Records, AT&T-TX.

154. J. A. Stewart, "A Short Review of the Progress Made by the New York Telephone Company since 1892," *Telephone Review* 3 (December 1912): 278.

155. Wanamaker Store, "Half the Comfort of Summertime Depends on Having the Right Things," *New York Times,* July 26, 1900.

156. "Expansion," *Chicago Tribune,* June 4, 1901.

157. "The Way Out of a Social Dilemma," *Chicago Tribune,* October 28, 1909.

158. *Telephone Review* 2 (December 1911): back cover.

159. Cited in Diane Zimmerman Umble, "Sinful Networks or Divine Service: Competing Meanings of the Telephone in Amish Country," in Lisa Gitelman and Geoffrey B. Pingree, eds., *New Media, 1740–1915* (Cambridge, Mass.: MIT Press, 2003), p. 145.

160. *Telephone Review* 3 (April 1912): front cover; *Telephone Review* 3 (September 1912): front cover; *Telephone Review* 8 (October 1917): front cover.

161. Roland Marchand, *Creating the Corporate Soul: The Rise of Public Relations and Corporate Imagery in American Big Business* (Berkeley: University of California Press, 1998), chap. 2.

9. Gray Wolves

1. Ivy L. Lee, "Telephone Publicity—Appealing to Public Opinion," *Sound Waves* 11 (August 1906): 304.

2. *Wall Street Journal,* May 1, 1907; Albert Bigelow Paine, *In One Man's Life: Being Chapters from the Personal and Business Career of Theodore N. Vail* (New York: Harper & Brothers, 1921), pp. 229–230.

3. J. P. Morgan & Co. to Vail, August 9, 1915, in Federal Communications Commission, *Accounting Department: Telephone Investigation,* vol. 3 [Washington, D.C.: Federal Communications Commission], 1936–1937.

4. Vincent P. Carosso, *More than a Century of Investment Banking: The Kidder, Peabody & Co. Story* (New York: McGraw-Hill, 1979), pp. 30–31.

5. "Judge Thomas on Independent Telephony," *Electrical World* 37 (June 8, 1901): 979.

6. "Independent Interdependence," *Transmitter* (Fort Worth, Tex.) 5 (August 1907): 16.

7. Hugh Dougherty to Henry A. Barnhart, February 15, 1902, Barnhart Papers, Indiana State Library and Archives, Indianapolis.

8. Cuyahoga Telephone Company, *A Little Talk on Talk* (Cleveland: Cuyahoga Telephone Company, [c. 1900]), subject file, Ohio Bell Telephone Company Records, AT&T Archives and History Center, San Antonio, Tex. (hereafter AT&T-TX).

9. Frank R. Colvin to Winfield S. Hutchinson, October 27, 1900, Colvin letterbook, Colvin letterbook, AT&T Archives and History Center, Warren, N.J. (hereafter AT&T-NJ).

10. *Electrical World* 39 (May 10, 1902): 809.

11. Charles T. Smiley to H. Linton Reber, January 29, 1908, Kinloch Telephone Company, *Annual Report* (1907).

12. Smiley to Reber, January 14, 1907, Kinloch Telephone Company, *Annual Report* (1906), Southwestern Bell Telephone Company Records, AT&T-TX; *Druggists' Circular* 56 (January 1912): 34.

13. "Value of Party Line Service," *Sound Waves* 10 (September 1905): 322.

14. "Independent National Telephone Convention," *Electrical World* 35 (June 23, 1900): 936.

15. Ibid.

16. Harry B. MacMeal, *The Story of Independent Telephony* (Chicago: Independent Pioneer Telephone Association, 1934), p. 130.

17. Ralph L. Mahon, "The Telephone in Chicago, 1877–1940," typescript, p. 17, AT&T-TX.

18. *Western Telephone Manufacturing Company v. Swedish-American Telephone Company*, U.S. Circuit Court, no. 28,994, pp. 2–3, RG 21, National Archives, Great Lakes Branch, Chicago.

19. Western Telephone Construction Company, *Price List* (Chicago, n.p. [1896]).

20. MacMeal, *Independent Telephony*, p. 68.

21. *Western Electric v. Western Telephone Construction Co.*, 81 F. 572 (1897); MacMeal, *Independent Telephony*, p. 85.

22. Gansey R. Johnston, "Comments on the 1907 Report of the A. T. & T. Co.," *Telephony* 16 (October 24, 1908): 409–411; A. C. Lindemuth, "The Legal Status and Relationship of Independent Telephone Companies," *Telephony* 15 (December 5, 1908): 577–581.

23. James E. Keelyn, "A Letter on the Proposed Telephone Consolidation," *Electrical Review* 35 (November 1899): 293.

24. "Conflicting Telephone Service," *Telephone Magazine* 21 (May 1903): 207.

25. Charles A. Pleasance, *The Spirit of Independent Telephony* (Johnson City, Tenn.: Independent Telephone Books, 1989), p. xiv.

26. J. Warren Stehman, *The Financial History of the American Telephone and Telegraph Company* (Boston: Houghton Mifflin Co., 1925), pp. 309–311.

27. *Cumberland Telephone Journal* 1 (May 15, 1903): 2.

28. New Orleans Board of Trade, *Telephone Conditions in New Orleans, La.: Being a Report Presented by a Special Committee of the New Orleans Board of Trade, Approved, April 8th, 1908* (New Orleans: n.p., 1908), p. 133.

29. Edwin W. Gorom to Burleson, February 2, 1914, Office of the Solicitor, Department of Justice, RG 60, National Archives, Washington, D.C. (hereafter DOJ-NA).

30. Stehman, *Financial History*, p. 83.

31. "Opposition for Bell Concern," *Chicago Tribune*, November 10, 1899.

32. "The Telephone Convention," *New York Times*, June 29, 1899.

33. "A Big Telephone Combine," *New York Times*, February 28, 1900; Stehman, *Financial History*, p. 97.

34. Colvin to Hutchinson, January 29, 1901, Colvin letterbook, AT&T-NJ.

35. Stehman, *Financial History*, pp. 100–104; Carosso, *Kidder, Peabody & Co.*, p. 31.

36. Stehman, *Financial History*, pp. 80–81.

37. John P. Boylan, *A History of Telephony in Rochester, N.Y.* (n.p., 1953), p. 8.

38. "Opposition Telephones," *Wall Street Journal,* February 1, 1907; *Public Service 5* (November 1908): 151.

39. *Wall Street Journal,* April 18, 1907.

40. Richard Sylla, "The Progressive Era and the Political Economy of Big Government," *Critical Review 5* (1992): 531–557.

41. MacMeal, *Story of Independent Telephony,* p. 122; James E. Caldwell, *Recollections of a Life Time* (Nashville, Tenn.: Baird-Ward Press, 1923), pp. 174–177.

42. "Opposition Telephones," *Wall Street Journal,* February 1, 1907.

43. Clarence W. Barron, *More They Told Barron,* ed. Arthur Pound and Samuel Taylor Moore (New York: Harper & Brothers, 1931), pp. 12–14.

44. Theodore N. Vail to L. G. Richardson, September 10, 1908, president's letterbook, AT&T-NJ.

45. Colvin to John E. Hudson, July 28, 1896; Colvin to Winfield S. Hutchinson, December 28, 1899; both in Colvin letterbook, AT&T-NJ.

46. Colvin to Hutchinson, December 28, 1899, Colvin letterbook, AT&T-NJ.

47. "Telephones and Politics," *The Voter 9* (August 1912): 33–34.

48. "Aldrich Denies a Sale," *Chicago Tribune,* March 24, 1899; "New 'Phone Company in Field," *Chicago Tribune,* May 20, 1899.

49. *Chicago Tribune,* May 20, 1899.

50. Kempster Miller, *Report on the Automatic Telephone Situation in the City of Chicago* (Chicago: n.p., 1915), p. 11.

51. C. O. Frisbie to Charles G. Dawes and David R. Forgan, March 19, 1912, box 58, Dawes Papers, Northwestern University, Evanston, Ill.

52. Frederick P. Fish to W. Murray Crane, October 19, 1906, president's letterbook, AT&T-NJ.

53. "Will Buy 'Phone Tunnels," *Chicago Tribune,* July 9, 1901; Bruce G. Moffat, *The Chicago Tunnel Story: Exploring the Railroad "Forty Feet Below"* (Chicago: Central Electric Railfans' Association, 2002), chaps. 1, 4.

54. Charles Merriam, "Public Utilities," box 94, Charles E. Merriam Papers, University of Chicago, Chicago, Ill.

55. Edward W. Bemis to Thomas W. Gregory, August 2, 1916, section 3, box 46, DOJ-NA.

56. "Automatic Electric," *Economist* (Chicago) 55 (March 18, 1916): 556; Merriam, "Public Utilities."

57. Hugo S. Grosser, "Report," Chicago City Council, *Proceedings* (1907), p. 1396.

58. C. O. Frisbie to Dawes, January 1, 1910, box 58, Dawes Papers.

59. Miller, *Automatic Telephone Situation,* p. 32.

60. _____ to Fish, December 30, 1902, box 65, AT&T-NJ.

61. *Chicago Telephone v. Illinois Manufacturers' Association,* 106 Ill. App. 54 (1903).

62. "The Telephone Rate Case," *Economist* (Chicago) 29 (February 21, 1903): 292.

63. George V. Leverett to Charles S. Holt, October 17, 1903, Chicago Telephone Company files, Sidley Austin Archives, Chicago.

64. "The Telephone Rate Case," *Economist* (Chicago) 29 (February 21, 1903): 232.

65. "Important Telephone Decision in Chicago," *Electrical World* 39 (January 18, 1902): 127; *Western Electrician* 30 (February 22, 1902): 128.

66. *Western Electrician* 38 (February 24, 1906): 165.

67. "Victory to City in Telephone Fight," *Chicago Record-Herald,* February 16, 1906; "Phone Controversy Is at End," *Chicago Record-Herald,* April 12, 1906; "Phone Refund Begins," *Chicago Record-Herald,* July 21, 1906; *Western Electrician* 38 (March 10, 1906): 204; *Western Electrician* 39 (July 28, 1906): 69; Dugald C. Jackson, William H. Crumb, and George W. Wilder, *Report on the Telephone Situation in the City of Chicago* (n.p., 1907), p. 49.

68. *Wall Street Journal,* December 11, 1907.

69. Grosser, "Report," p. 1396.

70. Allen T. Burns to Chicago City Council, November 4, 1907, Chicago City Council Records, Northeastern Illinois University.

71. "Mayor Dunne and Public Service Affairs," *Public Service* 2 (March 1907): 69; Maureen A. Flanagan, "Gender and Urban Political Reform: The City Club and the Woman's City Club of Chicago in the Progressive Era," *American Historical Review* 95 (October 1990): 1032–1033.

72. Edward F. Dunne, "Advantages of Public Ownership and Operation of Utilities," March 29, 1902, in *Dunne: Judge, Mayor, Governor,* ed. and comp. William L. Sullivan (Chicago: Windermere Press, 1916), p. 137.

73. "The Public Wins," *Chicago Tribune,* July 26, 1907.

74. *Sound Waves* 11 (November 1906): 398.

75. Angus Hibbard, *Hello Goodbye: My Story of Telephone Pioneering* (Chicago: A. C. McClurg & Co., 1941), p. 222.

76. Ibid.

77. "Take up Phone Rates of Proposed Measure," *Chicago Record-Herald,* November 22, 1906.

78. "Flat Rates Conceded in Chicago Telephone Negotiations," *Western Electrician* 41 (August 3, 1907): 92; "Chicago Pays Tribute," *Chicago Tribune,* September 8, 1907; "Clubs in League for Phone Veto," *Chicago Tribune,* November 8, 1907.

79. "Chicago Telephone Annual," *Economist* (Chicago) 35 (January 20, 1905): 203; "Chicago Telephone Ordinance," *Economist* (Chicago) 36 (November 10, 1906): 723.

80. "Chicago Telephone," *Economist* (Chicago) 35 (February 17, 1905): 357.

81. "Chicago Telephone Rates," *Public Service* 9 (July 1910): 6.

82. *Wall Street Journal,* July 17, 1907.

83. Jackson, Crumb, and Wilder, *Telephone Situation,* pp. 5–16, 22, 35.

84. "Competition and Measured Rates," *Public Service* 2 (April 1907): 116–117.

85. "Clubs in League for Phone Veto," *Chicago Tribune,* November 8, 1907.

86. Charles E. Merriam, *Chicago: A More Intimate View of Urban Politics* (New York: Macmillan, 1929), p. 225.

87. "I Hope Our Bell Boy Hurries with That Ordinance—I'm Getting Nervous," *Chicago Tribune,* September 12, 1907.

88. Richard L. McCormick, "The Discovery That Business Corrupts Politics: A Reappraisal," *American Historical Review* 86 (April 1981): 247–274.

89. "The Chicago Telephone Situation," *Sound Waves* 11 (May 1906): 167.

90. "250,000 Telephone Users," *Chicago Record-Herald,* November 24, 1906.

91. David Nord, "The Experts versus the Experts: Conflicting Philosophies of Municipal Utility Regulation in the Progressive Era," *Wisconsin Magazine of History* 58 (Spring 1975): 219–236.

92. Delos F. Wilcox, *Municipal Franchises: A Description of the Terms and Conditions upon Which Private Corporations Enjoy Special Privileges in the Streets of American Cities,* vol. 1: *Pipe and Wire Franchises* (Rochester, N.Y.: Gervaise Press, 1910), p. 322; "Competition and Measured Rates," *Public Service* 2 (April 1907): 116–117.

93. "Ultimatum Talk Stirs Phone Co.," *Chicago Tribune,* November 18, 1906.

10. Universal Service

1. American Telephone and Telegraph, *Annual Report* (1910), pp. 23, 43, 44, 53.

2. "Will Seek to Amend the Utilities Law," *New York Times,* September 24, 1907; Richard L. McCormick, *From Realignment to Reform: Political Change in New York State, 1893–1910* (Ithaca, N.Y.: Cornell University Press, 1981), p. 238; "Public Ownership," box 101, National Civic Federation Records, Columbia University, New York.

3. Richard L. McCormick, "The Discovery that Business Corrupts Politics: A Reappraisal," *American Historical Review* 86 (April 1981): 247–274.

4. "Roosevelt Message Stirs Up Congress," *New York Times,* October 9, 1908; "Federal Control of the Telegraphs," *New York Times,* December 10, 1908; "President Writes Commerce Message," *New York Times,* December 19, 1909.

5. Arthur Stedman Hills, "The Origin, Growth, and Work of Public Utility Commissions," *Public Service* 13 (February 1912): 61.

6. "An Act Relative to the Supervision by the Massachusetts Highway Commission of All Companies Engaged in the Transmission of Intelligence by Electricity," in *Acts and Resolves Passed by the General Court of Massachusetts,* chap. 433 (Boston: Wright & Potter, 1906), pp. 448–451; "An Act . . . Giving the Wisconsin Railroad Commission Jurisdiction over Public Utilities," in *Laws of Wisconsin,* chap. 499 (Madison, Wis.: Democrat Printing, 1907), p. 1130.

7. "An Act to Amend the Public Service Commissions Law, in Relation to Telegraph and Telephone Lines and Companies," in *Laws of the State of New York,* vol. 2, chap. 673 (Albany, N.Y.: J. B. Lyon, 1910), pp. 1929–1945.

8. "An Act to Authorize Cities to Acquire, Construct, Own, and Lease or Operate Public Utilities," and "An Act to Provide for the Regulation of Public Utilities," both in *Laws of the State of Illinois* (Springfield: Illinois State Journal, 1913), pp. 455–459 and 460–502.

9. H. D. Critchfield to Frank H. Woods, May 18, 1915, box 21, AT&T Archives and History Center, Warren, N.J. (hereafter AT&T-NJ).

10. J. C. Kelsey, "The New Decade," *Telephony* 70 (January 1916): 36.

11. "Regulate the Telephone Companies," *Wall Street Journal,* April 20, 1909; "Morgan in Phone Quiz," *Chicago Record-Herald,* February 10, 1910.

12. "Will Seek to Amend the Utilities Law," *New York Times,* September 24, 1907.

13. "An Act to Create a Commerce Court," *Statutes at Large of the United States of America,* chap. 309, June 18, 1910, pp. 539–557.

14. Morton J. Horwitz, "The History of the Public/Private Distinction," *University of Pennsylvania Law Review* 130 (June 1982): 1427.

15. Wickersham to Samuel Hill, January 24, 1913, box 39, U.S. Department of Justice, RG 60, National Archives, Washington, D.C. (hereafter DOJ-NA).

16. Alexander M. Bickel, *History of the Supreme Court of the United States,* vol. 9: *The Judiciary and Responsible Government, 1910–1921* (New York: Macmillan, 1984), pt. 1, p. 125; Burton J. Hendrick, "James C. McReynolds," *World's Work* 27 (November 1913): 31.

17. Vail to E. C. Bradley, [January 1909], president's letterbook, AT&T-NJ.

18. "Vail Looks for National Public Utilities Commission," *Wall Street Journal,* June 11, 1911; *Central Telephone News* 1 (October 1911): 17; "Monopoly of Utilities Proved to be in Public Interest," *Wall Street Journal,* July 25, 1914.

19. American Telephone and Telegraph, *Annual Report* (1907), p. 28.

20. American Telephone and Telegraph, *Annual Report* (1910), p. 43.

21. Leonard S. Reich, *The Making of American Industrial Research: Science and Business at GE and Bell, 1876–1926* (Cambridge: Cambridge University Press, 1985), p. 158.

22. Frisbie to Krauthoff, December 30, 1910, box 58, Dawes Papers, Northwestern University, Evanston, Ill.; "Chicago Hearings in the Government-Bell Trust Suit," *Telephony* 65 (November 29, 1913): 23.

23. L. D. Kellogg to William Howard Taft, December 9, 1911, box 37; John H. Wright to Woodrow Wilson, March 11, 1913, box 38; both in DOJ-NA; "Phone Merger Plan Told," *Chicago Tribune,* November 21, 1913.

24. C. O. Frisbie to L. C. Krauthoff, December 30, 1910, box 58, Dawes Papers; "Chicago Hearings in the Government-Bell Trust Suit," *Telephony* 65 (November 29, 1913): 23.

25. R. Morgan Olcott to H. D. Critchfield, September 30, 1910, box 1375, AT&T-NJ.

26. Ibid.

27. *Telephony* 65 (November 29, 1913): 22–23.

28. Wright to Wickersham, November 4, 1911, box 37, DOJ-NA.

29. Ibid.; Manford Savage to Wickersham, November 28, 1911; both in box 37, DOJ-NA.

30. "Independents Seek to Have Government Bring Suit against Bell Telephone Companies," *Electrical World* 59 (January 20, 1912): 129.

31. Wright to Wickersham, March 19, 1912; Wright to Wickersham, November 4, 1911; both in box 37, DOJ-NA.

32. Wright to J. P. Tumulty, March 11, 1913, box 38, DOJ-NA.

33. Kenneth J. Lipartito, "'Cutthroat' Competition, Corporate Strategy, and the Growth of Network Industries," *Research on Technological Innovation, Management, and Policy* 6 (1997): 1–53.

34. Vail to John A. Moon, December 30, 1918, *Government Control of the Telegraph and Telephone Systems: Hearings on J. J. Res. 368 . . . ,* 1919, 65th Cong., 3rd sess., pt. 1, p. 57.

35. Terrestrial Globe, 1916, ART-0016-009217, AT&T-NJ.

36. W. F. Brown, "Our Relations with the Western Union," *Transmitter* (Denver) 5 (February 1911): 3.

37. *Chicago Telephone Directory* (June 1910), p. 648; Newcomb Carlton, "Putting Western Union on Its Feet and How Vail Did It," *Printer's Ink* 79 (November 5, 1914): 8.

38. "Telephone Wires for Telegraphing," *Transmitter* (Denver) 5 (February 1911): 11.

39. Cited in Marshall Cushing, *The Story of Our Post Office: The Greatest Government Department in All Its Phases* (Boston: A. M. Thayer & Co., 1893), pp. 1000–1003.

40. Charles Van Hise, *Concentration and Control: A Solution of the Trust Problem in the United States,* rev. ed. (New York: Macmillan, 1914), p. 192b.

41. Charles N. Fay, *Big Business and Government* (New York: Moffatt, Yard, and Co., 1912), p. 11.

42. Fay, *Too Much Government, Too Much Taxation* (Garden City, N.Y.: Doubleday, Page & Co., 1923), p. 11.

43. Lyman Abbott, "Telegraphs and Telephones," *Outlook* 93 (November 27, 1909): 640.

44. Bertie Charles Forbes, *Men Who Are Making America* (New York: B. C. Forbes Publishing Co., 1922), p. 381.

45. Arthur Brisbane, "Warning to Combinations! Do Not Benefit the Public!" *Chicago Examiner,* December 22, 1913.

46. James E. Caldwell, *Recollections of a Life Time* (Nashville, Tenn.: Baird-Ward Press, 1923), p. 209.

47. Caldwell to Vail, August 2, 1913, in Caldwell, *Recollections,* p. 227.

48. Alan L. Seltzer, "Woodrow Wilson as 'Corporate-Liberal': Toward a Reconsideration of Left Revisionist Historiography," *Western Political Quarterly* 30 (June 1977): 200.

49. Woodrow Wilson, "The New Freedom," *World's Work* 26 (June 1913): 185.

50. Frederick P. Fish deposition, pp. 8–9, 15, June 25–29, 1914, *William Read et al. v. Central Union,* box 8, AT&T-NJ; L. D. Kellogg, memorandum on meeting at Blackstone Hotel, [1910], Box 37, DOJ-NA.

51. Wickersham to Nathan C. Kingsbury, January 3, 1913, box 38, RG 60, DOJ-NA.

52. *Wall Street Journal,* December 17, 1909.

53. Wickersham to Kingsbury, January 3, 1913, box 38, RG 60, DOJ-NA.

54. J. P. Morgan & Co. to Vail, August 9, 1915, in Federal Communications Commission, Accounting Department, "Telephone Investigation," vol. 3, typescript, Baker Library, Harvard University, Boston, Mass.

55. Harry B. MacMeal, *The Story of Independent Telephony* (Chicago: Independent Pioneer Telephone Association, 1934), pp. 183–187.

56. Wright to Wickersham, November 4, 1911, December 26, 1911; both in box 37, DOJ-NA.

57. Frisbie to Dawes, December 28, 1910, box 58; "Early History," p. 19, box 62; both in Dawes Papers; *Electrical World* 62 (August 2, 1913): 223; Kingsbury to McReynolds, September 24, 1913; Morton L. Johnson to Thomas W. Gregory, November 21, 1914; both in box 38, DOJ-NA.

58. "Secret Bell War on Rivals Told," *Chicago Tribune,* November 22, 1913.

59. Hubbell to McReynolds, June 29, 1913, box 38; Morton L. Johnson to Thomas W. Gregory, November 21, 1914, box 46; both in DOJ-NA.

60. "Chicago Hearings in the Government-Bell Trust Suit," *Telephony* 65 (November 29, 1913): 44.

61. "The Government Hearing in Chicago," *Telephony* 65 (November 29, 1913): 17.

62. "Government Asks Phone Dissolution," *Oregonian* (Portland, Ore.), July 25, 1913.

63. Cited in John E. Tuhy, *Sam Hill: The Prince of Castle Nowhere* (Goldendale, Wash.: Maryhill Museum of Art, 1992), p. 122.

64. Cited in ibid., p. 120.

65. "The Postal Telegraph Company's Announcement," *Telephony* 60 (June 24, 1911): 739; Home Telephone and Telegraph Company (Portland, Ore.), *Annual Report* (1912), pp. 4, 7; "Postal-Telephone Merger Projected," *New York Times,* December 6, 1913; Tuhy, *Sam Hill,* p. 122.

66. Tuhy, *Sam Hill,* pp. 122–123.

67. John McCourt to Wickersham, February 27, 1913, box 39, DOJ-NA.

68. *Wall Street Journal,* August 22, 1913.

69. "Home Phone Campaign," *Oregon Voter* 8 (March 3, 1917): 23.

70. Tuhy, *Sam Hill,* p. 6.

71. MacMeal, *Independent Telephony,* p. 210.

72. C. M. Keys, "The Rulers of the Wires," *World's Work* 19 (March 1910): 12726–12729.

73. "Extends Telephone War," *New York Times,* December 21, 1911; MacMeal, *Independent Telephony,* p. 211.

74. "Wickersham to Act in 'Phone Inquiry,' " *New York Times,* December 29, 1912.

75. Ibid.

76. *Wall Street Journal,* December 11, 1911.

77. *Postal Telegraph* (March 1912): 4, 5.

78. Kingsbury to attorney general, December 19, 1913, in American Telephone and Telegraph, *Annual Report* (1913), pp. 24–26.

79. "Bell Telephone Litigation with Government Settled," *Electrical World* 63 (April 4, 1914): 744.

80. American Telephone and Telegraph, *Annual Report* (1913), p. 24; Angus Hibbard, *Hello Goodbye: My Story of Telephone Pioneering* (Chicago: A. C. McClurg & Co., 1941), pp. 239–240.

81. E. Kinney to William W. Cook, December 20, 1913, William W. Cook Papers, University of Michigan, Ann Arbor.

82. Wright to Cook, December 20, 1913, Cook Papers.

83. Joseph Harris, *Automatic Electric Company* (n.p., 1914).

84. "A Gift from Santa Claus," *Telephony* 65 (December 27, 1913): 17; "The Bell Company Relinquishes Its Monopoly Methods," *Telephony* 65 (December 27, 1913): 20.

85. Wright to G. Carroll Todd, October 8, 1917; Wright to Kingsbury, December 4, 1917; Kingsbury to Todd, December 5, 1917; all in box 38, DOJ-NA.

86. Thomas W. Gregory to Woodrow Wilson, January 27, 1917, box 38, DOJ-NA.

87. Wright to Kingsbury, December 4, 1917, AT&T-NJ.

88. MacMeal, *Independent Telephony*, pp. 75, 175.

89. "Home Phone Campaign," *Oregon Voter* 8 (March 3, 1917): 23–27.

90. "Home Property Is Sold," *Oregonian*, February 18, 1919.

91. George E. McFarland to Nathan C. Kingsbury, December 8, 1918, Pacific Telephone and Telegraph Company Records, AT&T Archives and History Center, San Antonio, Texas.

92. Walter S. Allen, "Plan for a Telephone Magazine," 1909, p. 2, box 1317, AT&T-NJ.

93. Edwin Seligman, testimony, December 6, 1899, in *Report of the Industrial Commission on Transportation, Including Review of Evidence, Topical Digest of Evidence, and Testimony So Far as Taken May 1, 1900,* vol. 4 (Washington, D.C.: U.S. Government Printing Office, 1900), p. 612.

94. A. N. Holcombe, *Public Ownership of Telephones on the Continent of Europe* (Cambridge, Mass.: Harvard University Press, 1911), pp. 442, 462–463.

95. *Government Control of the Telegraph and Telephone Systems,* pt. 3, pp. 308, 319.

96. Ellen Nore, *Charles A. Beard: An Intellectual Biography* (Carbondale: Southern Illinois University Press, 1983), chap. 4.

97. *Arthur Norman Holcombe, Memorial Minute Adopted by the Faculty of Arts and Sciences, Harvard University,* Holcombe file, Archives, Harvard University, Cambridge, Mass.

98. Post Office Department, *Annual Report* (1911), p. 14.

99. Theodore Roosevelt to William Allen White, July 6, 1914, in *Letters of Theodore Roosevelt,* vol. 7, ed. Elting E. Morison (Cambridge, Mass.: Harvard University Press, 1954), p. 773.

100. Frederick Upham Adams, ed., "Are Great Fortunes Great Dangers?" *Cosmopolitan* 40 (February 1906): 399.

101. David J. Lewis, speech to the Maryland Grange [c. 1914], p. 10, Lewis Papers, Duke University, Durham, N.C.

102. David J. Lewis, *The Postalization of the Telephone and the Telegraph* (Washington, D.C.: n.p., 1914), p. 11.

103. *Congressional Record,* January 16, 1914, 63rd Cong., 2nd sess., 1769.

104. *Congressional Record,* March 4, 1915, 63rd Cong., 3rd sess., 849.

105. *Congressional Record,* December 29, 1914, 63rd Cong., 3rd sess., 689, 694, 695.

106. American Telephone and Telegraph, *Annual Report* (1911), p. 37.

107. American Telephone and Telegraph, *Annual Report* (1913), p. 37.

108. *The Postalization of the Telephone: Hearings before the Committee on the Post Office and Post Roads, House of Representatives, Sixty-Third Congress, Third Session, on H.R. 20471* (Washington, D.C.: U.S. Government Printing Office, 1915), p. 29.

109. A. Lincoln Lavine, "Review of the Government Ownership Situation during 1916," box 23, AT&T-NJ.

110. Lewis, *Postalization,* p. 9.

111. Burleson testimony, *Federal Control of Systems of Communication: Hearing before the Committee on Interstate and Foreign Commerce of the House of Representatives,* 65th Cong., 2nd sess., 1918, p. 35.

112. Burleson to Thomas R. Marshall, March 14, 1918, box 38, DOJ-NA.

113. Burleson testimony, *Federal Control of Systems of Communication,* p. 34.

114. *Government Ownership of the Electrical Means of Communication,* 63rd Cong., 2nd sess., 1914, Sen. Doc. 399 (serial 6576), pp. 8, 10, 12.

115. Ibid., pp. 12–13.

116. Daniel C. Roper, *The United States Post Office: Its Past Record, Present Condition, and Potential Relation to the New World Era* (New York: Funk & Wagnalls, 1917), pp. 79, 287, 317–319.

11. One Great Medium?

1. "A Real Investigation by the Government Expected," *Transmitter* (Fort Worth, Tex.) 14 (April 1913): 9; "Government Ownership," *Transmitter* (Fort Worth, Tex.) 16 (November 1913): 7; "Government Ownership," *Transmitter* (Fort Worth, Tex.) 16 (March 1914): 11–12.

2. Eli Noam, *Telecommunications in Europe* (New York: Oxford University Press, 1992), p. 4.

3. Wilson to Burleson, April 4, 1913, in *Papers of Woodrow Wilson,* vol. 25, ed. Arthur Link (Princeton, N.J.: Princeton University Press, 1978), p. 260.

4. Woodrow Wilson, "The New Freedom," *World's Work* 25 (June 1913): 185.

5. Winsor to Gaspard Farrer, March 6, 1914, box 45, Kidder, Peabody & Co. Collection, Historical Collections, Baker Library, Harvard Business School, Boston, Mass.

6. Burleson to Wilson, with enclosure, November 29, 1918, in *Papers of Woodrow Wilson,* vol. 53, ed. Arthur Link (Princeton, N.J.: Princeton University Press, 1986), pp. 247–249.

7. Petitions, House Committee on Interstate and Foreign Commerce, HR 63A-12.10, RG 233, National Archives, Washington, D.C. (hereafter NA); *Congressional Record,* 63rd Cong., 1st sess., May 5, 1913, p. 1088; Chester I. Barnard, "Report on Government Ownership," May 15, 1914, box 23, AT&T Archives, Warren, N.J. (hereafter AT&T-NJ).

8. William Jennings Bryan to Albert S. Burleson, July 23, 1918, Burleson Papers, Library of Congress, Washington, D.C.

9. Barnard, "Report on Government Ownership," AT&T-NJ.

10. Arthur Brisbane, "Government Ownership of Telephones and Telegraphs Desirable and Inevitable," *Chicago Examiner,* December 20, 1913.

11. "A Bill to Enable the United States of America to Acquire, Maintain, and Operate Electric Telegraphs, and So Forth," H.R. 464, 59th Cong., 1st sess., HR 59A-D22 RG 233, NA.

12. Herbert H. Rosenthal, "William Randolph Hearst and Municipal Ownership," *Tamkang Journal of American Studies* 1 (1984): 6–36.

13. Sydney Brooks, "The Politics of American Business," *North American Review* 193 (May 1911): 717; Brooks, "Aspects of Public Ownership," *North American Review* 194 (November 1911): 737–747.

14. *Wall Street Journal,* October 8, 1918.

15. "Government Ownership Near," *Lincoln Daily Star* (Neb.), December 20, 1913.

16. Elbert Hubbard, *Our Telephone Service* (East Aurora, N.Y.: Roycrofters, 1913), p. 27.

17. "Holland's Letter," *Wall Street Journal,* December 9, 1911; "'Holland' on Federal Ownership of Telegraph and Telephone Systems," *Wall Street Journal,* November 12, 1913.

18. Vail to F. L. Spaulding, February 18, 1914, box 47, AT&T-NJ.

19. "Vail's View of Wire Plan," *New York Times,* October 3, 1913; "Vail on Telephone Legislation," *Wall Street Journal,* October 3, 1913.

20. "Federal Ownership of the Telephone a Costly Affair," *Wall Street Journal,* October 4, 1913.

21. *Bell System Statistical Manual* (New York: American Telephone and Telegraph, 1946); J. Warren Stehman, *The Financial History of the American Telephone and Telegraph Company* (Boston: Houghton Mifflin Co., 1925), p. 217.

22. Charles M. Saltzman to Daniel C. Roper, December 9, 1913, box 38, Office of the Solicitor, Post Office Department Records, RG 28, National Archives, Washington, D.C. (hereafter POD-NA).

23. Bernard E. Sunny to Kingsbury, December 4, 1912, box 13, AT&T-NJ.

24. Walter S. Allen, "Public Service Corporations and the Government," 1914, p. 1, box 1067, AT&T-NJ.

25. DuBois to Vail, November 11, 1913, box 47, AT&T-NJ.

26. Ibid.

27. Ibid.; DuBois, "Plan Suggested for a Federal Administration of the Telephone and Telegraph Business of the United States," November 10, 1913; both in box 47, AT&T-NJ.

28. Gaspard Farrer to Robert Winsor, November 11, 1913, box 45, Kidder, Peabody & Co. Collection.

29. Barbara H. Fried, *The Progressive Assault on Laissez-Faire: Robert Hale and the First Law and Economics Movement* (Cambridge, Mass.: Harvard University Press, 1998), chap. 5.

30. "Progress Made," *Wall Street Journal,* March 21, 1908.

31. Frank Riblett to William C. Langdon, February 25, 1928, box 1019, AT&T-NJ.

32. Theodore N. Vail, "Lest We Forget!" box 49, AT&T-NJ.

33. Theodore N. Vail, "State Control of Public Utility Companies," *Public Service* 11 (July 1911): 10.

34. Nathan C. Kingsbury, "Wrong Ideas about the Bell System," *Public Service* 17 (August 1914): 46; *Wall Street Journal,* May 26, 1913.

35. *Wall Street Journal,* February 3, 1914.

36. Vail to R. C. Clowry, June 1907, president's letterbook, AT&T-NJ.

37. David F. Weiman and Richard C. Levin, "Preying for Monopoly? The Case of Southern Bell Telephone Company, 1894–1912,"*Journal of Political Economy* 102 (February 1994): 103–126.

38. Walter S. Allen, "The Post Office and the Telephone System," box 47, AT&T-NJ.

39. Henry C. Adams, *Description of Industry: An Introduction to Economics* (New York: Henry Holt and Co., 1918), p. 258.

40. Chicago Telephone Company, *Report* (1901), pp. 7–8.

41. Chesapeake and Potomac Telephone Company, *Report* (1906), p. 10.

42. Colorado Telephone Company, *Annual Report* (1910), p. 9.

43. Chester I. Barnard to David J. Lewis, December 10, 1918, box 102, Office of the Solicitor, POD-NA.

44. Nathan C. Kingsbury, "Telephone Problems of the Present and the Future," *Public Service* 15 (December 1913): 205.

45. Nathan C. Kingsbury, *Address . . . before the Cleveland Chamber of Commerce, December 30th, 1913* (n.p., 1914), pp. 24–25.

46. E. K. Hall, "Address," March 3, 1913, box 2061, AT&T-NJ.

47. A. Lincoln Lavine, *Circuits of Victory* (New York: Doubleday, Page & Co., 1921), p. 22.

48. "Marconi Wireless Telegraph Stock," *Reformed Church Messenger,* March 22, 1906.

49. "Marconi Telegraph," *Los Angeles Times,* January 31, 1904.

50. "Marconi Wireless Telegraph Stock," *Reformed Church Messenger.*

51. *Literary Digest,* October 18, 1913, pp. 663–664, in Katherine B. Judson, ed., *Selected Articles on Government Ownership of the Telegraph and Telephone* (New York: H. W. Wilson Co., 1914), p. 4.

52. "The Government Telegraph Prospects," *New York Times,* October 4, 1913, p. 12.

53. Reuben Dean Bowen to William A. Bowen, April 19, 1915, box 2, Reuben Dean Bowen Papers, Duke University, Durham, N.C.

54. Leonard S. Reich, *The Making of American Industrial Research: Science and Business at GE and Bell, 1876–1926* (Cambridge: Cambridge University Press, 1985), chaps. 7–9; Reich, "Industrial Research and the Pursuit of Corporate Security: The Early Years of Bell Labs," *Business History Review* 54 (Winter 1980): 504–529.

55. *Wall Street Journal,* March 30, 1912.

56. William G. Scott, *Chester I. Barnard and the Guardians of the Managerial State* (Lawrence: University Press of Kansas, 1992), pp. 68–72.

57. Robert J. Chapuis, *One Hundred Years of Telephone Switching (1878–1978)* (Amsterdam: North-Holland Publishing Co., 1982), p. 251.

58. Angus Hibbard, *Hello Goodbye: My Story of Telephone Pioneering* (Chicago: A. C. McClurg & Co., 1941), p. 141.

59. Kenneth Lipartito, "Component Innovation: The Case of Automatic Telephone Switching, 1891–1920," *Industrial and Corporate Change* 3, no. 2 (1994): 325–357.

60. "Tests of the Strowger Automatic System in Chicago, Illinois," October 18, 1904, 11-07-01-02, AT&T-NJ.

61. Delos F. Wilcox, *Municipal Franchises: A Description of the Terms and Conditions upon Which Private Corporations Enjoy Special Privileges in the Streets of American Cities,* vol. 1: *Pipe and Wire Franchises* (Rochester, N.Y.: Gervaise Press, 1910), pp. 5, 87, 227; "Fraud on Telephone Subscribers," *Chicago Tribune,* January 19, 1900, "Way to Reduce 'Phone Charges," *Chicago Tribune,* July 28, 1901.

62. *Chicago Electrical Handbook* (n.p., 1904), p. 100.

63. M. D. Fagen, ed., *A History of Engineering and Science in the Bell System: The Early Years (1875–1925)* (New York: Bell Telephone Laboratories, 1975), p. 584.

64. Bert G. Hubbell to Woodrow Wilson, July 28, 1913, box 45, DOJ-NA.

65. "The Story of Telephone Competition," *Public Service* 5 (November 1908): 152.

66. American Telephone and Telegraph, *Annual Report* (1915), p. 51.

67. J. L. Turner, "The Invisible Servant," *Public Service* 24 (March 1918): 77.

68. "Effects of Technology on Telephone Operator's Employment," 1940, pp. 7, 9, Women's Trade Union League Records, Schlesinger Library, Harvard University, Cambridge, Mass.

69. _____ Fassett to James D. Ellsworth, October 2, 1906, box 1317; Vail to Walter H. Page, July 13, 1908, president's letterbook; both at AT&T-NJ.

70. "The Telephone Question: The Effect of the Berliner Decision on the Industry," *Electrical Review* 25 (December 26, 1894): 320.

71. Vail to Henry M. Watson, November 11, 1907, president's letterbook, AT&T-NJ.

72. James D. Ellsworth to W. J. O'Connor, January 17, 1929, Box 1066, AT&T-NJ.

73. R. T. Barrett, "The Start of an Advertiser: How the Bell System's Institutional Advertising Developed," *Printers Ink Monthly* 22 (June 1931): 54.

74. Roland Marchand, *Creating the Corporate Soul: The Rise of Public Relations and Corporate Imagery in American Big Business* (Berkeley: University of California Press, 1998), p. 51.

75. "Roosevelt Message Stirs Up Congress," *New York Times,* October 9, 1908; "Federal Control of the Telegraphs," *New York Times,* December 20, 1908.

76. Nathan C. Kingsbury, *The National Advertiser* (n.p., 1916), p. 11.

77. Vail to Henry M. Watson, March 26, 1908, president's letterbook, AT&T-NJ.

78. American Telephone and Telegraph, "Twenty Million Voices," 1908, box 2061, AT&T-NJ.

79. Emerson McMillan to Seth Low, January 3, 1914, July 8, 1913, July 21, 1913, National Civic Federation Records, Columbia University, New York.

80. James E. Caldwell, *Recollections of a Life Time* (Nashville, Tenn.: Baird-Ward Press, 1923), p. 197.

81. "Theodore N. Vail: The Commander of a $500,000,000 Service Organization," *Public Service* 4 (June 1908): 164–167; Herbert N. Casson, *The History of the Telephone* (Chicago: A. G. McClurg & Co., 1910), pp. 66, 171; "Theodore N. Vail: President of the American Telephone and Telegraph Company and of the Western Union Telegraph Company," *Harper's Weekly* 54 (December 17, 1910): 6.

82. "Theodore N. Vail," *Harper's Weekly,* pp. 6–7.

83. E. J. Edwards, "Holland's Letter," *Wall Street Journal,* December 15, 1909.

84. John D. Rockefeller Jr., to Frederick T. Gates, July 27, 1912, in John M. Jordan, ed., "'To Educate Public Opinion': John D. Rockefeller, Jr., and the Origins of Social Scientific Fact-Finding," *New England Quarterly* 64 (June 1991): 293–295.

85. Evelyn B. Longman to Marc Eidlitz & Son, December 7, 1914, AT&T-NJ.

86. Ada Rainey, "American Women in Sculpture," *Century* 93 (January 1917): 438.

87. William Wells Bosworth to Evelyn B. Longman, April 20, 1914, Archives, Loomis Chaffee School, Windsor, Conn.

88. *Government Ownership and Taxation: The High Cost of Governing* (n.p., [1914]); *Government Ownership and the Farmer* (n.p., [1914]); both in box 47, AT&T-NJ.

89. James D. Ellsworth, "The Twisting Trail," box 1066, AT&T-NJ.

90. "Minutes of Advertising Conference, Bell Telephone System, Philadelphia, Pa., June 28, 1916," pp. 4, 10, box 1310, AT&T-NJ.

91. "Engineering Improvements and Publicity," *Electrical Review* 67 (October 9, 1915): 650.

92. Lavine, *Circuits of Victory,* p. 21.

93. "Making a Neighborhood of a Nation," *Telephone Review* 6 supplement (January 1915), inside front cover.

94. Edward W. Gorom to Albert Sidney Burleson, February 2, 1914, box 39, Office of the Solicitor, POD-NA.

95. Arthur T. Hadley, "Some Difficulties of Public Business Management," *Political Science Quarterly* 3 (December 1888): 587.

96. *New Nation* 1 (February 7, 1891): 28.

97. "Western Telephone News," *Electrical Review* 11 (December 17, 1887): 6.

98. Hibbard, *Hello Goodbye,* chap. 8; "Long Distance Telephoning," *Electrical Review* 14 (August 3, 1889): 6.

99. "Phone to Pacific from the Atlantic," *New York Times,* January 26, 1915.

100. Vail to F. L. Spaulding, box 47, AT&T-NJ.

101. *Brief of Arguments against Public Ownership,* 3 vols. AT&T-NJ; Barnard, "Report on Government Ownership," box 23, AT&T-NJ; Barnard, *Governmental and Private: Telegraph and Telephone Utilities—An Analysis* (New York: American Telephone and Telephone Co., 1914).

102. Barnard to Harry B. Thayer, May 15, 1914, "Status of Government Ownership Movement," box 47, AT&T-NJ; Scott, *Barnard,* p. 65.

103. Walter S. Allen, "Twenty Five Reasons Why a Privately Owned Telephone System Is Better for the Users than a System Owned and Operated by the United States Government," box 1135, AT&T-NJ.

104. John J. Carty, "What Political Ownership of Telephones Offers," *Public Service* 22 (January 1917): 6–7; "John J. Carty Not the Author," *Public Service* 22 (February 1917): 38.

105. David M. Grossman, "American Foundation and the Support of Economic Research," *Minerva* 20 (Spring–Summer 1982): 76–77.

106. K. Austin Kerr, *American Railroad Politics, 1914–1920: Rates, Wages, and Efficiency* (Pittsburgh: University of Pittsburgh Press, 1968), chap. 3.

107. Christopher N. May, *In the Name of War: Judicial Review and the War Powers since 1918* (Cambridge, Mass.: Harvard University Press, 1989), pp. 32–33.

108. Cited in Stephen H. Norwood, *Labor's Flaming Youth: Telephone Operators and Worker Militancy, 1878–1923* (Urbana: University of Illinois Press, 1990), p. 159.

109. May, *In the Name of War,* pp. 39, 51–52.

110. Ibid., p. 43.

111. Ibid., pp. 30–37; quotation on p. 31.

112. Ibid., pp. 40–47; "Basis for Metering Service," *Telephony* 17 (November 15, 1919): 11.

113. American Telephone and Telegraph, *Annual Report* (1917), p. 50.

114. Nathan C. Kingsbury, statement before the Senate interstate commerce committee, 1919, box 37, AT&T-NJ.

115. "Mr. Burleson," *Baltimore Sun,* April 24, 1919.

116. Vail, "Memorandum," p. 1.

117. Daniel R. Headrick, *The Invisible Weapon: Telecommunications and International Politics, 1851–1945* (New York: Oxford University Press, 1991), chaps. 7–8.

118. Press release, December 9, 1918, box 294, Office of the Solicitor, POD-NA.

119. Theodore N. Vail, "Memorandum," December 8, 1918, pp. 5, 8, box 38, Office of the Solicitor, POD-NA.

120. Vail, *Wire System: Discussion of Electrical Intelligence: Letter of Theo. N. Vail in Response to a Request of Hon. John A. Moon . . .* (n.p., 1918), p. 26.

121. Press release, December 9, 1918, box 294, Office of the Solicitor, POD-NA.

122. Vail, "International Intercommunication," pp. 2, 10, box 14, AT&T-NJ.

123. Michael J. Hogan, *Informal Entente: The Private Structure of Cooperation in Anglo-American Economic Diplomacy, 1918–1928* (Columbia: University of Missouri Press, 1977), pp. 108, 118.

124. Hugh G. J. Aitken, *The Continuous Wave: Technology and American Radio, 1900–1932* (Princeton, N.J.: Princeton University Press, 1985), chaps. 5–8.

125. Vail, "Memorandum," p. 13; Vail to John A. Moon, December 30, 1918, in *Government Control of the Telegraph and Telephone Systems* (Washington, D.C.: U.S. Government Printing Office, 1919), pt. 1, p. 52.

126. Caldwell, *Recollections,* p. 196.

127. "Would Put Wires under One Head, Cables Likewise," *New York Times,* December 9, 1918.

128. "Sherman Assails Vail," *New York Times,* January 21, 1919.

129. Vail to Henry L. Higginson, June 18, 1919, president's letterbook, AT&T-NJ.

130. *Government Control of the Telegraph and Telephone Systems,* pt. 2, pp. 75–105.

131. Norwood, *Labor's Flaming Youth,* p. 158.

132. Henry A. Barnhart to Claude R. Stoops, February 15, 1919, box 9, Barnhart Papers, Indiana State Library and Archives, Indianapolis, Ind.

133. Clippings file, box 160, DOJ-NA.

134. Norwood, *Labor's Flaming Youth,* chap. 5; Maureen Weiner Greenwald, *Women, War, and Work: The Impact of World War I on Women Workers in the United States* (Westport, Conn.: Greenwood Press, 1980), chap. 5.

135. Norwood, *Labor's Flaming Youth,* pp. 198, 208.

136. *New York World,* April 19, 1919; "Wire Rate Legislation Necessary," *Telephony* 76 (May 19, 1919): 16–18.

137. "Popular Mr. Burleson," *Cleveland Plain Dealer,* April 30, 1919.

138. Joseph Tumulty to Wilson, April 25, 1919, in *Papers of Woodrow Wilson,* vol. 56, ed. Arthur Link (Princeton, N.J.: Princeton University Press, 1987), p. 146.

139. *Government Control of the Telegraph and Telephone Systems,* pts. 1–4.

140. May, *In the Name of War,* pp. 41, 50.

141. Wilson, special message to Congress, May 22, 1919, in *Papers of Woodrow Wilson,* vol. 59, ed. Arthur Link (Princeton, N.J.: Princeton University Press, 1988), p. 296.

142. *Government Control of the Telegraph and Telephone Systems: Hearings on H.J. Res. 368 before the Committee on the Post Office and Post Roads,* 65th Cong., 3rd sess., 1919, pt. 1, p. 16.

143. Nathan C. Kingsbury, statement before the Senate interstate commerce committee, 1919, box 37, AT&T NJ.

144. Harry B. Thayer to Walter Berry, January 5, 1922, box 1, AT&T-NJ.

145. Thayer, "Confidential to the Directors: Federal Control," box 1, AT&T-NJ.

Epilogue

1. Michael K. Kellogg, John Thorne, and Peter W. Huger, *Federal Telecommunications Law* (Boston: Little, Brown and Co., 1992), p. 4.

2. Walter S. Gifford, "Bell System Policies and Objectives," in *Proceedings of the Bell System Operating Conference, Absecon, New Jersey, May 1928,* box 185 06 03, AT&T Archives and History Center, Warren, N.J.

3. Neil H. Wasserman, *From Invention to Innovation: Long-Distance Telephone Transmission at the Turn of the Century* (Baltimore, Md.: Johns Hopkins University Press, 1985); Robert W. Garnet, *The Telephone Enterprise: The Evolution of the Bell System's Horizontal Structure, 1876–1909* (Baltimore, Md.: Johns Hopkins University Press, 1985); George David Smith, *The Anatomy of a Business Strategy: Bell, Western Electric, and the Origins of the American Telephone Industry* (Baltimore, Md.: Johns Hopkins University Press, 1985).

4. Thomas P. Hughes, *American Genesis: A History of the American Genius for Invention* (New York: Penguin Books, 1990), p. 2.

5. George L. Priest, "The Origins of Utility Regulation and the 'Theories of Regulation' Debate," *Journal of Law and Economics* 36 (April 1993): 289–329;

Werner Troesken, *Why Regulate Utilities? The New Institutional Economics and the Chicago Gas Industry, 1849–1924* (Ann Arbor: University of Michigan Press, 1996); Robert Britt Horwitz, *The Irony of Regulatory Reform: The Deregulation of American Telecommunications* (New York: Oxford University Press, 1989).

6. David A. Moss and Michael R. Fein, "Radio Regulation Revisited: Coase, the FCC, and the Public Interest," *Journal of Policy History* 15, no. 4 (2003): 389–416.

7. Philip T. Rosen, *The Modern Stentors: Radio Broadcasting and the Federal Government, 1920–1934* (Westport, Conn.: Greenwood Press, 1980), pp. 175–178.

8. "Secretary Roper's Report on Communications Study," *Wall Street Journal,* January 30, 1934.

9. Alvin von Auw, *Heritage and Destiny: Reflections on the Bell System in Transition* (New York: Praeger, 1983).

ACKNOWLEDGMENTS

In the course of researching and writing this book, I have accumulated numerous debts. For fellowship support, I am grateful to the Smithsonian Institution's Woodrow Wilson Center, the John M. Olin Foundation, the Newberry Library, the Humanities Institute at the University of Illinois at Chicago, the Great Cities Institute at the University of Illinois at Chicago, and the National Endowment for the Humanities. Among the administrators who smoothed my way were Gene Ruoff, Michael Lacey, James Grossman, David Perry, and Francesca Gaiba. For research assistance, I am grateful to the Stuart Rossiter Trust and the Campus Research Board at the University of Illinois at Chicago.

The research on which this book is based is dependent on the many archivists and librarians who collect, catalogue, and preserve the records of business corporations and government agencies. For particular favors, I am grateful to Alison Olwald at the Smithsonian Institution's Archives Center; William Caughlin at the AT&T Archives and History Center in San Antonio, Texas; Sheldon Hochheiser, Chip Larkin, and George Kupczak at the AT&T Archives and History Center in Warren, New Jersey; Laura Linard at the Harvard Business School; Rodney Ross and Fred Romanski at the National Archives; Jan Hilley at the New-York Historical Society; Martin Tuohy at the Great Lakes Branch of the National Archives; Bruce Abrams at the New York County Archives; Steve Hallberg at the Oregon Historical Society; Pegeen Bassett at the Northwestern University Law School; Jean Barr at the Sidley Austin Archives; and Margaret Leary at the University of Michigan Law School. Tom Morsch helped me gain access to the Sidley Austin Archives, and Bernard Finn led me on a tour of the Smithsonian's remarkable collection of telegraph and telephone artifacts. Ana Ortiz and John Mathews proved indispensable in securing materials via interlibrary loan at the University of Illinois at Chicago.

For research assistance, I am indebted to Clarissa Ceglio, Justin Coffey, Addie Compton, Cory Davis, Michael Davis, Tom Dorrance, Joshua Fennell, Raymond Lohne, Sarah Moskowitz, Joshua Salzmann, Jordan Stalker, Dylan Steinberg, Christopher Tassava, Elizabeth Tieri, Lee Vinsel, and Mark R. Wilson. I owe special thanks to Sarah Rose for the ingenuity with which she completed several specialized research projects, and for coordinating for several years the flow of books in and out of my office.

Various individuals helped bring my story to life. Beatrice Manx led me on a memorable tour of the home of her great grandfather, American Bell president William H. Forbes. Kim Hoeveler accompanied me on an unforgettable trek to Maryhill, the palatial estate of the eccentric telephone promoter Samuel Hill. Marian Shaw generously shared her recollections of the nickel-in-the-slot telephone that graced the front hall of her family's Chicago apartment during the 1930s. Seven decades later, she retains a vivid memory of the pink quartz dish that her parents brought home as a souvenir from a summer vacation to the Black Hills of South Dakota in which her mother kept the nickels that she deposited in the telephone coin-slot to make an outgoing call.

Colleagues who have read and commented on chapter drafts include Christopher Beauchamp, Michael Les Benedict, Richard Bensel, Menahem Blondheim, Robert Bruegmann, Louis Carlat, W. Bernard Carlson, Carolyn Cooper, Jonathan Coopersmith, Jonathan Daly, Perry Duis, Tom Eisenmann, Leon Fink, Bernard Finn, Walter Friedman, David Gabel, Edward Gray, Robert Dalton Harris, Daniel Headrick, David Hochfelder, Sheldon Hochheiser, Derek Hoff, Robert Horwitz, Thomas P. Hughes, Jane Kamensky, Morton Keller, Richard B. Kielbowicz, Maury Klein, Pamela W. Laird, Kenneth Lipartito, Robert MacDougall, Deirdre McCloskey, Thomas K. McCraw, John McVey, Stephen Mihm, Milton L. Mueller Jr., David Nelson, Keith Nier, Tomas Nonnenmacher, William J. Novak, Walter Nugent, Andrew Odlyzko, Edwin J. Perkins, Michael Perman, George L. Priest, Mark H. Rose, Sarah Rose, Dan Schiller, Jonathan Silberstein-Loeb, Kenneth Silverman, Bartholemew Sparrow, Michael Stamm, John Staudenmaier, Christopher Sterling, T. J. Stiles, Susan Strasser, Stanley Swihart, Joel Tarr, Tamara Thornton, David Weiman, Mark R. Wilson, and Joshua Wolff. For special favors I am grateful to Eric Arnesen, Richard Bensel, Burton J. Bledstein, William K. Bolt,

Diane DeBlois, Vice Admiral George W. Emery, James Garde, Robert Dalton Harris, Paul Israel, Christine MacLeod, Gregory Mark, Jerry Meites, Jeffrey Nichols, Tomas Nonnenmacher, Gautham Rao, Kenneth Silverman, Mark W. Summers, Stanley Swihart, and Ross Thomson. While these individuals have saved me from many missteps, responsibility for all errors of fact and interpretation remains mine alone.

My editor, Joyce Seltzer, has been a loyal champion of this project from its inception; her perceptive editorial suggestions improved the manuscript in numerous ways. So, too, did the anonymous referees for Harvard University Press.

Special thanks to Dennis McClendon for expertly drawing the map on page 325; to John Donohue for skillfully coordinating the production of the manuscript; to Colin Agur and Lynn Berger for diligently reading the proofs; and to Jeannette Estruth for the cheerful professionalism with which she assisted in the production process.

Chapter drafts were previewed at the Hagley Museum and Library, Harvard Business School, the Miller Center at the University of Virginia, the Newberry Library, the University of Maryland, and Willamette University. Some material in Chapter 3 appeared in "Private Enterprise, Public Good? Communications Deregulation as a National Political Issue, 1839–1851," in Jeffrey L. Pasley, Andrew W. Robertson, and David Waldstreicher, eds., *Beyond the Founders: New Approaches to the Political History of the Early American Republic* (Chapel Hill: University of North Carolina Press, 2004), pp. 328–354. Certain themes in Chapters 5, 8, and 9 were sketched in "Telecommunications," *Enterprise and Society* 9 (September 2008): 507–520.

The preparation of this book has been a major event in the life of my family. It has benefited from the thoughtful critiques of Richard R. John Sr., Suzanne H. John, and Thomas Reimer. My children, Rodda and Emery, have been a constant source of encouragement and support. Rodda remains convinced that the Morse code was really a cipher, and Emery would like it to be duly recorded that Alexander Graham Bell's first telephone resembles Abraham Lincoln's stovepipe hat. This book could not have been completed without the loving assistance of my wife, Nancy John, who has read every chapter numerous times and been its most unwavering champion and perceptive critic.

INDEX

Note: Page numbers in *italics* refer to illustrations.